Love On Line?

A Tale Of Internet Dating

NICHOLAS TOMBS

Disclaimer

The story you are about to read is true. It took place in the Fall of 2011. I exercised my creative license to help the flow of the story. For the most part the conversations are word for word from how they originally happened. Some words or phrases in parentheses weren't part of the original conversation and are there to clarify the abbreviation. I changed names to protect the identities of family and friends.

All opinions expressed herein are strictly my own.

No part of this book may be reproduced, or stored in a retrieval system, or transmitted in any manner, electronic, mechanical, photocopy, recording, or otherwise without the express written permission of the author.

All rights reserved 2020 Nicholas Tombs

Copyright © 2020 Nicholas Tombs
ISBN 978-1-7782177-0-8 (hard cover)
ISBN 978-1-7782177-3-9 (audio Book)
ISBN 978-1-7782177-1-5 (paper back)
ISBN 978-1-7782177-2-2 (ebook)

With special thanks for all their help.

Krista Wallace
Jonathan Lyster
Samantha VanIngen

Introduction

It's been said one in three relationships starts from an online dating site.

I've thought of trying it but wondered — how safe is it? Meeting someone through a computer screen seems sterile and emotionless. I enjoy meeting people in person. But, who's to say where you'll find that one person, who every time you see them you feel all warm and fuzzy inside, your heart flip flops and the world disappears.

That feeling of unconditional love from a partner is ultimately what we'd all like to have — isn't it? I believe being loved is a big part of happiness. Love is more fun than anything you can imagine. Nothing can touch that feeling. Some people spend their entire life searching and never find it. They say the best way to find it is to stop looking. Maybe it only exists on television or in the movies?

Being skeptical I'll still give it a shot. I'll keep it casual and reserve a little of myself just to be safe.

Chapter 1 September 30 - October 2

I hope to meet someone who sees and appreciates the little things the world has to offer as well as the complex. She'll be strong and independent. She can be a goofball sometimes and not take herself too seriously. Content with who she is, knows where she's going in life and has a plan on how to get there. She'll know how to define happiness and she'll always have my back.

I'll start with a free site. A little something to get my feet wet, it's free so why not? I'm sure you've heard of it, something to do with fishing. I'll give it a month and if there's no real connections then I'll cancel my account and try another.

First off a screen name?... I'm drawing a blank... I'll come back to that one. I'll do the easy ones first. Age: 39, Height: 6' 3", Hair Colour: Bald/Shaved, Eye Colour: Blue, Body Type: Athletic. Hmm... screen name, oh I know, LeftCoast72 and I'll go with this for my bio;

"Thanks for stopping by. I'm a jeans and T shirt kind of guy, shorts and flip flops in the summer but I don't mind getting dressed up on occasion. I don't like drama or mind games and I don't like to be strung along. I am an artist in my spare time but I do have a regular job so I'm not starving. Being an artist I work in whatever medium will get me the end result whether it be steel, wood, fabric, clay.... I enjoy working with my hands. I'm also an inventor of sorts. My friends say I'm easy to be around, very creative, open minded and detail oriented.

I lead a healthy lifestyle without it leading me. I enjoy cooking and I try to eat healthy. I'm pretty down to earth, out going, laid back and a people person. I'm very independent, gentle, caring, passionate and enthusiastic while maintaining a masculine demeanor. I am not easy to anger. I enjoy meeting new people and trying new things. I respect others opinions even if I disagree with them. I try not to be wasteful. I'm clean cut and I take care of myself. I take pride in my appearance without being overly obsessed.

My dream is to one day own a home and have my creative design studio close by so I can design and build my projects from home.

Music Interests; Everything between the extremes. I have a soft spot for the roots of rock n roll; Buddy Holly, Elvis, Jerry Lee Lewis and the '60's; The Beach Boys...

Favourite Band: The Doors.

Favourite Movies: Shawshank Redemption, Red Dawn.

My busy schedule does have room in it for someone special but a serious relationship has to start from somewhere. If something more develops from friends then I'm open to it. Thanks for stopping by and enjoy your day.

I know this was a lot to read but, (*) if you've made it this far maybe you're willing to come a little further, so don't be shy and drop me a line and say hi or tell me how you're doing, I wont bite. No expectations, no pressure."

*A quote from the The Shawshank Redemption. I hope someone will see this detail as those are the things I notice.

A couple of photos when I was in Mexico and I'm done.

I surfed the site and sent out a few messages but received no replies. It seems women don't make first contact. Some would add me to a favorites list yet say nothing — is this my cue to approach them? Some profiles state they are, "Not looking for sex.", "Not interested in anyone that says, 'Sup baby." or "U lookin' fine." Some even asked what the deal is with guys taking shirtless bathroom photos. It's difficult to come up with something that'll catch their attention. Hopefully the women I do message will read my profile and see I put some effort into it. That I was there to make a real connection and no shirtless bathroom photos lol.

I think it's time to move onto the sites with a fee. If I, like others have to pay to be on it then maybe it'll weed out the riffraff.

The first one turned out to be a scam. It took my money then sent random messages from bogus profiles claiming to be so interested in me and just couldn't wait to get to know me better. When I replied to these messages I never received a response. I did some research, something I should have done in the first place and I was right, it was a scam, lesson learned.

The next site was a popular one and I did arrange a date with a woman who surprisingly approached me. We decided to meet in the West End of Vancouver and go for a walk. She was very nice and the conversation was natural and relaxed. We had a good time but didn't feel a close connection so we didn't arrange a second date.

After experiencing the online dating world for a few months the profiles are very repetitive, soul mate... partner in crime... blah blah blah — very boring. In reality they're just words on a page till you meet in person, that's when it becomes real. You enter your search criteria and there are thousands of profiles to choose from. I sent messages but again no replies — it seems I'm attracted to the not interested lol.

I wonder how long it takes to find a connection or just someone to chat with? About this time a friend told me about the site she was on. I let my existing account expire and I opened one on Lava Life.

Lava Life has three different levels — Friends, Relationship and Intimate. There's also a section in your profile that's your "Back Stage". This is where you post photos you don't want everyone to see, just the people you allow. You don't have to post a profile in all three if you don't want to and you can use different wording for each of them. I started in Friends and eventually posted in the other two.

The Intimate section — WOW! People are really honest with what they're looking for or more so what they're willing to do in the bedroom, or out of it! I'm pretty open minded but it's quite shocking. I guess that's one of the benefits of online dating, it gives you a certain anonymity and people feel more audacious because of it.

Now here's one...

We're on the 15th floor of an executive high rise apartment building. The windows are floor to ceiling with a beautiful view of the evening city below. The lights are low and music is softly playing in the back ground. You are the host of the party but you don't know who I am and we haven't been able to meet yet. I have warm dark honey coloured skin. I'm wearing a form fitting dress and my long silky dark hair flows when I move. Throughout the evening you've been trying to figure out who I am, then I catch you watching me. You smile inquisitively and when I smile back my face lights up and my warmth shows through. As you're mingling with your guests, still unable to talk with me you sense you're being watched and looking around the room you notice I am now watching you. Again we exchange warm smiles. With the party winding down and people leaving I purposefully make sure I'm the last guest to leave. You hold my coat to help me put it on. I slip my arms into the sleeves and you lean in close to softly whisper in my ear "Don't go". The coat falls to the floor and I turn to face you. You pull me close. I stand on the tips of my toes and wrap my hands around the back of your neck and we embrace in a long passionate kiss...

That's where the scenario ends and I guess we make up our own ending?

I need to say something! I'm not sure what but I have to say something! She hasn't posted a photo — I wonder why? It would be funny hitting it off never knowing what she looked like until later.

LEFTCOAST72

Sept 30 2:17 AM

Subject : Wow!

Wow! Your bio is really cool. Very creative. How are you? Can I see you please? You can see me seems fair... yes?

An hour passed and much to my surprise I received a reply!

SENSUALSEDUCTION

3:48 PM

Subject : Re:Wow!

Hi there ... thankyou, glad you enjoyed reading my profile.
I enjoyed reading yours as well.
Iam working the next 2 days ... i work odd hours ...so i wont be around til sunday. So it would be nice to connect with you online and exchange bs (Back Stage). Id rather exchange while we are online.
Dont worry ... i described myself exactly as in my story.
Have a good next 2 days ... and i look forward to chatting with you !!
Cheers ~N~

I have goose bumps wondering what she looks like. I hope she's as excited as I am.

She works odd hours, I thought, *Maybe she's a nurse? Caring and compassionate by nature, that's a good start.*

It's difficult to not let my emotions or doubts get the better of me. I'll take a step back. I'll put it out of my mind and let the weekend pass.

Finally Sunday evening, I can't stand it any longer.

LEFTCOAST72

Oct 2 3:37 PM

Subject : Hey!

Hi there. Are you back from work yet? I'll be in for the evening. If you feel like chatting send me a message.

SENSUALSEDUCTION

6:30 PM

Subject : Re:Hey!

Ok i will be on later tonite ... im just heading out to meet some friends for dinner ... just checking for messages for now

Hope ur having a good weekend

Talk to you soon !!

~N~

LEFTCOAST72

okay cool. have fun

Only ten minutes later I received another message!

SENSUALSEDUCTION

Ok I have a few mins here... if you wanna chat !

I jumped at the opportunity!

LEFTCOAST72

okay. will you grant me access to your back stage please? so I can put a face to your words

SENSUALSEDUCTION

Hehe ... ok ...here goes ...

Name is Namita.

Sign : Pisces

Are you interested in indian women?

LEFTCOAST72

I have no restrictions about race

"Oh my fucking god! Are you kidding me! She's beautiful!"

She's lying on her tummy with her chin resting on the bed, the camera at arms length. She has a beautiful smile, pretty brown eyes and dark hair. The second photo looks like it should be in a magazine. She's sitting on a bay window seat, legs crossed with her hands one on top of the other on her knee and she's looking out the window over her shoulder. She's wearing jeans and a brown long sleeve form fitting shirt.

SENSUALSEDUCTION

What exactly are you looking for from Lavalife ? Franky i sometimes dont know what im doing here in this section ... i find that i get more responses this side.

I do have a profile in the relationship section ... im hoping to find something more meaningful ...and have a better connection with someone on many different levels.

I admire everything youve mentioned in ur profile ...and i feel it does reflect the person iam as well.

What are your thoughts ?

~Namita~

LEFTCOAST72

To be completely honest I'd like to find a woman of substance. Someone I can always be myself around. She fits seamlessly into my life and I hers. I'll want to give her my heart and she'll hold it close to protect and cherish it. When I'm with her I feel a warmth deep inside. A warmth that radiates throughout my body to where I feel an invincible happiness. It's the way I feel on a crisp spring morning or when the summer sun warms me. The way I feel when I hear a favourite song or I see the beauty nature has to offer. When she looks at me the rest of the world disappears and I feel like I'm floating. I want to feel all that all at the same time.

SENSUALSEDUCTION

I do understand what ur saying ..and thats what i appreciate too ...someone, where we can complement each other ...

Im a very passionate person that way !!

I am the kind of person that give 200% in a relationship

Unfortunatley im only 5'7 ...hehe ...

But i think i make it up in other ways

So by the looks of ur pic ... looks like you have nice travel stories ...

Have you been anywhere exotic ??

I love travelling ,... but havent done enough of long distance exotic locations much.

I do enjoy spontaneous road trips ... i love what BC has to offer.

Im loving recieving ur emails ... in fact i got another ..now ... so im going to go open the other one ...hehe

LEFTCOAST72

I'm so beside myself I forgot to tell you my name.

It's sooo nice to meet you Namita I'm Nicholas. I'm really enjoying reading your emails too. I hope we can reach a point where we're comfortable to meet in person. I look forward to that day!

5' 7" is perfect! That's just what I wished for.

SENSUALSEDUCTION

Hehe ... very pleased to meet you Nicholas !!!!

Ahhhh i see wish granted again !! Now you have one more !! Hehe

Im glad we've got in touch ..in fact while i was at work ...i kept checking to see if you wrote back to me ...but alas ...no

But i moved on ....hehe ... im coping.

Im sure we will have nice long chats soon !

Im a very playful ,easy to get along with person. People say im pretty funny ... i dont have any hangups.

Never married ...no children.

But i dont mind if whoever i end up with has children ...as long as he is not married ..that is ... lol

Hope im not rambling here ...

This is too good to be true. No kids, never married and 5' 7 ?! That's exactly what I wished for.

It seems I have this ability to wish... no that's not right... connect with the world around me? Just passing thoughts to make my life more enjoyable or a friend I haven't talk with for a while. Sometimes it's a scene from a movie I haven't watched for a long time or a song that pops into my head. For some mysterious reason, at times only minutes or hours things... happen. I get a call or text from that very person, I see the movie on TV or I hear the song on the radio. It happens far too often to be dismissed as coincidence. I still haven't been able to make the Lotto numbers happen but I keep trying lol. Okay, maybe it is a wish.

My wish went something like this. Keep in mind it's a wish and you need to be specific:

I'd like to meet someone tall, no shorter than 5' 7", confident, enjoys her job or career, is financially stable, has no debt, physically fit, eats healthy and takes pride in her appearance without being obsessive about it, is just as attracted to me as I am to her and has a healthy sex drive. Preferably with no kids. Perhaps someone exotic with an unusual name.

LEFTCOAST72

You're not rambling but if you want to ramble go right ahead I love reading what you've written. You were in my thoughts all weekend but I knew you were at work so I patiently waited for this evening and my patients were rewarded.

I'm going to save my last wish because it's an important one. Do you have any wishes I can help you with. I'd be more than happy to see what I can do to make them happen.

I'm glad you're open to someone with kids. I have 2 daughter from a previous marriage. They're 11 and 13. They live with their mom but I see them often. And I am happily divorced just to be clear.

I see another message from you.

SENSUALSEDUCTION

Yes i do enjoy being around kids of all ages- i volunteer doing Burn Camp for kids anually ...used to work with burn victims a few yrs back . I have a neice and nephew...whom i adore and love !!

You must have ur hands full with 2 daughters ... granting their wishes ...hehe ... i find the neice can more work than the 3 yr old nephew.. neice is 7yrs

I have no wishes at this time ... but i will hold it to you for my 3 ...hehe !!

What else would like to know about me Nicholas ?

LEFTCOAST72

Anytime you want to make a wish you just let me know and I'll do what I can for you. What do you do in your down time? What's your schedule like? What are your plans for the long weekend? Do you like cake or pie? Chocolate or vanilla? I could go on and on just to keep talking with you ;)

What would you like to know about me?

SENSUALSEDUCTION

LOL !! Downtime ... i love going to the beach in white rock ...even if it just to sit around and watch the ocean waves ...or the clouds roll in !!

Watching the waves?! Or the clouds roll in?! I love doing that stuff.

Dad has a boat ..so sometimes i tag along to go fishing off the coast of whiterock ... last time we made it to Galiano Island !!

I loveee going on road trips and just exploring... love camping too ...lots of outdoorsy stuff !!

i model sometimes ...and a have portfolio with a one of my girlfriend she is studying fashion design and photography !

I also love spending time with my dog !! Hes a golden retriever ... i loveeeeeeeee animals !! Except cats ... ok they are cute ...but not my animal of choice ...hehe

Hey i do have to run soon ... getting hungry ... lol

But heres my msn ...if you wanna chat for free ...

namita_007@******

LEFTCOAST72

okay. If you want to text you can I don't mind giving you my number. Or is it to soon for that? I don't know what the protocol is here.

Have fun with your friends. Again it's so nice to meet you.

Chapter 2 October 3

Last night was the first thing that popped to mind when I opened my eyes — *Was it a dream?*

I imagined what it would be like waking up next to her. What a life with her would be like. I know it's only been a couple of days but I can't help but wonder. She's intoxicating my thoughts. Part of me is trying to believe what's happening while the voice in my head keeps telling me to slow down. I can't wait to talk with her again.

Oct 3 8:39 AM

Subject: Good Morning

Good morning Namita. I trust you slept well? I hope you didn't have to get up too early as I kept you up quite late. You were the last thought I had before I fell asleep and you were the first thought I had when I awoke this morning. I want to tell you again how nice it was to meet you and I hope this is the start of something very special and long term. I'm willing to take things as slowly as we see fit as the best things are worth waiting for. I think you're worth the wait... I'm off to start my day. I just wanted to say good morning and let you know I was thinking about you. Enjoy your day and I look forward to your reply.

I hope this finds you well,

Nicholas

2:46 PM

Subject: Re: Good Morning

Hi Nicholas... WOw nice email to wake up to !! I just opened it at 2:35 pm... I did sleep well last night... although I was up by 2 am ish... couldn't sleep... thought about you too !! Hehe... Yes I'm very excited about meeting you online finally... and our conversations so far.

I still didn't close my MSN page where we were MSN-ing... so I could re-read our conversation last night. You must be at work by now... another week of hard work. How was your first part of the day ? I've been running errands here and there... also went for a walk with my dog... then he had a regular vet appointment. I love your line "you were the last thought I had before I fell asleep and..." hehe

I will be around later tonite... after you get home... if you want to chat some more on MSN. Hope you have a good day at work Nicholas !! Will look forward to chatting again.

Talk to you soon !! xo

~Namita~

    I got home about 11:30, showered, logged into messenger and turned on the TV. It wasn't long before I heard the bing from Messenger — someone's logged on. I grabbed my laptop.

Start Time: 12:12 AM

Nicholas: Hello there!

Namita: helllooooo !!

Nicholas: hi!!

Namita: How was work ?

Nicholas: I've been waiting for right now all day! was okay

Namita: hehe .... sorry i took awhile

Nicholas: totally fine

Namita: im just slipping into bed here but keep talking

Nicholas: mmm I like the sound of that 😀

Nicholas: what kind of schedule are you on?

Namita: hehe... usually im 4 on 5 off

Nicholas: ah yes

Namita: this week is pretty hectic though

Nicholas: 12 hr shifts?

Namita: yeah 12.5 hrs

Namita: day and night shifts

Nicholas: I remembered from when I was in the hospital

Nicholas: 2 years ago

Namita: what happened to you then... if i may ask ?

Nicholas: I had aortic valve replacement again... and an aortic graft

Nicholas: I had it when I was 24... well the valve replacement and the valve wore out so I have a metal one now

Nicholas: the graft was new.... and you can ask me anything anytime

Namita: oh wow ... did you stay in hospital long?

Nicholas: 6 days this last time

Namita: hope they treated you well !

Nicholas: they did. My nurses were great

Nicholas: I like that your a nurse

Namita: really ?

Nicholas: tells me a lot about you

Namita: how so?

Nicholas: tells me you're caring and compassionate by nature

Nicholas: which I really like

Namita: thx hehe... you know i never really knew that that was what I wanted to do... most of my friends thought id go the creative route... with my drawings and paintings

Nicholas: people thought I'd join the military

Namita: yes at work i totally dedicate myself to my patient and their families ... in icu (Intensive Care Unit) i take care of one patient who is on life support and cardiac monitoring

Namita: WOW military ... why did they think that?

Nicholas: I remember that when I was in icu

Nicholas: not sure

Namita: yeah it can be a little hazy being in the icu .. with all the happy drugs

Nicholas: clean cut and a bit of a military history buff

Nicholas: morphine! potent stuff

Namita: ahhh i see... what kind of history in particular fascinates you?

Namita: Hehe... yes good old morphine... some of my patient are on morphine infusions

Nicholas: canadian mostly but I like to learn about all types of history

Nicholas: I always wanted to be an astronaut when I was a kid. So the lunar landings are a huge thing for me

Namita: ahh...yes i love reading about world history... esp (especially) european history

Nicholas: oh yah

Namita: So what does your work involve Nicholas?

Nicholas: okay I'll start from the beginning

Namita: oh ok

Nicholas: is that too much or do you just want to know what I do? nutshell?

Namita: no no tell me... i loved to know

Nicholas: okay

Namita: im always a good listener

Nicholas Tombs   17

Nicholas: me too

Nicholas: okay, so we process railway castings

Namita: ok i checked that off in my list... hehe

Nicholas: I've got compassionate, caring, how can I forget beautiful, tall and independent checked off... I'm almost out of list lol

Namita: LOL !!!

Namita: Ohhhh Nicholas !!!

Nicholas: what? what did I do?

Namita: i thought you were writing about ur (your) work... hehe

Nicholas: oh right sorry side tracked

Namita: is my pic distracting you ?

Nicholas: that's been happening a lot since yesterday

Namita: lol... can you see a pic on msn?

Nicholas: I have been looking at that... I can do this bare w me

Namita: haha

Nicholas: I most defiantly can

Namita: should i change it back to the flower i had

Nicholas: my mind has been intoxicated with thoughts of you lately

Nicholas: no no please don't

Nicholas: okay work

Nicholas: lol

Namita: hehe... uh ohhh... please pay attention... lol

Nicholas: we process railway castings

Namita: uh huh ...we got that far!

Namita: hahaha

Nicholas: they come in from the foundry

Nicholas: lol

Namita: k

Nicholas: brat lol

Namita: go on... hehe

Nicholas: we air arc the flashing off

Nicholas: this may sound like pink bunnies that's if you're not familiar w the process names

Namita: ok... no not really... but do go on

Nicholas: the castings get pressed to make them straight

Nicholas: then machine the running surfaces where the train wheels run on them

Namita: ohhh cool ... I get it now

Namita: does that get shipped somewhere eventually ?

Nicholas: then the sharp edges from the machining get blended in by grinding

Nicholas: we'll get there, yes they do

Namita: lol ... oops im getting ahead of myself

Nicholas: then they get sent out to be blasted

Namita: uh huh

Nicholas: they come back to the plant and the dimensions get checked, that's where I come in

Nicholas: then they go to QA (Quality Assurance) and shipped out

Nicholas: tah duh!... thats it

Namita: ohhh wow that is some work there

Nicholas: it's big heavy things

Namita: how long have you been doing this nicholas ?

Nicholas: I started there july 22th this year. I got the job through a friend of mine I use to work w before my surgery

Nicholas: you see there use to be a middle man between the foundry and the place I'm at

Namita: ohhh cool !! Good for you !!

Nicholas: the place I'm at now decided to do all the work in house so it eliminated the middle man

Nicholas: thanks

Namita: Wow that is good for the company then and works out for you too!!

Nicholas: so I'm familiar w the product, it's quite easy work and they pay me very well too

Nicholas: okay more about you

Namita: being in a union also helps too ...you have ur benefits

Nicholas: which hospital do you work at?

Nicholas: my benefits kick in soon I think

Namita: i work in Vancouver

Nicholas: the union is why we have the high wages I think

Namita: yes that is soo true

Nicholas: oh yah... that's a long drive no?

Namita: yes it is ... i usually take the tunnel... Alex Fraser is wayyyy too busy in the mornings

Namita: do you live in Vancouver ?

Nicholas: Port Moody remember lol

Namita: ohhh yesssssss

Nicholas: what makes you live in White Rock?

Nicholas: so your at St Paul's?

Namita: well i love being near the water... and its a small community... like Port Moody

Namita: yes i am

Nicholas: I hear it's a great hospital

Namita: yes its a good hospital ... and i love the ppl (people) i work with too

Nicholas: I like living near the water too. I use to live on a sail boat that my dad built

Namita: omg ...cool !!! my dad is crazy about boats too... but i don't think he can build one

Namita: that must have been quite nice to live in one... the rocking would put you to sleep

Waiting for ~Namita~ to accept the file "IMG_1458. JPG" (1203 Kb). Please wait for a response or

Cancel (Ctrl+C)

the file transfer.

Transfer of file "IMG_1458.JPG" has been accepted by ~Namita~. Starting transfer...

Cancel

Nicholas: i just sent a pic of my hot rod, its a 1927 Roadster Pickup I built, it's commonly referred to as a T Bucket

Namita: ok its getting loaded... one sec

Nicholas: I see that

Namita: ohhh hehe

Nicholas: I thought it was on my LL (Lava Life) profile but I guess not

Nicholas: I'm trying to figure out how to put my profile pic up on here

Transfer of "IMG_1458.JPG" is complete.

Nicholas: I'm going to my mom's for the long weekend to work on it

Nicholas: and to see her too

Namita: Ohhh my... that is very cool!! i can't begin to think of how to put one together if i had to

Namita: does she live close by ?

Nicholas: Parksville

Namita: ohhh beautiful place

Namita: is that where you grew up too?

Nicholas: it is

Nicholas: it's nice to visit but my life is here

Namita: ohhh wow... now i see why you love being near the water as much as i

Nicholas: yes yes

Namita: better opportunities here on the mainland for younger ppl like us

Nicholas: yes... it's a retirement community over there and I want to live! to enjoy life

Namita: hahaha... yes so true

Nicholas: so you know, I'm not searching the dating site I'd like to see where things go with you. Thought you should know

Nicholas: so far I like where things are going

Namita: ohhh so sweet... well i haven't been on it either... except to check to see if you wrote the other day... im tired of the 60 plus year olds trying to talk to me or get my attention.. or sending me pics of their ummm ahem "you know what"

Nicholas: that's really sad

Nicholas: first contact is so important

Namita: hehe... YES... sooo gross... my dad is 66... and i have like 68 year olds trying to get my attention

Nicholas: that is gross

Namita: well even the younger ones or our age group... they are doing the same thing

Namita: it's a total turn off for me

Nicholas: I don't think like that and I'm looking for a deeper connection

Namita: there's nothing to the imagination

Namita: yesssssssssssssssssssssss me too !!!!

Namita: hehe

Namita: did you find women do it too... on LL?

Nicholas: you wouldn't walk up to someone and just flash your unit so why would you on a site? I don't get it

Nicholas: not at all... I sent out a lot of "hi there's" or "you have a nice smile" and got nothing back

Nicholas: your profile stood out to me. I admire the creativity

Namita: aweee thanks

Namita: one time i was chatting to a guy not long ago on LL ... and he asked to see my bs (back stage)... so eventually i gave it in exchange for his... and all his pics was of him and his unit... i didn't even know what he looked like... so i told him, thanks but no

Nicholas: if you want to see my creative side check out MySpace and look me up and you can see some of my projects halloween costumes, hot rod etc

Namita: ohhh ok cool ! ive never been to that site before

Nicholas: I figured it was a free website to show what I do

Nicholas: I had people asking if I have a website and I felt bad saying no so I opened an account, its free so why not

Namita: ohhh nice you must love what you do. i know... once an idea gets into ur head... i know i just want to get down to it

Nicholas: exactly!

Nicholas: my ideas start as a fuzzy ball in my mind then the more I work it out the clearer and closer it gets until it's right in front of me in my mind. Or I picture what I want then I reverse engineer it

Namita: yes i totally know what you mean!!

Nicholas: is tomorrow your last day off? then you're back on for 4?

Namita: no ... back on friday

Nicholas: oh wow

Nicholas: 4 on 5 off right?

Namita: hehe... yes 4 on DDNN then 5 off... if they dont call me on OT... or if im on call for emergency cases where they need extra nurses

Nicholas: i see

Namita: we deal with a lot of transplant cases... mostly liver or lung transplant... and those patients are usually pretty sick... where there are 2 nurses assigned to that one patient

Nicholas: how do you like the 12.5 hr shifts?

Namita: i actually prefer it cause then i get the 5 off... if i had to work 7.5 then it ends up that i have to work 5 or 6 to make up the workweek... it doesn't hurt to stay the extra 4 hrs then go home.... plus traffic is better too

Namita: i just dont like night shifts

Namita: or days for that matter ...hehe ...yes im difficult

Namita: im not a morning person... and on nights id rather be in bed

Nicholas: I can't imagine you being difficult. You seem very easy going... oh there's another check list item lol

Namita: do you guys have other shift times too?

Namita: LOL

Nicholas: oh yah. we run 24/7

Namita: No really im not a difficult person... im a pretty laid back person

Namita: i dont sit there and stress about trivial things

Nicholas: I sensed that... me either

Namita: wow we're both in a 24/7 business!! hehe

Nicholas: they're talking about different shifts at my work... talk is 10 hr days

Namita: you mean for you? or everyone?

Namita: ohh i see

Nicholas: we have collective bargaining talks coming up

Namita: i think it's better... then ur downtime is longer... or balances out at least

Nicholas: everyone

Nicholas: I dont mind either... though it would be nice to have fri nights back

Nicholas: you've got quite the slide show going w (with) your pic

Namita: lol .... yes i do get jealous of ppl being off on the weekends

Namita: hehe

Namita: thanks... im keeping you entertained

Nicholas: distracting but keep it up

Nicholas: yes you are

Namita: so which one is me in the pic ?

Nicholas: and I'm enjoying it too

Namita: lol

Nicholas: good question I thought that when I first looked

Nicholas: you're in the red

Namita: YES !!

Namita: thats my sister n my dad

Nicholas: details are my thing

Namita: and for that you get free steak knives

Nicholas: lol

Namita: yes i can see that... hehe... you are quite observant

Namita: and intuitive

Nicholas: for only $19.95 but wait we'll send you 2 sets for the price of 1

Namita: YES OMG (oh my god) how did you know !!!!!

Namita: we will double it !! or ur money back !!

Nicholas: intuition my dear

Namita: and we will throw in a snuggie too

Nicholas: or the slap chop?!

Namita: awwe i liked how you called me dear

Namita: ohhh yes slap the chop !! hahahahaha

Nicholas: interesting because i dont usually use pet names

Nicholas: oh wow. now that photo i like!... i like the others but this one wow!

From her Lava Life profile, the one with the jeans and brown long sleeve form fitting shirt.

Namita: hehe... i use it to annoy

Namita: you like !!

Nicholas: I do!

Nicholas: I feel a little bad that I don't have more for you

Namita: my friend and i... the one that is doing her fashion design... her name is Miranda... she did me up like a 60's gogo dancer... and i did her photo shoot for her portfolio

Namita: no don't worry about it Nicholas!!

Namita: im liking the one im seeing right now

Nicholas: you'll just have to see me in real life lol I'll let you take pics if you want

Nicholas: I'm so glad

Namita: yes from every angel

Namita: angle i meant

Namita: lol

Nicholas: whatever pleases you

Namita: how tall are you again ?

Nicholas: 6' 3"

Namita: OOOooOo

Nicholas: and shaved not bald lol

Namita: eye color ?

Nicholas: blue

Namita: lol... I loveeeeeeeeeeeee it !!!!!

Namita: the shaved look

Nicholas: again I'm sooo glad

Namita: ooooOOoo blue

Namita: actually i always found that look very sexy... ever since i was a kid... in my teens at least

Nicholas: that works for me

Nicholas: I like that you like it

Namita: use to watch old movies of an old actor Yul Brynner and i thought he was hot

Nicholas: cool

Nicholas: been rolling your name through my mind all day

Namita: lol

Nicholas: I love it

Namita: it is tattooed yet ?

Nicholas: lol into my brain? yes

Namita: lol

Nicholas: speaking of tattoo's do you have any?

Namita: no i don't... but i like them

Namita: i don't know if i would get one

Nicholas: I have one

Namita: you do ??? where ?

Nicholas: on my back

Namita: i wouldnt mind a small one for myself

Namita: ohhh niceeee

Nicholas: I'll send you a photo of it or my future company logo which is what my tat' is of

Namita: ahh i see... im sure it is cool!! i love looking at other ppl's tattoos ... some of them being works of art

Namita: theres my baby ive ... had him since he was a pup at 12 weeks old ... he is 8 now

Nicholas: what's your dogs name?

Namita: baloo

Nicholas: like from the jungle book?

Namita: hehe YES... i was going to ask if it rings a bell with you... but waited for ur response

Nicholas: I can't seem to get a file of my tat so I'll just have to show you one day

Namita: in person

Nicholas: yes

Namita: heheh

Namita: how long have you had it?

Nicholas: the middle part for 9 years and the rockers for 3

Nicholas: it's kind of a long story for on here.... I'll explain it to you in person

Namita: it is finished ?

Nicholas: yes

Namita: ahhh ok

Namita: what do you do in ur spare time ?

Namita: hey let me know if ur tired and need to go... ok?

Nicholas: you're killing me w the slide show. my heart skips every time you change it

I guess when you model you have a lot of photos of yourself.

Namita: lol

Nicholas: I could talk w you all night my dear

Namita: aweee thanks nicholas

Nicholas: made me forget what you asked lol

Namita: hehe

Nicholas: I remembered

Nicholas: work out when I can. work on which ever project motivates/inspires me

Namita: do you like watching movies?

Namita: do you like music ?

Nicholas: I love music!

Nicholas: you?

Namita: Me toooo!

Namita: any fav bands

Nicholas: everything between the extremes

Nicholas: fav band the Doors

Namita: yes!!

Nicholas: love the roots of rock n roll

Namita: uh huh

Nicholas: elvis, buddy holly, jerry lee lewis

Nicholas: the beach boys

Namita: i was just thinking of Elvis just now

Namita: beach boys are good too

Nicholas: Love him... been a fan of him since I was about 7

Namita: i loveeee... ok don't laugh

Namita: i loveee many 80's music… rock

Nicholas: I would never

Nicholas: i like the '80's

Namita: G&R (Guns & Roses) fan... the old school stuff

Namita: hehe

Nicholas: Lover Boy, Head Pins

Namita: yes those too... creed, brian adams

Nicholas: yes G&R

Nicholas: not a big creed fan

Namita: stone temple pilots , depeche mode

Namita: i like one or 2 songs of theirs

Nicholas: I like pretty much 50's through to modern day

Namita: eagles are good

Nicholas: STP (Stone Temple Pilots)!!! YES love them

Namita: HA !! Yes

Nicholas: love Scott Weiland's voice

Namita: yes me tooo

Nicholas: have all their albums

Namita: cool !!

Nicholas: did you hear him w/ Velvet Revolver?

Namita: i loveee old bands like puddle of mudd, stained

Nicholas: yes

Namita: no I haven't ..really ??

Nicholas: It's harder, like work out music

Nicholas: its Scott w G&R members

Namita: ohhh cool... i will have to listen to it sometime

Nicholas: like Slash

Namita: wowwwww... love slash !!!!!!!!

Nicholas: I really like it

Nicholas: have some songs on my workout play list

Namita: on ur ipod ?

Nicholas: on a disc... don't have an iPod yet

Namita: ahhh ok

Nicholas: looking at getting an iPhone soon though

Namita: i had one... till it was stolen from my car at work

Namita: arghhhhhh

Nicholas: I have a Mac laptop... I like Mac

Namita: my workout list was on it

Nicholas: damn

Nicholas: I hate, and I don't use the word hate often, when ppl steal

Namita: it wasn't even in site... it was in a compartment... and those idiots broke into it

Namita: yessss... me too

Namita: i have an iphone though... it is a 3G

Nicholas: my contract is almost up w Rogers so im thinking of switching to Fido (I know rogers owns it) and getting an iPhone and a cheaper phone bill

Namita: oh i love INXS, U2, Default, Blue Rodeo

Nicholas: I saw BR (Blue Rodeo) at the Orpheum

Namita: im with telus

Namita: i hate em !!

Nicholas: was great

Namita: Ohhh cool... i totally missed them

Nicholas: I havent heard good things about telus

Namita: i love concerts

Nicholas: seen them once, that was enough

Namita: hehe

Nicholas: I took my girls

Nicholas: did you see Bon Jovi when they were here?

Namita: no I didn't... you took ur girls to Bon jovi?

Nicholas: to BR

Namita: ohhh did they enjoy it ?

Nicholas: my ex took them to Bon Jovi

Namita: that is cool that they're exposed to music from the past

Nicholas: at BR my youngest fell asleep. It was late and the music is relaxing

Namita: hehe

Namita: uhhh ohhh

Nicholas: I'm their music history teacher like Jack Black in School of Rock

Namita: lol... well it is good that they grow up with a wide range of music

Namita: my range is pretty diverse too... there is a mix of indian... from classical indian to pop to Bollywood music

Nicholas: okay don't laugh but I like Gordon Lightfoot, Simon n Garfunkel and Neil Diamond

Namita: i know the last one... heard of Simon... but not the other

Namita: id have to look them up

Nicholas: Simon and Garfunkel from the 60's Scarborough Fair, Mrs Robinson? sound familiar now

Namita: im not laughing

Namita: yeah kinda... but id have to hear it

Nicholas: yes you are... lol

Namita: hehe

Nicholas: it's okay laugh away 😜

Namita: im giggling but not laughing

Nicholas: I can't wait to here you laugh, sorry giggle

Nicholas: or your voice for that matter

Nicholas: it will be nice to put a voice to these wonderful words

Namita: hehe... yess... im a pretty giggly person

Nicholas: thats a cool pic

So many photos it's hard to keep track of them all.

Namita: thanks

Nicholas: I love laughter

Namita: i hardly get mad or annoyed at things... except bad drivers

Nicholas: as I said in my bio I'm not easy to anger

Namita: that was a couple of months ago

Nicholas: I have great people skills. been told im very articulate too

Namita: ohhh phew !!

Nicholas: and can usually defuse a tense situation

Nicholas: I dont like conflict

Namita: good... but there wont be any defusing with me

Namita: me either... i hate it

Nicholas: i like that

Nicholas: nor me...

Nicholas: you're in bed still yes?

Nicholas: you must be fading?

Nicholas: I don't want to go

Namita: yes I'm in bed with my laptop... lights out... on my tummy

Namita: you must be tired too?

Nicholas: mmm I like the word tummy

Namita: hehe

Namita: is that ur fav part ?

Nicholas: I am but I've waited all day to talk w you

Nicholas: actually I'm a legs n bum guy

Namita: ahhhhhhh

Nicholas: I like the rest of what I've seen of you too though don't get me wrong

Nicholas: tummy's just a cute word

Namita: ohhh nooo... hehe... i always say that

Nicholas: tummy? fine w me

Namita: or belly

Nicholas: mmm that too

Nicholas: you could pretty much say anything and I'd like it

Namita: lol

Namita: you would just agree with everything i say?

Namita: hmmmmm

Namita: hehe

Nicholas: right now w how tired I'm getting I probably would but when I'm rested look out missy lol

Namita: hahaha ...now i know ur weakness

Namita: legs, bum, and lack of sleep

Nicholas: yup

Nicholas: put those all together w you and im yours

Namita: lmaooooo

Namita: NICeeeeeee !!

Nicholas: 😀

Namita: hmmm now i know what i have to do to seduce you

Namita: 😀

Nicholas: seduce away. I'd be putty in your hands

Nicholas: then you can be putty in my hands

Nicholas: it's only fair

Namita: hehehehe... hmmmm it wont take long for me

Namita: yes yes

Nicholas: in your bio it says you're passionate n sensual yes?

Namita: yes I very much am

Namita: its the pisces in me

Nicholas: I'm a gentle passionate lover who knows his way around a women's body

Namita: around all bends and curves ?

Nicholas: I hope one day I can show you so you can enjoy every second of it

Nicholas: every curve... every bend

Namita: mmmmm yesss

Namita: hehe

Nicholas: 😀

Namita: i am pretty in tune to a guys body as well... having said that... it doesn't mean that ive slept around enough to know that

Namita: i know my profile can be misleading in some ways... esp with the way ive written it... ppl think... that im solely there to sleep around with as many ppl as i can

Nicholas: that's not what i thought ... nor have i

Namita: in fact that is not my mission at all... and in reality i have not met one person from that section

Namita: no... i know you didn't... cuz our conversations has been based to get to know one another... i know that about you

Namita: youre genuine

Nicholas: I would much rather be with 1 that I have a deep connection w, a connection that grows after being intimate, than to have sex just for the sake of doing it

Namita: YES exactly !!!

Namita: its just not in me to do otherwise

Nicholas: I have quite a low # of partners compared to most

Nicholas: I like to think sex is more of a journey w someone. something to take a relationship to another level

Namita: yes and grow and explore each other... enjoy each other pleasures... even if it is just cuddling... and watching tv

Nicholas: yes!

Nicholas: I knew you got it

Namita: doing the simple things can evoke sensuality

Nicholas: yes yes

Namita: holding hands

Namita: a smile across the room

Nicholas: I love holding hands

Namita: in a room full of ppl

Namita: me too.... or laying a hand on ur guys leg as he's driving

Nicholas: yes, the little things

Nicholas: you just get it. I love that!

Namita: yes !!

Namita: im all about that!!

Nicholas: cool

Namita: or a wink from across the room... that gets me!!

Namita: i melt!!

Nicholas: I'll keep that in mind

Namita: hehehe

Namita: i dont need materialistic things to keep me happy... ive never been like that

Nicholas: the "I'm here and I'm right where I want to be, with you" kind of things

Namita: i can buy those myself if i wanted to

Namita: YES !!!

Namita: totally YES !!!

Nicholas: I think the little things mean so much more

Nicholas: there goes my heart again... every time you change your pic

Namita: yes... it sure does... cuz you remember those things the most... the memories

Nicholas: yes

Namita: building on the memories

Nicholas: life is a journey... the ride is part of that not the destination

Namita: if ur not around... ur at work or something... i can think back how you winked at me... or ur smile

Namita: those things make me smile

Nicholas: I love everything you say

Namita: Yes Omg... that is totally true

Namita: of course i do like the occasional flower... hehe

Nicholas: I'll bring you flowers just because I can and to say "hey I was thinking about you n thought you'd like these"

Namita: hehehe ...aweee thanks !!

Namita: i loveee flowers

Namita: i go crazy sometimes w/ the flowers that is... i even have a flower garden in the front of my place

Namita: all kinds of stuff in it

Namita: Nicholas ...are you tired yet ?

Nicholas: not just flowers? what kind of stuff?

Namita: huh?

Namita: lol

Nicholas: I am exhausted but as in said your bio.... "don't go"

Namita: ok

Nicholas: when can we chat again?

Nicholas: tomorrow?

Namita: yes tomorrow is good

Nicholas: or later today as it's 3:19 in the am lol

Namita: but im taking my mom to a doctors appointment

Nicholas: family first

Namita: how about 4am ?

Nicholas: okay

Namita: so you have like 40 mins

Nicholas: lol

Namita: hahaha

Nicholas: is that when you have to be up?

Namita: no no... i was kidding

Nicholas: okay good

Namita: i will be up around 10ish

Nicholas: messing w the tired guy funny

Namita: hehehe... too cute

Nicholas: I'll email you when I'm up. sound good?

Namita: yes sounds good Nicholas !!

Nicholas: okay then

Namita: ok... sleepy head

Nicholas: Good night Namita. Sleep well and I will talk with you later today lol. Thanks for sharing w me tonight... xo

Namita: hehe... enjoyed every minute of it!! we talked like 3 hrs straight!!!

Nicholas: yes we did

Namita: good run for the first time

Namita: i will be around tomorrow... you have a good sleep now... pleasant dreams always

Nicholas: it was well worth the wait as I knew you would be

Namita: aweee thanks Nicholas ... its been a pleasure!!

Namita: sweet dreams !!

Nicholas: you too

Namita: i will log off now... and let you go

Nicholas: ok

Nicholas: ☺

End Time: 3:26 AM

    I can't believe this amazing connection and she's putting in the same effort I am! I don't know if I can shut my brain off so I can sleep.

Chapter 3 October 4-5

Oct 4 7:35 AM

Subject: Gmorning

Good morning my dear,

I fell asleep about 3:30.... couldn't stop thinking of you and our wonderful conversation.... wide awake at 7... again thinking of you.... with "The Bear Necessities" running through my head lol.... I couldn't stop thinking of exploring your body.... if someone had told me that I'd be feeling the way I'm feeling I wouldn't have believed them... I feel as though me feet have been swept out from under me.... like I'm walking on 6 inches of air and I can't touch the ground... like I'm floating.... I don't want to touch the ground... I like this feeling.... it's because of you... it would have been so nice to have you curled up in my arms when I woke this morning.... one day ;)

So looking forward to talking with you again. Enjoy your day and I'll keep an eye out for you.

Nicholas

8:20 AM

Subject: RE: Gmorning

Good morning Nicholas !!! Wow that doesnt sound like much sleep !! I sure hope you get a nap in before work. Imagined if we both napped together before work...that would be cool !!

Yes i was thinking of you last night as well... imagined you sleeping next to me....hehe

I didnt fall asleep til 4am .... was listening to the rain for a bit ... which i find sooo relaxing.

I did wake up a few times afterwards ..and wondered what you must be doing?

Hope ur having a good day. Do you have to cook for ur take to work meal ...or do you grab something on the way?

Hmmm what do you mean by the "BAre Necessities" ....hehe ...please elaborate ....do tell !! Hehehe

Have i given you impure thoughts ?

Will look forward to our next chat ... if you have any questions that pop up into ur mind ...dont hesitate to ask tonite ok ?

I will be around roughly the same time ....

Have a great evening at work ... if i dont back again to you ...

Talk to you soon Nicholas !! Namita xo

12:27 PM

Hello there!. I love getting messages from you... I just woke from a nap.... I would so love to nap with you... I too have been imagining you next to me sleeping.... me listening to you breath thinking "she's really in my bed and in my world".... at 4 am I was asleep... the thoughts of you were relaxing and put me right to sleep... I baked a lasagna yesterday for my lunches. I make 4 loaf pan size ones at once and freeze them then bake one when I need to. I prefer to bring dinners as it's cheaper, easier and more healthy that way. Bare Necessities hmm... you lying next to me... under the covers.... me exploring your body.... with my hands.... with my body... touching you.... kissing you.... on your neck.... just between your shoulder and neck.... kissing your ear ever so gently... you can heard my breath... feel my body pressed to yours.... Yes on the naughty thoughts.... yes... yes... yes.... it'll be so much easier to show you ;) one day.... If you have any questions please ask... I want to tell you everything....

I will come and find you tonight. xo

Nicholas

3:37 PM

Heyyy there ...

i just got back from Langley running errands and so !! Traffic was getting so bad - but im back safe and sound... i didnt want to be there after 4pm. It just gets worse !

I loveeeee the fall weather ...seeing all the pumpkins out and the corn mazes.

Wow you sound like quite the cook - ya i agree its wayy better to make ur own meals, i do it most of the time too- hardly buy stuff in the cafeteria. Ive never made lasagna before. Thats something i should accomplish one of these days.

Yesterday i made baked salmon on cedar plank... garlic mashed potatoes... some veges/pasta with some garlic bread for our dinner with the sisters.

I still have leftovers ... so i dont think i will be cooking tonite.

Do you like east indian food ...namely the famous butter chicken ... i can make a killer butter chicken !!

Hehehe

Ive been cooking up a storm since i was 13. Some baking too. Ive always enjoyed it !

I think we should have our own cook off competition one day ! LOL

Hope ur having a good shift !!

Look forward to our chat tonite !

Namita xo

Oct 5:34 PM

Hi there. I was hoping I'd have a reply from you. Yes I'm at work. I read our LL conversation again today and looked at your photos. I can't believe how lucky I am to have found such a beautiful women with the same type of values. Our conversations keep playing through my head. I'm home about 11:30. By the time I'm showered its usually 11:45ish. I will of course look for you. ;)

Nicholas

Sent from my BlackBerry device

6:13 PM

Almost off !! Hehe ... I have my sisters over for dinner so i wont be around til about 12ish ... I hope you will be around for a bit. You must be tired too from ur long evening.

I will be on msn at that time....after i kick my sisters out !!

Hehe Talk to you soon !

Namita

Start Time: 11:49 PM

Nicholas: yes!

Nicholas: there you are

Namita: heyyy there

Nicholas: hey you!

Namita: sorry to keep you waiting

Nicholas: how are you?... you're worth it

Namita: im good... just jumped into bed

Nicholas: cool

Namita: aweee thanks !!!

Namita: hehehe

Nicholas: would be nice to be having this conversation with you, physically

Nicholas: did you see my email from dinner time?

Namita: we'd be awake all night... giggling and talking and talking

Namita: yes i did !!

Nicholas: fine w me

Nicholas: oh good

Namita: sorry didnt reply... was on a phone call one after the other

Nicholas: sokay... it didn't need a reply

Nicholas: I know you got it that's all that matters

Namita: how was work tonight ?

Nicholas: and the slide show continues

Nicholas: yes

Namita: hehehe

Nicholas: was okay... time goes by quickly

Namita: do you think i did justice with a description of myself to my profile... now that you see the pics

Nicholas: Oh my did you ever

Namita: well im glad to hear it... esp when time flies quickly

Namita: hehe

Nicholas: I'm very pleased that you're so beautiful

Namita: good genes i guess

Nicholas: and not a 65 year old man lol

Nicholas: very good jeans!

Namita: from both sides of family

Namita: hahaha

Namita: do you wear jeans to work too ?

Nicholas: I came up w a couple of questions for you

Namita: ok shoot

Nicholas: I wear black ones

Namita: hmmm nice

Nicholas: what perfume do you wear?

Nicholas: did you come up w any for me?

Namita: ah haaaa... i wear Miss Dior sometimes

Nicholas: hmm I'm not familiar w that one

Namita: other times it can be pink sugar

Namita: it was out a couple of years ago

Nicholas: have you heard of Givenchy Organza?

Namita: the first one is from Dior obviously

Namita: yes i have

Namita: is that ur fav?

Nicholas: pink sugar that must smell sweet

Nicholas: one of

Nicholas: I'm a sucker for Body Shop White musk

Namita: it is... but i have to be careful sometimes... in the spring it aggravates my allergies... but it smells sooo nice

Nicholas: I bet... I'd like to smell your sent. I'm sure it's lovely

Namita: i used to wear that body shop musk... when was in my 20's and early 30's

Namita: then i grew out of it

Nicholas: I see

Namita: is it still out there?

Namita: but i do like the musk smell

Nicholas: it is... I'm sure I'll like whatever you wear when you're w me

Nicholas: I'm open to new ones though

Namita: i see that a nice smell must be a turn on for you!!

Nicholas: very much

Namita: IT IS FOR ME TOO!!! HUGELY!!!

Nicholas: do you want to know what I wear?

Namita: yes pleaseeeeeeeeee !!!!

Nicholas: its called Nautica Voyage

Nicholas: it's light blue and a light sent

Namita: Ohhhhhhhhhhh nice .... sounds delicious!!

Nicholas: I like it

Namita: where do you get it?

Nicholas: I like to smell nice

Nicholas: I got it at London Drugs

Nicholas: I like to get a different one each time I run out

Namita: ahhhh... my other fav for myself is Shisedo's Energizer... it is japanese

Namita: yeahhh me too... i like to change things up a bit... season to season

Nichola: Shiseido I remember that name from when I was a make up artist in the film industry

Namita: OMG you were a makeup artist ????? YOu didn't tell me that!!

Nicholas: just did 😀

Namita: what kind of makeup did you do?

Namita: hehee

Nicholas: yup. Special Make up effects

Namita: WOWwwwww sooo cool!!

Nicholas: still do for halloween of course

Namita: so you're not afraid of makeup on a woman... not that i put on gobs of it

Namita: WOw that is quite the talent!!

Nicholas: not at all

Nicholas: I like it when you can't tell a women has it on

Namita: i usually just accentuate what i have

Nicholas: then of course you don't wear a lot

Namita: hehe yes true !!!

Nicholas: you probably don't need any as far as I can see

Nicholas: those good jeans and nature

Namita: well i do usually put on liquid eyeliner on top lid most times... and mascara... and some lipgloss... but if my lipgloss come off at some point during my day i dont put on more... and its not something i carry in my purse ever

Namita: lol love ur words !!!

Nicholas: my words? how so?

Waiting for ~Namita~ to accept the file "IMG_0617JPG" (1608 Kb). Please wait for a response or

Cancel (Ctrl+C)

the file transfer.

Namita: i meant when you said ... those good jeans

Transfer of file "IMG_0617.JPG" has been accepted by ~Namita~. Starting transfer...

Cancel

Nicholas: I'm sending you my halloween costume pics

Nicholas: I figured

Namita: ohhh ok

Waiting for ~Namita~ to accept the file "IMG_0621.JPG" (476 Kb). Please wait for a response or

Cancel (Ctrl+C)

the file transfer.

Nicholas: those are the 2 finished costumes

Namita: ok almost done with loading... is it for this year ?

Nicholas: this next one is a side shot of the army ant

Waiting for ~Namita~ to accept the file "IMG_0618.JPG" (1832 Kb). Please wait for a response or

Cancel (Ctrl+C)

the file transfer.

Transfer of file "IMG_0618.JPG" has been accepted by ~Namita~. Starting transfer...

Cancel

Nicholas: hopefully they don't take too long to load

Transfer of file "IMG_0621.JPG" has been accepted by ~Namita~. Starting transfer…

Cancel

Namita: ok one sec

Transfer of "IMG_0617.JPG" is complete.

Nicholas: is your mom still alive?

Nicholas: you've mentioned your dad but not your mom

Transfer of "IMG_0621.JPG" is complete.

Namita: yes mom is around... both and dad are married... they just celebrated their 43rd anniversary last week

Namita: OMG im looking at ur combat suit !!!

Nicholas: wow that's great... my parents were married for almost 41 years before my dad died

Nicholas: that's the Army Ant. its an amalgamation of a solder and the insect

Namita: Ohhh sorry to hear about ur dad... how long ago was that?

Nicholas: just over 3 years. he had CML (Chronic myelogenous leukemia)

Transfer of "IMG_0618.JPG" is complete.

Namita: Ohh yes the ant !!

Nicholas: I was sewing as Tony my best friend came in so we could go to a party that night

Nicholas: talk about down to the wire

Namita: hehehe... was it a staff party or friends party ?

Nicholas: I re-read our convo from last night and I missed one of your questions

Namita: CML? I've heard of AML (Acute Myeloid Leukemia)

She's an ICU nurse but hasn't heard of CML?

Nicholas: it's a type of leukemia

Namita: ohhh what was that ?

Nicholas: it was the Blarney Stone pub down town party

Namita: ahhhh ive heard of the place but never been there

Nicholas: we know the manager so when Tony is in town that's where we go

Namita: ohhh... ive taken care of a lot patients with AML... but rarely CML

Namita: where does He live ?

Nicholas: Armstrong

Namita: im sorry i don't even know where that is

Nicholas: we like to people watch. I like to watch the dynamics of people socializing

Nicholas: its near Penticton, Kelowna, Vernon

Namita: ohhh ok ... its been awhile since I've been to Penticton !!

Nicholas: I've ever been

Namita: i was going to go there this summer but i ended up sick and in hospital

Nicholas: oh geeze

Nicholas: from what?

Nicholas: I'm glad you're better

Namita: it is beautiful near the lakes

Nicholas: I think it's close to a lake. Tony keeps trying to get me up there and he talks of boating on a lake

Namita: i ended up with a cut on my foot the became infected to the point of me having a high fever

Nicholas: oh my god... you're better now though?

Namita: then nausea and vomiting... and that has never happened with me... that was a first time in my adulthood

Nicholas: that's a sign of something bad going on

Namita: yeah by then i knew something is not right

Namita: yes im better now

Nicholas: good

Namita: they put in an IV and gave me antibiotics for a week

Nicholas: wow!

Namita: mom and dad took me

Nicholas: oh good. to the hospital in White Rock?

Namita: to Surrey Memorial... one place i hate the most

Namita: but thank god i knew one of the doctors there... he took care of me

Nicholas: yah I've never heard good things about that place

Namita: lol

Nicholas: well I'm glad you're better

Namita: i forgot to get that tattoo... not to take me to Surrey Memorial in case of emergencies

Nicholas: lol good one

Nicholas: last night you asked me about movies? i like to watch them

Nicholas: fav (favourite) movie Shawshank Redemption

Namita: yesss

Nicholas: what's your fav movie?

Namita: hmmm... i love horror movies... so last year i watched Paranormal Activity... omfg (oh my fucking god)... i didnt sleep for a few days unless my dog was in the room with me

Nicholas: i wanted to see that

Nicholas: do you want to see the new PA? (Paranormal Activity)

Namita: i do like lord of the rings

Namita: both of the PAs... were good... you have to watch the first though

Namita: there's a third?

Nicholas: I guess I'll have to catch up then

Namita: lol

Nicholas: they've been advertising it

Nicholas: I thought the Ring was scary

Nicholas: good story to it too

Namita: yes that scary too... and the Grudge!!

Namita: i love action movies too

Nicholas: didn't see the Grudge

Namita: that is a bad one... the Grudge

Namita: im trying to think of an action movie

Nicholas: I like most movies. I'll even watch a chick flick

Namita: i also like period piece movies. based on actual events are good too

Nicholas: yes

Namita: or history

Namita: hehe a chick flick

Namita: id watch if its good

Namita: i loveeeeee the hangover... both of them

Nicholas: really? I didn't see it

Nicholas: another question

Namita: yes go ahead

Nicholas: what do you sleep in? and don't say a bed lol

Namita: hehehe... i sleep in a short nightie most times... ive never been a pj kinda girl... i find it too retractive

Namita: if its really hot... in the summer... im in the buff

Namita: lol

Namita: what about you ?

Nicholas: that id like to see

Nicholas: boxers and a t shirt most nights... in the summer just the boxers

Namita: ahhh nice

Nicholas: I like the sound of you in the buff

Namita: hehehe... i can't stand being hot... id rather be cold

Namita: does lingerie turn you on ?

Nicholas: oh so very much

Namita: any fav color ?

Nicholas: yes... satin blue

Nicholas: my fav color is blue

Nicholas: would love to see you in something satin blue

Namita: omg my fav color is blue as well... and greens

Nicholas: seriously?!

Namita: yes seriously!!!... ever since i was kid

Nicholas: like peas in a pod we are

Namita: it just reminds me of the ocean

Namita: i always gravitate towards blue

Nicholas: me too

Namita: hehehe

Nicholas: it's a calm color too

Namita: yes it sure is... i always think maybe im a pisces... and that's why i loveee blue so much

Namita: what sign are you nicholas?

Nicholas: good thing i have a strong heart, coz it skipped again

44   Love On Line? A Tale Of Internet Dating

Photo change

Namita: hehehe

Nicholas: cancer

Nicholas: July 2

Namita: another water sign !!!

Nicholas: your feb to march

Namita: there you go!!!!

Namita: well 2 of my sisters are cancer

Namita: march

Nicholas: cool... march what?

Namita: march 4

Nicholas: cool... you're 4 months older than me

Namita: omg am i older than you !!!?...ARGHHHHHHHHHHHHHHHHH !!!!!!!

Nicholas: I like older women lol

Namita: lol

Nicholas: only in months

Namita: nice one !! butter me up !!... hehehe

Nicholas: we're the same age really

Namita: yes yes !!! i can bug you about it !!

Nicholas: you have so many different looks I'm looking at yet another profile photo

Namita: you can be my slave for 4 months

Nicholas: oh yah?... what would you have me do?

Nicholas: each pic of you is a different look... I like them all

Namita: hehehe... pamper me... rub my feet... carry me to bed... tuck me in... make me breakfast... actually carry me to the breakfast table in the morning

Namita: hmmmmm im thinking

Nicholas: I can do that lol

Namita: hehehe

Namita: im sure you wont be complaining anytime in that 4 months

Nicholas: I can give you the best body massage ever

Namita: Mmmmmmmm nice

Nicholas: I would have nothing to complain about being with you

Namita: hehehe you'd be loving every minute of it

Nicholas: yes I would

Namita: i had a question... kinda off topic though

Nicholas: okay

Namita: do you have any siblings?

Nicholas: yup a sister. 2 years older. lives with her girl friend in Vancouver

Nicholas: see I said you could ask anything

Namita: ahhh ok... so just the 2 of you... are you close to her?

Nicholas: as close as we need to be

Namita: ohh thats good !!

Namita: does she have kids?

Nicholas: nope

Nicholas: my 2 are the only grandkids

Nicholas: really there's me, my sis, my mom and my grampa thats pretty much it for close by

Namita: ahhh... do your girls get to see grandma often?

Namita: aunts and uncles ?

Nicholas: I have rellies in England but I rarely see them

Nicholas: they dont see my mom as often as we'd like as she's in Parksville

Namita: what is your background Nicholas ?

Namita: yes thats understandable

Nicholas: I have an aunt and uncle in Sask (Saskatchewan)

Nicholas: background? as in heritage?

Namita: yes

Nicholas: my dad was canadian and my mom's british

Namita: ohhhhh ok... have you been to england ?

Nicholas: last time I went to England I was 14

Namita: ahhhh

Nicholas: it was my granny and granddad's 50 wedding anniversary... they were married for 52 years before my granddad died

Namita: aweeee thats so sweet !!

Nicholas: you see my grampa isn't a blood relative but he's the only grampa I know

Nicholas: my dad's dad died a long time ago fortunately. he was a poor excuse for a human being. then my gramma married my grampa and the rest is well history

Namita: ohhh good to hear that ur grandma was able to have a better life for herself

Nicholas: she was. I've thanked my grampa for marrying her and giving her a better life

Nicholas: before my dad died I made sure I didn't leave anything left unsaid

Nicholas: so I still do that w family and friends

Namita: that is sooo good of you to say that... when time slips away... it is hard to convey what is in ones heart

Nicholas: it is

Namita: did you have a good relationship with ur dad?

Nicholas: I did... the best

Namita: that is good !!

Namita: yes im sure that void will be there for a long time

Nicholas: forever

Namita: im really close to my parents too... and i don't know what id do should something happen to them

Nicholas: you never get over it you just find ways to keep moving forward

Namita: i always give them a hug

Nicholas: yes

Namita: yes i understand what you are saying

Nicholas: tell them how much you love them always

Namita: yes i always do... and how much i appreciate them

Nicholas: yes

Nicholas: I'll do anything for them

Namita: we`ve always had a good relationship... i was never a problem child... lol

Namita: yes me too !!

Nicholas: my dad wasn't able to do much near the end so i did it for them

Namita: that is so good Nicholas!! im sure he was proud of you and still is!!

Nicholas: my mom said that he was, that they both are

Nicholas: side note, this new pic doesn't look like you?

Namita: awweee so nice! does ur mom live by herself?

Namita: hehe yes new pic

Nicholas: she does

Nicholas: doesn't look like the last one

Nicholas: I still like it it's just different

Namita: ohhh the new pic is me... no makeup probably

Nicholas: ah... not to worry coz I still like it

Namita: hehehe

Nicholas: I don't want to rush things but when can we exchange phone numbers?

Namita: it was taken around new years 2011

Nicholas: when was the pic in your LL profile taken? the one in the jeans and the snug brown long sleeve top?

Namita: how about tomorrow... my cell isnt charged properly right now... and the cord is too short for me

Who needs their phone to give out their phone number?

Nicholas: that's cool... just wondered... eventually I get to see you in real life yes?

Namita: hehe you like the jeans one... that was almost exactly last year... the pic where im looking away... with brown hair... is from last october

Namita: yes of course

Nicholas: I can hardly stand the anticipation now I'm going to be a basket case when I can see you... I'll keep it together

Namita: lol

Nicholas: yes I like the jeans pic. its very classy

Namita: you can see the curves too

Namita: do you like long hair ?

Nicholas: very much so... love those curves... cant wait to explore them all!

Namita: hehehe... hope you dont get dizzy... ohhh to hell with it... i know cpr... so ur good !!

Nicholas: I like your hair... up... down... as long as it's part of the package then I'm in

Nicholas: cpr... maybe a little mouth to mouth too?

Namita: hehehe... ive always had it longer... and its kinda black- brown color

Nicholas: I love it

Namita: yes i know a little mouth to mouth action !!

Namita: long lashes... the big eyes... well what do you think so far?

Nicholas: as I said in my last email 90% of my brain is currently being taken up thinking of you

Namita: lol !!!

Namita: you know sometimes i found on LL if ppl heard that im east indian... they would say... ahhh no thanks not into indian women... or they are just not open to women of other races... they were specifically after blondes

Nicholas: their loss and my gain

Namita: hehe... that sums it up right there!!

Nicholas: I've had a silly little grin on my face since Sun night after our first chat that hasn't left

Nicholas: sometimes i giggle to myself and catch myself so ppl don't think I'm crazy

Namita: ahhh i can imagine!!! i really thought you were cute when i first saw ur pic on LL

Nicholas: well thx

Namita: loveed ur eyes... ur shaved head... ur smile... ur arms... the little glint in ur eyes

Nicholas: they're even better in real life

Namita: hehe im sure they are !!!

Nicholas: glint?! really no one has ever seen that

Nicholas: I'm so glad you're as into me as I'm into you

Namita: lol...no really !?!?!... i said to myself... Omg who is that !!!!

Nicholas: seriously, no one has ever seen that in me... I'm glad you can

Nicholas: that's so nice to hear

Nicholas: when I saw your pics for the first time I said... oh my f**kin' god, she beautiful! you've got to be kidding me

Namita: aweeee well it is true from my end

Namita: Lmaoo (laughing my ass off)

Nicholas: I think I was actually shaking too

Namita: thats why i waited to give them to you... i didnt want to miss ur reaction... its not that im high on my looks... in fact ive never been that way

Nicholas: again, I'm so glad that the feelings are mutual

Namita: ohhh noooo u were shaking !!?

Nicholas: I was. I was able to calm down... I didn't want to start rambling

Namita: lol ...oh Nicholas !!... you crack me up!!

Nicholas: you see this kind of thing doesn't happen to me. women I'm attracted to don't usually give me the time of day so when you responded I was a little taken back

Namita: hehe well rest easy... im here

Nicholas: I'm still holding my breath a little. I'll be fine once I can touch you... well I might skip around a little at first lol kidding, that's the goof ball in me

Namita: hahahaha... maybe touch me... or ask me to pinch you!!

Nicholas: sure that works

Namita: hehe... ohhhh myyyy

Nicholas: I'm down right giddy at times. if someone told me I'd feel this way I'd have said they were crazy. I've never felt this way before

Namita: i can almost hear you giggling!!

Nicholas: I feel like life has just said "hey you can go to the front of the line" or something like that

Namita: lol

Nicholas: I burst out in a big smile at work walking across the yard

Nicholas: and thought I hope the guys can't see me. they're going to think I'm loopy

Namita: ohhhh Nicholas... well you sound like a wonderful person!! and we share so many qualities and similarities

Nicholas: so do you... and yes we do

Namita: or they would have thought... oh he got some tonight !!

Nicholas: I can't wait to see you

Nicholas: lol

Namita: hehehe

Nicholas: I'm pretty quiet at work

Namita: really ? is it because ur newish ?

Nicholas: I don't think so. it's just the way I am... and most of the conversations aren't that stimulating so I just read my book... I'm friendly and out going Im just not splashy about it

Namita: you know im kinda like that too at work... i dont get involved with drama... i do my work... and occasionally i will go out for breakfast or dinner with staff after work... i dont drink so i dont feel i have to entertain ppl in that sense

Namita: i keep to the patient and omg the family drama... and thats enough for me

Nicholas: yup... this job is something to do and the checks clear, is what I always say

Nicholas: for me I'm usually doing the work but my mind is working on one of my projects

Namita: ur creative juices flowing in a project !!

Nicholas: I have trouble shutting my mind off at night. I have to mentally slow down in order to sleep

Nicholas: they are or do

Nicholas: I can visualize things to the point of being able to walk around it and be able to hear the stones under my boots

~Namita~ would like to send you the file "NP~august.jpg" (122 Kb). Do you want to

Accept

(Ctrl+G) or

Decline

(Ctrl+C) the invitation?

Transfer of file "NP~august.jpg" from ~Namita~ has been accepted. Starting transfer...

Cancel

You have successfully received NP~august.jpg from ~Namita~. Before opening this file, you may want to scan it with a virus-scanning program.

Namita: yes i can understand what ur saying

Namita: just sent a pic of a wedding i went to this august

Nicholas: I dont have the means to build it here so I have to work out all the details in my mind so when I can build it the trouble shooting is mostly done

Nicholas: I'm trying to look

Namita: im wearing a traditional indian sari

Nicholas: wow! still can't believe this is you. it'll take some time to sink in but I'll get there

Namita: lol

Namita: hehehehe... are u kinda familiar to a sari

Nicholas: sounds familiar but not really

Nicholas: it looks shear in places

Nicholas: like the sleeve

Namita: its usually a half top... something sexy... and a wrapped around in a long silk or satin... or see thru sari fabric... with lots of embroidery work on it

Namita: the entire thing is sheer... but the bottom half you wear a thin skirt to tuck the sari into and make the folds

Namita: i was trying to give you the most recent pic of myself

Nicholas: shear... sexy

Namita: hehe

Nicholas: you look wonderful

Namita: aweee thanks Nicholas

Nicholas: so I've been thinking that for our first date I was hoping to not have any time restrictions if that's okay.. As in meeting for lunch but I have to go to work kind of thing

Namita: ohhh yes not a problem... keep it casual !!

Namita: and relaxed

Namita: we will let things flow

Nicholas: yes but not quite what I mean

Nicholas: it sounded diff (different) in my head

Namita: ohhh i missed the point... hehe

Nicholas: I want to spend as much time w you as possible especially after waiting so long... with out having to rush off to something like work

Namita: ohhh i see... yes that is cool with me !!

Nicholas: I know it hasn't been that long yet but it might be once our schedules jive

Nicholas: I do like that photo

Namita: ur fav ? hehe

Nicholas: could be though the one in the jeans is hot too

Nicholas: fav head shot ok

Namita: ohhh yesss the jeans !!!

Nicholas: jean fav body shot

Namita: hehehehe

Nicholas: it's really more the top and the smile

Namita: most ppl say i have a nice smile!

Nicholas: yes you do

Namita: and a killer body

Namita: hehe

Namita: hehe aweee thanks... i dont do a lot though... running around at work is sometimes enough for me

Namita: both of our work is quite physical i believe

Nicholas: really? heavy women must hate to hear that

Nicholas: I don't have any trouble w my weight

Nicholas: I like were I'm at

Namita: ohhh good !! it is just better to be content with what you have and lead a happy healthy life

Nicholas: yup

Namita: you look like you have strong arms though!

Nicholas: I gained about 25-27 lbs since high school mostly muscle from working out since I was 15

Nicholas: well shaped and toned i guess

Namita: Mmmmmmmmm niceeee

Nicholas: which is what I've always tried for

Namita: i love strong arms !!

Nicholas: good to know

Namita: whats ur fav part of a woman's body?

Namita: oh never mind you answered that yesterday

Nicholas: legs

Namita: and bum ?

Nicholas: strong shapely smooth legs

Nicholas: yes bum too

Nicholas: ok so here's something you don't know yet

Nicholas: and I hope you like it too

Namita: ok tell me !!... 😀

Nicholas: my head and face aren't the only thing that are shaved

Namita: hehehe... omg you shave ur legs ???

Nicholas: lets just say the longest hair on my body is my eye brows... I use clippers and do my entire body

Nicholas: it's cooler in the summer and easier to get clean w/o hair

Namita: ahhhh i see... sounds reasonable !!

Nicholas: I use to use a blade on my body but it was too much trouble

Nicholas: oh and I don't have hair on my back

Nicholas: and I don't snore

Namita: hehehehe

Namita: yayyyy score !! no snoring

Nicholas: I sleep with my mouth closed

Namita: i dont shave ANYTHING

Nicholas: jungle women?!

Namita: i alway sleep with my mouth open... with drool running out

Nicholas: haha... liar

Namita: yes of course the only way to go !!

Namita: NOPE !! hehe

Nicholas: that is sooooo hot

Namita: yes and im missing a chicklet tooth and i carry a snuff box

Nicholas: also if men expect their women to be shaved then they should reciprocate I think

Nicholas: lol

Namita: UH huh !!

Nicholas: n spit

Namita: we put so much work into making ourselves presentable

Namita: yes i spit too ... so pls have a spit can ready for me

Nicholas: lol

Nicholas: we have so much in common

Nicholas: i like to whittle too

Namita: hehehe yes we do

Namita: what habits turn you off ?

Nicholas: poor table manners

Nicholas: rude people

Namita: thats the first thing i thought of just now... ppl chewing with mouths open is one

Nicholas: ignorant ppl

Namita: yes yes !!!

Nicholas: elbows on the table. when ppl hold their fork like it's a shovel

Namita: uh huh !!!

Nicholas: especially when they put something in their mouth

Namita: lol... i hate ppl who smoke

Namita: i just cant breathe properly being around them

Nicholas: I don't like it when ppl smoke around me

Nicholas: yes smoking is a deal breaker when it comes to dating

Namita: for me too... it just wont work for me

Nicholas: it's gross and stinks

Namita: total turn off for me !

Nicholas: I find it offensive when someone in the car in front of me is smoking and I smell it

Namita: me too ...or they blow the smoke into my face

Namita: hence why ive never been a clubber type of person... cuz i dont drink or smoke

Nicholas: being on blood thinners I don't drink

Namita: ohh yes... i forgot... you must be on coumadin

Nicholas: I may have one drink when out w Tony but I drive too so 1 is all I'll have

Nicholas: warfarin... same thing

Namita: yes same... its the other name for it

Nicholas: right

Namita: it is also rat poison in a different dosage

Nicholas: yup

Namita: hehe

Nicholas: my kids didn't like it when they heard that

Namita: I SO HATE RATSSSSSSS !!!!!

Nicholas: ew

Namita: if im grossed of anything its rats... and sometimes those big spiders

Nicholas: oh those f**ckers can get big

Namita: i saw one rat one time last year.. that my dog found... i almost became physically sick... i couldn't eat for days

Nicholas: geeze

Nicholas: we're just about up all night again talking only diff is I'm not in bed w you

Namita: yessss those spiders are huge... i found one last week in my living room... i put a jar onto it... and was going to pick it next day... and my sister knocked it over... she didnt see it... so we`re both screaming and running around again

Nicholas: lol that's too funny

Namita: hehehe... you must be tired

Nicholas: I capture them and let them go outside

Namita: i try to

Nicholas: I am but this is my "you" time. I wait all day for this

Namita: please let me know if have to go... i dont want to keep u up all night

Nicholas: and I need to get my fill of you, if that's possible until I can have some physical time too

Nicholas: I will.... a little longer please 😊

Namita: hehe no worries

Namita: any other pressing questions you have… im a pretty open person

Nicholas: we'll have plenty of up all night talking I'm sure of it

Namita: you dont have to refrain from anything with me

Namita: ohhhhh yesss we will

Nicholas: okay here goes

Namita: ok

Nicholas: do you like to be on the top or bottom?

Namita: i like both actually

Nicholas: me too!

Namita: i love variety

Nicholas: though I prefer the bottom that way I have better use of my hands

Namita: where would ur hands be then

Nicholas: but top is good too

Nicholas: holding your hips so I can press myself deeper inside you... maybe touching your breasts too

Namita: mmmm niceee

Nicholas: I cant wait to show you

Namita: i would love ur big hands on my breasts... im a very sensitive person... that would turn me on

Namita: would you like to know the size?

Nicholas: I'd have you lean forward so we're chest to breasts and all you'd have to do is feel me sliding in and out of you pausing ever so slightly at the tip

Nicholas: let me guess

Nicholas: 36 CC

Namita: ok guess... and omg ur turning me on already

Namita: yesss they are!!

Nicholas: I'm all ready there

Nicholas: really?!

Namita: WOw you are quite observant

Nicholas: bang on?!

Namita: BANG ON !

Nicholas: that's a perfect handful for me

Nicholas: I think

Namita: small nipples... but not too small

Nicholas: silver dollar size yes?

Namita: yes

Nicholas: oh my god

Namita: what ?

Nicholas: talk about a wish come true

Namita: hehe really?

Namita: why ?

Nicholas: you're perfect as far as I'm concerned

Namita: hehe

Namita: can i ask you a question

Nicholas: of course

Namita: do you enjoy oral?

Nicholas: giving or receiving. or both?

Namita: yes both

Nicholas: yes... especially if you're shaved

Nicholas: I'd go down on you with the appetite of a starving man

Namita: yes i thought i told you im shaved... ohhh oops... no i said it was a jungle

Namita: OMG Nicholas

Namita: for a long time ?

Nicholas: long time?

Namita: i mean would you go down for awhile ? You wont tire of it?

Nicholas: I wouldn't stop till you pop

Namita: MMMMMMMMMM WOW !!!

Namita: you wont be disappointed in that department

Nicholas: oh my

Namita: I can orgasm multiple times

Nicholas: oh good

Namita: im gifted in that sense... hehe

Nicholas: I know what will happen for me so getting you off as many times as you can handle is part of the turn on for me

Nicholas: good to know... can't wait

Namita: ohhhhhhhh Nicholas !!! that is soooo sweet !!

Namita: But i loveeeeeeeeee recuperating the love

Namita: i love going down too

Nicholas: mmm

Namita: enjoy hearing the moans of pleasure

Namita: then coming up and kissing u

Namita: if u dont mind that

Namita: then going back down again

Nicholas: not at all

Namita: paying attention to every sensitive area

Nicholas: we're going to need 5 or 6 hours the first time around

Namita: hehehee... lol... yesssssss

Namita: what would be ur fav position?

Nicholas: you on top as I described

Namita: ahhh ok

Nicholas: w my hands on your hips

Nicholas: you like it from behind too?

Namita: my hands on ur chest

Namita: yessss i loveeeeeeeeeee it !!

Nicholas: you sitting up yes

Namita: its a deeper penetration

Nicholas: it so is

Nicholas: we'll add that too

Namita: hehe

Namita: are you getting hot? or already there?

Nicholas: and hit the G spot just diff

Nicholas: oh I'm way past hot

Namita: hahaha

Nicholas: you?

Namita: yes the G spot is very sensitive for me

Namita: so much that

Namita: yes im getting there tooo

Namita: may i ask what you look like down there

Nicholas: you can

Namita: hehe

Namita: brat !!

Namita: now im shy

Namita: so ur cut ?

Nicholas: yup

Namita: ohhh ok

Nicholas: that okay?

Nicholas: almost 7 inches and thick

Namita: ohhh yesss of course it is

Namita: ohhh myyyyy

Namita: thicker is good

Nicholas: I think you'll be pleased w size and how I use it

Namita: can you tell im shy

Nicholas: maybe a little

Namita: hehe

Nicholas: shy is cute

Nicholas: I dont mind

Namita: not all the time though

Namita: how open are you sexually?

Nicholas: you'll be more comfortable once you know my body better

Nicholas: pretty open

Namita: in what way... give me an example

Namita: you dont have to answer anything if ur not comfortable though

Namita: maybe you can tell me what's ur idea of being open?

Nicholas: hmm open to suggestions while in the moment, able to improvise, able to listen to you and adjust when needed

Nicholas: what's your idea of open?

Namita: using other means like toys to our sexual relationship... or different places

Namita: toys for ur pleasure too

Nicholas: oh most defiantly

Nicholas: my pleasure like what?

Namita: hehe

Nicholas: outdoor sex is so much fun!

Namita: im sure there must be things out there for guys

Namita: yes outdoor sex is cool

Nicholas: not as much as for women

Namita: they do have those vibe rings for guys to put around their cocks

Namita: sorry have to put it that way

Nicholas: they do n I have one

Namita: you have one?

Nicholas: I do

Namita: do you like it?

Nicholas: the vibe sits right where the clit should be

Namita: ive never seen one

Namita: ohhhhhh

Nicholas: well you can see mine lol

Namita: hehe

Nicholas: it's more for your pleasure

Namita: ohhh

Namita: i didnt know that

Namita: oops... hehe

Nicholas: we can go to a sex shop one day if you like

Namita: whats ur take on multiple partners

Namita: yes yes would love to

Nicholas: never had the opportunity and would be more comfortable with a 2nd women. not big on another man in the room

Namita: lol

Namita: so you would go for a second woman... what would you do to her ? or is she an accessory

Namita: im open to ideas... im not closed to any

Nicholas: I'm not really sure as I've never had the opportunity

Namita: ahhhh ok

Namita: ive never been in a situation like that either man or woman

Nicholas: I guess it would be finding the right 3rd and going from there

Namita: but i get asked that

Namita: yes true .... and alot of trust

Nicholas: yes

Nicholas: I sometimes think it would be easier when you're not involved w one of them but I don't know... depends how strong the relationship is

Namita: yes... it all boils down to trust and comfort level

Namita: i wont even consider if i wasnt committed to my partner

Namita: for all i know he can run off with the other

Nicholas: it sound like a great fantasy but once you do it you cant take it back and I wouldn't want to hurt you

Nicholas: that's right... there's so much more to consider emotions wise

Namita: yes... it is such a fantasy... and you have to be 100 percent sure of what ur doing and what the mindset is of one another

Nicholas: yes

Namita: yes sooo true again... theres the whole emotional investment

Nicholas: saying you're okay watching me have sex w someone else is way diff when you're right there

Namita: are you still HOT?

Nicholas: that's how open I am to talking about everything

Nicholas: I can't wait to... excuse the wording, burry myself deep in side you till you pop!

Namita: OMG

Namita: you would be one wet guy then

Nicholas: that's how hot I am right now

Namita: ohhh god !!!

Nicholas: mmm love the sound of how wet I'm making you

Namita: and what if i squirt if ur doing that?

Namita: are you ok with it?

Nicholas: of course... you're a squirter? I've never been with anyone that did

Namita: yes i am... if you get me going... hehe

Nicholas: we'll just put down some towels

Namita: ever since the beginning of my thirties i have been

Nicholas: cool

Namita: Nicholas i know ur fading... you should go to sleep

Nicholas: I looked at the time earlier too

Nicholas: before I forget and once your phone is charged

Nicholas: here's my phone #***-***-****

Nicholas: shoot me a text when you can so I can save your number okay?

Namita: ok got it

Nicholas: I'm so looking forward to seeing you

Namita: lol

Nicholas: whenever that may be

Nicholas: are you around in the morning-ish

Nicholas: these late nights are fun but they're going to be the death of me

Namita: yes i may be around for a bit

Nicholas: ok

Namita: im so sorry

Nicholas: I'll email or text if i have your # by then and say hi

Namita: we`re so opposite in that sense

Namita: ok i will be in touch

Nicholas: ok gnght XO

Namita: sweet dreams

Nicholas: you too

Namita: XO

Nicholas: XX

Namita: OO

End Time: 3:58 AM

Chapter 4 October 5-7

Oct 5 2:35 PM

Subject: Heyyyy

Heyyyy Nicholas ... I finally have a few minutes to say hi... I've been quite busy all morning. I had a call this morning... my sister fell or slipped down her stairs at home and busted her knee. So I've been running around dropping the kids off to school and daycare. Her hubby is at work and can't get off right now. So off to the hospital I go with her... she will need surgery now. Geeze what a morning.

Hope things are well with you. You must be off to work by now. I will try to be in touch with you. But I have to again pick up the kids and maybe look after them. Long story... will tell you later.

Talk to you later...

Ciao Namita

5:34 PM

Subject: Re: Heyyyy

Oh geeze! I'm sorry to hear that. She's going to be okay though right?

Do what you have to. Family first. I can catch up w you later.

Thinking of you xo

Nicholas

Sent from my BlackBerry device

7:57 PM

Hey.... just a crazy day on my end !! Hope work is going well for you.

I haven't forgotten about you... hehe

I will be around tonight... the usual time.

We can catch up then.

Yes I've enjoyed our chats also last night... I didn't sleep till about 4 am... but was up by 7:30-ish when i got the dreaded call.

Oh well... hehe

Did you have your break yet ? What did you have for dinner?

Cheers ~Namita~

PS thinking of you too!!

8:39 PM

I do love talking with you :) just on break now. I hope you've had time to come down from your whirl wind day. How is your sister doing? Looking forward to chatting later.

xo Nicholas

Sent from my BlackBerry device

8:47 PM

She just came out of surgery about an hour ago now... and waking up. I'm taking care of the kids right now... and will be dropping them to school in the morning... well at least the niece. The nephew is only 3 yrs old right now.

Her husband cant get time off work due to some important meeting so I'm taking over the day tomorrow.

I just had some dinner not long ago... yeah a late dinner. The kids are in bed... dog has been fed... thank god! Hehehe... but generally they have been good... usually they behave with me.

I'm unwinding a bit... I hope I don't crash !

But don't worry i will be around when ur home.

Hope you have a good break... how long is it anyway? Like 30mins ?

Talk to you soon !

xo Namita

Sent from my iPhone device

Oct 6 12:45 AM

Glad to hear your sister is going to be okay.... You had a busy day today and you have to be up to get your niece to school on time.... we've had a couple of late nights and we're both a little deprived of sleep.... I waited for you but you've probably fallen asleep... not to worry I'm not going anywhere.... I will be here tomorrow... and the next day....

Sleep well my Indian princess...

xo Nicholas

1:46 AM

OMGGG so sorry ...its like 1:45 right now... and I just woke up from a deep sleep. I did wake from a nap... but don't remember falling back to sleep again. I'm sorry if I kept you waiting Nicholas.

But I'm sure you must have been tired too from a long shift at work. By the end of the work week I'm sure you must be extra tired.

I think in one of our early conversations I missed a question from you that didn't get answered... ur question was "what does my name mean" ...well there is not a direct meaning ...but it was once a name of a indian princess back in the mogul times in india... I'm talking wayyy back in the 1300's to 1400's time period ....

I also found out that it was once a name of a perfume from Guerlain a french brand. I have yet to get my hands on it!!

Have a great sleep Nicholas... pleasant dreams to you.

Send me a pic of urself... hehe

xo Namita

I bet I can find this perfume she's talking about.

8:48 AM

Good morning.... I hope you slept well....not to worry.... I waited till 12:45 so not too late.... I imagined you sleeping so beautiful and peaceful.... I was pretty exhausted.... was nice to catch up on my sleep.... though I prefer talking with you.....

If my calculations are correct our schedules should jive on the 22nd... if so, would you like to do something?.... I don't mind what just as long as can I see you... let me know... I'll see what I can do about your photo request 😊.... how about a shirtless bathroom pic? lol.... that is the norm isn't it? lol... though I would do something more creative... talk to you soon

xo Nicholas

11:26 AM

Hey Nicholas...yes I did sleep well last night. I'm glad you were also able to catch some sleep as well.

I've been running all over the place again today... hehe… doing this and that... taking care of the 3yr old.

You must be back to work again... I was online earlier hoping to chat with you for a little bit when I came home briefly... but then had to go away soon.

On October 22nd ...im working that weekend on shift trades i did like 6 months ago...ARghhh !! if i had known id be spending that weekend with you... I would never have done it. I cant even undo it !!

I'm sure something else will come up ...will let you know ok ? Hmmm even so ...what would we do... I'm curious... hehe... evening out in the city? walking at Rocky Point Marina? love that area

Would love to see a pic of you for myself... I don't want to go to LL to see it. I start to get hounded with the sleazy ppl... and then they get mad when I don't respond to them... lol I will be online tonite... for sure... will try to aim for bed earlier... as I have work in the morning...

So maybe we can chat for a bit before sleep...

Look forward to it...

Talk to you soon .... xo

~Namita~

Start Time: 11:56 PM

Nicholas: hey you!

Namita: heyyyyyyyyyyyyyyyy

Nicholas: it's soooo good to finally talk with you

Nicholas: i missed you last night

Namita: yes me too !! How was work ?

Nicholas: was okay... as usual

Nicholas: how was your day?

Namita: ok ... was able to kinda unwind for a bit

Nicholas: thats good

Namita: although it was busy

Nicholas: how is your sis (sister) doing?

Namita: she had surgery last night ... they put in some metal hardware into her knee ... she having lots of pain... taking her meds

Nicholas: what happened? like how did she fall?

Namita: she slipped at the end of her landing coming down the steps with the kids and her knee smashed onto the floor

Nicholas: is this the sis that was over for dinner the other night?

Namita: yes she is one of them... i have 3 sis

Namita: they were all over

Nicholas: 3 sis and 1 bro right?

Namita: no brothers

Nicholas: oh

Namita: hehe

Nicholas: for some reason i thought there was a bro mixed in there

Namita: just 5 women in the house plus poor dad... growing up

Nicholas: your dad must really feel out numbered lol

Namita: oh he is outnumbered for sure... and he knows not to argue

Namita: he always had a dog though... male of course

Nicholas: smart man

Namita: yes... hehe... but he always says he is glad to have all girls

Nicholas: i can understand that

Namita: well if he knows what is right for him... hehe

Nicholas: i much prefer having girls than boys

Namita: really ...why is that ?

Nicholas: there's so much alpha male crap that goes on w boys as they're growing up

Nicholas: girls mature faster too

Namita: yes true ... girls are much more fun too

Namita: yes i was going to say that too

Nicholas: ive always related better w girls/women

Namita: aweee cute... are you close to ur girls?

Namita: do they enjoy their time being with you ?

Nicholas: oh yah.

Namita: were you guys married ?

Nicholas: yes

Nicholas: officially happily divorced as of April the 8th 2010

Namita: good for you nicholas !!

Namita: does she live in lower mainland too ?

Nicholas: they do. they're about 10 mins away

Namita: talking about kids would you want more... i know... kinda loaded question... hehe

Nicholas: i dont. i think im too old for more. i dont want to be the old guy at my kids graduation

Namita: lol

Nicholas: is that something you've wanted?

Namita: im not so sure anymore either

Namita: if it happens it happens... if not then im not going to regret it either

Nicholas: that's good. lol if it happens it happens... you either make it happen or you don't

Namita: hehehe

Namita: yes true

Nicholas: im very careful and have alway practiced safe sex

Namita: yes me too

Nicholas: and never had any STD's

Namita: me either... NEVER !!

Nicholas: how long have you been on LL?

Namita: I've always been super super careful about that

Nicholas: good to know

Namita: hmmm over a year... on and off

Nicholas: as a teenager i use to have dreams that I'm about to have sex but i was too busy running around looking for a condom... hows that for being careful? lol

Namita: and ive never met anyone from that site just purely for sex... its just not my thing

Namita: lol... even in your dreams ??

Nicholas: I only asked because I saw on your other profile today that it had a 2008 date on it. I know you were waiting for me and I'm sorry it took me so long to find you

Namita: its now engrained into you to have a condom

Namita: hehe... yes the relationship one has been on there longer

Nicholas: i dont do random. i never go home w anyone i meet the first time

Namita: and ive just activated it... so you could read the bio the other day

Nicholas: it took time for me to zero in on where to look

Namita: yes i was patiently waiting

Nicholas: thank you

Nicholas: I'll make up for lost time

Namita: do I get a coupon of a slurpee just for waiting that long

Namita: coupon or a slurpee... that should read

Nicholas: slurpee coupon? hell i'll give you the full meal deal honey

Namita: hahahaha

Namita: do i get a toy too

Nicholas: theres lost time to make up for so its hammer down

Nicholas: yes you can have a toy

Nicholas: how long have you been single?

Namita: we can both use the toy

Nicholas: we can

Nicholas: im jumping right into more questions

Nicholas: didnt think i needed to ask

Namita: last bf was in 2009... then he decided i wasnt enough for him

Nicholas: stupid guy but lucky me

Nicholas: how long was your longest relationship?

Namita: he was Indian too... he just wasnt being honest to me about what he wanted

Namita: hmmm 5 yrs

Nicholas: wow

Nicholas: did you live together?

Nicholas: was that the last one?

Namita: then he moved away to the states... and expected me to drop everything and go along with him

Nicholas: im glad you didnt

Namita: the 5 yr one was before that indian one

Namita: yes... i had a life... going through my career

Nicholas: i think you'll like white guys lol at least this one lol

Nicholas: you know I hope you

Nicholas: oops... wrong button

Namita: establishing things in my life... but he was adamant that i just throw everything away

Namita: hehe actually i only prefer white guys now

Nicholas: i hope you'll be my last first... everything... i hope thats not putting too much pressure on you

Namita: it took me awhile to get over it

Namita: no no... no pressure... lol

Nicholas: i bet. it hurts when someone you care about puts that on you

Namita: im not afraid of committing to the right person

Nicholas: me too!

Namita: yes the last one... even said that he wasnt sure if he wanted to be with me... he wanted to know if there was other beautiful women out there... and that he was never serious about me... and this after i finally confronted him... with what he was doing

Namita: arghhhh... now when i think about it... i want to strangle him

Namita: heheh

Namita: im sooo over it

Nicholas: if I had been told not too long ago that I would find someone special, i wouldn't have believed it. I thought that the love train had passed me by and forgot to stop and pick me up

Namita: aweeeeeeeeeeeeeeee Nicholas !!!!!!!

Nicholas: and I was okay w that because I'm not going to settle

Namita: good for you... you've been there done that !!!

Nicholas: But the way I've been feeling lately

Namita: hehehe ...giddy ?

Nicholas: but I've always wanted someone special to share my life with

Nicholas: yah giddy

Nicholas: was smiling like an idiot on and off all day... again

Namita: hehe... its nice to share ur life with someone who totally understands you... even in silence... i think im pretty gifted in the sense that i can pick up the unspoken words

Namita: if that makes sense

Namita: has anyone asked you why you look so happy?

Nicholas: it does make sense

Nicholas: not yet

Namita: well i hope i dont hurt anyone tomorrow

Nicholas: I haven't said anything to anyone about you yet... don't want to jinks it *shakes head* I know that sounds silly but on the other hand I want to shout it from the roof tops about you and how good you make me feel.... again no pressure

Namita: hehe

Namita: well we will have to climb one of those rooftops with a ladder

Namita: dresses in black

Namita: and look like some robber

Namita: then get arrested

Namita: sorry my mind is going away in this scenario

Nicholas: lol

Namita: omg... I'm being silly

Nicholas: have you seen in our other convo's the spelling and grammar mistakes? it's quite funny

Namita: do you own ur own place ?

Namita: yesssssssssssssssss I have !!

Namita: hehe

Namita: and im such a sticker for grammar and spelling

Namita: at least fro my end

Namita: lol ... ``fro``

Nicholas: I rent a basement suite. its still the place I moved into after the separation. now that I have a good job I'd like to find a house w a garage so I can set up my studio/shop and make some side money w my projects

Nicholas: and have the hot rod here to work on and drive

Nicholas: you own your place yes?

Namita: wow sounds good... yes have my own place... its a house... a one level house

Nicholas: nice

Nicholas: garage?

Namita: with a decent size lot... both front and back... double garage

Nicholas: cool

Nicholas: what part of WR (White Rock)?

Namita: tool shed in back too

Namita: after crescent beach

Nicholas: wow

Namita: wow what ?

Namita: hehe

Namita: the tool shed ?

Nicholas: wow it sounds nice

Namita: ohhhh heheh

Nicholas: the whole picture

Nicholas: I can see it in my mind

Namita: hehe... i loveee it

Nicholas: what do you drive?

Namita: i drive a mid size SUV... a honda pilot 2006

Nicholas: oh yah

Namita: just paid if off last month

Namita: phewwww !!!

Nicholas: good for you

Namita: what do you drive ?

Nicholas: a dodge SX 2.0 '04

Namita: actually i bought the honda from Westwood honda and still take it there for maintenance

Namita: is that a truck ?

Nicholas: car... id like to get a dodge Dakota... thats a mid size 4 door truck

Namita: yes loveeeeeeeeeee those

Namita: im beginning to love the trucks too

Nicholas: lots of room and a box to haul stuff

Namita: yes yes !!

Namita: the inside is pretty good

Nicholas: I'd like an automatic. my car is a stick which is okay I just get tired of shifting especially in the city

Namita: the reason i have an suv is cuz i commute long ways for work ...so i thought it would be safer being a suv rather than a car ... esp in winter and driving with the big rigs

Nicholas: good idea

Namita: ahhhhhhh ...automatic is wayyyy easier

Namita: i wont know what to do with a stick

Namita: yes i know... i'll make popsicles !! hehe

Nicholas: lol

Nicholas: there's an '08 Dakota on the lot at Parksville Chrysler, where my mom is and the sales manager we've known for years so I may go and visit him and see what kind of a deal I could get

Namita: wow yes go for it if you get a good deal !!... do you like sports ?

Nicholas: its a bigger engine so the gas milage wouldnt be that great but its 4 wheel drive for those winter days

Nicholas: I love sports

Namita: yes... but it is safer in a way

Nicholas: to watch but prefer to play

Namita: what do u like to watch ?

Nicholas: it is.. higher up which i like

Nicholas: Canucks, Drag racing, building shows

Namita: the higher the better... plus you are tall too

Namita: yes me too... love hockey... esp in the playoffs

Nicholas: that I am... cant wait to see where you come up to on me

Namita: never been to a game though

Nicholas: really?

Namita: hehe

Nicholas: I went to 3 last year reg season games tho

Nicholas: we'll have to go. Its soooo much fun

Namita: ohhh... man it was such a close game !! (referring to the 2011 Stanley Cup Playoffs)

Nicholas: it was

Namita: to bad it ended the way it did

Namita: i was supposed to be working

Namita: but i called in sick... ahem ahem... cough cough... 2 days in a row in advance of the final game

Nicholas: yah. good teams know how to put a team away when they have the chance and Van (Vancouver Canucks) needs to figure out how to do that if they want to win

Namita: and i wasn't even sick... alas they lost

Nicholas: you can't miss a game like that

Namita: and i felt like a sore loser too

Nicholas: I have a #35 Richard Brodeur jersey

Namita: i knowwwwwwwwww i really had to fake it... cuz i got called in anyway

Namita: after the riots broke out

Nicholas: I've been a fan since the early '80's

Namita: we were on disaster alert

Nicholas: the riots were awful

Nicholas: I bet. oh yah you would have been right in the thick of the treatment

Namita: ive been a fan since their other finals... in the 90`s with the rangers

Nicholas: '94

Namita: yes thats right

Namita: i was still living in coquitlam then

Nicholas: that's cool. glad to hear you're not a band wagoner

Namita: hehe

Nicholas: I lived down town in '94

Nicholas: Denman and Barclay

Namita: ohhhhh

Nicholas: when they scored i could hear the city roar. was sooo cool

Nicholas: thats when I tried the film industry

Namita: i remember that too... cuz i was coming back from Downtown after picking up my sis from school

Nicholas: oh my favourite show is on! I think you've seen it. It's called the Namita Slide Show More profile photo's

Namita: lol !!!

Nicholas: it's soooo good. I love it

Nicholas: I am such a lucky guy

Namita: yeah i thought i should change it... didnt want to bore you

Namita: hehe

Nicholas: yah right. I don't think I'll get bored

Nicholas: I'm working on some photos for you. that way you can avoid the site

Namita: hehehe... just making sure ur awake

Namita: lol... thank u

Nicholas: oh I'm awake

Namita: is it a surprise ?

Namita: the pics i mean

Nicholas: umm I don't know. wasn't going to show any nudity if thats what you're getting at lol. I want to leave some up to the imagination

Nicholas: I have other surprises for you

Nicholas: I feel kind of silly taking those kind of photos even as tastefully as I would

Namita: no i wasn't getting at nudity... but u want to... im ok with it... but i will use my imagination... we will leave the real surprise for later

Nicholas: I have a couple of poses in mind

Namita: lol

Nicholas: I defiantly thought nudity. maybe another shoot

Namita: hehe no worries

Nicholas: have you ever thought about video tapping having sex?

Namita: you can send me what ur comfortable with... sex appeal for me lies in the persons eyes... their smile...

Nicholas: I don't know if I want to see myself like that

Namita: hmmmm yes... but keep it to ourselves

Namita: i cant say no

Nicholas: yes to ourselves and I don't really want video like that lying around

Namita: its not something that i lust after to do

Nicholas: would have to keep it locked up

Namita: its a fleeting thought

Nicholas: yah

Namita: it should be in a safe Nicholas not just locked

Namita: lol

Nicholas: lol yes a safe

Namita: so how would that happen... someone actually tape us... or set up a tripod ?

Nicholas: tripod

Namita: and the safe should be underground somewhere

Namita: hehe

Nicholas: maybe some hand held action

Namita: ahhh... imagine having some one else film that

Namita: AWKWARD !!!!

Nicholas: yah

Nicholas: okay here's one for you... you don't have to answer if you don't want to... have you tried anal? or would you like to?

Nicholas: I don't think the video would capture the emotional ride we'd be on

Namita: no i havent tried it... and im ok to try it

Nicholas: okay

Namita: have you?

Nicholas: I have... it's different for me... suppose to be fantastic for you.. hits the g spot from the back side so I've been told

Namita: really ?? wow didnt know that

Nicholas: especially from behind

Namita: Ohhhh

Nicholas: how many partners have you had?

Namita: how is it for you ?

Namita: 4

Namita: i wasnt sexually active till i was 20ish

Nicholas: just different... more pressure at the base and not as much head stimulus

Nicholas: I lost my virginity when I was 19

Namita: its not something i sought after in my teens... just to do it

Nicholas: yess

Nicholas: I was building my hot rod and playing sports

Namita: a girlfriend ?

Namita: or an older woman ?

Namita: hehe

Nicholas: co-worker. she was 22

Namita: how was it ?

Nicholas: was fun. she knew i wasn't experienced so she showed me how to please a women

Namita: aweee thats good !!

Nicholas: I pick things up quickly and I'm pretty body aware to begin with, I can pick up on even the littlest things with a women's body. I listen and feel her so I know that she's getting exactly what she wants. and if I miss something then she can tell me but I don't usually miss much

Namita: WOwwwww that is incredible Nicholas !! you're stirring me up inside already

Nicholas: just imagine how stirred up inside you'll be when you're with me

Namita: hehe ...usually im pretty in tune with my partners needs too... i feel im a pretty sexually happy person... meaning my appetite for it can be high

Namita: can do it everyday if i want

Namita: or several times... alas but work gets in the way

Nicholas: oh me too!

Namita: hehe

Nicholas: a quickly for me is about 45 mins

Namita: hehe me too... nothing less

Nicholas: yes

Namita: i also love to take my time exploring ur body

Nicholas: foreplay is the best part

Namita: finding out what make you excited and crazy

Namita: mmmmmm yes me too

Namita: loveeeeeeeeeeeeeeeee KISSING

Nicholas: I like to use my body as well as my hands

Nicholas: yes yes

Nicholas: kissing you all over!

Namita: mmmmmmmmmm yessssssss

Nicholas: rubbing my body all over yours... that's part of my full body massages

Nicholas: that pic is very cute, the one in the hat

    She's wearing a winter coat with fur around the collar and a black toque with bold white and grey horizontal stripes.

Namita: sucking on ur fingers... taking in the wonderful aroma of ur body

Namita: ohhh thanks

Namita: its from last fall

Nicholas: kissing... tongue or no?

Namita: yesssssss running my tongue all over ur body too

Namita: trailing little kisses along the way

Nicholas: well yes... I'm not a big fan of touching tongues or having a tongue in my mouth other than my own

Namita: would love the feel of ur whole body weight on top of me... pinning me down

Nicholas: trailing kisses yes yes

Namita: ohh sorry i didnt see ur question

Nicholas: that can be arranged my dear

Namita: a little tongue is ok

Nicholas: but all of what you said I'm all over

Nicholas: yes a little

Namita: but the entire thing is weird

Nicholas: I agree

Namita: what about biting

Namita: i love little nibbles along the way

Namita: on yOU !!

Namita: hehe

Nicholas: not big on biting but nibbling yes please giving and receiving

Namita: hehe ... yes no chomping down here !!

Namita: nibbles are good

Nicholas: my god I can hardly stand this!

Namita: like would you nibble on my breasts

Namita: lol

Nicholas: oh very much so

Namita: are you getting aroused ?

Nicholas: its one thing to see pics of you and talk this way but not being able to have you is driving me crazy!

Nicholas: way passed aroused over here

Nicholas: you?

Namita: lol... seriously... you are at attention ?

Namita: for how long ?

Nicholas: I'd say about half mast

Namita: hehe

Nicholas: it wouldn't take long to be at full attention

Namita: mmmmmmmm

Nicholas: and thinking about how wet you are.... mmm mmm mmm

Namita: mmmmmmm ohhhh yesssssss

Nicholas: this is torture

Nicholas: taking matters into my own hands just will not satisfy the craving for your body!

Namita: one thing i have to tell you

Nicholas: yes

Nicholas: the suspense is killing me

Namita: i sometimes get exceptionally turned on during my time of the month... and sometimes depending on the person im with... i craveeeeeeeeeeee sex... would you do it ? or would it be a turn off for you ?

Nicholas: I'd be totally in!

Namita: seriously ??

Nicholas: yup

Nicholas: we'll just put down towels or something

Namita: i am like a witch then !!

Namita: hehe

Namita: im giggling here

Namita: its not funny !! hehehe

Namita: don't laugh... i can hear you

Nicholas: most women go and hide when they're on their cycle

Nicholas: I want to spend as much time as I can w you

Namita: aweeee thanks

Namita: yes my body is pretty different

Nicholas: I'll say... I've never been w someone that has such a perfect body

Namita: we shower together afterwards

Namita: lol... awee thanks

Nicholas: "we shower together afterwards"?

Namita: hehe i mean after sex... we can shower together

Namita: or lovemaking

Namita: sex sounds too harsh for me

Nicholas: oh yes love to shower w you!

Nicholas: lovemaking sounds classier... which you are

Namita: awee thanks... i just make myself say it that way... sex to me is not enlisting the emotions... and togetherness... whereas lovemaking does

Namita: just cant* i meant

Nicholas: yes i totally hear you

Nicholas: with our schedules the way they are we may just have to fit each other in when we can. I don't want to have to wait too long to see you... not saying we're going to jump into bed right away. but the suspense of seeing you is killing me

Namita: lol ...yes same here on my end too

Namita: im sure things will work out for us in the end

Nicholas: oh good.. well not good but you know what I mean though

Namita: yes i do

Nicholas: yes they will... we've waited this long, 39 years what's another few days

Namita: hehehehe... yes we have wasted 39 yrs we should have been together since we were like 5

Nicholas: yes exactly!

Namita: would have made more sense

Nicholas: it would have

Namita: lol

Namita: geeeeeeeeeeeeez

Nicholas: I've imagined getting off work and instead of going home I driving straight over to your place

Namita: i would have pulled you into my arms

Namita: welcomed you home

Nicholas: and I would have inhaled you

Namita: lol

Nicholas: you intoxicate my thoughts

Nicholas: your name passes my lips about a thousand times a day

Namita: hehehe ohhh nooo

Namita: seriously ?!

Nicholas: that glint in my eye... is the though of you

Namita: do you go by nicholas or nick

Nicholas: makes you sound more real when I say it out loud

Namita: mmmmmmmmmmmnu

Nicholas: I introduce myself as Nicholas that way it doesn't get confused with anything else that ends in i c k

Namita: mmmmmmmmmmmm n

Namita: mmmmmmmmmmmmmm nice i meant to say

Nicholas: sokay

Namita: oh ok

Namita: hehe

Nicholas: can see the tiredness in our convo's when you read these the next day

Namita: heheh

Nicholas: okay so are you going to give me your phone number soon.. I'LL CONTINUE TO EMAIL

Namita: yeah i should head off soon nicholas... i wake up in a 3 hrs

Nicholas: OOPS sorry for the caps lock... good timing though lol

Namita: no worries

Namita: i loveee talking to you

Nicholas: me too

Nicholas: so no # tonight?

Nicholas: 3hrs geeze

Namita: k here you go... hehe... ***-***-***

Nicholas: oh thank you

Namita: ur welcome

Nicholas: that way I can send you little text smiles

Namita: yes... i will have my phone with me at work

Nicholas: okay cool

Nicholas: as much as I want to keep talking you need your sleep

Namita: tomorrow nite ?

Nicholas: will you be around?

Nicholas: oh right you're on days

Namita: in between day shift

Nicholas: so yes of course!

Namita: lol

Namita: ok deal

Nicholas: about what time do you think?

Namita: when ur around ?

Nicholas: usual time then or during the day?

Namita: im going to be in bed by 1030

Nicholas: am?

Namita: well im not home till like 8:45 pm

Nicholas: sorry really tired now cant think

Namita: i start at 7 am

Namita: no worries

Nicholas: so tmw when?

Namita: well when you get home

Namita: like tonite

Nicholas: but you'll be in bed at 1030?

Namita: i know... so i will wait

Namita: hehe

Nicholas: just not sleeping

Nicholas: oh okay

Namita: no not sleeping

Namita: just in bed

Nicholas: yes tmw same time

Namita: ok... deal

Nicholas: i like the sound of you in bed

Nicholas: deal

Namita: mmmmmmmmmmmmmmmmmmm

Nicholas: I'll come look for you

Namita: ok babes

Nicholas: okay gnight Namita. love talking with you

Nicholas: sleep well

Namita: goodnite nicholas

Nicholas: 💋

Namita: thank u for another great conversation

Nicholas: and you

Nicholas: 😊

Namita: sweet dreams

Nicholas: night

End Time: 2:26 AM

Oct 6 00:45 PM

Hello there my Indian princess. I hope you don't mind me calling you that? seems fitting.

I was hoping to catch you online earlier. I did get your return smile from LL. I'm working on a photo or 2 for you. Will take them tmw n send them off asap.

A night on the town with you sounds wonderful!! Or Rocky Point. I live just up the road from there. We'll figure something out. I'm not going anywhere xo.

I'll be patently waiting for you on msn tonight. Same Bat time same Bat channel lol.

Back to work.

Xoxo

Sent from my BlackBerry device

6:13 PM

Hehehe... always good to hear from you Nicholas !! You put a smile on my face when I read ur emails !!

Yes you can call me whatever pleases you... hehe... I don't mind the little things.

Did you get my pic on ur BB (Blackberry)?

Wow then you must have good view of the inlet... or being close around to the water.

Living and growing up in Coquitlam… I always used to go down to Rocky Point... or Buntzen Lake area... it is sooo beautiful... just to get away for a bit.

Im just on my way to make some dinner for myself... i usually make something from scatch rather freezing it. But i will make enough for work tomorrow... I'm thinking butter chicken and some salad… but my colleagues are going to kill me for sure and run away with my butter chicken !! They absolutely LOVE IT... and say it is the best butter chicken they have ever tasted !!

During the Xmas holidays when im working... we usually have potluck... and that's the only thing I'm allowed to bring to work. People even come in on their day off to have the chicken. Im sure you will hold me up it too... one day !! LOL !! Hope work is going well so far !! A few more hours to go !! Yayyyyyy

Xo- Namita…

I love how both of our names start with "N"… most names don't start with N

Chapter 5 October 8

I looked up the perfume and found it on Amazon for about $70.00. I decided to buy it and surprise Namita on our first date.

I went to Parksville for the weekend to visit my mom.

Start Time: 11:29 PM

Nicholas: hey you!

Namita: heyy

Namita: how are you ?

Nicholas: was just napping while i waited

Nicholas: im good now! how was work?

Namita: ohhh sorry i woke you up !!

Nicholas: any time

Namita: hehe

Namita: work was busy

Nicholas: just napping and I've been waiting to talk w u

Namita: as i was leaving the sirens and helicopters were pulling in

Namita: i made a beeline to the exit door as soon as i could

Nicholas: oh good. Do you usually have to deal w them?

Namita: well things do happen in the last possible minute

Nicholas: the helicopters n sirens that is

Namita: yes and we have a landing pad on top the roof of one of the buildings

Nicholas: but is that part of what you deal w?

Namita: emergency is just below us

Nicholas: oh I see

Namita: yes we do

Nicholas: oh wow

Namita: we get a lot of the traumas ...or ppl coming in from the interior... being flown in

Namita: or sometimes it is an organ being dropped off

Nicholas: thats too bad really. not good for so many ppl to be getting hurt

Namita: a lot of the times i see them coming in for the landing... i can see right thru to the pilot... and gives me a wave

Nicholas: that sound so mad scientist "organ drop off"

Namita: lol

Nicholas: wow

Namita: it is cool in the night... then the landing pad is lit up in blue

Nicholas: I bet

Namita: and you can see the North shore mountains in the background

Nicholas: cool

Nicholas: what time do you start your night shift?

Namita: ive thought about becoming a flight nurse... i have the credentials

Namita: but its always been a thought... never really acted on it

Nicholas: you'd make an excellent flight nurse from the sounds of it

Namita: hehe

Nicholas: you can be my nurse anytime

Nicholas: lol

Namita: one of my colleague volunteered last spring ...and she was flown in a private plane to mexico to pick a patient up

Nicholas: holy sh**

Namita: Hehehe... of course you will have ur own private nurse

Nicholas: awesome!

Namita: yes... then i was talking to her one day

Nicholas: I don't get sick very often but I think I might be coming down w something *cough cough*

Namita: and it turns out... the pilot was one of my neighbors... who does contract flights for these very scenarios

Nicholas: that's stuff u see in the movies cool that it actually happens

Namita: i see him just about everyday... our dogs are friends... and i never knew he was a pilot... nor did he know i was a nurse

Nicholas: really?! small world

Namita: lol .... i can hear ur "cough" already

Nicholas: yah I think my head is a little stuffy too

Namita: you may need a physical

Nicholas: I think so too

Namita: are you serious? or pulling my leg here... lol

Nicholas: pulling your leg but anytime you want to check me out you go right ahead

Namita: hehehe

Nicholas: so you liked my photos?

Namita: ohhh yes... thank u so much

Nicholas: I thought of you for my smile and poof

Nicholas: ur quite welcome

Namita: hehe... it looks like you took it in a studio

Nicholas: just my living room

Nicholas: I know how to do it up right

Namita: ahhhh ok

Namita: are you into photography ?

Nicholas: into? I don't know. I like to take good pics though

Nicholas: I can get a little artsy fartsy w the camera sometimes

Namita: ive been meaning of taking some good photography classes... dad was and still is a wonderful photographer... it is his hobby

Nicholas: but I never seem to do things simple. I always find a more creative way of doing something like my portfolio I made it into a slide show w music

Nicholas: cool. I learned some things from the still photographer on the first film I worked on

Namita: yes i sense ur creativity

Nicholas: 😄

Namita: ohhh wow... maybe we can share some ideas

Nicholas: absolutely!

Namita: hehe

Nicholas: when I take pics I usually think hmm what would I see in a magazine

Namita: well that a good way of thinking about it... i know dad has taught some basic thought process into composing a good picture... ie balancing the pic with the picture composition

Nicholas: yah and filling the frame that's the biggest one I learned

Namita: sort of like framing a scene and balancing the subject

Nicholas: yah

Namita: yes... we were thinking on the same wavelength... hehe

Nicholas: but of course

Nicholas: like minds

Namita: lol... yes our creative minds that is !

Namita: hows ur mom doing ?

Nicholas: she's good. we spent the day talking n catching up

Namita: how old is she... if i may ask

Nicholas: she's still pretty lonely n trying to put her life back together. My dad was the world to her. only guy she'd ever been w

Nicholas: n you can ask me anything coz I want to tell you

Namita: ohhh... that must be hard for her... to try to move forward... does she have friends or know ppl around there

Nicholas: I couldn't stand it anymore I had to tell someone about you so I told her, I hope you don't mind

Namita: oh... no i dont mind

Nicholas: she has friends but it's just not the same for her so she tries to stay busy

Namita: its all good

Nicholas: have you told anyone about me?

Nicholas: just curious

Namita: i cant imagine being in that position

Namita: hehe... no not yet

Nicholas: nor can I. I try to cheer her up and just let her talk things out

Nicholas: she's the only one though

Namita: what did you tell her ?

Namita: lol

Namita: that you found this crazy nurse online

Nicholas: just that I met this wonderful women and think the world of her but I have yet to meet her lol

Namita: ohhh my nicholas... hehe

Nicholas: I showed her your photo coz I wanted her to see how beautiful you are. n told her what an awesome person you are

Nicholas: no pressure. I played it cool

Namita: hehehe... which photo did you show... and what did she think ? now im curious

Nicholas: the one you sent me on here the other night

Nicholas: she thinks your beautiful and hopes things work out

Namita: i thought you showed the LL one

Namita: aweeeeeeeeeeee

Nicholas: was too much trouble to get to. I have that one n the wedding pic closer n easier to pull up

Namita: yes... can you imagined if she read my profile... hehe

Nicholas: lol.... we talked a lot about how the internet plays a big part in our society and how so many ppl are meeting on there... it's just finding the right person... goes to show you never know where you'll find someone

Namita: that is sooo true... these days the internet plays a huge role... i know some ppl who have met online... coworkers, friends... some are married... some are together... if anyone would have told me about internet dating like 10 or 15 yrs ago... i would have laughed !!

Namita: but now it seems the norm

Nicholas: it does... I don't mind where I found you just that I finally did ☺

Namita: hehe... did you get back into the swing of things pretty quickly after ur divorce or did you find it hard

Nicholas: not hard... I took a lot of time to reflect and figure out what I learned from it... I don't date a lot to begin w... I'm not usually in a position to meet new ppl and it seems I'm attracted to the not interested, not available... usually both... but it did take time to figure out what I wanted in a partner and from a relationship

Namita: yes i guess it does give you the opportunity to seriously think of what it is you want out of life and a potential partner... expectations, and really brings forth ones values as well

Nicholas: I'm curious to know when you're going to tell someone about me? and who the first person will be?

Nicholas: it does

Namita: probably my sister... the youngest one... cuz im closer to her

Nicholas: again no pressure

Nicholas: I see

Nicholas: all in due time of course

Namita: my friends have deserted me

Nicholas: deserted you? how come?

Namita: yes ...unless ur psychic abilities kick in

Nicholas: kick in?

Namita: deserted me... cuz Ashley one of my best friend is off on a safari trip in africa... Jessica... is now living on Bowen Island with her young family

Nicholas: I find when ppl mention meeting someone online there's this stigma that goes w it. do you find that too?

Namita: and the others are busy right now too... lol

Nicholas: aww I'll keep you company and will NEver desert you

Namita: no i don't find the stigma or generalization ...mainly cuz it is so mainstream nowadays

Namita: hehe

Nicholas: hmm maybe it's just me

Namita: yeah its just YOU... hehe

Namita: or Port Moody

Nicholas: lol brat

Namita: geeeeeeeeeeez

Nicholas: lol

Namita: did you grow up in the same house that ur mom is living in now

Nicholas: so what's on the Namita side show for tonight?

Nicholas: nope

Namita: hmmm one sec

Nicholas: 😋

Nicholas: not that I don't like the opening photo... one of my fav's actually

Nicholas: oooohhh i like that one! n thank you

Namita: oh really ...what do like about it

Namita: hehe

Namita: thanks

Namita: this pic is pro shot

~Namita~ would like to send you the file "Lady Red.jpg" (21 Kb). Do you want to

Accept

(Ctrl+G) or

Decline

(Ctrl+C) the invitation?

Transfer of file "Lady Red.jpg" from ~Namita~ has been accepted. Starting transfer...

Cancel

You have successfully received Lady Red.jpg from ~Namita~. Before opening this file, you may want to scan it with a virus-scanning program.

Nicholas: the pose, your hair... the way it falls down your back... the look you have... the over all look to it... the beauty in it

> She's wearing a summer dress. It's red satin but more pink. I'm seeing her right side from mid thigh up, she's looking over her shoulder toward me. Her right arm is relaxed at her side, left arm across her

front, hand gently on her right elbow. Her hair is wavy, off her shoulder and down her back.

Namita: i have a feeling you like it !

Namita: hehe

Nicholas: oh my that's sooo hot again thank you... i'll add it to my collection

Nicholas: do I ever!

Namita: ur getting a close up view now ?

Nicholas: I leave them up while I'm talking to you so I end up w a Namita collage on my screen

Nicholas: yes I am and loving it!

Namita: hehe... there goes ur creative side

Nicholas: absolutely beautiful!

Namita: aweeee thanks

Nicholas: defiantly have some juices flowing that's for sure

Namita: lol

Namita: ohhh nooo dare i ask

Nicholas: creative juices that is

Namita: hehe ... im teasing you

Nicholas: you are just too delicious... can't wait to eat you up

Namita: hehe .... you wont need whip cream

Nicholas: mmmhmm

Namita: lol

Nicholas: you are the whip cream and the cherry

Namita: are you in bed with ur laptop

Nicholas: sure am. you?

Namita: yes so am i... other wise i would have fallen over a long while back

Namita: usually im on my tummy

Nicholas: now I'm picturing you in your little nighty looking all hot in bed

Namita: with laptop in front of me

Namita: black one tonite

Nicholas: fallen over?

Nicholas: mmm tummy more specifically your tummy mmm

Namita: i meant fallen over from tiredness... i needed to be in bed... i wouldnt have functioned

Namita: hehe

Nicholas: your hair is naturally curly?

Nicholas: thats what i thought you meant

Namita: yes naturally wavy

Namita: sometime i have dead straight

Namita: ahhh i see

Nicholas: I like naturally wavy

Nicholas: oh I see n thx for filling in that image.. mmm mmm mm

Nicholas: oh I wish I was there... to see it unfold

Nicholas: black satin?

Namita: yes black satin

Nicholas: so G-string? thong? T back?

Namita: with a little lace

Nicholas: oh damn very hot!!

Namita: this is getting really sexy

Nicholas: you're killing me

Namita: hehe

Nicholas: that sounds soooo hot!

Namita: up to my knees

Nicholas: mmm just as I imagined

Namita: lace around the bodice

Nicholas: damn

Namita: with some ribbon effect too

Nicholas: like a crisscross ribbon action in the back?

Nicholas: its like you reach into my mind and pull out my fantasy

Namita: no... but i have ribbon straps... and ribbon weaved into the bodice... like a edging along the cups

Nicholas: mmm

Namita: hehe

Nicholas: I cant wait to see that!

Nicholas: I love a women that dresses sexy even when she's alone

Namita: i have a trunk of just my fav nighties... and lingerie... everyday stuff... and nighties... bras sets... etc

Nicholas: very tasty!

Namita: some women like their purses... i like my lingerie

Nicholas: mmm mmm mmm

Namita: i do like purses and shoes too though

Nicholas: I love that you like lingerie

Namita: ive always wore nice stuff... even under my scrubs

Nicholas: have you been to a store on Granville st called Dare To Wear?

Nicholas: I like that

Nicholas: what you just said about dressing nice

Namita: no... but i think ive heard of it... in the Georgia Strait paper

Nicholas: it has some really hot outfits in there let me tell yah

Nicholas: and would look sooo hot on you

Namita: yes i do take pride in how i dress... it doesnt have to be name brand... but ive never been the type to hang around in jogging pants like many do these days

Namita: i like to look classy... even if its jeans... then i wear it in a classy way

Namita: i hate when women looked like they crawled out of bed... when out and about

Namita: are you there ? or have i put you to sleep !!

Nicholas: yup

Nicholas: had to use the bathroom

Namita: ohhh

Namita: hehe

Nicholas: god no... no sleeping here

Namita: i just wrote like a story above and you went to the bathroom

Namita: hehe kidding

Nicholas: I like the sound of that... how you dress... I like to look put together and dress age appropriate too

Nicholas: Oh I was not to worry... was just to grab a klenex

Namita: yes age appropriate is also big too

Nicholas: I see so many older men dressing like a 20 year old n think "who do you think you're kidding?"

Namita: when you look at some of the women... they are just as bad sometimes

Nicholas: or dressing like a thug w their big gold chains... looks ridiculous

Namita: lmao

Nicholas: they are

Namita: gangsta`d out !!

Nicholas: they scream diva from a mile away

Nicholas: yes

Nicholas: I don't get the chain look

Nicholas: I don't wear jewelry

Namita: hehe...you mean the thick gold chain around their neck ?

Nicholas: I have medical ID that looks like dog tags

Namita: i wear jewelry... hehe

Nicholas: lol yes! those ones

Namita: yes ive seen those

Namita: OMFG... yes i don't get it either !!!!

Nicholas: I bet you do... lucky jewelry

Namita: awee thanks

Namita: do you have piercing?

Nicholas: at the fireworks one year I saw a young muscular kid but w little chicken legs wearing a huge chain w a huge cross that hung down to his waist. Not to mention the attitude he had. Though he was so cool.

Namita: i can only imagine... if i saw that... i would have been rolling my eyes

Namita: come on i bet you do !!!

Namita: hahahhaha

Nicholas: use to have one ear ring but took it out years ago

Nicholas: you have your ears pierced yes anything else?

Namita: why did you do that ?

Namita: Yes ears are pierced

Nicholas: took it out? for a change

Namita: nothing else yet

Namita: hehe

Nicholas: yet? what else would you pierce?

Namita: my ears were pierced since i was like 2

Nicholas: belly button?

Namita: no I'm kidding

Namita: i thought about my nose... so i can wear a small tiny white stone in it

Nicholas: that would look so hot on you... I like the sound of that

Nicholas: a friend of mine I've known since we were kids has her clit done

Namita: i did pierce my nose when i was a teen... when it was not the norm thing to do

Namita: and she told you about that ???

Namita: i dont know about the clit... cuz i would think the chances are great that you can damage ur nerve endings... and that would be the end of it

Nicholas: yah, we've known each other since I was 7 n she was 5 so we go way back

Namita: wow... cool... you guys must be close

Nicholas: yes don't want to mess w the clit... well not like that... can think of other ways to stimulate it though

Namita: ive seen some patients who come in who have had piercing down there

Nicholas: on n off for years

Namita: mainly guys...

Namita: and most of them OLD ....like in their 60`s or 70`s

Namita: eweee

Namita: hehe

Nicholas: that's wired I think... like a ring right through the end.. the pee goes all over I bet lol

Nicholas: eww old sausage gross

Namita: lol !!!

Namita: ewee i dont want to know... they need a diaper

Namita: ur grossing me out

Nicholas: why mess w something that works pretty darn well in the first place. the old saying if it aint broke don't fix it

Nicholas: any idea when we might be able to see each other?... maybe lunch one day just to get some face time

Nicholas: as much as I'd like to spend more than a couple of hrs w you I'll take what I can get though

Namita: i remember... being fresh out of school nurse... total rookie... i had a patient... and 80 or 90 yr old... with a much younger 40`s girlfriend... and when we went to help him coming back from a hip surgery... covers go down... and viola... this penis is sticking straight up... but unusually so... he had a massive penal implant... i almost screamed... totally scared me

Nicholas: lmao too funny!

Namita: i will let you know nicholas... im coming off tuesday... but have an OT shift... followed by a shift trades as well... its my screwed week right now

Nicholas: ok

Namita: hehehe... but i will keep you posted

Namita: yes i have many stories to tell

Nicholas: cool... I know you will

Nicholas: I can't wait to hear them all

Namita: hehe... you will be in tears

Nicholas: we have 39 years to catch up on lol

Namita: lol... thats right !!!

Nicholas: Stories Of The ER?

Namita: yes... some gross, many funny

Nicholas: and I want to learn everything about you

Namita: aweeeeeeeeeeeeeeeee nicholas

Namita: what would have been ur very first job when you were first employed

Nicholas: I was a bus boy at a restaurant that was close to where we had our sail boat we lived on. the owner was our waiter n he asked me if I was looking for work in the summer. I said sure

Nicholas: bused the whole place myself. made good money too

Nicholas: what was your first job?

Namita: omg ... i was a bus girl... in a restaurant

Namita: actually it was down on north road

Nicholas: cool

Namita: where they have the Price Mart foods i think now

Namita: they tore down that building i worked in

Namita: i hated bussing

Nicholas: eventually I'll bring you over here and on our tour I can show you the restaurant

Namita: so i started making salads and desserts in the back... rather than be in the front

Nicholas: I was the only buser n there were 2 servers one male n one female. the guy was the owner and he showed me how to be efficient at my job.... I made good tips being the only buser

Nicholas: Uncle Willys?

Namita: the restaurant was called... ok don't laugh... Uncle Willys

Nicholas: I remember that place

Namita: why did you say Uncle Willys?

Namita: was that ur guess

Nicholas: yah

Nicholas: I use to live close to there when I was married

Namita: omg... for a moment i thought that was the restaurant you worked in too

Nicholas: n sort of still do live close

Namita: i used to work there in the early part of the 90`s

Namita: last winter i had just finished a book about Willy Pickton .... sort of a bio

Nicholas: lol I worked at a place called the French Creek House in French Creek harbour where we kept the boat

Nicholas: wow they have a book about that already

Namita: and in it it described how he frequented that very restaurant i worked in... in the same years i worked

Nicholas: scary

Namita: yes the book is pretty interesting

Namita: it is called On the Farm

Namita: i know... gives me the creeps !!!

Nicholas: you weren't in his target range n you worked in the back too so you should have been okay

Namita: and to think i might have laid eyes on him

Namita: yes so glad i worked in the back !!!

Namita: and mom always picked me up too

Nicholas: Clifford Olson was captured in Campbell River, so he travelled right through Parksville... spooky

Namita: OMG !!!

Nicholas: yeah

Namita: that guy lived on Foster i think... in coquitlam

Nicholas: was quite the talk around town

Namita: i must have been around 10ish... when he was prowling

Nicholas: the world is a better place now that he's dead

Namita: yes thats for sure

Nicholas: what time do you start tmw (tomorrow) for your night shift?

Namita: i used to live right on Como Lake Ave... between Schoolhouse Road and Poirier Street

Nicholas: oh yah I know where that is

Namita: i start at 730 pm

Namita: went to Parkland elementary

Namita: then Charles Best Middle School

Nicholas: I like the pic that's currently up btw... if I didn't already say so

Namita: then Centennial Senior Sec

Nicholas: know them both

Namita: hehehe

Namita: thanks

~Namita~ would like to send you the file "2010-04. bmp" (695 Kb). Do you want to

Accept

(Ctrl+G) or

Decline

(Ctrl+C) the invitation?

Transfer of file "2010-04.bmp" from ~Namita~ has been accepted. Starting transfer...

Cancel

Namita: my best years was in Centennial Senior

Namita: grades 11 and 12

Nicholas: it amazes me how often "wow" comes out of my mouth when I see photos of you... so beautiful

Nicholas: oh yah

You have successfully received 2010-04.bmp from ~Namita~. Before opening this file, you may want to scan it with a virus-scanning program.

In black & white — She's laying on a chair very relaxed, resting on her right elbow with her head gently laying on the back rest casually looking at me from the side, her left arm draped across her body.

Nicholas: oh my.... god... wow

Namita: lol

Nicholas: I am beside myself with how beautiful you are... that will ever get old

Namita: awee thanks nicholas

Nicholas: can I have my own special portfolio of you one day?

Namita: of course you can

Namita: we can add our own together

Nicholas: I hope you don't tire of me telling you how beautiful you are?

Nicholas: cool... that would be awesome

Namita: no i dont get tire of it... but also i dont go fishing for it either... i am not conceited... ever... hehe

Nicholas: another thing I love about you

Namita: im humble about things like that

Namita: in fact if u had said that to me in person ... i might turn a shade pinker

Nicholas: yes you are... another great quality.... which makes you than much more sexy... if that's possible

Namita: ohhh myyyy... hehe... the list is getting longer

Nicholas: I think we'd look great together

Nicholas: or should I say we'll look great together

Namita: yes we would

Nicholas: ppl will wonder who the good looking couple is and what to know how they can be like that

Namita: yes they would wanna know our secret

Nicholas: I know I've seen couples like that n wondered the same thing

Namita: hehe i like that !! to see couples who are sooo compatible like that and so into each other

Nicholas: yes they just ooze confidence and compatibility w/o being conceited... and they look so happy together... like there's no other place they'd rather be than w each other

Namita: yesss loveeee that !!

Nicholas: can you believe that it hasn't even been a week since we first talked?.... it seems like forever and just yesterday all at the same time

Namita: yes a week has gone by so fast

Namita: it seems like we've been talking for a month now

Nicholas: it does

Nicholas: I don't think... no thats not right... I've never felt this way before about someone

Nicholas: you're awesome and wonderful n all those other words I cant think of right now all at the same time

Namita: hehe aweeee ur sooo sweet nicholas

Namita: its been a pleasure talking to you too

Nicholas: I cant wait to give a big hug

Namita: and envelope me ?

Namita: heheh

Nicholas: yes

Namita: i can imagine it

Nicholas: that's when I can exhale and it makes this more real for me... I sometimes think I'm dreaming... then I talk w you and realize I'm awake

Namita: hehehehe ...do you need me to pinch you?

Nicholas: I think so just not too hard as I do bruise easy lol

Namita: lmao ... ok precious one

Nicholas: I might need you to pinch me everyday

Namita: actually i bruise easily too

Namita: ur butt might be one red butt by the end of the day, week, month

Nicholas: I decided on another name for you, other than my indian princess... came up w it today on the ferry... your my indian rainbow... rare special and beautiful

Nicholas: was the Rolling Stones song Blinded By RainBows that made me think of it

Namita: ohhh myyy ... ur mind is bombarded with thoughts of me

Nicholas: blinded by your beauty

Namita: even on the ferry

Namita: hehe

Namita: did you even get out of ur car ?

Namita: aweee nicholas

Nicholas: yah... have a bit of a soft spot for a women named Namita Puranjay

Namita: lol

Nicholas: I did. I usually sit upstairs n watch a movie on the lap top

Namita: what movie was it

Nicholas: thought about you being w me and ppl thinking wow look at that couple they look so happy together

Nicholas: the Replacements w Keanu Reeves

Namita: hehe... I'd be on the deck most of the time... looking at the ocean

Namita: ohh never seen that movie before

Namita: hoping to see a whale

Nicholas: we'll have to watch it

Namita: ok

Nicholas: in all the times I've been on the ferry I've never seen whales

Nicholas: there's so many things I look forward to doing w you

Namita: last year when i went boating with dad off Tsawwassen... we were in close proximity with a pod of killer whales... id say 20 ft away

Namita: it was absolutely beautiful

Nicholas: snuggling together watching a movie or dinner down town or a walk somewhere

Nicholas: that's cool

Nicholas: I've always loved the ocean and the animals in it... love the sea otters at the aquarium.... in the wild too

Namita: then soon afterwards there was a pod of pacific white side dolphins swimming and jumping out of the water... within 15 ft... i was like a kid in a zoo... soooooooooooooo excited

Namita: me too the otters are sooooo cute

Nicholas: that's always cool when the dolphins come to play

Namita: they are sooo social

Namita: i love their little happy faces... the corners of their mouth turned at the edges

Nicholas: and the only other animal to have sex for pleasure

Nicholas: so they say

Namita: really... didnt know that tidbit

Nicholas: yup

Nicholas: also that orcas are dolphins

Namita: yes knew that

Nicholas: are you pretty tired from work?... im finding im not nearly as tired as i usually am... though i did sort of power nap waiting for you lol

Namita: lol... youve got the advantage tonite... i am tired... but still ok right now

Nicholas: okay. let me know when you've had enough

Namita: yes will let you know

Nicholas: tmw we'll have to be content w texting as you'll be working at this time

Nicholas: will do

Namita: yesss

Namita: arghhh

Namita: are you there ? Pee break ?

Nicholas: just admiring your pics

Namita: what did u have for dinner

Namita: hehe ohhh

Nicholas: we went to A&W. we usually make our way there at some point. my mom doesn't cook n we find it easier to just go out to eat. what did you have for dinner?

Namita: ☺

Namita: i had chicken ...and salad

Namita: i dont eat beef

Namita: so chicken and fish and eggs

Nicholas: you don't... religious beliefs?

Namita: yes... although im not a religious person

Namita: been brought up not eating it... so it stuck with me

Namita: i dont think i'll ever will try it

Nicholas: ah... I'm spiritual not religious

Namita: yes im spiritual... but not religious... that was my next thing to say before you said it

Nicholas: I make a pretty mean rib eye steak... just melt in you mouth goodness

Namita: hehehe

Nicholas: like minds

Namita: what meats do u eat

Nicholas: all of them

Namita: i will eat pork sometimes... but that is occasional

Nicholas: though I don't eat glands as in liver or kidneys

Namita: and sometimes lamb

Nicholas: ok I don't do lamb

Namita: YUCk !!! i dont eat any of that either !!!

Namita: lol

Nicholas: chicken beef pork white fish

Namita: very occasional for me on the lamb

Nicholas: I don't like the taste of it, lamb

Namita: will eat turkey

Nicholas: never tried nor really wanted to try rabbit or goat... I figure there's enf (enough) beef chicken n pork to go 'round

Namita: lol.... never tried those either

Nicholas: oh yes turkey that's one of my fav food groups at thanksgiving or christmas, turkey stuffing n gravy lol

Namita: mmmmmmmmmmmmmm

Namita: xmas time its my job to make the turkey

Nicholas: cool

Namita: and i think i do a good job of it

Nicholas: I bet you do

Namita: i season it... and stuff herbs and a large onion plus garlic in the cavity

Namita: i make the stuffing separate though

Nicholas: mom n I were just talking about what we're dong for christmas. my sis n her partner aren't going to do the dinner this year so we're figuring what we'll all do

Namita: mmm thats a tough one

Nicholas: I go w Stove Top. now is a good time to get it on sale

Namita: are their restaurants open for xmas dinner

Nicholas: oh yah. we've been to them before

Nicholas: most offer an xmas dinner

Namita: if you do stove top... i add additional veggies... like diced celery, peppers, onion, and sliced shiitake mushroom

Nicholas: how big is your family? it's you 3 sisters mom dad... any other rellies here?

Namita: then add a chicken stock to simmer it

Namita: 2 of my sis are married... so their spouses... and niece and nephew

Namita: if my cousins are in town... then their family too

Nicholas: I'm not a big fan of mushrooms. can't see the point of eating a fungus lol

Namita: lmao

Namita: i like it if its cooked down

Nicholas: so there's quite a few of you when you're all together

Namita: yes a roomful of ppl

Namita: actually both mom and dad side of family is huge

Nicholas: and I need someone to explain the nutritional value in a fungus too

Namita: dad was 10 siblings... mom side 12 sibling

Namita: hehehe one day nicholas... one day i will

Nicholas: how do you think your family more specifically your mom n dad would react if you brought a white guy around?

Namita: so i have many cousins here and there ...some of them i dont even know what they look like

Nicholas: wow big family

Namita: my youngest cousins are 2 yrs old

Nicholas: that's quite the age spread

Namita: i knowwwwwwwww isnt it... my uncle who is 60... just now had his first children... they are twins... by accident

Namita: with his common law wife

Namita: lol

Nicholas: 60 geeze!

Namita: i tease him about it now

Namita: he lives in Australia

Nicholas: he's going to be the old guy at grad lol

Namita: he called today after a year... and chatted with mom and dad

Namita: i misses him... while i was at work

Namita: ohhhh yessssss he is and will be the old guy at the high school grad

Nicholas: cool... my mom is going to Australia to visit a friend she hasn't seen in 50 years

Namita: omggg wowwww

Namita: well its good that she is getting away for a bit

Nicholas: did you miss my question?

Namita: yes i think so

Namita: what was it ?

Nicholas: how do you think you're family more specifically your mom n dad would react if you brought a white guy home?

Nicholas: and is there any pressure from the family for you to find someone?

Namita: i know they will be alright with it... cuz they've told me so... they dont care one bit if he is white... they are accepting of the fact... they just want me to be happy

Namita: thats what counts

Nicholas: good answer... another check list item checked

Nicholas: lol

Namita: no big pressure to find someone... they know im a late bloomer in that regards... so they've been patient

Nicholas: not to toot my own horn but parents like me

Namita: hehehe good to hear

Nicholas: ☺

Namita: checked off

Nicholas: lol

Namita: hehe

Nicholas: you're awesome

Namita: one thing i will clarify... not that it matters

Nicholas: yes

Namita: when ppl think of east indian... they automatically think im Sikh which im not

Nicholas: really? i don't know the difference

Namita: im hindu indian... the true indian heritage from india

Nicholas: my sisters girls friend is indian

Nicholas: you seem pretty pure to me

Namita: sikh ppl wear the turbans... where as hindu Indian do not

Namita: hehe

Namita: good answer

Nicholas: ☺

Namita: can i ask u one thing

Namita: pls dont laugh

Nicholas: ask away my dear

Namita: and i dont want to put my foot in my mouth on this... or offend

Nicholas: it takes a lot to offend me

Namita: when you say ur sisters partner... do you mean her bf (boyfriend) ?

Nicholas: nope her girl friend

Namita: ohh ok

Nicholas: that okay?

Namita: i wasnt sure if that what you meant... i kinda though so but wasnt so sure

Namita: most ppl say partner in that respect

Nicholas: sokay

Namita: is she happy

Namita: and settled

Nicholas: yah I mean it the gay way lol

Namita: lol

Namita: ok

Namita: OHHHHHHHHHHHHHHHH MYYYYYYYYYYYYYYYYYYYYYYY

Nicholas: what?

Namita: nice pic

Nicholas: thx... I can switch things up now that I have some photos

Nicholas: oooooo damn... now that's an oooohhhh mmmyyyy from here

Namita: ohh ok... well that is good

Namita: well hot damn !!!

Namita: hehe

Nicholas: if it's a battle of the photos you'll win coz I'll vote for you and you have way more... well I'll let you win so I can celebrate w you

Nicholas: speaking of dancing do you like to dance?

Namita: yes i do... ive got the moves like jagger

Namita: hehe

Namita: im being silly

Nicholas: I like to dance especially with the right women... lots of bumping n grinding

Namita: yes one of one is very nice and sensual

Nicholas: tastefully of course

Nicholas: I'd hold you so close our bodies would move as one

Namita: mmmmm i like the sound of that

Nicholas: you'll like the feel of it too... i know i will

Namita: esp when ur tall... and i can look up at you

Nicholas: that you can... you'll fit perfectly in your spot.... that's in my arms

Namita: aweee... i can imagine the feeling

Nicholas: I can't wait to hold you... n never let go

Namita: hehe

Namita: take me in drink in my scent

Namita: as i would you

Nicholas: oh you know it!

Nicholas: I would bath in your sent n have it on me so when I was away from you I could still smell you

Namita: hehehe... i think you will also like smelling my hair... im one of those ppl who is a stickler to making sure my hair smells wonderful ...its from the shampoo i use

Namita: and i always get commented on how nice my hair smells from ppl at work

Nicholas: I like the sound of that... I'm a very touchy guy.. I like to touch a lot

Namita: no worries here

Nicholas: sent n touch are huge for me

Nicholas: I cant wait to show you

Namita: mmmmmmmmmm nice

Nicholas: I take it all in... the touching... your sent your look... they way you look at me... it's a complete experience... I use all my senses

Nicholas: it's most satisfying and complete

Namita: yes it is an overall experience... i love using all my senses to explore and appreciate my partner

Nicholas: that way I get to experience you completely

Nicholas: we're going to have sooo much fun. in and out of the bedroom

Namita: god i didn't even finish reading ur previous sentence to mine... and we said the same thing

Namita: about using all the senses

Nicholas: like minds honey

Namita: hehe !!

Nicholas: just fantasizing about being w you, not just under the covers

Namita: mmmmmmmm cool !!

Namita: watching tv together

Nicholas: imagining being out in public w you holding hands walking down the street feeling so content

Nicholas: yes

Namita: hehe

Namita: yes that tooo

Nicholas: watching peoples reaction when we enter somewhere .. the looks on there faces.. they look so happy together looks

Namita: hehe... turn their heads

Nicholas: showering together... waking up next to you

Nicholas: yes

Namita: omg yessss

Namita: shower sex

Namita: no not sex

Nicholas: hearing you fall asleep

Namita: lovemaking

Nicholas: shower love making yes

Nicholas: all wet n slippery

Nicholas: me washing your body... my hand gliding all over you

Namita: then we turn off the shower and u pick me up and walk back to the room

Namita: mmmmmmmm niceeeeee

Nicholas: lay you on the bed n we don't even dry off

Namita: and dry me off with a towel

Namita: like minds eh

Nicholas: ever so gently dry you off

Nicholas: or I just lick the water off you

Nicholas: or better yet kiss the water off you

Namita: mmmmm omgggg I was just thinking of that

Nicholas: those minds of ours

Namita: i prefer to dry off with our tongues

Nicholas: I would lick you like a man dying of thrust

Namita: ohh myyy

Namita: id be urning for more and more

Namita: pressing myself up to you

Nicholas: you say you're shy but I'll help you release the vixen I know wants to come out of you

Namita: omg

Namita: yessss

Nicholas: wow is it hot in here?! my god

Namita: hehe

Nicholas: mmm mmm mmm

Namita: i would climb up on top of you... the sight giving a image of a goddess

Namita: my breasts ... full and around ... ready for picking

Namita: water dripping down my naked body... in beads

Namita: would that turn you on

Nicholas: ooohhhh hhhheeeellll yes

Nicholas: I'm very visual and I am soooo there

Nicholas: my god

Namita: ur hands on my waist

Namita: steadying me

Nicholas: pressing myself deep inside you

Namita: yes ur wayyyyyyy deep inside of me... you don't even remember how you slipped inside of me

Nicholas: slowly grinding my hip so you can feel every inch of me

Namita: mmmmmmm yessssss

Nicholas: it just knew where to go

Namita: i lean forward my hands on either side of your head bracing myself on the bed

Nicholas: my hard cock touching every inch inside you... hitting all the spots you just cant reach by yourself

Namita: im rocking my hips

Namita: mmmmmmmmmm

Nicholas: nice n slow

Namita: oh god

Nicholas: I can feel you tense n relax w every stroke

Namita: then i sit up again... continuing my slow rhythmic rocking of my hips on you

Namita: as you take one of ur hands... and start rubbing my clit as i grind into you

Nicholas: me touching your breasts then sitting up to inhale you

Namita: ooooooh god

Nicholas: I use my thumb to work your clit till you pop

Namita: you can feel the hot juices flowing inside of me

Nicholas: as they run down my hips

Namita: some of it trickling out from around ur hard cock

Namita: you want me to work and grind faster

Nicholas: was just thinking that

Namita: but im too slow... so you grab me in ur arms

Namita: with me still on ur hard cock

Namita: and stand up

Namita: and you start walking around the room

Nicholas: you wrap your legs around me

Namita: every so often... you stay in one spot and thrust into me deeply

Namita: making me moan loudly

Namita: yes my legs are wrapped around you

Namita: clinging onto you

Nicholas: as you flip your hair around

Namita: when you walk it drives me wild... as i can feel the vibrations from every step you take

Nicholas: and press you against the wall to slowly thrust into you

Namita: ommmg

Nicholas: n when my legs tire i flip you around onto the bed and take you from behind

Nicholas: you on your elbows n knees

Namita: omggg nicholas

Namita: i offer myself up to you

Nicholas: thrusting deeper inside you till you want to scream

Nicholas: you claw at the sheets in ecstasy

Namita: you can feel the tension inside of me

Namita: yesssssssssss ur drivng me wild

Namita: im clutching on to the sheets

Nicholas: pressing yourself against me tying to feel me as deep as you can

Namita: mmmmmmmmm yesssssssssss

Nicholas: as I pound you from behind you asking for more n don't stop... please don't stop

Namita: yesssssss i want more of you

Namita: feel ever inch of you

Nicholas: I lean over you and reach around n massage your swollen clit till you cum again

Namita: ommmg nicholas

Nicholas: just you wait honey

Namita: are u hard?

Nicholas: we'll do all this in real life

Nicholas: way past hard

Nicholas: oh my god

Nicholas: you've worked me up in to a frenzy

Namita: cum for me

Nicholas: as long as you cum for me

Namita: yes yes

Nicholas: okay

Namita: as ur pounding me hard... from behind

Nicholas: it's urning for your tight wet pussy

Namita: mmmmmmmm yesss

Nicholas: my god I cant wait to do this w you

Namita: you slip ur cock out for a moment

Nicholas: just to linger my tip at your opening

Namita: and then i turn around to suck on it long and hard

Namita: tasting myself on you

Nicholas: oh yesss

Namita: then i would come up to kiss you

Nicholas: tell me your playing w your wet pussy

Namita: yes i am

Nicholas: that's soooooo hot

Nicholas: in that black satin nightie

Namita: its sooo wet

Nicholas: I can almost feel it

Namita: yesss pulled it up

Nicholas: so hot

Nicholas: ohhhh god

Namita: what about you

Nicholas: i can just imagine you stroking me

Nicholas: cock in hand wishing it was you doing this

Nicholas: lying in bed sitting up

Nicholas: looking at your pics

Nicholas: fantasizing about you

Namita: as you slide ur cock into me again... it's sooo engorged... i gasp at the growth in size

Namita: i have to have a moment to get used to it

Nicholas: I feel you quiver

Nicholas: are you going to pop for me?

Namita: yes i will if u are

Nicholas: almost there

Nicholas: now I hold you by the hips n drive myself into you

Namita: mmmm

Nicholas: I can feel you starting to cum as I tell you I'm going too go off

Namita: im already shaking

Namita: i can feel the tension building

Nicholas: you feel me getting bigger as I pause ever so slightly... then I slam myself deeeep inside you as I go off with an explosive contraction

Nicholas: as I contract over n over inside you making you shake w ecstasy

Nicholas: all you can do is ride it out

Namita: i hold on to ur cock with my pussy... milking everything you got

Nicholas: squeezing every last drop from me

Namita: yesssss

Nicholas: you lay face down on the bed catching your breath... me still inside you

Nicholas: you can feel my pulse

Namita: mmmmmmmmmm pleaeeeeeeeee nicholas

Nicholas: still throbbing ever so slightly inside you

Nicholas: hitting you with an after shock one after another

Namita: ohhh god

Namita: you will make me go again

Nicholas: sure

Namita: yessss

Nicholas: now that we've gone off you want more ... I slip out of you

Nicholas: you roll onto your back and I make my way to our throbbing pussy

Namita: ohhh god

Nicholas: trailing kisses all the way down

Nicholas: you can feel my breath on your body

Namita: mmmmmmmmm

Nicholas: I blow gently on your pussy sending goose bumps up your tummy

Namita: ur driving me wild

Nicholas: I kiss you gently

Nicholas: on your lips... yes the ones down there

Namita: ohhhhh nicholas

Nicholas: I spread your lips apart and gently lick your throbbing clit

Nicholas: flicking it w my tongue

Namita: mmmmmmmmmmmmmmmmmmmm

Nicholas: sucking on it then dipping my tongue inside you feeling how hot you are

Nicholas: n how wet you've become

Nicholas: again flicking n sucking your clit faster n faster

Nicholas: listening to you moan w pleasure

Namita: im wet for you nicholas

Nicholas: I can feel your tension building

Nicholas: you want to explode

Namita: yesssssss I do

Nicholas: I burry my face in deeper n lick faster

Nicholas: just before you cum I suck on your clit to push you over the edge

Nicholas: as you cum all over me

Namita: ohhhhhh babyyyyy

Nicholas: shaking n moaning w ecstasy

Nicholas: I gently kiss you all over working my way back up to kiss your lips... you can taste n smell you on my face n lips

Namita: i came sooooooooooo hard again

Nicholas: oh good

Nicholas: just wait till I'm inside you

Namita: i could have screamed

Nicholas: hehe

Nicholas: excellent!

Namita: wake up the neighbors

Namita: do u like to be vocal during?

Nicholas: I'm not usually

Nicholas: not a lot of talking I don't think

Namita: i dont mean talking

Nicholas: oh god comes out a few times

Namita: i mean like moaning

Nicholas: I try to convey that I'm enjoying it

Namita: and groaning

Nicholas: oh yes definitely lots of moaning n groaning

Nicholas: Im guessing you are

Namita: turns me on even more

Nicholas: me too

Nicholas: I love to hear my partner... that way I know I'm in the right spot too

Nicholas: its very hot

Namita: yes that is a good indicator... lol

Nicholas: I guess we just had cyber-sex

Nicholas: never done that before

Namita: hehe yes we did

Namita: how it started i dont know

Nicholas: was very hot

Nicholas: we were talking about doing things together

Namita: yes it was

Nicholas: then we went off on the showering together

Namita: now i have to go back and look what happened

Namita: hahhaha

Nicholas: yah it's all there

Namita: next time we are not going to talk about showers

Nicholas: nope

Namita: taboo

Namita: hehe

Nicholas: algebra & calculus

Namita: yes thats it !!!

Nicholas: my god its after 4

Namita: omg !!

Namita: i didnt even notice

Nicholas: me either

Namita: time just flew

Nicholas: that's like 4 n a half hrs

Namita: oh and please dont mention shower in ur text when im working

Nicholas: longest stretch yet

Namita: it will be an embarrassing mess

Nicholas: lol can't promise anything lol

Namita: hehehe

Nicholas: I'd love to just fall asleep next to you right now

Nicholas: in due time

Namita: mmmmmmmmmmmm it would be sooo nice

Namita: and sleep in on a sunday morning

Nicholas: yes!

Nicholas: being w you everyday would feel like sunday morning

Namita: laze around all day

Nicholas: go for breakfast

Namita: lol aweeeeee... never even thought of that... like how ur mind works

Namita: come back for more

Namita: then go for dinner

Namita: and finish the rest of the evening off

Nicholas: yup work up an appetite

Namita: lol

Nicholas: what time do you start tmw?

Namita: 730pm

Nicholas: ah yes right

Nicholas: well I'll keep my phone w me in the garage n keep an eye out for your text

Namita: ok

Nicholas: as I'll be most of the day working on the hot rod

Nicholas: and thinking of you of course

Namita: oh you will be working on ur car

Namita: got it

Nicholas: yup, thats primarily why I come over (to Parksville)

Namita: ohh yes i see

Nicholas: the biggest reason I want it over there (on the mainland)

Namita: how much more work is there left

Nicholas: hard to say, a true hot rod is never finished lol. but I think it's about 90%

Nicholas: I've driven it before

Namita: ahhhh i seee

Nicholas: now I'm making it exactly as I want it

Nicholas: when I started it I sort of skipped the mock up stage as I wanted to just drive it

Nicholas: now I can see it in my head I just have to make it that way

Namita: well you have a vision

Nicholas: I do

Nicholas: well my dear... I think i need to sleep... as much as I want to keep talking... u must be fading too

Namita: yes im fading here too

Nicholas: I should be up in 4 hrs

Namita: omg

Nicholas: don't want to sleep the day away

Nicholas: only have 2 days here so need to make the most of them

Namita: no dont waste it ... and pls dont fall asleep under ur hot rod

Nicholas: lol I wont... thoughts of you keep me wake

Namita: hehehe

Nicholas: I bid you good night fare maiden. thank u again for a wonderful chat and the play time

Namita: it was a pleasure chatting with u nicholas

Nicholas: and you Namita sleep well

Namita: i will thank u for a great night ... chatting and otherwise 😜

End Time: 4:31 AM

Chapter 6 October 11

At times I have trouble believing Namita is real, even though I have her photos and our conversations. I saved each of them after we were done chatting. I like going through them again, that way I can see things I might have missed the first time and it makes her feel closer. It took some time but, I finally let myself fully commit.

I usually went to bed around 12:45 after a shower and a snack. Before I met Namita I didn't have any reason to stay up late. These days I've been staying up till about 4 am. I was really tired the next day and I was falling asleep during my dinner breaks at work. I figured Namita was worth it and things would change once we were able to spend physical time together.

Start Time: 12:25 AM
Namita: good morning
Nicholas: heeeellllooooo!!!!
Nicholas: was starting to worry
The following message could not be delivered:
"was starting to worry"
Nicholas: hey!
Namita: are you asleep
Nicholas: nope
Nicholas: was waiting for you
Namita: ohhh sorry didnt notice you wrote back
Nicholas: sokay
Namita: i was having issues signing in
Nicholas: ah... you're here now
Namita: how was your day
Nicholas: how was your sleep?
Nicholas: was long
Nicholas: up at 7:30
Nicholas: home about 1 then off to work
Namita: i got up around 8 pm... was out all day... next thing i know it is dark

Nicholas: wow

Namita: when its busy at work... i crash when i get home

Nicholas: is that usually what happens on your work schedule?

Namita: no no tall the time

Namita: not all the time i mean

Nicholas: it must take some time to re coupe to go back on days?

Namita: sometimes you do a set of shifts that are quite challenging both mentally and physically

Nicholas: I bet

Nicholas: that's a long time to be on your toes

Namita: give me a day and im good

Nicholas: have you always worked that kind of schedule?

Nicholas: cool

Namita: yes... ive always worked pretty much the same schedule

Namita: i can work a mon to fri job 8 hrs

Nicholas: I was wondering if one day when our schedules jive and there's a hockey game on if you'd want to go?

Namita: in nursing but i find that 2 days isnt enough for me

Nicholas: I see

Namita: of course i would !!

Nicholas: thought you might

Namita: what time did you get back

Nicholas: about 1

Nicholas: then off to work at 2

Namita: did you go straight to work then ?

Nicholas: yup

Namita: ohh myyy

Nicholas: I thought about how peaceful you must have looked when you were sleeping

Namita: aweee ... even if i had drool coming out the corner of my mouth ?

Namita: hehe

Nicholas: well maybe if its just a little lol

Namita: im kidding of course

Nicholas: I'm sure you are

Namita: hehe... trying to make myself unsexy

Nicholas: not gonna happen

Namita: hehe

Nicholas: I think you'd look sexy right out of the shower and mad as hell at me

Nicholas: lol

Namita: hahaha... mad because ??

Nicholas: no idea

Namita: you didn't join me

Namita: or didnt pass me my towel

Nicholas: like that would ever happen lol

Namita: or maybe flushed the can

Namita: lol

Nicholas: lol

Namita: yes that would never happen... what am i saying

Nicholas: thats my gauge on weather or not I could be w someone

Namita: what ?

Nicholas: if I still think she's sexy even when she's right out of the shower n mad as hell at me

Namita: ahhh i see

Namita: hehe

Nicholas: just something i thought of

Namita: hehe... then watch i might throw something... at you

Nicholas: I'm quick

Namita: like my towel

Namita: lol

Nicholas: mmm

Namita: or hmmmmm

Namita: im thinking... my soap

Nicholas: oh and there we go again talking about showering

Namita: lol

Nicholas: I was good and didn't mention it while you were at work

Nicholas: thought about it

Namita: if i was mad... which rarely happens... what would you do ? RUN the other way ?

Nicholas: nah

Namita: hehe

Nicholas: I'd ask what's wrong

Nicholas: still have the image of you lying in bed... your black satin nightie pulled up... playing with yourself... thinking of me

Namita: hehe... tonight it is blue

Nicholas: mmmm my fav color!

Namita: hehe

Nicholas: is it short or long?

Namita: thanks... yes it is just above the knee

Nicholas: just how i pictured it

Nicholas: n body hugging yes?

Namita: hehe

Namita: yes body hugging... hugging in the right places

Nicholas: of course on you... again just how i imagined it

Nicholas: you defiantly have all the right places

Namita: hehe

Namita: aweee thanks

Namita: i work out every once in awhile

Nicholas: oh yah

Namita: but not fanatically

Nicholas: I try to lead a healthy life style w/o (without) it leading me

Nicholas: I work out about 4 x week

Namita: well put !! ... that is very good !!

Nicholas: n take weekends off

Namita: yeah weekends you have to enjoy and take time for urself for ur mental health

Nicholas: life is too busy to be fanatical about it

Nicholas: yup

Namita: yess sooo true

Nicholas: its 90% nutrition so you can eat right most of the time

Nicholas: n indulge once in a while

Namita: yesss that what keeps us happy

Nicholas: yup

Nicholas: what are your thoughts on marriage? not that I'm asking

Namita: hehe

Nicholas: just curious

Namita: well id love to settle down someday... but doesnt mean i want some huge wedding like every women thinks of

Namita: i just want to be with the right person

Nicholas: yes good answer

Nicholas: being w the right person makes everything else right

Namita: many ppl i believe put sooo much emphasis on the wedding itself... but very little effort in the marriage

Nicholas: yes!!! I totally agree!

Nicholas: thats what I've always thought

Namita: and i feel the importance of why they were together gets lost

Nicholas: yes

Namita: yes me too !!

Nicholas: I want a solid relationship w the right person then the rest is easy

Namita: hehe yessss !!

Namita: im wayyy past doing a big wedding thing

Namita: its just not me

Nicholas: as I said before I'm not willing to settle

Namita: me either

Nicholas: when I got married we didn't have a huge wedding

Nicholas: if my partner and I are happy and we're right for each other then the rest will fall into place

Namita: were you pressured into it ? when you say you settled

Namita: pressured into marriage

Nicholas: I feel like I settled coz there were issues about her that I knew I wasn't comfortable with

Namita: yesss that is so true... im not a worry wart type of person

Nicholas: the marriage was just "what you do" when there's a baby on the way

Nicholas: sometimes I feel like I was trapped

Namita: ohh i see... now i understand

Nicholas: have you ever lived w anyone?

Namita: hmmm would it be wrong if i honestly said no

Nicholas: all i want is for you to be honest

Nicholas: so no its not wrong

Namita: most times ive been with someone they lived away from me

Nicholas: which I know you have been

Namita: yes i know you wont judge... but ppl automatically think stupid things when i say ive never lived with anyone

Nicholas: that's strange

Nicholas: that ppl would think that... you're allowed to be w someone n not live together

Namita: i dont feel i have to... just to prove i did... but also i havent met anyone where ive gone to that level to do that

Nicholas: its a big step n if you're not ready then thats fine

Namita: yes... i am not afraid to though either

Nicholas: whatever you're comfortable w/ is what's important

Nicholas: thats good... you're just waiting for the right person and situation

Nicholas: and whom ever you're w should respect your decision

Namita: yes thats it !! hehe

Namita: oh im not saying thats something i would never do... its just that i havent met someone that i would take that step with

Nicholas: you have such a calming effect on me

Namita: awee thanks nicholas

Nicholas: so you're back to work sat this week?

Namita: im back to work tomorrow for a shift trade

Nicholas: day or night?

Namita: than back again fri and sat

Namita: im working night shift

Nicholas: thats right you said this was your crazy week

Nicholas: I see

Nicholas: any hint as to when I might be able to see you?

Namita: yeah quite gross

Namita: im thinking next thurs or fri

Nicholas: okay let me check my schedule

Namita: ok

Nicholas: during the day coz i'll be working in the afternoon

Namita: k... will let you know

Nicholas: coz sat is the 22nd n you'll be working

Nicholas: I can work around whenever day I can see you. I'll figure something out

Namita: yes... also next week sometime is our festival of lights... in the indian culture

Nicholas: oh cool

Namita: so i may get busy... its like our xmas

Nicholas: that sounds like fun

Namita: some family might be coming in from calgary

Nicholas: I see

Namita: yes it is busy october

Nicholas: do you celebrate xmas?

Namita: first the festival of lights... then halloween

Namita: yes we celebrate xmas too... with a tree

Nicholas: ah

Namita: and turkey and all the trimmings

Nicholas: yah we do too but it's not a religious thing

Nicholas: it's a time for family

Namita: yes i do it for family... although im not religious either

Nicholas: like that photo ... such a pretty smile n cute dimple

Namita: hehe

Namita: thanks

Namita: you have dimples too right ?

Nicholas: yup

Namita: on both sides i see

Nicholas: I think so

Namita: hehe tooo cute !!

Nicholas: thx

Nicholas: we'll look good together dimples n all lol

Namita: yes we will match !!

Nicholas: people wont be able to look away lol

Namita: hehee... nooo it will be the invasion of the dimples

Nicholas: lol

Nicholas: how's that for a close up? I changed my profile photo to a head shot I took the other day so I could mix up things up

Namita: ohhhhhhhhhhhh myyyyyyyyyy

Nicholas: I take it you like?

Namita: yes i think i can see it... in fact maybe i should have a closer look when i see you in person

Nicholas: you can get as close as you like

Namita: hehe... yes with a magnifying glass

Nicholas: now you're just being silly lol

Namita: hehe !! ohh noo my silliness has got me now

Nicholas: lol

Namita: do you wear glasses ?

Nicholas: I do. how'd you guess?

Namita: sorry random question

Nicholas: contacts most of the time

Nicholas: sokay i can keep up w random

Namita: hehe... just thinking

Nicholas: do you?

Namita: own teeth ?

Nicholas: yup

Nicholas: lol

Namita: no i dont... i have good eyesight

Namita: for now that is

Nicholas: lucky

Namita: my entire family wears eyeglasses except me

Nicholas: wow

Namita: or they wear contacts

Namita: i have my own teeth too

Namita: just in case ur wondering

Nicholas: good to know n you don't put them in a jar at night right?

Namita: well i do soak em in baking soda

Namita: hehe

Nicholas: lol brat

Namita: and i have my own boobs too

Namita: hehe

Nicholas: I kind of figured and thats soooo awesome!

Namita: really ??

Nicholas: which part?

Nicholas: me figuring or that being awesome?

Namita: the part that you thought it was awesome

Namita: well both actually

Namita: you must have studied the pics quite well

Namita: you did ur homework

Namita: hehe

Nicholas: just sensed it and not a big fan of fake ones

Namita: eweee me either

Nicholas: I may have had a few looks at your pics not gonna deny

Namita: lol

Nicholas: and 2 more check list items

Namita: what is that ?

Nicholas: real boobs

Namita: check

Nicholas: I guess thats only 1 but there is 2 of them

Namita: yes you count it as 2

Namita: hehe

Nicholas: so it can be worth 2 checks

Namita: yes two checks... i could have had one real boob and one fake !!!

Namita: im just saying

Nicholas: lol

Namita: hehehe

Nicholas: you see I have this mental wish list that I put out to the universe and so far its all in you

Namita: you didnt think that far did you ??

Nicholas: thats why all the check list items

Namita: uh huh

Nicholas: I did not but so far my wish list is being filled

Namita: hmmmm... anything else in ur wish list

Nicholas: not that I can think of at the moment

Nicholas: your comment this morning about taking in all the details that one put me over

Namita: ohh really !!

Nicholas: it's like you knew what I was looking for without me saying it

Nicholas: n its soo awesome that we think alike

Nicholas: now thats not something that i thought would happen

Namita: wowwwww !!

Nicholas: that was one of the little detail things that made me say wow

Namita: ive always been like that... i could pick up a leaf and marvel at it

Namita: i look at birds out my window... which i was doing this morning

Namita: those things make me smile

Nicholas: that's the way I've always been n no one ever seemed to see things the way I do or think the way I do

Nicholas: me too!

Nicholas: its like you get me n no one has ever been able to do that before

Namita: ive always been fascinated with birds since i was a toddler... and now colorful fish

Nicholas: oh yah

Namita: hence why i have an aquarium

Nicholas: oh right salt water reef

Namita: i loveeee looking at the mountains or watching a sunset

Namita: yes it is saltwater

Namita: and ive created a little reef

Namita: with live rocks and coral

Namita: anemones

Nicholas: cool I cant wait to see it

Namita: crabs and shrimp which feed right off my hand

Nicholas: that is cool

Nicholas: I see things that most ppl don't n I can't understand how they can miss them

Namita: and clown fish

Nicholas: Nemo!

Namita: yessss me too

Namita: i am mesmerized by the beauty of nature... no matter what the season

Namita: i even love it when it snows

Nicholas: me too!!

Namita: and cant wait to go drive in it

Namita: it is soooo relaxing

Nicholas: I've looked at the snow as its falling n seen individual snow flakes

Namita: watching it come down as you drive in it

Namita: yessss me too

Nicholas: when they land on a window

Namita: ok like the other morning

Nicholas: mmhmm

Namita: when i was coming home from work... i think it was sunday morning

Namita: i was driving home... and it was pouring rain... they were playing crap music in the radio channels i listen to... so I turned it off so i could just listen to the rain pounding on the wind shield

Namita: it was super relaxing just listening to it

Nicholas: cool

Namita: those are the things i loveeeeee doing

Namita: or getting wet in the rain too

Nicholas: I have a cd that has just waves on the beach and i use it to fall asleep sometimes

Nicholas: yes

Nicholas: watching the clouds

Namita: mmmmmmmmmmm wow sooo nice

Nicholas: the way the wind blows them around n the shapes they make

Namita: have you ever been to Tofino ?

Nicholas: hell yes many a time surfed n camped there lots

Namita: omg the first time i went there with my girlfriends... we were in a bed and breakfast near the ocean... listening to the waves crash in and the lull of the ocean was sooo relaxing and peaceful

Namita: ommmg i loveeeeeeeeeeeeeeeeeeee that place !!!!

Namita: can you imagined if we lived there

Nicholas: it's really cool

Nicholas: that would be cool

Namita: they even have a tiny hospital

Nicholas: long way away from everything

Namita: yeah thats the drawback though

Nicholas: different life style that's for sure

Namita: yes a peaceful one though

Namita: laze around all day... hehe

Nicholas: nice to visit yes very peaceful

Nicholas: I find I sometimes turn the radio off n just listen

Namita: i know i wouldnt survive a month... it would be too peaceful

Nicholas: lol yes

Namita: yessss me too

Nicholas: my sis n her gf were just there this last weekend w friends

Namita: ohhhh cool !! !

Nicholas: have you been to Harrison?

Namita: yessss but ... just a day trip

Nicholas: me either

Namita: would be nice to stay there

Namita: my best friend got married there

Nicholas: driven the scenic route... was cool

Namita: at the hotel grounds

Namita: ive been both ways... the old mission route too

Nicholas: yes drive up n stay the night then come home sometime the next day

Nicholas: yah that's the way I've been

Namita: it is long but nice to go that way

Nicholas: yes yes

Namita: but very picturesque

Nicholas: sometimes the journey is the best part

Namita: yes very true indeed

Nicholas: gives you lots of time to talk and be together

Namita: so ur saying you wont tire of me being a chatterbox all the way to our destination ?

Nicholas: never!

Namita: lol

Nicholas: you can talk my ears off if you like

Namita: what if ur ears start to bleed ?

Nicholas: I want to know everything there is to know about you n I want to hear everything you have to say

Nicholas: your a nurse so problem solved

Namita: hahahahah good one !!!!!!!!!!!

Namita: you're in good hands !!

Nicholas: that's what I hear

Nicholas: can't wait to try them out lol

Namita: hehe... sometimes they can get cold though

Nicholas: quite all right I can warm them up

Namita: mmmmmmmmmm nice

Namita: so what colour is ur hair... if you didn't shave it ? random question

Nicholas: blonde at least it use to be

Nicholas: not sure now

Namita: how long have you shaved it

Nicholas: hmm since '05

Nicholas: do yo like cake or pie? speaking of random questions lol

Namita: hmmm id lean towards cake... i do like pie... my fav would be apple

Namita: only cuz ive never tried any other type

Namita: well i have had pumpkin

Namita: both are good

Nicholas: stick w me kid n I'll show you the world

Namita: hehehe

Namita: do u bake cake/pies ?

Nicholas: strawberry rhubarb pie is my fav as well as coconut cream

Nicholas: I've baked both before

Namita: mmm sounds good

Namita: never had either

Nicholas: I usually turn cakes into cupcakes that way they're easier to eat

Namita: mmmmmmm yummm i loveee cupcakes

Namita: have you ever been to that cupcake store ?

Nicholas: price mart carries a good s/r (strawberry rhubarb)

Namita: called cupcakes

Nicholas: yes i have

Nicholas: Save On has a great coconut cream pie, strawberry rhubarb pie too

Namita: you know... i have never even been to price mart

Nicholas: the cupcake store is a little pricey but they're good

Nicholas: hmm

Namita: i do love lemon meringue pie

Nicholas: smaller version of Save-on

Namita: had one in the states... it was sooo good

Nicholas: yes those are good

Nicholas: chocolate or vanilla?

Namita: yes the cupcake store is pricey but i dont like their cupcakes much cuz the sponge cake is dry

Nicholas: you seem like you can keep up though

Nicholas: hmm

Namita: ive discovered a new place in white rock

Nicholas: oh yah do tell

Namita: ooohhhhhhhhh CHOCOLATE !!!!!!!

Namita: mmmmmmmmmmmm

Nicholas: lol

Namita: this place is called Tracey Cakes

Nicholas: have you been to the Valley Bakery on Hastings?

Namita: in the white rock town overlooking the ocean

Nicholas: oh yah you'll have to take me there one day

Namita: they serve high tea with little sandwiches and scones

Namita: but their cupcakes are to die for

Nicholas: cool

Namita: no ive never been to valley bakery

Nicholas: its a great bakery

Nicholas: wicked chocolate eclairs

Namita: ohhhhh cool

Nicholas: love apple turn overs too

Namita: i went to Fratellis... on commercial drive like 2 weeks ago for the first time

Namita: omg everything looked good

Nicholas: oh yah how was it?

Nicholas: what did you have?

Namita: it is an italian bakery ....all sorts of stuff

Namita: eclairs... cookies... bars

Namita: cakes

Namita: pies

Nicholas: wow

Namita: loafs

Nicholas: not the place to go when one is hungry

Namita: i loveed their pistachio cake

Namita: nooooooooo

Namita: hehe

Nicholas: have you had gelato?

Namita: or get a job there

Nicholas: dangerous was just thinking that

Namita: yes first time this year

Namita: and it wasn't good

Nicholas: I'd be 300 lbs if i worked at a bakery

Namita: hehehe

Namita: i went to that italian gelato house in Vancouver

Nicholas: on Venables?

Namita: and everything looked good but the gelato tasted like ice

Namita: yes thats the one

Nicholas: noticed that too

Namita: it wasn't creamy

Nicholas: i'll take you to Camparis down the road from me. it is to die for

Namita: ohhhhhhh wowwwwwwww

Namita: yayyyyyyyyyyyyyyy

Namita: i loveeeeeeeeeeee ice cream

Nicholas: last time I had strawberry cheesecake n it tasted just like it even though it was gelato

Nicholas: good to know

Namita: my fav this year was creme brulé ice cream

Nicholas: there's a place near Parksville called Whiskey Creek and the gas station/connivence store serves huge ice cream cones w Island Farms ice cream. a one scoop is like 2 reg scoops

Namita: ohhh myyyy

Nicholas: I like pralines n cream

Nicholas: a 3 scoop looks like about a half liter of ice cream

Nicholas: all stacked onto a waffle cone

Namita: there is like tons of ice cream shops in white rock along the beach... every other shop is either fish and chips or ice cream

Namita: mmmmmmmmm we could share one then

Nicholas: I was down there years ago

Nicholas: yes we should

Nicholas: to WR it's been a while since I was there

Nicholas: I have a feeling I'm going to be going to WR more often in the near future lol

Namita: i love this one ice cream shop... it is italian

Namita: they have the coolest flavors

Namita: like pear... lavender

Nicholas: oh yah

Nicholas: wow lavender that's different

Namita: and baci

Namita: they make it on the premises

Nicholas: Camparis makes all there own gelato too

Nicholas: they even have some cakes n pastries too

Namita: wow cool !!! we will have to check it out

Nicholas: yes we will

Nicholas: its open late too

Nicholas: an Italian man owns it

Namita: ohhh nice... for us night owls!!

Nicholas: lol yah

Namita: i will go in my nightie and robe with you

Nicholas: well not this late but they're open till 11 or 12 i think

Namita: after you come back from work

Nicholas: ok but if you're in your nightie I might not be able to go out I may just keep you all to myself

Nicholas: I like the way you think though

Namita: hehehe ...yes im sure you will opt for a different dessert !!

Nicholas: you know it!

Namita: lol

Nicholas: I could pick some up on the way home then we wouldn't have to leave again lol

Namita: ohhh yes !! we can just dig in

Nicholas: yup

Namita: hey how was ur grandpa doing ?

Nicholas: he's okay

Nicholas: he's pretty lonely since my gramma died

Nicholas: I know he liked having me there for dinner

Namita: ohhh... does he live by himself?

Nicholas: which is one of the reasons I visit him

Nicholas: he lives in an assisted care place

Namita: ohh... im sure he enjoyed ur company !!

Nicholas: yah we have a special bond. shortly before my gramma died i wrote him an email where i thanked him for being my grampa and for giving my gramma a better life

Nicholas: so he knows i do what i can for him even if its just sitting n watching baseball.

The following message could not be delivered:

"yah we have a special bond. shortly before my gramma died i wrote him an email where i thanked him her being my grampa and for giving my gramma a better life"

The following message could not be delivered:

"so he knows i do what i can for him even if its just sitting n watching baseball"

Namita: my dads side of grandparents passed away a while back

Namita: i have one grandma left

Nicholas: I don't know why but messenger keeps kicking me off

Namita: yeah i noticed too

Nicholas: I'm sorry to hear that

Namita: it did that to me when i logged on

Nicholas: I love that photo!!! thats wow w a capital WOW!

She's wearing a black sequinned strapless top in this a medium shot. Her hair is down slightly wavy with a smokey eye makeup and full lips. Definitely shows her curves.

Namita: hehe... thanks... it was taken this spring... or june i think... when i went to see Wicked the musical at the QE (Queen Elisabeth Theatre) with friends

Nicholas: I heard about that. my sis n a bunch of her friends went

Nicholas: that is a very hot photo

Nicholas: I don't have very many pics so I'll just bounce back n forth with the ones I've got

The following message could not be delivered:

"that is a very hot photo"

The following message could not be delivered:

"I don't have very many pics so I'll just bounce back n forth with the ones I've got"

The following message could not be delivered:

"I heard about that. my sis n a bunch of her friends went"

Nicholas: stupid messenger

Namita: lol

Namita: they dont want you to talk to me

Nicholas: I thought when i up dated it wouldn't do that anymore

Nicholas: I guess not

Nicholas: I know it's only been a week n a half

Namita: yes it does actually

Nicholas: its very cool to have this strong a connection w someone after only a week n a half which says a lot

Nicholas: I feel an undeniable chemistry w you... I anticipate sparks or fireworks or even time standing still when we finally meet

Namita: i know it sometimes hard to find a person that one is compatible with and share the same values, thoughts and feelings as one another... so having connected like this is still almost surreal to me too... we've made a connection on every level here

Nicholas: yes surreal is a good word for it. almost too good to be true. I think that's why I love talking with you because it makes you that much more real to me. instead of feeling like I'm dreaming you.

Namita: no ur not dreaming... i guess i will have to pinch you when we first meet

Nicholas: okay

Namita: lol

Nicholas: I've been walking on about 6 inches of air since our first conversation

Nicholas: I never would have guessed that I'd meet someone as special as you... I had pretty much given up looking... then out of the blue you showed up and whisked me off my feet

Namita: yes i noticed ur pic first on LL... thought you were cute... but hoped you would notice me too

Namita: and you did

Nicholas: and it was your story that caught my attention

Namita: did you have any conversations with other women on LL

Nicholas: nope

Namita: could you picture urself in my scenario ?

Nicholas: oh hell yes

Nicholas: was like a movie playing out in my head

Namita: lol

Nicholas: when I saw your photo i was able to put you in it too

Nicholas: n it was so cool n hot all at the same time

Namita: yes i tried to describe myself as i went along in my scenario

Namita: ohhh woww really ?

Nicholas: you did a fabulous job

Nicholas: yes

Namita: ohh thanks... hehehe... at least it caught ur attention

Nicholas: that it did

Nicholas: I was getting tired of reading the same things over n over. Thats why it was so refreshing to read yours

Nicholas: and it spoke to my creative side

Namita: what do the other women write ? Im curious now

Nicholas: I'm easy going family oriented fit blah blah blah lol

Nicholas: like walks on the beach

Nicholas: like my life

Namita: hehe... that is soooo cliche... like dont you think the beach would be a crowded place by now if everyone did that

Nicholas: one day I'll show you my whole write up. there's way more but LL would only let me put so much

Nicholas: yah thats what I mean just boring stuff

Namita: or i like it when they write ...lets take a walk on the beach and see where it takes us... ummm my answer is... it will take you to the other side !!!

Nicholas: lol

Namita: hehe

Nicholas: I don't know what other guys write but I wanted to be honest and let my personality come through

Nicholas: I know there is a lot of deception on there

Namita: yess me too

Nicholas: and instead of making a list of all the things I don't want like a lot of bio's do I wanted to stay on the positive side and write about what I am looking for

Namita: yesss that is sooo good !! i hate it when there a list of negative ideas on ppl's bio's

Namita: i remember one time ... a guy was chatting with me ... an older fellow

Nicholas: a friend of mine saw my bio on LL and she said this sounds like Nick n then she saw the pic was like omg it is him lol

Namita: hehehee that is sooo cool !!

Namita: well this guy showed me his pics

Namita: he wasnt anything to look at

Namita: good thing i didnt show my pic

Nicholas: disappointing

Nicholas: no kidding

Namita: but i made a comment to him... about his nice boat or yacht ... he told me it wasnt his

Nicholas: I find there's a lot of desperation on there too, like they're looking so hard that its the last thing they'll do

Namita: and the conversation goes downhill very very quickly

Nicholas: oh geeze

Namita: by him asking me ...HOW MUCH !?!?! ... he wanted a high end escort

Nicholas: OMG what an asshole

Namita: or something i dont know

Namita: i was stunned at first and then i said you have it all wrong

Namita: then he started calling me names like a whore, tramp...

Nicholas: jerk

Namita: still thank god he didnt get my pics

Nicholas: yah

Namita: beforehand

Namita: i was sooo glad i didnt... and held off

Namita: i ended up reporting him to LL

Nicholas: ppl take it way too serious. I was looking to make some friends and if one of those friendships turned into something special than great. I gave it a month then I deleted my account

Nicholas: good you reported him

Namita: yes there are the usual harassing men on LL

Nicholas: I'm amazed 2 ppl that are honest good hearted found each other through all the crap that goes on on those sites

Namita: hehehehe

Namita: yes we sifted thru the thick sludge

Nicholas: I could never understand that online or in real life. slobbering all over women isn't going to get you anywhere

Namita: lol

Nicholas: yes we did and I'm pretty pleased with who I came up with

Namita: no it wont !! in fact it makes us run the other way

Nicholas: or calling them names either

Namita: ommggg that is a really stupid move

Namita: unless ur calling out dirty names in a heat of passion

Namita: thats different

Namita: hehehe

Nicholas: I knew or hoped one day that the right person would come along and I'd be waiting for her and everything would fall into place. little did I know it would take 39 years

Nicholas: yes heat of passion, very different

Namita: its never too late for anything

Nicholas: that's right

Namita: uh huh

Nicholas: are you fading?

Namita: hehe... are you ?

Nicholas: a little... I don't want to go though

Namita: you've had a long day too

Namita: it's almost 4 now

Nicholas: yah but I waited all day to talk w you

Namita: lol

Nicholas: wow time flies

Namita: i knowwwwwwww

Nicholas: promise me that if I am dreaming you wont wake me up

Namita: i wont... and i wont wipe that smirk off ur face either

Nicholas: okay good

Nicholas: with you in my life it'll be a permanent smirk

Namita: hehehe

Nicholas: let me know as soon as you have an opening in your schedule ok?

Namita: ok i will

Nicholas: and I'll try to make it work

Namita: are you in bed ?

Nicholas: not yet

Nicholas: was going to be

Namita: arent you cold ?

Nicholas: was going to follow your lead

Namita: hehe

Nicholas: just my feet

Namita: ohhh geeez

Namita: are you in ur boxers ?

Nicholas: sweat pants n t shirt

Nicholas: I know very sexy lol

Nicholas: and socks

Namita: ahhh   ok... yessss sooo sexy

Nicholas: lol

Namita: even better

Nicholas: I'd love to be in your bed right now

Nicholas: I know my feet wouldn't be cold

Namita: mmmmmmmm yesssss

Nicholas: you in your nightie mmm mmm

Namita: no i would keep them warm

Nicholas: I can almost feel the heat coming from your body

Namita: mmmm im nice and warm

Nicholas: I bet you are

Nicholas: my place is always a little cool

Namita: i like that though

Nicholas: the heat doesn't stay very long in my place n I don't have control of it either

Nicholas: it's okay when in bed n to sleep

Nicholas: suppose I could put a sweater on

Namita: i know basements are hard to maintain the heat in

Nicholas: it's nice in the summer

Namita: plus ur dependent on ur landlord to keep warm

Nicholas: yes

Namita: yesss summertime its nice and cool

Namita: nicholas im seriously fading ...and my right shoulder is hurting me

Nicholas: ok im fading too

Namita: probably with the lifting done at work

Nicholas: don't want you in pain

Nicholas: oh sorry to hear that

Namita: yeah i think i will take some Advil

Namita: no i will be ok

Nicholas: you know best

Nicholas: I hope so

Namita: yes it will... just needs a little tlc

Namita: and Advil

Nicholas: okay I'm going to log off brush my teeth n go to bed. you know I want to stay but you need to sleep too

Nicholas: thanks for another great session Namita

Nicholas: just to clarify in case it wasn't obvious

Namita: yesss you go get some rest too... i know we always have cool things to talk about

Nicholas: I really like you n can't wait to know more

Namita: hehe thanks nicholas!!! you are an awesome person too

Nicholas: thx. gnight my sweet

Namita: good nite nicholas !! pleasant dreams

Namita: have a good day tomorrow

Nicholas: you too

Namita: thanks

Nicholas: night

End Time: 3:58 AM

Chapter 7 October 13

I finally feel I'm living life instead of this "Look but don't touch world" I've been in for so long. I'm constantly smiling, it wells up from emotions deep inside.

Start Time: 12:20 AM

Nicholas: hey!!!

Namita: hey there

Namita: how have you been ?

Nicholas: not bad. you?

Namita: sorry i didnt get back to you with the text... in fact i just saw them now

Nicholas: sokay. as long as everything is okay

Namita: was busy all day

Nicholas: was starting to worry but I know you were probly sleeping most of the day

Namita: yep things are good

Nicholas: good

Namita: actually didnt get much sleep at all today

Nicholas: aw how come?

Namita: i went Chilliwack... one of my friends is getting married and im one of the bridesmaid... so i had to go for a dress fitting

Namita: i didnt even know about it till i go the message in my email

Nicholas: oh I see... that's a long way

Nicholas: oh geeze

Namita: i hadnt even checked my email for a while

Namita: yeah i made it there and back in one piece

Nicholas: good

Namita: hehe

Nicholas: are the dresses nice?

Namita: meh... its good

Nicholas: I know most brides maids aren't usually

Namita: they are orange... autumn colours

Nicholas: orange wow bold

Nicholas: form fitting? or loose?

Namita: hehe... its a sleeveless... and come up to the knees

Namita: yes form fitting

Nicholas: hmm

Namita: hehe

Nicholas: I guess as long as the bride is happy that's all that matters

Namita: but the fabric is layered on top of each other ...in tiers

Namita: yes true !!

Nicholas: hmm

Namita: is that a good hmmm or a bad hmmm?... hehe

Nicholas: hmm just letting you know I'm listening

Namita: ohhhh hehe

Nicholas: the bride doesn't usually want her maids looking better than her

Nicholas: random question

Nicholas: did you have braces when you were younger?

Namita: yes you're right... so we have to look as hideous as possible

Namita: no i didnt

Namita: do they look crooked ? ... hehe

Nicholas: they're really gonna have to work at that to make you hideous

Namita: did you have braces ?

Namita: hahahaha

Nicholas: I did... no its just I haven't seen a toothy smile yet

Namita: well the color orange does complement my skin tone

Namita: ahhhhh

Nicholas: you could wear a garbage bag n it would look good on you lol

Nicholas: are you back on days tmw?

Namita: aweee thanks... hehe... or a burlap sack

Namita: im back on days...yes

Namita: i hate the short turnover

Nicholas: oh wow.. all I have to do is ask n you answer

Namita: what do you mean ?

Nicholas: I bet... messes w the body

Namita: ohhhhh ...lol

Nicholas: I love your smile!!!!

Namita: hehe... thanks

Namita: it sure does mess with the body

Nicholas: I mentioned not seeing a toothy smile n poof there's one

Namita: a few weeks ago... i got quite nauseated finishing off a nite shift

Namita: hehe

Nicholas: how come?

Namita: and my friend Ashley and i were coming down the elevator and here i am retching every now and then... that never happens to me

Nicholas: wow was so bad you spewed?

Namita: i dont know why it happened but i know sometimes working night shifts can make some nurses nauseated cuz ur entire food and sleep schedule is out

Nicholas: I can see that.. if I'm up too early my body doesn't want to eat

Namita: i had to breath really deeply and close my eyes... as it was coming

Nicholas: damn... I hate that feeling.. knowing it's coming n there's nothing you can do about it

Namita: that was weird... ive been doing this for 15 yrs and that was the worst

Namita: yeah i knowwwwww

Nicholas: one xmas at my parents house we all got sick

Nicholas: like really sick which never happens

Nicholas: I found out years later that it was Norwalk

Namita: omg !! that really takes the energy out of you

Namita: it happened to me too back in 2006

Nicholas: there were 8 of us n the only one that didn't get it was my youngest as she was in bed early and no one had any contact w her till morning

Namita: i survived on jello... if at all

Nicholas: I was able to fight it till the bitter end but finally it won

Namita: she lucked out !!

Nicholas: she did

Namita: were u down with a fever too ?

Nicholas: after I ate freezies sitting against the fridge

Namita: hehehhehhee

Namita: i can just picture that

Nicholas: nope no fever just the runs and the spewing

Namita: lol

Nicholas: they tasted soooo good... the freezies that is lol

Namita: ohhh i had the fever and rigors

Namita: lol

Nicholas: oh geeze

Nicholas: do you get sick often?

Namita: i was on my bedroom floor when it first hit

Namita: no otherwise im pretty healthy and tough

Nicholas: me too

Namita: i will get the yearly cold but that is it

Nicholas: if I do get sick it's just a cold n only about 2 per year

Namita: hehe

Nicholas: let me guess... you're the type of person to just suck it up and push on through when you have a cold rather than wallowing in your own misery right?

Namita: hehe... how did you guess !!! But when i do succumb to it... im a baby !!

Nicholas: just like me sept for the last part lol

Namita: by then i am sooo calling in sick to work

Nicholas: yah... I don't usually call in but you kind of have too

Namita: actually we are not supposed to be at work if we're sick with a cold

Nicholas: that's what I thought

Namita: but then at the same time if ur sick often like 10 percent of the year then they call us in to ask us why we are sick often

Nicholas: I can see that

Namita: it is soooo annoying... you sit down with the union , ur manager , and someone from health & wellness

Namita: arghhhh

Nicholas: you've had to do it?

Namita: so far no yet

Nicholas: just what u heard?

Namita: ive been careful plus i try to keep a good attendance

Nicholas: me too

Namita: and i have good work ethics

Namita: i dont call in sick just because its a weekend or friday

Nicholas: yes!!! I show up when I'm suppose to n do the best I can which is usually more than what's expected

Namita: well i did for the hockey game ... i told you ... but that was it

Nicholas: playoffs are way different

Namita: yesss... im a very concientious person... i know i spelled that wrong

Namita: conscientious i mean

Namita: hehe yesssssss playoffs... im sorry you cant drag me to work

Nicholas: totally fine I didn't notice the spelling... I knew what you meant

Nicholas: so I have to tell you.... today is the first day that I let myself completely believe that this with you is really happening

Nicholas: oh and I get a little mushy when I get tired

Namita: hehe... mushy is all good with me

Nicholas: but you've probly noticed the last part

Namita: and what exactly do you do ? in person

Nicholas: when I get mushy?

Namita: yes

Nicholas: mmm more touchy feely if that's possible... not that I'm in your back pocket... I just like to reach out n touch to let you know that I'm there n thinking of you and that I'm happy

Nicholas: and touch you because I can

Namita: aweeee sooo cute... i am touchy feely too... love holding hands... just to know that ur there

Nicholas: makes you more real... I've always been a physical contact type of person that's why online dating is so strange to me

Nicholas: yes!!!

Nicholas: I once read that we touch our partner the way we want to be touched

Namita: or even its like we're working side by side in the kitchen perhaps... every once in awhile I like to touch... like a pat on the shoulder... or a kiss

Namita: yes I would agree with that

Nicholas: yes!! or a hand brushes your back

Namita: yesss !!

Nicholas: unreal!.. if someone told me I'd meet someone like you I would have said not a chance... call it fate or coincidence... call it whatever you want, I'm just glad.. no that's not the right word... ecstatic we found each other

Nicholas: I know I keep bringing that up but sometimes I'm just beside myself with it all

Namita: hehe... we have so much in common and similarities... it is quite amazing

Nicholas: it is

Nicholas: opposites attract but similarities bind

Namita: hehe that is sooo true... never really thought of it that way

Nicholas: I heard that a long time ago... now I really understand it

Namita: yeah it doesn't make sense at that time till you experience it

Nicholas: yes!! you have to experience most things to really get them

Namita: i was going to ask a random question and forgot

Nicholas: sokay

Nicholas: it'll come back

Namita: ohhhh so were you born in Parksville too ?

Nicholas: nope Vernon

Namita: ohhhhh cool !!

Namita: ive been there once

Nicholas: my parents lived on a ranch in Falkland. I don't remember it, just seen pics. and Vernon was the closest hospital

Nicholas: it's not much to see from what I've heard

Nicholas: where were you born? new west?

Namita: ahhhh I see ...so what made them move to the island

Nicholas: after Falkland we lived in Edmonton and Ft McMurray. we visited parksville a couple of times then finally my parents said lets move there

Namita: hehe... nooo I was born New Zealand

Nicholas: really!!! that's sooo cool... I have rellies there

Namita: omg ive been to Ft McMurry !!

Nicholas: do you have double citizenship?

Namita: yes my parents were there for awhile ... and we moved in the early 70's here

Nicholas: cool!

Nicholas: where were they before NZ (New Zealand)?

Namita: no i dont have double citizenship

Namita: i have relatives there too

Nicholas: just Canadian?

Nicholas: neat

Namita: hehe yes just a Canadian... they were in Fiji before that

Nicholas: lol well not "just" canadian

Namita: and before that India

Nicholas: geeze they really travelled

Namita: hehe... yes they've been around

Nicholas: so they're landed immigrants?

Namita: lol

Nicholas: I'm very patriotic

Nicholas: love being Canadian

Namita: no they are full Canadian citizen since the late 70's

Nicholas: I see

Namita: yes me too... i am soo canadian... i cant think of being anything else

Nicholas: yup... when I was younger I looked into becoming a US Navy SEAL but you have to be a US citizen because of the security clearance issue

Nicholas: I like that photo... the camera loves you

Namita: ohhh geeez i can imagine !!

Nicholas: you're on the right. right?

Namita: awee thanks

Namita: yes

Nicholas: keen eye for detail

Namita: the other one is my sister

Namita: hehe... yes you can pick me out from a crowd now

Nicholas: that n I could spot that beautiful smile from a mile away

Namita: hehehee

Nicholas: younger sis or older?

Namita: younger

Namita: im the eldest on the totem pole

Nicholas: ohhh

Namita: that sounds like i am too old

Nicholas: I guess they would have to be younger if you're the eldest lol

Namita: lol

Nicholas: age is all a state of mind

Nicholas: sometimes I feel 14... 39 and 87

Namita: i knowww... i dont feel my age sometimes... most times i feel like a teenager

Nicholas: what matters is that you're young at heart and not to let the little things get in the way of the important things

Nicholas: totally w you on that

Namita: yessss that is very true indeed

Namita: tell me... i think i missed it... what were you doing in Ft M (Ft McMurry) ?

Nicholas: you didn't miss it... I didn't mention it

Nicholas: my dad was working at Syncrude

Namita: ohh yes the oil company

Nicholas: in the early 70's when they were building it

Namita: ohhh wow !!

Namita: it must have been quite desolate back then

Nicholas: yup... he was a self taught heavy duty mechanic

Namita: wow !! that is sooo cool

Nicholas: he was able to figure out how things worked and fix them

Namita: most of that kind of mechanical duties can only be learned by pulling things apart

Namita: im sure he was quite an asset for the company

Nicholas: I inherited a lot of his mind and abilities too except the mathematics part... im not great at math

Nicholas: he was

Namita: wowww

Namita: have you been back

Nicholas: when we lived in Ft Mac he challenged the heavy duty mechanics course and got such a high mark he was given the Red Seal or interprovincial cert (certificate) all that without taking a single class

Nicholas: you have to get above a certain score to be awarded the Red Seal

Nicholas: have not... I like BC too much to leave. that being said I do like to travel and experience the world

Namita: ohhh wowwww... good for him !!! he knew what he was doing... thats for sure !!

Namita: OMG !!

Nicholas: he learned to drive when he was 9

Namita: i loveeeeeeeeeeeee BC so much too !!

Nicholas: I love road trips

Namita: and im not just talking about the cities... I love everything from north to south... east to west

Nicholas: doesn't always matter where I'm going I just like to drive

Nicholas: yes

Namita: Yes me too... i love driving along scenic routes

Nicholas: yes! those are the best

Nicholas: random question, what color nightie are you wearing this evening?

Namita: my cousin used to live in Ft M and she and her bf worked for Syncrude...i cant remember which one cuz they sound similar

Nicholas: just filing in my image of you

Namita: lol

Namita: im wearing pink

Nicholas: lying in bed.. thought I should give you some clothes lol

Nicholas: thank you

Namita: hehehehe... yes you should esp since i was feeling cold

Nicholas: not that the nightie will stay on for long. but I'm getting distracted

Namita: hehe... it is pink with tiny black polka dots

Nicholas: cold gotcha... snuggling a little closer to help warm u up

Nicholas: mmm the details love it!

Namita: and black lace around the cups of the bodice

Nicholas: mmmm mmmm

Namita: with a pink ribbon in between

Nicholas: mmmhmmm

Namita: ohh and black lace edging at the bottom hem

Nicholas: perfect

Namita: heheh

Nicholas: so G-string thong or T back usually

Namita: hmmm I have a variety but would go for t back most times

Nicholas: sooo sexy

Nicholas: made me loose my concentration n forgot where I was going w my thoughts

Nicholas: do you have to be up early?

Namita: hehehehe... sounds like you loveeeeeeeee lingerie

Nicholas: it's very sexy on the right body and you definitely have the right body

Nicholas: lingerie was made for you

Namita: aweee thanks... yes I loveee lingerie

Namita: I have soo many in many colors

Nicholas: your body makes lingerie look good

Nicholas: I can't wait to see them all!

Namita: hehe... I like lace and different textures or patterns

Nicholas: I love a woman who likes to dress sexy even just everyday wear

Namita: hehe... yesss I even wear it to work... not to show off... it just makes me feel good under very "sexy" scrubs

Nicholas: the lingerie you wear to work for under your scrubs?

Nicholas: now that's hot!

Namita: yessss !!

Namita: I always wore lingerie ever since I could remember

Namita: I'm particular about those things

Nicholas: that's cool... there are so many options for women.. not much for men, we dress manly

Namita: I never buy cheap lingerie cuz I know I will end up paying for its cheapness in some way

Nicholas: so true

Namita: well I loveeeeeee a manly man !!!!

Nicholas: it doesn't last long and after a few washes the cheapness shows

Namita: one time I bought a bra from walmart ...cuz i thought it looked ok

Namita: brought it home... wore it all day and omg the inside was this cheap sheer meshy liner and it make me itch all day !!!

Namita: it was not fun at all

Nicholas: damn that sucks when you don't get your moneys worth out of something

Namita: it went into the garbage that day

Nicholas: not a place to be itchy either

Namita: hehe

Nicholas: so you have some Victoria Secret?

Namita: I was soooo sore and red

Nicholas: I bet, thats a tender sensitive place

Namita: yessss I do... they send me their catalogue every now and then

Namita: yes it was quite sensitive

Namita: I felt like someone put in some itching powder or something

Nicholas: lol

Namita: hehehe

Namita: I was squirming alot

Namita: I'm sure you can totally picture this

Namita: lol

Nicholas: it's hard to scratch when in public

Nicholas: mmmhmmm

Nicholas: your boobs sensitive... go on

Namita: yesssssssss wont be ladylike !!

Namita: hehe

Namita: so you grin and bear it !!

Nicholas: them in my face... definitely bare them

Nicholas: ☺

Namita: hehe

Namita: I didn't even see you wrote that above

Namita: yes I'm pretty sensitive

Namita: even in cold

Nicholas: that's what I've heard

Nicholas: even more so in the cold I bet

Namita: ohhh yess...

Nicholas: I could warm them for you... one in each hand

Nicholas: it's taking all my being to not let this scenario in my head turn into a full on porno lol

Namita: I remember one year... in the winter... whenever i went to work in the early wee hrs of the morning... no matter what i did... my nipples became extremely sensitive to the cold... so much that they hurt

Namita: hahahahaha ohhhhhhhhhhhh nicholas !!!!!

Nicholas: sorry to hear that

Nicholas: talking about your boobs will do it to me every time

Namita: i would stuff tissues in my bra to keep them warm

Namita: hehehe

Nicholas: do they still get sensitive in the cold like that?

Namita: then as soon as it started it went away... granted it happened that whole winter season

Nicholas: hmm

Namita: yes they do... but not till the point of hurting

Nicholas: well that's good... never fun when they hurt

Namita: yesss... that for sure !!

Nicholas: what time are you up in the morning?

Namita: im good... im up by 6 but i slept this evening for a bit

Nicholas: ok.. don't want to keep you too late

Namita: no no im good !

Nicholas: ok

Nicholas: my spelling blows when I get tired... not that I am or anything lol

Namita: i was wondering what you just meant but now i go tit

Namita: omgggggg i mean it !!!!!

Nicholas: lmaof

Nicholas: lol

Namita: hhahahaha

Nicholas: funny

Namita: ur talking about ur spelling !!!

Nicholas: yup lol

Nicholas: not tits

Nicholas: lol

Namita: that was such great timing !!

Nicholas: you couldn't plan that lol

Nicholas: as long as we know what each other means then it's all good

Namita: no im typing like a mad woman...and my fingers slipped

Namita: yes slipped... i will go with that

Namita: hehehe

Nicholas: I still look at the keys so sometimes I get a little dizzy when I type fast

Namita: yes me too

Nicholas: more of a hunt n peck approach

Namita: i have to look at the keys... typing was not my greatest subject

Namita: cuz i leaned on the creative side in school

Nicholas: me either... I took food or auto shop instead of typing in school

Namita: omg yes me too

Namita: i tried typing for a week then dropped it

Nicholas: I couldn't justify taking a class to learn to type when I could take PE or those others I mentioned

Namita: i took home ec, family studies, and art

Nicholas: I knew I wouldn't have a job that required it

Nicholas: art all the way... graduated top of the grade 12's in Foods n nutrition

Namita: yeah i hated the typing teacher too ...he was a loser... so i wasnt about to sit for entire year with him

Namita: WOWWWW cool Nicholas

Nicholas: visual arts to be exact

Nicholas: I do like to cook n bake

Namita: yes i took art all the way from 8 thru 12

Namita: my fav subject

Nicholas: cooking is more fun when cooking for someone

Namita: always got an guaranteed A in it

Nicholas: PE art n acting were my staple courses

Nicholas: yup my thoughts too

Namita: yes true... cooking for someone is wayyy more fun and you pay attention to the little detail and give 200 percent

Namita: what kind of sports do you play or enjoy

Nicholas: PE 11 n 12 was leisure activities... for PE 12 the 2nd week in we went to Long Beach to go surfing... was soooo cool

Namita: ohhh wow... that must have fun

Nicholas: beach volleyball, hockey... ice and ball

Namita: esp when ur closer to it

Namita: loveeeeee volleyball

Namita: tennis sometimes

Namita: used to play basketball in high school

Nicholas: we always had fun in PE... there were a few of us that had the same instructor since grade 4 so we had a bond w him

Nicholas: so it was always fun

Namita: i was not into the cheerleading stuff

Nicholas: soo good to hear

Namita: that was left to the blondes of my school

Namita: they had no skills

Nicholas: I've heard cheerleaders are retarded dancers lol

Namita: or had no other skills

Namita: LMAO !!!!

Namita: that should sum it up !!

Nicholas: I played high school volleyball n basketball too

Nicholas: lol

Namita: well most of the girls in my high school were like that ...sleeping around , smoking pot, cheerleading

Nicholas: when I play ice hockey I play left wing but when I play ball hockey I play goal

Namita: and im talking about Charles Best on Como Lake

Namita: up the hill from you

Nicholas: wow really?!

Namita: ohhh that is cool nicholas... do you still play hockey ?

Nicholas: not as much as I'd like

Nicholas: I go to stick n puck sometimes

Namita: the school is in front of Mundy park... so they would go into the woods and smoke pot... make out... hang out

Nicholas: I'd like to get back into ball hockey for sure

Namita: never heard of ball hockey...thats not grass hockey...is it ?

Nicholas: I guess that's how you become popular in school by putting out... such a shame

Namita: or is it floor hockey

Namita: yes I was one of the other girls

Nicholas: nope basically floor hockey sept played w a special ball

Namita: it wasnt till i was in grade 11 that i was more noticed

Namita: Centennial was a melting pot of so many ppl then

Namita: ohhh i see

Nicholas: good to know... I wasn't a big partier in school... I was too bust working on my hot rod

Namita: the sluts of CB (Charles Best) became the other girls !!

Namita: sorry have to put it like that

Nicholas: I graduated w a girl who was pregnant

Nicholas: sokay

Namita: how many hot rods have you made ?

Nicholas: just the 1

Namita: ohhh ... yes i remember one girl was preggars in grade 11 and brought her baby to school in gr 12

Namita: what a life

Nicholas: I have a design for a shop truck I'd like to build... I'd like to open my own creative design studio

Namita: that would be soooo cool

Nicholas: I have yet to tell you about Blueflame Creative.... that's what I call myself

Nicholas: that's what's tattooed on my back

Nicholas: my logo

Namita: you kinda mentioned it ...but didn't get into it

Namita: ohhh yesss the tattoo

Nicholas: I work in whatever medium gets me the end result

Namita: what mediums have you worked in so far... steel fabric clay wood plastic

Nicholas: I have T shirts printed that have the top 5 reasons welders make better lovers

Namita: LOL

Namita: wow cool !!

Nicholas: there are innuendoes that go w welding terminology so I put them on a shirt

Namita: can i hear them ?

Nicholas: you sure can

Nicholas: brb (be right back) I have to grab one I can't remember them off the top of my head lol

Namita: okay

Nicholas: 1 we always have plenty of rod for the job

Namita: lmaooo !!

Nicholas: 2 our rod is always hot

Namita: hehehe

Nicholas: 3 we can work in all positions, there's 4

Namita: hehehe

Nicholas: 4 we always work at the right temperature

Namita: check !!

Nicholas: 5 we always ensure maximum depth of penetration

Namita: hahahaha... check

Nicholas: I've had them for about 3 years now n sold about 50

Namita: wow !! that is pretty good !!

Nicholas: I guess it's more of a check list for you lol

Nicholas: thx

Nicholas: I have a couple of other T shirt ideas too

Namita: ohhh yesss a check list !!!

Namita: you should do a nurse one

Nicholas: most women like #5

Namita: the penetration one ?

Nicholas: yes

Nicholas: are there innuendoes that nurses say?

Namita: YESssss I got pretty excited over here !!!

Namita: yes we do... but more like phrases

Nicholas: too bad I'm not there to see just how excited you got

Namita: lemme think

Nicholas: I also want to have a line of Blueflame Creative clothing too... diff clothes w my logo on it

Namita: ok heres one... remember my name... cuz you'll be screaming it later !!

Nicholas: lol good one

Namita: ohhh wow !!! that is very cool

Nicholas: I bought a home screen print kit so I can print some... I did some screen printing in high school

Nicholas: just waiting for a rainy day to do it

Namita: i was going to ask you about that... if you've done silk screening and if thats what you had in mind to do ur logo with

Nicholas: yup

Namita: i did a bit silk screening... wayyy back when

Nicholas: I got the machine kit thing for like 70% off... so instead of 399.00 it was 139.00 couldn't pass it up

Nicholas: I'm pretty good at figuring things out too

Namita: wow you struck a deal... where did you get it ?

Nicholas: modification is always in the equation is one of my slogans

Nicholas: got it at Michael's.. it was just on sale so I bought it

Nicholas: I have some designs ready to be printed. it's just a matter of setting up n doing it

Namita: ohhh i didnt know Michaels carried that stuff !!

Namita: but mind you i havent been in Michaels in a long time

Nicholas: they seem to... I saw it on TV then at Michael's, I went to check it out n it was on sale so yah me!

Nicholas: I like that place... I get inspired in whatever store I go in... could be Windsor Plywood or Fabricana

Namita: i like the fact that you work in fabric too

Namita: would you design a dress too... if you wanted too

Nicholas: sewing is a good skill to have especially for a guy

Namita: yesss sounds like you have a good eye for that

Nicholas: I'm not great at it but it gets me the result I want

Namita: well ur better than what i could do with fabric

Nicholas: like the space suit I made I modified a pattern for coveralls so I would suit my needs

Namita: hmmm... a good hmm, that is very cool that you can do that

Nicholas: if I've never done something eg; using car paint to paint the hot rod then I read a lot about it then did it.. that way I get exactly what I want and the satisfaction of doing it myself

Namita: wow sounds like you have alot of patience too

Namita: did you use one of those spray guns for paint

Nicholas: I'm pretty good with my hands... the only way to get the ideas out of my head is to build them n I can't explain it to someone coz I change things on the fly if something isn't working

Nicholas: I did

Nicholas: I have a smattering of tools at my mom's place that I want to bring over here so I can finish the hot rod and make some side money doing projects for other people

Namita: yes i know what you mean... when ur working like that... ur mind starts creating and envisioning the finished product

Nicholas: yes

Nicholas: and if you have to change something coz its not working then you trouble shoot it n come up w something to fix it

Namita: uh huh... and keep working at it till ur satisfied with the end result

Nicholas: my mind works while I'm at work.. the body goes on autopilot my mind works on projects

Nicholas: yes! I knew you'd understand... no one has ever been able to relate to me that way

Namita: I can totally see what ur saying

Namita: really ???

Nicholas: yes

Nicholas: you are the first one

Nicholas: most ppl look at me w that deer in the headlights look then nod n smile

Nicholas: and say "let me see it when you're done"

Namita: ive sat down with a sketchbook ...wanting to draw something ... thats in my mind ....but you end up erasing and trying again with lines , angles, and proportions

Nicholas: yes... my problem is that I don't work in any one medium really well and if one medium isn't working then I change it

Namita: i close my eyes and envision where the angles should be or what i want this to look like in the end

Namita: it is good that ur comfortable in many mediums

Namita: ur a builder of sorts

Nicholas: I don't draw as well as I'd like I prefer working 3 dimensionally so I can see it from all angles

Namita: where as i have to have it down on a flat surface be it paper or canvas

Nicholas: you can draw the renderings and I can build them

Namita: ive drawn in chalk, pencils all the different hardness and softness

Namita: yes wouldnt that be great

Namita: i will create a template

Namita: and you bring it to life

Nicholas: yes I envision exactly as I want it

Nicholas: YES!!!!

Namita: hehe... we make a team

Nicholas: my imagination has no boundaries... sky's the limit when I'm figure out what I want

Nicholas: the best time for me to work something out is when i'm lying in bed waiting to fall asleep and when I first wake up... I have no barriers then n my mind is free to wander and find possibilities I hadn't thought of

Nicholas: yes we would

Namita: that is good that you have a great imagination... that means it carries over in aspects of ur life too !!

Nicholas: it does

Nicholas: one project I'd like to build and one day sell is an interactive spaceship bed for kids

Namita: woww that would be sooo cool !! im sure the kids would go crazy over it

Nicholas: the cockpit would open to access the bed n drawers along the sides to put socks n underwear in.. the landing gear would be the legs

Nicholas: I always wanted to be an astronaut when I was a kid and what kid wouldn't want a spaceship bed right?!

Namita: hehe... im sure that would keep em busy for hours on end

Namita: yesss so true

Nicholas: I'd like to donate one to BC Children's Hospital to the cancer recovery dept

Nicholas: I've also got an idea for a clamshell bed

Namita: aweeee thats sooo sweet Nicholas !!!

Nicholas: oh and a tree house double bed too

Namita: yes girls can pretend to be a mermaid

Nicholas: yes or the pearl but I guess that would be an oyster

Namita: OMG I WANT ONE NOW !!

Nicholas: lol

Namita: HEHE

Nicholas: that's why I 'm so passionate about having a house w a shop so I can get started

Namita: yes it makes sense !!! There is soo much more that you can do with a shop and its convenient

Nicholas: when I'm on the mainland my idle time seems wasted when I could be doing what I love to do... I've waited this long... other things are happening for me so I don't doubt that that'll happen too... all in due time I guess

Nicholas: yes and can write off a lot being a home based business

Nicholas: I have 2 projects w 2 friends and 2 of my own that I need to develop and get to market too

Namita: you've got more space... and no one bothers you... when you have ur own place to work

Nicholas: yes

Namita: you could make lots of money like this

Nicholas: that's the idea... passive income

Nicholas: I want to license the products to other companies so I can build my one off projects to show case what I can do

Nicholas: when ppl ask me "what do you do?" I answer with "what do you need me to do?"

Nicholas: I like that photo wow!

Namita: yes I was going to ask you that... but wasn't sure how to word it

Namita: oh thanks... it was at a wedding

Nicholas: so beautiful wow

Namita: I'm tired or weddings ...seems never ending ...hehe

Nicholas: sounds like it... when is this next one?

Namita: the first week of november... nov 5

Nicholas: I really rambled on there... you hit my passion button n it just came pouring out

Nicholas: that's soon

Namita: it will be one cold day

Nicholas: I bet

Namita: oh god no worries... i like listening to you

Nicholas: I'm glad

Nicholas: I'm a little animated too when I talk about the things I want to build

Nicholas: I can see it all

Nicholas: it's just a matter of making it happen

Namita: i see that... i can sense your passion and excitement in ur words

Nicholas: lol I wondered if that was coming through

Nicholas: I feel like a little kid when I tell ppl about it

Namita: yes I could tell... hehe

Nicholas: most just nod n smile coz they can't see it... which is sad coz I've just showed them lol

Namita: you mean being face to face with them and showing them ur passion... they don't get it

Nicholas: yes

Namita: and here I can tell what ur saying thru a pc screen

Nicholas: yes you can

Namita: hehe ...CHECK

Nicholas: first time

Nicholas: amazing

Namita: well that should be a big check mark for you

Nicholas: kind of near the top of the list!

Namita: aweee thanks,,, hehehe

Nicholas: those are check list items I didn't think I'd ever be able to check off n here you are

Namita: ohhhhhhhhh sooo sweet nicholas

Nicholas: life has a way of sorting itself out sometimes... I'm just glad it's my turn

Namita: well im pretty in tuned with things like that

Nicholas: I love how you say my name

Namita: you do ?

Nicholas: I do

Nicholas: well type it... can't wait to hear it... hehe

Namita: do you drink wine

Namita: random Q

Nicholas: nope

Namita: but finish what ur were writing

Namita: me either

Namita: never acquired the taste

Nicholas: I can keep up w random. Tony is all over the place when he talks so I'm well practiced

Nicholas: me either

Namita: im like that too... so random at times... that my friend Ashley teases me by saying ive got ADD or something

Nicholas: once in a while when Tony comes to town n we go out I'll have a kahlua n coke but I don't drink regularly

Namita: where does he live again

Nicholas: Tony can change topics mid sentence

Namita: hahahahhaah

Nicholas: Armstrong

Nicholas: he keeps me on my toes

Namita: oh god... where's that ?

Nicholas: he was in combat n had a head injury among others

Nicholas: near penticton kelowna

Namita: wait what do you mean in combat ?

Namita: ahhh k

Namita: yes remember you saying it

Nicholas: he was in the military

Namita: ohhh wow !!

Nicholas: 3 tours in Bosnia

Nicholas: was up close n personal combat too

Namita: wow !!! is he married ?

Namita: kids ?

Namita: what does he do now ?

Nicholas: nope

Nicholas: his wife n baby died in Bosnia both at the birth

Nicholas: he's a welder.. met him at BCIT welding program

Namita: whatttttttttttttt !!!

Namita: you mean during childbirth ??

Nicholas: yah he got the shitty end of the deal

Namita: ohhh nooo

Nicholas: he married a woman, she was their translator over there tried to get them back to Can (Canada) ended up doing 3 tours to be w her... complications w the birth n they both died

Nicholas: took him about a year or so to tell me

Namita: ohhh wow !!! going thru labor is no fun... i remember when i did labor and delivery... i was traumatized then

Namita: OMG

Nicholas: shook him to the core still bothers him... he's kinda rough around the edges but has a heart of gold

Namita: Poor Tony !! has he moved on in other ways

Nicholas: I think so

Namita: that is something you wont ever forget

Namita: it stays with you

Nicholas: I know I'm a big help coz he's told me I am, and I counsel him for lack of better words

Nicholas: stuff like that stays w him

Namita: yes sounds like ur a great friends !!

Nicholas: if he could have gotten them back here they both could have been saved

Namita: ohhh god !!

Nicholas: yah he's my best friend

Namita: that is good to hear !!!

Namita: what does he do now ?

Namita: work wise ?

Nicholas: I've never had one before n his best friend in the military stepped on a land mine

Nicholas: welder

Namita: omggg

Nicholas: took him quite some time to open up about that too

Namita: he's had a hard life !!

Nicholas: yah Tony saw it happen

Nicholas: that he has

Namita: wow !! Im still blown away

Nicholas: about 3 years ago he was being considered for the Victoria Cross for his actions during a rescue operation

Nicholas: they awarded it to another guy posthumously

Nicholas: he's very humble about his service

Namita: ohhh man !!! well i hope they consider him again

Nicholas: I wish they would

Nicholas: doesn't talk about his medal's coz he thinks it sounds like bragging

Namita: when i worked in the trauma unit... the head doctor... was in the navy and served in Bosnia

Nicholas: it would give him some peace n reassure him what he did over there meant something

Nicholas: oh yah

Nicholas: what dept do you work in again?

Nicholas: transplants?

Namita: wow ... well he did make a personal sacrifice ...as well as going thru so much mental trauma watching his friend die

Namita: i work in ICU

Nicholas: ah right

Namita: but we deal with everything

Namita: cardiac, transplant

Namita: trauma

Namita: spinal trauma

Nicholas: that's why you have the qualifications for flight nurse

Namita: head injuries

Nicholas: ok random ?

Namita: yes cuz we do everything

Nicholas: do you swim?

Namita: hehe

Namita: yes

Namita: do you ?

Nicholas: cool... yes... usually take the girls... they can spend hrs in the water

Namita: oh god me too

Nicholas: we love the water

Namita: in fact ive been infatuated with a hot tub

Namita: well ur a water sign too

Nicholas: my mom has one

Namita: ohhhhh reallllllllyyyyyyyyy

Nicholas: ah yes makes sense

Nicholas: yup went in it sunday night

Namita: omg arghhhhhhhh... im jealous

Nicholas: lookin' up at the stars... can see 5 satellites too

Nicholas: it's soo hot getting in but once you're in it's nice... I had to get out coz I could have fallen asleep n almost did

The following message could not be delivered:

"it's soo hot getting in but once you're in it's nice... I had to get out coz I could have fallen asleep n almost did"

End Time: 3:56 AM

I guess she got booted.

Chapter 8 October 15

The perfume arrived. I had it shipped to an address in Sumas Washington, it's just over the border in the US. It's about an hour and a half round trip though you can never anticipate how long the border wait will be. I mentioned nothing of it to keep it a surprise.

Our late night or I should say, early morning conversations were becoming a regular thing. We exchanged texts and emails throughout the day but it was our messenger conversations I looked forward to most.

Start Time: 11:52 PM

Nicholas: hey!!

Namita: hey you !!

Nicholas: how are you?

Namita: im ok... tired but still alive and kicking

Namita: im so sorry about last night i got booted

Nicholas: sokay that's what I figured

Namita: how was ur day ?

Nicholas: busy

Namita: I totally forgot my phone at home today

Namita: hehe

Namita: what did you do today ?

Nicholas: picked the girls up at 11... Amanda had this Apple sales thing w scouts from 1 to 230... I had a Standardized Patient training at 430 in Van then home for dinner

Nicholas: How was work?

Nicholas: you got my wink from across the room when you got home then lol

Namita: what does standardized patient mean

Namita: Hehe yes i did !!

Namita: and that nice smile too

Namita: sounds like you had a busy day too

Nicholas: it's a standardized roll play for Medical students...it's a part time acting job

Namita: ohhh cool !!

Namita: what do you have to do

Nicholas: been doing it for about 8 years now

Namita: so do you dress up like a patient... and act cick ?

Namita: sick i mean hehe

Nicholas: it's a confidential roll and there are 3 or 4 Sp's and we all do the roll exactly the same

Nicholas: depending on the roll yes

Namita: ahhh ok... you mean role ?

Nicholas: they cast for diff demographics and there are usually 12 cases per track

Nicholas: oops yes role lol

Namita: hehe

Namita: do you act like ur injured ?

Nicholas: yup depending on the role

Nicholas: or act sick... we have standardized answers we give when asked... basically we're dumb patients, when you go to your reg Dr you tell them everything that's wrong w you so they can diagnose but an Sp waits to be asked specific questions because the candidate is being marked by an examiner

Nicholas: I've worked w the Pharmacy Board and the nurse practitioners too

Nicholas: it's $18.00 hr it's fun and you meet so many diff ppl

Nicholas: training's are 2 hrs but if you're under the time you still get paid for 2 hrs

Namita: ahhh i see... when i did my advanced burn life support BCLS and advanced cardiac & trauma life support ACLS/ATLS we had live actors who actually had a pretty good makeup job and basically we had to assess them and try to get as much info from them to know what was going on and base our decisions on it

Namita: ahhh sooo cool... im sure its fun for you

Nicholas: yah sounds like you had Sp's

Namita: im sure urs is more advanced

Nicholas: we have to stay in character at all times so yah it's pretty strict

Nicholas: we sign confidentiality forms

Namita: Wow... that is very good... i dont think i could do as good of a job as you

Nicholas: some of the 4th year exams run across the country at the same time so there's no time zone cheating

Namita: what does the confidentiality pertain to ?

Nicholas: not discussing the case itself w anyone ever

Namita: ohh i see... so theres no cheating

Nicholas: yah

Nicholas: and that you'll keep the case in a safe place

Namita: ahhh make sense

Namita: do you do ur own makeup job then ?

Nicholas: No... Most roles don't need makeup and they have a woman that does it but she's more of a self taught theater person... she n her husband know I use to do it for a living so I think she gets a little nervous when I'm around

Namita: hehehehee

Nicholas: she knows the basics... would be nice to show her some things but as I said they don't use makeup very often

Nicholas: I used this money to buy my Oakley's... always wanted a pair so I finally splurged

Namita: oh... what are Oakleys Nicholas ?

Nicholas: sunglasses

Nicholas: I didn't go crazy on them... fortunately the pair I wanted were under $200.

Namita: ohhh i see ...never even heard of them

Namita: did you get a case with it... i hope ?

Nicholas: no case that was separate of course though they did come in a cloth bag/cleaning thing

Namita: ohhh wow ... at least they could give you a case if ur paying that much

Nicholas: I've always taken care of the things I buy n do the research on what I want n then wait till it's on sale

Nicholas: a case was another $30. crazy eh?

Namita: you've got patience then

Namita: omg

Nicholas: that I do

Namita: hehe

Nicholas: I still have the mask n fins I bought when I was 12 and they still work just fine

Namita: ohh myyy... like a diving mask ?

Nicholas: when I bought my goalie gear I checked out about 4 diff places

Nicholas: yah but I don't dive, I prefer to snorkel... took them to Mexico

Namita: yes it is better to shop around for things .. i do most of the comparing of prices online now

Namita: so much easier

Namita: did you see much when you went snorkeling in mexico ?

Nicholas: I check out a few stores to make sure I've covered everything, that way I'm always satisfied w my purchases

Nicholas: hell yah! just like on TV or the movies, was soooo cool!

Namita: realllllyyyy !!!

Namita: what did u see ?? tell meeee

Nicholas: I do that with parts for the Hot Rod too

Namita: that is ur pride and joy, a labour of love... so it has to be done right...

Nicholas: I saw parrot fish eating corral, a sting ray that was about 14 inches across, big grouper fish, so many other little fish like in Finding Nemo

Namita: yes the clown fish

Nicholas: and Dori too

Namita: im very familiar of most sea and reef fishes... i studied about 2 yrs before i started my aquarium

Namita: the blue tang... is Dori

Namita: loveeeeeee them... they are soooo cute

Namita: im sure it was amazing to see that in real life

Nicholas: it was and of course you'd know... you probly know the names of most if not all of what I saw I just know they're fish

Namita: hehe... did the stingray come close to you guys ?

Nicholas: it was really cool... the water was cooler than I expected but you warm up pretty fast n there's so much to look at you don't think about being cold

Nicholas: I swam over it in about 10 feet of water

Namita: oh wowwwwwwwwwwwwww... its an experience of a lifetime ...im sure

Nicholas: it was

Nicholas: I don't know if I told you but Tony has brain cancer from his time over seas... he told me yesterday that they might not be able to operate to remove it

Nicholas: he's doing chemo and radiation

Nicholas: talking about Mexico made me think of it

Namita: ohh nooo... no you didnt tell me... how long has he known ?

Nicholas: since august

Namita: ohhh geeez... so this is fairly new !

Nicholas: the military has narrowed it down to 5 diff bases they were on.... 18 of the 20 guys in his platoon have some sort of cancer... the other 2 took there own lives so they don't know about them

Namita: WOwww and i was thinking about ur friend today... about him losing his family

Nicholas: yah pretty new

Namita: Omg !! Wow !!

Namita: how are you doing with the news ?

Nicholas: if he didn't have bad luck he'd have no luck at all

Nicholas: a little worried but as my dearly departed dad use to say, worrying is like a rocking chair, gives you something to do but doesn't get you anywhere

Nicholas: so it's just a waiting game right now

Namita: thats a goood way to put it !!

Nicholas: we're suppose to be going to Mexico again in March, he's apid for it already so we'll see if that happens

Nicholas: *paid

Namita: sounds like he had a wonderful time... what area did you go to ?

Nicholas: we had a great time!! went to the Riviera Mayan, 20 mins south of Playa Del Carmen

Nicholas: this trip we're staying in Playa Del Carmen

Namita: wow... I've never even been close to mexico... everrr

Nicholas: I remember you said that

Namita: ive heard good things about playa del carmen

Nicholas: it's so much fun to get away n do whatever you want

Namita: hmmmm nice... and enjoy the beaches

Namita: and swim

Namita: watch a sunset

Nicholas: eat when you'er hungry sleep when you're tired n do whatever the hell you want

Nicholas: yes all the above

Namita: yesssssss !!! What a life huh ??

Nicholas: we went on 2 tours

Namita: really ?? was it good ?

Nicholas: it was... was sad to come back

Namita: ohhh im sure it was... how long did you go for ?

Nicholas: they were both fun but the 2nd one was awesome!

Nicholas: 7 days

Nicholas: I'll show you photos one day

Namita: ohh cool

Nicholas: we got some pics from the 2nd tour n there were a lot of extra pics on it so it was worth the $40.

Nicholas: I was the shutter bug

Nicholas: must have taken 400 or so pics

Nicholas: then the extra ones

Namita: mexico is quite picturesque... it must have been quite beautiful there

Namita: wowwww

Nicholas: it was... I tried to soak up as much of it as I could... n w my mind all I have to do is close my eyes n concentrate n I can put myself back there

Nicholas: I have an autobiographical memory, the ability to recall my life events with great detail n accuracy

Namita: hmmm i love it when i can just visualize all those places youve been to and imagine that ur back there again

Nicholas: yah helps me relax n turn my mind off so I can fall asleep

Nicholas: to meditate

Namita: hmmm yesss... do you really meditate ?

Namita: must be relaxing

Nicholas: I do it before I fall asleep every night... studied Tai Chi for a bit

Nicholas: also read about what they think our mind does while we sleep too

Nicholas: book was called The Mind At Night

Namita: ohhh ok

Nicholas: was really interesting... thought it might be dry to some but I thought it was really good read

Namita: never even heard of it before

Nicholas: I just stumbled upon it in the library one time

Nicholas: random ? what are your sisters names?

Namita: ahhh i see ... and you actually finished it from cover to cover ?

Nicholas: I did shocked me too

Nicholas: as I say it was really interesting

Namita: ohh Jaya, Sonia, Preeti, and myself

Nicholas: I do like the last one hehe

Namita: hehe

Namita: i was going to ask you

Nicholas: yes

Namita: when you did ur iron workers course ..where did you go to do it ?

Nicholas: it was a Welding program n I went to BCIT (British Columbia Institute Of Technology). they have an iron workers program too... those are the guys that build the big I beam buildings

Namita: ahhh I see

Nicholas: welders fuse metal together

Namita: it would be near the canada way side of the campus then ?

Nicholas: sure was, right on it

Namita: hehe

Namita: i went to BCIT ...for my initial nursing program

Nicholas: oh yah

Namita: did my diploma first then finished off with BSN at UVic... then back to Bcit for my critical care specialty training

Nicholas: I learned to weld when I was 15 to build the hot rod.. I went to school to fill in the blanks and to try to make a living at it too

Nicholas: wow that's a lot of schooling

Namita: just being a welder sometimes is hard to find a job i bet

Nicholas: which isn't really surprising though

Namita: you need additional training in other areas as a backup... am I right ?

Nicholas: it is n was... after my surgery I was out of work for a year which never happens to me

Namita: yes mine was 5 yrs in total

Nicholas: depends on where you work. It's usually certificates the shops are looking for

Namita: ICU nursing is wayyy different than regular ward nursing... you are "it" most times to make critical decisions for a patient... or guide the newbees to make a decisions sometimes

Namita: ahhh i see

Nicholas: all I really did was add welding to my repertoire, it's just one more skill I can pull out when needed

Nicholas: I can see that n be able to make those decisions quickly too I imagine?

Namita: yesss totally understand ... when ur in trades... im sure it is better to have more than one skills in that area

Namita: yes sometimes you only have a few seconds to a min

Nicholas: it is. you get treated you like you don't know anything anyway but that's the way things are in most places

Nicholas: at this job they find out that I built the hot rod. guys I haven't met yet are asking what I have n want to see pics of it

Namita: we do things like intubating a patient... where we put in a breathing tube into a patient... well the Dr does and our job is to drug the patient and sedate them with a sequence of anesthesia just so the patient doesn't crap out

Nicholas: wow

Namita: wowww really ?

Namita: hehe

Nicholas: yup

Nicholas: you seem like you'd be cool under pressure

Namita: they all start talking to you then ?

Nicholas: I know I am

Namita: hehe

Namita: yes i work well under pressure

Namita: im part of the code blue team as well

Nicholas: yah. they're all friendly it's just when the fellow gear heads find out what I have they want to talk n I can talk for hrs about my ride

Namita: we carry the code blue pagers for the day... and if there are any emergencies anywhere within the hospital then im one of those ppl responding

Nicholas: cool... and a code blue would be?

Namita: im sure you have piqued their interest on that

Namita: sorry code blue is when a patients stops breathing or has a cardiac arrest

Namita: and they need to deal with it... and brought to ICU

Namita: sometimes the case can be quite bad ...where the doc has to saw down their chest n open it to manually pump their heart

Nicholas: yah... the thing that makes my hot rod sooo diff is me... most guys building them are in there 50's and the fact I've had mine for about 24 years is a big deal too

Namita: as in the case last week

Nicholas: wow holly sh**!

Namita: wowwww

Namita: I love how we are having 2 different conversations

Nicholas: so you've seen inside some ones chest!?

Nicholas: that's not something ppl can do face to face lol

Nicholas: I figured a code blue was bad

Namita: yes... ive seen everything... the chest is opened up wide... right down the middle and across... all you see is organs... the respiratory therapist is blowing air into the lungs and the lungs rise and fall and the Dr is manually pumping the heart... blood pouring out down the sides of the stretcher and nurses and myself giving drugs to jump start the heart

Namita: its always a shit show

Namita: hehe

Nicholas: geeze!!

Nicholas: that's amazing!

Namita: scrubs covered in blood at the bottom

Nicholas: god!!

Nicholas: stuff most ppl see only on TV

Nicholas: n you can just leave that stuff at work when it's time to go home?

Namita: or if we have time to get the patient into the operating room... then the Dr is sitting on top of the stretcher pumping the heart with his hands as everyone else basically pushes the stretcher to the elevators and to the awaiting OR

Namita: yes you just have to leave it behind

Namita: we see wacky stuff nicholas

Nicholas: no kidding!

Namita: we harvest organs from ppl who wanted to donate

Nicholas: unreal my mouth is hanging open

Nicholas: how often do the shit shows happen?

Namita: so you could be taking care of a patient who is dying... could take hrs... then if they consent or family did... once they have died... off to the OR they go to have their chest sawed down with and electric saw and few hrs later ur taking care of another pt who is the recipient of the organs from ur other pt

Namita: shit shows happens almost everyday ...its one thing or another ... it could be anywhere within the 24 hr period

Namita: sometimes i miss it... cuz im home by then

Nicholas: my god! wow.. holy mad scientist stuff

Namita: hehe

Namita: sometimes you can dodge the bullet ...when ur shift ends

Namita: and you have to race out of there into the locker room

Nicholas: holy crap... I'm running out of words to describe my amazement

Namita: hehe

Namita: you'll be hearing a lot of these wacky stories

Nicholas: just so you don't get caught in in so you can go home

Namita: alot is what you hear on the news

Nicholas: can't wait, I'm all ears!

Namita: hell yess

Namita: i hope you have a strong stomach then

Namita: lol

Nicholas: I guess if you get caught in it as you're off then you're there for the duration?

Namita: yesss... sometimes you feel sorry for ur coworker coming on and there's no help around so you get caught up in the mayhem

Nicholas: I do... I'm more fascinated than anything n like to hear stuff like that... part of my character

Namita: hehe good !!

Nicholas: the things we see yet no one knows we see them

Namita: yesss so true...

Nicholas: that's so crazy... defiantly takes a certain type of person to be able to do that job... someone who reacts not runs away

Nicholas: so off topic... tonight's nightie is?

Namita: hehe... tonight's flavor of the nite is like a mauve color with darker purple ribbon edging around it

Nicholas: oooo I like the sound of that!

Namita: and ribbon woven into the edge of the cups

Nicholas: same type as last night? yes

Namita: knee length

Namita: yes it is

Nicholas: knee length very nice

Namita: hehe

Namita: do you get a good picture of it ?

Nicholas: I certainly do especially w my imagination very much so

Nicholas: sounds delicious

Namita: that imagination is running wild... i suppose

Namita: hehe

Nicholas: usually does when I think about you in bed lookin' all sexy

Nicholas: lying on ur tummy.... I can imagine slipping into bed w you n lying on top of you n pressing my body to yours... rubbing myself all over you

Namita: my hair in a pony tail right now... stupid msn is acting up again

Namita: do u like long hair, short hair ...open or tied ?

Nicholas: mmm sokay n thx for the pony tail image... details need the details

Namita: hehe

Namita: toes painted

Nicholas: I don't mind either hair style

Namita: im not fond of short hair

Nicholas: ohhh so cute... I like it when a woman paints her toes... shows me she cares about the details

Namita: hehe... i always do... i dont paint fingernails as much due to work

Nicholas: I think long hair on u is sexier

Namita: aweee thanks

Nicholas: I love the natural curl to it

Namita: i did have a hot pink bra on under my scrubs today at work though ... it had pink lace on the sides

Nicholas: oooo sexy

Namita: my hair is versatile... i can have it dead straight... curly in ringlets naturally... or naturally wavy

Namita: when i first wash it... it is in ringlets

Nicholas: very nice

Namita: hehe

Nicholas: cool I like curly hair

Nicholas: if u were my nurse when I was in the hospital I would never have gotten better just so I could spend more time w u. though I'd be sad when you were off

Namita: hehehheehehe

Nicholas: I like this situation better mind you

Namita: I can imagine all ur woe stories that you would make up

Nicholas: fantom aliments just to get you to touch me

Namita: lol

Nicholas: "oooo it hurts here could you please have a look at tit thx"

Nicholas: it* not tit see my mind is going there

Namita: yeah yeah... whateverrrrrrrrr

Namita: check you out again... listen to ur heart with my stethoscope again

Namita: hehehehehee

Namita: i pay extra attention to cute guys

Nicholas: awe shucks

Nicholas: slip of the fingers so to speak

Namita: lol uh huh !!!

Namita: its all about the boobies... I knowwwwww

Nicholas: listening to my heart you'd hear my valve

Nicholas: lol yahhh still a guy

Namita: hehe

Nicholas: lmaof

Namita: yes i think it has a distinct sound

Nicholas: you caught me

Namita: hehe

Nicholas: it sure does has a tick tick sound

Nicholas: listening to my heart you'd also hear it calling out to be loved... okay now I'm just being silly

Namita: hehehe... i guess i will have to go do the course on the hearts morse code

Nicholas: lol

Namita: hehe

Namita: and when i look up at you while listening to ur heart... you will just shrug ur shoulders

Nicholas: I hope the sound doesn't bother you, I'm sure you'll get use to it

Namita: no it does not

Namita: can you hear it too?

Nicholas: I'll tell you when I was a kid I swallowed a little clock n it got stuck in there n they couldn't get it out so they left it in

Namita: i should get to bed soon ...need to be up in few hrs again

Namita: hehee... sure that will do

Nicholas: I can hear it. its just diff than what you can hear

Nicholas: I thought you were on nights now?

Namita: no I have 2 n

Namita: 2 more day shifts then nights

Namita: I was doing the extra shifts first

Nicholas: oh right this is your wacky week

Namita: regular shifts start tomorrow

Nicholas: thought yesterday n today were your days n now ur on 2 nights

Nicholas: ohhh I see

Nicholas: gotcha

Namita: noooooo i wish it was

Nicholas: ok I'll let you go then

Nicholas: don't want you over tired for work

Namita: ok nicholas... it was a pleasure chatting with you again

Namita: yes i need to be alert

Nicholas: and you Namita

Nicholas: again tomorrow?

Namita: yes sure

Nicholas: okay I'll look for you

Namita: ok ... have a good sunday... will have my cell with me this time

Nicholas: gnight my sweet pleasant dreams... I'll send you a text at some point 😊

Namita: hehe ok... be in touch tomorrow

Nicholas: nite

End Time: 1:56 AM

Chapter 9 October 16

I'm excited to see where this deep connection leads. Hopefully the chemistry will still be there when we meet in person.

Start Time: 11:32 PM

Nicholas: hellooooo!

Namita: hey there

Nicholas: ur early tonight

Nicholas: not complaining

Namita: yeah i just crawled into bed... would have been the moment i got home after my shower but was on the phone with sis

Namita: how was ur day ?

Nicholas: was good...

Nicholas: went to Belcarra w the girls

Nicholas: how was work?

Namita: ohhh niceeeee... I heard it was a beautiful day

Nicholas: it was! so nice... we tried fishing but there were no fish

Nicholas: there was a seal swimming close by n popped up so we could see it... very cool

Nicholas: sat in the sun for a bit n just soaked up all nature had to offer

Namita: ohh geez work was a nightmare the moment i got in... one of the patients just got admitted... some gang member... after being beaten with a bat or something

Nicholas: oh god!

Nicholas: absolutely stupid, gang stuff

Namita: and he was screaming and yelling at us as we tried to stabilize him

Nicholas: let him suffer I say... u want in that life take your licks.. lol

Namita: then he made a direct threat to us that he made a call to his ppl ...to come and deal with us ...as in harm us

Nicholas: was he asian?

Namita: so next thing we know... the police VPD (Vancouver Police Dept) are there and we are under police protection for the rest of the day

Namita: yes he was

Nicholas: good... efn prick!

Namita: soon afterwards he deteriorated and we had to sedate and put in a breathing tube

Namita: i know... he was spitting too... told us that you bitches are going to get it !!

Nicholas: wow... threaten the ppl trying to help you... what an idiot... not thinking that his life is in ur hands

Namita: we deal with a lot of A$$ holes

Nicholas: he got beat up n felt like a pussy so he was trying to be tough n take it out on someone else

Namita: well outside ppl think we deal with ppl who are all sweet and appreciative with everything ...that is a breath of fresh air

Namita: many of the patients are tied down

Nicholas: wow! tied down?! geeze

Namita: we see a lot of pts (patients) who are combative

Namita: in the process... sometimes you get hurt

Nicholas: unreal... hope not hurt

Namita: id say 95% are tied down... tied down to the bed by their hands

Nicholas: wow!

Nicholas: life in the big city

Namita: no no im ok... the nurse they put there was 6 ft guy and big build so he manhandled him all day

Namita: although by then the pt was sedated

Nicholas: good

Namita: its just the fact ur working nearby and have to be on guard for anything suspicious

Namita: the ICU doors are locked down... cant get in unless ID is scanned

Nicholas: I don't feel bad he got beat up... acting like that... he probly mouthed off the wrong person n WHAM!, face meet baseball bat

Namita: hehe

Namita: yeah he totally deserved it

Nicholas: may I request a lovely photo from your collection, not that I don't like the flower but I'm pretty partial to the Namita Slide Show

Nicholas: did u have to deal w that guy all day?

Namita: it's not uncommon to have gang members come in after shootings or stabbings

Nicholas: I guess you had to till he was sedated

Namita: i did help to turn him... it took 4 ppl to do that

Nicholas: do u think he'll make it or are you allowed to tell me that?

Nicholas: oh thank you... for the photo change... love it!

Nicholas: is that from a runway shoot?

Namita: yes he will make it but will have some lasting effects too

Namita: yes it is... hehe

Namita: the is dress is black leather

Nicholas: cool... the run way part

Nicholas: I can see that, very hot!

Namita: with a zipper down the front

Nicholas: how long was it

Nicholas: mmm easy access

Namita: above my knees

Namita: hehe

Nicholas: just how I imagined it

Nicholas: I was thinking about you when we were out at Belcarra.... how much you'd have liked to be there soaking up the sun

Nicholas: that's very hot!

Nicholas: it was very peaceful out there

Namita: mmmm sounds so niceeeeee... love that area... did you go to Belcarra Park ? or just around there somewhere

Nicholas: yup to the park n out on the dock to fish

Namita: ahhh cool

Nicholas: water was really calm

Nicholas: it was a lovely afternoon

Namita: are you allowed to crab there anymore ?

Namita: im sure it was !!

Nicholas: yah, every time we go there are ppl crabbing

Namita: ive been crabbing with dad on his boat

Nicholas: thats cool

Nicholas: the girls wanted to go swimming at the indoor pool... I mentioned that this might be the last good day we have for awhile so we might want to spend it outside

Namita: there's another park... ur girls will love... its on Barnet hwy... off on ur right... going towards vancouver ...but i forgot the name to it

Namita: it's very beautiful... i discovered just last yr... didnt know it existed... unless its new in the last several yrs

Nicholas: I think we've been there before... right at the cement plant yes?

Namita: yes thats the one

Nicholas: it's been there for quite some time

Namita: ohhh

Namita: do you eat crabs oe seafood ?

Namita: or*

Nicholas: some... I like more bottom fish, crab, scallops

Nicholas: I like catching salmon when I was a kid but I prefer halibut or cod or sole

Namita: bottom fish as in halibut ?

Nicholas: yup

Namita: lol

Namita: my dad is a halibut freak... thats all he wants to do... catch halibut

Namita: he always looking for someone to go w him

Namita: those things can smack the living daylights out of you when you catch it

Nicholas: today I pulled a styrofoam flat from between the docks... it had been in the waters so long that there were muscles growing on it... I pulled them off n let them sink to the bottom then tossed the styrofoam in the garbage

Nicholas: I've heard commercial halibut fisherman shoot them w a shot gun to put them out

Nicholas: I haven't been out on a boat fishing for a long time... I'd probly get sea sick

Namita: who is looking after the area i wonder ? Unfortunately other ppl end up doing the cleanup job for the careless ppl

Namita: and ignorant

Nicholas: who knows how long that garbage was in there or where it came from

Namita: im environmentally conscious and i hate when garbage doesnt make it in the garbage

Nicholas: me too... yet another similarity

Namita: dads boat is a leisure boat... its a 21 ft Bayliner

Namita: seats 4 i think

Nicholas: some ppl just don't think about things like that

Nicholas: wow 21 feet that's pretty big

Nicholas: I guess he goes out in it often then?

Namita: last year we went out towards Tsawwassen Ferry terminal... past Point Robert's and we saw a pod of killer whales within 15 or 20 ft away

Namita: and dolphins too

Nicholas: when we lived on our sail boat we use to borrow my dad's friends boat n go salmon fishing all the time

Namita: yeah in the summer he got out 1 or 2 times a week

Nicholas: cool

Namita: but he brings his boat back home

Nicholas: ah... so he stores it at home then

Namita: wowww cool...did you have to use down riggers for salmon or just regular fishing lines

Namita: yes... he likes to see his pride and joy when he's not on the water

Nicholas: sometimes we used down riggers but most times we didn't... the shelf off Qualicum wasn't too deep so we didn't always need the down rigger

Namita: ohhh that's good

Nicholas: I told you before about the sail boat my dad built n we lived on for 2 n a half years right/

Nicholas: suppose to be a ? not a /

Namita: hehe... got it

Namita: yess I remember... must have been quite fun !!

Nicholas: it was okay very tight for space even though it was 53 feet x 16

Nicholas: it was fun but I'm glad we moved off it

Namita: did ur mom live on it too?

Nicholas: sure did.. the 4 of us... actually we moved off it coz my mom got really seasick especially when it was stormy... she stayed w friends a couple of times

Namita: lol poor mom !! I can only imagine !!

Namita: my mom refuses to step into the boat

Nicholas: yah she wasn't too impressed when she found out just how sick she could get lol

Namita: hehehehe

Nicholas: really? how come?

Namita: she is scared she will be sick too

Nicholas: ah

Namita: esp when the boat is moving

Nicholas: they do have a tendency to do that lol

Namita: i almost puked the last time

Nicholas: not a nice feeling

Nicholas: nor is the puking lol

Namita: we were out in early August and did a trip to Galiano Island... omg... i was in the back facing backwards... cuz my dads neighbor came with us and he and dad were in the front

Nicholas: I call puking feeding the fish coz that's what my dad use to call it

Namita: i got tired of looking at the waves and wake created by the engine that i kinda got green for a bit

Namita: EWEeeeeeeeeeeeeeeee

Namita: thats soooo grosss... lol

Nicholas: the smell of the gas n the smell of the boat itself makes me queazy

Namita: yesssss... i think that was it too plus i looked down on the floor of the boat looking for something while we had the engine turned off... so the gentle rocking and up and down motion triggered me

Nicholas: when I was younger my dad use to go fishing a lot n I'd go w him... we'd have to gey up really early... this one morning my dad had pineapple upside down cake n coffee for breakfast, he had an iron stomach. so I thought I could have what I wanted too n he let me, so I had the same w Kool Aid instead of the coffee lol... well out on the boat guess who fed the fish... learned my lesson

Nicholas: for me it's the combination of all of it... haven't been around it for so long that I have no tolerance for it anymore

Namita: lmaooooooo... i know ...sometimes you think ur invincible and immune to those things... thats what i thought... that i had an iron stomach... however i managed not to puke

Namita: drank some ginger ale

Namita: and it subsided

Nicholas: good old ginger ale

Namita: hehe

Namita: i love raspberry ginger ale

Nicholas: must be the ginger coz they have non drowsy Gravol that's made from ginger

Nicholas: you do, creating mental note

Namita: yess... i have some too but never used it yet

Namita: hehe

Namita: do you like chocolate or candy or do you crave salt ?

Nicholas: I find it gives me burps n they taste like ginger... sorry for the image

Namita: hehe its ok

Nicholas: hmmm don't crave salt... do like good milk chocolate now n again... depends on the candy

Nicholas: don't have a big sweet tooth but I do like it once in a while

Namita: yes love choc milk

Nicholas: I keep some Nestle Quick the syrup on hand at all times

Namita: im not a salt craver either

Namita: mmmm

Nicholas: I don't add salt to food either

Nicholas: unless I'm cooking that is

Namita: me very rarely

Nicholas: but I don't use it on my plate

Namita: no I don't do that at all

Nicholas: it surprises me when I see ppl add salt to their plate before they even try it.... crazy.... at least try it first

Namita: lol... like salt to their fries before trying it

Namita: i do like pepper though

Nicholas: yes! mmm not big on pepper... I use it to cook w like chicken soup but I don't add it to my food

Namita: im particular to what i add it to... like a bowl of soup or stir fry... i will add on my plate

Nicholas: ah

Namita: other times i used it to marinate while cooking

Nicholas: yah using it to flavor your dishes I do

Nicholas: I thought of another question for you

Namita: ok ... go ahead

Nicholas: what have you learned from your past relationships?

Nicholas: n what is the most important thing u learned?

Namita: hmmm... im thinking thru my daze here

Nicholas: ok... ur probly pretty tired... nderstandable

Nicholas: understandable*

Namita: well to be supportive of the person im with ... in whatever the endeavor he chooses

Namita: im not here in his life to change the person he is ...

Namita: he is what he is... his own person

Nicholas: interesting... good answer, I like that one

Namita: to which it kinda goes to what i was saying the other night ... that you dont want to lose urself in a relationship by giving to much and losing ur identity in the process

Nicholas: so true

Namita: give to what ur potential is and have a balanced relationship

Namita: reciprocate where needed

Namita: nothing should be one sided

Nicholas: yes

Namita: and appreciate each other

Nicholas: yes

Namita: appreciate his mind his happiness ... the relationship itself

Namita: and things will come back to you too

Nicholas: that they will... letting him be him is so important

Namita: also i know never to embarrass ur partner... show respect

Nicholas: have u embarrassed a partner before?

Namita: i dont do it on a one to one level and certainly wont do it when other ppl are around either

Namita: no never

Nicholas: didn't think so

Namita: no guy... i dont think... wants to be embarrassed in front of his friends

Namita: for instance ... talking in a rude, condescending manner

Nicholas: there's a fine line between laughing w him and laughing at him

Namita: calling him names

Namita: yes

Nicholas: oh yes

Nicholas: talking down to him or treating him like a cat that shit on the carpet

Namita: basically treating him like a dog... its a total no no for me... if i dont want to be treated that way... why should I do it

Nicholas: tone is so important

Namita: lol or a cat yes

Namita: yes

Namita: and i also dont like sarcastic undertones

Nicholas: yes do unto others... that's the way I've always treated everyone

Namita: sarcasm with humor is fine

Nicholas: yup

Namita: i hope i answered as best as possible

Nicholas: was very thorough, thank you

Namita: what about urself Nicholas ?

Nicholas: I learned that marriage doesn't solidify a relationship and neither do kids not that I ever thought that

Namita: ohhh god... noooo it doesnt... ever

Namita: sooo agree with that statement

Nicholas: I learned or figured out what it is I really want in a partner

Nicholas: and to never settle... it always comes back to bite you if you do

Namita: yesssss true

Nicholas: OMG that's hot WOW!

    A day at the beach catching some rays. Lying on her tummy, looking at me, resting her chin on her clasped hands.

Namita: hehehe... i didnt want to distract you !!!

Nicholas: is that a bathing suit shot?

Namita: yes it is

Nicholas: too late... I can refocus though

Namita: lol

Nicholas: yummy... nice bare shoulder

Namita: hehe... back to earth nicholas

Nicholas: haven't seen that one before

Nicholas: I'm back maybe a little whoozy

Namita: no you didnt... I held back on you

Namita: lol

Nicholas: yes you did... can u send that one to me pls? I promise to stay focused

Nicholas: were you modeling the bathing suit or you in the photo?

Namita: no its just a pic my friend took while we were all out at the beach

Namita: this was 2 yrs ago i think

Namita: so not recent

Namita: and for some reason its not in my backup files

Namita: so i will try to retrieve it later and get it for you

Nicholas: just casual on the beach wow! looks like a photo shoot

Nicholas: ok

Namita: yes just a casual shot

Nicholas: my my my

Namita: hehe

Namita: this one really got you !!

Nicholas: hot even when casual check

Nicholas: did so

Namita: lol

Nicholas: my mind evaporated on me... may take a sec to reboot

Nicholas: I'm good

Nicholas: I can do this lol

Namita: yes recover nicholas... hehe

Nicholas: do you tan or burn/ I'm guessing tan a nice golden brown

Nicholas: which beach was it taken at?

Namita: i tan... never burned

Namita: but i dont stay too long either

Nicholas: those good jeans again

Nicholas: me either

Namita: this was in Penticton

Namita: at Okanagan Lake

Nicholas: oh wow that's a long way from here

Namita: yesss but it is sooo beautiful over there... its 6 hrs drive Six hours?

Nicholas: im pretty sure its only 4 hrs

Namita: oh… ok

Namita: sandy beaches... palm trees

Nicholas: I bet the guys were slobbering all over themselves trying to get ur attention?

Nicholas: palm trees really?!

Namita: lol... yes even the young ones

Namita: yesss you should go... it feels like paradise

Nicholas: u must have carried a big stick? lol

Namita: we were camping though

Namita: hehe

Namita: yes baseball bat

Nicholas: I'd defiantly go w you

Namita: lol

Nicholas: so ur on nights now right?

Nicholas: n ur done wed? or do you have shift exchange again?

Namita: noooooooo still day shift nicholas

Namita: then the nite shifts begin

Nicholas: ohh but I thought you did 2 days then 2 nights?

Nicholas: oh right

Nicholas: you've only done 1 day reg shift duh

Namita: yess

Namita: hehee

Namita: this is the start of my regular now

Nicholas: and ur the one who's been up for longer

Nicholas: right

Nicholas: I'll get it down soon... it's the extra shifts that threw me

Namita: hehe... ohhh its throwing me to... i dont know if im coming or going sometimes

Nicholas: I like how we can work around our schedules... I was a little nervous about that

Nicholas: it's not something everyone is willing to do

Namita: yesss well we both work shift work ,,,and odd hours ... so something will eventually work out

Nicholas: it will n as I said I'm willing to wait for you coz I think ur worth it

Namita: aweee thanks nicholas

Nicholas: it enables us to build a solid foundation w our conversations

Namita: yes it sure does !! we talked about almost everything under the sun now... even salt and pepper !!! Hehee

Nicholas: a bit of an inconvenience but also keeps things to a stable pace... if that makes sense?

Namita: yesss it does makes sense

Nicholas: lol and talked just about every night n it's only just 2 weeks today

Namita: hehee yesss

Nicholas: do you fall in love easy?

Nicholas: or do you take a step back n take things slow?

Namita: hehe... sometimes i wear my heart on my sleeve... lets just say

Namita: but im cautious too

Nicholas: again just like me

Namita: hehe

Namita: and if im madly in love... ohhh it will be known !!

Nicholas: I'll keep my eyes open for it

Namita: hehe

Nicholas: they say you just know when it happens but until you experience it it's hard to relate to

Namita: i should get to sleep soon nicholas... but write what ur writing

Namita: yess ssooo true

Namita: it hits you like a ton of bricks

Nicholas: that was it

Namita: hehe

Nicholas: I don't want to sleep deprive you

Nicholas: at least not chatting online that is hehe

Namita: tomorrow being a monday I think... traffic will be busy

Nicholas: probably... hopefully work wont be too busy for you

Namita: it was soooooo foggy this morning when i was out the door

Namita: and it was only 2 degrees... BURrrrrrrrrrrrr !!

Nicholas: unless it goes by faster for u in that case i hope it will be busy lol

Namita: yesss i hope it doesnt drag

Nicholas: geeze 2 degrees

Namita: yessss 2 degrees !!

Namita: my tire pressure was out on my rear tires

Namita: cuz of the cold

Nicholas: ooh

Nicholas: u gat it fixed though?

Nicholas: got*

Namita: so on my way home... i had to check all the pressures

Namita: and add air

Nicholas: ur handy like that?

Namita: yeah i did it

Nicholas: cool

Namita: i have a tire gauge in my glove compartment

Nicholas: that's awesome.... part of being independent... check

Namita: hehehehe

Namita: dad even had me trained to change a tire but i havent done one in a longggggggggg time

Namita: so im rusty on that

Nicholas: I could refresh ur memory.

Namita: plus i have wheel locks so tires cant be stolen so i havent even ventured how to change or unlock it

Namita: hehe i think i may need some lessons

Nicholas: I'm a good teacher... very patient... like to take my time n be very thorough

Namita: hmmm yesss thats what i need

Namita: i god im fading

Namita: oh god im fading i mean hehe

Nicholas: okay, as much as I could keep u up all night I better let u go

Namita: hehe ..we will keep each other up in other ways

Nicholas: yes we will!!

Namita: goodnight nicholas... hehe

Nicholas: I'll talk to you tmw at some point... nite Namita

Namita: take care... chat tomorrow ?

Nicholas: sleep well

Nicholas: yes please!!!

Namita: will have cell phone

Nicholas: same timeish?

Namita: hehe

Namita: yes same time

Nicholas: cool.. nite

Namita: gnite

Namita: btw... all black

Nicholas: xo lol thx like minds xo

Namita: with small lace detail

Nicholas: mmmmmmmm

Namita: xo ...hehe

End Time: 1:34 AM

Chapter 10 October 17

Start Time: 12:19 AM

Nicholas: good evening my sweet

Namita: hi there !!

Namita: sorry to keep you waiting

Nicholas: excellent still w the bathing suit

Namita: hehe

Namita: i didnt change it from yesterday

Nicholas: totally fine you're.. right on time actually

Namita: ohh good

Nicholas: u don't have to change it

Namita: seems like you have a new favorite

Nicholas: ur usually on at 12:20

Namita: yes... i am

Nicholas: they're all my favourites that one might just be first lol

Namita: hehehe

Namita: what do you like about it ?

Nicholas: besides everything?

Namita: hehe... yes

Nicholas: the over all look to it. it's very classy n sexy

Nicholas: I can't put it into words really... it's artful

Namita: ahhhhh i see... i even have class on a normal day ?!

Namita: ohhh thanks nicholas

Nicholas: u seem classy to me all the time

Nicholas: thx for the message this morning... made my heart melt knowing u took time out of ur morning to tell me u were thinking about me

Namita: ohhhh ur sooo welcome... i sat in front of my patient outside the room ... we're supposed to be sitting and working at the bedside at all times ... so before i went in to tackle the day i texted you beforehand and left you a wake up message... i was also very tired and sleepy still... so really wasnt awake to make the move over to the bedside... im glad to hear that it was a pleasant surprise for you

Namita: did you have a good sleep too ?

Nicholas: it was... it made my day

Nicholas: it was okay

Nicholas: did u get enough sleep?

Nicholas: I feel bad keeping you up so late when ur on days but that's the only time I get w you so I take what I can get... I give as much too lol

Namita: this morning as i was brushing my hair in my stupor ... i accidently grabbed the hot iron with my left hand but at the hot part and omg i burned my thumb slightly

Namita: noooooo don't feel bad... i was ok really

Nicholas: ooohhh I'm sooo sorry to hear that, are you okay?

Namita: hehehe... it totally woke me up

Namita: its better now... i dont even feel it

Nicholas: I bet... not the nice way to wake up

Nicholas: do you skate?

Nicholas: random I know

Namita: but at least i looked good !!!

Nicholas: as per usual... I can only imagine

Namita: ummm im not that good... havent skated since i was a kid

Nicholas: ah just wondered about it today

Nicholas: I can't stop w 2 feet but I can stop n play hockey a little

Namita: id be at a childs level skating... with one of those bar thingys... hehe

Nicholas: I see... I could help

Namita: do you play ice hockey?

Nicholas: not often but I can

Nicholas: very novice though

Namita: ahhhh

Namita: do you go out with work friends ?

Nicholas: I love to play... always wanted to play as a kid but my parents didn't want to commit to the early mornings... I wanted to play goal

Namita: you could probably still get into it even now

Nicholas: depends... I don't actually have a lot of close friends, never have... I see hear n feel things others miss... ever since I was young so I found other things to occupy my time

Nicholas: I could I just don't have the time

Namita: yes true... with the evening schedule it is pretty hard to do so

Nicholas: the friends I did have in school were my sisters age, 2 years older

Namita: yes i know what you mean... when being choosy about friends and other ppl... a good friend is hard to find... esp ones that have the same views as you do

Nicholas: when I was in school I wasn't into getting smashed on the weekends... I started building my rod at the beginning of grade 11 so I had that to work on

Namita: i have 4 good friends... 3 of them younger than and one a bit older

Nicholas: yes the same views for sure, very hard to find in friends

Nicholas: that's cool. women?

Nicholas: or both?

Namita: ahhhh good... i have a feeling you've never been drunk in ur life... am I right ?

Namita: yes all women

Namita: i do have a lot acquaintances though

Namita: men and women... like light friends

Namita: not ppl who i would pour my heart out to

Nicholas: oh no been pretty smashed in my past... was the result of social drinking though, not just to get drunk

Namita: you have ...hehe

Nicholas: yah we usually have friends we can count on one hand n the rest are acquaintances

Namita: yesss true

Nicholas: hell yah! I learned where my limit was pretty quick so I knew not to go over it

Namita: lol

Namita: im sure the feeling wasnt ever great

Namita: i am proud to say... ive never been drunk in my life

Nicholas: I remember my first party, it was w the friends that were 2 years older. they were friends w my sister as well. before I left the house my sister said "nobody likes it when there's a falling down drunk younger kid at the party"

Nicholas: never... wow! a little buzzed though yah?

Namita: yes a little buzzed... i hardly ever drink... and if i did... it would be one drink

Nicholas: I suffered from migraines since I was 4 n a hangover is a lot like a migraine so why inflict that type of pain on myself

Namita: im satisfied with the one... i dont crave another... I dont know how other women or younger ppl drink one drink after another and get wasted... or crash...or pick up some stranger... lol

Nicholas: I've never liked the taste of alcohol in the drinks.. I like the flavour of say Kahlua but I can still taste the alcohol

Nicholas: yes

Namita: wow... migraines at 4... that's pretty young

Nicholas: I limit myself to 1 coz of the blood thinners i take n I also like to know that I'm a safe ride home

Nicholas: it is... my mom got 1 type n my dad got the other n I inherited both

Namita: yes that a good practice... i usually am the designated driver for friends

Namita: ohhhh nicholas... sooo sorry... do you still get them even now?

Namita: you must know by now what would trigger them

Nicholas: I've usually drive when we go out so I can leave whenever I want

Namita: thats good to hear !!

Nicholas: I do still get them but not as often as when I was younger. the change in the weather can bring one on... my triggers are going too long w/o food, not enough sleep n after I've been worrying about something

Namita: ohhh... i hope youve been getting enough sleep

Nicholas: I get a diff type now that I'm older, more like my dad's type.. when I was younger it was my mom's type

Nicholas: oh yes not to worry

Namita: ohhh geeez

Namita: once in a while i do get a headache ... im not sure if it is a migraine.... i take an aspirin and go to sleep

Nicholas: after my first surgery I discovered Diclofenac or Voltaren so if my vision goes I can take one n I don't get the headache

Namita: next morning i may feel lightheadedness but ok afterwards

Namita: yess voltaren is a good anti-inflammatory

Nicholas: migraines feel like there's a clamp on ur head n it keeps getting tighter

Namita: OUCH !!!

Namita: thats no fun !

Nicholas: I wish I'd known about Voltaren when I was younger, could have saved me so much lost time

Namita: i sometimes take it for back pain from lifting at work... my upper back and shoulders get sore... my parents take it... so i steal one from them when I need it

Nicholas: nope... I've had them so bad about 4 times where I laid on the floor n cried.. if someone put a bullet through my head it probly wouldn't have hurt as much... I know that sounds extreme n doesn't sound great in type

Namita: wow... i can only imagine how it must feel

Nicholas: I haven't had one that bad for about 2 years now

Nicholas: they just build and get away on you so quickly sometimes

Namita: my mom used to have them but now its not as bad

Nicholas: my mom too

Namita: i think women are more prone to it too

Nicholas: they say they subside as you get older. I'm noticing that now

Namita: hormones have something to do with it

Nicholas: I think so too

Nicholas: I use to get them in clusters too... would come on at the same time everyday once for 5 days I think was one... had one last 7 days before, both were when I was in high school

Namita: wowww... yes i think it even termed cluster headache migraine

Nicholas: it seemed like when I went through puberty I got all the types of migraines. not fun missed quite a few days of school

Nicholas: how was work today?

Namita: ohhh thats not good !!

Namita: work was ok... i had a pt with a double lung transplant

Namita: who is not waking up

Nicholas: holy god that's amazing!

Nicholas: damn

Namita: she has not come out of her consciousness

Nicholas: what are some of the reasons someone would have a lung transplant?

Namita: is dependent on the breathing machine

Nicholas: it's fascinating what we can do these days medically

Namita: you can have a condition called pulmonary hypertension... where the main artery going to the lungs has narrowed for some reason and it causes the blood to slows down... leading to poor oxygen/carbon dioxide exchange

Nicholas: oh yah

Namita: so the pressure in the lung becomes sooo great... you can manage for a few yrs (years)... while waiting for AN EXACT DONOR TO BECOME AVAILABLE

Namita: sorry for caps

Nicholas: lol

Nicholas: good placement on the caps lock lol

Namita: most patients have to be on viagra to control the pressure of the lung

Namita: heheh

Nicholas: viagra as in the erectile disfunction meds

Namita: yes viagra is an erectile dysf (disfunction) med but originally it was used for treating pressures in the vascular system... well namely chest pressure... before they discovered the more obvious use

Nicholas: I guess they discovered that side effect when they gave the med to men... here you go mr smith this should relieve ur discomfort n your wife should like the side effect... lol

Namita: hehehe... yes and im sure they get told !!

Namita: my patient was a 40 something yr old female

Nicholas: oh geeze close to home

Namita: other reasons... cystic fibrosis

Nicholas: ah

Nicholas: I'm fortunate I don't have anything major n don't get sick often

Namita: yes... it is pretty sad... they are giving her another week... if she doesn't wake up... well in her case it is the lights are on but nobody home

Namita: then we will go to comfort care

Namita: let her pass away

Nicholas: just make her comfortable till she passes u mean?

Namita: yes

Nicholas: mind reader

Nicholas: lol

Nicholas: I can read between the lines

Namita: we wont escalate her care and we wont do CPR should a crisis occur

Namita: hehehe

Nicholas: DNR (do not resuscitate) order then

Namita: yes ur getting the hang of the medical world

Namita: OMG yess

Nicholas: I know some

Namita: yes DNR

Nicholas: I'm holding back

Namita: yes I'm sure you do

Nicholas: not bragging though

Nicholas: I have a steel trap memory

Namita: hehe I can tell

Nicholas: there's a lot of stuff stored in here let me tell yah lol

Namita: how was ur work ?

Nicholas: was ok went by quickly which was nice

Nicholas: thx for the pre-work message... they're like little surprises throughout my day

Namita: hehe

Namita: ur welcome

Namita: do you guys just work and do ur job that ur assigned for or do you get to chat while doing ur job... is it a noisy place ?

Nicholas: its pretty noisy so earplugs n fresh air respirators too... we work in our own booths too coz we're welding n grinding

Namita: ahhh i see

Namita: i hate those respirators

Nicholas: I listen to a little radio w headphones to help pass the time n listen to the hockey games

Namita: we do wear them too... they're called N95 masks... esp when dealing with unknown airborne diseases

Namita: like H1N1

Nicholas: these ones are nicer than the half mask resp (respirators)

Namita: ohh good... so you dont get completely bored !

Nicholas: those N95 are a dusk mask I think

Namita: ohhh

Namita: i think i know which ones ur talking about

Nicholas: we have full on respirators. the one I wear has a hard hat w a face shield. a little motor at the back of a belt around your waist that pulls air through filters through a flex tube into the back of the hard hat n over ur face

Nicholas: it's kinda like a space helmet lol

Namita: ohh must be nice that they can do that... i practically suffocate in my mask... i hate them

Nicholas: I use to work at a safety supply company

Namita: ohhh wow

Nicholas: yah I'm not big on the dust masks

Nicholas: they fog my safety glasses

Namita: yeah i can imagine

Namita: it happens to me too... than i bump into things in the room

Nicholas: I don't need to wear the glasses w the fresh air resp

Namita: can i ask you a funny question

Nicholas: sooo not that I don't like the photo thats up n not getting tired of it by any means but what else have you got that you've been holding out on me? hmmm

Nicholas: sure can

Namita: hehe

Nicholas: as I've said before u can ask me anything

Namita: ok question first... in ur work bathroom... are the walls covered in... ummm ahem... playboy pics ... the reason i ask is cuz when i was a teen... i used to team up with other ppl and we used to go clean offices... to earn money... and one time we went to this steel company... once i went to the back warehouse... i accidently went into the mens washroom... thank god no one was in it ... the walls were covered with playboy pics from magazines

Namita: i was soooo embarrassed and flew out of there

Nicholas: ours is not. most places dont

Namita: hehe... now when i look back... it was a pretty funny site

Nicholas: I totally know what u mean though. I remember those days too

Namita: the managers crunched down ?

Namita: omg good !!

Nicholas: yah that n it's just not acceptable these days especially in a big company like this one

Nicholas: u might find that in a little hole in the wall shop

Namita: ohhh wow ... so they have evolved !!

Nicholas: oh very nice... my typed words just don't give you the total experience of my reactions to your photos

Namita: yes i remember my reaction... i was stunned at first... with my mouth open... then ran out of there... bumping into someone

Namita: what mouth open ?

Namita: hehe

Namita: hehe thanks

Nicholas: mmm more sounds I make... love those legs

Nicholas: I mean the rest is fantastic! but your legs mmm mmm mmm

~Namita~ would like to send you the file "nmp-2011-3. jpg" (55 Kb). Do you want to

Accept

(Ctrl+G) or

Decline

(Ctrl+C) the invitation?

Transfer of file "nmp-2011-3.jpg" from ~Namita~ has been accepted. Starting transfer...

Cancel

You have successfully received nmp-2011-3.jpg from ~Namita~. Before opening this file, you may want to scan it with a virus-scanning program.

A Sepia photo this time. She's wearing a form fitting black nighty, lace top and bottom with spaghetti straps, high on the thigh, accentuating her smooth shapely legs. She's turned slightly to the left toward me on the edge of a fancy white scrolled metal chair. Knees together, left hand on her knee. Right hand sensually touching her neck, hair down and wavy. Looking down like she's pondering something important.

Namita: sounds like ur going to chomp on them ...hehe

Nicholas: I do love the art of the photos too if that makes sense?

Namita: yess i know what you mean

Nicholas: it's hard to explain but I'll give it a shot

Namita: ok go for it

Nicholas: I don't look at them n think "I want a piece of that" like I don't get turned on sexually. I look at them and see the artful beauty in it... the model... the lighting... the way it accentuates your body... the look on your face... what you might be thinking... the sepia colour to the photo.... I appreciate it for the beauty

Nicholas: and it's a big turn on... not sexually... just hits me in the chest

Nicholas: my screen is very full at the moment w all your pics

Namita: ohhh Nicholas... and thats why i do it... it is the beauty of the lines the angles... the lighting... for me too and its not because im in the pic... it could have been any subject in this pic

Nicholas: how old or recent is that one?

Namita: it is how the picture captures the imagination and beyond

Namita: this is from june this year

Nicholas: it does... it's really lovely

Namita: actually i didnt even know the pic was going to turn out like that

Nicholas: june this year wow... I knew I was a lucky guy but I don't think I quite knew how lucky

Namita: hehe

Nicholas: it's very very nice!

Nicholas: I love it!

Namita: ur welcome nicholas

Nicholas: thank you

Nicholas: I want to frame that one

Namita: hehe... and put it on ur nite stand ?

Nicholas: yes or over the fire place

Namita: hehehee

Namita: ur too funny

Nicholas: lol

Nicholas: that ones nice too. Is it from the same shoot?

Namita: yes it is

Nicholas: very lovely

Nicholas: I'm running out of words lol

~Namita~ would like to send you the file "nmp=2011-2. jpg" (32 Kb). Do you want to

Accept

(Ctrl+G) or

Decline

(Ctrl+C) the invitation?

Transfer of file "nmp=2011-2.jpg" from ~Namita~ has been accepted. Starting transfer...

Cancel

You have successfully received nmp=2011-2.jpg from ~Namita~. Before opening this file, you may want to scan it with a virus-scanning program.

Same nighty, she's leaning her bum against maybe our dining room table? Turned slightly at the shoulders looking at me from in the other room. One hand resting on the table. Hair down and full, with a "What are you waiting for?" look.

Nicholas: absolutely stunning!

Nicholas: I hope I'm not slobbering too much lol

Namita: the one i just sent you?

Namita: lmaoo

Nicholas: yes

Namita: do you need a bucket ?

Nicholas: as I say I love them all but damn woman! I'm speechless

Namita: hehhehe

Nicholas: maybe not a bucket but close

Namita: lmao

Namita: im sooo giggling here

Nicholas: lol

Nicholas: you must be pretty special coz now I've covered my entire screen w your photos... n covered my desktop of the hot rod

Namita: omg... have i surpassed ur hot rod now ?? Well you can have the best of both worlds

Nicholas: I like the last one coz it gives me a great view of your face

Nicholas: you have n that's sooo awesome

Namita: this is one of them too... from the same day

Namita: i think you may have seen this one before

Nicholas: you know while I was in my happy place, working on the hot rod, it truly was my happy place coz while I was working on it I was thinking about you

Nicholas: best of both worlds that's so great

Nicholas: have I told you lately how awesome I think you are?

Namita: hehe aweee so sweet nicholas... im glad to bring a smile to ur face

Nicholas: you sure know how to make me smile

Namita: hehe

Nicholas: your very photogenic

Namita: am i provoking impure thoughts now ?

Nicholas: not gonna lie I have impure thoughts of you quite often honey

Namita: yes ive been told that since i was a baby... my dad was into photography when i was a baby and took a lot pics... one of which... a portrait he sent to LA wayyy back when... in a contest and he won !!!

Nicholas: that's so cool... not surprising though

Nicholas: I might need a cold shower

Namita: i must have been 1 yrs old... with a white baby dress on... curly ringlet hair... and its a close portrait pic... and I have this grin... with one or 2 teeth

Namita: its one my fav pics

Nicholas: I can imagine... very cute

Namita: the pic was black and white too but it captured my babyness

Nicholas: cool

Namita: Ohhhhh poor nicholas needs a cold shower ??

Nicholas: lol not poor nicholas... lucky nicholas!

Namita: lmaooo !!!

Nicholas: it's like I won the lottery but didn't know I was playing

Namita: hehehe that a good way to put it

Nicholas: I thought so

Nicholas: all this because of your story/scenario on your profile... who'd a thought

Namita: hehee... i hope i do justice to the profile

Nicholas: I do feel like I've won... from what I know about your personality n seen from your photos you definitely do justice!

Namita: aweee thanks Nicholas !!

Nicholas: I hope I do the same too

Nicholas: I don't have sexy photos to show you but you might be a little concerned if I did I bet?

Namita: heheehehehehehe... no i dont think id be too concerned...

Namita: so are you into sexy pics... i mean say how about doing sexy pics together

Nicholas: you wouldn't? well maybe I'll let you take some if you wanted to

Namita: hehe

Nicholas: oh very much so

Nicholas: mind reader

Namita: now this is only for our pleasure... something personal

Nicholas: I've always wanted to do a project w someone

Nicholas: yes

Namita: mind reader ?

Nicholas: about the pics

Namita: ohhhh I see

Namita: lol

Nicholas: it involves paint

Namita: ohhhhh

Namita: edible paint ?

Nicholas: I'd like to make love on a canvas with primary colour paints so not only would you get body shapes you'd get all the colours when they mix

Nicholas: I'd call it the Colours of Love

Namita: hmmmm never even thought of that

Namita: then we frame it and put it in the room

Namita: over the bed

Nicholas: yes!

Namita: hehe

Namita: i remember you saying something about filming

Namita: filming making love

Nicholas: lol I think you mentioned it first but yes

Namita: omg I did !!

Namita: hehe

Namita: yesss blame me !!

Nicholas: I think so... was your vixen coming out

Namita: would you do it

Namita: not that ive ever done it

Nicholas: I sense a sexy vixen just dyeing to come out of you

Namita: what about watching those kinds of movies ?

Namita: lmO

Nicholas: never done it either but I'd try it w you

Namita: LMAO

Nicholas: I've seen porno's before. have you?

Namita: yes i have ... what do you think about it ?

Nicholas: I find it hard to find a porno that has a good story n is classy. I don't like the ones where they role credits n they start banging away

Namita: theres no right answer i am not testing you

Nicholas: I like sensual n erotic

Namita: lol

Namita: yes me too

Nicholas: what do I think about us making our own? I'm in!

Namita: most porn is based on a mans point of view

Nicholas: yes

Namita: im good too but whos going to film it ?

Nicholas: would prefer a woman's point of view

Nicholas: tripod n some hand held by us

Namita: womens point of view is more sensual

Nicholas: very much so

Namita: not that ive seen a lot

Nicholas: nor have I

Nicholas: I've seen enough though

Nicholas: I don't own any either lol

Namita: i think most porn out there... it is all about the mans pleasure

Nicholas: so true

Nicholas: it's a mans world

Namita: yess ... how the man wants it to be

Namita: no i dont own any either

Nicholas: from what I've seen about the industry there are mostly men directors... n the style n proceedings are all the same

Namita: yesss soo true

Namita: i sometimes cant believe why guys dont get tired of it the same ol' same ol'

Nicholas: it seems in porn women are there just to satisfy the men n that's so not cool

Nicholas: I do. It gets very boring

Nicholas: n not a turn on at all after awhile

Namita: hehee im sure !!

Namita: its very predictable

Nicholas: it is... I like a good story w cool sensual music n actors that look like they're enjoying what they're doing not just banging away n faking it

Nicholas: I guess that's why it's predictable coz they are faking it

Namita: yesss sooo true

Namita: i am all about sensuality... and romance

Nicholas: I'd like to see the man pleasuring the woman rather than just banging away

Nicholas: yes I know... another check list item

Namita: yesss i knowww... too many times it is the woman pleasing from beginning to end

Nicholas: yup

Nicholas: I'm not big on seeing a guy in the first place. I'd rather see her n how she's being pleasured n how she's enjoying it but again I know she's faking

Namita: hehe... wow just those words of urs... turned me on !!

Nicholas: mmmm

Namita: how shes being pleasured

Nicholas: I'm more than a little hot n bothered myself

Nicholas: I can't wait to pleasure you

Namita: hehe

Nicholas: I do love those sepia photos

Namita: is ur laptop sitting balanced on ur lap... or crooked ?

Nicholas: lol

Namita: hehe

Nicholas: balanced but out on my thighs so I have room so to speak

~Namita~ would like to send you the file "nmp 2011. jpg" (26 Kb). Do you want to

Accept

(Ctrl+G) or

Decline (Ctrl+C)

the invitation?

Transfer of file "nmp 2011.jpg" from ~Namita~ has been accepted. Starting transfer...

Cancel

You have successfully received nmp 2011.jpg from ~Namita~. Before opening this file, you may want to scan it with a virus-scanning program.

    Now she's lying on the table, on her tummy, up on her elbows, knees bent. Wearing a short black skirt and a black halter strap top with strapped black heels. Looking over her shoulder with a beautiful full smile, she's waiting for my response.

Namita: hahaha... i like the picture you painted

Nicholas: you're killing me here

Nicholas: I'm very visual

Nicholas: I could almost fly to you right now

Namita: hehehe... I sure hope you can think straight

Nicholas: I can

Namita: last one of the series

Nicholas: I think our first meeting should be something other than getting naked, as nice an idea that would be

Nicholas: ah was gonna say

Nicholas: oooohhh topless? yes

Namita: hehe yesss

Nicholas: oohhh mmmyyyyyyy

Namita: but i think you can do without this one ... 😊

Nicholas: that's mean

Nicholas: lol

Namita: lol

Nicholas: I'm not going to beg!

Namita: you dont need this one... it doesnt show my legs

Namita: hehe

Nicholas: brat!

~Namita~ would like to send you the file "nmp-11- 06. jpg" (74 Kb). Do you want to

 Accept

(Ctrl+G) or

Decline

(Ctrl+C) the invitation?

Nicholas: pleeeeease

Transfer of file "nmp-11-06.jpg" from ~Namita~ has been accepted. Starting transfer...

Cancel

Namita: ok ok

You have successfully received nmp-11-06.jpg from ~Namita~. Before opening this file, you may want to scan it with a virus-scanning program.

 She has her back to me, only this time she's topless looking over her left shoulder, arms crossed. Hair down and full.

Nicholas: thank you 😊

Namita: i have pity on you... lol

Nicholas: oh wow it shows up big excellent!

Namita: oh really ?

Namita: hehe

Nicholas: yup. its about a 3rd of my screen

Namita: lol

Namita: another screen saver

Nicholas: I've got a whole collage going on here!

Namita: hehehe...

Nicholas: random... you're 5'7" right?

Namita: yes

Nicholas: mmm I could just eat you up!

Namita: really ? where would you start ?

Nicholas: 5' 7" that's perfect!

Namita: sometimes i do wear heels

Nicholas: I'd start at your legs n slowly work my way up

Namita: so i can be a little taller

Nicholas: even better

Nicholas: you can wear heels anytime you want

Namita: makes up the difference

Nicholas: they do

Namita: hehe

Nicholas: could almost look you in the eyes

Namita: yesss ... or i can look up into urs ... innocently

Nicholas: n bat those eye lashes I bet

Namita: yesss bat those long lashes at you

Nicholas: mmm I can see them now

Namita: hehehe

Nicholas: so what's the word on seeing you?

Namita: im thinking more like fri

Namita: cuz im coming home on thurs

Nicholas: the girls have a pro-D day friday so thurs would be better if that works for you

Namita: morning

Nicholas: oh right

Namita: and would be tired after night shift

Nicholas: yes you would

Namita: ohhh

Nicholas: what about sat morning?

Namita: well weekend is good too

Nicholas: are you on nights for sat?

Namita: yes

Nicholas: I'm kid free this weekend

Namita: ahhh ok... do you have them over every other weekend ?

Nicholas: I don't want to take away from your sleep time during the day if you're on nights though

Nicholas: I do

Namita: we will work something out im sure

Nicholas: I may not have them the Halloween weekend coz Tony is going to try to come so we can go out

Nicholas: oh yes we will

Namita: what are the plans with Tony ?

Namita: a halloween party ?

Nicholas: we're planning to dress up and go to the Blarney Stone

Nicholas: yes

Nicholas: you're more than welcome to come if you like

Nicholas: my friend Diana is going to try to come too

Namita: hehe... ohhh cool... do you have ur costume together ?

Namita: Blarney Stone is irish ?

Nicholas: I have 2 costumes they're my back ups

Nicholas: it is... we know the owner too

Nicholas: so we don't have to wait in line

Namita: ive heard of it

Namita: never been though

Nicholas: it's fun, we like it

Namita: im sure it is !!

Namita: im supposed to be trick or treating with niece and nephew cuz sis cant walk properly yet and her husband doesn't get home til' after 630 or 7ish

Nicholas: halloween is on sunday this year, we'd be going out sat night

Namita: yeah i think he is still out

Nicholas: it's on monday

Namita: thats what i thought

Namita: are ur girls excited too ?

Nicholas: sort of... Isabel is getting to the age where she's deciding if she's still going out. Amanda is still into it though

Nicholas: oh haven't seen that one yet... just saw it now

Namita: geeez pay attention !!!

Nicholas: lol distracted by the topless pic sorry

Namita: ur going to have an oral exam soon !

Namita: lol

Nicholas: oral?! is that right? well then I better get ready then

Nicholas: I bet I can get an A

Namita: lmao

Nicholas: I'll be the teachers pet

Namita: hmmmm dont be too sure of urself... you'll be tested on technique, creativity, endurance

Namita: hehehe

Nicholas: I think you'll be very satisfied

Namita: mmmmmmmmmmmmmm

Namita: i will have my marking book/ pencil in hand and list to check things off

Nicholas: thorough I like that

Nicholas: you may want to jot down a few notes

Namita: lmao

Nicholas: though I'm good at remembering what pleases my partner

Namita: yes of course !!

Namita: ur making me hot over here

Nicholas: I dont think you'll have any complaints

Nicholas: over there?! you should be here then we could take care of this sexual tension that's building

Namita: we'd be up all night long ... releasing tension after tension !!!

Nicholas: we're almost there now

Nicholas: it's a bit like chinese food very satisfying not real filling and you want more in an hour or so

Namita: would you like if i was laying on top of you... my long silky hair around ur face

Namita: hehehe sooo true

Nicholas: I really would

Namita: you can take in the fragrance of my hair

Nicholas: feeling the heat from your body

Namita: my hands running up and down ur chest

Nicholas: the softness of your skin

Nicholas: mmmm

Namita: then in circles on ur stomach

Namita: my head on ur chest

Nicholas: mmmm

Namita: i can hear ur heart beating

Namita: ur one arm around me

Namita: ur trying to concentrate

Nicholas: I'd run my hands over ur back down to ur bum

Namita: mmmm

Namita: then i move over directly on top of you

Nicholas: n ever so gently down ur sides causing goose bumps

Namita: mmm yess

Namita: my hair spilling across my face onto ur chest

Namita: you loveee the feel of it

Namita: sooo silky

Namita: adding to the exoticness

Nicholas: one of my hands finds its way to the back of ur head n I lace my fingers into ur hair

Namita: mmmm

Nicholas: n caress the base of your neck n scalp

Namita: you hold my face in ur hands and bring me closer to ur face

Nicholas: running my fingers up into your hair

Namita: we make eye contact

Nicholas: you see right into me

Namita: so far so good ?

Nicholas: sounds fantastic!

Namita: i drown into the big pools of blue eyes

Nicholas: mmm

Namita: as you meet the big brown eyes

Nicholas: so not helping the horniness over here

Namita: lmao

Nicholas: well its helping there's just no happy ending for both of us

Namita: no dont think that way

Nicholas: so what are we going to do for our first meeting?

Namita: hmm anything goes

Namita: we can keep it casual

Nicholas: I haven't really thought about after I hug you n not want to let go

Nicholas: mmm casual eh?

Namita: we dont have to spend a lot to make our evening memorable

Nicholas: that we don't

Namita: i dont think that going somewhere fancy is the way to please me for first impressions

Namita: thats just not me

Nicholas: good to know. me either

Namita: i hope whatever im saying is making sense

Nicholas: walking n talking

Nicholas: yes

Nicholas: totally with you

Namita: im slowly fading... heheh... hope im not blabbering

Namita: yes walking and talking is good with me

Nicholas: ur not... I can see that you are

Namita: and just go with the flow

Namita: how can you tell? lol

Nicholas: should we meet somewhere or me pick you up or you pick me up?

Nicholas: I can... you can probly tell I am too

Namita: hmmm i can come over and we can meet

Namita: yes i think i can

Namita: hehe

Nicholas: ok

Nicholas: you could leave for work from here if you want

Nicholas: we could go to Rocky Point?

Nicholas: it's close n we wont burn up too much time driving anywhere

Namita: yess... thats a good idea

Nicholas: okay

Nicholas: so saturday then?

Namita: yes that is fine with me

Nicholas: okay cool. we can figure a time when we're both more coherent

Namita: heheh

Nicholas: you're fading my dear I'll let you sleep okay

Namita: ohhh geeze im sorry nicholas

Nicholas: it's totally fine

Namita: i went from seducing you online to fading

Nicholas: you've had a long day

Nicholas: save it for saturday

Namita: that's what going to happen... i will try to seduce you for real... then fall asleep with my head on ur chest before we've done anything

Namita: lol

Nicholas: lol

Nicholas: just getting to touch you will make my day!

Namita: lol

Namita: omg i almost fell asleep on you just now

Namita: i think we should call it a nite

Nicholas: ok go to sleep I'll talk to you tomorrow

Namita: ok

Nicholas: sleep well

Nicholas: xo

Namita: good nite

Nicholas: thx for a wonderful night

Namita: yes you too

Nicholas: nite

Namita: logging off

End Time: 3:35 AM

October 22 is the big day. We finally see each other for the first time. I can hardly stand the excitement. I just wont think about it and the days will fly by — I hope.

Chapter 11 October 20

Start Time: 12:59 AM

Nicholas: hey!!

Namita: hey there... sorry i havent been in touch with you

Namita: how has your day been ?

Nicholas: sokay I figured you were busy

Namita: ive been more than busy... im exhausted

Nicholas: I'm good... a little Namita withdrawal lol

Namita: ohhh sorry... hehe

Nicholas: so what's happened?

Namita: a close uncle of mine had a heart attack last night and he is in hospital

Nicholas: it's okay I figured its part of the independence and I'm still getting use to it

Namita: in intensive care

Nicholas: OMG

Nicholas: is he going to be okay?

Namita: yess... i just saw him in july

Namita: he and his family live in san francisco

Nicholas: oh geeze

Nicholas: San Fran? you've been there n back in the last couple of days?

Namita: im not sure if he is ok... i havent spoken to family... except got the info from my own parents

Namita: they left a message around midday... while i was sleeping

Namita: no i havent been there... hehe

Namita: im planning to go Nicholas

Nicholas: hopefully he'll be okay... my thoughts go out to him n his family

Namita: yes me too

Nicholas: when are you able to go?

Namita: well the only flight i was able to get was on saturday morning

Namita: im so sorry to bail out on you like this

Nicholas: it's okay... family first

Namita: the flight is at 10 am

Nicholas: disappointing yes but your family is more important

Namita: i phoned work to cancel my shift on that day and i got a special leave

Nicholas: we'll have plenty of time when your back

Namita: m sooo sorry

Nicholas: it's okay please don't worry about it

Nicholas: we'll work something out

Namita: the news came to my parents last nite while i was at work... my parents and one of other sisters is going too

Nicholas: you need to be w ur family

Namita: thank for understanding Nicholas

Namita: ive been running around and getting things in order

Nicholas: there's one thing I learned when my dad died is to leave nothing unsaid... you need to be w ur family n I understand

Namita: sorry didnt get a chance to text you

Nicholas: it's okay really

Namita: yesss that is such a good advice

Namita: it is sooo true

Nicholas: I figured something was up coz ur not the type of person to just disappear

Nicholas: I was starting to worry about what might have happened to you

Namita: well you thought right !

Nicholas: when will you be back?

Namita: i didnt forget about you

Nicholas: didn't think so

Namita: im not sure... right now... i might be there for a week

Nicholas: but thx for saying it

Namita: one of my cousins works for West Jet so she can book in my flight form the other side using a buddy pass

Nicholas: take ur laptop n we can still keep in touch that way if you have time. texting international is expensive

Namita: yess i will !

Nicholas: cool

Namita: i thought of that already

Namita: hehe

Nicholas: I don't know if I could go a week w/o talking to you lol

Namita: hehehe

Namita: youd be in serious withdrawal then

Nicholas: 3 days was a challenge... I didn't want to seem clingy though

Nicholas: yes I would

Namita: lol

Namita: sounds like someone missed me ?!

Nicholas: or needy either

Nicholas: YES he did!

Namita: hehe

Namita: was he curled up in a ball in a corner ?

Nicholas: went 2 solid weeks of chatting n then cold turkey... was tough

Nicholas: no he wasn't that bad

Namita: hehe ... he needs an antidote !!

Nicholas: yes he does... or yes I do lol

Namita: hehe

Nicholas: side note: you're my home screen on my phone now

Namita: which pic ?

Nicholas: it's a head shot of your topless photo

Namita: ohh nooo... i hope no one else sees it ! lol

Nicholas: it's very nice... and a surprise every time I open my phone

Nicholas: it's just from the shoulder up

Namita: it is the black and white pic?

Nicholas: yes

Namita: the one im looking back ?

Namita: or sideways ?

Nicholas: I'm kinda hoping someone will see it n ask who the beautiful woman is

Nicholas: looking back

Nicholas: I love them all but I really love that one the most

Namita: this one ?

Nicholas: YES!!! that one

Namita: hehe

Nicholas: that is just sweet perfection

Namita: oh please dont show it to anyone... ur a select few that have seen it

Namita: hehe

Nicholas: no one has seen it n it's not something I'd show around... I keep to myself most of the time

Namita: ohh phew !! hehe ... i know you wont be doing that though

Nicholas: it's a little you time every time I open my phone

Namita: hehe

Namita: makes ur day... i bet youve been staring at it for the last 3 days since youve had it !

Nicholas: I've been straightening up around here for our saturday meeting but now you wont be here

Nicholas: lol I have... I open my phone just to have a look

Namita: hehe ...are your girls over tomorrow too ...they have that pro-D day tomorrow

Nicholas: for a little while. I'll pick them up at 11... they'll say something about me having company over coz it's clean n tidy

Nicholas: I'm pretty clean anyway

Namita: hehe... me too... i try to keep thing in order at my place

Nicholas: n a bit of a germaphobe too

Nicholas: I do have projects on the go but I try not to let them get away on me n take over the place

Namita: except when im doing my shifts my bed doesnt get made... when i leave at 6 am and come home by 9 pm theres no point

Nicholas: I rarely make my bed

Namita: did you say ur a bit of germaphobe ?

Namita: ahhhh GOOD !!

Nicholas: I did

Namita: hehe

Namita: what makes you a germaphobe?

Nicholas: mmm not touching the escalator when I'm on it... I open doors away from where ppl usually touch them... washing my hands regularly

Namita: ahhh i see

Namita: i hate touching a shopping buggy

Nicholas: I'm not over the top but I'm aware of what I touch

Nicholas: yes that too

Namita: but i make sure i wash my hands too

Namita: at work esp

Nicholas: I don't put my grocery bags on the ground coz I'll end up putting them on my counter

Namita: i have to touch an escalator or i will surely fall flat on face

Namita: hehe

Nicholas: lol

Namita: no i dont do that either w groceries

Namita: heyyy its almost happened to me...hehe

Nicholas: I like to wear gloves in the winter so

Nicholas: I'm not OCD about it

Namita: hehe

Nicholas: what's almost happened to you?

Namita: thanks for clearing that up !!

Nicholas: lol

Nicholas: didn't want you to think I was a freak or something

Namita: ive almost fallen on an escalator before... cuz i was toooo confident

Namita: hehehe

Namita: thanks

Nicholas: hmmm no comment lol

Namita: of course i didnt think that!

Nicholas: ☺

Namita: yes it would have been one embarrassing day if that had happened

Namita: hehe

Nicholas: anything in particular that would have made it embarrassing?

Nicholas: u were wearing a dress?

Namita: just falling down like that in front of ppl

Nicholas: ah

Nicholas: do you wear dresses? skirts?

Namita: no i was wearing a black pant suit and heels

Nicholas: pant suit cool

Nicholas: I bet heads turned when you wore that

Namita: it almost happened when i had landed in calgary at the airport and i was going thru their moving sidewalk

Namita: the horizontal escalator walk

Nicholas: those things are neat

Namita: and at the end i tripped

Namita: and almost fell flat on my face

Namita: hehe

Namita: of course my sister had to laugh about it

Nicholas: that wouldn't have been good

Namita: noooooooo

Nicholas: side note: at least you'll be in the same time zone while ur away

Namita: sorry answer to ur question ...yes i love wearing dresses, skirts and pants , jeans

Nicholas: cool

Namita: yes true !!

Nicholas: random: the following sat is the halloween party n Tony will be in town. My friend Diana is going to try to come with us... as I said ur more than welcome to come but I don't know if it's too early to be meeting the friends yet?

Nicholas: the convo the other night was pretty funny to re-read

Nicholas: Oh my point

Nicholas: I'll be kid free that weekend coz Tony will be in town

Namita: thank you for the invite Nicholas! ill keep that in mind

Namita: ahh i see

Nicholas: I would like to see you just the 2 of us before that though

Namita: yes it might be better that way

Nicholas: as I've said before I don't want to rush things

Namita: yes

Nicholas: we've waited 39 years what's another couple of weeks... I hope it wont be weeks

Nicholas: I had thought we could got n get gelato then go to Rocky Point

Namita: yes that sounds like fun !

Namita: and watch the occasional boaters

Nicholas: yes

Nicholas: n talk n spend time together

Namita: the park is beautiful

Nicholas: I like the sound of that

Namita: yess

Nicholas: that's something we could do during the day too if we're in a time pinch

Nicholas: I mean if we can't work a weekend visit in

Namita: yess and it is close by to you too

Nicholas: or just a more time visit

Nicholas: yes the gelato place is too

Namita: ive never even seen the gelato place

Nicholas: it's where the Burger King use to be on North rd

Namita: ahhh ok ... even that i dont remember,,, hehe

Nicholas: lol

Namita: i hardly go to Burger King

Nicholas: I never do

Nicholas: I don't do McDonald's either... haven't eaten there since grade 11

Nicholas: I'm not big on that type of fast food

Namita: me either... id rather make my own food

Nicholas: I like A&W though

Namita: i never even worked in a fast food place

Nicholas: DQ (Dairy Queen), Subway, Quizno's

Namita: A&W is good... i like the grilled chicken sandwich

Namita: Quiznos is good too

Namita: never tried DQ

Nicholas: I hope this doesn't sound uppity but I always told myself that I'd never pump gas or work at a fast food place

Nicholas: you've never had DQ?!

Nicholas: never had their ice cream?

Nicholas: or a Blizzard?

Nicholas: or u mean the food?

Namita: yeah me either working in a fast food place was enough of a deterrent for me to go school and get a better job

Nicholas: no kidding

Namita: ive had the ice cream... mmmmmmmmmmm but not the burgers before

Nicholas: ah

Namita: i loveeeeeeeeeeee ice cream

Nicholas: I've heard lol

Namita: how can i not set foot in DQ ?!?!?!

Namita: lol

Nicholas: what's your fav flavor ice cream?

Namita: that is ice cream heaven

Nicholas: it is

Namita: ummm chocolate

Namita: mmmmmmmmmmmmmmmmmmmm

Nicholas: hmm

Namita: but I love the soft serve

Namita: what is yours ?

Nicholas: Tiger n Pralines n cream... not together mind you

Namita: whats tiger ?

Nicholas: liquorice and orange

Namita: oh ... never heard of it

Nicholas: it's a good thing I have spell check coz my spelling tonight is terrible

Namita: i dont like too many nut or peanut in my ice cream

Namita: i do like caramel though

Nicholas: no peanuts

Nicholas: mmmm caramel... love it!

Namita: i lovee caramel

Nicholas: tis very delish

Namita: yummm !!!

Namita: hehe

Namita: i love their ice cream cakes too

Nicholas: I like the cakes but I prefer to not have the fudge stuff inside them

Namita: ohhh i loveee it !! Hehehe

Namita: you can give it to me then !

Nicholas: I like the crumbly bits just not the fudge or whatever it is

Namita: lol

Nicholas: I will

Namita: yesss lovee the crumbly bit too

Nicholas: I'll let you scrap it off my ice cream cake

Nicholas: scrape*

Namita: mmmmm yesss !!!

Namita: hehe

Namita: sounds like we are having sex !! with our conversation here

Namita: lmao

Nicholas: it crossed my mind

Namita: hahahhaha

Namita: you too ?!?!?!

Nicholas: I wondered if it would come a cross sounding like that lol

Namita: i was thinking the exact same thing !!!!

Nicholas: great minds

Nicholas: I can't not help thinking naughty thoughts when I think about you

Nicholas: looking at your wonderful photos puts me over the edge

Namita: like what !! do tell !!

Nicholas: like how I can't wait to rub my hands all over your smooth naked skin

Nicholas: to drown in those beautiful brown eyes

Namita: hehe... slowlyyyYYYYyYYYyyy

Namita: do you like brown ?

Nicholas: ever so slowly

Nicholas: I like YOU!!!

Nicholas: n yours are brown so YES!

Namita: did you ever have a type in ur mind.... most guys like blondes

Nicholas: I never had a particular woman in mind just qualities I wanted

Namita: i understand

Nicholas: I can't help who I'm attracted to

Namita: so go on... hehee... what else did you have in ur mind

Nicholas: N let me tell you Namita you fit them ALL!

Nicholas: lol

Namita: wowwww thanks

Nicholas: the thought of feeling your body next to mine

Nicholas: smelling your sent

Namita: mmmmm niceee

Nicholas: rubbing my body over yours

Nicholas: touching you all over

Nicholas: from your legs

Nicholas: to your thighs

Nicholas: your tummy

Namita: sound like you are going to devour me

Nicholas: I will lol

Namita: hehe

Namita: i will loveee every min of it

Namita: hehe

Nicholas: how I want to kiss you just between your shoulder n your neck

Nicholas: you feeling my breath on you

Nicholas: kissing your ear lobes

Namita: mmmmmmm and you feeling my breath on ur skin as you do that

Nicholas: you can hear me smelling you ever so gently

Nicholas: mmhmm

Namita: driving you wild !

Nicholas: mmm

Nicholas: me listening to your body

Namita: you can hear my heart beat a little faster

Nicholas: feeling you tingle

Namita: sending shivers up my body

Nicholas: kissing you ever soooo gently on the lips

Namita: mmmmmmmmmmmmm niceeeeeee

Namita: and you can feel me wanting more

Nicholas: there are just some things I just can't explain in type

Nicholas: I can't wait to show you

Namita: yessss me either

Nicholas: there is sooo much more to this than just words

Namita: yesssss i can sense that

Nicholas: I'm anticipating pure magic when I see you

Nicholas: and a physical connection like no other when I make love to you

Namita: i think we will be ripping each others clothes off right at rocky point

Nicholas: lol

Namita: on the bench!!!

Namita: hehe

Namita: hey can u do me a favour

Nicholas: being with you will feel like there's no one else around

Nicholas: anything

Namita: change ur pic

Namita: hehe

Nicholas: k hold on

Namita: would you really make a move of me in public

Namita: without public knowing of course

Nicholas: sure would!

Namita: ohh nice

Nicholas: there is soooo much we'll experience my dear just you wait

Namita: how would you do it ?

Namita: hehe

Nicholas: depends where we are n what's going on around us

Namita: yess im sure the possibilities are endless

Nicholas: maybe I reach up your skirt n finger you in public

Namita: OMG !!

Namita: woww

Nicholas: or maybe while your driving

Namita: we would need to pull over soon !!!

Nicholas: lol

Namita: what if i did that !!

Nicholas: would probably be on the way to a room

Namita: while ur driving in the night perhaps

Nicholas: pulled over?

Namita: i cant wait to get home

Nicholas: I'd totally let you!!

Namita: id would unzip ur pants

Namita: slowly

Nicholas: button fly

Namita: hehe

Namita: oh right button fly

Namita: and i would slip my hand into ur pants

Nicholas: ohhh yes!

Namita: and trying to concentrate on the road

Nicholas: trying yes

Namita: but you can feel urself getting really hard

Nicholas: oh I'd already be there before you got ur hand in there

Namita: hehehe

Namita: ok... i would start massaging you... up and down

Nicholas: oh I like that

Nicholas: playing w the tip

Namita: making you all slippery with ur precum

Nicholas: mmmhhmmm

Namita: yes rubbing my thumb over ur tip

Nicholas: yes!

Namita: we are almost home

Namita: into the driveway

Nicholas: mmm mmmm

Namita: and you cant wait to get out of the car

Nicholas: I can't wait to get your clothes off

Namita: lol

Namita: you get out of the car in the garage

Nicholas: mmmhmm

Namita: and run around the car... open my door

Namita: and pull me out of the car

Nicholas: with my pants open

Namita: yess pants open

Nicholas: n I pick you up

Namita: n sit me on the hood of the car

Namita: then lift up my skirt

Namita: i pull ur jeans down

Namita: got rid of my boots long ago

Nicholas: yes

Namita: hehe

Nicholas: then I slip your panties off

Namita: mmmmmmmmmmmmmmmmm

Nicholas: then go down on you

Nicholas: kissing n licking your throbbing clit

Nicholas: right there on the hood of the car

Namita: omg

Nicholas: dipping my tongue into you hot wet pussy

Namita: i would be trying to squirm away

Namita: but you have GOOD grip on me

Nicholas: I'm holding your legs with my arms wrapped around them

Namita: ohhh myyy... i can feel ur power... it feels like im being punished for my doings while we were in the car

Nicholas: hehe

Namita: hehe

Nicholas: flicking ur clit w my tongue

Namita: and im writhing underneath you

Namita: telling you im sorry that i provoked you

Namita: and you tell me its wayyyy to late

Nicholas: faster n faster till you squirt all aver the hood of the car

Namita: ohhh yes

Namita: yes ... you feel hot liquid squirting out of me

Namita: onto ur face and running down the hood of the car

Nicholas: yes I do

Nicholas: mmhmm

Namita: but you know its not the end... you know my body can go on for hours

Namita: this was just the beginning

Nicholas: now that you've gotten off it's my turn

Nicholas: to play

Namita: ohh yesss

Nicholas: I bend you over the car

Nicholas: n I take you from behind

Nicholas: easing myself into you ever so slowly

Namita: hmmm yes

Nicholas: leaning over you

Namita: omg nicholas !!!

Nicholas: so I can massage that clit yet again

Namita: ohhhh god !!! thats totally going to make me wild

Nicholas: one holding your hip the other reaching around you to pleasure your clit

Nicholas: while I'm been deep inside you

Namita: hmmm ur all about pleasuring me... its not all about you... i like that !!!!!!!

Nicholas: thrusting into you

Nicholas: just you wait

Namita: oh god .... im going to go crazyyyy

Namita: im holding on for dear life

Nicholas: I know what will happen for me so getting you off as many times as you can handle is what I really love

Nicholas: slowly pulling out

Namita: you wont be disappointed in that department

Namita: hehe

Nicholas: you think I'm done w that until I ever so gently slide myself back into you

Nicholas: I pause as you catch your breath

Namita: ohhh god nicholas !!!

Namita: yes and i try to get accustomed to you

Nicholas: then I thrust deep inside

Nicholas: all the way to the very end

Namita: i soooo want you deep inside of me

Namita: i can feel you hitting the end

Nicholas: hitting spots you never knew you had

Namita: ohhh wowwww

Nicholas: then slowly rolling my hips

Nicholas: so you can enjoy every inch of me

Namita: ohhhhh Nicholas !

Namita: mmmmmmmmmmmm

Namita: you tighten up the union... between ur hard cock and my wet pussy

Namita: i can feel every inch of you

Namita: making you crazyyyyy

Namita: you want to get in sooo deep

Nicholas: there couldn't possibly be any more so I slide out a little then back in

Namita: hehe

Namita: am i making you hard

Nicholas: circling my hips

Nicholas: I've been hard since we started

Namita: hehee

Namita: do you feel like ur going to cum ?

Nicholas: am I making you wet?

Nicholas: I have good control of that

Namita: i am sooooooooooooooooooooo sexed up right now... hehe...yes im wet

Nicholas: It'll only go off if it's stroked

Namita: wowwww

Namita: then you pull out completely

Nicholas: I could drive to you?

Namita: no my sis is staying with me tonite

Namita: the youngest one... Jaya

Nicholas: but we should meet outside the bedroom first

Namita: hehe

Nicholas: all in due time

Namita: yes

Nicholas: don't want to rush things

Namita: no me either

Nicholas: we'll have plenty of time to live these words

Namita: buts its all in fun here... with our hot steamy scenarios

Nicholas: yes

Nicholas: I guess you know a photographer or 2?

Namita: no just one and shes a woman... hehe

Nicholas: defiantly hot that's for sure

Namita: i would not pose like this for a man behind the camera

Nicholas: would she be into photos of both of us

Namita: im sure she would be

Nicholas: no kidding

Namita: shes done it before for other ppl

Nicholas: been thinking of poses for us

~Namita~ would like to send you the file "january-2011.jpg " (49 Kb). Do you want to

Accept

(Ctrl+G) or

Decline

(Ctrl+C) the invitation?

Transfer of file "january-2011.jpg" from ~Namita~ has been accepted. Starting transfer...

Cancel

~Namita~ says: tell me what you think ?

You have successfully received january-2011.jpg from ~Namita~. Before opening this file, you may want to scan it with a virus-scanning program.

    A colour photo. She's lying naked, on the bed, the sheets and pillows are white, a beautiful contrast with her warm dark honey coloured skin. She's on her tummy, propped up on a pillow, her hands loosely crossed. Looking down the smoothness of her back, one of the sheets is casually covering her bum. Her hair is down and slightly in her face.

Nicholas: I think I'm speechless... n what a lucky guy I am

Namita: lol

Nicholas: you have so many different looks... they're all fantastic!!

Namita: aweee thanks Nicholas

Nicholas: I've run out of room on my screen to fit all of them on

Namita: hehehehe

Nicholas: I love them all!

Namita: make this ur wallpaper

Nicholas: I have you as a slideshow screen saver

Namita: lol

Namita: even better

Nicholas: another week eh?

Namita: hehe yes

Nicholas: just teasing

Namita: this is my come hither pic

Nicholas: it works!

Namita: lol

Nicholas: I'll never tire of seeing it that's for sure

Nicholas: it's titled January is it for a calendar?

Namita: now this pic really goes with our explicit story

Namita: hehe

Nicholas: or just taken in Jan

Namita: hehe... yes it is for our work calendar... I am MISS JANAUARY

Nicholas: OMG!!!!

Namita: it is the nurse calendar

Nicholas: Hello Miss January!

Namita: hot nurses of course

Namita: hehe

Nicholas: hot yes

Nicholas: interesting I wondered if you had something like that

Namita: NOOOOOOOOOOOOOOOoooooooooooo im kidding Nicholas

Namita: i would get so fired for that!!!

Nicholas: oooohh?!

Namita: it would be end of my career

Namita: hehe

Nicholas: you had me going lol

Namita: it was just taken in january

Nicholas: ah... still sexy as all hell

Namita: i nice chilly day and me naked

Nicholas: mmmhmmm

Nicholas: hard little nipples

Namita: ohhh yessss

Namita: what do you like about the pic ?

Nicholas: hmmmmm

Nicholas: I'll try to put in words

Namita: hehehe

Nicholas: the way your hair falls over your face but not too much so I can still see your eyes n smile

Nicholas: seeing the small of your back

Namita: hehe ... you studied the pic very very well

Nicholas: seeing your skin...

Nicholas: just glanced at it really lol

Nicholas: let me take a closer look

Namita: yeah right you did !!!!

Nicholas: lol

Namita: hehe

Namita: yes get the magnifying glass out

Nicholas: I've always preferred photo's that leave things up to my imagination.... naked is good but imagination is better

Namita: yes me too... i dont think ur seeing everything here... it still leaves enough to the imagination...

Nicholas: it does

Namita: would you pose nude... if you had the chance ?

Nicholas: it's way more classy n artful

Nicholas: sure

Namita: awwee thanks

Nicholas: as long as you couldn't see my scars

Namita: what scars ? if i may ask

Nicholas: especially if I could pose nude w you

Nicholas: on my chest, from my surgery

Namita: ohh yesss

Namita: so if you posed nude with me... would you show ur bits tooo ?

Namita: hehe

Nicholas: I hate them... I don't use the word hate very often but I hate my scars

Nicholas: of course

Nicholas: I'd probly look like a sun dial but sure

Namita: nooooo don't hate them... they are ur battle signs... it gives you character

Nicholas: lol

Namita: lol... sundial cuzzz?

Nicholas: posing nude w you I'd have a huge hard on!!! ... I'd really have to think about calculus n algebra

Nicholas: lol

Namita: huh ? ... about what ??? calculus n algebra how come ??

Nicholas: I think that would be fun though, posing nude w you

Nicholas: calculus n algebra... to curb the erection?!

Namita: yes it would be...

Nicholas: coz there's nothing sexual about calculus n algebra

Namita: ohhhh lmaooooooo

Nicholas: guys need a thought to prevent the chub from happening

Nicholas: for me calculus n algebra seems to help

Namita: well what if i dressed up all sexy n and i umm ... go down on you ?

228   Love On Line? A Tale Of Internet Dating

Nicholas: that would totally blow, pun intended. the whole thing

Namita: hahahhahahhahahahhahahhahahha !!!!!!!!!!!!!

Nicholas: nice set up to that too

Namita: hey im trying to help you get rid of ur phobias ok ??

Nicholas: oh it's not a phobias just a thought

Nicholas: and gave you a umm? you don't want to say that word?

Namita: the phobia was being hard in public esp in front of a camera ... i meant

Nicholas: oh I see

Namita: noooo i dont

Namita: hehe

Nicholas: okay then

Nicholas: that's cool

Nicholas: you're being shy again are you?

Namita: i wanted to say a blow job... but to me that sounds sooo crude and cheap

Nicholas: I see

Namita: esp when i care about someone

Nicholas: that's cool

Nicholas: you just made me smile... you just said you care about me, that's soooo sweet thanks

Namita: aweee ur welcome

Namita: yes i can be shy too

Nicholas: we'll have to come up w another word for it

Nicholas: I've seen that... totally cool

Namita: you have ?

Nicholas: your shyness

Nicholas: yes

Namita: how ? hehe

Nicholas: just w how you word things... can't think of anything for an example but I've seen it

Namita: yes i sense that you sense those things... hehe

Nicholas: interesting how we can sense things w each other n it's all in written form

Nicholas: must be those great minds

Namita: i knowwww... it's almost as though we can see thru each other

Namita: read our minds

Nicholas: or know what the other is going to say

Namita: ive caught that many times

Namita: yessssss

Nicholas: me too!

Namita: hehee

Nicholas: I've never had that before

Namita: me either... it is sooo new

Nicholas: as I've said that's one of the many many reasons you excite me

Nicholas: n quite refreshing

Namita: aweee thanks nicholas

Namita: you excite me too... i look forward to ur texts

Nicholas: I didn't think I would ever find someone like you n poof here you are

Namita: hehe

Nicholas: smiling again!

Nicholas: I love getting texts from you

Namita: hehe me too

Namita: are you in bed ?

Nicholas: in my chair

Namita: ohhh... i hope ur are comfortable

Namita: im in bed... on my tummy

Nicholas: it's ma comfy chair so yes

Nicholas: as usual

Namita: talking to some crazy guy

Namita: ok good

Nicholas: that's how I picture you

Nicholas: lol

Nicholas: yah well let me tell you about this nurse I met

Namita: imagine if you crept up behind me as i was lying in bed like this

Namita: hehe

Nicholas: ohhh mmmm

Nicholas: n just slide in on top of you

Namita: you creep up... omg yesssssssssss i was just typing that

Namita: creep up on top of me

Nicholas: you've got quite the naughty little mind tonight

Namita: ohhh i can be... watch out those quiet ones... theyre the naughtiest

Nicholas: I hold your legs together n slide myself into you that way

Namita: yesssssssssss that too

Namita: my arms spread out in front of me grasping the bed sheet

Namita: eyes closed head tilted back

Nicholas: mmmmm mmmm

Nicholas: kissing your neck

Namita: and you start to rhythmically move ur hips

Namita: yes... kissing me on my neck

Namita: and gently nibble

Nicholas: n up your neck to our ear

Namita: mmmmmmmmmmm yesssssssssss

Nicholas: as I nibble on your ear lobe

Nicholas: brushing the end of my nose all the way down your neck to your shoulder

Nicholas: smelling you the whole way

Namita: mmmmmmmmmmm nicholassssssssss !!!!!!!!!!

Namita: you're freshly showered

Nicholas: nice n clean

Nicholas: you can feel my weight on you

Namita: and i can feel ur dewy skin against mine

Nicholas: you can smell the fragrance of my body wash

Namita: i loveeeeeeeeeeeeeeee that... feel ur weight on me

Namita: mmmmmmm niceeeeeeee

Nicholas: moving my body all over you

Nicholas: touching you with my hands... my legs... my face... my body

Nicholas: making sure I feel every part of you

Namita: mmmmm nicholas !!!

Namita: then you turn me over... and let me get on top of you

Namita: you want to enter me

Nicholas: yes

Nicholas: I want to see the look on your face when I do

Namita: as you try to get me into position

Namita: i reach down and hold ur cock in my hands... feeling it throb

Nicholas: I want to see the look you have while I make love to you

Nicholas: yes it does

Nicholas: you can feel me throbbing w every heart beat

Namita: I gently dip ur hard cock into me then lean down and gently guide ur cock into my waiting mouth

Nicholas: ooooohhhhhh yyyeeeesssss!!!!

Namita: i take in the tip a little at first

Namita: then suck on it... feeling the juices flow

Nicholas: mmmmhhmmmmm

Namita: running down ur cock and down my chin

Namita: then i take it in a little further into my mouth

Namita: tasting myself on you...

Namita: but its ur taste im after

Nicholas: I'm moaning w pleasure

Namita: i want ALL OF YOU !!!

Namita: inside my mouth

Nicholas: mmmm mmmmmm

Namita: i take you ALL THE WAYYYYYYYYYY INTO MY MOUTH

Namita: suck on ur cock deeeeeeeeeeep and long

Namita: making you even harder

Namita: i look up to you as i do to see ur reaction

Namita: ur hands are in my soft silky hair

Nicholas: it could explode in your mouth at any second

Namita: urging me to go on

Namita: i run my hand up and down ur cock

Namita: stroking it

Nicholas: yes please my god that feels good

Namita: as i go back to suck the tip

Namita: as i stroke the rest with my hand

Nicholas: ooohhh mmmyyy GOD!

Namita: running my tongue over and over it

Nicholas: I want to cum in your mouth but you wont let me

Namita: mmmmmmmmmmmmm

Namita: you can hear my moans of pleasure ... as thats what i want... to taste you

Namita: i am totally eating you up

Nicholas: mmm it's all there for you

Namita: i reach down further beyond ur cock

Namita: and taste ur balls... take one into my mouth

Namita: would you like that ?

Nicholas: yes

Nicholas: I know you'd be gentle

Namita: as i keep stroking ur hard cock

Namita: yesss i can only be gentle

Namita: are you sensitive ?

Nicholas: stroke my hard cock n you can do just about anything

Nicholas: when it comes to my balls I'm very sensitive!

Namita: if i came up to kiss you afterwards... is that ok ?

Nicholas: totally okay my dear

Namita: do you like having attention to it though during love making?

Namita: i mean to ur balls ?

Nicholas: hmmm depends

Namita: ok

Namita: what if i sucked on it gently... not like a mad woman !

Namita: or just licked it

Nicholas: it's not like you need to pay attention specifically.... just do what feels good to you n what your comfortable with

Nicholas: sure

Nicholas: I want you to do what you like too

Namita: ohhh ok

Namita: yes i would enjoy it if i knew you enjoyed it

Namita: its not fun if its one sided

Nicholas: you'll be able to tell what I like I'm sure of it

Namita: hehe ok

Namita: would you tell me if you didnt like something

Nicholas: we both seem to be pretty body aware n in tune to our partners so we'll be just fine I'm guessing lol

Nicholas: yes I would

Namita: hehehe of course... we are both conscious of that

Namita: i agree

Nicholas: or help change it if there's something that I like

Namita: yes im all for it

Namita: mmmm are you still hard ?

Nicholas: it's an adventure and it's more fun to tell or help my partner

Nicholas: lol yes

Nicholas: semi

Namita: ohhh yesss... its all part of exploring each other

Nicholas: it never really goes away when I talk with you

Nicholas: it just gets harder when we talk naughty

Namita: heheh

Namita: i loveeee being naughty and unpredictable

Nicholas: as I said before when we do finally make love we're going to need some time

Nicholas: me too!

Namita: ohhh yesss... like a whole day perhaps

Namita: hehe

Nicholas: yes my thoughts exactly a whole day

Nicholas: just to get naked n explore each other

Namita: not even going out to see the light of the day

Nicholas: nope

Namita: hehe

Nicholas: we'd bring supplies i.e. food drinks n just be naked together

Namita: ohhh yesss... everything within our reach

Nicholas: n do it in any or every room

Namita: on the floor !

Nicholas: kitchen table

Namita: yesss

Nicholas: couch

Namita: in the bathroom

Namita: yess

Nicholas: where ever we felt like jumping one another

Namita: lol

Nicholas: in the garage bent over the car

Namita: ohhh yesssssssssss

Namita: one leg up on the car and you behind me

Nicholas: oohh yes

Namita: on the pool table

Nicholas: you have a pool table?

Namita: yes

Nicholas: coooool!

Nicholas: yes on the pool table then

Nicholas: sweet!

Namita: i dont play it often... kind of rusty

Namita: but when i get the hang of it im ok

Nicholas: I'm not to bad n I like to play

Namita: hehehe deal then !

Namita: one question... i have

Nicholas: "rack em" will have a new meaning once we christen the pool table lol

Nicholas: yes

Namita: hehehhehehe

Namita: didnt even think of that

Nicholas: lol

Nicholas: what's ur question

Namita: ohhh

Namita: if we are together... i know its kind of jumping the gun

Namita: what contraceptive would you be willing to use

Nicholas: I use condoms always

Nicholas: what were you thinking?

Namita: ok... yes thinking the same

Namita: ive never been on oral contraceptives

Nicholas: never been on the pill?

Namita: no never

Nicholas: is it something you'd want to try ?

Nicholas: you've never had any scares

Namita: ive been careful... so no never

Nicholas: coz I use condoms regardless

Namita: yes me too

Namita: ive been pretty good about not putting myself in that position where im doubting myself

Namita: i can go on it... if i needed to

Nicholas: it's your body do what you think is best for you. I'll support whatever you decide

Namita: oh god have i scared you

Nicholas: no. I'm trying to get a thought out

Namita: ohh ok... hehe

Nicholas: I'm not searching for anyone else n I'm not looking to date anyone else... by sleeping with you I would be exclusive with you.... I want to have a relationship with you n only you... again take things slow but I want to see where things go with you

Nicholas: I hope that makes sense

Nicholas: n I hope you feel the same

Nicholas: again no pressure

Namita: yessss it totally does... im not into dating multiple ppl at once... i want to be exclusive to one person. ..that's the only way to know what the other is all about and who they are... i find it respectful if it is exclusive

Nicholas: yes

Nicholas: so we'll take things slow and go from there... agreed?

Namita: yes agreed

Namita: that has always been my thing... is to be exclusive to that person

Nicholas: I see others but all I think about is how amazing you are

Nicholas: me too

Namita: hehe

Namita: you see other women ...you mean in public ?

Nicholas: yes in public

Namita: phewwww !!

Namita: lol

Nicholas: sorry for not being clear on that

Namita: i knew what you meant... i was teasing you

Nicholas: my world is a little brighter having you in it. I never thought I'd feel this way but here I am

Nicholas: it's a pretty cool feeling

Namita: mmmm yesss it is

Nicholas: we just need to get this whole face to face thing out of the way lol

Namita: even though it is fall and dark out there

Nicholas: yes

Namita: hehehe yes

Nicholas: I always thought a relationship would be long lasting when you meet someone in the fall

Namita: really ?? thats a good thought !

Nicholas: spring is when everyone is horny... winter is when ppl want a snuggle buddy

Namita: yes ppl do say... spring fling or summer fling alot

Nicholas: summer can be just a fling

Namita: hehe

Namita: same thoughts again

Nicholas: spring is when all the other animals are looking to mate so we're no diff

Nicholas: like minds

Namita: yesss true... we have too many wild rabbits in my neighborhood and in my garden

Nicholas: lol

Namita: everyday theres one or two in my front and back lawn

Namita: ive named them too

Nicholas: lol

Namita: hehe

Nicholas: my mom has deer in her yard

Nicholas: she feeds them

Namita: ohhhh cool

Namita: that can be dangerous

Nicholas: she doesn't hand feed n they move away when she comes out

Namita: aweee must be cute to watch

Nicholas: I'm trying to get a pic of them

Namita: nicholas brb

Nicholas: k

Waiting for ~Namita~ to accept the file "IMG_1248.JPG " (2215 Kb). Please wait for a response or

Cancel (Ctrl+C)

the file transfer.

~Namita~ has canceled the file transfer.

Nicholas: you got kicked off?

Namita: are you there ?

Nicholas: yup

Namita: no i didnt get kicked off

Nicholas: strange

Namita: i didnt get what you sent

Nicholas: you signed back in

Nicholas: hold on

Namita: no i didnt... hehe

Waiting for ~Namita~ to accept the file "IMG_1248.JPG " (2215 Kb). Please wait for a response or

Cancel (Ctrl+C)

the file transfer.

Transfer of file "IMG_1248.JPG" has been accepted by ~Namita~. Starting transfer...

Cancel

Nicholas: this pic was taken from my mom's back window. they're about 10 feet away

Namita: ohhh cool

Nicholas: you got it?

Namita: no i didnt... still loading

Nicholas: ok

Nicholas: it just says missing plug in so I don't know if that's relevant

Namita: where does it say that

Nicholas: just below the transfer message

Nicholas: side note: so we're officially seeing each other then? so to speak

Transfer of "IMG_1248.JPG" is complete.

Namita: i dont see it from my end

Nicholas: hmmm

Nicholas: strange

Nicholas: there's no pic on ur end?

Namita: we can make it official when we see each other

Namita: you mean my pic is gone

Nicholas: ok

Nicholas: weird

Nicholas: about the pic

Namita: whattttttttttttttttt ?!

Namita: hehe

Nicholas: oh well I'll show you another time

Namita: what happened ?

Nicholas: no idea

Namita: whattttttttttttt... i got ur pic

Nicholas: it's a pic of a Doe n her 2 fawns

Namita: you cant see my pic now?

Nicholas: no no

Nicholas: crossed messages I think

Namita: yesssssssssssss... they are soooooooooooo cuteeeeeeeeeeeee

Nicholas: ok you did get it cool

Namita: look at the babiesssss !!!!!!!!!!!

Namita: they must be sooo soft

Namita: it must be hard not to go up to them

Nicholas: they run away when we go out

Nicholas: they're pretty sketchy

Namita: what are they eating ? grapes ?

Namita: why ?

Nicholas: probly the food my mom puts out for them

Nicholas: coz they're wild animals

Namita: yes so true

Nicholas: they're on guard all the time

Namita: i used to see them all the time in high school

Namita: when i used to go jogging

Nicholas: oh yah... I find it strange to see them here in the city

Namita: really ?? there are some around... i see some on way to work every once in a while

Namita: near burns bog area

Nicholas: they just seem like something you see in the country is all

Namita: yesss true

Nicholas: have you seen that it's 20 to 5?

Namita: hmmmmm are you tired ?

Namita: hehe yes

Nicholas: a little more... I don't want to go

Nicholas: I missed you the last couple of day so I need to get my fill

Nicholas: if that's possible lol

Namita: hehe... drink me up

Nicholas: I am n will

Namita: what would do if im working the shifts ? hehe

Nicholas: if you were here on sat you mean?

Namita: i know alot of married nurses or newly married ones... it is hard on the husbands to be alone on nights

Nicholas: oh I see

Namita: no i mean in general

Nicholas: I work nights too so no problem

Namita: yes it would work out in our sense

Namita: do you guys work other shifts too ?

Nicholas: I work around your schedule n you work around mine

Namita: yes sure will

Nicholas: not a big deal as far as I can see

Namita: it's give and take

Nicholas: you love your job n I'll support you... I'll see you when I can

Namita: does ur work have other shifts as well?

Namita: ohhh thanks nicholas

Nicholas: they do but it's union n seniority rules

Namita: ahh i see

Namita: so you have to wait ur turn

Nicholas: I do

Namita: they should mix it up like we do

Namita: so it is fair

Nicholas: yah... I'm not keen the day shift anyway

Nicholas: so afternoons work

Namita: not a morning person ?

Nicholas: doesn't matter really

Namita: i hate getting up in the mornings esp in winter

Nicholas: once I'm up, I'm up

Namita: when its snowing

Nicholas: I do like not getting up w an alarm

Namita: just to go to work i mean

Nicholas: yes

Nicholas: way more fun when your doing something you want to

Namita: i rather be home and enjoy the snow

Nicholas: I'm not big on driving in the snow. I do it because I have to

Namita: i lovee it but of course with due care

Nicholas: I prefer the summer but being born in July they say that makes a difference

Namita: i like to drive in fresh snow... not when it looks all messy and black though

Nicholas: you love driving in the snow? really?

Nicholas: hmmm

Namita: yes i love it cuz it is sooo relaxing and peaceful... i mean when it snowed buckets and the road isnt cleaned yet

Nicholas: hmmm

Namita: i loveee how quiet and serene everything is

Namita: looking at the trees laden with snow

Nicholas: I don't mind walking in the snow

Namita: looking at the glow... esp in the evening or night

Nicholas: as long as I don't HAVE to go somewhere in it I guess

Namita: the glow from the snow reflecting off

Namita: hehe

Nicholas: so your off tmw right?

Namita: to me it looks soo magical

Nicholas: it does

Namita: yes i am... running a few errands and getting things together

Nicholas: right

Nicholas: will you be around at our regular time?

Namita: yes i will !!!

Nicholas: or maybe a little earlier?

Nicholas: okay cool

Namita: yes earlier would be good

Nicholas: a particular time work better for you?

Namita: i will try to aim around 1130

Nicholas: I can't believe its 5 in the morning

Namita: are you working tomorrow ?

Nicholas: I am

Namita: ok then ill will be around

Namita: hehe

Nicholas: I'll be home n showered by 11:45

Namita: omg im delirious

Nicholas: me too

Namita: ok works

Nicholas: I need to sleep

Nicholas: text me if you can n tell me how your doing

Namita: ok i will

Nicholas: time to sleep

Namita: work with me nicholas

Namita: hehe

Nicholas: I'm trying

Namita: hehe stay focused

Nicholas: okay my sweet I need to sleep

Namita: ok you need to go to bed before you root urself in that recliner

Nicholas: I haven't been up this late in a very long time

Namita: me either

Nicholas: but it's always fun talking w you

Nicholas: time just evaporates on me

Namita: yes time just flies between us

Namita: hehe

Nicholas: okay time to say "until we talk again"

Namita: k

Namita: goodnight

Nicholas: nite

Namita: nite nite

Nicholas: sleep well

Namita: you log off first

Nicholas: no you hang up

Namita: hehe

Nicholas: lol

Namita: no youuuuuuuuuuu

Nicholas: nnnnnooo youuuu

Nicholas: lol

Namita: hehe

Nicholas: okay nite my sweet

Namita: ok ill take orders only this time

End Time: 5:00 AM

Chapter 12 October 21

Start Time: 12:26 AM

Nicholas: good evening!

Nicholas: or should I say morning?

Namita: hehe... hellloooo

Namita: have i kept you waiting ?

Nicholas: was just reading our convo from last night

Nicholas: only about 5 mins

Nicholas: you have a lot going on so not to worry

Namita: hehe did something make you smile... or did something stand out

Nicholas: stand out yes, you saying you care about me... the naughty stuff we got into

Namita: hehe... we had a fun time last nite id say

Nicholas: I like to re-read our convos in case I missed something

Nicholas: yes we did

Nicholas: my tiredness hit about 2:30 on my drive to work

Namita: when did you get up this morning ?

Nicholas: about 9

Namita: omg... that's not a good feeling

Nicholas: I know, that's not much sleep

Namita: are ur eyes red now ?

Nicholas: meh... it's not like I had to operate heavy machinery or anything

Namita: esp when u wear contacts

Nicholas: no red eyes

Namita: ahhh good

Nicholas: my eyes don't do that

Namita: sometimes mine do

Nicholas: do you remember when I asked you about dancing?

Namita: yes that was a while ago... right ?

Nicholas: n you said you got the moves like Jagger

Nicholas: yup

Namita: hehehe yesssss

Nicholas: I just got that ref (reference) the other day when I heard Maroon 5's new song

Namita: ohhh you didn't know then ?

Nicholas: I'd heard it before but I didn't know what he was saying

Namita: i thought you didn't... cuz i didnt think you caught that

Nicholas: till I saw the video

Namita: hahahaha

Namita: that is toooo funny

Namita: nice video eh ?

Nicholas: so do I get stuck w the starfish photo tonight?

Nicholas: it is

Namita: hell yess ... it's starfish nite tonite !!

Namita: lol

Nicholas: awe too bad

Nicholas: lol

Nicholas: hey, what do you do w Baloo when you go away or at work?

Namita: hehe... my parents take care of him... they come over to get him or i drop him off

Nicholas: is your back yard big enough for him to be outside while your gone?

Nicholas: I see

Nicholas: just random questions I thought of today

Namita: ohh yess... it is big enough for him to run around... from one end to the other... i just cant leave him alone in the yard by himself cuz he loveeees digging and rolling in the grass

Namita: i even have a vegetable garden

Nicholas: you do?! that's cool

Namita: an apple, peach, cherry , and banana tree

Nicholas: wow!

Namita: and some flowering trees... like wisteria and gold-chain tree

Nicholas: you've got quite the little oasis

Nicholas: I can see why you love it there

Namita: google it and you will know what i mean

Nicholas: I will but later

Namita: i loveeeeee plants and trees and flowers

Namita: i even have 3 different types of Clematis flowers

Nicholas: wow

Namita: and a tool shed too

Namita: hehe

Nicholas: how big is your property?

Nicholas: ah yes you've mentioned the shed before

Namita: there is also a cement patio and a deck that is covered with a roof

Nicholas: so you're serious about tonight being a starfish night?!

Namita: the front lawn is bigger than the back

Namita: i really cant remember the size

Nicholas: I can picture it all... sounds wonderful

Namita: lmao

Namita: one sec... geeeeeeeeeeeez !!!

Nicholas: don't laugh too hard I don't want that ass falling off

Namita: hehe... yesss you love ur ass

Namita: yes sir... whatever you say

Nicholas: I love YOur ass

Nicholas: wow taking orders again... that's 2 nights now

Nicholas: lol

Namita: hehee

Namita: its ur lucky nite

Nicholas: it is how so?

Nicholas: naked pic's... kidding... sort of lol

Namita: hold on ...geeeeeeez ...lol

Nicholas: still holding on lol

Namita: hehe good

Nicholas: wow

Namita: ohhhhhhhhhhhhhh niceeeeeeeeee

Nicholas: another one

Namita: when was that one taken ?

Nicholas: 3 years ago

Nicholas: was the ferry ride to the Island the day my dad died

Namita: ohhh sorry... 1 day no one can forget

Nicholas: kind of a morbid tone but it's a pic you haven't seen before

Nicholas: as I said I don't have a lot of photos of me

Namita: no i havent... you do look nice in it

Nicholas: well thanks

Namita: can u send me that one pleaseeeeeeee

Nicholas: sure

Waiting for ~Namita~ to accept the file "IMG_0568.JPG " (1161 Kb). Please wait for a response or

Cancel (Ctrl+C)

the file transfer.

Nicholas: there you go

Transfer of file "IMG_0568.JPG" has been accepted by ~Namita~. Starting transfer...

Cancel

Namita: aweee thanks

Nicholas: ur quite welcome

Nicholas: I'll see if I can find others

Namita: oh thanks nicholas

Nicholas: anytime my dear

Namita: still waiting for it too load here

Nicholas: all you do is change your eye make up n you have a totally new look

Transfer of "IMG_0568.JPG" is complete.

Nicholas: I see that... oh... there you go

Namita: yes do you like that ?

Nicholas: I do. it's very cool

Namita: hehe... thanks for the pic... yes many ppl say I look like a totally different person... hmmm maybe ppl will think that you are with a different woman every time we're out

Nicholas: maybe lol

Namita: they will be quite jealous of you !!

Namita: hehe

Nicholas: Yes they will

Nicholas: they'll wonder how 2 such beautiful ppl found each other

Namita: hehe... yes it was the unconventional internet dating site... go figure

Nicholas: we'll hear them whispering "wow they look so happy together" or " look at them they look so into each other"

Nicholas: lol yah no kidding

Nicholas: not typical results and results may ver

Namita: hehehe... yes results may vary

Namita: i loveee that

Namita: hehe

Nicholas: chalk it up to fait or coincidence I guess. call it what you want all I know is that it happened n I'm so happy it did

Namita: awee sooo sweet... the internet dating is sooo hit and miss

Nicholas: I would have never thought in a million years that I would have found someone like you on through internet dating

Nicholas: well my good luck finally came in and it was a hit as far as I'm concerned

Namita: hehe ... was that ur first time w internet dating ?

Nicholas: mmm first time but 3rd site I think

Namita: ohh which others have you been on ? I've only been in LL

Nicholas: I decided to give each one a month

Namita: ahhh i see

Nicholas: I tried Plenty of Fish

Nicholas: this other one that was just a scam

Nicholas: then Match

Namita: ive heard of Plenty of Fish

Namita: a scam how so?

Nicholas: then LL, so

Namita: are they all similar ?

Nicholas: they are

Nicholas: they sent messages saying they were interested but when I contacted them I never heard anything back

Namita: that's disappointing

Nicholas: I didn't take them very seriously... I was really just looking

Namita: similar as in having an intimate section, relationship or dating ?

Namita: yeah more like browsing

Nicholas: there were a lot of repeat women on both POF (Plenty Of Fish) and LL

Namita: ohhh ... can you really tell ?

Nicholas: oh no there was just one profile and you decided what you were looking for ie friends. relationship blah blah blah

Nicholas: some had the same pic and profile up

Namita: ahhh i see and said the same words blah blah blah

Namita: hehe

Nicholas: I tired LL coz my friend is on it and it was time to try a new site

Nicholas: my profile was kind of long n LL would only let me put up so much so I posted a cut down version

Namita: ohhh... i hope i didnt talk to ur friend... hehe... no that I would say anything stupid

Namita: ahhh i seee

Nicholas: not to worry she's a woman lol

Nicholas: I doubt you say anything stupid lol

Namita: LOL ok phewwwwwwww !!!!!!!!

Namita: good to know that ur friend is a woman

Nicholas: ooohhh I like that one... tis very Hot!!

She's looking straight at me, wearing a strapless black and silver sequinned top. Her hair is down and slightly full, draped over both shoulders with a beautiful smokey eye make up.

Nicholas: lol

Nicholas: very sexy

Namita: hehe another different look

Nicholas: yes it is

Nicholas: your so awesome you know that right?!

Nicholas: I can't believe there are so many beautiful women inside just one woman

Nicholas: I'm so lucky

Namita: i was going out with friends to a stagette then dancing ... we met at Miranda's place ... the photographer and she took pics of us together and individually against her background screen

Nicholas: cool

Namita: so we were trying to be the vixens of the night

Namita: hehe

Nicholas: I'm trying to guess which look is the first one when I meet you in person

Nicholas: you nailed it! total vixen!

Namita: hehe... you think so ????

Nicholas: I'm sure I'll love which ever one shows up

Namita: hehehe yessss me and my multiple personalities

Nicholas: oh yes definitely a come hither look

Nicholas: lol multiple looks not personalities lol

Namita: hehe ...you want come hither to come to you ?

Waiting for ~Namita~ to accept the file "IMG_0561.JPG " (1413 Kb). Please wait for a response or

Cancel (Ctrl+C)

the file transfer.

Transfer of file "IMG_0561.JPG" has been accepted by ~Namita~. Starting transfer...

Cancel

Nicholas: this is another one form the same day

~Namita~ would like to send you the file "img1101103057_1_1.jpg" (47 Kb). Do you want to

Accept

(Ctrl+G) or

Decline

(Ctrl+C) the invitation?

Nicholas: I hope you like it

Nicholas: some of the others have the girls in them so I'll need to edit them out so it's just me

Transfer of "IMG_0561.JPG" is complete.

Namita: ok ... no worries ...thanks for the pic

Namita: did you accept mine ?

Transfer of file "img1101103057_1_1.jpg" from ~Namita~ has been accepted. Starting transfer...

Cancel

You have successfully received img1101103057_1_1.jpg from ~Namita~. Before opening this file, you may want to scan it with a virus-scanning program.

Nicholas: just did... I didn't see the file at first

Nicholas: OOOhhh MMyyyy!

Namita: lol

Nicholas: you went out looking that smokin" damn. you musta had guys falling all over themselves for your attention

Namita: hehee... I kept them at bay... don't worry

Nicholas: I bet you did

Namita: even young ones... they crack me up

Nicholas: I'm sure your friends helped too

Nicholas: yah they have no style

Namita: yes they are not a bad bunch either

Nicholas: I would hope so if they're ur friends lol

Namita: they were just as beautiful... inside and out

Nicholas: I can imagine

Namita: whenever i do go out like that with friends... its just not my thing to leave with a guy... no matter what

Nicholas: now that would be funny to see... me out w you n your friends... the looks on those guys faces... priceless lol

Namita: its better to get to know someone... at least for me

Nicholas: I didn't think you would

Namita: hehe

Nicholas: I never go home w anyone I meet for the first time

Namita: yeah i just cant do it

Nicholas: I've never understood that, picking up a stranger, if they go home w me then how many others has she gone home with?

Waiting for ~Namita~ to accept the file "IMG_0569_3. JPG" (688 Kb). Please wait for a response or

Cancel (Ctrl+C)

the file transfer.

Nicholas: I've never gotten that far w anyone in the first place

Nicholas: I sent you this new one too

Namita: yesssss i knowwwwwww... plus it looks and sounds soooo cheap !!! i dont know how one sleeps with another and then go their separate ways in the morning. Not even knowing ur names

Transfer of file "IMG_0569_3.JPG" has been accepted by ~Namita~. Starting transfer...

Cancel

Nicholas: yes it's quite sketchy I just shake my head at it

Transfer of "IMG_0569_3.JPG" is complete.

Namita: aweeee cute... i love how ur daughter has her arms around you You can see Amanda's arm in this photo but not her face.

Nicholas: I definitely need a bigger screen to fit all your photo's on

Nicholas: thx

Namita: hehehe

Nicholas: one day you'll see what they look like... of course

Namita: they must be cute !!

Nicholas: they've changed so much in 3 years since those pics were taken

Namita: in what way ?

Nicholas: they've gotten taller n leaned out

Namita: hehehe... tall is good... are they active ?

Nicholas: they are

Nicholas: Isabel is definitely turning into a young woman. you can see the changes almost overnight sometimes

Namita: what was moms physique ? if i may ask ?

Namita: how old is Isabel again... 13?

Nicholas: you may lol

Nicholas: yes 13

Nicholas: she's 5' 11" and heaver than she'd like... has been since I met her... I was never physically attracted to her... she presented herself as someone I thought I could be with just in a diff wrapper so to speak

Namita: ohhh... now i understand what you mean by you settled

Nicholas: Isabel broke her finger playing volleyball on Wed... random I know

Nicholas: yes

Nicholas: I dated outside my type n got burned

Namita: omggg really ??? did she get a splint ?

Namita: well at least you tried Nicholas !!

Nicholas: you're attracted to your type for a reason... I strayed ... momentary laps of judgment

Namita: you gave her a chance and in the end she blew it

Nicholas: god how I tried

Nicholas: that she did... n fortunately for me lol

Nicholas: yes she's splinted

Namita: yesss a blessing in disguise for you

Nicholas: it's the tip of her R ring finger

Namita: did she go to RCH (Royal Columbian Hospital) for it ?

Namita: well at least she can say she's got battle wounds

Namita: hehe

Nicholas: It really was... it was a huge relief

Nicholas: I think they went to RCH

Nicholas: yah it's a total volleyball injury too

Namita: yesss sometimes you really have to step out of the circle to see what is really happening... see it in a different light

Namita: its a whole different world from a different angle

Nicholas: went for a set n the ball came down right on her finger.... this is the first season she's played so her skills need some work n she'll probly never have that happen again

Namita: yesss she has learned... hehe

Namita: have you ever broken bones ?

Namita: yours I mean... not others !!

Nicholas: lol I had a green stick fracture on my L wrist when I was about 10

Nicholas: have you broken anything?

Namita: ohhh poor nicholas

Namita: no ive never broken anything on me ... thank god

Namita: how did you meet your ex anyway ?

Nicholas: I did some SPFX make up for a life guard competition n met her there

Nicholas: as she was a life guard

Namita: ohhh you were a life guard ??? Cool !!

Nicholas: no not me her

Namita: ohhhh i see... got it

Nicholas: I just did some make up effects for their competition

Namita: oh ok... i understand now... i read it wrong

Nicholas: I was looking for something to do... she was from here the mainland n me from Parksville... so when she invited me n a couple of other guys over to the mainland of course I said sure

Nicholas: I hope that makes sense?

Namita: yes it does makes sense

Nicholas: I get into trouble w being so friendly n easy going that some women get their signals crossed n think I'm interested when I'm really just being friendly

Namita: how long have you been in the mainland now ?

Namita: ohhh nicholas !!! Poor you !!

Namita: i know i hate when that happens... when ur just being friendly and next thing you know...

Nicholas: I lived here in '92 - '95 for the film industry then moved back... came here w the family in 2001

Nicholas: so 11 years... wow hadn't thought of it like that before

Nicholas: yes exactly

Namita: wowww

Nicholas: just being friendly n BAM!

Namita: 92 to 94... i was working in a minimum wage job

Nicholas: wow

Namita: waiting to get into nursing school

Nicholas: I was a starving make up artist lol

Nicholas: well not starving

Namita: you must have met quite a array of different ppl in that market

Nicholas: I worked in a logging camp to save for the move to the big city

Nicholas: I did

Nicholas: one guy I met on my first film was a set decorator... he became a good friend

Namita: ohhh cool !!

Nicholas: his name was Justin he was gay so that was a hole new world

Nicholas: new world to see not partake just to be clear

Nicholas: lol

Namita: hehe ...phewwww !!

Nicholas: too each they're own but I'm definitely not gay

Namita: i dont know how ppl decide that thats what they want... not to pass judgement or anything

Namita: my best friend is gay too but i have never had the courage to ask her

Namita: what precipitates the change to want the same sex partner... ive never even thought of playing the same field

Namita: im a mans lady... hehe

Nicholas: my friend Justin said he tried so hard not to be gay. he even lived w a girlfriend for 9 months... finally he made the switch n he was so much happier

Nicholas: you've got a man here that's willing to play

Namita: yes if you have the tendencies... then its best not to fight the inevitable

Namita: did it come as a surprise to you about ur sis ?

Nicholas: I've always been attracted to women ever since I can remember

Namita: hehe ... really ???

Nicholas: she was listening to a lot of Melissa Etheridge and the Indigo Girls so I started to wonder

Nicholas: yup always liked the ladies... n always been very selective... don't date much either

Nicholas: that's so cool that you can relate... most ppl would have said who?

Namita: you mean the Indigo Girls ?

Nicholas: yes

Namita: hehe yeah ive heard of them !

Nicholas: same generation n like minds lol

Namita: yes i was going to say... we are 39 !!

Nicholas: yes we are

Nicholas: you really don't look 39

Namita: hehehe... thanks you're my new bbf !!

Nicholas: not that I know what 39 is suppose to look like lol

Nicholas: lol

Namita: i guess cuz i take care of myself

Nicholas: good jeans

Nicholas: yes you do

Namita: yesss good fitted jeans helps too

Nicholas: not quite what I meant but sure lol

Namita: hehe... i know what you meant !! im teasing

Nicholas: I figured

Nicholas: its a real shame we can't be lying in bed talking right now

Namita: do you wear jeans most of the time too ?

Nicholas: I do

Namita: loveeee jeans

Nicholas: shorts in the summer n jeans any other time

Nicholas: Levis 501

Namita: you look like you have an easy style

Nicholas: I do have dressy clothes too n do like to dress up

Namita: mmmm niceee

Nicholas: T shirt n jeans or long sleeve shirt n jeans

Nicholas: love to go commando in jeans too

Namita: ohhhh niceee... i love the look

Namita: seriously ????????

Nicholas: yup

Nicholas: don't do it all the time but now n again sure

Namita: so i can really pull ur zipper down... while ur driving !!!

Nicholas: was fun n Mexico

Nicholas: button fly my dear

Namita: why was it fun in mexico ?

Nicholas: n yes

Nicholas: coz it was hot out

Namita: button fly ?

Namita: is that what we call it ?

Namita: im behind my times i think

Nicholas: n we couldn't wear shorts to the evening restaurants

Namita: ohhhh niceee

Nicholas: well my jeans have a button fly not a zipper

Namita: whats that ?

Nicholas: buttons instead of a zipper

Namita: ohhhhhhhhhhhhhhhhhhhhhhhhh !!!!!!!

Nicholas: just like the top button the fly has like 4 or 5 too

Namita: then i would have to cut ur buttons off with my dagger... hehe while ur driving

Nicholas: so really you could slide a finger between the buttons n have a touch

Nicholas: lol it opens pretty easy, you'll see lol

Namita: touch but not peek !?!

Nicholas: just an appetizer then you can open n peek

Namita: hehehehehe

Namita: i have to make sure it is there !

Nicholas: lol oh you'll know its there even before you open it

Namita: hahhahaha

Nicholas: it'll be like a jack in the box

Namita: hahahhahaa

Namita: that is sooo true

Nicholas: open the fly n out pops the

Nicholas: surprise

Namita: the weasel... ohhh sorry... yes out pops the surprise

Namita: oops

Nicholas: lol

Namita: hehe

Nicholas: I'm sure it wont be a surprise coz you'll know what's in there

Nicholas: oh well hello there!

Namita: hehe ... im sooo giggling here

Nicholas: you are. how come?

Namita: well the we are talking about ur surprise

Nicholas: ah I see

Namita: im over it now

Nicholas: so... whatcha wearing?

Namita: im wearing black

Nicholas: nice

Nicholas: we didn't get that far last night

Namita: hehe no we didnt ..we were busy in the garage !!!

Nicholas: we got pretty far but not w your nightie

Nicholas: lol mind reader

Namita: hehehe

Nicholas: thought about that a few times today

Namita: yeah we never even made it past the garage

Namita: you did !!

Namita: what were ur thoughts

Nicholas: yup

Nicholas: just replaying the scenarios again

Namita: over and over again !!!

Namita: i can just imagine it

Nicholas: keeping in mind that it'll be another week till I might be able to see you... or longer

Nicholas: it was pretty vivid n explicit

Namita: yes it sure was

Nicholas: n with my imagination very real!

Namita: hehe... imagine when you come home from work

Nicholas: n your waiting for me in nothing more than a cute little nightie of your choice

Namita: yesss sprawled on the bed... freshly showered

Nicholas: niceeee

Namita: sorry msn is being slow for me... for some time now

Nicholas: I love freshly showered

Nicholas: sokay

Namita: my skin is still dewy

Nicholas: yessss

Namita: you notice me in bed as you walk by

Nicholas: I do

Namita: after a hard day of work

Namita: and you head straight into the shower

Namita: but on ur mind is me on that bed waiting ...in a red almost see thru nightie

Nicholas: niceeeeee

Nicholas: mmm mmm mmm

Namita: you try to hurry up

Namita: you are lathering urself up

Nicholas: showering as fast as I can

Namita: when you notice

Namita: a hand reach up behind you and starts to lather ur back and shoulders... you never heard me come in

Nicholas: mmmm sooooo nice

Nicholas: hello nurse

Nicholas: how yoouu doin'?

Namita: you turn around quickly and see me right there behind you in my red see thru nightie

Namita: hehehe

Nicholas: ooohhh myyyy

Namita: well helloooo to you too !!!

Nicholas: all wet in your nightie

Namita: and is clingy to my every curve

Nicholas: mmm mmm mmm I could just eat you up!

Namita: it is just pasted on me

Nicholas: love those curves

Nicholas: painted on

Namita: you can see my erect nipples thru it as the water hits me

Nicholas: yes I can

Namita: maybe sort of looks like this

Nicholas: OMG!

Namita: you cup my breasts in ur hands ... i tell you not to hurry

Namita: hehe

Nicholas: holly sh**!

Nicholas: oh so very slowly

Nicholas: I need a copy of that pls

Namita: what now ?? NAHHHHhhh !!!

Namita: you dont need it !

Namita: lol

Nicholas: nooo? brat!

Nicholas: now what? I pull you close

Nicholas: wrap my arms around you n press myself against you

Namita: one sec im sending... have to look for it... u continue

~Namita~ would like to send you the file "nmp-drench ed.jpg" (46 Kb). Do you want to

Accept

(Ctrl+G) or

Decline

(Ctrl+C) the invitation?

Nicholas: you can feel my hard cock pressing against you, searching for that hot moist opening

Transfer of file "nmp- drenched.jpg" from ~Namita~ has been accepted. Starting transfer...

Cancel

You have successfully received nmp- drenched.jpg from ~Namita~. Before opening this file, you may want to scan it with a virus-scanning program.

    Framed to her belly button. She's standing in front of a mauve and turquoise blended back drop. She's wearing a white dress shirt tied in the front accentuating her breasts. There's water raining down soaking her through. Her eyes are closed, chin up ever so slightly. Arms at her sides slightly bent. And did I say soaked through... I think I did... lol.

Namita: mmmmmmmmmmm ohhh god

Nicholas: holly F***ing hell that's hot!

Nicholas: steamed up my glasses you did

Namita: hehe i did that one a couple of years ago... forgot i had it... came in handy tonite

Nicholas: it sure did. almost spot on

Nicholas: n thx

Namita: so now you know !!

Nicholas: know what?

Namita: now you know... that I have an innie !! LOL

Nicholas: oh um yah looking at your belly button, right

Namita: so if i was in front of you in the shower like this ... would you faint ?

Namita: hehee yeah right you are !!

Nicholas: no no would stay conscious, my pulse would kick into over drive

Nicholas: you have really nice boobs.... I'm sooo lucky!

Namita: and I would whisper in ur ear ...don't keep me waiting

Namita: they are a nice handful i guess

Namita: what do you like about them ?

Nicholas: yes they will be

Nicholas: how round n firm they look

Namita: mmmmmmmm yesssss

Nicholas: how inviting they look

Nicholas: can't wait to touch them, to taste

Nicholas: to massage my face w them

Namita: is this the first time ur seeing a good pic of them ?

Nicholas: it is

Namita: ohhh !

Nicholas: it's so awesome you have all these photo's

Namita: hehe... yesss i held out on you again

Nicholas: you did but that's okay

Nicholas: leaves me to my imagination

Nicholas: you don't want to show all your cards at once

Namita: nooooo you have to leave something to the imagination

Namita: thats where many women get it wrong

Namita: they bare it all !! and it backfires

Nicholas: yes they do

Nicholas: okay so excuse the crassness of this question but I don't know how else to word it... have you ever been tit f**ked?

Namita: no i havent actually

Namita: but im open to it

Nicholas: I think you'll like it

Nicholas: you know how it's done right?

Namita: would love to see ur hard cock coming towards my mouth

Namita: how does it feel to you ?

Nicholas: amazing

Namita: how is it done... from ur words

Nicholas: you press your boobs together with my cock between them n then I proceed to make love to your boobs till I cum between them... you feel every contraction... you can either let it go off in your mouth or let it go off between your boobs

Nicholas: or if you're on top then I press them together n you rock back n forth till i cum

Namita: mmmm niceeee !!! Do you feel any tightness from being between the boobs... cuz boobs are soft

Nicholas: yup you just press them together more

Namita: ahhhh i seee

Nicholas: you on top probly works better

Namita: the sensations must be quite wild !!

Nicholas: you can lube it up w your saliva or w my precum

Nicholas: it is

Namita: mmmmmmm yum

Nicholas: my hard cock sliding between your boobs mmmhmm fun for both of us

Namita: do you enjoy if i lowered myself onto ur face... while ur on ur back...

Nicholas: sometimes a nice alternative when your on your cycle

Namita: yessss true

Nicholas: ooo like 69? yes like that very much

Nicholas: or even just straddling my face

Namita: yes face sitting

Namita: yes 69 is good too

Nicholas: this talk isn't helping my hornyness

Namita: would you enjoy something like that

Namita: hehehhehe

Nicholas: I've been horny now for weeks

Namita: are you hard ?

Nicholas: I would

Nicholas: semi hard

Nicholas: it seems to think that your here n gonna get in the game

Namita: you mean ur cock ?

Nicholas: yes

Namita: hehehe... so where were we ?

Nicholas: naughty talk n it perks up

Namita: we were in the shower and im lathering you up

Nicholas: but actually doing something is when it likes to preform

Nicholas: yes the shower

Namita: i lather up ur hard cock... stroking it

Nicholas: mmmhmmm

Namita: watch as the bubbles slip away

Nicholas: as the water rinses it off

Namita: you can see the water running down my body and in between my breasts

Namita: i look up at you ... with those big brown eyes

Nicholas: I kiss you

Nicholas: long slow n passionate

Namita: mmmmmm yesssssssssss

Namita: i reach up behind ur neck and press ur lips to me

Namita: my other hand is on ur cock

Nicholas: I reach around n slide my hands dwn ur back to ur bum

Namita: rubbing my thumb over ur tip as u kiss me

Nicholas: n squeeze ur cheeks

Nicholas: mmmhmmm nice

Namita: mmmmmmmm yeeesssssssss

Nicholas: I'm moaning w pleasure

Namita: you cant take this anymore

Namita: you can hear me moaning tooo

Nicholas: mmm

Namita: i can feel ur precum

Namita: you say something under ur breath... sounds like... "oh god"

Namita: we step out of the shower n I go down on all 4s presenting myself to you

Nicholas: mmm

Namita: you peel the short hem up off my ass and pull the G-string aside

Namita: and you first insert one finger into me

Nicholas: lingering at ur opening

Namita: mmmmmmmmmm yesssss

Namita: to feel how wet i am

Nicholas: touching ur clit

Namita: mmmmmm yesssss

Namita: the water is dripping off us

Nicholas: making you shudder with anticipation

Namita: mmmmm yesssssss... i dont know what ur going to do

Nicholas: you're loosing control of your body

Namita: then you insert another finger into me

Nicholas: n massage your G spot

Namita: making me moan so badly

Namita: mmmmmmmmmmmm yesssssssss

Nicholas: using that come hither motion w my fingers to please you

Namita: my back is arched towards you... ass in the air

Namita: omg

Nicholas: you beg me to fuck you form behind

Namita: you can see clear fluid on ur fingers... like honey

Namita: i lick ur fingers

Nicholas: mmmm

Namita: yesss im moaning and squirming begging you not to stop

Namita: yessssss

Nicholas: but I'm not done

Namita: ur cock is soooo hard

Nicholas: I don't stop n w my fingers i make you pop

Namita: desperately wants to be inside of me

Nicholas: then I mount you n press myself all the way deep inside you ever so slowly

Namita: mmmmmmmmm yesssssssss

Namita: you hold on to my hips

Nicholas: yes

Nicholas: so deep that there isn't any more

Namita: and start pounding me

Namita: mmmm oh god yesssssss

Nicholas: driving my hard cock into you

Nicholas: making you shake w ecstasy

Namita: you leaning down to kiss the back of my neck

Nicholas: I pound you harder n faster till u can't take it anymore

Namita: mmmmmm.... im gasping at ur every thrust

Nicholas: I can feel you getting closer to cuming

Namita: you reach down with one hand and cup my breast lightly grazing my nipple

Namita: making it rock hard

Nicholas: rolling it between my fingers

Namita: mmm yesss

Namita: im begin you

Nicholas: I can feel you urning to cum

Nicholas: you want me to explode inside you

Namita: noooooooo i cant

Namita: i quickly move away

Namita: and turn around to suck on ur cock... tasting our intertwined juices

Nicholas: oohhh yes!

Namita: then i get up and lead you away from the bathroom... to the bedroom!

Nicholas: mmmhmm

Namita: as you finally get close to the edge of the bed

Namita: i push you down onto the bed... both of us dripping wet in every sense of the word

Nicholas: niceeeee

Namita: i climb on top of you

Namita: still wet with the nightie pasted on me

Nicholas: I admire the site before me

Namita: you cup my breasts ... rub my nipples

Namita: im towering over you like some goddess

Namita: bronzed and wet

Nicholas: was thinking that

Namita: seriously ?

Nicholas: yup

Nicholas: like a goddess

Nicholas: the goddess of love

Namita: im sitting on top of you... ur cock still hard as ever just at my tummy

Nicholas: mmhhmmm

Namita: and i slip off my nightie

Nicholas: exposing your now naked breasts

Namita: you watch me and think youve died and gone to heaven

Nicholas: so perfect n beautiful

Namita: im totally exposed... you can see my every curve

Namita: the curve of my hips sitting on top of you

Nicholas: my hands on ur hips

Namita: you pull off the G string

Namita: and now there is nothing between us

Nicholas: just our nakedness

Namita: i reach down and shuffle down ur body

Namita: till my mouth reaches ur manhood

Nicholas: nice

Namita: and i start feeding on it

Nicholas: mmmm

Namita: running my tongue over the full length of it

Nicholas: I thrust gently onto ur mouth

Namita: i can feel ur urgency

Namita: you want me sooo desperately

Nicholas: u feel my cock get a little bigger

Namita: yessssss ...mmmmmmmm

Namita: i loveeeeeeee the taste of it

Nicholas: I ask you where you want it

Namita: hehe... i want it in my mouth

Namita: would you like that ?

Nicholas: oh hell yah

Namita: does it turn you on even more ?

Nicholas: yesssssss

Namita: but you need to fuck good first

Nicholas: yes mamm

Namita: hehe

Namita: sorry for being dirty

Nicholas: no need to apologize

Nicholas: its part of the moment

Nicholas: whatever turns you on honey

Namita: so i turn myself around facing away from you... still on top

Nicholas: reverse cowgirl

Namita: and lower myself onto ur hard cock

Namita: yesss

Namita: i start riding ur cock

Nicholas: u lean back

Namita: taking it as deep as i can

Namita: mmmmmmmmyesssssssssss

Nicholas: so ur back is on my chest

Namita: oh god yes... i want to be close to you

Nicholas: I grab u by the hips n slide my cock in n out

Namita: OMG

Nicholas: one hand on ur hip the other reaching up to play w your breasts

Namita: mmmmmmmmmmm yesssssssssss

Nicholas: then gently down to massage ur clit

Namita: i want to screammm

Namita: i can feel all ur force inside of me

Nicholas: I want u to cum for me so I massage u faster

Namita: still pounding me

Nicholas: yes

Namita: you reach down and grab hold of my thighs and use that as leverage to pile drive into me

Nicholas: yesssssss

Namita: im moaning in ecstasy !!!

Namita: arching my back

Nicholas: ur ready to cum?

Namita: yesssssss

Namita: are you ?

Nicholas: then lets bring it on home

Nicholas: I'm close

Namita: yessss now pleaseeeeeeeeee

Nicholas: I pound you faster n harder

Namita: im playing with my clit as you drive into me

Nicholas: yes

Namita: pushing me upwards on you

Namita: my other hand is reached toward ur face

Namita: it is such a site

Namita: you wished you filmed it

Nicholas: yes

Namita: mmmmmmmmm yesssssssssss

Nicholas: cum for me!

Namita: ohhh the noises you hear as you slam me

Nicholas: rub that clit of urs

Namita: mmmmm yesss it is sooo swollen

Nicholas: the smacking of flesh

Namita: mmmm nicholas

Nicholas: I'm pounding you so hard n fast that ur pussy feels numb

Namita: omggg

Nicholas: ur wanting so bad for me to explode inside you

Namita: yesssssssss plssss

Nicholas: u feel me grow bigger

Namita: omggg yessss

Nicholas: u know the end is near

Namita: oooooooooo

Nicholas: I cant take anymore as I EXplode inside u!!!

Namita: OoOOooOoOOoOooooOooo nicholas !!!!!!!!!!!!!!

Namita: omgg

Nicholas: ohhhh myyy godddd Namita

Nicholas: wow

Nicholas: it was like riding a bucking bronco

Namita: omg wowwwwwwww is right... i would totally enjoy that with you

Nicholas: if that's any indication of the proceedings

Namita: hehe

Nicholas: mmmmhmmm

Namita: did you cum nicholas ?

Nicholas: I did n thank you

Nicholas: did you?

Namita: i would loveee to make this a reality one day

Namita: oh yes!!

Namita: hehe

Nicholas: my god yes

Nicholas: n we will

Nicholas: all in due time

Namita: i think i would enjoy that position

Nicholas: that's why we'll need some time

Namita: hehe

Namita: i would taste ur cum afterwards

Nicholas: would you? as in swallowed?

Namita: yess i would

Nicholas: mmmhmmm

Namita: would you enjoy that?

Nicholas: I most defiantly would

Namita: its not something i do all the time but i would like to do it

Nicholas: whatever you're comfortable with

Namita: yes i would be comfortable

Nicholas: I'd like the first time to be really special... not just do it coz we're so hot for each other.... we only get one first time

Nicholas: the first time we sleep together that is

Namita: yess that's right... i totally agree

Namita: i feel the same way

Nicholas: and hopefully the last first time

Nicholas: cool

Namita: the lust for each other can come afterwards

Nicholas: yes

Namita: along with playfulness

Nicholas: we'll have plenty of other times to play

Namita: hhehe yesss

Nicholas: n do it coz we're so hot n just want to rip each others clothes off

Namita: oh god yesss

Namita: i would rip it off the moment you stepped into the door

Nicholas: 😀

Namita: lol

Nicholas: you have to be at the airport for 7 yah?

Nicholas: I know random

Namita: yes soon

Namita: i should go to sleep

Nicholas: u pulling an all nighter

Namita: nooo hehhee

Nicholas: yes you should

Namita: i will save it for later

Namita: the all nighter

Nicholas: now that we've taken care of some business so to speak

Nicholas: ah yes

Nicholas: you'll need one of those unless we got an realy start

Namita: hehehe.. .yes ?

Nicholas: my spellimg blows right now

Namita: i knew wahty maent

Nicholas: was agreeing to saving the all nighter

Namita: i kne wwhat u meant i mean

Namita: hehe

Nicholas: lol

Namita: we are soooo screwed

Nicholas: so tomorrow?

Nicholas: lol

Nicholas: I need to be in bed early

Namita: sure

Nicholas: coz I have an Sp gigsun morning

Namita: will be around

Namita: a what ?

Nicholas: Standardized Patient

Nicholas: exam sunday

Namita: ohhhhhh yeassss

Nicholas: n need to be well rested so I don't forget anything

Nicholas: I've done them on little sleep n it's not fun

Namita: good luck on that exam nichals

Nicholas: we could chat earlier if you want?

Namita: nicholas

Nicholas: but ur w ur family so I don't want to pull u awa from that

Nicholas: the exam isn't for me I just play a roll

Namita: i will try to get on msn ... i dontknow how my day will be there

Namita: ohhh i seeee

Namita: oh god ...sorry got heavy on the key there

Nicholas: lol

Nicholas: was just looking at my spelling wow

Nicholas: really bad

Namita: hehe

Namita: we are soooo bad

Nicholas: u knew what I meant so that was good

Nicholas: yup

Namita: yes i can between the lines now

Namita: hehe

Nicholas: another up till 4:30 session

Nicholas: if we started earlier we'd probly still be uo late

Namita: ohhh geez

Nicholas: we'd just have talked longer

Namita: i knowwww

Namita: theres no stopping us

Nicholas: nope

Nicholas: I'm fading

Nicholas: zoning out

Namita: im soooo falling into dreamland tight noe

Nicholas: u need some sleep too u have a big day tmw

Namita: i mean right now

Nicholas: lol

Namita: hehe

Namita: tight noe.. like wtf (what the fuck)??

Nicholas: thx for another wonderful chat

Namita: ok ttyl (talk to you later) ... tee hee hee

Nicholas: gnight my sweet

Namita: i lovedddddddddd our chat

Namita: goodnite

Nicholas: night

End Time: 4:27 AM

Chapter 13 October 22

Start Time: 11:51 PM

Nicholas: hey!

Namita: hello

Nicholas: you made it

Nicholas: cool

Namita: yes i did

Nicholas: didn't know if you'd have time

Namita: how have you been ?

Nicholas: good, slept till 10

Nicholas: how was the flight?

Namita: yes i hit the bed early.. .had a tiring day

Nicholas: n how are you?

Nicholas: how's your uncle?

Namita: the flight was good... i forgot that sometimes being in high altitude makes me have a headache

Nicholas: awe sorry to hear that

Nicholas: did you get my text this morning?

Namita: he is still in the icu... sedated and on many different drugs

Nicholas: what's the word on him?

Namita: i didn't see them... cuz i was rushing out the door and my cell fell under my bed

Nicholas: oh no

Namita: at present they are doing everything for him... only time will tell

Nicholas: I sent it just before 10 so I didn't think u'd get it coz u were already on the plane

Namita: hehe... ohh well... i will see it when i get home

Nicholas: you didn't bring ur phone?

Nicholas: ah

Nicholas: you don't really need it there anyway... not like you can use it

Namita: no i didnt... i left it home... should have brought it... actually i kinda forgot

She forgot her phone?

Namita: yes true

Nicholas: it's expensive to use out of country

Namita: no one is going to phone me here anyways

Nicholas: yah

Namita: yes its more than an arm and leg

Namita: i didnt even see u come online

Nicholas: are you staying w family while ur there or a hotel?

Namita: ive been in bed since 1130ish

Namita: im staying with my uncles family

Nicholas: I opened msn about 11:30ish

Namita: ohhh ok

Nicholas: probly easier that way

Namita: hotel would have been expensive too

Nicholas: I heard you come on

Namita: hehe

Namita: you heard the ding ?

Nicholas: that's why I came on when I did coz we didn't really decide on a time

Nicholas: I heard the ding

Namita: hehe... how was ur day ?

Nicholas: the opening page of msn is buried under all ur photos

Namita: was it still raining all day over there

Nicholas: was okay... didn't get as much done as I would have liked

Namita: hehe... ohhh my... ur collage is getting bigger

Nicholas: been raining on n off all day

Nicholas: yes it is... some creative shuffling to fit all of you in

Nicholas: my screen saver is pretty cool too

Namita: hehe... hmmmm im sure its looking wonderful... any fav pics in the front ?

Nicholas: I tried to put u on as a desk top but the pics are too big n I can't see all of u in them

Namita: ahhhhhhhh

Nicholas: they're all seeable

Nicholas: they all have beautiful qualities

Namita: ohhh cool

Nicholas: I can't really pick just one

Namita: hehehe

Nicholas: they all invoke different feelings when I look at each of them

Namita: aweeee !!!

Nicholas: and there's so many diff looks too!! love it

Namita: i know everyone of them is different... hard to pick a fav

Namita: hehe true

Nicholas: so are you going to be staying for the week?

Nichola: it's probly cheaper to stay longer

Namita: yes for a week... for now

Nicholas: or more cost effective

Namita: i will see how things go

Namita: my parents are here too

Nicholas: yah I guess you can only stay for so long before u need to come back

Nicholas: thought so... any of ur sisters come too?

Namita: well one of them is going to come over in a couple of days

Nicholas: ah

Namita: did you get enough sleep last nite ? hehe

Nicholas: I did... slept like a baby... woke up w a smile too.... once my brain turned on it flipped to you and poof instanta smile

Nicholas: did you get enf? u probly slept on the plane?

Namita: hehee... that was some conversation last nite !!!

Nicholas: yesssss it was

Namita: i tried to sleep but i get so self conscious of it sometimes

Namita: lol

Nicholas: was like a create-ur-own-porno in my head lol

Nicholas: ah no sleeping in public... mental note

Namita: it was quite HOT !!!!!

Namita: i was still having wave after wave of the big O... even after we signed off

Nicholas: it was extremely HOT!!

Nicholas: oh wow cool... can't wait to experience that

Nicholas: I'm able to climax so intense sometimes that it feels like an outer body experience

Namita: yesss maybe another 3 or 4 times more

Nicholas: wow, cool

Namita: but the weird thing was ... i hope it doesnt gross you out

Namita: when i woke up this morning... i had a shower... after i came back into my room i felt like i was still cumming... as in the clear honey like cum... i wasnt orgasming though

Nicholas: hmm... no that doesn't gross me out

Namita: thats never happened before

Nicholas: I wonder if it was left over from last night it just didn't come out till this morning

Namita: like it was a little bit more to cum

Namita: yes thats what i thought tooo

Nicholas: it may have thickened as you slept but couldn't come out till u changed positions

Namita: hehe yes maybe

Nicholas: maybe ur body forgot to turn off the juices

Namita: imagine if we both woke up in the morning and we were still wet or at least me from the nite and we get it on again

Nicholas: oooh myyyy

Namita: hehe yess maybe... or i was dreaming

Nicholas: u didn't really have much time from when u went to sleep till u got up so I'm thinking it was left over love juice

Namita: hehe yess true !!

Namita: does that turn you on ?

Nicholas: I know waking up next to you we'd more than like likely go at it again

Nicholas: hell yah!!!

Namita: hehe

Nicholas: talking about how turned on you are n thinking about you n ur body... huge turn on!

Namita: mmmm yessss

Nicholas: lying next to you... feeling ur heat my god! we'll be lucky if we ever see the light of day again lol

Namita: i think yesterdays storytelling really got me soooooooooooo turned on esp the last bit

Namita: lmao

Nicholas: I can't think of a better way to start the day

Namita: ohhh Nicholas !!

Nicholas: yes last night was esp hot!

Nicholas: just think how hot we'll be when we do it for real! ... we might just burst into flames

Namita: i was soOoOOoOOoOOoo horny... i couldnt believe it !! ... i could just picture the whole scenario

Nicholas: me tooooo

Namita: hehehe

Namita: yes spontaneously combust

Nicholas: as I say I'm very visual n have a great imagination so I can put all the aspects into it

Nicholas: after all this chatting being w you will seem like a dream come true

Namita: Hmmmm yesss me tooo... i find i am very sensual when it comes to making love... i like to pay attention to detail

Namita: and take my time to tease and seduce

Nicholas: I carry those details in my imagination too

Nicholas: I love foreplay

Nicholas: long slow sensual foreplay makes the finish so much more intense for me

Namita: i dont like doing it with no emotion or feelings its just not me... not that ive done it that way before

Nicholas: me either

Nicholas: it's not as complete esp for me if I just get on n get off so to speak... not that I can or do that

Namita: well actually it is all part of tantric sex... the ancient indian way of sex... or Kama Sutra as ppl know it

Nicholas: I don't want to do it just to climax coz it's not fulfilling

Nicholas: yes love the Kama Sutra

Namita: yesssss it is not all about the climax... it's everything before and after that

Namita: have you heard of it or the movie ?

Nicholas: I only get one climax per, so knowing that I can get you off many times is part of the journey for me

Nicholas: heard of the books but didn't know there was a movie.... I have the New Joy of Sex somewhere

Namita: ohh god... you would enjoy that ? WOuldn't you be tired after ur climax ?

Nicholas: I don't fall asleep

Namita: really ???

Nicholas: I'm a chatter

Namita: wowwww cool !

Nicholas: have a tendency to ramble actually

Namita: And really to the book too?

Nicholas: pillow talk

Namita: ahhhhh cool !

Nicholas: yah it's here somewhere

Namita: why did you buy it ?

Nicholas: pillow talk is when you really get to know someone

Namita: uh huh true !!

Nicholas: for the information... I eat up info on pretty much everything

Nicholas: ur totally open... naked you just freed ur mind so to speak

Namita: wowww cool

Nicholas: so you talk about everything

Namita: is it more to understand a womans body too?

Nicholas: it's one of the few times we really get to think about nothing and clear our minds

Namita: yessss soooo true !!

Nicholas: hmmm I guess so

Namita: hehe ...good for you !

Nicholas: I'm fascinated w learning how to please a woman so I read n listen as much as I can

Nicholas: it's just nice to be able to put it into practice lol

Namita: wowww sounds like ur a good learner and teacher tooo

Namita: hehe... im sure i can give you some tutorials

Nicholas: gentle passionate and I know my way around a woman's body

Nicholas: I look forward to them

Namita: hehehe

Nicholas: I'm pretty sure you wont be disappointed

Namita: wowww ur already making me feel hot !

Nicholas: I have the skills and the tool so to speak lol

Namita: lmao !!!

Nicholas: just wait till I touch you n make you hot

Namita: cant wait for the tools to come out !!!

Nicholas: you'll be able to feel the energy radiating from me onto you

Nicholas: lol I'm very good with my tools... I know how to make them work very efficiently

Namita: yes you will sure transfer ur energy into me... thats for sure !!

Nicholas: mmmhmmm

Namita: hehe

Namita: we are soooo bad !!

Nicholas: yes we are n so naughty

Nicholas: have you told anybody about me yet?

Nicholas: just wondering

Namita: no not yet... i havent had the chance really... havent seen my sis and my friends are out of town

Nicholas: ah

Nicholas: no pressure

Namita: have you? bedsides ur mom

Nicholas: my grampa and my friend Diana... she's the one that told me about LL

Nicholas: I'm even keeping it from Tony

Nicholas: just till we meet in person though

Namita: lol... what did ur grampa say ?

Namita: and diana?

Nicholas: he said it's so wonderful that I found someone and there's no better feeling than to have someone that warms ur heart

Nicholas: Diana thought it was cool

Nicholas: she actually found someone too... there talking n have been out on a couple of dates

Namita: good for her !!!!

Namita: hope things work out for her

Nicholas: I sent my grampa the photo of you in the long sleeve n jeans n he replied w "she's just as beautiful as you said she is"

Namita: the very first pic ?

Nicholas: me too

Nicholas: I think so

Nicholas: moving day... looking out the window

Namita: does diana have kids too ?

Nicholas: love that look

Namita: ohh yesss

Nicholas: she does

Nicholas: same age as mine but boys

Namita: ohh woww !!

Nicholas: met them when the kids started school

Namita: meaning that they are same age as urs

Namita: ahhh i see

Nicholas: yes same age

Nicholas: she's a singer n damn good

Namita: wowww cool ...good for her !! If i may ask what does she do for a living ?

Nicholas: she's an actress... I'm not sure what she's doing for work at the moment

Namita: is ur ex with anyone ? if i may ask ?

Nicholas: you know it's really cool being able to talk to you even though ur in San Fran

Nicholas: don't think so

Namita: yeah i made sure my laptop was tucked under my arm

Nicholas: cool

Namita: the mom automatically gets more custody right ?

Nicholas: not always

Nicholas: we have joint

Namita: i see

Nicholas: they live w her coz it was the least disruptive to the girls lives

Nicholas: it is shitty that the mom usually gets the kids in some cases coz the mom's not always the better parent

Namita: omg... i know sometimes these judges are effing retarded

Namita: do they live in an apartment ?

Nicholas: town house... she rents

Namita: ohhh i see

Namita: did u move out of there ?

Nicholas: I did

Nicholas: I'd like to be in a house of my own so when or if the girls decided to live w me they could

Nicholas: but right now I'm still in my transition place

Namita: how old is that in BC ?

Nicholas: 12

Namita: ahhh i seee

Nicholas: It's hard to save when you have a big leak in your bank account ie child support

Namita: yess i understand... i dont know how you guys do it !!

Namita: does she work ?

Nicholas: a friend of mine is paying support and he doesn't even get to see his kids

Nicholas: she does now

Nicholas: she didn't when we were together

Namita: now she has to suck it up !!

Namita: you know i always thought... being a parent and esp a mom to girls you need to set a good example and show them what life is all about... teach them what they need to do to stand on their own 2 feet

Namita: these are the times that is crucial for them... you are never going to get it back

Nicholas: yes

Nicholas: my mom would like me to be w someone who is a good example for them.. a role model... someone they can look up to

Namita: when young girls go awry... its not cuz they are rebellious... i dont believe in that... its cuz they didnt get direction from who they needed it the most from

Namita: i believe in discipline at a young age ... they are ur friends when they are older

Nicholas: yup

Nicholas: it's a balancing act most times

Namita: it is a balancing act

Namita: and as a parent it should naturally come to you

Nicholas: I don't ever want to be that parent that's always slagging the other parent in front of the kids

Nicholas: it should

Namita: i know i dont have children but being the eldest i looked after my sisters

Namita: i was the responsible one ....the one that looked out for them

Namita: yes slagging in front of the kids is a no no

Namita: i was the one that kind of forged my way in the world ... my parents were working most of the time... my mom sometimes had 2 jobs

Namita: so it was me and the other ones at home... alone and we didnt rebel or created problems or go awry and its cuz we werent afraid of anything... i guess we were achievers in some way

Namita: busy doing schoolwork and stuff

Nicholas: that's good

Nicholas: my youngest has asked me before why I moved out

Namita: really ?

Nicholas: I told her that wasn't something I was able to tell her yet but it was better that I left and when she's old enough I'll tell her everything

Nicholas: yup

Namita: good Nicholas... she is too young to understand and dont ever feel guilty of anything... you did the right thing... this is one example you are setting for the girls

Namita: that they should know when to walk away from a relationship... INTACT

Nicholas: thx that's what everybody says

Nicholas: yup

Namita: and have their sanity and self worth too... many girls and women... around the world get sooo tangled in a bad relationship that they lose themselves

Nicholas: your awesome you know that?!

Namita: really?

Nicholas: you are

Namita: hehe... how is that ?

Nicholas: just wanted to tell you that

Namita: aweee thanks

Nicholas: just being able to talk about everything w you... you're just awesome

Nicholas: anyway sorry to distract

Namita: oOOoOooooOoo thanks nicholas !!

Namita: im all ears here

Nicholas: it takes so much longer to type all this lol

Namita: hehhe

Namita: no worries

Namita: ur fingers must be bleeding by now

Nicholas: lol

Nicholas: I'm definitely faster at typing that's for sure

Namita: i know im getting better too... in an unconventional way

Nicholas: mmmm nice pic

Namita: lol

Namita: you like ?

Nicholas: lol yes hunt n peck

Nicholas: I do

Nicholas: I like them all

Namita: i was with friends last year near Chilliwack Lake... out in the boonies

Nicholas: that one really shows ur smile n dimple

Namita: and we were sitting in the water ...or river ... in our small lawn chairs and cowboy hats

Nicholas: cool... I like to camp too just haven't taken the time lately

Namita: water rushing around us

Namita: sipping beer

Namita: well i wasnt

Namita: not a beer person

Nicholas: n a cowboy hat really?

Nicholas: I don't like beer

Nicholas: drank a little when I was younger but can't stand it now

Namita: yeah me n a bunch of other girls... and guys... all camping

Nicholas: cool

Namita: its nice sitting in the water like that

Namita: beer in the water cooling

Namita: have you seen the Chilliwack river ?

Nicholas: nope... been to the water slides at Cultis lake tho

Nicholas: I'm sure that's spelt wrong

Namita: ohhh yesss that is nice

Namita: Cultis

Nicholas: I did get it right lol

Namita: hehe

Namita: i knew what u meant

Namita: i didnt have my cowboy hat on in this pic

Nicholas: sweetie.... I should really go to bed I need to be up at 5:30

Namita: ohh ok ... no worries

Nicholas: I don't want to but I'll be a zombie tmw if I don't sleep

Namita: hehe ...ohhhhh come on ...cant you be a little festive ????? GEeeeezzz

Nicholas: lol

Namita: i loveee zombies

Namita: hehe

Nicholas: good to know

Nicholas: then I'm your guy

Namita: lol

Nicholas: same time tmw? or earlier?

Namita: ok ... ill be around

Nicholas: same time?

Nicholas: as usual

Namita: im not sure about tomorrow... how the day will end

Namita: yes i aim for 1130

Nicholas: ok that's cool

Nicholas: I'm not going anywhere so I'll be here

Nicholas: if that makes sense?

Namita: ok... tomorrow is better for you... have fun tomorrow

Namita: yes it does

Nicholas: I will

Nicholas: I wont have to get up early monday so we can talk till reg time lol

Namita: hehe ok

Nicholas: ur awesome

Namita: goodnite... so are you !!

Nicholas: okay gnight

Nicholas: sleep well n positive waves to your family

Namita: ohhh thanks nicholas

Nicholas: night xo

Namita: nite nite

End Time: 1:46 AM

Chapter 14 October 23

Start Time: 12:32 AM

Namita: hey there

Nicholas: hello there!!!

Namita: arghhhhh i cant sign into msn properly !!

Nicholas: oh no

Namita: ive been trying to sign in since 11:30

Nicholas: I'm glad you made it

Nicholas: I see

Namita: well i still dont have my regular window up... im going thru my inbox

Nicholas: ah that's a small window too

Nicholas: well I'm glad you found a back door

Namita: i have to get it fixed somehow... it wont let me sign in but i can get into my msn inbox with the same password

Namita: lol... thanks for the backdoor

Namita: it tells me a system error or something

Namita: argghhhh

Nicholas: hmm

Namita: anyways how was ur day ?

Nicholas: was long

Nicholas: up at 530

Nicholas: stopped for an energy drink on my way n sipped it all day

Nicholas: it helped

Namita: ohh myyy

Nicholas: I don't usually drink them

Namita: ive never ever had an energy drink before

Nicholas: how was ur day?

Nicholas: I couldn't drink one all at once that would make me sick

Namita: ohhh... my day was ok

Nicholas: the one I like doesn't taste like others

Namita: spent part of the day at the hospital... then we went out to get some fresh air and clear our heads... went for dinner

Nicholas: most energy drinks taste like cough syrup

Namita: eweeeeeeeee !!!

Nicholas: how's ur uncle?

Namita: you can never get me to drink cough syrup !!

Namita: i hate it !!

Nicholas: hahaha

Nicholas: I haven't had it since I was little

Nicholas: I found other ways to medicate for colds

Namita: he is doing pretty much the same... no real improvements... its a good thing i can understand in a medical way what is going on... so i explain alot of it to family

Nicholas: that's good

Namita: the most i will ever have is halls ... the cough drops

Nicholas: good u can explain it

Namita: yess true

Namita: when did you get home after ur stint ?

Nicholas: I'm not a big believer in Halls... I'll use Cepacol if I have a really sore throat

Namita: did you get any more sleep?

Nicholas: about 6ish... I went for groceries after

Namita: i like the lemon/honey halls... its the only one i will take

Nicholas: nope... thought I might nap while I waited for you but got busy around here

Namita: ahhh... grocery shopping... it must have been busy

Nicholas: a little bit... I try not to go on weekends for just that reason

Namita: ohhh what have you been doing ?

Nicholas: got my laundry done and made dinner

Namita: i always pick up things on the way or as i need it esp produce

Namita: hehe... wowwwww quite the domestic man you are !!!

Nicholas: produce usually goes bad before I can eat it

Namita: is laundry included ?

Nicholas: yup very independent

Namita: hehe

Nicholas: in my rent you mean?

Namita: yes in your rent

Nicholas: the thought crossed my mind about how to wash sexy nighties

Nicholas: yes I have a washer n dryer here

Namita: lol ?? would you wash them for me ? the delicates i mean

Nicholas: I sure would! if laundry needs to be done then i do it

Namita: ohhh good !! it is such a hassle when it isnt

Namita: aweeeeeeeeeee soooo sweet !!

Nicholas: yah that was one of the things I liked about this place compared to others I'd seen

Namita: usually wash my lingerie separately

Nicholas: probably hand wash only

Namita: yes... sometimes i do it by hand ... hate ruining a good bra or some lacy stuff

Namita: aweeeee seriously ur too sweet

Nicholas: thx

Nicholas: don't want to ruin your delicates

Namita: hehe

Namita: no we wont want that happening

Nicholas: no we don't

Namita: hehehehe

Namita: or off to the lingerie shop we go !!

Nicholas: though you'd be naked more often but I like the idea of you in lingerie

Nicholas: oh that would be fun

Nicholas: seriously would love to shop for lingerie w you

Nicholas: we'll have to check out that store down town Dare To Wear

Namita: ive never been there before

Namita: hehe... wouldnt it be cool if we stopped by my favorite lingerie shop and you could pick out some cool lingerie... then we both go in the fitting room and i could try it on... with you right in there with me

Nicholas: ooohhhhh mmmyyyy that would be fun!!!!!!

Nicholas: I love how you think!

Nicholas: it's pretty cool judging from the displays they put in the windows

Namita: i usually go to La Vie en Rose and ive seen boyfriends and hubbies go in with the women

Nicholas: I know that store

Namita: i think the staff encourage it... and dont mind at all

Nicholas: they probly spend more when the bf n hubbies go in

Namita: yeah i like that store... the one i go to is in Langley

Nicholas: oh yah

Namita: hehehe yessss probably cuz the bf or hubbies talk the women into it

Nicholas: I guess

Namita: they do have cool stuff though

Nicholas: I bet they do... can't wait to see some of it... in the store n in your bedroom

Namita: lol... im sure it will look good on the floor for you !!!!

Nicholas: lol

Namita: lol

Nicholas: I'm trying to figure out which of your looks I'm going to get the first time I see you... I'll love which ever you choose

Nicholas: I have 11 of them on my screen n it's hard to choose the best one... I love them all

Namita: hehehe... i will come wearing all leather and boots

Nicholas: oooOooo

Namita: looking a bit harsh

Namita: hehe

Nicholas: sexy harsh?

Namita: but then it will only fuel you !!

Namita: yes sexy harsh

Nicholas: that it will

Nicholas: ooohhh damn

Namita: maybe wear a getup from that place you mentioned earlier

Namita: hehe

Nicholas: mmmmhmmm

Namita: lol

Nicholas: we're trying to stay out of the bedroom for first meeting thought right?

Namita: you will lose consciousness i think !!

Namita: yes out would be better for first time

Nicholas: might stop my heart or blow my pulse through my neck

Namita: hahaha

Namita: i can take ur blood pressure

Nicholas: yes... gelato n a walk at Rocky Point

Namita: and will do a checkup afterwards and make sure ur ok before i leave

Nicholas: oohh right you can take care of me if I need medical attention like mouth to mouth

Nicholas: or a secondary body check

Namita: ohhh yessss... i will take ur breath away... ur in good hands... just trust me !! Hehe

Nicholas: Oh I trust you my dear

Namita: hehe

Nicholas: your photos take my breath away I can only imagine what will happen to me when I see you in real life

Nicholas: I'll probably mention more than once that I can't believe ur right here w me

Namita: lol... i can pinch you if you want me too

Nicholas: please do

Namita: or tickle you ? if you dont like pain

Nicholas: anytime you want to touch me you go right ahead

Nicholas: I'm a little ticklish not big on pain but a little pinch is okay

Namita: im a touchy person but not clingy... i love holding hands

Namita: hehe... hmmm i guess i have to find those special spots

Nicholas: me too... I know I'll love holding ur hand

Nicholas: I just love talking w you

Namita: me too... i hope i havent ever bored you at any time

Nicholas: your photos are amazing

Nicholas: never

Namita: during the day i think about our sometimes wacky conversations

Namita: lol

Nicholas: I hope I haven't bored you

Nicholas: lol me too

Namita: nooo never

Nicholas: I read them over again too

Namita: the start of ur day ?

Namita: it is too funny sometimes

Nicholas: I don't start my day reading them but whenever I have time or I'm looking for something you've said that made me smile I'll look at them again

Nicholas: our spelling is hilarious the more tired we get

Namita: hehe.. for me it plays in my head like a tape recorder... with our chatter... my response and urs... the funny things you say

Nicholas: when I read it it makes you more real... when I just think about what you've said it sometimes feels like I've dreamt it

Namita: lol

Namita: i knowwww sometimes i think to myself... did i really say that to him

Nicholas: 😃

Nicholas: yes you did... n I love how open you are w me

Namita: aweee thanks... most times i can be reserved

Namita: but if i get to know a person better im more playful and open

Nicholas: I can see that... I can be like that sometimes too

Namita: ppl are sometime astonished what can come out of my mouth sometimes... hehe

Nicholas: yes you are... I think that's why this chatting is so great... we become comfortable w each other and we can talk about things we might not say in person... though I'm pretty open in person too

Nicholas: well I feel lucky coz I know I'm the only one that hears some of the things you say

Nicholas: esp open w someone I'd like to have a relationship with

Namita: lol,,, yesss ur getting the naughtier version of it !!!

Nicholas: communication on all levels

Nicholas: n that's so cool... n thank you for it as well

Namita: yess i think being open in terms of communication in a relationship is not only key but very very important ... talk things out rather than playing mind games

Nicholas: yes I agree... speak your mind... some ppl don't for fear of upsetting or loosing their partner... if u do loose them then it wasn't a healthy relationship to begin with

Namita: i hate the idea where one partner sulks or gives you the cold shoulder... hoping that the other can read ur mind... like wtf is that all about !! Sorry for the swear

Nicholas: your partner should love you on all levels and take you for who you are and not try to change you into someone they want you to be

Nicholas: sokay I totally agree

Namita: yessssssssss totally agree on that

Namita: being open like that... opens doors on being comfortable and honest with each other... if that makes sense?

Nicholas: some ppl like the idea of being in a relationship that they settle for someone that they're not really happy with

Nicholas: it totally does

Namita: yes and eventually you are going to hit a roadblock with that

Namita: you shouldnt have to sacrifice and make do

Nicholas: I've always longed for that deeper connection w a woman... someone who doesn't try to change who I am n loves me for who I am

Nicholas: someone that just gets it on a deeper level.... n so far you seem to be.... another exciting aspect I see in you

Nicholas: as you said compliment one another

Namita: yesss totally... ppl are going to be different and different views/opinions/the way they dress or talk or walk or anything ... if you want to be with that person... accept them for who they are !!

Nicholas: yesssss

Namita: they dont need to be an exact mold of you

Namita: that would be totally boring !!

Nicholas: if there is any doubt right from the start then ppl shouldnt pursue a relationship w that person

Nicholas: yessss

Namita: exactly !!!! omg amen !!!

Namita: lol

Namita: ppl in relationship spend most of their energy ... trying to make the other into something they are not !! i totally hate that

Nicholas: another aspect I see is I don't have any reservations or red flags when it comes to a relationship w you... having never experienced that it makes it a little scary n exciting all at the same time... scary coz I don't want to have my heart broken n exciting coz it could be something I've searched a very long time for.... no pressure

Namita: yes i understand... i feel the same way too

Nicholas: oh good

Namita: its like being cautious and excited at the same time

Nicholas: yessss exactly what I've been thinking all along... I'm still holding my breath till I finally meet you... that's when I can exhale n know that it's real

Namita: hehe... i think its like that every time though

Nicholas: so we proceed w caution, not rush things and do it all for the right reasons n see what happens

Namita: yess right

Nicholas: every time? or just w someone new?

Namita: i dont want to rush into things either

Nicholas: I've never felt like this before

Namita: i meant when i was on LL a few yrs before... meeting ppl from the relationship or dating section... first contact was always nerve wracking

Nicholas: ah

Namita: for me... a few times i didnt even know what the other person looked like till i met them

Namita: so it was like a blind date

Namita: omg never doing that again

Nicholas: you were able to meet ppl face to face before from LL

Namita: yes... now this is when i was first on it a few yrs ago... i would meet for lunch or coffee

Nicholas: I guess you had a longer time on there than I did... I just got really lucky when I found you

Nicholas: yah I can see that would be nerve racking

Namita: and sometimes it would be the first time seeing them ... not knowing what they looked like... cuz they didnt have a pic but they sounded good thru messaging

Nicholas: ah yah im a visual person n I think everyone needs that physical attraction.

Namita: lol

Nicholas: that's the first thing we notice... I don't think it's shallow I just know what I'm attracted to... I know you don't think I'm shallow

Namita: watch us... we say it is going to be no rush and keep it civil and we end up making out in the park in front of the boathouse !! Hehee

Nicholas: lol yah that's crossed my mind too

Namita: noo i dont think ur shallow... it never crossed my mind... its just you know what you want in a partner and in ur life !!

Nicholas: though I guess if it's meant to be it will happen

Namita: yess true !!

Namita: hehe

Nicholas: though I still want our first time to be special... the second time we can devour each other lol

Namita: lmaooo... yes and rip our clothes off too !!!

Nicholas: not that anytime wont be special w you

Nicholas: yup

Namita: buttons flying everywhere

Nicholas: we'll have had weeks to build up to the first time

Namita: hair disheveled

Nicholas: buttons flying lol button fly jeans good one lol

Namita: yess of course we would !!

Namita: hehe

Nicholas: just being w you will be special

Namita: i was remembering today how u liked one of my texts

Namita: about how hot it might get in the kitchen if we were to cook together... about me putting the rub on ur meat while you have me marinating in my juices

Nicholas: lol yes I did

Namita: hehe

Nicholas: I also liked it when you said I can have the best of both worlds

Namita: i dont know how i came up with that one... it just came to me... i started madly texting you before it was out of my head

Namita: best of both worlds... meaning ? i cant remember what i was saying in reference to ?

Nicholas: My passion for my hot rod has been an issue for others I've dated... they felt they had to compete w it for my attention

Nicholas: best of both worlds, the hot rod n a wonderful partner

Namita: omg !! seriously ?? that is an interest ...a hobby

Nicholas: yah I knew you'd get it

Namita: my passion is reef keeping... i sure dont want someone to feel that theyre competing with fishes

Nicholas: those were the clingy n emotionally needy women though

Nicholas: I like that you have hobbies

Namita: ohhh geeeez... that and probably they didnt have a life of their own or a hobby or friend for themselves on their own time

Nicholas: at the hospital today, that's where the Sp gig was, there was a salt water tank there n I immediately thought of you n went to have a look

Namita: well i could go shop for live corals or fishes all day... love doing that

Nicholas: thats right they didn't, I was their hobby

Nicholas: cool

Namita: which hospital was it ?

Nicholas: this tank had a clown fish n i just stared at him

Namita: aweeeeeeeeee soooooooooo cuteeeee

Nicholas: Children's in vancouver

Nicholas: in the ambulatory care building

Namita: ohhh yesss... im sure they would have one

Nicholas: though I'm usually thinking of you

Namita: did they have live rocks with corals ?

Namita: lol

Nicholas: was just gonna tell you what they had

Nicholas: mind reader

Namita: lol

Namita: ok tell me

Nicholas: about 5 or 6 diff fish n just plastic coral n rocks

Nicholas: I can't wait to see your reef

Namita: ohhh i guess someone would have to upkeep the corals and rocks but it would have been cool of everything was real

Nicholas: yes it would have

Namita: i have all sorts of stuff

Namita: its a total conversation piece

Nicholas: I think it's pretty cool watching fish... very relaxing

Namita: at night its even cooler

Nicholas: I bet

Nicholas: we could make love on the floor in front of the reef... if there's room

Namita: cuz certain creatures come out that i didnt buy... usually they are the hitchhikers on the rocks i bought

Nicholas: oh cool

Namita: so i would sit there with a flash light

Namita: OMG yesssssssssss

Nicholas: so glad you think so too

Namita: i always thought it would be cool to have a huge tank in the BR (bedroom) and make passionate love in the background

Namita: its my fantasy

Nicholas: well we'll do our best to make that happen

Namita: hehe

Namita: and flood the room

Namita: yess sure

Namita: hehe

Nicholas: flood the room *shakes head* the only liquid we'll spill is our own

Namita: lmaooo

Namita: then i will put on my snorkel equipment before i go down

Nicholas: lol good one

Namita: hehe

Nicholas: I'll provide you w the snorkel okay? hehe

Namita: ok deal

Nicholas: lol

Namita: lol

Nicholas: I think it'll be long enf n its definitely a mouth full

Nicholas: lol

Namita: hahahaa...very funny

Nicholas: lol

Namita: do you have a preference ?

Nicholas: preference to what?

Namita: hehe... if there is a mouthful

Namita: would you want me to spit it out or do you want me to... take it in

Nicholas: totally up to you... whatever you're comfortable with... you decide

Namita: would that turn you on even more ?

Nicholas: the mouth full ref (reference) wasn't the deposit, was more the unit

Namita: ohhhhhhhhhhhhhhhhh hehehehehhe

Nicholas: it is a turn on n I'm not sure why but whatever you're comfortable with is okay w me

Namita: geeeeez my mind is in the gutter !!!

Namita: hehehe

Nicholas: the deposit isn't that much... it's not like a milkshake lol

Namita: lmaoooooooo

Namita: phewwwwwww glad you cleared that up !!!

Nicholas: I've seen some porn where it looks like a fire hose going off... not sure if its real but looks pretty damn real

Namita: lol... yesss one has to wonder sometimes

Nicholas: not that I've seen a lot of porno's just to be clear lol

Namita: yah right lol... just teasing hehe

Namita: if it was me... that came... what are you comfortable doing... just wanna know... it is not a judging question

Nicholas: lol

Nicholas: it's been the black guys too n some don't look natural they're so big... you'd think they'd pass out when they get hard if it was really that big

Namita: hahahhahahaha !!!

Namita: ohhhhhhhhhhh Nicholas !!!

Nicholas: what am I comfortable with? I'm pretty open n never been w someone that can squirt so it would be new for me... kind of interested to see it actually

Namita: ohh yessss I see

Nicholas: I certainly wouldn't say or do anything that might make you feel uncomfortable that's for sure... I know you know I wouldn't but I needed to say it

Nicholas: when I get you to go then I know I've hit the right spots too so I think it's cool

Nicholas: it's just part of the moment

Nicholas: I wouldn't react to it in a negative way... maybe that's a better way of saying it

Namita: ohhhh it takes a lot to get me annoyed and plsss we have to be open minded to each other

Nicholas: of course

Namita: are you referring to making me feel uncomfortable in a general sense of the word or in a sexual manner ?

Nicholas: if you squirt then that's cool w me... just part of the package

Namita: lol

Nicholas: was more of not making you feel uncomfortable if or when you were to squirt... I'm okay with it

Nicholas: kind of excited to get you to go off like that

Nicholas: then I know I've pleasured you

Namita: ohh... im comfortable with myself when it happens... its only been in my 30's that it's been happening

Nicholas: either way I'm totally cool w it

Nicholas: not that I would but I would never intentionally do or say anything to make you feel uncomfortable

Namita: I've come to enjoy it and now I know that not everyone is programmed like me... squirt... so I take it in stride and consider it a privilege in sorts that I can do that

Nicholas: yes it is

Namita: ohhhh I know Nicholas... you are a sweet person and I know you would never hurt me or make feel uncomfortable

Nicholas: I know u know that I just wanted to say it

Namita: thank you so much for saying it Nicholas... it does mean alot to me

Namita: it is another caring attribute of you

Nicholas: awe thanks

Nicholas: n I do care about you... a lot!!!

Namita: the first time it happened... with me

Namita: was on my own... hehe

Namita: awee thanks

Nicholas: oh yah

Namita: oh nooo... hehe i perked ur interest now

Nicholas: yes u have

Namita: ur totally awake now

Nicholas: lol

Namita: ears and eyes wider slightly

Nicholas: always when talking w you

Namita: lol

Nicholas: a little

Namita: shaking his head again

Nicholas: nope

Namita: lol

Nicholas: anyway go on you were pleasuring urself the first time, do go on pls

Namita: hehe

Namita: yes i was .... and next thing you know im totally gushing and i think i might have hit that gspot... i was astonished at first... i thought... ok dont laugh pls

Namita: i thought i had peed

Nicholas: that's what I've heard it feels like

Namita: but when i looked closer... it wasnt... I didnt even know anything about women squirting then

Nicholas: I think I know where to rub n pleasure to get you to go so I'm gonna do my best at some point to get you to go off

Nicholas: hmm.... I've looked into n the experts don't know what it is

Namita: ohhh god !! ur turning me on again

Nicholas: hehe

Namita: it is still a mystery... i think

Nicholas: it is

Nicholas: they don't know what it is or where it comes from

Namita: yesss... ive thought of that... it boggle me

Nicholas: so ur very privileged to be able to do that

Namita: the smell is even more arousing... i hear

Nicholas: what does it smell like?

Namita: well sweet

Nicholas: I wouldn't think it would have a smell

Namita: it turns me on even more... i suppose even the partner

Nicholas: guess we'll find out

Namita: lol... we sure will

Nicholas: mmmhmm

Nicholas: the first time I see you I'm gonna have a hard time keeping my hands off you... don't want to maul you lol

Namita: lmao !!!!!!!!!!!!!!!

Nicholas: all this talk is just adding to my arousal

Namita: i could handcuff you... so ur restrained

Nicholas: hmmm never been tied up... have you?

Namita: hey would you be open to being handcuffed while i... ahem perform my seduction

Nicholas: hell yah!!

Namita: hehe

Namita: blindfolded?

Nicholas: sure

Nicholas: would you like to be?

Namita: lights off or on

Namita: ohhh yessssss

Nicholas: we'll add that to the list then

Namita: as far as being tied... yess i would but not my feet... i dont like being completely restrained

Nicholas: good to know

Namita: i like a dim glow ... maybe candles

Namita: or how about if we go away together... maybe to whistler or some other retreat... and we book a room with a jacuzzi tub in the room beside the bed

Nicholas: oooh yessss!

Nicholas: or a room down town n we could make love like in ur scenario

Namita: ohhh yesssssss

Namita: by the fireplace

Nicholas: pressed against the window while we make sweet passionate love to each other

Namita: mmmmmmm yessss

Nicholas: side note; been thinking of some poses for our photo shoot

Namita: really ??? what ??

Nicholas: one is me w my back to the camera feet together arms out to the sides... you in front of me w ur arms wrapped around me... not sure where to put ur hands yet

Namita: hmmm niceee

Nicholas: black n white, both of us naked, of course me sideways to the camera in a half squat, u straddling me your legs wrapper around my hips holding urself close

Namita: mine would be we are in bed naked... you on bottom and Im on top but draped across ur body... both of us looking up at the camera... so the shot is taken from above

Nicholas: I'm still thinking about one w you the focal point n me wrapped around u some how

Namita: yes b/w or sepia is more sexy i think

Nicholas: cool

Nicholas: I like that one

Nicholas: I'm sure we'll come up w more once we're in the moment n w the photographers suggestions too

Namita: yesss possibilities are endless

Nicholas: how much is the photographer?

Namita: nicholas my msn is crapping out on me

Nicholas: okay

Namita: she is free for me

Nicholas: ah

Nicholas: so do you want to call it a night then?

Namita: one of my good friends

Nicholas: cool
Namita: is that ok ?
Nicholas: of course
Nicholas: same time tmw?
Namita: i have a pause on the return message... will try to fix it tomorrow
Nicholas: hopefully ur msn will be sorted out by then
Namita: yes
Nicholas: sleep well my sweet
Namita: byeeee
Nicholas: nite
End Time: 3:02 AM

Chapter 15 October 24

Start Time: 12:47 AM

Nicholas: yes! you made it!

Namita: yes i did... i was hesitant to say hi... cuz i thought you were asleep

Namita: sorry to keep u waiting nicholas

Nicholas: nope been waiting for you

Namita: my msn has been giving me grief

Nicholas: I don't usually go to bed these days till 3:30 or 4 am lol

Namita: lol... thanks to someone !!

Nicholas: ah I figured msn was giving u trouble

Nicholas: anytime

Namita: hehe... how was ur day ?

Nicholas: you can keep me up till the wee hrs of the morning anytime

Nicholas: work went by really fast, thankfully

Namita: aweee nicholas

Nicholas: how was ur day?

Namita: that is good to hear... its nice when the workday goes by fast and pain free

Nicholas: yes it is... it's something to do n the checks clear... lol

Nicholas: how is ur uncle doing?

Namita: my day was ok ... its always at the hospital or finding ways to keep everyones minds off the obvious

Nicholas: yah it must be tough

Nicholas: are they keeping him sedated so he can heal?

Namita: he is pretty much the same... it seems like he had another attack last nite but it is too risky to take him in for surgery now

Namita: yes he is still sedated for now

Nicholas: oh n please don't ever feel hesitant with me okay

Namita: hehe thanks... i know... i just didnt want to wake you up from your slumber ...esp since we havent been having enough sleep lately ...hehe

Namita: i have this song stuck in my head right now

Nicholas: sokay... I slept till 10 this morning

Namita: driving me crazy... hehe

Nicholas: AND I look forward to my talks w you

Nicholas: what song?

Namita: ohh niceee... was it enough though?

Nicholas: it was

Namita: it is a new song... i think and it is called all or nothing... from theory of a deadman... one my fav groups

Nicholas: I'll get my sleep when I can, not to worry

Nicholas: theory of a dead man? really?

Namita: good im glad

Namita: what ?? Have you heard of them ?

Namita: lol

Nicholas: of course

Namita: are you laughing ?

Namita: hehe

Namita: cuz i can feel it !!!

Nicholas: I find them a little too much like Nickel Back

Namita: yes true

Namita: cuz they are related

Nicholas: Not a fan of NB (Nickel Back)

Namita: no im not either

Namita: but i do like theory of a dead man

Namita: both of the lead singers are cousins

Nicholas: are they!!! didn't know that

Namita: i was listening to it on the radio today ...came up twice ...and now its stuck in my head

Namita: yes they sure are

Nicholas: Theory is okay but I find their songs kinda sound the same

Namita: thats why they sound alike

Namita: yes true ....see you learned something today !!

Namita: lol

Nicholas: I thought they sounded alike coz NB produces Theory

Namita: yes... i think the frontman from NB ...helped the other out

Namita: i have to find another song to get stuck in my head now

Nicholas: I had heard that Theory approached NB n said we think you should record us n NB said you need a little tweaking n ended up making them sound like NB

Namita: hahahhaha

Namita: hmmmmm nooo wonder they sound alike

Namita: actually at first i thought that song was sung by NB

Nicholas: I heard Count on Me by Default the other day n thought of you... I really like that song... cool lyrics n great sound

Namita: i loveee default

Namita: thats one of my fav songs too

Namita: and live a lie... is the other

Namita: they are local too... from delta

Nicholas: the first time I heard Theory I thought it was NB but it sounded better so it couldn't be NB

Nicholas: Default is from Langley

Namita: they are ...maybe they moved ?

Nicholas: haha

Namita: hehe

Nicholas: don't know I heard Langley but you beat me to a reply

Nicholas: lol

Nicholas: I'm a big fan of pretty much all music except thrasher speed metal

Namita: whats is an example of thrasher ?

Nicholas: Anthrax

Namita: never heard of them

Nicholas: any "music" that doesn't really sound like music I don't like

Nicholas: but there is so much out there that I do

Namita: yes me either

Namita: rap ?

Nicholas: I'm big on the 60's music coz they experimented w so many diff sounds

Nicholas: some rap... Eminem... I like how he rhymes, not big on gangsta' rap

Namita: hmmm im not too familiar with the 60's but i do like some of the Beatles, elvis,

Namita: yesss love eminem

Namita: i think eminem is probably the best rap artist i have ever heard

Nicholas: well stick w me n I'll show you the way into the world of the late 50's and 60's music

Namita: hehe

Nicholas: I agree... I like Eminem's messages in his rhymes too

Nicholas: I'm Not Afraid is such an excellent song

Namita: yessssss that is such a good song

Namita: he is very gifted young man

Nicholas: I love the lyrics

Nicholas: have you seen 8 Mile?

Namita: and im glad he found an avenue to show the world what he can do

Nicholas: yes

Namita: loveeeeeee 8 mile

Nicholas: great film!!

Namita: all his songs are in my ipod

Namita: never seen the movie though

Nicholas: cool... I don't have any of his, though I should

Nicholas: 8 Mile is a song too?

Namita: yesss the title song

Nicholas: I was referring to the movie

Nicholas: oh

Namita: can i send it to you?

Nicholas: the movie is great

Nicholas: sure

Namita: youve probably heard it but cant remember

Namita: one sec

Namita: the song was called Lose Yourself... does it ring a bell ?

Nicholas: oh yah I've herd that one

Nicholas: great song

Namita: yess it was from 8 Mile

Namita: i always crank the dial up in my car with these songs

Nicholas: loose urself in the music you own it u better never let it go!

Namita: yesssss

Namita: hehehe

Nicholas: do not miss ur chance coz opportunity goes but once in a life time

Namita: yesssssssssss

Nicholas: yup I know that one lol

Nicholas: but u haven't seen the movie?

Namita: hehehe... it is great song... i have so many eminem favs but another is a more playful one its Slim Shady

Namita: nooo never saw the movie... booo

Nicholas: yup know that one too

Namita: and the other song i loveee is i'll Be Your Superman !!

Nicholas: we'll have to add that one to the list then

Namita: hehe yesss

Nicholas: we'll stock up on supplies n just watch movies n play!

Namita: lol... sounds like a plan

Nicholas: cool

Namita: i dont even mind his swearing in his music either

Namita: hehe

Nicholas: I try not to swear that way when I do ppl know Im serious... but I've been known to drop a few F bombs now n again

Namita: do you like going to concerts nicholas ?

Nicholas: I try not to sound like a sailor on shore leave though lol

Nicholas: I do!

Namita: lol ...yes me too... when i do its serious... i do it at work too

Nicholas: last one was Bon Jovi

Nicholas: excellent as usual.. the concert

Namita: something like ..."for fucks sake" ..."are you kidding me" is usually what i say

Namita: ohhh yesss ....days of glory or was it blaze of glory ?

Nicholas: I 'll keep an ear out for it u know so I know you're not f***king around lol

Namita: hehehehe... i am sooo giggling here

Nicholas: lol blaze of glory is the song... days of glory is a Will Ferrell movie

Namita: hahahah

Nicholas: sarcasm is just one of the many features I have to offer lol

Namita: or was it Blades of Glory ??? on the Will Ferrell movie ?

Namita: HA !!!!!

Nicholas: yup Blades of Glory is a movie too

Namita: Loveeeeeeee Will Ferrell !!!!!!!!

Namita: he is awesome !!!

Nicholas: I can take him or leave him... not big on his movies like Anchor Man or Days of Glory... no wait Days of Glory is a Tom Cruise movie about car racing

Namita: do you have any fav movies ? in different genres ?

Namita: hehe... i never watched Anchorman

Namita: but his blades of glory was good !!

Nicholas: fav movie of all time Shawshank Redemption and a close second is Red Dawn

Namita: neither of which i have seen

Namita: Red Dawn... who was in it ?

Nicholas: didn't see Blades n Anchor Man I turned off coz I thought it was really dumb... I liked him in Bewitched

Namita: Ahhh... never seen Bewitched either... never even heard of it

Nicholas: Red Dawn; the UN falls and the US gets invaded by Cuba who are backed by the russians. a bunch of kids head for the hills n become rebels n fight the bad guys. Patrick Swayze n Tom Howell, Charlie Sheen are in it. they're really young

Namita: ohhhh

Nicholas: so u like Will Farrell but haven't see any of his movies, well except for Blades of Glory?

Namita: the other day... i watched texas chainsaw massacre- the beginning ... again

Nicholas: I saw that was on

Namita: hehehe... noo ive seen Elf

Nicholas: didn't watch much of it only about 5 mins

Namita: and there was this other one i think called Stepbrothers

Nicholas: oooohh Elf is really great love that one!!

Namita: yes that ones good

Nicholas: great message in Elf!!

Namita: yess true

Namita: he did a good job in that one

Nicholas: have you seen Corina Corina? w Ray Liotta n Whoopi Goldberg?

Nicholas: yes he did but I think the story was really strong so that helped him out

Namita: yes omg like a lonnnngggggg time ago

Nicholas: I love that movie... I like Ray Liotta a lot, great actor

Nicholas: Goodfellas is one of my fav mob movies... I own it

Nicholas: based on a true story too

Namita: i agree... he is really a good actor... one of his movies i really liked was several years ago... it was a thriller called The Skeleton Key with Kate Hudson

Namita: never seen that movie !! Ahem... i guess i better get up to the times !!

Nicholas: I didn't see that one but I'd like too

Namita: it is a good story line

Nicholas: lol we'll add that to the list as well... not to worry we'll have plenty of time for u to catch up

Namita: hehee

Nicholas: it's a great story n to think that that's what the guy went through... it's pretty neat

Nicholas: have you see Blow w Johnny Depp?

Namita: hmmm im sure we will have a melting pot sort of good movies to watch

Nicholas: we will

Namita: never seen Blow ... but i do like Johnny Depp

Nicholas: I do. he's great actor

Nicholas: do u like him?

Namita: sometimes movies come out i dont get a chance to see it ... then i forget about them

Nicholas: yesss me too

Namita: yess he is a great and versatile actor

Namita: i dont swoon over him like a school girl

Namita: ive never been like that

Nicholas: then next thing I know it's in the bargain bin at Walmart n I think hey I was gonna see that

Namita: nor do i find Brad Pitt handsome

Namita: like many women

Nicholas: lol not quite what I meant

Namita: lmao

Nicholas: Brad Pitt is good too

Namita: he is good !

Nicholas: they're ok looking I guess

Namita: i like Leo Dicaprio

Namita: sans Titanic though

Nicholas: I saw Shutter Island

Namita: what did you think ?

Nicholas: was good, predicted it from the start

Namita: really... maybe i was tired but i seriously didnt see it coming !!! Hehehe

Nicholas: I liked it but I called the twist before we went in

Namita: OHHhhhhhhhh crap... glad i wasnt with you then

Nicholas: ppl were like hey you called it

Namita: i would have been pouting all the way home if you blew the story

Namita: lol

Nicholas: mental note keep the predictions to myself lol

Namita: hehehhe

Namita: i did like Inception too

Nicholas: didn't see that one

Namita: omg... that was a good movie

Nicholas: the new one w JT looks good

Nicholas: inception is the dream one right?

Namita: who's JT ? hehe

Namita: yes thats the one

Nicholas: Justin Timberlake

Namita: ohhh yesss

Namita: he's kinda up and coming as an actor

Nicholas: didn't feel like typing out his full name.. that kinda back fired lol

Namita: lol

Nicholas: he's got a few movies on the go

Namita: his music is good

Namita: not the teeny bopper stuff though

Nicholas: as long as he's collaborated w someone I don't mind it

Nicholas: yes don't like his Instink days

Namita: hehehe ... yess true

Namita: Hahahhahahahah

Namita: my tummy hurts now... never heard of that before !!

Nicholas: don't like Backstreet Boys either

Namita: noooo me either

Nicholas: yuck

Namita: omg nooooooooooo

Namita: or NKOTB (New Kids On The Block)

Nicholas: I basically don't like any music that sounds like simplistic regurgitated repetition

Nicholas: EEEEWWWW grosss NKOTB

Nicholas: poor excuse for music

Namita: yes me either... hehehe... yesssssss eweeeeee grosss is right

Namita: i dont know what the girls saw in them

Nicholas: I also don't like it when an artist takes an old song n samples it then loops it n puts their own lyrics to it

Namita: omg i hate that

Nicholas: come up w ur own sound

Nicholas: Kid Rock did that w the Warren Zevone's song Ware Wolves of London

Namita: there is this recent song... i think i told you... cant remember... its one of fav 80 song... called Alone by Heart and some artist... i think Carrie Underwood totally ruined and mutilated the song

Namita: ohhh yessss i remember that Kid Rock song

Namita: yeah i hATE IT

Namita: i dont like country so much either

Nicholas: YES!! me tooo!!!

Nicholas: talk about simplistic repetition!!! my god

Namita: what in the world is that all about ?!?!?!

Namita: lol

Nicholas: n the rhythms are soooooo simple it makes me queazy

Nicholas: I don't mind some Dwight Yoakam... I like the covers he did of Elvis

Namita: hmmmmm i dont remember those ones he did... the only time i listened to country is when i was stuck the car with mom when i was a kid ... she listened to country

Namita: omg i know all the old time country singers

Namita: the songs were always about the same things

Namita: my ears would start to bleed !! heheheh

Nicholas: ah yes listening to whatever the parents have on I remember those days but my Dad listened to the oldies so I was exposed to good music early on

Nicholas: lol

Namita: ohh good for ur dad !!

Namita: he saved you !!!

Nicholas: he did

Nicholas: I like the oldies n how the songs weren't too long n they were light in sound and lyrics

Nicholas: I have a lot of oldies CD's

Namita: yesss... im sure we will be listening to alot of music together

Nicholas: yes we will

Namita: lol

Nicholas: so hears a question for you... I know it's getting way ahead of things but could you see us living together? way down the road that is

Nicholas: I know it's a deep question

Namita: hmmm yes... if things are serious... then why not !!

Nicholas: okay good

Namita: no reason to commute back and forth

Nicholas: thought of that today n just wanted to put it out there

Namita: you work in richmond right ?

Nicholas: I do

Namita: what are your thoughts on the matter ?

Nicholas: I've been thinking the same thing

Nicholas: that's what I mean when I say I can see a future w you

Nicholas: and I've never seen that w someone before

Nicholas: it just fell into place in my mind n that's never happened

Namita: yes it makes sense

Namita: well i guess when it come down to it we will sort the logistics out

Nicholas: great answer, again another reason I really like you

Namita: hehe seriously !

Nicholas: yup

Namita: half of the time I'm wondering if im making any sense here !!

Nicholas: you are

Nicholas: I've imagined living w you... being in your life and you in mine... I think you have to to see if that's where you want to be n I'd be totally comfortable doing that

Namita: im open to any possibilities... you only live once

Namita: although i do take things with due caution... if that makes sense.

Nicholas: I think that way I'm being completely honest w myself and I want to share those kind of things w you to see if we're thinking a long the same lines. Weather it happens or not it's something I've thought about

Nicholas: yes it does I'm w you there

Nicholas: I think that's why it's important to take things slow to make sure things are being done for the right reasons

Namita: i totally agree with you... we have to be on the same page with each other and have a good understanding of each other

Nicholas: the other thing is I really have nothing to loose by being completely honest n up front and I have everything to gain

Namita: yes i totally understand what ur saying... i feel the same way too

Nicholas: cool

Nicholas: wow we really got deep there but I needed to put it out there

Namita: hehe yes we did !!!

Namita: but im sure alot has been circling in each others minds too

Nicholas: I guess that's what it's all about communication n being open

Nicholas: I think so too

Namita: lol

Nicholas: from what we've talked about n you've mentioned I figured you might be thinking the same

Namita: yess... what else have you been thinking?? Sounds like the the gerbils are running overtime in ur head... hehe

Namita: i would loveee to know

Nicholas: lol.. that was pretty much the last of the big things really

Namita: hehehe

Namita: yeah right !!

Nicholas: my hope is that things work out for us n we live happily ever after so to speak lol

Nicholas: again no pressure

Namita: yesss there is no harm to think that and look into the future

Nicholas: but you can't help but imagine those things

Namita: yesss true !!

Namita: here's a question ...would you settle again ?

Nicholas: it's just where the mind wanders... I think it's healthy that way there are no surprises later on

Nicholas: never! and I would never think that I was settling with you in my life

Namita: yesss i agree... its good to talk things out together even if its just ideas ... its healthy and no one is in the dark about it

Namita: noooooOoOooo... hehe... i mean settle down in life as in getting married ?

Nicholas: you are exactly who I wished for which makes me a little cautious as I explained before

Nicholas: oooooohh sorry

Namita: lol

Nicholas: with the right woman I would

Namita: no worries... i should have been more clear... hehe

Nicholas: do you think settling down is getting married?

Namita: well yes i thought of it that way but also yes... settling down means a lot of things these days

Nicholas: I just didn't really think of getting married as settling down

Namita: lol

Nicholas: yah I don't know how to explain that anymore

Namita: hmmm come to think of it... its not settling down... it's living it up more !!! enjoy the life with a good partner

Nicholas: for me marriage or settling down is more of a state of mind

Nicholas: yesssss

Nicholas: that's it!!! well said!!

Namita: hehehe

Namita: i cant believe im even making any sense to yah

Nicholas: lol u are

Nicholas: great minds

Namita: lol

Nicholas: I think it's feeling this same way how ever many years down the road... the feeling of excitement n content

Nicholas: those feeling form being w someone special

Namita: yesss and it is a good feeling !!

Namita: you know when ur home ...when you have that feeling

Nicholas: yesss

Namita: home not in the literal sense

Nicholas: yes, I knew what u meant

Namita: hehehe

Nicholas: holding you n knowing that this is right where I'm suppose to be

Namita: yesss that's right !!! And no worries in the worldly kinda of feeling ... everyone else admire what we have!!

Nicholas: Yesssss!!

Namita: it's the silent understanding between us

Nicholas: they want to know our secret

Nicholas: yyesssss

Namita: its knowing who each other is !!

Namita: no one can say otherwise

Nicholas: and who we are inside our own selves

Nicholas: that's right

Namita: yesss

Nicholas: as I said before my life and world is so much brighter knowing that you're there

Nicholas: It's like the lights came on for me n the world opened up n let the sunshine in

Namita: yesss so true

Namita: hehe

Nicholas: when I can touch you then I'll know it's real... I know I've said that before... it's such diff territory for me to have this kind of connection w you even though I haven't seen you... said that before too

Nicholas: I would love to be in bed right now talking with you

Nicholas: or just sleeping next to you

Namita: yes it is kinda opposite... cuz we have connected on an emotional level first... not physically. Where many do it the other way around and still never get a clear understanding of the emotional aspect, or the thoughts, values or the true meaning of that person in the first place

Nicholas: yes so true... which is the start of a great foundation

Namita: mmm yesss... im sure we would be talking for hours on end being in bed together

Namita: yes very true indeed

Namita: cuddled under the blankets

Namita: with a dim light on

Namita: i always believe in laying down the foundation first

Namita: or another analogy i use... a chair cannot stand on 3 legs

Nicholas: having a great foundation to start off w is something I don't think many ppl have maybe because they didn't take the time to get to know the other person

Namita: so it is imperative to set that foundation first

Nicholas: yes

Namita: sooo true

Nicholas: we've had a great opportunity w modern technology on our side

Nicholas: lol

Namita: lol... yessss we do !! like how we are sooo open with each other

Nicholas: me tooo!!

Nicholas: I love that about you

Nicholas: I love being able to talk about everything w you

Namita: aweeee thanks nicholas

Nicholas: I'm like that so it's nice to find that in a partner... figure of speech, not jumping the gun lol

Nicholas: I love how you know exactly what I'm saying even though I'm typing it

Namita: lol... i had to read that a few times to see what u were talking about

Namita: lmao

Nicholas: lol I should have held off on the second part lol

Namita: i guess you should have waited

Namita: hahahhahaa

Namita: ok i did get you though !!

Namita: eventually

Nicholas: I had to read it again coz it looked like babble

Namita: god im hungry !!

Nicholas: I could eat

Namita: i knowww i never get hungry at this hour

Namita: i can feel my tummy growling ...hehe

Namita: sorry to change the subject

Nicholas: I usually have a snack when I get home n I've been having something before bed these days too coz my after work snack has worn off by the time I go to bed

Nicholas: totally fine. I can keep up w random

Nicholas: mmmm your tummy

Namita: what do you usually have ?

Namita: i know why i suddenly got hungry

Namita: hehe

Namita: mmmm tummmmmmyyyy !!

Namita: sounds like ur hungry for my tummy... hehe

Nicholas: bowl of cereal or milked down yogurt before bed... that way I don't have to chew lol

Nicholas: I am. I could just eat you UP!

Namita: hehehhee

Nicholas: why did you suddenly get hungry?

Namita: hmmmm maybe you can put ur yogurt on my tummy and then eat it !!!

Nicholas: ohhhh yes n lick it off you!

Namita: for some reason i randomly thought of chocolate cake... no reason... it just popped into my head !

Namita: lol

Nicholas: hmm

Namita: yes lick it off... no spoons allowed

Nicholas: spoon phf

Namita: hmmm what ??? What is nicholas thinking ???

Nicholas: I don't know how to spell that sound

Nicholas: was just thinking of things popping up lol

Namita: pfttt ?? this one ?

Nicholas: that's it! thank you

Namita: hehehe

Nicholas: great minds

Namita: hehe yesssss yet again !!!

Nicholas: do you like stand up comedians?

Namita: yes i do !!

Nicholas: cool

Namita: but never been to one

Nicholas: a friend of mine is a comic, he graduated w my sis so she's friends w him too

Namita: who is the comic ?

Namita: the friend ?

Nicholas: I've seen him and Jeff Dunham the ventriloquist... separately not together lol

Namita: ohhh cool !!!

Nicholas: what do your sisters do?

Nicholas: random I know

Namita: well Jaya is training for rcmp... Priya works as a bank manager and the other one works as a pharmacy technician

Nicholas: cool

Namita: and of course then there's ME

Nicholas: yes then there's you my favorite!!

Namita: lol

Nicholas: my favourite

Namita: hehe

Nicholas: what's the pharmacy tech's name?

Namita: her name is Preeti... that's what we call her

Nicholas: so Preet, Jaya, and Priya

Namita: we are all very close to each other

Namita: yes

Nicholas: taking note for the test later

Namita: Preeti

Namita: hehe

Nicholas: I thought that's just what you called her

Namita: you just have to put the names to the faces... hehehe

Nicholas: yes I do

Nicholas: I still need to put a touch you lol

Namita: yeah we do have a name for her too

Namita: huh ??

Nicholas: was trying to be funny guess that didn't work

Namita: lol

Nicholas: I'll have something better give me a sec or 2

Namita: ok... lol

Nicholas: it's late n the brain isn't working so great at the moment

Nicholas: names to faces... was trying to come up w some sort of funny comment for seeing you

Nicholas: I got nothing lol

Namita: lmao !!

Namita: that totally backfired on you !!

Nicholas: are chats will be even more interesting once we know each others mannerisms

Nicholas: that it did

Namita: hmmm do you have any quirks

Namita: or habits

Nicholas: that's sooo funny was just thinking that today

Nicholas: asking about quirks

Namita: lol

Nicholas: probably I just can't think of them at the moment

Nicholas: do you?

Nicholas: oh here's one

Nicholas: the toilet paper roll has to feed from the top... I'll change it if I see it backwards... at other ppls houses

Namita: usually quirks stand out to others ... i guess ... i do have a habit to swing my one leg ...when cross legged

Namita: hahahahaha

Namita: omg seriously !!

Namita: so the paper comes over not under

Nicholas: I've seen the leg swing before

Nicholas: yes

Nicholas: yah there's probly a bunch of them someone else could list off but I'm drawing a blank

Namita: and then i keep changing my hair... put it up in a ponytail while watching tv or sometimes it is down

Namita: at work sometimes i stick pencils or pens I'm my hair then look for them a while later, get mad !! then say "are you fucking kidding me, where is that pencil. i just had it here a moment ago !!!"

Nicholas: lol funny

Namita: one time i had a red ink pen explode in my hair and i didnt even know it !!!

Namita: Omg what a day that was !!

Nicholas: OMG that's awful

Namita: hehehe

Namita: i was already a redhead and then i get a red pen ink in my hair

Nicholas: on Friday after break I turned my radio on but couldn't hear it. I'd been having trouble w it thinking the battery was dead.. nothing was happening.. tried tuning it... nothing... am to fm…nothing.. what the hell is wrong w it damn it... Oh i guess I should put the head phones on lol

Nicholas: red head cool

Namita: hahahahaaaa !!!!!!

Nicholas: yah felt a little stupid

Namita: my hair has been black to a redhead to auburn

Namita: right now its auburn color

Nicholas: wow... ur naturally black though right?

Nicholas: sounds nice

Namita: yes kinda like deep brown

Namita: not quite black

Nicholas: I like to play w hair... not having any it's nice to run my fingers through

Namita: i go back to my natural too

Namita: mmmmmmmmm niceeeeeeee

Nicholas: start at the top n let my fingers glide through to the end then start all over again

Nicholas: would you like that? he asks knowingly

Namita: yessss she says its soo relaxing

Nicholas: thought you might

Nicholas: yah sitting together just running my fingers through ur hair

Namita: mmmm would love that

Nicholas: mmmhmmm

Namita: it is pretty silky and i take good care of my crowning glory

Nicholas: so I've heard. I'm looking forward to playing w it

Namita: lol

Namita: its playable i think

Namita: and always smells nice

Nicholas: I think so too. I'll let you know when I get to touch it

Namita: heehee

Nicholas: that's what I've heard too can't wait to smell it

Namita: nicholas i am really starting to fade here

Nicholas: okay it is late

Namita: yawning nonstop

Nicholas: you should get some sleep

Namita: hehe

Nicholas: you must be exhausted during the day

Namita: yes i will... you must be tired too?

Nicholas: I am

Namita: after a long day

Nicholas: but I love talking w you

Namita: me too

Nicholas: same time tmw then?

Namita: yes i will be around

Nicholas: okay

Nicholas: talk to you tmw... good luck w the family

~~positive waves~~~

Nicholas: gnight you... sleep well

Namita: yesss thank u soooo much nicholas it means alot

Nicholas: anytime my sweet

Namita: sweet dreams

Nicholas: night

Namita: goodnite nicholas

Nicholas: night Namita

End Time: 3:42 AM

Chapter 16 October 26

I've gotten use to chatting each night but, last night Namita wasn't around. I hope everything is okay. We've only known each other for a couple of weeks and I want to be respectful of her space. She has a life and that's important. We'll eventually make room for each other as we move forward.

Start Time: 12:26 AM

Nicholas: hello there!!

Namita: hey there !

Nicholas: how have you been?

Namita: how are you doing?

Nicholas: im good

Namita: im well thanks... sorry i wasnt around last nite... i didnt get back till around 130 am ish

Namita: how was work ?

Nicholas: its totally fine.... we've had a few late nights so it was probly for the better you have a lot on your plate down there

Namita: hehe... yes i guess it kinda was a good break ...so to speak

Nicholas: work was slow today but yesterday i got to trade in my green hard hat for a white one. green for being new n white for passing probation

Namita: ohhh cool !!! now ur really part of the gang !!

Nicholas: much as i missed u we needed to catch up on our sleep

Nicholas: yes i am

Namita: how long have you been on probation ?

Nicholas: I also got a compliment from one of the guys

Namita: what was the compliment ?

Nicholas: probation is like 3 months I think

Namita: that you looked well rested for once ?

Namita: lol

Nicholas: haha very funny

Nicholas: I fell asleep at dinner

Namita: wow thats not bad... hehe... ours is 6 months i think

Namita: ohhh myyy... you really must have been tired

Namita: so what was the compliment ?

Nicholas: he said that my work was good and when I get faster then I'll have more slack time, though I don't need slack time at work... I'm there to work n I like to be busy

Nicholas: I only closed my eyes for a minute n next I know one of the guys is tapping me telling me it's time to go back to work

Namita: ohh good for you !! i guess as you grow into ur duties ... then things become routine, plus you gain experience

Nicholas: did u get my email last night?

Namita: i just got it now... i havent been around my pc at all today

Namita: well first of all it was acting up

Nicholas: was just a little something to say I was thinking of you n I hope everything is okay down there

Namita: and i couldnt get into my msn

Nicholas: that darn msn giving you trouble tisk tisk

Namita: yes right now things are pretty much the same... my uncle is still on the breathing machine and kept sedated... they tried turning down the sedation but things didnt work out... so it has gone back up again. tomorrow they will do a n ultrasound of his heart again

Nicholas: what's ur uncles name?

Namita: last nite i was out with my cousins, his kids and we just went out to clear our heads ... ended up getting back about 1 am

Nicholas: I've been thinking about him n sending positive waves

Namita: thank you sooo much Nicholas

Namita: that is very thoughtful of you

Nicholas: I remember those times w my dad

Namita: im sure it was scary and stressful time for you too

Nicholas: I want you to know that I don't want you to worry about me if I don't hear from you like last night... I want you to take care of what you need to n I'll be here when you need me

Nicholas: the worst thing I've ever gone through

Namita: being in hospital... esp being on the other side of the table... is never fun !!

Namita: Aweee thank you soo much for saying that Nicholas... your a kind man.

Nicholas: it's never nice to go through anything like this w a loved one

Namita: so what else have you been up to these days ?

Nicholas: you're very welcome Namita

Namita: it is raining still over there ?

Namita: is it ? i mean... geeezzz

Nicholas: well I worked out yesterday n I hit my legs a little harder than usual n my Hamstrings are a little on the sore side today

Nicholas: lol yes on n off since you left

Namita: ohhh noooo !!! was it at the gym ?

Nicholas: no I work out at home

Namita: hehe

Nicholas: I have enf stuff here to get a full body work out

Namita: i remember i was on the treadmill at my house one time and i was watching tv too and next thing you know my foot touches the edge of the treadmill... i went flying back and put 2 holes on the wall directly behind me with my feet

Nicholas: I've been working out since I was 15 so I have a good back ground on how to work the body

Nicholas: OMG! you must have turned a lovely shade of red

Namita: on the drywall... it is still there... i covered it with a shelf... i didnt know how to fix drywall ... hehhehe

Namita: yes my feet hurt sooo much !!

Namita: so im living with 2 holes in the wall

Nicholas: well we can fix that one of the days when I come over... it's an easy fix

Namita: serious ??

Nicholas: yup

Namita: ur such a handyman !!

Nicholas: u wont even know there were holes there

Nicholas: as my dad use to say "if I can't fix it, it aint broke"

Namita: im embarrassed to even show it to anyone... none of my family knows cuz 1st they will laugh and secondly they will make fun of me forever !!

Namita: Good for your dad !!!!!!!

Namita: Thats a good one !!!!

Nicholas: then we'll fix it on the QT (quiet) n no one will know

Namita: hehe deal !!

Namita: is ur leg still sore even now ?

Namita: can you ice it ?

Nicholas: both legs... not really... lactic acid build up... it'll pass in a few days... goes with the territory

Namita: well i hope it will pass !

Nicholas: when they hurt like this then I know I hit them enf to make them stronger

Namita: i had a question that just popped in my head here

Nicholas: shoot

Namita: yesss that is sooo true

Namita: ok ... random ... if you can put a hotrod together ... can you fix cars too ?

Nicholas: depending on the problem w the car sure

Namita: like brakes

Nicholas: I can defiantly look at it ... if I can't then I have a great mechanic that's really inexpensive

Nicholas: oh I can do a brake job

Namita: dad used to fix a lot of his cars at home... brakes, fuel pump... or the alternator

Nicholas: my mechanic can do that for about $200

Nicholas: n $200 is way less than the dealer

Namita: he also used to do some body work too so im familiar with some of the things

Nicholas: ur car is pretty new... you shouldn't need brakes yet?

Namita: yes the dealer charges an arm and a leg

Nicholas: are they squeaking?

Nicholas: or grinding?

Namita: no not yet

Nicholas: that's good

Namita: and my tires are new too

Namita: from last year

Nicholas: do you rotate them

Namita: if you ever need new tires i know a good place to get them ?

Nicholas: okay cool

Namita: yes whenever i go to the dealer... they rotate them as necessary

Nicholas: thats good

Namita: it is called national tires wholesale on river road going towards delta/richmond

Nicholas: I was talking about you today to my friend Diana

Nicholas: I know where they are

Nicholas: she was down the road at Starbucks so I joined her

Namita: yess it is a big yellow building

Namita: cant miss it

Nicholas: she asked me how LL was... soooooo I told her about you

Nicholas: yes thats the place

Namita: ohhh... hehe... what did she say ?

Namita: have you been there before ?

Nicholas: just asked how things were going

Nicholas: I haven't, just heard good things about them and know where it is

Nicholas: she hopes things go well w you n it sounds like I'm really happy

Namita: yeah i paid 700.00 last year for all 4 brand new tires

Namita: i thought id have to fork out over a grand

Nicholas: 700 wow

Namita: my best friend told me about that place and they were sooo good

Nicholas: I think I paid $400 for 4 new ones

Namita: the job was done in 30 mins

Nicholas: you needed tires already

Namita: ohhhh is that too much then ??

Namita: hehehe

Nicholas: depends on the type of tires

Namita: well last year was my 4th year for the tires ... since i bought the car

Nicholas: you really only need to change them when they're worn

Namita: yes true... plus i guess it depends on the car or suv or truck too

Namita: yes i did ... cuz of them kept giving out on me ... the air would run out ... so i had to keep filling it

Nicholas: ah

Namita: and this is exactly last year at this time too

Namita: so it was best to change all of them

Nicholas: funny this time last year was about when I got tires too

Namita: the tire would be quite flat when i would get back to the car from work

Namita: lol ...no way !!

Nicholas: I did

Namita: then a few months later i had to change the batteries

Nicholas: or maybe it was 2 years ago this time coz it was around the time I got my tattoo so it would have been 2 years

Namita: ahhhh

Namita: did it hurt getting the tattoo?

Nicholas: you had the change the battery?! you should have gotten at least 5 to 7 years out of a new battery

Namita: yes even the battery had given out on me !!

Nicholas: near the end it did only cuz she was using the 5 needle gun

Namita: OOoOoo ..ouch

Nicholas: hmmm got to wonder about those Hondas lol

Namita: hehehehe

Namita: thanks !!

Nicholas: my back started to feel like hamburger near the end

Nicholas: I'm a domestic vehicle person

Nicholas: Ford Dodge not big on Chevy

Namita: what would be a good brand

Namita: noooo eweeee chevy ....nooooo

Nicholas: well the hot rod is a Ford n I drive a Dodge

Namita: fords i do like

Namita: and dodges look good too

Namita: what about gmc ?

Namita: i always like the ford and dodge trucks ...they are quite cool

Nicholas: GM=chevy GMC pontiac

Namita: ohhhh ok

Namita: didnt know that

Nicholas: I like the pre-WW2 fords

Nicholas: Model T's and model A's, they made lots of them, good hot rod foundations

Namita: the antiques

Namita: hmmmm will have to look it up

Namita: hehe

Nicholas: the Model A was the first ford car to have a V8 engine

Namita: ohhh cool !!

Namita: im sure they are hard to find these days

Namita: i loveee looking at old unique and antique cars and trucks

Nicholas: so the hot rodders would put the V8 Flat head as it's called into the Model T's to make them go faster

Nicholas: you're a woman after my heart

Namita: in fact every september ...in white rock they have a old car/truck show at crescent beach

Nicholas: I love going to car shows

Namita: near the water ... meeeeeeeeee tooooooooo i loveeeeee looking at cars

Nicholas: I can't wait to get my hot rod over here n drive it all over

Namita: ive been to the white rock one

Namita: it is sooooo coool

Nicholas: ur awesome!!!!

Namita: ive always had an eye for unique and cool cars

Nicholas: I like to dress up like I'm from the fifties, jeans white T shirt n my black canvas shoes

Nicholas: play the part so to speak

Namita: ask my friend ashley ..we always car pool together ...and if i see something old and fancy ... i stop our conversation to have a double take

Namita: wowowww sooo cool !! Im sure you look quite good in them too

Nicholas: that is just music to my ears!!

Nicholas: thx

Namita: ive always loveee looking at cool old cars !!!

Nicholas: you could dress up in a poodle skirt or even better like Olivia newton john from grease n come w me... if you wanted too that is

Namita: i remember going to the beach in late august ...and there was this old antique car parked in the parking lot ... and i was walking around it having a closer look .... i dont know what it was ... it almost looked like an old porsche ...but i couldnt tell

Nicholas: we'd be quite the pair

Namita: hehehe ... yesss and in a the fifties hairstyle too with a scarf around my neck

Nicholas: yesss!!!

Namita: hehe

Namita: have you ever been to the car show they have in BC Place ?

Nicholas: w the new cars?

Namita: yes

Nicholas: I have

Nicholas: was okay

Namita: it is good ?

Namita: yes ive never been

Nicholas: I find there's not a lot of character in new cars

Namita: im not sooo fond of the new futuristic cars as i am with the oldies

Nicholas: there's always a story that goes w a hot rod and it's a reflection of the builder

Namita: yesss true

Nicholas: I have a few photos of some pretty cool ones

Namita: wowww niceee

Nicholas: let me see if I can send you a pic

Namita: ok

Nicholas: ok hang on

Namita: k

Namita: my dada used to have an old little Dustan .... i begged him to keep it when i was a kid ...but alas he sold it to this young man who happened to see it and bought it on the spot !! ARghhhh

Nicholas: it's from a contest that peugeot had n this was the winner

Namita: i meant my dad ...geez i cant spell

Nicholas: sokay, I'm seeing past the spelling

Waiting for ~Namita~ to accept the file "peugeot-vers-city-roads-futuristic-car-03.jpg" (49 Kb). Please wait for a response or

Cancel (Ctrl+C)

the file transfer.

Transfer of file "peugeot-vers-city-roads-futuristic-car-03.jpg" has been accepted by ~Namita~. Starting transfer...

Cancel

Transfer of "peugeot-vers-city-roads-futuristic-car-03.jpg" is complete.

Namita: ohhh myyyyy ... it is sooo beautiful !!!

Nicholas: pretty cool eh?

Namita: yesssss it is gorgeous ... loveeeeeee the wheels

Nicholas: I'd like to build it day. I think it's be sooo cool to drive around

Namita: wow !! So 2 ppl can sit in it ?

Nicholas: yup 2 ppl

Namita: OoOOoo sooo cool !!

Nicholas: I think it's suppose to lay back when you're hiway driving and it sits up when driving in town or parked

Namita: ohhh my ... is it legal to drive it then ...on our roads ?

Namita: ahhhh i seee

Nicholas: there aren't a lot of concept cars that get nbuilt

Nicholas: built... not sure where that stray "n" came from

Namita: ahhhhh ok

Namita: hehehe

Nicholas: do you like lounge music?

Namita: yesss i do

Nicholas: I dug out a 2 disc set I bought a couple of years ago

Namita: oh cool !!

Nicholas: I had forgotten how much I enjoy it

Namita: is it plain music ...or someone singing too ?

Nicholas: though listening to it now all I can imagine is you n I making sweet passionate love while it plays in the back ground

Nicholas: it's 2 discs w diff artists, there's 20 songs

Namita: mmmm that would be sooo nice .... music and making love

Nicholas: yess it would

Nicholas: it's very nice back ground music

Namita: wow we would be making love all nite with those 2 cds

Nicholas: yes we would hehe

Namita: lol

Nicholas: I was thinking, you haven't seen the Shawshank Redemption, we'll have a movie date so you can... I think you'll like it

Namita: yess

Namita: are you a popcorn person ?

Nicholas: sure am!!! home made though

Nicholas: no microwave for this guy

Namita: hehe ... ok i will try the homemade popcorn

Namita: do you just put it in a pot ?

Nicholas: you've never had home made popcorn?

Namita: and close the lid ?

Namita: no never

Nicholas: pop corn maker, hot air popper

Nicholas: wow.. I'll bring my popper w me then too

Namita: im not a huge popcorn person ... but ive had popcorn

Namita: hehehe

Nicholas: sometimes the girls n I will drive to the theater buy pop corn then come home n watch moves

Nicholas: I like pop corn but I don't like the husks in my teeth n gums

Namita: so you go there just to buy popcorn ?

Nicholas: sometimes

Namita: nooo me either

Namita: i can eat a handful of popcorn

Nicholas: I don't need pop corn to watch movies though

Namita: most times i might munch on some candy in theatre or just a drink

Nicholas: I find the concession is a little pricey at the theatre so we sneak snacks in sometimes

Namita: lol .... me too ... i cant believe how much they charge for a little thing ...such a rip off !!!

Nicholas: it is... $12 to $14 to see the movie then gouge you more to have a treat while you watch

Namita: hehehehe ... thats why i stick with the drink ...but even that it like a 3 bucks for a little cup ... !!!

Namita: or 4 i think

Nicholas: yup

Nicholas: *shakes head*

Nicholas: what's your uncles name?

Namita: one day last year i just walked into the theater with my sis jaya .. both of us with a cup of starbucks hot chocolate ....they looked at us but didnt say anything

Namita: my uncles name is vijay ...it is an indian name

Nicholas: really that's surprising coz you're not usually allowed outside food or drink

Nicholas: I suppose it would be an indian name lol

Namita: i guess we gave them the look ...like dont fuck with me man !!! LOL !!

Namita: hehe yes i suppose

Nicholas: lol

Namita: plus most times they are young kids

Nicholas: if it was me I wouldn't have said anything to you, I'd be too stunned

Namita: doing their after school or weekend job

Namita: hehehe

Namita: you would be ushering me in ... without me paying for it

Nicholas: yah as I tell the girls, when you walk w purpose ppl usually leave you alone

Namita: yessss that is sooo true !!

Nicholas: I'd usher you to the back office n do a strip search to see what else you were bringing in

Namita: you have to let ppl know with ur body language ... like dont mess with me

Namita: LMAOOOOOOOOOO

Nicholas: that's right

Namita: OMG ...of course you would I think thats why ppl don't mess w me

Nicholas: if they only knew lol

Namita: good ...and thats the way it should be

Nicholas: yup

Namita: i remember ...at work ...one time i patient told me to fuck off

Namita: that usually makes my blood boil ... to hear it from a patient

Nicholas: also when you carry urself w confidence ppl listen to you when you have something to say

Nicholas: wow form a patient very uncool

Namita: i just told him ... "not now honey" and that kinda shut him up

Nicholas: lmaof thats funny

Namita: Nicholas ... that is not the worse thing ive heard

Namita: being a nurse is not as glamorous as it is made out to be

Nicholas: unreal when you're trying to care for them

Namita: hehehe glad i could make you laugh

Namita: i just tie them down tighter

Nicholas: I'm sure it's not

Namita: and if they kick ... then the feet are tied down too

Namita: just before i left work ... a week ago

Namita: a nurse got kicked in the head 5 times

Namita: her lip was swollen all night

Nicholas: I know when I was in hospital I had a male nurse n I needed suppository pain killers so lets just say that he n I got to know each other better than we both would have liked. though I'm sure he didn't like it any more than I did

Namita: she wasnt ok ... had a headache all nite ... but still worked her entire shift

Nicholas: in the head!!! my god!

Namita: ohhhh thats sooo uncomfortable im sure

Nicholas: damn she may have had a concussion?

Nicholas: it was

Nicholas: I try not to think about it lol

Namita: yessss she was hit quite hard !!

Nicholas: all part of the hospital experience

Namita: one side of her face was bruised !!

Nicholas: geeze poor woman

Namita: it looked like someone had totally beat her up ... we called security and had to hold him down till we could chemically sedate him

Nicholas: damn!

Namita: ive been hit a couple times too

Namita: but that was long while back

Nicholas: awe poor thing... I don't like hearing that my sweet

Namita: i was slapped across the face

Namita: hehe

Namita: im ok now

Nicholas: okay good

Namita: and ive been kicked in the tummy

Namita: not good either time

Nicholas: its like these ppl don't realize you're there to help them

Nicholas: gggrrrrr not on that cute tummy of urs

Namita: well the sad part is they know perfectly well what is going on

Namita: they knew what happening ...and they have intention to harm

Nicholas: n you can't do anything to harm them... as much as you'd like in those cases

Namita: ive been cornered by a patient with a knife demanding a dose of morphine .... this patient was a crack head too ...this was early on in my career

Nicholas: holly sh**!

Namita: no we cant harm them ...as much as i like to sock it to them

Nicholas: what did you do when the knife came out?

Namita: in that scenario i had to talk the person out of it... i remember he got out of his bed and came at me with a knife and good thing i could back into the hallway into my coworkers view but it take a while to even get their attention too

Nicholas: wow

Nicholas: welcome to the wild world of dwntwn nursing

Namita: but he kept advancing on to me knife held up to stab and one of the male coworkers walked by and i told him to go and call security

Namita: when they came those idiots were too afraid to approach him

Nicholas: how did he get the knife in there in the first place?

Nicholas: oooohhh geeze pussies

Namita: i was soooo mad cuz im the only female to 5 guys on the opposite side

Nicholas: duh what do they think they're suppose to do

Nicholas: idiots all of them

Namita: this crackhead went out to get some drugs ... so probably got it from another crackhead

Namita: my heart was thumping like crazyyyy

Namita: and i told myself to calm down and think ... what i should do next

Nicholas: I bet but no one pats them dwn when they come in

Namita: well one reason they stalled was cuz this crackhead was butt naked and comin at me

Namita: nooo no one pats them down

Nicholas: oh geeze but still... no punn intended lol

Namita: hehe

Namita: so finally i bargained with him

Nicholas: hmmm wonder where he hid the knife if he was naked but on the other hand I don't want to know lol

Namita: told him if he puts the knife down then i will promise to give him his morphine

Namita: HAHha

Nicholas: and did he

Namita: it did take awhile to convince him

Namita: i mean it wasnt like he wasnt getting morphine ....i was giving it to him every hour

Namita: down his IV

Namita: which has an immediate effect

Nicholas: yah but you just want to tell him what he wants to hear to defuse the situation

Namita: yeah i dealt with a lot of crazies

Namita: yesss exactly

Nicholas: you're a strong woman

Namita: although i dont know why it took a lot of convincing

Namita: meantime the dumb idiots security just stood there

Namita: i was sooo mad at them

Nicholas: oh god fire the lot of them I say

Nicholas: not the type of security ppl you want around

Namita: told them it is quite ok they can go deal with more serious issues around the hospital cuz knives are not a big deal

Namita: well come to think of it

Nicholas: now Tony on the other hand would have had him on the ground n subdued in seconds

Namita: another time a crackhead woman ... in the middle of the nite goes berserk on us

Nicholas: geeze just out of the blue?

Namita: this is a few yrs ago too

Namita: and again she wants her drugs

Namita: and she start ripping her IV out .. blood everywhere

Nicholas: oh god biohazard!!!

Namita: the nurse with her is brand new a rookie

Namita: and so being the charge nurse that nite i go over to subdue her with words and talk her out of her craziness

Namita: i call security ...they tell me they wont be there for another 10 mins

Namita: OMFG anything could happen in 10 mins

Nicholas: oh my god!! they need a new security company coz these guys are useless

Namita: so next thing i know ... she flings her IV pole at me ... and it comes barreling down towards me ... and hits my leg

Namita: i was fuming and in soooo much pain !!!!!!!!

Namita: no sign of security

Nicholas: unreal!

Namita: the reason they are such dumbass ...is cuz they are privatized a few years ago

Nicholas: ah so they hire any old hump

Namita: when we had our own hospital security ... they were really good and u could rely on them

Nicholas: "no experience necessary"

Namita: yessssssssss ever since gordon campbell started privatizing support staff in the hospital

Nicholas: *shakes head*

Namita: yesss just off the street ppl

Nicholas: that's really sad

Namita: most of the security ppl are thin scrawny asians ... no offense ... but their tool belt is heavier than themselves

Nicholas: none taken

Namita: how are they supposed to help me

Namita: hehehe

Nicholas: you need big burley guys

Namita: yesssssssssss

Nicholas: no kidding

Nicholas: do you get less of those situations now that ur in ICU?

Namita: if you look at them ...you would be shaking ur head

Nicholas: I can picture them

Namita: in icu ...we do see violence still

Nicholas: n i am shaking my head

Namita: patients fighting us

Nicholas: omg

Namita: just in september ... i was treating a burn victim ... and he went berserk on me

Nicholas: when I think icu I think everyone is asleep, I know I was

Namita: and kicked my coworker ... and nearly got me

Nicholas: damn!

Namita: we called the team over the speaker system

Namita: and 10 ppl came running

Nicholas: good old security to the rescue?!

Namita: it took all of us to get this patient down for the count

Nicholas: wow!

Namita: no we skip the security in icu for patients

Nicholas: ah

Namita: we do see violence from families too

Nicholas: they're not much help from what I hear lol

Nicholas: omg!

Namita: sometimes they dont like to hear that their family member is dying

Namita: and they go berserk too

Nicholas: I don't think that way so I can't understand how others do

Nicholas: ohhh I see but still

Namita: a couple of months ago a patients son decided he was going to throw a chair at a nurse

Nicholas: jesus!

Namita: and she was pregnant too !!!!!!!!!!!

Nicholas: OMG!!

Nicholas: what an idiot

Namita: that would have been a disaster !!!

Nicholas: no kidding

Namita: we have a zero tolerance policy in our hospital

Namita: so we can press charges

Nicholas: so did you get to stun him? now that would be fun

Nicholas: nice

Namita: against family members

Nicholas: did he throw it?

Namita: he did ... it missed her !!!

Nicholas: god! unreal

Namita: we called security right away and our docs were on top of him too

Nicholas: good

Namita: she was on stress leave for a bit

Nicholas: I bet... she could have lost the baby!

Namita: i remember hearing the crash

Namita: yesss she very well could have !!!

Nicholas: wow unbelievable

Namita: ppl on the streets dont know what we have to deal with ...till you spend a day with us

Nicholas: no kidding

Namita: and it is not just in icu ...it could be anywhere in the hospital

Nicholas: *shakes head*

Namita: but i still love my job ... we do see the other side of it too

Nicholas: you're a brave strong woman Namita

Namita: oh thanks nicholas !

Nicholas: yah I bet the other side makes it worth it

Nicholas: mental note; brave n strong... you know you're really racking up the points w me

Namita: it is nice to hear words of thanks ... or even a thumbs up from a patient

Namita: hehehe ohhhh myyy !!!

Nicholas: I know I was thankful for the main nurse I had... it's funny coz I thought we were going to but heads at first but she turned out to be really great

Nicholas: east indian woman too

Nicholas: go figure

Namita: hehe ... sometimes it feels that way that ur butting heads

Namita: wow cool !

Nicholas: it's always nice to know that you're appreciated

Namita: sometimes i feel like im butting heads with families

Namita: too

Namita: and it looks like im not making any progress

Nicholas: yah, you're a care giver but also a messenger too

Namita: so i usually go away ... take a deep breath ... and think how else can i approach this ... i really have to think where they are coming form

Nicholas: n if they don't like or want to hear what you have to say then it can get difficult

Namita: and get down to their level and i never get short with them nor dismissive

Namita: i always try to give them the impression that they can approach me with anything

Nicholas: patient, thought full, works well under pressure n up go the points

Namita: give them opportunities to ask questions ... address their comcerns

Namita: concerns*

Namita: hehe

Namita: are you adding more points now ?

Nicholas: good communicator, just as you said.. I love that

Nicholas: you are I'm just taking them in lol

Nicholas: yes ... I'm listening too so pls go on

Namita: hehe ... yess i do work well under pressure ... usually im calm, cool and collected ... someone could be in cardiac arrest .. and i tend to work quite calmly

Nicholas: I do too

Nicholas: when I took my OFA1 last year the woman I was partnered w asked if I'd done this before

Namita: i think i am good at diffusing bad situations ...and i think i am good at conflict resolution as well

Namita: good for you NIcholas !!!

Nicholas: she noticed how I worked under pressure n how thorough I was

Namita: that is a great quality !!

Nicholas: me too!

Nicholas: I always try to see all side to every situation

Nicholas: usually ppl are saying the same thing just w diff words but they can't see what the other is saying

Namita: i dont like confrontations ... but rather i like to resolve things in a timely and calm manner

Namita: yesss sooo true !!!

Nicholas: me too! we said that before

Nicholas: I find a lot of ppl don't have good ppl skills

Namita: although with the crackheads sometimes ... you just have to get down to their level

Nicholas: ture

Namita: ohhh god ... we study ppl skills as a nurse

Nicholas: I watch for them everywhere I go

Namita: their nonverbal and verbal cues

Nicholas: I should have studied sociology

Nicholas: I love reading body language

Namita: basically we have to have a sixth sense

Namita: lol

Nicholas: I have one of those too

Namita: i did do sociology ... it is quite interesting course to do

Nicholas: I bet

Namita: yayyyyy good !

Namita: meaning ur 6th sense

Nicholas: I love watching ppl interact w each other

Namita: yesss !!

Nicholas: we'll be able to be in the same room n not say a word to each other but know what we're thinking or wanting

Namita: hehee ... yesss ... i will see if you could read my mind !!

Nicholas: I think you'll be pleasantly surprised

Namita: hehehe

Nicholas: give us some time n there will be no stopping us lol

Namita: hehe .... we wont even have to say a word to each other ...things would just happen !!!

Nicholas: yesss!!

Namita: we would just know the looks

Nicholas: yup

Namita: i might give you the look ... and lift an eyebrow .... and you would know wha tit would mean

Namita: omg !!!!!!!!!!!

Nicholas: lol there's that tit again!!

Nicholas: subliminal message?

Namita: i mean .... what it would

Namita: hahahhahahhaaa

Nicholas: lol

Namita: that was a total typo

Nicholas: yah yah sure lol

Namita: hahahhaha

Nicholas: you've done that before

Namita: im lying on my side and typing ... so my fingers slipped

Namita: hehehehehhehe

Namita: ok ? SO there !!!

Nicholas: lol

Nicholas: I read that as "you're lying on MY side n typing w your fingers"

Nicholas: thinking u were imagining lying in bed w me

Namita: yes of course you did !!! LOL

Namita: spooning ?

Nicholas: mmm

Namita: would you like that ?

Nicholas: just being w you

Nicholas: YESSSSS!

Nicholas: OMFG YES!

Namita: hehehee

Namita: which do you prefer ...me behind you or you behind me ?

Nicholas: I can hardly stand it sometimes

Namita: lol

Namita: hehehe

Nicholas: you in front of me

Namita: think nicolas think

Nicholas: that way I can wrap my arms around you n not let go

Namita: ahhhh ok

Namita: pull me in closer to you

Namita: covered with a heavy blanket

Nicholas: was imagining both n couldn't concentrate

Namita: lol

Nicholas: yes so our bodies are touching as much as possible

Namita: mmmmmmmmmm

Namita: yesssssss

Nicholas: this is probably the hardest thing I've had to do

Namita: whatttt ?

Nicholas: waiting to see you!!

Namita: ohhhhh ...hehe

Namita: i thought you were going to say something else

Nicholas: n all the naughty talk is sooo hot but such torture

Nicholas: I did

Namita: hehehe ... giggling here

Nicholas: the waiting to see you is torture

Namita: are you a warm person ... sorry random ... or do you like to be cool

Namita: when in bed

Nicholas: I have to keep it under control so I don't loose my mind

Namita: hehehe

Nicholas: I like warm in bed

Nicholas: can always fling the covers open if things get too hot.. so to speak

Nicholas: which do yo like?

Namita: lol

Namita: i like to be covered .... but most times i like it a little cooler

Namita: i try to keep my window open a crack

Nicholas: oh yah, even in the winter?

Nicholas: I like the room a little cool but warm under the covers I need to be warm

Namita: yes most times .... just a crack ...if its getting too chilly then i will close it

Nicholas: hmmm

Namita: hehehe

Namita: it that a good hmmm or bad hmmmm ?

Namita: is that ... i mean

Nicholas: never a bad hmm when it comes to you

Nicholas: always a good hmm

Namita: lol ... good answer !

Nicholas: it's hard to convey my sounds over this thing

Nicholas: well its true

Namita: yes thats true ... i agree

Nicholas: there is so much to learn from each other when we're together... as in our mannerisms n gestures

Nicholas: how we say things w our bodies

Namita: yesss we were talking about that just that the other day

Nicholas: yes we were

Namita: yess true

Namita: i dont think i have any bad mannerisms

Nicholas: I want to learn everything your body has to tell me

Namita: i dont bit my nails

Namita: i may play with my hair once in a while

Nicholas: I wouldn't think you would

Namita: bat my eyelashes sometimes

Nicholas: playing w your hair isn't bad... it's quite attractive actually

Namita: make my eyes grow big ...so i get what i want ...hehehe

Nicholas: mmmm

Namita: really?

Nicholas: yes

Nicholas: body language .... play w hair = I hope you see me

Namita: hehehehe

Namita: i usually do it while watching tv or something ...or if im deep in thought

Nicholas: mental note

Namita: heheheh

Nicholas: so any idea what day you're coming back?

Namita: it was a great habit of mine when i was studying

Nicholas: oh yah did it help you retain info?

Namita: right now im thinking around tuesdayish

Namita: of course not

Nicholas: tuesday wow, okay then

Namita: is that a stretch for you ? soooo sorry

Nicholas: its okay, I'll make it lol

Namita: please dont spontaneously combust ....hehe

Nicholas: it is a stretch but as I said take care of what you need to

Nicholas: lol

Nicholas: I'll keep it together

Namita: hehe

Nicholas: and I've waited 39 years what's another few days

Namita: aweee thanks nicholas

Nicholas: what's the weather like dwn there?

Nicholas: anytime. as I said before I think you're worth the wait

Namita: its been cloudy ... a few showers here and there

Nicholas: really? though i guess thats typical for that area

Namita: yesss kinda like us ... home away from home

Nicholas: and really there's nothing I can do to speed up when ur back so I'll just ride it out

Nicholas: what do you get up to when ur not at the hospital?

Namita: what do mean ? didnt understand ur question

Namita: you mean in free time ?

Nicholas: yes

Nicholas: though I'm sure ur at the hospital most of the time

Nicholas: that takes quite a toll on you emotionally being at the hospital n there's nothing you can do but wait

Namita: i like browsing thru places ... ..exploring ... going for a car ride...it is harder to do things with this weather ...but like hanging around with friends too

Nicholas: I remember when the ex's grandfather was in hospital we circled the wagons n waited for 3 or 4 days. was really hard

Namita: well i try to keep my work life and personal life balanced .... that why i like going on little road trips ..even if its just to squamish .... to clear my head ...and appreciate whats around me

Nicholas: I like the sound of that

Namita: i love browsing to unique stores ... looking at antiques ... or unsual furniture

Namita: i just found this place a couple months ago ... it has unique old indian carved furniture

Nicholas: there's a cool beach out in Horseshoe Bay I'll take you to one day

Namita: like tables and cabinets

Nicholas: cool

Namita: some were like a 100 yrs old

Nicholas: wow!

Namita: some were used as dowry furniture

Namita: so it was my first time that i ventured and let alone even knew something like that existed

Namita: it was soooo cool

Nicholas: neat

Namita: i fell in love with this one cabinet

Namita: it was priced at 1200 dollars

Namita: well the owner came down on the price

Nicholas: hollycrap !

Nicholas: to what a 1000?

Namita: it would look so cool as a buffet table in the dining room ...i thought

Namita: hehehe

Nicholas: how big is it? what does it look like

Namita: now the original price was 1700

Nicholas: oh geeze

Namita: he came down to 1200

Namita: i told him i will think aboutit

Nicholas: thats quite the dowery

Namita: omgggg there i go again !!!

Namita: hahhahaa

Nicholas: go again?

Namita: yessss it is quite dowry

Nicholas: go where lol

Namita: the tit 6 sentences ago

Nicholas: oh damn I missed the tit

Namita: lol

Namita: anyways it was my first time even venturing so ... i held off

Nicholas: good for you

Namita: but they did have some cool pieces

Nicholas: wont power another good quality

Namita: hehe thanks

Namita: i like looking at decorating ideas

Nicholas: I like wandering n looking around

Namita: now that the car is paid off ...i can think about other things

Namita: yes me too ... i love wandering around

Namita: and finding things

Nicholas: Steveston is a cool place to wander

Namita: yesss true

Nicholas: I haven't been there in years

Namita: i venture out there every once in a while

Nicholas: cool

Namita: for no reason

Namita: i love getting in the car ...having no idea where id end up

Nicholas: I usually like to go on sunny days but now that i've met you the weather doesn't matter to me as much

Nicholas: me too! love to drive

Namita: i discovered a few months back Whole Foods in vancouver

Namita: it is a organic store

Nicholas: oh yah... yes it is

Namita: have you been ?

Nicholas: my sis n her gf are into organic

Nicholas: nope

Namita: hehhehe

Namita: are you ?

Nicholas: not really

Nicholas: I eat healthy though

Namita: yeah me either ... i am not a freak about it

Namita: geeeez

Namita: but i loveee that store

Nicholas: I think our bodies need a little of the reg food so our immune systems can fight off bad stuff

Namita: the produce is pretty expensive sometimes

Namita: yesss

Nicholas: it usually is for organic

Nicholas: I find ppl that are freaks about everything needing to be organic are usually sick more often

Namita: last time i was there ... i bought a papaya ... which i loveeeeeeeeee .. and when i got to the till ... with my other stuff .... they charged me 23.00 dollars just for that

Namita: lol ...so true !!!!

Namita: i made them take it out of my bill !!

Nicholas: $23 for one piece of fruit!

Nicholas: that's crazy

Namita: yessssss .... i was like .."are you fucking kidding me " !!!!

Namita: it was not worth it ... i could have gone to Kim's market and bought 4 of them for that price

Nicholas: thats ridiculous

Namita: lol

Nicholas: yes yes

Namita: what ur fav fruit ?

Nicholas: fav friut? hmm...

Namita: hehe

Nicholas: I like so many but my system doesn't like too much of it

Namita: dont say a peach

Nicholas: when they're in season blueberries or cherries

Namita: i think im allergic to cherries ....cuz my mouth gets itchy

Namita: not a good sing

Namita: sign

Nicholas: some of the exotic fruits pineapple papaya

Namita: i used to loveeee cherries

Nicholas: yes that's an oral allergy...when your mouth gets itchy

Namita: hehe thanks !!

Nicholas: I get that itch when I eat too much pineapple

Namita: really ?

Nicholas: yup

She doesn't know when your mouth gets itchy from certain foods that it's an oral allergy?

Namita: i loveeee pineapples

Nicholas: why couldn't I say peaches?

Namita: esp with a dash of salt ... and cooled down in the fridge

Nicholas: salt really hmmm never thought of that before

Namita: ahem never mind ... im not going there

Namita: every guy says that

Nicholas: oh

Nicholas: I don't eat a lot of fruit. I have a sensitive system

Nicholas: lol

Namita: yes try it with a little salt ...but what you do ...when youve cut the pinapple then add a little salt and put it back in the fridge ...to marinate ...it is sooooo goood !!!!!!!!!!

Nicholas: I love it but I have to be careful w it

Namita: hehehe ...i think you know

Namita: ur pulling my leg

Namita: lol

Namita: or no?

Nicholas: pulling ur leg? I'm lost

Namita: i meant eating a peach ... guys always say that ... to a woman

Nicholas: oh

Namita: you dont know what it means ?

Nicholas: there's a meaning behind eating peaches?

Namita: yesss .... when guys say i could eat a peach for hours they usually mean ... they could go down on a woman for hours

Nicholas: ooohhh never heard that before

Namita: dont worr i learned that too in the last couple of yrs

Nicholas: I just say I could go dwn on you for hrs

Namita: hehehe good

Namita: would you ?

Nicholas: I would... esp knowing you enjoy it and you shave dwn there... that's very hot

Namita: yeah i dont know why it cant be just said ... rather than using terms

Namita: turns you on ?

Nicholas: makin' me smile here

Nicholas: oh very much soooo!!

Namita: i would totally loveeee it too

Nicholas: I hope you don't find me prickly

Namita: on ur face ?

Namita: no it is a total turn on for me

Nicholas: cool

Namita: on ur face you mean ? or down there ?

Nicholas: I'm talking about my entire body lol

Nicholas: lets just say the longest hair on my body are my eyelashes n eyebrows lol

Namita: you shave all over ?

Nicholas: yes I told you that before lol

Namita: hehehe ... maybe i forgot

Namita: tell me again

Nicholas: I just did lol... I use clippers on my body n a blade on my head n face

Namita: ahhh ok

Nicholas: I use to use a blade on my body but it grows back so soon that it's hardly worth the effort so I just use clippers n keep it really short

Namita: otherwise ... excluding ur face and head ... do you find the hair is longer on ur body ?

Nicholas: I'm not a hairy guy to begin w i just like no hair

Namita: ok got it

Nicholas: it's earier to get clean n it's cooler in the summer

Namita: im sure it is

Nicholas: I also think that if guys want their woman to be shaved then they should reciprocate

Namita: yes esp down there

Namita: i dont anywhere else

Nicholas: have you ever been w a guy before who shaved his body?

Nicholas: not ur arm pits? or ur back? lol

Namita: but i hate that we have to go to all the trouble of looking good and guys dont reciprocate

Nicholas: you tried to put me on about shaving before

Namita: no i havent ... not the entire body

Nicholas: so I'm not sure I believe you now

Namita: huh ? im lost

Nicholas: you said you don't shave anywhere else but dwn there n I asked about ur arm pits

Namita: ohhh .... yesss i shave my armpits ... omg ... lol ... yes of course i do

Namita: and my legs too

Nicholas: lol

Namita: i cant not do it

Nicholas: too funny

Namita: i wont feel comfortable otherwise

Namita: legs ... all the way up

Nicholas: mmmm I like the sound of that!!

Namita: lol

Namita: maybe you can do it for me ?

Nicholas: Oh Yes I could

Nicholas: I'm pretty handy w a razor

Namita: would you enjoy that ?

Nicholas: sure would

Nicholas: spending time w you like that-priceless

Nicholas: I take it you'd like that?

Namita: it is quite intimate i think

Namita: yesss of course ... never done it before ... but it is an idea

Nicholas: that it is

Namita: mmmmmmmmm yesssssss

Nicholas: working my way up your legs

Namita: then you creep up further

Namita: hehe

Nicholas: n sweet kisses when I'm done

Namita: mmm nice

Namita: what about shaving me between my legs ? Would you ?

Nicholas: mmm mmm mmm so not helping the hornyness over here

Nicholas: HELL YAH!!

Namita: wowwwww it turns you on ???

Nicholas: yes of course!

Namita: me laying on my back ... naked

Namita: never had someone else shave me before

Namita: yesss i would

Nicholas: well it sounds like we've got a few firsts

Namita: maybe we are in the shower together

Namita: and you decide to shave me

Nicholas: mmm there we go agin in the shower hehe

Namita: hehehe

Nicholas: do you have a stand up shower or one w a tub?

Namita: i have both

Nicholas: cool!!

Namita: hehehe

Namita: what about you ?

Nicholas: just a little standup

Nicholas: I bump my elbows all the time

Namita: ahhh little is good

Namita: ohhh sorry about that

Nicholas: one of the things I don't like about here but as I said before it's my transition place

Nicholas: it would be very up close n personal

Namita: hehe ohhh yesss

Namita: my tub is separate from the shower ... i have 2 bathrooms

Nicholas: we'd just be able to shower n play though, not enf room to shave you

Namita: hehe ohhh damn

Nicholas: i figured you had 2

Nicholas: we'll do the shaving at ur place

Namita: k

Namita: you dont like a small trim dowm the middle

Nicholas: we still need to get this Gelato Rocky Point date out of the way first

Nicholas: a little landing strip is cool

Namita: it wouldnt get in ur way ?

Nicholas: nope

Namita: i dont mind either

Nicholas: the good bits are below the landing strip anyway

Namita: mmmmmm really ??? ur getting me hot here

Nicholas: it's ur body n whatever you feel comfortable doing is what I'll respect

Nicholas: honestly I've been hot form our first conversation Namita

Namita: aweee thanks nicholas

Namita: soooo sweet

Namita: hehehe

Nicholas: there hasn't been a day go by that I haven't thought of you at least a billion times

Namita: aweeee soo sweet

Namita: can i ask u a personal question

Nicholas: anything

Namita: have you thought about me and played with urself ?

Nicholas: yup

Namita: when we're not talking

Nicholas: mind reader

Nicholas: was just gonna say that

Nicholas: yes a few times

Namita: omg seriously ?

Nicholas: have you?

Nicholas: yes!

Namita: i mean the mind reader part

Nicholas: ah

Namita: yes i have

Nicholas: I don't usually take matters into my own hands but when I think of you n after we've talked I can't help it

Nicholas: you have... cool... now that makes me smile

Namita: so even after we logged off you have ?

Nicholas: yup

Namita: me too

Nicholas: nice

Nicholas: smiling agin

Namita: one time i remember telling you i didnt sleep for another hour after we logged off

Namita: remember ?

Nicholas: yes

Namita: hehe

Nicholas: OMG that's so hot.. thank you for telling me

Namita: hehe .... i thought you should know

Nicholas: I've imagined you doing that after we've said our gnights

Nicholas: I'm so glad, both that you do n that u told me

Namita: well i have !! a few times actually

Nicholas: that's a huge turn on

Nicholas: mmm

Nicholas: I have too

Namita: would it turn you on ... if i was right beside you and played with myself ... and you watch me for a bit

Nicholas: OOOHHH MMMYYY GGGOOODDD it would!!

Nicholas: ur killing me here

Namita: lol

Namita: and maybe ur trying to read in bed

Namita: but im distracting you

Namita: then you decide to watch me

Nicholas: hell no I couldn't read while ur doing that. I couldn't even pretend to read w u doing that

Namita: lmao

Nicholas: decide? there's no decision I'm in!

Namita: hahhaha

Namita: hmm maybe you can hold my one leg apart ... so you can watch me

Namita: sorry im getting really kinky here

Nicholas: mmmm

Nicholas: quite alright

Namita: mmmmm would be nice

Nicholas: that it would!

Namita: to watch you watch me

Namita: im laying on my back ... you on ur side watching

Nicholas: I'd be ready to pounce at any second

Namita: holding my leg .... slightly bent at the knee

Nicholas: mmmhmmm

Nicholas: are you flexible?

Namita: watching me playing with my clit .... making it super swollen

Namita: yes im flexible

Nicholas: cool

Namita: what did you have in mind ...hehe

Nicholas: I can almost feel that swollen clit of yours

Namita: then i grab ur hand ... and run ur fingers over it too

Nicholas: you on ur back me holding both ur legs up n together 90 degrees to ur body n make love to you that way

Namita: OMMGGG

Namita: Yessssssssssss

Nicholas: I sooo want to feel it

Namita: the penetration would be deep!!!!

Nicholas: yes it would

Namita: would loveee to feel your entire cock inside of me like that

Namita: feeling ur balls too

Nicholas: what you need to do is get ur sexy little ass back here so we can make all these words a reality

Namita: my legs eventually thrown over ur shoulders

Namita: mmmmm yessss

Nicholas: I would be, excuse the expression, balls deep inside you

Namita: oooooooooooooh god Nicholas !!!!!!!!!!!

Nicholas: yes ur legs bent at the knee over my shoulders n me sliding in n out of you making you moan w ecstasy

Namita: yesssssssssss

Namita: ohhhhhhhhhhh god !

Nicholas: I press myself so deep inside you n roll my hips to touch all those spots only I can reach

Namita: nicholas im gushing a little

Nicholas: cool

Namita: that took me over the edge

Nicholas: n it'll all be a reality one day just you wait

Nicholas: I'm glad I could help

Namita: i am sooooooooooooo turned on right now

Nicholas: u n me both Namita you n me both

Namita: im sooo wet

Nicholas: glad I could help make you wet.... though ur all wet but don't have my hard cock to put it there

Namita: mmmmmmmm

Namita: ohhh nicholas

Nicholas: I could push it in there n try to stop the gushing but I think it would just make up wetter

Nicholas: you*

Namita: nooo you can ... but it will be contained behind ur cock

Nicholas: then it would spill out over my hard cock n get all over us

Namita: yess ...would u enjoy that ?

Nicholas: yes!!

Nicholas: damn!

Namita: the warm hot clear liquid ... engulfing ur cock

Namita: while still inside of me

Nicholas: gliding in n out of you feeling and hearing how wet I've made you mmm mmm mmm

Nicholas: mmmhhhmmm

Namita: mmmmmmmmm yessssssss

Nicholas: tell me ur playing w urself

Namita: then you turn us on our sides

Namita: omg yes i am

Nicholas: good

Namita: are you ?

Nicholas: yup

Nicholas: i spoon you from behind

Namita: yesssssss

Nicholas: n slide myself into you form there

Nicholas: holding u close

Namita: ohhh yesss

Nicholas: pressing myself into u

Namita: and then i look back at you ... to kiss you

Namita: so we are joined together in 2 ways

Nicholas: I have one hand under ur head the other reaching around ur front massaging ur clit

Namita: OMGGG Nicholas

Namita: yessss

Nicholas: I've got u locked onto me

Namita: ommg

Namita: i start to writhe underneath you

Namita: soooo erotically

Namita: making you wannna get deep inside of me even more

Namita: im pleading with you

Namita: calling out ur name

Nicholas: I push myself deep inside you

Namita: im grabbing the sheets in front of me

Namita: mmmmmmmmmmmmm

Nicholas: I'm riding you faster n faster

Namita: ohhhhhhhhhhhhh baby

Nicholas: I can feel ur hot wet pussy screaming to cum

Namita: yesssssssssssssssssssss pleaseeeeeeeee

Nicholas: you tense gripping my hard cock

Namita: yesss ... you feel me tighten around ur cock

Nicholas: squeezing it trying to milk it

Namita: not wanting to let go

Namita: hmmmmmmmm yesssssss

Namita: yessss every drop !!

Nicholas: you want desperately for it to explode inside you

Namita: ohhhh yesssssssssssss

Nicholas: soooo deep

Namita: omggggggggggggg

Namita: i can feel you exploding

Namita: hear ur moans

Nicholas: i can feel u tense n contract

Namita: mmmmmmmmmmmmmmmmmmm

Nicholas: oh my god Namita

Nicholas: wow

Namita: baby pleaseeeeeeeeeeee

Nicholas: omg!!!!

Namita: nicoholas pleaseeee

Nicholas: my god that was intense

Namita: i am soooooo squirting here

Nicholas: can only imagine the magic that will happen when we do this for real... my god!!

Nicholas: just ride it out baby

Namita: omg im still going

Namita: i want to scream

Namita: i cant

Nicholas: best not to

Namita: no

Namita: but what if i did when we're together

Namita: would u mind

Nicholas: nope

Nicholas: I can never remember how to spell the ppl that live next door

Namita: spell what ?

Namita: neighbors?

Nicholas: the word for ppl who live next door

Nicholas: YES!!

Namita: hehhehehe

Nicholas: my god duh

Namita: e before the i

Nicholas: n my spell check doesn't give me any suggestions

Namita: so would u mind if i screamed

Namita: hehe

Nicholas: nah

Nicholas: whatever pleases you

Namita: and more importantly did u cum sweetheart ?

Nicholas: as long as the neighbors don't come running lol

Nicholas: oh my did I ever

Namita: hehehe ... they will think im getting murdered or something

Nicholas: that's the first time you called me sweetheart.... made me smile

Nicholas: oh geeze I hope not lol

Namita: if i licked it off ur tummy would u mind

Nicholas: nope

Nicholas: had a kleenex handy tho

Namita: ohhhhh nicholas ur welcome

Nicholas: you are quite the little vixen... love it!!

Namita: hehe ... i can be bad

Namita: but good for ur health

Nicholas: yes u can hehe

Nicholas: very

Namita: hehehe

Nicholas: my god it's 5 am thats a new record!

Namita: omg yesss it is !!!!!!!!

Nicholas: didn't even notice

Namita: neither did i

Nicholas: time evaporates when I'm w you

Namita: yes it sure goes away ...we just chew it up

Nicholas: yes we do

Namita: but i loveeeee chatting with u

Nicholas: and me w you my dear!!

Namita: enjoy every min of it

Nicholas: yes yes

Namita: aweeee

Namita: thanks

Nicholas: it's the only time I get

Nicholas: you are quite welcome, anytime

Namita: yesss true

Nicholas: there are a lot of hrs in the day I have to wait for this

Nicholas: makes for a long day

Namita: hehehe

Namita: i do look forward to it too

Nicholas: as do I

Namita: lmao

Namita: yesss our computers thank us too

Nicholas: I think about you n wonder what you're doing at that very moment

Nicholas: lol yes they do

Nicholas: and hope that you're safe and well

Namita: hmmmm i look at the time and think the same thing ... like ...ohhh he must be on his way to work

Namita: or he must be working

Nicholas: *smiling*

Namita: hehe

Namita: im sure ive tired you out tonight

Nicholas: sokay we're still making up for lost time

Nicholas: if I was working days I'd be getting up in a half hr

Namita: hahhahaha ...never thought of it that way .... i guess so

Nicholas: sooooo glad I work afternoons

Namita: omg ...and me too ...come to think of it

Nicholas: one day we'll catch up

Namita: yes we will

Namita: and go all nite and all day

Nicholas: and we'll still be just a smitten w each other when we are caught up

Nicholas: yes

Namita: hehehe yesss

Nicholas: I am so glad I have you in my life Namita

Namita: aweeee thanks nicholas ... nive to hear

Namita: nice i meant

Nicholas: lol

Namita: hehehe

Namita: ur spelling is suffering

Nicholas: yup

Namita: again

Namita: ohh god im falling alseep on you

Nicholas: I'm startng to zone out

Namita: hehe

Nicholas: lol

Namita: me too

Namita: call it a nite ?

Nicholas: we should call it a night or rather a morning

Nicholas: mind reader

Namita: LOL

Nicholas: too funny

Nicholas: so tmw again?

Namita: we cant spell but at least we can read minds

Nicholas: that we can

Nicholas: okay then

Namita:

Nicholas: until tmw

Namita: goodnite nicholas

Namita: have a good day

Nicholas: sleep well. I hope you're able to get enf sleep

Nicholas: you 2. good luck at the hospital

Namita: hehe ... i will try

Namita: thankyou

Namita: sweet dreams

Nicholas: gnight my sweet

End Time: 5:14 AM

Chapter 17 October 27

Start Time: 12:38 AM

Namita: hellooo

Nicholas: there she is!!! my favouratist woman in the whole wide world!!

Namita: hehehe... how have you been ?

Namita: i sure hope you had a good sleep

Nicholas: I've been good

Nicholas: and you?

Namita: or enough even

Nicholas: I did

Namita: ive been cat napping here and there

Namita: hehe

Nicholas: woke w a nasty migraine though

Nicholas: ooo that sounds nice

Namita: ohhh im sorry to hear that ...most probably for lack of sleep then

Nicholas: once my T3's kicked in I almost dozed off

Namita: ahhh i see

Nicholas: probly but I shook it off

Nicholas: only had to medicate twice

Namita: that was some record we set last nite

Nicholas: when you deal w them since ur 4 you learn how to treat them

Nicholas: YES it was

Namita: oh yes ...of course ... by then you know what works and what doesnt

Nicholas: looked at the time last night at one point n it was 4 something n the next thing i know its 5

Nicholas: I hit it pretty hard w the T3's

Namita: yes i remember the last time i checked it was around 4 ish ... time just flew by

Nicholas: I try not to over medicate when I get them so I judge how painful it will be n go from there

Namita: yes thats a good idea ... ur probably the best judge of what it is like

Nicholas: well I guess when we're wrapped up in the moment n visualizing our scenario time just disappears

Nicholas: most times I guess wrong but today I guessed right

Namita: hehe ... thats for sure ... man we end about talking about everything and anything

Nicholas: yes we do... I love it!!

Namita: hehehehe

Namita: i was thinking about our last conversation ... the hot and steamy one ...and i felt really hot in the face today ... as in shy ... im sure you are getting a good picture of that

Nicholas: I am

Nicholas: I was thinking about it too

Namita: i cant believe how open we are to each other in that department

Nicholas: does it surprise you? how open you are or both of us?

Nicholas: thats how open I am in the bedroom

Namita: no not really ... i think a lot of times ... things just flow from us ... for me literally ...lol

Nicholas: lol

Nicholas: thought of that a few times today too hehe

Namita: really?? What did you think exactly

Nicholas: hehe how wet I made you... how you've played w urself after we've logged off.... made me smile.... how much I'm looking forward to holding you close n feeling the heat from ur body...

Namita: mmmmmmm yesss

Namita: i would love to see the effect i have on you

Nicholas: inhaling you till I'm intoxicated w ur sent n I have my Namita buzz on

Namita: lol

Nicholas: just u wait honey just you wait

Namita: you might be unconscious then if you do that

Nicholas: I thought of that on the drive home.... how you give my a buzz just from thinking about you

Namita: OOOooOoo must have been a good drive home !!

Namita: hehe

Nicholas: lol it would be worth it though... I'll pace myself

Namita: i heard that there was a plane crash over there

Namita: in richmond?

Namita: sorry random ...hehe

Nicholas: I heard that too but didn't hear anything else

Namita: so you were able to get to work alright ?

Nicholas: I can sooo keep up w random lol not to worry

Nicholas: oh yes

Nicholas: traffic was pretty good actually

Namita: ahhh ... i know my hospital called a code orange ...which is a disaster alert

Namita: ahhhh ok

Nicholas: OH really

Namita: yeah some of the passengers were critical

Nicholas: even though ur hospital is in Van?

Nicholas: I bet

Nicholas: wouldn't they go to the Richmond hospital?

Namita: yes ... richmond hospital is a community hospital .. not a specialized hospital

Namita: they would go there for minor stuff

Nicholas: that's what I thought of after I sent my last

Namita: hmmm glad i was not there otherwise i would have got called in

Nicholas: from home? really?

Namita: dodged that bullet !! Pheww

Namita: yessss you get called while ur at home ... for a disaster alert

Nicholas: wow

Nicholas: so you're pretty much on call 24/7?

Namita: you just drop everything ... and it is mandatory to go in

Namita: yesss

Namita: even if there is an earthquake

Nicholas: wow. has that happened to you before?

Nicholas: so by the time you'd get there they'd still need you?

Namita: hehe .. yesss ... i dont know if you remember a few years ago ... there was this hot air balloon accident out in abbotsford

Nicholas: i do

Namita: i think 2 ppl died ... and 3 ppl jumped off the firey balloon

Namita: and that night i got called in .... i was at a friends party

Nicholas: so when we're making love n you feel the earth move you'll be waiting for the phone call about the earth quake? lol

Namita: and once i got there in my finery ... i have to change into scrubs and worked all nite

Namita: lmao

Namita: yesss

Nicholas: lol

Namita: the other time was in the Stanley cup riots

Nicholas: oh right i remember you telling me about the riot

Nicholas: you were already at work though right?

Nicholas: you get called because ur part of the Code Blue team or does everyone get called in?

Namita: no i wasnt ... i was sick at home .... but got called in anyways

Namita: no everyone gets called in on an orange

Namita: code orange i mean

Nicholas: geeze... so because dwntwn was closed do u show ID to get to the hospital?

Nicholas: oh I see

Nicholas: past the police I mean

Namita: the code blue is when theres a designated nurse at every shift to be the code blue nurse to respond to any cardiac arrest or respiratory arrest within the hospital

Nicholas: ah gotcha

Namita: usually there is an alarm ... followed by an announcement to where in the hospital the code blue is

Namita: yes i have to have my id handy at all times

Namita: a hospital id

Nicholas: cool... so you're pretty important to other ppl too not just me

Namita: hehee ,,, i try to keep a low profile

Namita: when im the code nurse i carry all the important drugs with me at all times with a pager

Nicholas: switching gears... I talked to Tony n he said his cancer has to shrink before they can operate and its shrunk a half mm (millimeter) in a month

Namita: most of the drugs paralytic agents , sedation, and powerful painkillers, drugs to keep the BP (blood pressure) up too

Nicholas: wow

Namita: ohhh wow

Namita: does he have to come down here for treatment ?

Nicholas: he has a tendency to not get all the info out at once

Namita: or is there a cancer clinic there?

Nicholas: nope he gets treatment up there

Nicholas: he's coming dwn tmw.... I'm going to tell him about you... finally... hope you don't mind

Namita: well thats good to hear... if he does get his surgery... where would he have it ?

Namita: oh i dont mind

Namita: is he going to stay with you ?

Nicholas: even though he's my best friend I'm only going to show him one or two of your photos.... none of the special ones

Nicholas: he is. he sleeps on the couch

Namita: yes thank you

Namita: i trust you

Namita: which one will you show him i wonder

Nicholas: I respect you far too much to do other wise

Namita: aweee thank u sooo much for saying that nicholas

Namita: how long have you been friends ?

Nicholas: probably the one in the brown long sleeve shirt and maybe the one where ur sitting on the edge of the table in the black dress... is that okay?

Nicholas: since BCIT in '04

Namita: im thinking which one ... in the second pic ... hold on

Nicholas: ur leaning/sitting against a table sepia color

Namita: the sepia one?

Namita: ahhh ok ... yeah thats fine

Nicholas: okay cool. wanted to make sure ur okay w my choice

Namita: yep im ok with it

Nicholas: I'm the only one that gets to see any of the others

Namita: hehehe... good !

Nicholas: you're far too special to me to flaunt your photos like that

Namita: awee thanks nicholas ... sooo sweet

Nicholas: and as I said I respect you immensely

Namita: when is tony coming again?

Namita: does he fly over ?

Nicholas: tomorrow... he's driving dwn w his parents then probly busing back

Nicholas: sometimes he flies dwn... his dad use to work for Air Canada so he still gets deals on flights though u fly stand by

Namita: ahhh ok ... how long is the drive ?

Nicholas: w his treatments he doesnt like to drive for long periods

Namita: oh well thats good too

Nicholas: it's a 4 hrs drive

Namita: yes he has to be careful ... needs to conserve his energy

Nicholas: he's been wanting me to go up there n visit but I just cant get enf time to go away

Nicholas: yes... I notice a big change in his energy level

Namita: really ?

Nicholas: can you hold on a sec? I need to get my tea.... its Chi tea btw

Nicholas: yes

Namita: yeah i know cancer can take that toll on ppl

Namita: yes i can

Namita: chai tea ?

Nicholas: I'm back

Nicholas: yah Chi it's indian I think

Namita: yayyy

Nicholas: lol

Namita: never heard of chi tea

Namita: but chai tea... yes

Nicholas: hair splitter!!

Nicholas: yes that one lol

Nicholas: brat

Namita: lol

Nicholas: I brew it in milk... I forgot how much i like it

Namita: well i thought maybe you have some special tea or something

Nicholas: w a spoon full of sugar

Namita: mmmmmm

Nicholas: its the only type of tea I'll drink

Namita: does it haVE SPICES in it

Nicholas: it's good even as it turns cold

Nicholas: YES lol

Namita: opps sorry for the caps.... hehe

Namita: i wonder what it has

Nicholas: its the Teatley brand... I think that's how you spell it

Nicholas: sokay

Namita: i can make good chai tea from scratch

Nicholas: the ingredients just say spices n flavor

Namita: yes thats right

Namita: ahhhh ok

Nicholas: I bet you can... I'd love to try yours

Namita: i make it in water ... but finish it off with evaporated milk ... to give it flavor and make it milky

Namita: i add crushed cardamons, or fresh ginger, sometimes cinnamon

Nicholas: cool... I tried making it by the direction, then ended up using more n more milk till I didn't use water anymore

Namita: hehehhe

Nicholas: this one has cinnamon in it too

Namita: ohhh nice

Nicholas: and I don't think there's caffeine in it either coz that makes me nauseous

Namita: yes i dont like caffeine either .... caffeine is not good for migraine sufferers anyways

Nicholas: and I don't want to be drinking caffeine this late

Namita: its one of the triggers i think

Nicholas: is it?

Namita: im sure it is

Nicholas: I guess it depends on the person... diff ppl diff triggers

Nicholas: sounds familiar

Nicholas: chocolate too

Nicholas: or dairy for some

Namita: caffeine is a blood vessel constrictor

Namita: so if you have a headache caffeine is not a good thing

Namita: it will make ur headache worse

Nicholas: really? I know it's a bata blocker or diuretic... prevents the body from absorbing water

Namita: i dont think it is a beta blocker

Namita: and i dont think its a good diuretic either

Nicholas: isn't that what it does to prevent ur body from absorbing water?

Nicholas: a bata blocker I mean

Nicholas: not a good diuretic nope

Namita: hmmm will have to look it up

Nicholas: pls do n get back to me... don't want to be spreading info thats not accurate

Namita: a beta blocker is something that would help you constrict ur blood vessels by blocking ur beta receptors in your body

Nicholas: oh

Namita: caffeine does not work on those receptors ..but can constrict ur vessels in other ways

Nicholas: i thought a bata was the thing that lets ur body do something

Namita: so therefore caffeine is not a considered a beta blocker

Nicholas: hence block the bata n it can't do what it's suppose to

Namita: theres no such thing as bata

Namita: there is such thing as beta blocker

Nicholas: oh hmm then why do they call it a bata blocker?

Namita: i think you heard it wrong

Nicholas: ggggrrr you knew what it meant though yah

Namita: are you on medications that are beta blockers ?

Nicholas: beta not bata duh... stupid spelling again lol

Namita: hehe

Nicholas: you know more about it than I do lol

Namita: hehehe

Namita: you cant win with me in that department

Nicholas: I'm just blabbering I guess... talking out of my a**

Nicholas: don't need to

Namita: we as nurses have done extensive pharmacology in school

Namita: heheheh

Nicholas: I was more inquisitive about it was all lol

Nicholas: and I should hope so

Namita: im just correcting you

Nicholas: okay

Namita: hehe

Namita: i hope u dont mind

Nicholas: that's what I was looking for the right info thank you

Nicholas: not at all my dear

Namita: ur welcome ... anytime

Nicholas: as I say I don't want to be talking about something that's wrong

Nicholas: n when I said bata I meant beta but it still didn't matter coz I was wrong either way lol

Namita: hehehe .. im sure there would be many instances were ur going to enlighten me as well

Namita: lol

Nicholas: meh

Nicholas: lol

Nicholas: anywho... how's ur uncle?

Namita: do you take BB (beta blockers)?

Nicholas: don't know are my thinners a beta blocker?

Namita: he is doing the same... it is guarded though ... i think in a few days they will meet with us

Namita: the docs i mean

Namita: no ur thinners are blood thinners

Nicholas: what kind of time frame do they have or is there a DNR ?

Nicholas: oh I see... that's all I take

Nicholas: or is he going to be on life support indefinitely? or is this something you're okay talking about right now?

Namita: its hard to say ... they work kinda differently in the states ...but he is not a dnr right now

Nicholas: if not we can talk about something else

Namita: yes sure

Nicholas: so they're waiting for him to get stronger?

Nicholas: talk about something else?

Namita: yes ... he has a balloon pump in his heart right now ... to bypass the blockage and keep it open ... thats never really good

Namita: in the first place ... if they could they would have had him in surgery

Namita: to fix the problem ... but his heart is weak to do that

Nicholas: ah

Namita: yes talk about something else

Nicholas: okay

Nicholas: did you find any cool shops while you has some free time today?

Namita: oh god tooo many cool shops here ... lots of good clothes shop

Namita: and shoes

Namita: hehe

Nicholas: cool

Namita: i love good shoes and bags

Nicholas: has any body noticed you were up late last night?

Nicholas: you're a woman ur suppose to like shoes n bags lol

Namita: oh yessss ... i was yawning a lot during the day.... and one of my cousins asked ...what the hell is wrong with me ?? in front of everyone ...hehehe... are you not getting enough sleep for some reason ?

Nicholas: lol

Nicholas: ahhh yah I am not

Nicholas: lol

Namita: it was in a restaurant we went into

Nicholas: talking w a guy I met on the internet lol

Namita: there was like 6 of us

Nicholas: oh no!!

Namita: yes can u imagine if i had said that

Nicholas: and you replied with ???

Nicholas: omg they would have flipped lol

Namita: i said ... oh nooo im ok ... but they all looked at me and there was a silence followed after it .... and then im trying to convince my bratty cousin

Nicholas: "just had a little cyber sex last night w a guy from the internet" lol

Namita: hehe

Namita: lmao

Nicholas: lol

Nicholas: "but you should hear the things he says OMG"

Namita: ohhh yesss thats what i should have said ...and then asked them "WHy havent you guys had cyber sex"?

Namita: lmaooo

Nicholas: lmao

Namita: yessss and he is sooooo good too !!!!!!!

Nicholas: too funny

Nicholas: awe shucks thx

Nicholas: you're pretty damn good urself

Namita: really ? heheh

Nicholas: yes u are

Namita: i hope i had you whirling

Nicholas: I'm right there w you in the moment

Namita: mmmmmmm yessss

Nicholas: my god yes... you're very good... great imagination and great descriptions too

Namita: really ?? i always say what comes to mind

Nicholas: me too

Nicholas: and it's all things I plan to do w you

Namita: and go with the flow and instincts ...do what i would do in real life basically

Nicholas: Yes that's what I do!!

Namita: hehee

Nicholas: listen n feel my partner n go w the flow

Namita: hmmmm yesss

Namita: evereything falls into place

Nicholas: yes it does esp when we're open w each other

Nicholas: as we are

Namita: yesss sooo true

Nicholas: it just sort of happens though we're always in control

Namita: uh huh ... well it is healthy too

Nicholas: but you can let go n feel safe too

Nicholas: cuz you're never as exposed as you are when u make love to ur partner

Nicholas: I think that's the biggest turn on for me, being totally exposed n open n safe all at the same time

Namita: that is true ... but this way ..we kinda have a feeling of what we like and what we dont

Nicholas: and there's only one person in the whole world that gets to see you like that

Namita: yesss me too ... i love feeling safe in my partners arms

Namita: yessss soo true

Nicholas: yes we really do have a head start on it dont we

Namita: it is the only person that would see you in that light

Namita: everyone else can wonder ...lol

Nicholas: yes... was gonna use the word light

Namita: lol ...touch

Nicholas: those great minds again

Namita: hehe

Nicholas: so what's ur work schedule when you get back?

Nicholas: are you going to have to pick up shifts to make up for the ones u missed?

Namita: hmmm im still off for a few days

Namita: no i took special leave so i dont have to make it up anytime

Nicholas: oh yah. when are you scheduled to start again?

Nicholas: I see

Namita: i have to look at my schedule ... im not sure right now

Namita: i dont have it with me

Nicholas: yes of course

Nicholas: has the sun come out there?

Namita: hehe no ... still cloudy

Namita: and cool

Namita: what about over there?

Nicholas: a little rainy here though it seems to stop while I'm at work

Nicholas: the sun pokes out a little just before it goes dwn

Namita: hehe ... of course ... thats the way it always is ... when ur stuck in some building then the rain stops

Nicholas: yup.... I had to switch tasks today which makes the day er shift go by a little quicker

Nicholas: yesterday it really dragged n I'm not sure why

Namita: what does that mean ?

Nicholas: did diff jobs today

Namita: i mean what did you do today that was different

Nicholas: I started the shift gouging, the first step in the process then switched to my reg job after dinner

Namita: ohhh was it cuz there was no one to do it ?

Namita: what does gouging mean ?

Nicholas: sort of. the guy that does the gouging doesn't always show up

Namita: ohhhhhhhhhhh thats not good !!

Namita: you mean he is a no show ?

Nicholas: yes. he does that a lot

Nicholas: not good

Namita: wow ... that asking for trouble man!!

Namita: but then he is in a union

Namita: he is totally abusing the system

Nicholas: gouging is 3/4" carbon rod has almost 2000 amps running through it and high air pressure blowing out under the rod, the work piece is grounded and when the rod touches the work piece the rod & the steel it touches melts and blows away like lava

Namita: ohhhh wowww

Nicholas: yes he is... he's missed a lot of time

Namita: ohhh ... no it makes sense ... he doesnt have his priorities straight

Nicholas: you are amazing you know that? i will never let you forget it.im such a lucky guy

Nicholas: i know random but what can i say was distracted by ur photos

Namita: hehe what did i say ??

Nicholas: what did what say?

Nicholas: nothing particular

Namita: i was saying what did i say to garner that response of being amazing ... that was soooo random !! HEhhehehe

Nicholas: it was... I just had a reality moment was all

Namita: lol

Nicholas: uummm so where was i lol

Nicholas: the guy at work right

Namita: hehehe you are tooo funny

Nicholas: lol

Namita: ahem ...yess right ...work

Nicholas: I'm not sure what he thinks

Nicholas: he use to do the same thing when I worked w him at the other place. he got away w it there n they keep letting him here but I think they're tired of it n going to go through proper channels to get rid of him... though he's really good at what he does. faster that anybody thats been there

Nicholas: side note; I got a burn on the back of my hand

Namita: yeah those ppl usually know how to squeak by and get away with things

Namita: ohhhhhh how did you do that ?

Namita: from work ?

Nicholas: it's a little bit bigger than the size of a pin head, thought it burned a little hole in my skin

Namita: side note for me ... im in meat withdrawal ...hehehe

Nicholas: hot orange spark jumped into my glove

Namita: ohhh geeeeeez

Nicholas: meat really?

Namita: does it sting

Nicholas: a little

Nicholas: meat like form chicken?

Nicholas: or my kind of meat ? lol

Namita: yes yesterday was our festival of lights ... called diwali ... and usually most ppl dont eat meat for that week

Namita: lmaoooooooooooooooo

Namita: nice one nicholas !!!!!!

Nicholas: damn I couldn't do that

Nicholas: just checking lol

Namita: as in chicken

Nicholas: yahhhh

Namita: well that too ... ok will give it to ya

Nicholas: hehe I'll give it to you lol

Namita: hehehehe ... ok i totally walked into that one !!! OMGGG !!!!!!!!!!!!

Namita: cant say i put my foot in my mouth ... cuz guess what you will come up with next ???!!

Nicholas: yes you did walked in chin up n everything lol

Nicholas: lmao

Nicholas: hehe yes i would lol

Namita: lmaooo

Nicholas: going back to the edible meat lol i figure if you want to try beef or a hamburger I'll take you to Five Guys. they make great burgers

Nicholas: nothing I've ever had compared

Namita: ohhh wow ... ive never tried beef... i dont think i really want to venture to eat beef ....but im sure they have other stuff too

Nicholas: oh well the point was if you wanted to try beef n I know you haven't tried it thats why I suggested it

Namita: hehe ok

Nicholas: totally up to you though

Nicholas: I cant imagine not trying beef though I know what it tastes like so having never tried it I just don't know that side

Namita: yes i understand ... im sure you love ur beef !! hehe

Namita: i would never ask you to give it up ... the thought never crossed my mind

Nicholas: Oh I didn't think it would... you're not like that but thx for saying it

Namita: lol ur welcome

Nicholas: I'm sure you'll love my beef too hehe

Namita: lmao

Nicholas: not the same beef? lol

Namita: i like it tough and hard though

Nicholas: figure of speech I know

Nicholas: hmmm I think that can be arranged

Namita: so i can have it welll done later !

Nicholas: well done for the pretty lady coming right up, pun intended lol

Namita: hehehhe

Nicholas: it will definitely be cooked thats for sure lol

Namita: hehehhe ... i do love the dessert that is offered afterwards

Nicholas: mmmm good to know

Nicholas: you need to work to get it but i think it's worth it

Namita: ahhhhh im sure it is ... it would be just perfect ...after the main course

Nicholas: ANd its not too filling so you have room for more

Namita: lol

Nicholas: I love the way you think

Namita: i loveee seconds

Nicholas: mmmhmmm me too!!

Namita: and thirds

Nicholas: that can be arranged

Namita: hehhe

Nicholas: hhmmm hhmmm

Namita: yummmmy

Nicholas: so not helping the hornyness

Nicholas: that is suuuuch a turn on, I dont know why but it is

Namita: seriously ??

Nicholas: yup

Namita: are you hard right now ?

Nicholas: can't explain it

Nicholas: lol not completely

Nicholas: it comes n goes as we talk

Namita: hmmmm niceeeeee

Nicholas: it gets harder when we get raunchy then settles when the convo changes

Namita: hehehe

Nicholas: it really has a mind of it's own sometimes

Nicholas: esp talking w you

Namita: what if i was there while ur sleeping and lounging on ur recliner

Nicholas: mmhmm

Namita: and i come up to sit over u kinda straddling u

Nicholas: I'm pretty sure I wouldn't be sleeping w you here

Namita: hehe

Nicholas: in my chair! yes talk about deep penetration!! we'll try it so you can see er feel for urself

Namita: ohhh myyy

Namita: do u think you will have enough room ?

Nicholas: all ur weight pressing dwn on my unit

Nicholas: oh yes

Namita: mmmmmmmmm yessssss

Nicholas: you don't take up much room

Namita: i can rock back and forth on u

Nicholas: oh n it's a rocking chair too

Namita: with my weight on ur ahem... meat

Namita: ohhh cool

Nicholas: I can just rock the chair n you can just ride all you want

Nicholas: this ride is free

Namita: ohhh my

Namita: is it all day rides ?

Nicholas: yup

Namita: no height restriction ?

Namita: hehe

Nicholas: well you must be at least 5'7" to ride this ride

Namita: ahhhhh i see ... i pass then

Namita: does ur rocker have speed control?

Nicholas: I think ur 5' 7" aren't you?

Namita: yes

Nicholas: its manual speed control

Namita: lol

Nicholas: oh you pass ur in... I thought you were passing to not ride lol I got it now

Nicholas: lol

Namita: hehe ...focussss !!

Nicholas: it's late n the brain doesn't work so well esp when I'm thinking of being balls deep inside you on sitting in my fav chair

Namita: mmmmmmmmm ur making me sooo horny again

Nicholas: sorry shall we talk about algebra n calculus instead? lol

Namita: lol

Namita: noooooooo

Namita: i loveeeeeee the feeling of you saying balls deep

Nicholas: sounds like your horny button has a hair trigger

Nicholas: I thought you might

Namita: hehehe ... it doesnt take much

Nicholas: good to know

Nicholas: maybe just a look or a touch hmmm

Namita: yesss or it could be something you say

Namita: not even sexual either

Nicholas: thats when you know you've reached the end when u bottom out on the balls

Nicholas: cool

Namita: mmmm yesss

Namita: then you slam again ... oh god ... that would drive me wild

Namita: hehehehe

Nicholas: just you wait sweet heart just you wait

Namita: MMmmmMmmMmmm yessss

Namita: give us 24 hours

Namita: all day and night

Nicholas: we'll go to Rocky Point then plan for our special night n yes we'll need quite a length of time

Namita: hehehe ... i will bring a pen and paper with me

Nicholas: to just be naked n explore each other

Namita: lol

Nicholas: I'll take mental notes... mind like a steel trap I have

Namita: hehehe ...uh ohhh

Nicholas: the wait between Rocky Point n our special time will be torture but Sooooooo worth it!!

Nicholas: uh ohh? what?

Namita: uh ohhh that i wont be able to get away with anything if you've got a steel trap mind

Namita: hehe

Nicholas: lol I wont hold you to anything... except my body

Nicholas: I'll bring a big box of condoms

Namita: hehehe

Nicholas: and I'll let you get away w whatever you want!!

Namita: yesss get the bulk boxes

Nicholas: I'll get the box of 28, that enf?

Namita: nooo get like 10 boxes pleaseee

Nicholas: lol

Namita: lol

Namita: thats like 280 condoms

Nicholas: thats a lot of sex in a 24hrs

Nicholas: yes it is!!

Nicholas: er love making I mean

Namita: hehheehe

Nicholas: I could wear them 2 or 3 at a time

Namita: yessss i think you should ... it will be sexy

Namita: put them on ur ears too

Namita: just to look sexy

Nicholas: that might be a good idea come to think of it because of the back pressure i may just blow through just one lol

Namita: back pressure ?

Namita: no we dont want that to blow either

Nicholas: how hard im going to explode inside you after all this time n build up

Namita: ohhhh hehhehe

Namita: omg ...ur making me hottttt again

Nicholas: maybe thats why I got a headache today, it was SRH

Namita: SRH ?

Nicholas: Sperm Retention Headache

Namita: hehehehehhehehehhehehhehehehehhehehehhehehe

Nicholas: did that on purpose hehe

Namita: i would want to feel u explode inside of me

Namita: do u cum a lot ?

Nicholas: taking matters into my own hands is one thing but doesn't compare to exploding inside you

Namita: mmmmmmm yessssss

Nicholas: a lot? not volume wise but I think you'll enjoy the ride

Namita: mmmm yesss ..sounds sooo good

Nicholas: it's pretty intense for me n there's a lot to it.... it'll be easier to show you

Namita: tell me a little

Namita: im getting super horny here

Nicholas: I don't know how to describe it

Namita: pleaseeeeeee....hehe

Nicholas: that makes 2 of us then

Namita: hehe

Nicholas: hmm

Nicholas: it's not just one contraction, it's a whole bunch n I grow a little bit too

Namita: ohhh god !!!!!!

Namita: im going to go crazy now thinking about it

Nicholas: if ur on top you'll be lifted off the bed a few times while I'm going off

Namita: OMGGG !!! !

Nicholas: I'll hold you by ur hips n I'll press myself into you as I go off

Nicholas: would you like that?? he asks knowingly hehe

Namita: OMG Nicholas !!!!!

Namita: YESSSSSSSSSSSSSSSsssssssss

Nicholas: hmmhmm

Nicholas: though u might

Namita: and im sure im going to be contracting to hold on to ur cock and milk its every last drop

Nicholas: it will be quite a ride

Nicholas: for both of us

Namita: mmmmm yessss

Nicholas: esp after all our foreplay

Nicholas: so does any of this answer ur question form long ago about how open am I in the bedroom?

Nicholas: you just took a moment to play w urself didn't you?

Namita: mmmm .... yesss

Namita: nooooooo

Namita: i mean

Namita: nooo i didnt

Namita: hehe

Nicholas: no? really?

Namita: well im very wet

Nicholas: I hoped you would be

Namita: but im thinking of ur sentence

Nicholas: though I can't imagine why

Nicholas: hmm which one?

Namita: my clit's swollen

Nicholas: mmmm I bet

Namita: was imagining ur mouth on me

Nicholas: sucking on ur swollen clit

Namita: biting a little

Namita: then sucking

Namita: ohh god

Nicholas: flicking my tongue

Nicholas: dipping it into ur hot wet pussy

Namita: ohhh myyy

Namita: nicholas !!

Nicholas: not helping?

Namita: yes and no

Namita: do you like going right into me with ur tongue ?

Nicholas: yes keep helping n no don't stop?

Namita: or would you ?

Namita: heheh yesss

Nicholas: I would dip n lick while I'm dwn there sure

Namita: ohhh goddd !!!!!!!!

Nicholas: all part of the experience

Namita: id be going super crazyyyyy then !!!!!!!!

Nicholas: maybe even get my thumb into you while I'm licking n sucking ur clit

Namita: arching and offering myself to you even more

Namita: mmmmmmmmmm

Nicholas: I'm going to explode inside u n ur going to explode all over me

Nicholas: then we'll shower to clean up n start all over

Namita: yesss we will

Namita: or i will climb on top of you while in shower

Namita: facing each other

Namita: and you insert ur cock deep inside of me

Nicholas: mmmhmmm

Namita: i hold onto ur shoulders n neck

Nicholas: that's one of the best parts... when I enter you

Namita: and we both rock up and down to each other

Nicholas: and it glides all the way in

Namita: while in ur arms ... ur holding me ... my legs wrapped around ur hips

Nicholas: mmmm

Namita: then we come out of the shower like that

Namita: and we can both feel the vibrations coming into our bodies

Namita: and you going deeper

Namita: im basically attached to u by ur cock

Nicholas: if you don't mind me asking how much do you weigh?

Nicholas: yes

Namita: hehe

Nicholas: like a Namita pole

Namita: i fluctuate around 125 to 130 lbs

Nicholas: cool

Namita: you?

Nicholas: just right

Nicholas: 190

Namita: mmm niceee

Nicholas: I'm glad u think so

Namita: i like the namita pole

Namita: hehe

Nicholas: wasn't sure if that made sense

Nicholas: I like it too

Namita: no it did

Nicholas: are you ready to cum while you're playing w urself?

Namita: lol

Namita: how did you know

Nicholas: or have u already?

Namita: no havent yet

Nicholas: 6th sense

Namita: lol

Namita: niceee

Nicholas: I can feel you all the way up here

Namita: are u still hard ?

Nicholas: yes n playing here too

Namita: ohhh good !!! ... hehe

Namita: would lovvvve to suck on ur hard cock

Nicholas: really wish it was you doing this

Namita: and then look up at u while doing it

Nicholas: OMG would I love that!!

Nicholas: mmhmm

Namita: mmmmmmmmmmmmm yessssssssss

Namita: is that hot for you?

Nicholas: I'd reach dwn behind you n massage ur clit for you

Namita: mmmmmmmmmmm

Nicholas: yes it is

Nicholas: I can feel ur hand on my cock n ur lips on the tip

Namita: my tongue flicking the tip of ur cock

Nicholas: feeling how wet I've made you

Namita: then my tongue would press down on ur opening

Nicholas: dipping my fingers inside you

Namita: with the tip of my tongue

Nicholas: mmmm

Namita: mmmm yesssssss

Namita: playing with the edge of ur opening

Nicholas: rub that clit for me Namita

Namita: then taking ur entire cock into my mouth

Namita: mmm yessssss

Nicholas: feel how wet it is under ur fingers

Nicholas: yess

Namita: yeesssss it is

Nicholas: mmm I can feel it too

Nicholas: omg

Namita: ooooooo god

Nicholas: i just want to explode in ur mouth!!!!

Namita: yessss plssss

Nicholas: omg I'm gonna explode

Namita: i want to frink you up

Namita: drink i mean

Namita: cum for me

Namita: cum for me lots

Namita: i want to taste you

Nicholas: here it cums !!!!

Namita: ur nice fat juicy cock in my mouth

Namita: me sucking on it hungrily

Namita: like ive been starving for it

Nicholas: oh god

Namita: pleasssssssssssssse give it to me

Namita: nowwwww

Nicholas: just about went all over

Namita: mmmmm yesssssss

Nicholas: oh yess

Nicholas: there u go!!!

Namita: mmmmmmmmmmm luvvvvv it

Nicholas: sweet Nicholas explosion!!!

Namita: im still sucking ur cock

Namita: cleaning u up

Nicholas: made me like jello

Nicholas: n I'm squeezing it all out for you

Namita: ohhh god !!!

Nicholas: I am Jello my god

Namita: im massaging ur balls too

Namita: as i do that

Nicholas: oh man

Nicholas: pfewwww damn

Namita: glad u came good !!!

Nicholas: oh did I!! wow .... did you?

Namita: no not yet

Nicholas: not yet oh geeze

Namita: im good though

Nicholas: well think of me dipping my tongue into you n

Namita: ohhhh nicholas

Nicholas: flicking ur clit

Nicholas: faster n faster

Namita: you dont have to nicholas

Nicholas: wasn't coz I have to

Namita: k

Nicholas: has the moment passed?

Namita: nooo

Nicholas: cuz i can keep going

Namita: k

Namita: go

Nicholas: sucking ur clit as you moan for more

Nicholas: you can see the top of my shaved head

Namita: ommg

Nicholas: dedicated to your swollen clit

Nicholas: wrapping my arms around ur legs so you can't get away

Nicholas: I insert a finger into you

Namita: ohhhhhh babbbyyy

Nicholas: n make the come hither motion on ur g spot

Nicholas: as I keep licking n sucking you

Namita: mmmmmmmmmmmmmmmmmmmmmm

Nicholas: then its 2 fingers

Namita: oomgggg

Nicholas: n make the same motion

Nicholas: reaching deep inside you

Nicholas: rolling my fingers around

Nicholas: touching all of you

Namita: mmmmmmmmmmmmmmmmmmmmmmmm

Nicholas: faster n faster I work u into an unstoppable frenzy

Nicholas: the only way to end it is to cum all over me

Nicholas: but you don't

Nicholas: I wont let u

Nicholas: I kiss you as I work my way up to ur lips

Namita: nooooo plsssss

Nicholas: I kiss you softly

Nicholas: as my hard cock finds is way into you

Namita: mmm

Nicholas: it just sides effortlessly into you

Nicholas: I press myself slowly all the way deep inside you

Nicholas: n pause ever so slightly at the end so you can catch ur breath

Namita: nicholas plssssssssssss babyyy

Nicholas: then I slowly roll my hips in big circles

Nicholas: touching all the wonderful spots

Nicholas: sending waves of pleasure up n dwn ur body

Nicholas: u can hear someone screaming then realize its you!!

Namita: yesssssssssss

Nicholas: you can't take it any more

Namita: im going to cummmm

Nicholas: u beg me to fuck you as hard as I can

Nicholas: n I pound you

Namita: yesssssssssssssssssssss

Nicholas: bringing u to the end of the journey

Nicholas: u shutter w pleasure again n agin as u cum

Namita: omggg im sooo tight

Nicholas: ur body vibrating w after shocks

Namita: ohhhh nicholas

Nicholas: I got you then?

Namita: yesss

Namita: you did

Nicholas: didn't want to leave you hanging

Nicholas: good!!

Nicholas: don't ever want to leave you hanging

Namita: aweee nicholas thanks

Nicholas: you are very welcome Namita

Nicholas: and thank you

Namita: thats sooo sweet

Nicholas: not sure where all that comes from but you seem to bring that out in me

Nicholas: though I'm imagining it as I'm typing

Namita: hmmmm yesss ... i was wracked with another orgasm

Nicholas: cool... can only imagine what we'll be like in real life

Namita: i am going to be so out of breath like this

Nicholas: hmmm breathless not a bad way to leave you

Namita: are u ok?

Nicholas: yup

Nicholas: why?

Namita: hehe

Nicholas: very tired all of a sudden though

Namita: from our round of cyber love making

Namita: no worries ... me too

Nicholas: yup!!

Nicholas: i bet you are!!

Nicholas: you had quite a work out

Namita: i bet you are too

Nicholas: yes I am

Nicholas: starting to zone out... just think when we do this for real we'll be able to just sleep

Namita: im dozing ... so sorry

Nicholas: sokay

Namita: ahhh yessssss total bliss

Nicholas: tmw Tony is here so i'll have to see how chatty he is as to weather or not u n I can chat... can you give me till 1 pls? if I'm not on by then then he n I are still chatting

Namita: ok no worries ... totally dont mind at all

Nicholas: n if he's sleepy then I'll come look for you

Namita: ok deal

Nicholas: thats cool?

Nicholas: cool

Nicholas: ur awesome

Namita: so are you

Nicholas: I'll never let you forget that

Nicholas: thx

Namita: mmmmm awwweee thx

Nicholas: so until tmw... don't want u over tired tmw

Nicholas: u need to be sharp

Namita: oh god thats for sure !!

Nicholas: yes yes

Namita: or will be teased again

Nicholas: okay... gnight my sweet pleasant dreams

Namita: goodnite nicholas and thank you for a wonderful nite

Nicholas: night

Namita: byeee

End Time: 4:24 AM

Chapter 18 October 28

Start Time: 12:44 AM

Namita: how's it going

Nicholas: hello

Nicholas: Tony says hello

Nicholas: thx for waiting

Namita: awee thanks ...say hello to him for me

Namita: is he around too ?

Namita: no worries

Nicholas: he's in the living room... I'm in my bedroom

Namita: ohhh ok ... did you work today too?

Nicholas: I did

Nicholas: was home at reg time

Namita: when did tony arrive ?

Nicholas: then I caught up w him

Namita: ohhh i see

Nicholas: this afternoon

Namita: how is he doing ?

Nicholas: I leave my keys for him when I leave for work so he can get in

Nicholas: seems okay

Nicholas: trying to stay positive

Namita: ahhh ok

Nicholas: its good for him to hang out w me

Namita: yes im sending good vibes over to ya guys

Namita: hehe

Nicholas: thx that means a lot

Namita: im sure its nice for him to catch up on things with his ol buddy

Nicholas: how are things on your front?

Nicholas: lol easy on the old part eh lol

Namita: its ok ... kinda stressful at times but ok

Namita: hehee

Nicholas: w your family that is

Namita: i didnt mean it like that !! lol

Namita: yes thats right

Nicholas: not the front of your body lol

Nicholas: just teasing you

Namita: hehehe

Namita: well last time i checked everything is still in place

Nicholas: good to know

Namita: nothing sagging or out of order

Namita: hehe

Nicholas: though I'll do a thorough check for myself, not that I don't believe you

Nicholas: I'm a hands on kind of guy

Namita: hehhe .... yes you can do an inventory for urelf

Namita: hehe

Namita: im sure you are !!

Nicholas: thx

Namita: does tony know that we're chatting right now ?

Nicholas: hands face body whatever I need to do a thorough job hehe

Nicholas: he does

Nicholas: he's totally ok w it

Namita: hehe ... plus you make sure they are the right size and dimensions

Nicholas: he can see how taken I am w you n would never get in the way

Namita: hehehe... i assume he saw my pics

Nicholas: that I will... I've already thought about what 36CC will feel like

Namita: hehe.... you do eh ?

Nicholas: yes I showed him the ones I said I would n nothing more

Namita: have you done some studying and researching on that already ?

Namita: what was his thoughts?

Nicholas: yup just looking at your photos though

Namita: lol

Nicholas: I told him what I said the first time I saw them, then showed him n he said pretty much the same thing... "oh my Fucking god dude! wow! you're really lucky"

Namita: lmaooo !!!

Namita: you guys are sooo funny !!

Nicholas: he's happy for me

Nicholas: we are quite the pair

Namita: im sure you are !!

Nicholas: ppl gravitate to us when we're out

Nicholas: its pretty funny and fun

Nicholas: we're just really friendly to everyone

Namita: that is cool to hear !!

Namita: thats how friends should be !!

Nicholas: and include everyone

Nicholas: yup

Namita: the more the merrier ... i say

Nicholas: we take each other as we are, we both have flaws n we appreciate each other regardless

Nicholas: yes the more the merrier

Namita: yesss that is good to hear ... no one is perfect in this world !!

Namita: how was work today ?

Nicholas: was okay. went by quickly so that was good

Nicholas: jumped between both jobs again

Namita: hmmm yessss ... quick and painless ... love those kind of days

Nicholas: as long as there's something to do and the checks clear I'm good

Namita: ohhh again a no show !!?

Nicholas: oh he showed up but I think he got his final warning

Namita: well at least they know ur a hard worker and ready to adapt to changes and duties

Namita: ohh i see

Nicholas: that they do... it's good to be diverse, makes you indispensable

Nicholas: did you get enf sleep last night?

Namita: yesss true ... kinda here and there ... but still tired

Namita: made it thru the day

Namita: what about you ?

Nicholas: I got up about 10 had breakfast then had a little nap about 2 hrs later

Namita: ohh good !!

Namita: i finally had some meat today !

Nicholas: wasn't very long a nap. kinda startled myself awake then couldn't go back to sleep

Namita: some scrambled eggs

Nicholas: napped in my chair

Namita: why did you startle urself ?

Nicholas: yeah!!! meat

Namita: hehehe

Nicholas: just startled myself out of my sleep... not sure I think I though it was later than it was n I might be late for work but it was an hr before I needed to be awake

Nicholas: what meat did you have?

Nicholas: bacon?

Namita: ohh i see ... i hate when that happens ...working shift work ...when i come home ... i sometimes wake up in the middle of the nite ... not knowing where i am for a min or what time it is ... am i suppose to be somewhere ... i hate that feeling

Nicholas: yah me too

Namita: i had scrambled eggs one bacon

Nicholas: mmmm bacon

Namita: i chewed til i couldnt anymore !!!

Namita: i was sooo infatuated with the taste of meat finally

Namita: hehe

Nicholas: scrambled eggs are good too

Namita: i love bacon ...mmmm

Nicholas: I do that to bacon too

Namita: how do you like ur eggs ?

Nicholas: the more u chew it the more flavor u get

Nicholas: scrambled

Namita: mmmm   yesss

Nicholas: I cook them in a pot w no milk added n you whisk them till they're done... they're really fluffy that way

Nicholas: u like scrambled too?

Namita: you whisk them as they are cooking ?

Nicholas: yup

Namita: yes i love scrambled too

Nicholas: saw it on a cooking show

Namita: oh cool !!!

Nicholas: the french way is to cook the yolks first in the same way then add the whites

Nicholas: using the whisk method

Namita: ohhh wow

Namita: never even heard of it

Nicholas: I don't usually cook them any other way now

Namita: what else you like for breakfast

Nicholas: I'll cook them for you one day

Nicholas: my usual breakfast is a bowl of oatmeal slice of toast w strawberry jam n a small glass of Sunripe wildraspberry juice

Nicholas: what do you have?

Namita: nice... i vary with alot of things... sometimes it is just fruits, other times it may be toast with marmalade or raspberry jam. Other times cereal with banana... or yogurt. If i get fancy then it could be pancakes or french toast... bacon and eggs.

Nicholas: cool

Namita: the latter i dont have very often ..cuz im working most times ...and if im off .. i couldnt be bothered

Nicholas: I make crepes for the girls n I for dinner sometimes

Namita: ohhh cool !! Like dessert crepes ?

Nicholas: yah its hard to cook for one

Nicholas: yup

Namita: what do you put in them ?

Nicholas: we put all kinds of things in them but usually fruit n yogurt

Namita: ohhh sounds sooo good !

Nicholas: there's this crepe place dwntwn thats really good. you can get just about anything in it

Nicholas: they're big n quite filling

Namita: hmmm never even heard of it ?

Nicholas: I usually make 2 batches and we end up eating them all

Namita: im sure it is quite good !

Namita: hehee

Nicholas: I forget what its call but I'll take you there one day

Namita: they sound just too good

Nicholas: I like the chicken n feta crepe

Nicholas: or is it chicken n spinach

Nicholas: cant remember

Namita: ohhh my ... they even have savory ones ?

Nicholas: or all 3? lol

Nicholas: yup

Namita: ohhh

Nicholas: they've got quite a menu

Nicholas: w lots of options

Namita: wow ... im sure it hard to pick what you want to eat

Nicholas: sometimes it is

Nicholas: though I do like the one I mentioned. you can get them to go so you can walk around and still enjoy it

Namita: ive had crepes before... a longgggggg time ago ... mom made them ... i think she stuffed them with some spinach mixture

Namita: ohhh niceee

Nicholas: cool. this place makes the crepe about 20 inches across then fold it into a cone n stuff everything into it

Namita: ohhh my ... sounds like one is enough to feed both of us !!

Nicholas: how often do you eat in a day?

Nicholas: almost but I can finish one all on my own, though I'd share anything w you

Namita: 2 when im home ... and snacks ... and i try to aim for 3 at work

Namita: i dont eat tons ... if ur worried !! lol

Nicholas: lol not worried lol

Namita: hehehe yeah right !!

Nicholas: just wondered. i eat about 6 or 7 times. thats meals and snacks combined

Namita: oh...but ur a guy

Nicholas: just wondered if you eat like a bird or if you have a healthy appetite

Namita: so thats good you eat ... and eat healthy

Namita: no i have a healthy appetite

Nicholas: I sometimes have trouble eating enf to keep the weight on

Namita: i can eat a sandwich or chicken burger

Namita: hehe

Nicholas: oh good

Nicholas: it's good for the brain to eat often, keeps the blood sugar consistent

Namita: well you probably burn alot of it off at work

Namita: yes very true

Nicholas: yah. I have my moms metabolism which is fast so I burn calories quickly

Namita: ohhh thats good !! YOu got good genes from mom

Nicholas: My dads size n my moms metabolism makes for a good combo

Nicholas: lol thx

Namita: heheh

Namita: how tall are you again ?

Nicholas: 6' 3"

Nicholas: just perfect for 5' 7" to fit in

Nicholas: 6' 4" w my boots on

Namita: hehehe ... im sure you measured the 5``7 out too

Namita: mmmmmm nicee

Nicholas: lol maaaaaybe

Namita: yeah you haVE !!! SAY IT !!!

Namita: LOL

Nicholas: lol i did

Namita: hehehe

Nicholas: was part of my wish

Namita: i knew it

Nicholas: 5' 7" was the minimum height I wanted

Namita: hmmm poor nicholas ... he goes to work wondering 5`7 would be like on him ... so he goes to the back of the workplace in a corner ... with a measuring tape ... when no one else is looking he whips out his tape to see where the 5`7 would come up on him !!!

Namita: to is astonishment ... he was pleasantly surprised to see that it would all work out in the end

Nicholas: lol did not lol I used my own tape measure at home so there 😜

Namita: heheheheh

Nicholas: I knew it would before hand lol

Namita: no you hid in a corner at work ... with the their measuring tape ... to get a second opinion

Nicholas: nope

Namita: just in case ur tape at home was faulty

Namita: hehe

Nicholas: though I did check it at home a couple of times just so I could visualize you better

Namita: hehhee ... too funny !!

Nicholas: when you put a wish out there you have to be precise in what you want... I was n look who I found? a perfect match

Namita: hehehe ... poof ... there i was !!

Nicholas: yup there you were... n I'm soooo glad

Nicholas: the proportions work. when we hold hands it's comfortable for both of us. when I put my arm around you while we're walking it feels right again for both of us... it just works

Namita: yesss ... i know what you mean ... if i was any shorter ... id have to get a ladder ... it makes kissing easier too

Nicholas: yup I can just lean over n kiss you... easy access

Namita: hehehe

Nicholas: when you said poof I got an image of spontaneous smoke n there you are

Namita: you can get me quickly and easily too ... the kisses that I don't see coming

Namita: hehe

Nicholas: yes I can

Namita: POOF ... i imagined some pink smoke ... and then i appear

Nicholas: the ambush kisses

Namita: hehe

Nicholas: cool, pink smoke it is

Namita: ahhhh ambush ... eh ??

Nicholas: like a genie from a bottle

Namita: i will have to keep my guard up and sleep with on eye open

Namita: uh huh ... yesss a genie

Nicholas: yup those are the ones that catch you off guard

Namita: or the morning ones !!

Namita: the morning ambush

Nicholas: no no pls don't sleep w one eye open that would look strange lol

Namita: kisses while the other is still asleep

Namita: Lmao

Namita: ok i will tape that one shut !!! GEEEEz

Nicholas: yes morning ambush kisses where I wake you gently w little passionate kisses till ur awake

Namita: mmmmmmmmmmmm nice

Nicholas: the height thing makes love making better too that way when I'm on top I can look right into ur eyes

Namita: Mmmmm yessss .... you can watch me ... watch what you do to me

Nicholas: or when ur on top you can lean over n kiss me easier

Nicholas: Yessss!!

Namita: mmmm yess for that too

Namita: easy to connect

Nicholas: everything is in better proportion

Nicholas: yess

Namita: with the eyes and sexually

Nicholas: connect n not just the physical way hehe

Nicholas: like minds

Namita: yesss of course ... the minds as well !!

Nicholas: it's like u read my mind

Nicholas: oh yes didn't think of that one

Namita: ohhh i get what u wrote

Nicholas: lol

Namita: love making goes beyond words and the usual ... it a deeper connection

Namita: hehe

Nicholas: like minds coz we wrote the same thing

Namita: hehe i see that !!

Nicholas: but yes we'll connect on so many levels

Namita: 2 peas in a pod again

Nicholas: looking forward to it!!

Nicholas: yes we are

Namita: hehehe

Nicholas: one day we'll be 2 naked bodies in a bed

Nicholas: or peas in a pod but I like my analogy a little better

Namita: what size is ur bed É

Namita: ?

Namita: lol

Nicholas: queen

Nicholas: yours?

Namita: i will take ur analogy

Nicholas: oh good

Namita: arghhhhhhh

Nicholas: I knew what you meant

Namita: hehe

Nicholas: what's w the E w the thing over top of it?

Namita: mine is queen too

Nicholas: excellent

Nicholas: just enf room to not get lost

Nicholas: king is too big I think

Namita: my question mark key at the bottom right on my keyboard stops working ... and give me the E when i hit it

Nicholas: ah

Namita: it is some second function of the key ... i dont know how to reverse it

Nicholas: is your bed on a frame?

Nicholas: soaky no to worry

Namita: it corrects itself on it own if i log off

Nicholas: sokay*

Nicholas: oooh don't log off pls

Namita: it is a wooden carved bed

Nicholas: it might not let u back on

Namita: 4 posters

Namita: dark wood

Nicholas: cool

Nicholas: mmm I can picture it now.... nice

Namita: i think 4 feet high

Nicholas: posts like to tie someone up? hmmm

Namita: but it is high off the ground

Namita: i cant touch the floor if i was sitting on the edge of it

Namita: ohhh nooo im giving someone ideas

Nicholas: cool... I think I'll be able to

Namita: hehe

Nicholas: yes you have

Namita: able to what ?

Namita: hehe

Nicholas: touch the floor w my feet while I'm sitting on the edge

Namita: and there are no notches in my bed post ... hehe

Nicholas: I like a high bed

Nicholas: lol good one

Nicholas: n good to know lol

Namita: yes you will able to ... but i wont

Nicholas: you wont need to

Namita: yes then you can stand and lean over me while i lean back from the edge ... and start making love

Nicholas: the only post you'll be touching is mine

Namita: lmaoooooooooooooooo

Nicholas: thought of that too

Namita: hehe

Nicholas: a high bed makes for good positions

Namita: yesss very true .... ive always envisioned that

Namita: but no face

Nicholas: we'll make that happen

Namita: to my visions

Namita: hehe

Nicholas: now you do hehe

Namita: what about urs ... your bed frame ?

Nicholas: it's on the ground unfortunately. I have a bunk bed over mine so when the girls stay over I sleep on the couch, one of them sleeps in my bed the other in the bunk bed

Nicholas: my place isn't real romantic

Nicholas: I kind of envision our first time at your place

Nicholas: if that's ok w you

Namita: well at least ur bed wont creak !!

Namita: hehe

Namita: or break

Nicholas: lol nope it wont

Namita: no i dont mind at all

Nicholas: cool

Namita: i do like the king size beds too ... but they are quite big

Namita: one can get lost in it

Nicholas: that they are n heavy to move

Namita: hehe

Namita: ohhh yesss didnt think of that

Nicholas: you can... maybe king size for at a hotel?

Namita: hmm yess

Namita: with a hot tub

Namita: mmmmmmmm

Nicholas: yes

Namita: and a nice view out

Nicholas: yessss

Namita: that would be quite something

Nicholas: yes it would not to mention the stunning woman I'll be with

Nicholas: thats a view to behold

Namita: hehehe ... sounds like you will never come up for air

Nicholas: nope

Nicholas: I'll survive on the my intoxication for you

Namita: captivating ... that you would forget everything else outside of the door

Namita: the bedroom door i mean

Nicholas: yup... I knew what you meant... an escape from reality... a time to forget about everything and just be together

Namita: hmmm yesss ... that would be sooo cool

Nicholas: physically, emotionally, mentally

Namita: yesss

Nicholas: just enjoy each others company, minds and bodies

Namita: yess lather our bodies ... run our hands thru every area ... and sweet spots ...or oil it up for a nice massage ...

Namita: i think i can give a good massage

Nicholas: ooooh yes

Nicholas: that sounds wonderful n I'll give you one too

Namita: oh god i could do for one anytime

Namita: hehe

Nicholas: I'd love to give you a massage

Namita: mmmmm niceeeee

Nicholas: I'll turn you to jello from your head to your toes

Namita: oh god !!

Namita: i hope i dont fall asleep on you then

Nicholas: ur skin will be tingling all over

Nicholas: if you do then I'll kiss you awake

Namita: mmmmmm yesssssss

Namita: i`ll be moaning lightly

Namita: do you like kissing deeply ?

Nicholas: I'm pretty sure you wont fall asleep.... when I give a full body massage I use my whole body

Nicholas: yesss

Namita: ohh myyy

Nicholas: I bet you do too

Namita: i can just imagine that scenario

Nicholas: hehe me tooooo

Nicholas: I can't wait to rub my body all over you

Namita: nicholas ...can i ask a personaL question ...hehe

Nicholas: thx for the pic change

Nicholas: yes

Nicholas: u can ask anything

Namita: what size are you ?

Nicholas: my unit?

Namita: ohhh were you getting tired of my clownfish ...hehe

Namita: yes ur equipment

Nicholas: you don't remember?

Namita: i think i do

Namita: i didnt jot it down

Namita: i think you said 7

Namita: ahhhh

Namita: there i did remember

Nicholas: I don't think you'll be disappointed

Namita: hehe ...thick too

Nicholas: yup

Namita: mmmmmm

Nicholas: it'll take ur breath away

Namita: i loveee that

Nicholas: thought u might

Namita: hehe

Nicholas: ANd I know how to use it

Nicholas: everything I've said on here isn't just words

Namita: ahem... im getting my measuring tape out ...oops did i say that !!?

Nicholas: lol

Namita: hehehe

Nicholas: you'll wonder where it's been all ur life hehe

Namita: hehehe

Namita: it will fit in like it belongs there !

Nicholas: YES!!

Namita: hehe

Nicholas: it will feel like it's home

Namita: it will be one happy cock !!

Namita: heheh

Nicholas: n you'll have one satisfied pussy

Namita: LMAO

Namita: hehhee

Nicholas: it will be a round peg in a round hole so to speak but we wont need directions to put them together lol

Nicholas: they'll just fit perfectly

Namita: lol ..niceeeee

Namita: a nice and tight fit too

Nicholas: now I'm just looking for more creative ways to talk about ur privates

Namita: hehehe

Nicholas: ohhh I like tight... not too tight but just right

Namita: i had one ...but kinda sounds crude ...hehehe

Nicholas: I'm sure once you adjust to it they'll be inseparable

Nicholas: oh say it damn it!

Namita: mmmmm yesss

Namita: LOL

Nicholas: we're way past that lol

Namita: like a banana in a split

Nicholas: GOOD ONE!!! well said!!

Namita: actually ive never even had one ...LMAO

Namita: im sure you will take care of that one

Nicholas: you will when we're done lol

Namita: LMAO

Nicholas: lol like minds

Nicholas: too funny

Namita: we are sooooooooo BAD

Nicholas: yes we are!!

Nicholas: and we will be!

Namita: lickety split ...yes we are

Nicholas: bad and naughty

Namita: omg im on a roll !!!!

Nicholas: yes you are

Namita: LOL

Nicholas: I'll lickety ur split anytime

Namita: Ohhhhhhhhhhhhh myyyyyyyyyyyyyy

Namita: hehehhehehe

Namita: Naughty Nicholas !!!!!!!!!!!!

Nicholas: that's me

Nicholas: you bring out the naughty in me

Namita: hehhee

Nicholas: soooo whatcha wearing?

Namita: nothing !!

Nicholas: oh my god really?

Namita: nooo ...im wearing a dark pink nightie

Nicholas: nice

Namita: but i am kinda hot ...so who knows where things end up

Nicholas: though the image I had was better

Nicholas: I wish they'd end up on me

Namita: i wonder what you would do if i wake up the middle of the nite to take off what im wearing ..and u wake up from ur sleep to see what im up to ? ...LOL

Nicholas: I probly jump you

Namita: what you wanna wear my nightie . heheh

Namita: hahhahahha

Nicholas: lol ah no

Nicholas: lol

Namita: from ur slumber .... you would jump me ??

Nicholas: sure would!!

Namita: LOL

Nicholas: that's if you'd let me of course

Namita: then maybe id have to straddle you down ... and go down boy !! while i strip off due to being hot

Nicholas: and why not ur awake I'm awake, we're both in bed sounds like a good idea to me

Namita: lol ... oh i see you've already rationalized this

Nicholas: ooooo now thats an image I'll hang on to, you straddling me while u strip mmm mmm mmm

Nicholas: oh yah

Namita: ohhhhh i totally do it !!!!!!!!

Nicholas: I can't wait to see it

Namita: i will do it when you come home from work ...and i grab you like a mad woman ...from the door ... shove you down on the floor

Nicholas: cool

Namita: straddle you and start ripping my clothes off

Nicholas: nice!!

Namita: revealing my full breasts

Namita: and lingerie

Namita: while you laying down flat on the floor in bewilderment

Namita: id be wearing a racy red bra

Nicholas: sounds awesome to me

Namita: and there i am ...stripping

Namita: on top of you

Nicholas: what guy wouldn't want to be greeted that way

Namita: hehhee

Namita: ur hands on my thighs

Namita: inching ur way under my short skirt

Nicholas: oooo so nice

Namita: then you cup my breasts ..feel me thru the fabric of the lace

Nicholas: would you consider urself a nimpho? or you just like making love all the time?

Namita: rub and tease my nipples thru the lace

Namita: id say a nympho

Nicholas: soooo nice

Namita: isnt that the same thing though ?

Nicholas: not really

Namita: hmm maybe i dont know what a nympho is

Namita: hehe

Nicholas: nymph is someone who needs to do it all the time ... hang on let me look it up

Nicholas: I think you just have a healthy sex drive like me

Namita: lol ok

Nicholas: nymphomania |ˌnimfəˈmānēə| noun uncontrollable or excessive sexual desire in a woman.

Namita: a sex maniac ?

Nicholas: ooops that didn't really cut n paste well

Nicholas: yes

Namita: no i have a healthy desire

Nicholas: thought so. me too

Namita: ohhh phew ...thanks for clearing that up !! Hehhee

Nicholas: no problem

Nicholas: just wanted to make sure we were on the same page

Nicholas: esp when I'm attracted to my partner

Nicholas: I want to be naked w her as much as possible

Namita: well what if i craved sex all the time ... and was a nympo ...how would it be change things ... hehe

Nicholas: if u craved it? hopefully I can satisfy you, he says knowingly... wouldn't change a thing

Namita: hehehhe

Namita: youd be one tired Nicholas !!!

Nicholas: I know I can it was more being able to satisfy the nimph in you

Nicholas: yah the little Nicholas would be tired thats for sure

Nicholas: well not that little lol

Namita: lol

Namita: tired and hallucinating the old times

Namita: not eating ..cuz most of his time is taken up making love

Nicholas: yup

Namita: talking to himself... pushing marbles around on the floor lol

Namita: hehe

Nicholas: so for our 2nd date what would you like to do?

Namita: we can play snakes and ladders

Nicholas: if we do Rocky Point n Gelato for the first date

Nicholas: I'll bring the snake n you bring the ladder?

Nicholas: I know that doesn't sound like a great innuendo but I tried

Namita: yep ...and every time one falls down the ladder we have to strip one article of clothing

Nicholas: ok

Namita: lol

Namita: i just got it

Nicholas: it was a time joke, when you have time you laugh

Namita: nah i think you should bring the snake and the wood

Nicholas: that I will

Namita: lol

Nicholas: I was thinking for our 2nd date I could bring over the Shawshank Redemption n we could have a dinner movie night?

Nicholas: I guess I'd bring dinner too

Nicholas: kinda hard to have dinner when all I brought was a movie

Namita: no ...i can make dinner too ...movie nite sounds good

Nicholas: cool... now we just need to find the time

Nicholas: lol

Namita: yes

Namita: lol

Nicholas: we have the dates all planned just no time to do them lol

Namita: hehe ...im sure things will fall into place

Nicholas: yes they will

Namita: at least we're not at a loss for things to do

Namita: hehe

Nicholas: it will take time to open our lives for each other

Nicholas: yes we definitely have lots to do

Namita: hehe yesss

Nicholas: they're falling into place now

Nicholas: I had a bit of a reality check today

Namita: hows that ?

Nicholas: was all this w you just sunk in more

Nicholas: I smiled quite a bit today from it

Namita: ahhh hehehhe

Nicholas: maybe reality check isn't the right words

Namita: glad to put a smile on ur face

Nicholas: was more of the reality of you sinking in more

Nicholas: you DO make me smile Namita

Namita: aweee thanks nicholas

Namita: do you have plans tomorrow with tony ?

Nicholas: during the day?

Namita: well anytime

Nicholas: just going out to the Blarney for the Halloween party at night

Namita: ohh are you dressing up too

Nicholas: probly just hang out during the day

Nicholas: catch up

Nicholas: of course we're dressing up,, can't go not dressed up

Namita: i mean dressed up for halloween ...you goof !

Nicholas: that looks really silly to go to a halloween party not dressed up

Namita: hehe ...what are u dressing up as

Nicholas: yes... going in my Army Ant costume

Nicholas: still need to dig it out tmw

Namita: ohhhh

Namita: what about Tony

Nicholas: been trying to dig it out all week but didn't feel motivated to do so

Nicholas: he's going as a Highland Warrior

Namita: ohhh cool

Nicholas: yah should be fun

Nicholas: the last time I wore the AA (Army Ant) I got 4th place

Namita: ohh wow !! that is cool ...looks like you did a good job with the sewing

Nicholas: I don't look for the prises I just like to design, build and wear my costumes

Nicholas: prizes*

Nicholas: thx

Namita: thx for what

Namita: hehe

Namita: geez

Nicholas: saying it looks like i did a good job on the sewing

Namita: ohhh ur welcome

Namita: maybe one day ..you can go as a sexy nurse ..and i will go as a worker with hard hat on ...heheh

Nicholas: lol sure

Namita: lol

Nicholas: I still need to get my next costume done, the interstellar bounty hunter n you could go as an alien goddess that I've captured

Namita: ohhhhhhhhhhhh yesssssssss

Namita: that would be cool

Nicholas: yes it would

Nicholas: we'll have to keep an eye out for a direction to take the idea in.. if that makes sense?

Namita: hehe ...give me an idea

Nicholas: off the top of my head I'm thinking body suit maybe blue w some sort of markings on it

Namita: ohh yess ...i thought of that .... and big rounded boobs

Nicholas: scales or some type of print

Namita: uh huh

Nicholas: well we don't need to look for big rounded boobs, already have those

Namita: i was thinking of Katie Perry's song where she is an alien ...not that im a huge fan of hers

Namita: but the effect of her makeup was pretty good

Nicholas: meh but the idea could work

Namita: hehe thanks for the boob comment

Namita: do you like my boobs

Nicholas: yah the make up cary the same print onto ur face or up ur neck

Namita: yessssss cool

Nicholas: very much soo

Nicholas: and ur quite welcome

Namita: i could put in some contacts ...maybe black ... to add to the effect

Nicholas: I'll show you one day how much I like them

Namita: thanks

Namita: hehe

Namita: mmmmmmmmmm

Namita: would loveeeeeeeeee that

Nicholas: I'm sure you will

Namita: mmm yess

Nicholas: yah some type of alien that's not a copy of something that way it doesn't have to be accurate to anything

Namita: yesss true

Nicholas: I find that easier to do costumes that way

Nicholas: hhmmmm only a few more days till ur back... i can do it

Namita: oh god im falling asleep nicholas

Nicholas: not that I want u to rush while ur dwn there

Nicholas: ok

Namita: soo sorry

Nicholas: do you want to say gnight?

Namita: is that ok with you

Nicholas: sokay we've been racking up the late nights

Nicholas: sure

Namita: hehe ...yess

Nicholas: I don't want to keep you from getting enf sleep

Namita: i dont want u to feel im ignoring u

Nicholas: I don't

Namita: good

Nicholas: we've had a good chat n I got to talk w you

Namita: yesss its good that we can connect still

Nicholas: depending when I'm home tmw I may be able to talk but depends when I'm home

Nicholas: and we connect on sooo many levels my dear Namita

Namita: ya no worries ... you have a fun time ...dont rush for anything

Nicholas: I wont but thx for saying it... it'll depend on how much energy Tony has as to how long we stay out

Nicholas: oh one thing

Namita: yes

Nicholas: turns out Tony's cancer isn't operable till the mass shrinks

Namita: yes i remember you telling me about it

Nicholas: that's what I was gonna tell you yesterday but forgot

Namita: you did tell me

Namita: hehe

Nicholas: oh okay

Nicholas: wasn't sure

Namita: hehe no worries

Nicholas: anyway sleep well my sweet enjoy your day tmw

Nicholas: always a good time talking w you

Namita: thank you … you guys have a great day tomorrow

Nicholas: get ur sexy little ass back here so we can talk face to face hehe

Nicholas: we will thx

Namita: hehehe

Nicholas: gnight Namita

Namita: k goodnite nicholas

End Time: 3:28 AM

Chapter 19 November 11

For the next few nights I logged on and waited but again, Namita wasn't around. I was worried something happened to her uncle. As the days passed I worried something happened to her. I sent her an email to find out.

Hey you. I'm going through some serious Namita withdrawal. I miss you soooooo much. This has been the longest week of my life. I had a strange feeling Sunday evening that carried through to Monday. It was like someone let the air out of me. A feeling that something terrible has happened... like I've lost you. I never knew I could miss someone so much. I know you're not the type of person to just disappear. Which leads me to believe something has happened to your family or god forbid to you. I understand and respect if you need some time... though this waiting and not knowing anything is killing me!!! The not knowing anything is the hardest. I'll be here when you need me but please if your able send me something to let me know you're okay.... an email, a text or even a phone call... If there's anything I can do to help please let me know. I'll keep the msn light on for you and hope you can find your way back to me. "Hope is a good thing... sometimes the best of things"..... I hope this finds you well... I hope to see you... I hope you come back to me.... I hope whatever powers that brought you to me in the first place will bring you back again.

Patiently waiting,

Nicholas xo

If I still haven't heard form her by the end of the week I'll call St. Paul's hospital. Better yet, I'll go in but, what would I say? "Hey, I met Namita online and we're kind of seeing each other. I just wondered if you'd heard from her?" I don't want to look like a fool going in and her co-workers say, "Yah, she's fine." So, I decided not to call or stop by.

As the days passed my heart would sink a little deeper. How can I care so much for someone I've never met in person? She has to come back to me at some point!

If the girls didn't have that pro D-day the Friday before she left we could have met then. Though it would make this waiting a lot harder.

I'm now at the point where, if I have to, I'll delete all her photos and our conversations and convince myself she never existed.

I decided to give her one more night. I got home, showered, logged on and went to get my snack. I was winding down, thinking of heading to bed when I finally heard the Messenger bing!

Start Time: 12:28 AM

Nicholas: hello

Namita: omg it finally worked !!

Namita: hellooo there

Nicholas: omg I thought I'd lost you!

Nicholas: how have you been?

Namita: my computer is slowly dieing

Namita: im well ...im still not back yet though

Namita: and my pc has been giving me a lot of grief

Namita: im sorry for not being in touch

Nicholas: I figured... I tried calling but your phone isn't charged so it sends a message saying something like that

Nicholas: its totally okay you're here now

Namita: ohhh ... everything is dead ...hehe

Nicholas: how is your uncle?

Namita: im not back yet nicholas

Nicholas: I realized that

Namita: my uncle is still in grave condition ...and my aunt , his wife ...is taking it real bad

Nicholas: I've seen you trying to log in a few times but not being able to get on

Namita: i think it is better that there are ppl around her

Nicholas: I'm so sorry to hear that... my thoughts have been going out to you n ur family

Namita: i havent been able to access my email

Namita: finally i told one of my cousin ...so he looked into the problem

Nicholas: I figured something like that was happening w ur email that is

Namita: thank you soooo much nicholas for understanding

Nicholas: its so nice to hear from you my dear

Namita: how have you been ?

Nicholas: okay... not a day has passed that I haven't thought about you n what you must be going through

Nicholas: hmmm... I got a new fridge

Nicholas: lol

Namita: aweee thanks nicholas

Namita: a new fridge ...what kind ?

Nicholas: its a Danby.. the landlords bought it... I told them the old one was on its last legs so the got me a new one

Nicholas: took me 4 hrs to get the old one out

Namita: omgg ...the old one must have been a dinosaur !!

Nicholas: who ever built the dwnstairs here must have built the kitchen around the appliances coz there wasn't enf room to get the old one out

Nicholas: I ended up cutting part of the back out just to clear the counter

Namita: ohhh woww ... did you end up cursing a lot ??? LOL

Nicholas: lol I did

Namita: hehehehe

Nicholas: n lots of head scratching too lol

Namita: hehehe

Nicholas: the new one is so great though

Namita: i hare moving furniture

Namita: hate i mean

Nicholas: me too

Namita: cool !! do you have lots of room in it ?

Nicholas: I got stuck at one point

Namita: ohh nooo !!!

Nicholas: it's not as big as the old one but this one works, I even bought ice cream

Namita: wowwww it is time to celevrate

Namita: omg i cant spell !!

Namita: celebrate I mean

Namita: hehe

Namita: now you can buy produce without worrying about it going bad quickly

Nicholas: its totally fine... I've missed your misspelling

Namita: hehehe

Nicholas: I've missed you SO much!

Namita: well i missed talking to you too

Nicholas: I've been sending you emails every couple of day just to let you know I was thinking about you

Namita: how has work been for you ?

Nicholas: *smiling*

Namita: aweee soo sweet !!

Nicholas: work has been dragging a little.... I think mostly coz I haven't heard form you... but it's all good now

Namita: yeah ive been trying to sign in ... then get frustrated ...plus im tired ...so i gave up sometimes ... i wished i could throw the laptop out the window ....heheheh

Namita: ohhh good to hear ... do you work tomorrow too ?

Nicholas: no work tmw

Nicholas: Remembrance Day

Namita: ohh yesss remembrance day

Nicholas: dont forget to give your 2 mins at 11

Namita: yes i will ... ive been wearing my poppy too

Nicholas: I was leaving msn on when I could n I saw you trying to log on

Nicholas: good to hear

Namita: do you wear one ?

Nicholas: yes I make sure I've got mine on when ever I'm pot

Namita: huh ? im pot ?? Ur smoking pot now ???

Namita: hehehe

Namita: niceeeeeee nicholas

Namita: just niceeeeeee

Nicholas: I use to spend it w my grampa as he's a veteran from ww2

Nicholas: but the last few years the holiday has been during the week

Namita: ohhhh .... i totally respect ppl who served in any of the wars

Nicholas: that was suppose to be "out"

Namita: whenever i get a patient that i hear has served in the war ...they always get extra attention from me

Nicholas: nice to hear

Namita: oh yeah right !!!

Nicholas: Tony is a veteran too

Namita: hehe

Namita: yess how is he doing ?

Namita: has he gone back home ?

Nicholas: not bad... he got laid off from work, lack of projects... oh yes he left on sun of the same weekend

Namita: ohh i see

Nicholas: his mass has shrunk a millimeter

Namita: ohhh wow thats good news !!

Nicholas: it is

Namita: anything is better than nothing

Nicholas: yes

Nicholas: I guess the Dr's have been hitting his cancer pretty hard so its nice to hear its working

Namita: i know some of those chemotherapy drugs can be quite harsh to the body ... i give those to my patients too .... in IV form ....and have to take soo many precautions to protect myself too from any exposure to the drugs

Nicholas: have you been able to do anything else while ur there or has it just been circling the wagons?

Namita: esp to the nurses of child bearing ages

Nicholas: wow... are the drugs absorbed through the skin?

Nicholas: I mean can you get it in ur system if you just touch it?

Namita: hehe ... once in while we would go out to clear our minds ... maybe shopping or the other guys go for drinks ...but i usually opt out of it the drinking part of it

Namita: yes those drugs can be absorbed thru skin .... i have to double glove, wear eye shields and masks

Nicholas: wow, those are some potent drugs

Namita: yes you can get it into ur system ...and if one of us is pregnant it is not good .... cause it can cause birth defects

Nicholas: Tony's on IV chemo.... my dad had chemo pills

Namita: usually pregnant nurses are not assigned those patients

Nicholas: I bet it would

Nicholas: makes sense

Namita: did tony feel decreased energy ?

Nicholas: oh yah... I can see it in him too

Namita: im sure it was hard for you to see him like that ...

Nicholas: turned out in the morning after we went out that he was up most on the night throwing up.... they said no drinking while on the meds n now he believes it

Nicholas: a little

Nicholas: he was his usual self just less energy

Namita: ohh nooo ...poor tony !!

Namita: hehe i guess he pushed it a little

Nicholas: for a big guy he's pretty soft or easily knocked dwn

Namita: hehe

Namita: how was the halloween party ?

Nicholas: he likes to push things n live for the day

Nicholas: oh right

Namita: at blarneys ??

Nicholas: Blarney Stone yes

Namita: you dressed as the army ant ?

Nicholas: I came 2nd to a couple of store bought Angry Birds costumes

Nicholas: I did

Nicholas: Angry Birds from the iPhone game

Namita: ohh wow !!!

Nicholas: it would have been nice to win something but I just like to dress up n have fun

Namita: yes i had that on my phone too ... a little addictive i must admit

Nicholas: so I've heard

Namita: you can play it on my phone ...and i will sit back and watch you

Namita: hehehe

Nicholas: I'm looking at getting an iPhone soon.... I'll see what kind of sale Fido has closer to Xmas

Nicholas: okay deal lol

Namita: yes i think you can use it as an ipod too ..and download songs

Nicholas: I'll just be happy to be in the same room w you lol

Namita: id be wondering ...so i come in second to angry birds ?!

Namita: Geeeeeezzz !! !

Nicholas: you'd never come in 2nd w me my sweet!!

Nicholas: good one though lol

Namita: hehhee

Nicholas: I'll make sure you come first if not at the same time hehe

Namita: i tried ... i can just picture it ...ur playing like a mad man with angry birds ...and i sit nearby rolling my eyes

Namita: hehehehehe GOOD ONE !!!

Nicholas: thx

Nicholas: have I mentioned how great it is to talk to you again

Namita: my my someone is quick witted tonite !! lol

Namita: not that this second you didnt

Namita: hehe

Nicholas: been pent up for 12 days give or take... not like I was counting or anything

Namita: hehe ... ohhh nooo ... you sound like a lion in a cage !!! of course who's counting

Nicholas: I've been re-reading our conversations just to have some contact w you

Namita: ohhh .... did it keep u occupied?

Nicholas: my world was a little grey the last few days but POOF pink smoke n ur back lol

Nicholas: they did

Namita: hehe ... i can imagine the pink smoke !!

Nicholas: I'm amazed at how intensely HOT our convo's got

Nicholas: its like we were actually doing it then decided to write it out so we don't forget

Namita: hehe ..it didnt take much sometimes .. i think

Namita: hehehehe

Nicholas: no it didn't

Nicholas: those like minds

Nicholas: just a preview of what's to come... I think lol

Namita: yess it was quite intense too ... i could almost feel it

Nicholas: yes me too

Nicholas: I dreamt about you the other night... 2 nights in a row actually

Namita: REAAALLLY ??? what did you dream of ?

Nicholas: just goes to show where my thoughts have been

Namita: hehe

Namita: im in ur subconscious now too

Nicholas: you know how dreams jump around a lot.... well I dreamt that I was on top of you.... holding you close as we were doing it... was sooo cool...

Nicholas: a little disappointing when I woke n you weren't there

Namita: mmmmm wowwowowowoow !!!

Namita: i never have dreams like that !!

Nicholas: I could feel you... n smell you

Namita: its always something stupid

Nicholas: I don't usually remember my dreams

Namita: hehe ....wowww really ?

Nicholas: my dreams have a way of coming true

Nicholas: yes

Namita: very cool !!

Nicholas: once I dreamt that I had all the numbers in the Super 7 lotto.... when I checked my ticket later that day I had all 7 numbers they were just on different lines

Namita: i know the last dream i could remember was a lil disturbing mainly cuz i watched some halloween movies around that time ...and totally creeped myself out for days ...even now if i think about it

Namita: OMMG Nicholas !!

Namita: LOL

Nicholas: another time I dreamt about those red caps on a roll of paper that you put in a cap gun, you know the ones from when we were kids?

Namita: oh yes

Nicholas: in my dream I was standing at the counter in a corner store n looked down to my right n saw those Red Caps then the dream was over

Nicholas: then a day or so later I was at the gym talking to a woman about dreams and how some of mine come true and I told her about the dream with the Caps. She got this strange look on her face n from out of her purse she pulls out a box of those very same Caps!... she said she saw them the other day n didn't know why but she bought them... she gave them to me. I still have them

Namita: WOW !! now thats spooky !!!

Namita: well one time ...and this not a dream.... this is when i was a teen

Namita: my dad sent me to the corner store... to get a printout of the winning lotto numbers

Nicholas: ok

Namita: when i got the printout... it looked just like the ticket printout... on my way out the store i also grabbed the lotto news paper... to check past numbers

Namita: on my way home im walking down the street and im checking the numbers and the goofball that i am i take the lotto winning number printout and check those numbers against the same numbers printed on the newspaper and OMG I thought i won the lottery !!! I ran all the way home rushed into the living room screaming gave it to my dad showed the numbers

Nicholas: lol funny

Namita: and of course he is now jumping for joy too ... looking at the exact match

Namita: and then my sisters join in

Nicholas: tooo funny

Nicholas: lmaofl!!

Namita: my mom comes over from the kitchen ...looks at us and asks wheres our ticket

Nicholas: priceless!!

Namita: and i kept showing the winning printout ticket

Nicholas: lol

Namita: shes like noooooooooo wheres our 649 ticket

Namita: and im like here it is !!!

Nicholas: talk about a real downer

Nicholas: after you figured it out

Namita: she kept repeating herself.... and we were oblivious to what she was saying... so she let us whoop for joy a bit longer before she broke our bubble

Nicholas: lol

Namita: Yesssss that was the most downest time everrrrrrrrrrr

Namita: hehehhehe

Nicholas: too bad

Namita: my dad ran around the house to catch me so he could hit me over the head ...of course playfully

Namita: everyone was trying to catch me to whack me !!!

Namita: even the dog !!

Nicholas: damn eh... you could have been millionaires

Namita: Omggg !!

Namita: hey but i did win this past summer ...about 160.00 ...did i tell you ?

Nicholas: you didn't... that's cool

Namita: the most i ever won was 350.00 yrs ago !!

Nicholas: wow... the most I've won was $90.00

Namita: yesss that was a surprise when i was checkin that one ticket this summer

Namita: wowww that pretty good too !!!

Namita: Didnt you feel like grabbing the money before they say ...sorry that was a mistake !!

Namita: thats what i felt like !!

Nicholas: ooo which reminds me I need to get a tix for tmw Lotto Max n 649

Nicholas: yes

Namita: how much is it ?

Nicholas: the Lotto Max is $50 mil n 649 is $30 or $40 can't remember but they're both big

Nicholas: I usually get a tix when it's really big

Namita: wowwww i wonder who is going to win in Ontario ?? Hehhee

Nicholas: you can't win if you don't play

Namita: yes me too

Nicholas: yah no kidding

Namita: nooo i always do ... at least on the fridays

Namita: how much do u spend on it ..if u dont mind me asking ?

Nicholas: I play for fun

Nicholas: usually only 1 tix, sometimes 2

Nicholas: what do you spend?

Nicholas: or how much I should say

Namita: Hehehe .. i really dont know what i would do ... sometimes i think i will work casual .... i definitely dont want to gruel over my work

Namita: the most i spend is 20 bucks

Namita: i see ppl forking over like 100 bucks ... omg i would never do that

Nicholas: I would do what I was meant to do n what I love to do... design n build my projects

Nicholas: yah that's way too much

Namita: yessss that would be a life !!

Nicholas: n be able to just leave for a vacation whenever n where ever

Namita: ive never been in a casino before ... or ever played ... nor do i want to ... so this is my tops for gambling in a way

Namita: yesss that would be sooo nice

Namita: have you been to reno or vegas?

Nicholas: I went to a casino in the spring for the first time n blew $20.00 in about an hr on the slots... was so not fun... was quite boring I thought

Nicholas: never been to Vegas or Reno

Namita: hehehe ...was it a local casino ?

Nicholas: yup the Boulevard casino

Namita: yeah reno or vegas just doesnt appeal to me

Nicholas: Reno has a huge car show in August

Namita: ppl flock to those places ... like several times a year

Namita: oh really ??? Like old cars ?

Nicholas: its called Hot August Nights n there's about 3000 hot rods

Nicholas: I've wanted to go for years

Namita: ohhh niceeee ...ok theres a reason to go then

Nicholas: yup

Namita: hehe

Nicholas: would be cool to take mine though I'd trailer it down to the out skirts of town then drive into town

Nicholas: they shut dwn the main drag for the weekend n then it's just hot rods as far as the eye can see

Namita: hehe ... does it take gas ... i mean is it gas powered ??? excuse my ignorance on hotrods ?

Nicholas: sokay... yes

Nicholas: stick w me n you'll know more than you ever care to know about hot rods lol

Nicholas: and you don't know unless you ask

Namita: LOL

Namita: i would like to know everything about ur rods nicholas

Namita: hehee

Nicholas: I use to wonder how my dad knew all he knew about them n after a while you pick it up

Nicholas: lol

Namita: ahhh i see

Nicholas: ur still talking my custom car when you're talking about my hot rod right? lol

Namita: hehe of course i am 😜

Nicholas: coz I'm more than happy to tell n show you both lol

Namita: hehehhee

Namita: will you show me how they work ?

Nicholas: yes of course

Namita: can i run my hands down the smooth exterior

Nicholas: it'll be a hands on teaching

Namita: hahahahha

Namita: any refreshments that you will provide ?

Nicholas: hmm refreshments? maybe some oil you know to ensure proper lubrication

Namita: hehheehe

Namita: yesss we cant forget that !!!

Nicholas: though if I touch you the right way you can provide proper lubrication hehe

Namita: hehehe

Namita: yes no need for extra lub on ur part

Nicholas: my hot rod vibrates too

Nicholas: the car that is

Namita: ohhhh really !!! Can i feel it ??

Nicholas: while it's idling it does

Namita: hehehe

Nicholas: hell yah!!

Namita: does it warm up pretty quick ?

Nicholas: that it does

Nicholas: and has pretty big ties too

Nicholas: tires

Namita: ahhh i see ...can it give me a good ride ?

Nicholas: OOOOhhhh that it can, just you wait!!

Namita: hhhehehehheehehehe

Nicholas: you'll wonder how you ever got anywhere without it

Namita: hehehe... yes id be wondering…. what have i been missing !!

Nicholas: it is a stick shift so you'll have to learn quickly how the shift gears lol

Namita: ohhhh geeez !!!

Nicholas: I think you'll be just fine

Namita: i get to ride a stick shift !!

Nicholas: that you do

Namita: actually is it hard ... to drive in stick shift ?

Nicholas: not really just takes time, like most new things

Namita: ahh i see .... you will have to teach me then

Nicholas: I most certainly will

Namita: deal then

Nicholas: cool

Nicholas: any idea when you might be heading back?

Nicholas: it must be quite exhausting for you

Nicholas: I know it was for us every time my dad was in the hospital

Namita: im not so sure right now .... i actually have just over a month off ... i didnt want to tell u that earlier a week ago ...cuz i didnt want to get u excited or ur hopes up

Namita: i am exhausted ... tonight my back is killing me

Nicholas: I see

Nicholas: are you using ur holiday time for this?

Namita: yes i am

Nicholas: oh how I would love to give you a massage for ur back

Namita: it was already scheduled at this time ... so it was pure coincidence that things were happening at this time

Namita: with family

Nicholas: wow... not quite how you intended to spend ur holiday I bet

Namita: i loveeeeeeeee that too

Namita: i mean ur back rub

Nicholas: oh wow... funny how things happen for a reason

Namita: i knowwww

Nicholas: I knew what you meant

Namita: hehe

Nicholas: n yes that would have gotten my hopes up lol

Namita: i always find it soooo weird how things seem to sort themselves out

Nicholas: that they do... we just have to be open to them happening

Namita: i do plan to come back and have some time for myself ...and hopefully finally meet

Namita: hey how are ur girls ?

Nicholas: things might not always go the way we plan them but they do find a way

Namita: yesss they sure do

Nicholas: they seem okay.... there mom is still talking about moving to Maple Ridge so we'll see if that happens

Nicholas: I have Amanda this weekend as Isabel is going to a Pathfinder camp for the weekend

Namita: oh i didnt know that was in her plans

Namita: ahhh i see

Nicholas: my mom is coming to twn tmw too... she'll spend the day w the 2 of us then she's going to watch my sis dance in Richmond

Namita: do u have any plans with amanda ?

Namita: ohh cool

Namita: Ur sister dances ?? What kind of dance ?

Nicholas: Amanda has a Remembrance Day ceremony to attend for Scouts which I'm taking her to

Nicholas: my sis just got into Ballroom dancing

Namita: ohhh wowwww

Nicholas: so she's competing in her first competition this weekend

Namita: do you dance ?

Nicholas: my mom n dad use to compete too

Namita: wowwww that is very cool !!

Nicholas: I like to dance

Namita: OMG ur parents too !! I am impressed !!

Nicholas: they were quite good

Nicholas: my dad got into shape from all the dancing

Namita: wow... ur mom must be an expert

Namita: ive thought about taking dancing lessons

Nicholas: he was always a little heavy.. not over weight though

Namita: but never really got the chance

Nicholas: well maybe you will wink wink

Namita: plus the commitment ..and the shift work wont work

Namita: hehehhe

Namita: thanks nicholas

Nicholas: I like to dance when the mood hits

Nicholas: move how you want w the rhythm

Namita: yesss ...what kind of dance ?

Nicholas: me?

Namita: yess you ?

Namita: but i get what ur saying too

Nicholas: just bumpn' n grinding

Namita: move with the rhythm

Namita: hehehhe

Nicholas: feel the music

Namita: ohhhhh nicholas !!!

Nicholas: I have rhythm n can find the beat so not to worry I'm not a spaz lol

Namita: lol

Nicholas: I find it interesting watching others dance coz they say the way you dance is the way you are in bed

Namita: hehehe ..really ???

Nicholas: you never heard that?

Namita: what kind of dance would describe you ?

Namita: yes i guess i have heard of it .... in distant memory

Nicholas: depends on the music but mostly sensual

Namita: yess im like that too

Namita: one of my coworkers has been trying to get me into belly dancing ... and i was thinking of it too even before she said it

Namita: it really helps to strengthen the core muscles

Nicholas: as I say I like to feel the music... I've always been passionate about it... I've always felt the music if that makes sense

Namita: i like mostly the indian version of belly dancing

Nicholas: music for me invokes feelings

Namita: there are sooo many types

Namita: yesss me too ...i totally agree

Nicholas: there are? didn't know that

Namita: yes there is indian, arabian, lebanese and i cant remember the other ones

Nicholas: music that I really like has always made me feel all warm n fuzzy inside.... for lack of better terms

Namita: i know greece has their own too

Namita: yess i know what you mean

Nicholas: wow that's a lot of bellies dancing lol

Namita: hehehe

Namita: here i give u a link of the indian version

Nicholas: okay cool

Nicholas: I'm sure you'd be quite good at it

Namita: it is actually american ...but a fusion belly dancing

Namita: one sex

Namita: omg i mean one sec

Nicholas: lol sure

Namita: LOL

Nicholas: slip of the finger yah right lol

Namita: what has gotton into me !!

Namita: hehhee it wassssssssss

Nicholas: hopefully me

Nicholas: one day hehe

Namita: the girl that does this kind of belly dancing is american ....her name is rachel brice

Nicholas: oh yah

Nicholas: side note: is ur computer fixed now?

Namita: i hope so

Nicholas: cool

Namita: seems like its working ...so far so good

Nicholas: so we'll be able to talk tmw too, and the day after and so on? lol

Namita: hehe yess

Nicholas: excellent

Namita: lol

Nicholas: when you see my emails you'll see how much I missed you

Namita: http://www.youtube.com/watch?v=gnYYK07lGFc heres one of them ...not the one i wanted ...but it depicts more of a indian belly dancing

Nicholas: I was trying to figure out how I could miss you so much and be so attached to you w/o having met you in person.. what i came up with is because we've connected on so may levels that the physical is just the missing piece.... I hope that makes sense

Namita: hehehe it does totally make sense ...ive thought of that too

Namita: http://www.youtube.com/watch?v=lvpuMKCxDf4&feature=related

Nicholas: okay good... that you understand that is

Nicholas: there's a lot of body control in this first version.. very cool

Namita: i loveee how she has something tattoeed on her hip in indian ...and i dont know what it says

Nicholas: I saw that too

Namita: hehee

Nicholas: is it a competition?

Namita: i think it takes years and years of practice to get to that point

Nicholas: I agree

Namita: yes its a competition

Namita: the second one you can see how flexible one has to be

Nicholas: I'll check it out when this one is done

Namita: ok

Nicholas: looks like she has a couple of tatt's

Nicholas: on her hips

Namita: hehe yes she does

Nicholas: okay looking at the 2nd one

Namita: ok

Nicholas: she could use a tan lol

Namita: lol

Namita: like me ?

Nicholas: yes like you nice n golden brown

Namita: hehhe ... like honey

Namita: all u need is whipped cream

Nicholas: holly sh** talk about flexible wow!!

Nicholas: mmmmhmmm

Namita: hehehe

Namita: i wish i can do that type of belly dancing

Nicholas: imagine doing that on top of me

Namita: lmaooooo

Namita: we could achieve a lot of unthinkable positions

Nicholas: that we could

Nicholas: that was cool… thx for sending it

Nicholas: you could do that easy… you just need to practice

Namita: yesss she is my idol and im glad she is actually putting forth the difference of belly dancing from a diff part of the world

Namita: hehe thanks for the vote of confidence

Namita: you can stand there with a can of oil if i get stuck

Nicholas: I'm sure ur great at whatever you do

Nicholas: oooh yes I'll oil you anytime

Nicholas: I'll be ur oil boy

Namita: heheeeee

Nicholas: er man

Namita: thanks oil boy !!

Namita: or man

Nicholas: no problem

Nicholas: what's the weather been like dwn there?

Namita: its been cloudy and sometimes drizzling in the morning

Nicholas: whenever I think of San Fran I think of Alcatraz

Nicholas: hmm been rainy on n off last few days

Namita: yess me too ....that is the prison place ..right

Nicholas: was sunny this afternoon which was nice

Nicholas: yup

Namita: ohh nice

Namita: you know it is reputed to be haunted

Namita: hehe

Nicholas: I was there back when I was 11... the family drove to Disneyland n we stopped there

Nicholas: I've heard that too

Namita: oohhh really ?? why ? do they still use it ?

Nicholas: its worth the time to go n look... its got quite the history too

Namita: one of the shows i watch at home

Nicholas: no its a museum now

Nicholas: they give tours

Namita: is ghost hunters ...on channel 49

Namita: and they did an episode their with their cameras

Namita: at nite

Nicholas: when I was there we had a tour guide but now you get hand held thing that tells you the info

Nicholas: I saw that one too

Namita: ohhh i see

Namita: you watch that show too ?

Nicholas: Escape From Alcatraz w Clint Eastwood is a great movie n based on the true story

Namita: ohhh never heard of it

Nicholas: I did when it was first on but it got a little too repetitive after a while

Nicholas: well we'll just add the one to the list of movies to watch

Namita: hehe

Namita: yes we will

Namita: i do like clint eastwood

Nicholas: I watched Shawshank Redemption the other night... had a hankerin' to see it again

Namita: ohhhh ...is it a long movie ?

Nicholas: I like him too... I have a few of his old westerns, classics

Namita: i loveee his oldies

Nicholas: about 3 hrs but sooooo worth it

Namita: i think i used to have a crush on him too

Namita: hehe

Nicholas: A Fist Full Of Dollars, For A Few Dollars More and The Good The Bad and the Ugly

Namita: yes good bad ugly

Nicholas: great movies!!

Namita: they were all great movies

Nicholas: those are actually a trilogy which I didn't know until recently

Namita: heheh ... i found out a couple of years ago too

Nicholas: I own them... of course

Namita: even the good bad ugly ??

Nicholas: yup it's the last one

Namita: omg i didnt know that !!!!!!!!!!!

Namita: HAAAAA ive been watchin it for most of my life ...and didnt know that

Namita: that GBU (The Good The Bad and The Ugly) was always my fav one

Nicholas: I've used a few quotes from the good the bad n the ugly w the girls so they wanted to watch it, so we did... they thought is was cool

Nicholas: mine too

Nicholas: my dad introduced me to those movies too so it's a little dad time when I watch them

Namita: clint was my grandfathers fav too

Nicholas: cool

Nicholas: do you like his directing?

Namita: yes my dad too ...he introduced me to them

Namita: then later to james bond

Nicholas: another similarity

Nicholas: I can take or leave JB (James Bond)

Namita: i just watched GBU with dad like 2 months ago

Nicholas: lol

Namita: hehe

Namita: you dont like JB ?

Nicholas: I don't mind it

Nicholas: take it or leave it

Nicholas: I liked Roger Moore the best

Nicholas: do you like Clint's directing?

Namita: i dont like all of it ...but i did see most of them including the new ones with daniel craig

Nicholas: Bridges of Madison County?

Namita: yes he is good i think ..clint .... i mean

Nicholas: did see the new ones

Namita: he has a new one out too

Nicholas: he does looks good

Namita: based on some president

Nicholas: J Edger

Namita: story

Nicholas: Hoover

Namita: yesss thats the one

Nicholas: head of the FBI

Namita: ahhh i see

Nicholas: Leo's (Lenardo DiCaprio) make up is really good

Namita: yes i had to do a double take on that one

Nicholas: he's an actor that really came into his own

Nicholas: Catch Me If You Can was good too

Namita: yesss i never saw that one of his

Namita: brb

Nicholas: really? hmm... excuse me while I just write that one dwn on the list

Nicholas: k

Namita: keep typing

Namita: heheh

Nicholas: okay

Nicholas: pee break?

Nicholas: have you seen Fight Club?

Namita: well yess ..and i was parched ...lol

Namita: no i havent seen that one either

Nicholas: excellent movie!!!

Namita: who is in it ?

Nicholas: we'll have watch that one too

Nicholas: Brad Pitt n Edward Norton

Namita: ohhh

Nicholas: it's not what you might think it's about... definitely a pay attention movie

Nicholas: and sooo good... at least I think so

Namita: ahhh will have to wait and see

Nicholas: a little violent in spots but goes w the movie

Namita: hmmm ... i dont mind that

Nicholas: and the story is very well written

Namita: is it one of brads earlier movies ?

Nicholas: a refreshing new story

Nicholas: mmm I guess... came out mmmm 10 years ago I think

Namita: i know i heard of it ..but never really paid much attention to it

Nicholas: side note: don't suppose you'd want to accompany me to my work christmas party?

Namita: when is it ?

Nicholas: Dec 3rd I think

Namita: i will have to see what im up to then

Namita: mine is ...on dec 6th

Nicholas: that's if you're back n we've seen each other a few times in between

Namita: hehe ...no we will see each other first time at ur party ...lol

Nicholas: oh you do have an xmas party for work... cool

Namita: where is the party ?

Nicholas: yah right how strange would that be

Namita: yes ours it the annual icu xmas party

Nicholas: it's in Richmond at a hotel

Namita: hehe

Namita: ahhhhh

Namita: sounds niceee

Nicholas: the guys say it's usually pretty good... good food.. good prizes to win

Namita: really ??

Nicholas: I didn't want to go solo

Nicholas: that's what they're saying

Namita: ive been to one of the xmas parties that we throw ... and its pretty much the same as what u said ...good food ,dancing , door prizes

Nicholas: there's about 60 guys on the floor n I don't know how many are in the office... don't know how many are going either

Nicholas: that's pretty much what's happening at mine too

Namita: ahhh wow ...im sure lots of ppl will show up

Nicholas: dinner prizes dancing

Namita: free one bottle champagne at each table

Nicholas: I'm thinking so too... a lot of them have been there for 15+ years so they know each other well

Nicholas: cool

Nicholas: free stuff is always nice

Namita: ours is at the Dockside Inn restaurant in Granville island

Nicholas: oh yah... never been... to that restaurant that is lol

Nicholas: it would be nice to see work ppl dressed up and to dress up myself too

Namita: me either ..not to this one ... the one i been to as a xmas party was at the vancouver yaght club

Namita: i spelled that wrong and dont know how

Nicholas: wow cool

Namita: that boat thingy place

Namita: hehe

Nicholas: totally fine I got it

Namita: hehe

Nicholas: yacht

Namita: yesssss

Namita: at one time our parties used to be dressed to the nines

Nicholas: don't know why there would be a "ch" in yacht but oh well

Namita: as in ball gowns and black tie

Nicholas: really? wow

Namita: yess at the yacht club

Nicholas: that might be a bit much

Namita: the women would wear ball gowns

Nicholas: ooooh maybe it was dress code for the club

Namita: i remember i wore a red strapless ball gown to that one

Nicholas: they can be pretty uppity at times

Nicholas: hmmm now that I would have loved to see

Namita: yess i think so too ... it took me forever to find a something nice ...and not look like im going to my high school grad

Namita: had my hair up

Nicholas: was thinking that when you said ball gown

Nicholas: mmm mmm mmm

Namita: now we are more casual ....kinda clubby look to the party

Nicholas: I imagine you'd look good in just about anything

Namita: hehehehe

Nicholas: that's cool

Namita: ur mind is racing like a race horse

Nicholas: mmmhmmm

Namita: i still have the dress ...dont know what to do with it

Namita: hehehe

Nicholas: yah that's the thing w dresses like that, you ware them once, then what?

Nicholas: sell it?

Namita: hehehe ... i could cut it up for dish rag

Nicholas: or modify it

Namita: but said nahhhhhhhhhh

Nicholas: lol yah right

Namita: yes i could cut it short ...and make it a mini

Nicholas: mmmhmmm mini is good

Namita: the top part was fitting ... so it would work

Nicholas: imagining it now

Namita: lol

Nicholas: red... form fitting... touching all those curves of yours

Namita: hehe ... ur really got that imagination going

Nicholas: short... not too short but just right

Namita: it had a zipper up the back

Nicholas: doesn't take much

Nicholas: good to know... I like details

Namita: hehe

Namita: more A Line than poofy

Nicholas: nice

Namita: and i had black strappy heels ...shiny black

Nicholas: I can visualize my projects so well that I can walk around them in my mind and hear the gravel under my feet as I walk

Nicholas: mmmhmm

Namita: ahhhh niceeeee ...thats sign of a good mind

Nicholas: I'm imagining walking around you taking all of you in

Namita: hehehe

Nicholas: you waiting for me to touch you but I'm still soaking you all in

Namita: and if i remember correctly i had a red rose in my hair ... at the side

Nicholas: cute touch

Nicholas: I bet all the ladies secretly wished they were you… or that they looked as good as you did

Nicholas: did you go solo?

Nicholas: I wasn't even there n I can see you

Namita: hehehe ...i dunno about that ...but most ppl wore black .... and i thought why not wear something that is festive and not dull ...or similar as everyone else

Nicholas: yes good call

Namita: i went solo

Namita: i dont care ...hehe

Nicholas: good for you... shows confidence

Nicholas: oh how I would have loved to be on your arm

Namita: yes i was going to say something to that effect ... i felt comfortable

Namita: hehehe

Namita: looking over the inlet ...under the starry bot cool nite

Namita: but*

Nicholas: yes yes

Namita: ppl were dancing outside on the deck too

Dancing outside on the deck in the middle of winter?

Nicholas: cool

Namita: that would be fun to do too

Nicholas: band

Namita: you and me

Nicholas: yes it would

Namita: yes they had a live band

Namita: and a dj

Nicholas: cool love live bands

Nicholas: we could hold each other close to keep warm

Namita: the doctors usually pay for the venue and the menu

Namita: mmmm yessss

Nicholas: wow

Nicholas: is it a diff place each year?

Namita: they keep the place for a few years then change

Nicholas: that's cool

Namita: maybe every 2 to 3 yrs change

Nicholas: a change is as good as a rest as my dearly departed dad use to say

Namita: one time it used to be at the sky bar ...some club in vancouver

Namita: but some of the girls got their drinks spiked

Nicholas: oh no!!

Namita: and was sick ...so they cancelled that one off the list

Namita: good thing i didnt go

Namita: hehe

Nicholas: good

Nicholas: yah good thing

Namita: 2 or 3 of them were found passed out in the bathroom

Nicholas: side note: from work does the name Jody Turner ring a bell

Nicholas: oohh no!!

Namita: uhh noo ..why ...is she a nurse ?

Nicholas: geeze.... were they okay?

Nicholas: yah she was

Nicholas: its Tony's mom

Namita: yes they brought to our ER ..and treated

Nicholas: she worked there

Namita: tonys mom is a nurse ?

Namita: which area ?

Nicholas: she was she's retired now

Nicholas: area? hmm thinking

Nicholas: she was at St Paul's

Nicholas: post surgical I think

Nicholas: not ICU but after that

Namita: there are sooo many nurses in so many areas ..its hard to keep track of everyone ... i dont even know everyone in my own icu ....and ive been there for several years now

Namita: ahhh i see

Nicholas: sokay just wondered

Namita: hehe

Namita: no worries

Nicholas: I'm sure you'd remember her she stands out

Nicholas: big personality

Namita: heheehehe ... id have to see her

Namita: does tony have siblings ?

Nicholas: yup 2 bro's

Nicholas: he's the oldest

Namita: ahhh ok

Namita: 😊

Namita: lol

Nicholas: the middle bro has his masters in business, lives in Calgary works at a bank I think just married this summer.... the youngest is gay n I'm not sure what he's up to these days

Namita: what are u writing for soo long

Namita: hehe

Nicholas: sorry

Nicholas: Tony's bro's

Namita: hehehe .... i like how you said ur last sentence

Nicholas: unsolicited info

Namita: heheheh

Nicholas: how so?

Nicholas: was the nutshell version

Namita: i think it just me ... i sometimes dont know how to be politically correct when someone is gay

Namita: what is the correct or accepted way of saying it

Nicholas: having a gay sister I just say gay

Namita: she doesnt mind

Nicholas: or lesbian

Nicholas: nope as long as it's not in a derogatory manner

Namita: yes ..my good friend ashley is gay too

Nicholas: men are gay n women are lesbians

Namita: but she is an absolute great friend of mine

Namita: yes i knew that ...hehehe

Nicholas: yes you've mentioned that

Namita: thanks nicholas

Nicholas: she's your car show carpool buddy

Namita: yes

Nicholas: see good listener

Namita: she is supposed to be back from her africa trip by now

Nicholas: cool Africa

Namita: yesss i can see that ...check !!!

Namita: she is south america last year

Namita: she did i mean

Nicholas: miranda is the photographer right?

Namita: yes

Namita: correct

Namita: hehe

Nicholas: thought so

Nicholas: she's also the designer

Nicholas: fashion

Namita: yes she is ...she is taking the courses ...and is almost done i think

Nicholas: cool

Namita: havent talked to her in a long while

Nicholas: hmm

Namita: hmmm

Nicholas: you're a busy woman so not surprising

Namita: hehehe .... but i like to keep in touch with everyone ...im not usually like this though

Nicholas: you're under extenuating circumstances at the moment so not to worry

Namita: aweee nicholas thank you for understanding ...that what makes you so special

Nicholas: Baloo is going to be sooo excited to see you when you get home

Nicholas: *smiling*

Nicholas: I've been there n family comes first

Namita: omg he is going to go nuts ...then pick his stuff toys and offer me them to me as if he bought it for me as a present

Nicholas: lol

Nicholas: poor thing

Namita: hehee

Nicholas: well I think you're pretty special too

Namita: i cant wait till you meet him ... im sure he will love you to bits

Namita: nahhh i think you are special !!

Nicholas: I'm sure he will

Nicholas: we'll be 2 special peas in a pod

Namita: hehehhee

Namita: yes the special ppl

Nicholas: special not in the ware your helmet kind of special lol

Namita: hehehhee

Nicholas: I actually saw a woman in the mall one time warring a helmet crawling along the wall lol

Namita: with drool seeping down our face

Namita: ohhh noooo was she lost ?

Nicholas: there you go again w the drool

Namita: hehehe

Nicholas: nope it was special ppl day at the mall coz they were everywhere

Namita: hahahah

Nicholas: in wheel chairs n walking

Namita: and you didnt get the memo

Nicholas: I thought I was seeing things at first

Nicholas: I didn't

Namita: hehehe

Nicholas: maybe I was suppose to be part of the group but didn't know it

Nicholas: lol

Nicholas: though I did drive myself there

Namita: did they tie a handkerchief around ur neck to color code you

Namita: hehehe

Nicholas: lol nope

Namita: thats what they do usually

Nicholas: didn't know that

Namita: im serious

Namita: hehe

Nicholas: now I'll be looking for the coloured tie

Namita: hehehe

Nicholas: er handkerchief

Namita: yesss the kerchif

Namita: heyyyy that reminds me

Nicholas: my spelling is spot on... that's 2 big words that I nailed first shot yeah me lol

Nicholas: yes

Namita: watch this http://www.youtube.com/watch?v=bq2crPwz_N4

Nicholas: okay

Namita: yess im proud of you

Namita: im still struggling here

Namita: with spelling

Nicholas: OMG that's funny!!

Namita: hehe

Nicholas: that has to be the best condom commercial EVer!!

Nicholas: check this video out

Nicholas: its for the Axe washing ball

Namita: hahahhahahahaa

Nicholas: I can't stand the smell of any of the Axe products..... spend a little money n buy a real sent

Namita: ive never seen this one before

Namita: HA !!!!

Nicholas: good eh?

Namita: omggg

Nicholas: I've seen a tame-er version on tv

Namita: hahhaha

Namita: have u seen the durex balloon video

Nicholas: nope

Nicholas: n those are my brand Durex Love

Namita: http://www.youtube.com/watch?v=i-L06PfDF-M&feature=related

Nicholas: LMAOF!!!

Namita: hehehe

Nicholas: the bloobers!!!

Namita: i know i loveeeeeee em !!

Nicholas: still laughing here too funny

Namita: hehehe

Nicholas: I have to put that on my facebook

Nicholas: too funny not to share

Namita: hehehe

Nicholas: are you on facebook?

Namita: no im not ... hehe

Namita: im behind the times

Nicholas: can't be bothered?

Nicholas: oh

Namita: yes ... cant be bothered ... plus i keep in touch with ppl

Nicholas: I hardly ever go on it n when I do it's just to post something

Nicholas: like the inflated condoms bonking

Nicholas: OMG have you seen this one?

Nicholas: I just saw it now

Nicholas: it's a play on bathroom gratify

Namita: hehehe it totally cracks me ... i like the part where the third one is spying and looks the other way when he is noticed

Nicholas: yes

Nicholas: I like the balloon condom bloopers... the one where it floats away

Namita: LMAOoooooooooooooo

Namita: im watching urs

Nicholas: too funny

Namita: hahahahhahahahhahahahahahahhahahahahha

Nicholas: oh I have to share that one too

Namita: lol

Nicholas: oh my god that was funny

Namita: http://www.youtube.com/watch?v=gdjKVglUWlk

Namita: hehehe yesss it was ....my tummy hurts now

Nicholas: yogurt ? gross and funny

Nicholas: eeewwww

Namita: hehehehe

Namita: gotta watch those thai ppl

Nicholas: is surprising what's out there and what you find on the side bar

Nicholas: http://www.youtube.com/watch?v=8dwR-F79MjU&feature=youtu.be

Namita: i knowww !!

Namita: LMAO !!!!

Nicholas: the creamer one omg!!

Namita: hehheheeh just watched that one

Namita: hahahah the boob one !!

Nicholas: yes

Nicholas: it's amazing what the other countries put out there too

Namita: hehehe ...some of it is pretty funny

Nicholas: that it is

Nicholas: how many languages do yo speak?

Nicholas: random

Namita: i speak hindi fluently ...understand punjabi .... then english of course ... i took french in school for 7 yrs and forgot most of it ..cuz i didnt use it

Nicholas: wow

Namita: hehe and you ?

Namita: i took spanish too but alas forgot it too

Nicholas: I speak english and learned a little french from Sesame Street but have forgotten most of it

Namita: hehehe

Nicholas: oh n a little Spanish just to get by in Mexico

Namita: from sesame street ??

Namita: hehehe

Nicholas: nope they didn't teach Spanish on Sesame St back then

Namita: lol

Nicholas: today is 11/11/11 just noticed that

Namita: i knowww

Nicholas: and its almost 5 am... we certainly didn't miss a step w 12 days off

Namita: its supposed to be significant

Nicholas: my body didn't know what to do all the extra sleep I've been getting lol

Namita: hehee

Nicholas: didn't know that

Namita: you feel deprived ?

Nicholas: of you yes!!

Namita: lol of course

Namita: i missed you too

Nicholas: *smiling*

Namita: hehe

Nicholas: just think one day we'll be able to talk n make love all night then wake up n be right next to each other

Namita: mmmmmmmmmm yesssssssss

Namita: my one leg over ur body when we're asleep

Namita: and u holding on to it

Nicholas: snuggled together n we just fell asleep holding each other

Namita: uh huh !!!

Nicholas: do you like space while you sleep or a little of both?

Namita: a little of both

Nicholas: yes me too

Namita: hehe

Namita: you might have to pry me off in my sleep though

Nicholas: I wont try very hard

Nicholas: I want you right beside me

Namita: hehehe

Nicholas: once again you've calmed me

Namita: really ...how so ?

Nicholas: was worrying about you

Nicholas: and now we've talked I know you're okay

Namita: ohhh .... well the computer gods felt sorry for us

Nicholas: they must have decided I needed my Namita fix

Namita: lol

Nicholas: was a long time to go w/o.... I did it but I'd rather not go as long if I don't have too

Nicholas: though I kept reminding myself that you've got a lot on your plate dwn there and to respect your time there

Namita: yes will keep fingers crossed that things will work out

Nicholas: that we will

Namita: thank you for checking up on me ..and respecting what my family is going thru

Nicholas: you're quite welcome... I respect and care so much for you

Namita: awwwweee thank you nicholas

Nicholas: it will be nice to hear your voice one day

Namita: hehe yesss ...and urs as well

Nicholas: not to mention touch you

Namita: i wondered about that actually ...what u sound like

Nicholas: N I you

Nicholas: I hope you like my voice

Namita: ohh god sorry ...im struggling to stay awake

Nicholas: I don't know how to describe my voice

Nicholas: me too

Namita: ok describe it

Nicholas: searching for the keys

Nicholas: I don't know how

Namita: lets leave it at that

Namita: hehe

Nicholas: it'll be a surprise

Namita: tomorrow

Nicholas: I'm not a chipmunk on helium that's for sure

Nicholas: lol

Namita: heheh ok phewwww

Nicholas: okay

Nicholas: lol

Namita: thank heavens

Namita: hehee

Nicholas: tmw then same time or earlier?

Namita: i will try earlier

Nicholas: okay

Namita: if u plan earlier than thats ok tooo

Nicholas: I'll keep an eye out for you

Namita: okays

Nicholas: gnight my sweet... so nice to talk again

Nicholas: glad you're okay

Namita: goodnight nicholas .... pleasant dreams

Namita: muahhh

Nicholas: kisses

Namita: its supposed to be a kissing noise

Namita: hehe

Nicholas: I got it

Nicholas: night

Namita: night

End Time: 4:59:32 AM

Chapter 20 November 12

Start Time: 11:13 PM

Namita: helloo

Nicholas: hi there

Nicholas: I didn't hear you log on

Nicholas: how are you?

Namita: im sorry to keep u waiting ... was just hanging out with family

Namita: im ok

Nicholas: cool

Namita: not feeling to hot right now

Namita: hehe

Nicholas: sorry to hear that

Namita: how are you doing ?

Nicholas: any idea why?

Namita: just my lower back is hurting me

Nicholas: I'm good.... been napping on n off all afternoon n eve

Nicholas: awe wish I could massage it for you

Namita: ohhh niceee ..catching up on much needed sleep

Namita: hehe i could do with that

Nicholas: lol yah out of practice w the late nights

Namita: hehehe

Nicholas: how was ur Remembrance Day?

Namita: it was good ... we did have a moment of silence too

Namita: what about urself ?

Nicholas: good to hear

Nicholas: the ceremony was good

Nicholas: the rain held off too which was nice

Namita: what ceremony did you go to again

Namita: i heard it was quite windy there

Nicholas: the one in Burnaby w Amanda and her Scouts at the cenotaph in Confederation park in Burnaby

Namita: ohh yesss

Nicholas: the wind really pick up later

Nicholas: we even heard thunder twice

Namita: ohh wowww .. i missed it ... i love it when it is windy

Namita: ohh cool !!

Nicholas: the leaves blew from the trees near my place it looked like it was raining leaves

Namita: hehehe

Nicholas: we watched it as we drove back to my place

Namita: ohhh i loveeeeeeee that sooo much ...wish i could have seen it

Nicholas: oh and it hailed at the same time

Nicholas: it was pretty cool to see

Namita: ohh myyyy ...you had it all ...im jealous now

Nicholas: lol

Namita: hehe

Namita: ur like adding to the list of things i missed

Namita: what else did you do today ?

Nicholas: mmmm went to London drugs in Coquitlam center ... was looking for a dish set I saw in the Lougheed LD but that set didn't have bowls

Nicholas: the LD (London drugs) at CC (Coquitlam Center) didn't have the set at all

Namita: ohhh thats too bad !!

Namita: i hate when ur looking for something in particular ..it is not there

Nicholas: yah.... I decided to find a set of dishes that I like and get rid of the miss matched set I have now

Namita: hehee ... what did the one you were looking for look like ?

Namita: i always have mismatched stuff for everyday use

Nicholas: let me see if I can find a photo

Namita: ok

Nicholas: I have a particular bowl I use most of the time, just because it's the right size

Namita: ahhh ok ... so i wont take it away from you ... point taken

Namita: hehe

Nicholas: lol

Nicholas: I'll let u use it when ever you like

Namita: hehe ... are you sure ?

Namita: what if i drop it ?

Nicholas: yes

Nicholas: then I'll buy another one

Namita: you wont make me glue it together ?

Nicholas: god no!! silly lol

Namita: hehe ... im being silly !!

Nicholas: we'll just go to Ikea n see what they have

Namita: i havent been to ikea in a huge long time

Nicholas: I went a few weeks ago... I don't really need anything they have

Namita: im sure one can spend hours in there

Nicholas: I can't seem to drag n drop the image

Nicholas: oh yes

Namita: ohhh dont worry about it

Nicholas: it would be nice to go in n just take a whole room

Nicholas: I'll have to show you, that's if I can find the set

Namita: hehe yesss ...some things are nice ... but ive really only been in ikea maybe twice in my lifetime

Namita: send me the page instead

Nicholas: oh wow.... some stuff is cool... its nice to look n get ideas

Nicholas: okay I'll try

Namita: k

Nicholas: I'm not sure how to

Nicholas: help pls

Namita: ok stay on the page that has the dishes

Nicholas: k

Namita: go to ur toolbar above ur computer

Nicholas: okay

Namita: highlight it

Nicholas: yes

Namita: right click

Nicholas: www.londondrugs.com/Cultures/en- Detail/Homeware.htm?BreadCrumbs= Tableware; Dinnerware&ProductID= 5351887&ProductTab=3

Namita: and press copy

Nicholas: did that work?

Namita: yes it did

Nicholas: cool

Nicholas: I thought that's how but wasn't sure

Namita: ohhh nice colours ... i like the blue in it

Nicholas: me too

Namita: but thats a pricey set

Namita: the plates look nice too

Nicholas: I like that it has a couple of colours so one could match other stuff w it

Namita: yesss it is quite nice

Nicholas: the set at Lougheed was missing the bowls

Namita: someone just took the bowls out

Nicholas: I'm going to check other locations to see if maybe they have it

Namita: where on lougheed is LD ?

Nicholas: at the mall

Nicholas: or in the mall

Namita: it used to be on north road and lougheed before

Namita: i used to go there when i lived in coquitlam

Namita: which mall ?

Nicholas: yes I'm aware this is ur old stomping grounds lol

Nicholas: Lougheed mall

Namita: ohhhh so they moved into the mall .... ok cool

Nicholas: I like that everything is close by

Namita: yes ... me too .. i loved that about coquitlam

Nicholas: oh I didn't know they moved. they've always been there since I've been in the area

Nicholas: and dwntwn is so close too for hockey games or a night on the twn too

Namita: they used to be on north road and lougheed before

Namita: where all the korean stores are now

Nicholas: oh okay I know where u mean

Nicholas: I like the area on Como Lake rd further east

Nicholas: there are some nice homes w parks close by w trees

Namita: hehehe ... i used to live on como lake

Nicholas: I love being around green spaces

Nicholas: cool

Namita: which way is east ?

Nicholas: away from dwntwn

Namita: yessss thats why i loved it there so much ... it was a good area to grow up

Nicholas: dwntwn is west

Namita: hehe thanks

Nicholas: the mountains are always north

Namita: we used to live ..right on como lake ..between pororir st and schoolhouse

Nicholas: oh yah I know the area

Namita: yesssssssssss thats right ... i always loved the mountains

Namita: the original house was torn down ..and a new one sits there ... between my old neighbors

Namita: i still have dreams of going back in the house

Nicholas: growing up in a small twn and close to the ocean I appreciate and respect nature

Namita: yesss ...and that is a wonderful quality .... i do envy you for being close to the ocean

Nicholas: I think about the house I grew up in too... its the house where we built our sail boat

Namita: ohh cool

Namita: did you guys finish it and sail it

Nicholas: I decided a while ago that I'd like to live in house where I can see the ocean... I don't need to be right on the water but I'd like to see it everyday

Nicholas: we moved on it but never got a chance to rig it

Nicholas: we took it out under power a couple of times

Namita: omg thats how i am too ... i loveee just seeing the water ...at some point ... and be near it

Nicholas: like minds *smiling*

Namita: it is a privilege for me ... and i never get tired of seeing the ocean

Nicholas: I smiled a few times today thinking about you

Nicholas: totally agree

Namita: hehe you did

Namita: was it the balloons ?

Namita: hehe

Nicholas: made me feel all warm inside knowing you're there and okay

Namita: aweee thanks

Nicholas: lol.... I had a friend comment on those youtube posts I put on FB (FaceBook)

Nicholas: they are pretty funny

Namita: hahahha ...you actually did it !! what did they say ??

Nicholas: that they thought is was funny... nothing major

Namita: i loveeee them ... its on my youtube playlist ...ive had it for a few yrs now

Nicholas: wow

Namita: it always cracks me up !!

Nicholas: I didn't know you could have a play list on there... I knew you can subscribe to videos

Namita: i dont subscribe ... you use ur email as ur account ...and create a playlist

Nicholas: I get an image of the graffiti penis walking all dejected across the wall.. lol

Nicholas: oh neet

Namita: like find a video ...at the bottom of the video it says to add to playlist ..click it .,,,and it may prompt you to create one

Namita: ive saved all my fav songs here

Nicholas: oh okay

Namita: and funny stuff

Nicholas: ah

Namita: hehehe the graffiti penis was pretty funny

Nicholas: there's a site you can extract the song from youtube

Namita: are u asking me or telling me ?

Nicholas: it doesn't work very well for mac

Nicholas: telling

Nicholas: sorry

Namita: ohh ok

Namita: no worries

Nicholas: its called Listen to youtube or something

Nicholas: side note: how is the rest of ur family coping w ur uncle?

Namita: whats the sites name ?

Nicholas: I think so

Namita: they are doing ok ... my parents are worried though

Nicholas: for some reason that site wont dwnload the song to my iTunes

Nicholas: I bet

Namita: ohh i see

Nicholas: is ur uncle on ur mom's side or dad's?

Namita: dads side

Namita: here i will send a pic

Namita: one sec

Nicholas: ah

Nicholas: k

~Namita~ would like to send you the file "317765_10150317389464644_680624643_7703205..." (44 Kb). Do you want to

Accept

(Ctrl+G) or

Decline (Ctrl+C)

the invitation?

Transfer of file "317765_10150317389464644_680624643_7703205..." from ~Namita~ has been accepted. Starting transfer...

Cancel

You have successfully received 317765_10150317389464644_680624643_7703205_22 67 84412_n.jpg from~Namita~. Before opening this file, you may want to scan it with a virus-scanning program.

Nicholas: that's ur uncle n his daughter?

Namita: yesss the young lady on the left is my cousin ...his daughter

Nicholas: thought so

Namita: her name is komal

Nicholas: cool

Nicholas: where was the photo taken? or do you know?

Nicholas: looks like a party

Nicholas: how old is your cousin?

Namita: in the states i guess .. it was her birthday party ...she turned 21

Nicholas: you say young lady made me think way younger

Namita: hehe

Nicholas: wow that is young

Namita: i didnt mean it in a sarcastic way ... hehe ... she is young though

Nicholas: hard to believe we were that age once *shakes head*

Nicholas: oh no I didn't take it that way

Nicholas: I took it the way you meant it

Nicholas: I refer to ppl like that too

Namita: hehe i know u didnt ,.... i just wanted to clear it

Namita: hehe me too

Nicholas: sokay

Nicholas: I like to treat everybody w the same respect

Namita: yess me too

Nicholas: its up to them to screw that up.. if that makes sense

Namita: yes it totally makes sense... do you have any cousins

Namita: i dont know if i asked you that

Nicholas: I have one here but I don't see him and a few in england

Nicholas: about 7 over there I think

Nicholas: I have a small family

Nicholas: most live in england

Namita: ive lost count of how many cousins i have

Nicholas: I figure everyone has a bigger family than I do

Namita: id say a lot ... i will tally them up one day

Nicholas: lol

Namita: hehe

Namita: my guess is 30 ...but im not sure

Nicholas: have you all been together at least once?

Nicholas: 30!!! wow

Namita: no i havent even met some of my cousins at all

Nicholas: w 30 I'm not surprised

Namita: 2 of my uncles one from dad side one from mom have twin boys one set is 3 the other is 4 they are my youngest cousins

Nicholas: wow that's a big age range

Namita: the four yr olds are half indian and half caucasian .... and they look italian

Namita: lol yess

Nicholas: interesting

Nicholas: are you pretty handy? as in can you use tools?

Namita: yes i can use a screwdriver

Namita: hehe

Namita: a wrench

Namita: a level

Nicholas: would you consider urself a safe driver?

Nicholas: that's cool

Namita: i do have a power screwdriver

Namita: yesss im a safe driver

Namita: why ?

Nicholas: me too

Nicholas: just wondered

Nicholas: we're getting to the nitty gritty w the questions now lol

Namita: im extra safe ... not drinking counts for being safe

Namita: hehe

Namita: ok

Nicholas: me too

Namita: why did u ask about the tools ?

Namita: hehe

Nicholas: I try to drive the speed limit too w/o driving like an old man lol

Nicholas: just wondered

Nicholas: now you have me around so you don't need to use tools if you don't want to

Namita: hehe ... ok i will admit ..i have used a butter knife to screw things or unscrew

Nicholas: hmm good to know

Namita: ahhhh yesss i can rely on you now !!!

Nicholas: that you can

Namita: yes im fessing up to you !!

Nicholas: as I said my dearly departed dad use to say "if I can't fix it, it ain't broke"

Namita: hehehehe i lovee that saying !!!

Nicholas: most times I can figure out how to fix most anything... within reason that is

Nicholas: I have quite a few tools here... at my mom's I have all my dad's tools and my grampa's as well... quite a variety

Namita: ohhh thats good ... if ur handy like that ...then i make up for it in the kitchen and the bedroom ...hehe

Nicholas: a little wood working, metal fabricating, welders hand tools

Namita: ohhh cool!!!

Nicholas: cool

Namita: lol

Namita: you read every word of that ...didnt you ??

Nicholas: we'll both excel in the bedroom

Namita: heheh

Nicholas: I did

Namita: lol

Nicholas: one of the reasons why I'd like to get all those tools at my mom's over here as I said before so I can work on side projects to bring in extra money

Namita: yesss it make sense ... im sure those tools are quite valuable

Nicholas: I think there's about $10,000 worth of tools

Namita: OMGGG really

Nicholas: yup

Namita: do you have a compressor too ?

Nicholas: not yet.. that's one of a couple of things I still need

Nicholas: a compressor, a shear, lathe and a brake

Namita: my dad has one

Nicholas: cool

Namita: like new

Namita: he bought it brand new a few yrs back

Nicholas: nice

Namita: and kept it in good condition

Nicholas: they're handy to have

Namita: yesss thats why he doesnt want to part with it

Namita: lol

Nicholas: I have a few air tools, sanders n impact guns

Nicholas: even a little one is nice to have around, even just to fill a tire

Namita: ahh i see

Namita: yess true

Nicholas: other than the tools I mentioned I'd like to get I have enf equipment to build the projects that I want

Nicholas: well there equipment not tools

Nicholas: a space about 25'x25' would be good to start

Namita: yess its good to have those important tools ... that way you dont have to pester anyone to borrow it

Namita: good to have ur own

Nicholas: yes.. I don't like to borrow tools coz I don't lend mine out... just one of the things my dad passed on to me

Nicholas: "never lend your tools out, they never come back the way you loaned them out"

Nicholas: may sound selfish but it's true

Namita: hehe ..yes i understand ... some of those tools can cost a fortune ..when you add things up like that

Namita: yess so true

Namita: i seen it first hand when dad used to lend it out to friends

Nicholas: I prefer to build it myself anyway

Nicholas: yup

Namita: he hated how things weren't returned or they took awhile to return

Nicholas: yup or they come back broken

Nicholas: n don't get replaced or fixed

Namita: omg yesss

Nicholas: how many weeks do you have for holiday's?

Nicholas: and did you take them all together?

Namita: 3.5 weeks

Namita: i took it all at the same time

Nicholas: 3.5 weeks for 15 years of work? really?

Nicholas: thats a long time waiting for them to come around... though the only holiday I've really taken was w Tony to Mexico

Namita: well i have roughly 20 days of paid vacation

Namita: in 15 yrs

Nicholas: oh I see

Namita: i think u incur a day every 2 yrs or so

Nicholas: at my work I think 15 years gets you 6 weeks

Namita: i wish it was faster

Namita: ommg id be in heaven then

Namita: well actually it is more than 3 weeks

Nicholas: some guys take the 6 weeks all at the same time.... I wouldn't want to come back after that long lol

Namita: wait i have to think here ...cuz i took some holiday earlier tooo

Namita: lol

Namita: i think it works out to be 6 weeks too

Namita: for me

Nicholas: oh cool

Namita: sorry

Nicholas: totally fine

Nicholas: we all make mistakes

Nicholas: wasn't going to hold you to ur first answer lol

Namita: hehehe

Namita: are you in ur comfy chair

Nicholas: I am

Nicholas: you are?

Namita: in bed ...on my tummy

Nicholas: not beside me that's for sure lol

Namita: hehe

Nicholas: oh that tummy yes yes

Namita: good one ...nooo id be on top of you .... is there room beside you ?

Nicholas: had to keep my emotions under control today

Nicholas: I'd make room for you

Namita: why is that nicholas ?

Nicholas: I keep thinking about how I'm going to feel when I first see you and most times I can't hardly stand it

Namita: hehehe ... i will pinch you remember

Nicholas: I might just sweep u up n never let you go

Nicholas: yes you will n I do

Namita: and run into ur room ?

Namita: do the caveman thing

Nicholas: we'll just fly away together

Namita: hehe

Nicholas: knock you over the head n drag you away mmm don't think so lol

Namita: hehehe

Nicholas: more like hug you like I've never hugged anyone before and feel the world stand still

Namita: im sure there other ways of knocking me

Nicholas: and have that oh so important first last kiss

Namita: aweeee soooo sweet nicholas

Namita: hehehe

Nicholas: or last first

Namita: or first first

Nicholas: yes

Namita: no last

Nicholas: no no lol

Nicholas: it will be so hot that our gelato will melt just by being close to us

Namita: hehehe ... it will be milkshake by then

Nicholas: yes

Namita: i think we would melt a lot of things together

Nicholas: that we will

Nicholas: our hearts hehe

Nicholas: sappy I know

Namita: ohh yesss

Namita: noooo it is not sappy at all

Namita: hehe

Nicholas: it will be so nice to see you in person n not just in ur photos

Namita: someone real ...someone tangible

Nicholas: and hear ur words not just read them

Nicholas: yes well said... took the words out of me

Namita: really ?

Nicholas: and know that ur not a peg leg one eyed 73 year old man lol!!

Nicholas: yes

Nicholas: you have a way of doing that... finding my words that I can't always find

Namita: hahahaha ...nooooooo im a tobacco chewing ..beer belly... old man

Nicholas: lol lol

Namita: hehe

Nicholas: you're just as you described in our first contact

Namita: what do u mean ...just as i described

Nicholas: just as you described... in your scenario in ur bio from LL

Namita: ohhh i see ...hehhe

Nicholas: long silky dark hair.. curves in all the right places

Namita: well i tried to be true to the core of who i am

Namita: mmmm

Nicholas: yes you did

Namita: brown eyes ?

Nicholas: ohhh yes

Namita: full lips

Nicholas: mmmhmmm

Namita: lol

Namita: full perky boobs ?

Nicholas: ooohhh yess lets not for get those wonderful perky full rounded boobs

Namita: hehehehe

Namita: just enough to fit ur hands

Nicholas: have loved looking at those in ur Drenched photo

Nicholas: yes please

Namita: ahhh yesss .. i forgot about that

Nicholas: which takes me to our story of you loining me in the shower w ur red nightie still on

Nicholas: you joining*

Namita: mmmmmmmmmm yessssss

Namita: the fabric drenched and sticking to my every curve

Nicholas: clinging to those curves in all the right places

Namita: hehe yesss

Nicholas: or you straddling me while you strip for me

Nicholas: mmm mmm mmm

Nicholas: my god I can't wait to explore your body

Namita: yesss would you like that ...i strip for you while straddling you ..undoing the front buttons slowly

Namita: as i watch you

Nicholas: yes i would

Nicholas: you feeling my manhood trying to burst out of my pants

Nicholas: trying to find your moist wet opening

Namita: ommmgggg

Nicholas: touching you all over

Namita: yess all you can feel between my legs are my panties

Namita: and see me unbutton my shirt

Nicholas: mmhmmm

Namita: very slowly

Namita: my long hair all to one side

Namita: flowing down beside me

Nicholas: waiting for those wonderful boobs to pop out n say hi

Namita: hehehe

Namita: i peel away the white shirt ..which actually happens to be yours

Namita: and it reveals a red racy bra underneath

Nicholas: I think that's one of my fav parts... when you take ur shirt off n I see them being offered to me

Namita: that matches the panties

Namita: mmmmmm yessssssss

Nicholas: mmmhhmmm

Nicholas: that will never get old... seeing your brown naked body

Namita: hehe ... my skin catching the golden hues from the small candlelight beside the bed

Nicholas: yesssss

Namita: playing tricks on our bodies

Namita: casting shadows ...and flickering of lights

Nicholas: I have a song on that lounge music cd that sings about candle light on bodies

You missed a call from Namita

Nicholas: you called?

Namita: no i didnt

Nicholas: how did that happen?

Namita: i dunno what happened

Nicholas: that was strange.. it rang on my end

Namita: ohhh

Nicholas: said I missed a call from you

Namita: i didnt call you at all

Namita: thats sooo wierd

Nicholas: there's a call icon at the top

Nicholas: oh well

Namita: ok

Namita: weird

Nicholas: I didn't know there was that option

Nicholas: where were we?

Namita: hmmm hehe

Namita: my boobs i think

Namita: nooo... candlelight... yesss candlelight

Nicholas: candle light dancing across our bodies

Namita: thats it

Nicholas: it's so easy to get lost in these scenarios.... can't wait to play for real

Namita: hehehe me either.... im sure though we both have interesting ideas

Nicholas: music playing softly in the back ground

Namita: mmm yesss

Nicholas: yes... we'll play w them all

Nicholas: do yo u like to take charge in the bedroom? or go w the flow and let things develop? or let me take charge?

Nicholas: I like to be open n let us both let things go where they want or we want

Namita: i like a bit of everything ...go with the flow ..you taking charge ..and me turning the tables on you

Nicholas: just like me

Namita: hehe good

Namita: im having a hard time staying awake nicholas

Nicholas: oh okay

Namita: im soo sorry

Nicholas: good we started early

Nicholas: not to worry

Nicholas: you need ur sleep

Namita: i feel like ur doing all the talking

Nicholas: sokay

Namita: and im ignoring you

Namita: soo sorry

Nicholas: ur not or I don't feel like u are

Namita: i think im just feeling physically drained

Nicholas: if you want to say gnight we can

Nicholas: I bet you are

Nicholas: u have a lot going on there it gets draining at times

Namita: well with the back ache it doesnt help

Namita: i'll be ok though

Nicholas: wish I could help

Namita: hehe

Nicholas: I don't want to run you down

Namita: oh god no

Namita: i feel comfortable telling you

Nicholas: okay

Nicholas: do you want to sleep? it's okay if you do... we can chat tmw

Namita: ok ...yess im half sleeping anyways

Nicholas: okay

Namita: i hope u dont mind

Nicholas: do you want to chat same time tmw?

Namita: yes that would be great

Nicholas: nope... as much as I love talking w you, you need ur sleep

Nicholas: earlier is good, same time that is

Namita: yes i will be around for sure

Nicholas: okay. I'll look for you about 11. that work?

Namita: yes ...i will aim for 1030ish though

Nicholas: oh okay even better

Namita: hehe

Nicholas: gnight then my sweet.... pleasant dreams 😊 😊

Namita: sweet dreams... keep smiling 😊

End Time: 1:21 AM

Chapter 21 November 13

Start Time: 11:18 PM

Nicholas: hello there!!

Namita: heyyyy... how are you ?

Nicholas: was just checking something n there you were

Nicholas: I'm good and you?

Namita: im well thanks... what were you checking..am i interrupting?

Nicholas: not interrupting

Namita: hehe

Nicholas: was just looking to see what happened to the New Jersey Devils goaltender Martin Brodeur

Namita: ohhhh

Nicholas: how was your day?

Namita: what happened? did you find out ?

Nicholas: not yet still looking

Namita: hehe ... ok ...my day was ok ...just tired a bit

Nicholas: don't know if he retired or is just hurt

Namita: ohhh i see

Nicholas: still shows him on their roster so he must be still playing

Nicholas: did you get up to anything interesting?

Namita: hmmm i dont really know who he is anyways

Nicholas: lol

Namita: hehe

Nicholas: he's the reg goalie for the New Jersey Devils

Namita: hehe ...ok ok .... hehe

Namita: the highlight of my day was a nice long soak in the jacuzzi today

Namita: with the jets all going

Nicholas: oooo that would have been nice to share w you

Namita: mmmmm yess

Nicholas: Sara n I went swimming this afternoon

Namita: i had the full on bubble bath going

Nicholas: cool

Namita: i needed it ..esp my back being sore

Nicholas: hot tub at ur families place?

Namita: ohh where did you go swimming ?

Nicholas: do you think ur back is sore form sleeping in a strange bed for so long?

Namita: noo not hottub ... the bathroom jacuzzi

Nicholas: went to Chimo pool in Coq

Namita: hmmm maybe

Namita: omg i remember chimo pool

Namita: that was my childhood haunt

Namita: I used to go there in gr 3 to 7

Nicholas: I know when I stay at my mom's for too many nights my back gets sore as she has a hide-a-bed

Namita: and in the summer

Namita: ahhh i see

Nicholas: they've made a bunch of renos there

Namita: i heard ,,,, do you guys go to the library too

Nicholas: the annex was torn dwn and a new rink built on the other side of the complex

Namita: they built that library ...when i was in grade 11

Nicholas: I haven't been to the library

Namita: and i loveeed goiong across the street and studying there

Namita: or procrastinating

Namita: hehe

Namita: it is a good library

Namita: thats when i was in Centennial high of course

Nicholas: lol yah I didn't usually go to the library often when I was in school.... I'd rather be building something lol

Namita: i loveee that area cuz everything is sooo nearby

Nicholas: that would be nice n close then

Nicholas: I like it too

Nicholas: I found a house around that area that I like

Namita: i think the best years of my school days were right there in centennial ... gr 11 and 12

Namita: ohh really ??

Namita: cool

Namita: did you check it out inside ?

Namita: hehe

Nicholas: its not for sale

Namita: ohhhhhhh

Nicholas: but its a lot like what I'm looking for

Namita: well tell em to get out !!

Nicholas: its a smaller house w a big yard and a detached garage

Nicholas: lol tempting

Namita: ahhh i see ... i must have pasted by it quite a bit

Nicholas: probably

Namita: it is right on Poirier ?

Nicholas: I'm trying to find it again on google maps

Namita: i was just going to google map

Nicholas: like minds

Namita: lol

Nicholas: its across from Mundy Park on Hillcrest

Namita: hmm one sec

Nicholas: its *** Hillcrest coquitlam

Namita: ok ... i did probably pass it if i went to Spani pool in the summer

Nicholas: thats kind of scary being able to google map a strangers house

Namita: lol

Nicholas: yup same area

Namita: i knoww

Nicholas: its an older house but it looks like its been kept up nicely

Namita: ohhh cool ...is it one level?

Nicholas: looks like 3

Nicholas: its not a big house but just right I think

Namita: what color is the house

Nicholas: I don't need a big house just one that suits my needs

Nicholas: looks like light brownish w white trim

Namita: ok

Nicholas: try looking up *** Hillcrest in Coquitlam n it should come up

Namita: ok one sec

Nicholas: I think if I lived there I'd move the fence further out to the street though

Namita: is it beside the pink house

Nicholas: its a really nice area... I like that its not on a busy street and not on a hill

Nicholas: the older one to the left

Nicholas: or yes

Nicholas: didnt read that properly lol

Namita: yes a lot of properties are really nice in coquitlam ..plus they have back yards

Nicholas: yah I like a yard

Nicholas: nice to have ppl over and so the girls can use it too

Namita: so it the the pink house in between the tall brown house ...with white trim windows ?

Nicholas: I like that some of the properties have a bit of land for a yard as most places in the lower mainland are just houses squished together

Namita: no im wrong i think

Nicholas: its the tall brown house

Nicholas: would be nice to see inside

Namita: ohhhhhh i hate when the houses are squished together ... hated since i was a kid ... dad made sure when he bought our childhood house that it wasnt stuck to the house next to it

Nicholas: cool

Namita: ahhh ok .... the one with the cedar fence ?

Nicholas: too claustrophobic when they're squished

Nicholas: yes

Namita: yess we had a huge yard in the back ... it took forever to cut the grass

Nicholas: and the garage in the back to the left of the property

Namita: you could fit another house in the back

Nicholas: lol probably

Namita: hehe

Namita: yesss i like the garage too

Nicholas: as I say I think the fence could come out to the road more

Namita: the driveway is nice too ...not cracked

Namita: yes i agree with the fence

Namita: it also needs a flower garden

Nicholas: I like the idea of a detached garage so I can make noise n it doesn't bother anyone in the house

Namita: which i would go crazy over

Nicholas: yes flowers

Namita: hehe

Namita: i do like the little shrubs in the front too

Nicholas: yah.... there are a lot of nice houses in that area

Nicholas: I like the park being across the street too

Namita: it also needs some trees dividing to the left side of the yard for some privacy

Nicholas: only draw back is you can't see the water

Namita: yesss its like the park too

Nicholas: and the pool is within walking distance too

Namita: hehe

Nicholas: or a bike ride

Namita: hmm niceeee ... i can imagine long lazy summer days ... or going to all the amenities nearby

Nicholas: I just like to have nature close by so I don't feel so locked in by the city

Nicholas: yes

Namita: have you been in mundy park ?

Nicholas: its far enf off the main drag that it would be quiet too.. I think

Namita: to lost lake

Namita: yesss it is quiet there

Nicholas: not to the lake but to the lacrosse box... that's wear Isabel practiced last season

Namita: and you always get the a good dump of snow from the rest of the lower mainland

Nicholas: would be a nice adventure one day

Namita: since its higher elevation

Namita: ahhh i see

Namita: ive been a few times when i was a kid

Namita: inside mundy park

Nicholas: cool

Namita: lots of banana slugs

Namita: and some wildlife

Nicholas: looks like a big park

Namita: it is pretty big ...there is 2 lakes in it

Nicholas: really?! wow

Namita: yes Mundy lake and lost lake

Nicholas: oh yah one Mundy lake n one that doesn't seem to have a name

Nicholas: oh Lost lake okay

Namita: some areas are swampy

Nicholas: note to self wear boots lol

Namita: yess ...hehe

Namita: lots of ppl jog thru it though

Nicholas: its early and my spelling is already sucking lol

Namita: hehehehee

Nicholas: Amanda n I went out for dinner w my mom, sister n her girlfriend

Namita: ur mom is in town ?

Nicholas: yah

Namita: where did you guys go ?

Nicholas: she leaves for Australia monday night

Nicholas: Swiss Chalet

Namita: ohhhh cool !!! On a leisure trip ...or visiting someone ?

Nicholas: both

Namita: ohhh ive never been to swiss chalet before

Nicholas: she's visiting a friend she hasn't see in like 52 years...

Namita: ohhh well thats good ....it is something she can look forward too

Nicholas: they've kept in contact over the years

Namita: ohhh myyyy

Namita: thats is cool !!!

Nicholas: she has a sinus cold and is stressing a little

Namita: im sure she will have an awesome time

Nicholas: she's a worrier

Namita: oh noooo

Nicholas: its really prevalent now that my dad is gone... he really kept her grounded

Namita: im sure the trip will do her good ....she probably needs it

Nicholas: I think she's still figuring how to have a life

Namita: is this her first long trip ?

Nicholas: w/o my dad

Nicholas: yah

Namita: yesss ... i know it can be hard

Nicholas: she goes to Mexico w friends the past 2 years

Namita: but its good that she is venturing out

Nicholas: the friends son owns a house dwn there so they stay there

Namita: ohh good for her !!

Nicholas: she's going to go again for her B-day this next year

Nicholas: she turns 65

Namita: well its good that she is taking care of herself and treating herself ...she deserves it

Nicholas: it is good she's going out but she's still quite lost w/o my dad

Namita: wow ... i think my mom is going to be 63

Nicholas: he was the visionary... she took care of the money doing the books

Nicholas: ur dad is older?... than ur mom I mean

Namita: ohhh...im sure that feeling of being lost doesnt go away so easily and probably never will

Namita: yes dad is 66

Nicholas: ah

Namita: together and still strong

Namita: hehe

Namita: i love them to bits

Nicholas: I find it strange to see my parents as people... seeing them as the know all be all for so long n as you get older you see them as people and they're not invincible... I will always love her and my dad

Namita: ohhh I can only imagine how that must feel ... missing ur dad

Namita: you mean you didnt connect with ur mom so much as you did ur dad ?

Nicholas: when I talk about my future both of them usually throw in a good dose of reality

Nicholas: yes... or my sister

Namita: ahhh ok

Namita: so they dont see things how you see them ?

Nicholas: my dad n I could talk about a project and brainstorm... I can't do that w my mom or sister.... they seem to think that I'm going to quit my job and be a starving artist

Nicholas: that they don't

Nicholas: when I'm just talking things out n dreaming

Nicholas: or envisioning where I'd like to be

Namita: ahhh i see ... they are probably programmed differently in their thoughts and ideas ...whereas you and ur dad saw things in the same light

Nicholas: makes me wonder if they think long term when it come to their futures

Namita: yess i get what ur saying

Namita: im a dreamer too

Namita: and i understand exactly what ur saying

Nicholas: yah... so as I say I keep conversation w them light and not too deep or personal coz I don't like it when ppl step on my dreams esp when its family

Namita: you have to envision urself what ur going to be doing in 2 yrs 5 yrs ..or 10 yrs time

Nicholas: yes

Namita: yess good approach

Namita: that way you dont feel crushed when they dont understand what ur saying or doing

Nicholas: I read a book called "Why Small businesses Fail n What to do about it"

Nicholas: yes

Namita: uh huh

Nicholas: the book said you have 3 ppl inside you

Nicholas: which I can relate too

Namita: ohhh really

Nicholas: we have our Visionary our Manager and our technician

Namita: ahhh ok

Nicholas: and they can't do each others jobs

Namita: makes sense

Nicholas: the technician does the work... the manager makes sure the work is getting done and the visionary keeps looking to the future and dreaming

Namita: hehe thats a good way of thinking !!!!

Nicholas: I know I can do the work but I don't know how to run a business and I can certainly dream about the future

Namita: there is never harm in dreaming !! I don't think

Nicholas: so you find ppl that can fill the missing jobs for you

Nicholas: I sometimes feel like I can see this parallel universe where what I want is happening but I can't figure out how to get over there so I'm left watching from the outside

Nicholas: I can see Blueflame Creative, my company, being successful I just haven't found a way to kick it off

Nicholas: but all in due time

Nicholas: it's a big wish so it'll take time

Namita: well sometimes you just have to envision what you want to attain as ur goals in life ...and basically have to throw urself into finding and achieving those goals

Nicholas: I can see the projects, the clothing line all of it

Namita: yess everything is all in due time ...it will happen

Nicholas: yessss

Namita: i kinda know what ur saying

Namita: it was like that for me when i was working like a mad woman to just get into the waiting list for nursing school

Nicholas: wow look at me ramble... that's the passion I have for doing something I love and know I was meant to do

Namita: and i was madly trying to re do some of the courses to improve my high school standing ...just so they would consider my application

Nicholas: was nursing something that stood out to you?

Nicholas: I hear yah... my grades sucked

Nicholas: not saying ur did though

Namita: sort of ... i didnt know what else to go into ... i wanted something where i can go to school for as short as possible and be able to earn the money

Nicholas: yes me too

Namita: i did think of med school ...but i didnt want to commit the rest of my life to a profession like that

Nicholas: didn't want to be in school for years... I learn better by doing

Nicholas: yah and what if you didn't like it... then what

Nicholas: been there done that

Nicholas: well not a long time invested though

Namita: yess... i dont like all the drama of writing paper after paper ... and research ....although we did do that in nursing school

Namita: i just didnt want to do it for the rest of my life

Namita: doesnt appeal to me

Nicholas: I hear you

Nicholas: me either

Namita: and i hate being stuck on one place all day ..cooped up ...being forced to read something

Nicholas: it's pretty cut n dry when it come to health care yes?

Namita: yes and no

Nicholas: I like to be creative and work in diff mediums

Namita: going thru nursing school is not easy

Nicholas: I bet it's not

Namita: everything is taught right down to the cellular level

Nicholas: I can't imagine... I have a lot of respect for you when it comes to your schooling

Namita: you have to know ur chemistry, biology inside out

Namita: all ur diseases, conditions, pharmacology ...front and backwards too

Nicholas: you have way closer tolerances to work in

Namita: ur tested thru exams written , oral

Namita: thru clinical practice

Namita: you have to pass every aspect of it

Nicholas: if I'm a 1/32" out I can probably live with it.... wear as you have to be bang on every time

Namita: plus immunology, sociology, phycology, physiology

Namita: yesss it has to be bang on in everything

Nicholas: wow ur making my head spin hehe... I wouldn't know where to start

Namita: heheh

Namita: and if i was complaining about math in high school ...well it did come in habdy

Namita: handy*

Nicholas: I love that you're so intelligent and have such a rewarding fulfilling job

Namita: aweee nicholas ...thx

Nicholas: I bet... my math was terrible

Nicholas: YOu are quite welcome

Namita: it has its moments too ...where i wonder why couldnt i just do a paper route and just get it over with

Namita: hehe

Nicholas: I hear yah

Namita: hehehe

Nicholas: or win the lottery and do whatever you wanted lol

Namita: omgg yessss !!!

Nicholas: that's the dreamer in me lol

Namita: but its always the old folks or someone in ontario that win the lottery

Namita: lol

Nicholas: lol yah no kidding

Namita: hehe ...pisces are huge dreamers

Nicholas: I wouldn't work for someone else but I would definitely open Blueflame Creative n do it for fun

Nicholas: like minds another similarity

Nicholas: I'm a big dreamer

Namita: i can imagine ...and it is a good trait

Nicholas: I get the feeling my mom n sis see I'm not able to make it happen so why bother talking about it

Namita: ohh geeez

Namita: well they are not programmed to dream and dream big

Nicholas: that was a real round about conversation lol

Nicholas: guess not

Namita: hehe yes it sure was

Nicholas: that's why I keep my convo's w them light

Namita: hehe

Nicholas: I really enjoy talking about it and sharing my dreams with like minded ppl

Nicholas: sharing them w someone special.... like you

Namita: aweee thanks

Nicholas: welcome

Nicholas: complimenting each other in every aspect

Nicholas: building each other up and supporting

Namita: im the kinda person ...who likes sitting up at night ..and looking up into the summer night ... looking at the stars .... and dream big

Namita: if you can envision it ...it will happen ...and things will fall into place

Nicholas: mee too!!! knowing there so much more to life

Namita: yessss

Nicholas: just get lost in the big picture... I find it relaxing

Namita: dont fret the small things in life

Nicholas: it's about wanting more

Namita: yess

Nicholas: have you seen the movie The Rookie

Namita: i know when i did that ....things came true for me

Namita: no i havent

Nicholas: yes

Namita: who is in it

Nicholas: Denis Quade... its about a high school teacher baseball making a deal w his players that if they win state finals that he'd try out for the majors.... based on a true story

Nicholas: I own it n we'll add it to the list

Namita: lol ok

Nicholas: he talks about wanting more out of life

Nicholas: and trying to achieve it

Nicholas: it has some great lines in it that I love

Namita: woww sounds good

Nicholas: it is

Namita: our list is getting longer and longer

Nicholas: we're going to have quite the list

Nicholas: lol

Namita: we will need a huge bag of popcorn

Nicholas: took the words out again

Namita: and a huge bowl of candy

Nicholas: lol not too big coz you don't eat it lol

Namita: hehehe

Namita: yesss i will pretend

Namita: yes i eat popcorn

Nicholas: lol I don't want you to ever pretend with me okay? lol

Namita: lol ...ok

Nicholas: lol there's only so much I can eat of it too

Namita: hehe

Namita: hehe ... too funny

Nicholas: it's the husks in the gums I don't like

Namita: ohh yess me either

Nicholas: we can set up a bed near your tv or mine n we'll lay in bed n watch movies till we're caught up okay?

Namita: i dont like the microwave popcorn smell ...i get sort of breath ...as if im standing beside someone smoking a cigarette

Nicholas: me either

Namita: hmmm yesss deal

Nicholas: home made hot air popper

Namita: i do have a sofa bed in my living room

Nicholas: thought you'd be okay w that

Namita: yesss i remeber ur homemade popcorn

Nicholas: nicccceee!!!

Namita: lol

Namita: mmmmm

Nicholas: how has the weather been dwn there?

Nicholas: was raining a lot today n suppose to rain tmw too

Namita: im sure we can get thru all those movies without putting the moves on each other

Namita: im confident ...lol

Nicholas: yah right

Nicholas: lol

Namita: hehehe

Namita: i will have my corner and you will have urs

Nicholas: laying next to you n not jumping you I don't think I'll be able to keep my hands off you

Namita: in fact i will put a piece of tape right down the middle

Namita: so we wont disturb each other

Namita: lol

Namita: ohhhhhh nicholas !!!

Namita: hehehe

Nicholas: okay you do that n we'll see how we make out... punn intended

Namita: hahhahaa

Nicholas: we'll be lucky if we make it through one movie in a night lol

Namita: ok i will put up the barbed wire ... i guess

Nicholas: oooo kinky lol

Namita: hehe

Namita: heheheheh

Nicholas: we can build forts out of cushions n blankets then attack each others camps

Namita: im totally giggling here

Namita: yes with popcorn

Namita: meantime the movie is still running

Nicholas: yup

Nicholas: we'll watch something else while we're involved and while we're resting we'll watch the pay attention movies

Namita: hehehe ... what will we watch when we are involved ?

Nicholas: each other I guess

Nicholas: *shakes head* we'll just stop the movie and ravage each other then watch during intermission

Namita: lol ...ohhh yesss id be eyeing you ... wont take my eyes off you ...while im eating my candy ...cuz u never know when ur going to come after me

Namita: lol

Namita: RRrrrrrrr

Namita: supposed to be a growl

Nicholas: when you say eating your candy you're talking about?... the sweetness between your legs? hehe or the actual sweets

Nicholas: I got it

Nicholas: I can hear your sounds

Namita: hehehehe ...you really are reading between the lines arent you ?

Namita: lol

Nicholas: sure am or between your legs hehe

Namita: ommggg yessss

Namita: just saying that ur driving me wild

Nicholas: *giggling*

Namita: lol

Namita: yess i guess i can share my candy with you

Nicholas: well I have seen the movies... so you can watch n I'll play

Namita: if you share ur popcorn with me too

Nicholas: oh you're so thoughtful n thank you

Namita: lol

Nicholas: that I will

Namita: ur welcome anytime

Nicholas: *sighs*

Namita: lol

Nicholas: don't want to seem like I'm pestering you but any idea on when I'm going to get to see you?

Nicholas: take ur time dwn there but get back here woman!!

Namita: i wont be back till maybe first week of dec

Namita: lol

Nicholas: I see.. sokay

Namita: maybe sooner ...who knows

Nicholas: damn thats like 2 n 1/2 weeks away

Namita: soo sorry babes

Nicholas: sooner would be nice... sorry if I'm sounding selfish hehe

Namita: no no ur not

Nicholas: sokay... do what you need to

Namita: hey thanks for being patient and understanding nicholas

Nicholas: so I wont hand in the RSVP for my work Xmas party yet?... no pressure

Nicholas: any time my sweet

Nicholas: I think ur so worth the wait

Namita: ohhh i forgot about ur party

Nicholas: we'll have plenty of time to catch up.... family first okay

Namita: i know we chatted briefly about it

Nicholas: its okay if you cant make it... not to worry

Namita: do ppl usually bring dates to ur party ?

Nicholas: just thought I'd ask

Namita: i want you to go ...and have fun though

Nicholas: no idea... never been to one at this place but I think they usually bring their wives or gf's

Namita: ahhh i see

Nicholas: we're suppose to hand in the rsvp in on monday.... I thought it wasn't much time

Nicholas: as we only got them thursday

Namita: thats not enough time

Namita: grrrrrrr

Nicholas: the 3rd is 2 n a half weeks away

Namita: ohhhh

Nicholas: if it doesn't work out its okay.... I don't really know any of them very well to begin w so I wont be heart broken if I don't make it... there's always next year

Nicholas: you can come w me then... that way we'll have had more time to get to know each other better

Namita: yesss thats true !!

Namita: then you can show me around and introduce me to ppl you know and are comfortable with

Nicholas: so please don't worry about it.... you have bigger things to think about at the moment

Nicholas: yes

Namita: but i hope ur not missing out on anything

Nicholas: the only person I really know is Jim and I don't know if he's going

Namita: i do want you to get into the festive mood

Nicholas: never been so I wouldn't know

Namita: ask him if ppl usually brings dates

Nicholas: knowing you're in my life is festive for me

Namita: i think it is easier on women ...if they dont have a date... we go in groups ...its harder on guys

Namita: hehehe thanks

Namita: for placing me in the festive section ...lol

Nicholas: he's only been there for about 3 months longer than me

Namita: ohhh i see

Nicholas: welcome... you make me very festive inside hehe

Nicholas: I was smiling a few times today thinking about you

Namita: ohh really ??

Nicholas: yup... your photos rolling through my head... our conversation too

Namita: hehe ... our crazzy conversations

Nicholas: envisioning you with me through out the day

Nicholas: yes quite crazy at times

Namita: puttering around with you

Nicholas: yup

Namita: hehe

Namita: i like puttering around too

Nicholas: waking next to you... coming to the pool w us... just envisioning you fitting into my life

Nicholas: trying it on so to speak

Namita: hehehe ... yesss ive been thinking of similar things too

Nicholas: that's the visionary in me day dreaming.... no pressure of course

Namita: grocery shopping

Nicholas: yes

Namita: or doing mundane things

Nicholas: yup

Nicholas: just hanging out... being in the same room

Namita: going for lunch somewhere

Namita: yes just hanging out

Namita: and letting it all hang out

Nicholas: you know.... I've never thought like this before... or it never seemed so natural before

Namita: really ... well its good to think like that ...it is healthy

Namita: yess we fit right in

Nicholas: it's refreshing and liberating

Namita: like we've been doing it for years

Nicholas: we do

Nicholas: yessss

Namita: hehe

Nicholas: like you're just out of twn right now and I'll see you soon

Namita: hehe yessss

Nicholas: every scenario is really comfortable and works... that's never happened before

The following message could not be delivered

"every scenario is really comfortable and works... that's never happened before"

End Time: 1:48 AM

That damn computer of hers.

Chapter 22 November 14

Start Time: 11:13 PM

Namita: hellllllllllllooooooooooo

Nicholas: hello

Nicholas: you were having trouble logging in?

Namita: how are you doing ? did you get my message ?

Nicholas: I didn't

Namita: ohhhh

Nicholas: I'm better now

Nicholas: you got booted last night

Namita: so sorry about last nite

Nicholas: sokay

Namita: yesss ... it was getting tooo hot on msn !!

Nicholas: lol I guess

Namita: hehe ...how has ur day been ?

Nicholas: good... picked Isabel up at the ferry... came home n made french toast for lunch

Nicholas: how have you been?

Namita: ohhh yum !!!

Namita: its been a lonnnngggg while since i have had french toast

Nicholas: it was good... picked up some cinnamon bread from Cobs Bread n used that for the french toast

Namita: ive been good nicholas

Namita: ohhhh cool !!!

Nicholas: I'm glad to heard you're well

Namita: do you just dip it in eggs and cook it ?

Nicholas: I like it when you're good

Namita: my back feels better too

Nicholas: eggs milk n cinnamon

Nicholas: oh that's good

Nicholas: did you do anything diff for ur back?

Namita: ohhhh ..the last time ive ever made french toast was in my home ec ...cooking class i think ...hehe

Namita: yeah i soaked in the jacuzzi again

Namita: and used the jets

Namita: i like the water hot ..not warm ...so it helps my back

Nicholas: I used the recipe from the Chef at Home... 4 eggs to 1 cup milk n 1 teaspoon cinnamon

Namita: i stayed in it for a long while ...so i probably look like a prune

Namita: chef at home ?? His name is Michael something right??

Nicholas: yah I like to soak in my moms hot tub after working on the hot rod

Namita: ohhhhh she has a hot tub??? Now im jealous again !!

Nicholas: yup Michael Smith from PEI

Nicholas: yup... I mentioned that before n you said pretty much the same thing lol

Namita: ohhh he is from PEI ?? But he lives somewhere on the island right ?

Nicholas: PEI = Prince Edward Island

Namita: oh right ... duh

Namita: I loveee his show

Namita: mainly cuz he is cute ...lol

Nicholas: you think so?! ... I find him very tall n mostly legs lol

Namita: hehehe ... well he probably looks good on tv ... cuz the camera is always in his face

Nicholas: I sit in my moms hot tub at night when its dark n clear out n you can see the 5 satellites go over head

Namita: yeah he probably is tall

Namita: but ur cute too !!!

Namita: you can seriously see the satellites ??

Nicholas: lol awe shucks... thx... wasn't jealous

Namita: hehehe

Nicholas: yup they're moving stars

Nicholas: n they move quite quickly

Namita: ohhhhh cool ... ive never even noticed !

Nicholas: some nights you can see the space station too

Namita: it not a shooting star ?

Nicholas: nope

Namita: omg ..really ???

Namita: wowwww !!

Nicholas: seen them too but they go out quick

Namita: you must have good eyes !!

Nicholas: the satellites go from horizon line to horizon

Namita: ohhhh .... cool !!! Now ive learned something new

Nicholas: sort of but when it's clear they're easy to spot

Namita: im sure its harder to see it from our place then?

Nicholas: oh good... I have a lot of info stored my steel trap mind lol

Namita: hehehe

Nicholas: depends on how clear it is here n how many city lights are interfering

Namita: ohhh ok

Namita: i know the sky sure is beautiful at night from the island .... ive seen it when i was in tofino once

Nicholas: dwntwn might be more difficult to see but out here or where you are could be better

Namita: here ur lucky if you see the sun !!

Nicholas: tofino is a great place to star search

Nicholas: I was meaning White Rock

Namita: i remember when we had a meteor shower last summer ... i was out in the yard at night with my niece ...and we watched the shooting stars go by .... that was the first time i ever saw one too

Nicholas: cool!!

Namita: and we were sooo very excited .. i was more excited than my 6 yr old niece

Nicholas: when I was younger a bunch of us were at a friends house on the water n we watched a meteor shower.... about 1 every 5 seconds

Nicholas: lol

Nicholas: they are pretty cool to watch

Nicholas: I have a telescope too

Namita: it is soooo cool to see !! im sure it was just as mesmerizing to you as me

Namita: you do !!! That is sooo cool !!

Nicholas: it was... I love space

Nicholas: I'm still not very good at using it but maybe one day

Namita: did you buy it ?

Nicholas: the lunar landing and space travel, love it

Nicholas: I got it for xmas one year

Namita: are you a space junkie ?? hehe

Nicholas: I sort of picked it out though

Namita: wowww soo nice

Nicholas: I am

Namita: ive seen some telescopes ...but never been close to one ... and always wondered if it was worth the money

Nicholas: I have 2 news papers from July 1969.... ones from Seattle n the other is British

Namita: ohh wow !! They must be worth something in itself !!

Nicholas: I think w practice it would be pretty easy to find things in the sky

Nicholas: the one I have was about $300 I think

Nicholas: I also have the mission patches from the Mercury, Gemini and Apollo projects

Namita: wowww thats not bad for a small investment

Namita: is that something you collect ?

Nicholas: and an autographed photo of Tom Hanks from Apollo 13 w a piece of the film in it

Namita: ohh wow Nicholas !!!

Namita: you must have quite a collection there

Nicholas: the space stuff yah... depending what it is, I don't just buy anything

Nicholas: I have the Apollo patches mounted on the wall and the Tom Hanks photo n the Seattle paper are framed on the wall too

Nicholas: I have yet to mount the Mercury and Gemini patches

Namita: wowww cool !! Im sure i will get to see it one day

Nicholas: yes you will

Namita: you mounted them urself ?

Nicholas: I love showing them off

Namita: hehe

Nicholas: the patches yes but I bought the photo n news paper already mounted

Namita: ahhh i see ..did you pay a fortune for the other memorabilia ?? The newspaper one ?

Nicholas: not really... the news paper was about $150 n the photo was $125 I think

Namita: are they worth more now ? do you think ?

Nicholas: I originally was buying the photo then last minute I decided to get the news paper

Nicholas: no idea.... they mean more to me..... I'd never sell them

Namita: ahhh i see

Nicholas: maybe one day they might be

Namita: yes im sure they are probably priceless for you now

Namita: did u buy it on ebay or something ?

Nicholas: maybe not the news paper coz there were so many printed back then

Namita: ohhh i see

Nicholas: I bought both in a shop in Langley.... the shop has long since gone

Nicholas: was about 14 years ago I guess

Namita: ohhh wowww cool !!

Namita: so you lucked out when you did !!

Nicholas: I like them... I like to have different thing in my place

Nicholas: I did

Nicholas: do you collect anything?

Nicholas: besides the reef stuff

Namita: im sure it is quite unique too !! and a conversational piece

Nicholas: which I think is really cool n can't wait to see

Namita: hehe besides reef stuff ....hmmm i love unique jewelry

Namita: esp pendents

Namita: sometimes rings

Nicholas: cool

Nicholas: where are you finding them?

Nicholas: I noticed the ring in some of your photos you've showed me

Namita: it could be different semi precious stones ...like turquoise ...or garnet or whatever catches my eye

Namita: my sister Jaya likes to make jewelry ...as a hobby

Namita: so i do wear some of hers

Nicholas: i like finding things that stand out.... sort of speak to me

Nicholas: oh cool... so creativity runs in the family

Namita: the stones we buy from a place called country beads in near kitsilano i think and they get stones from india mostly

Namita: in a string ... in different cuts and angles or shapes

Nicholas: cool... there's a bead place in Port Moody New Port village

Namita: my sis has made an genuine emerald necklace for her best friends wedding ... ..with matching earrings

Namita: ohhh what is it called ?

Nicholas: that's cool!!

Namita: yes me too i like things that stand out and are unique to me

Nicholas: umm not sure.... my friend Melissa took me there last year around xmas when we were hanging out... it's easy to find... hopefully it's still there

Namita: hehe ... no worries !

Nicholas: there are a lot of places I'd like to take you

Namita: i have sooo many earrings that Jaya has made for me

Namita: aweeeeeeeeeee sooooo sweet

Namita: yes take me !!!

Namita: hehe

Nicholas: speaking of places to take you... there's a little beach out near horseshoe bay that's pretty cool

Nicholas: it's a park out on the other side of the point

Nicholas: there were divers in n out of the water when I was there last

Namita: hehehe ..Whytecliff park ?

Nicholas: ooohh maybe thats it

Namita: Yessssssssss its one of my fav hiding place !!!

Nicholas: I've forgotten what its called

Nicholas: lol so you've been... cool

Namita: yesss i know where ur talking about

Nicholas: it was really cool

Namita: its one my fave places ..cuz not very many ppl know of this place

Nicholas: yes

Nicholas: n lot to see

Namita: you can watch the ferries go from that point

Nicholas: was just going to say that

Namita: lol

Namita: hehe ... i loveee exploring things like that

Nicholas: me toooo!!

Namita: im sure you know some more hidden places ... like i do

Nicholas: I like to not always have a plan n just make it up as I go along

Namita: yessssssssss mee tooooo

Nicholas: probly

Namita: i love going where ever the day is going to take me ...no plan what so ever

Nicholas: have you been to loco beach n richmond?

Namita: even in the winter

Nicholas: yes

Namita: yesss discovered that one a couple of years ago

Namita: have you been to this park in Tsawwassen

Namita: forgot the name ..one sec

Nicholas: its really cool.... I walked the, whatever you call the long thing that goes out into the water, last year n my legs were sore for like 2 days after

Namita: hehehehe

Namita: i havent done that yet !!

Namita: maybe we can do it together

Nicholas: its a long walk

Nicholas: yes we can!!!

Namita: ok you can carry me then

Nicholas: piggy back you if need be lol

Namita: hehhee

Nicholas: we'd stay warm that way lol

Nicholas: you riding my back er on my back I mean lol

Nicholas: I think its about 4 km one way... they have the kms marked

Namita: ok the park im looking for in Tsawwassen is called boundary bay regional park ..have you been there?

Namita: hehehehe yess i'll be riding ur back ...

Namita: cowgirl style !!

Nicholas: mmm not sure, I know I've been to one out there

Namita: lol

Nicholas: yee hah lol

Nicholas: it is quite secluded out at the point n you can see if anyone is coming

Namita: hehe ...it is really nice ...good place to go for a picnic ..it is before point roberts on the canadian side

Namita: hehee ok i will keep my eyes open

Nicholas: lol

Nicholas: I'd have to see the Boundary Bay park to recognize if I've been there or not

Namita: theres another area in richmond ...where you go see the planes coming and going ...it is on river road ... but you have to take the number # 1 road to get there ... there is a nice walkway ..and picnic benches

Namita: google it

Namita: google map it i mean

Nicholas: I did but the over head isn't helping at the moment

Namita: the river road one is right in front of YVR

Namita: what overhead ?

Nicholas: the google maps over head

Namita: ohhh

Nicholas: there's a pub called the Flying Beaver where you can watch the float planes take off n land right beside the pub

Namita: i think ive seen it ... u cant remember the the pubs name

Nicholas: I've parked on the road at the end of the run way in richmond n watched as the planes take off or land right over your head

Namita: hehehe wowww cool !!!

Nicholas: its called the Flying Beaver

Namita: ohhhh ...hehe

Nicholas: so whatcha wearing?

Namita: lol

Namita: hmmm my black nightie

Nicholas: yeah funny name for a pub

Nicholas: satin black? nice

Nicholas: I'm delegated to sleeping on the couch tonight as both the girls are staying over

Namita: yesss i wonder who could name a place like that !! yes satin ...and some sheer around the cups

Nicholas: ooooo love sheer esp around the cups

Namita: ohhhhhhhhhh .... so ur in ur recliner right now ?

Nicholas: yup

Namita: are you comfortable ?

Nicholas: sure am

Nicholas: you? he asks knowingly

Namita: hehe yes you like sheer ...it is sheer black too

Nicholas: mmmhmmm

Namita: yes im comfortable too ...kinda cold

Nicholas: I can picture it now

Namita: but ok ... maybe its the sheer thats keeping me cold ..hehe

Nicholas: awe too bad.... you need a tall bald guy you keep u warm

Namita: and it has a sheer black trim at the hem too

Namita: hehehe

Nicholas: mmmhmmm nice

Namita: yes i do

Namita: what are u wearing ?

Nicholas: I wont be able to keep my hands off you

Nicholas: u don't want to know..... nothing as sexy as you

Nicholas: lol

Namita: hehehe

Nicholas: t shirt sweats n socks

Nicholas: n glasses on

Namita: yeah i dont think any nightie will last long on me

Nicholas: you have plenty of sexyness for both of us

Namita: hmmm sexy ...i can just picture it

Nicholas: not while I'm around u it wont hehe

Nicholas: lol

Namita: heheh

Nicholas: my place has a tendency to be a little on the cool side in the colder months so I wear more clothes

Nicholas: in the summer it's shorts n nothing else

Namita: i can do a fashion show for you ..while ur sitting on ur trusty recliner ...i can come up to you sit on ur lap .... and show the strings .... and then go change into another nightie ..come back sit on top again ...and show you the other one

Nicholas: oooo I would love that mmmhhmmm

Namita: i can imagine it being cold ...esp when ur in a basement ... all the hot warm air rises to the top floor instead

Nicholas: you might not escape my arms once you sit dwn on me though fyi

Namita: heheheheh

Nicholas: yah n it's not well insulated in here... its better since I stopped up the drafts

Nicholas: but can get cold at times

Namita: ur hands on my thighs ...steadying me as i sit down on ur lap

Nicholas: mmmm yesssss

Namita: hehe .. i loveee how we're having 2 different conversations here

Nicholas: multi tasking my dear.... one of the many features I have to offer

Namita: hehehe

Namita: niceee one !!

Nicholas: I think you'll like sitting on me in my chair.... all ur weight pressing dwn on me... talk about deep penetration... wow!!

Namita: i loveee a multi tasker ...like me !

Namita: ommmg wowww yesss

Namita: would you enjoy that too ?

Nicholas: cool.. definitely not a linear thinker here

Namita: i wonder what it feels like for you

Nicholas: OOOhh HHelll yes!!!

Namita: i multitask a lot with work ..so its not new for me

Nicholas: you would feel ALL of me... every inch my sweet

Namita: OMGGG

Nicholas: right dwn to the every end

Namita: OMG Nicholas !!!

Namita: i would go crazy !!!

Nicholas: it'll be your fav chair too

Namita: LMAO !!!!

Nicholas: then a little rocking to wind u up even more

Namita: one hears of chairs that give massages or reclines... but this one would give me a deep penetration... hmm ... ok deal !!!

Nicholas: hehe

Namita: lol

Nicholas: I thought about you while I was out in Horseshoe bay.... we were sitting on a bench looking out over the bay n I thought how much you'd have liked it

Nicholas: I think about you a lot like that actually

Namita: aweeee... horseshoe bay has been one of my fav places to go since i was a kid .... can never pass up to go there

Nicholas: cool

Nicholas: where's another place you'd like to take me?... other than your bedroom hehe

Namita: hehehe ...hmmm well another place i discovered last yr ..was ... i was on my way to Squamish one time ...and just at the light by britannica beach

Nicholas: thats a cool place

Namita: you turn right from the hwy at that light ..and follow the road up to the left of the lil town

Namita: have you been ?

Namita: if you keep going up ..and u can only go up

Nicholas: i've been to the mine before but not where ur talking about I dont think

Namita: you will cross a little bridge

Nicholas: I've only ever stayed on the hiway

Namita: and OMG the most beautiful waterfall comes down under the bridge ...one side comes from the top of the mountain...and if u walk to the other side of bridge ..you can see it go down to the ocean below

Namita: veer off the hwy ...it is quite beautiful lil nests of places

Nicholas: sounds absolutely amazing!!

Nicholas: cool

Namita: like the sunset marina ...take that road down ...to the marina ...and you may be surprised

Nicholas: do you realize we've been talking for about 7 weeks now?

Nicholas: cool

Namita: ohh the water fall ..pools several times as it comes down .then cascades down

Namita: yesss i do ...hehhe

Nicholas: it seems like just a day and forever all at the same time

Namita: hehehe .. i know what u mean !!!

Namita: i agree ..

Nicholas: have you said anything to anyone about me yet? .... or are you waiting till after we've met?

Namita: only my sis Jaya knows right now

Namita: ive shown her ur pics

Nicholas: it seems strange to tell ppl about you w/o meeting yet

Nicholas: cool

Nicholas: what did she say?

Namita: hehehe ... yes i know what u mean

Nicholas: but thats the day n age we live in though

Nicholas: *smiling*

Namita: she says ...u look like a nice handsome guy !!

Nicholas: lol

Namita: hehe what ??

Nicholas: handsome thats nice of her

Namita: hehehe

Nicholas: just that you told someone was all

Namita: she liked ur pic where ur sitting at the airport ... kinda sideways glance

Nicholas: makes "this" that much more real I guess

Nicholas: oh yah

Namita: my fav is that one ...and the one you had on LL

Namita: do you have that pic still ?

Nicholas: I do I have all of them

Nicholas: I sent them to you didn't I?

Namita: no

Nicholas: oh sorry

Nicholas: hang on

Namita: well not the one in LL

Waiting for ~Namita~ to accept the file "IMG_1906. JPG" (1776 Kb). Please wait for a response or

Cancel (Ctrl+C)

the file transfer.

Namita: or change ur profile pic here

Transfer of file "IMG_1906.JPG" has been accepted by ~Namita~. Starting transfer...

Cancel

Nicholas: I can't remember which one I had on LL

Nicholas: oh I do like that one!!

Nicholas: mm sooo sexy

Namita: its the one i think ur in the airport or in the plane ....and maybe you took the pic urself

Nicholas: makes me think I'm in the kitchen w you n we just caught each other looking at each other

Transfer of "IMG_1906.JPG" is complete.

Nicholas: that should be the one I just sent you

Namita: hehehe

Namita: mmmmmmmmmmmmmmmmmmmmm yummmm

Namita: i loveeeeee ur eyes !!!

Nicholas: that it?

Nicholas: thx I love yours tooo!!

Namita: no not that one

Namita: ur in the plane

Nicholas: ohhh that one ok let me get it for you

Namita: it seems ur arms is holding the camera to take ur own pic

Namita: nice leg !!!

Namita: just noticed !

Waiting for ~Namita~ to accept the file "DSC_9437_2.JPG " (1067 Kb). Please wait for a response or

 Cancel (Ctrl+C)

the file transfer.

Transfer of file "DSC_9437_2.JPG" has been accepted by ~Namita~. Starting transfer...

Cancel

Nicholas: maybe this one will tide you over while I find the other

Namita: hehe ok

Waiting for ~Namita~ to accept the file "IMG_1906_2.JPG " (1021 Kb). Please wait for a response or

Cancel (Ctrl+C)

the file transfer.

Nicholas: found it!!

Namita: ahhhhhhhhhhhhhhhh ok

Namita: yayyyyyyyyyyyyyyyyyyy

Nicholas: that one

Transfer of file "IMG_1906_2.JPG" has been accepted by ~Namita~. Starting transfer...

Cancel

Transfer of "DSC_9437_2.JPG" is complete.

Nicholas: I think thats it

Namita: lol ok

Transfer of "IMG_1906_2.JPG" is complete.

Nicholas: now I'm confused

Nicholas: thats not the same one is it?

Namita: thats the same pic as the first one u sent me

Nicholas: damn I thought so sorry

Namita: no it isnt

Nicholas: no?

Namita: noooooooooooooo

Namita: hehe

Nicholas: one's in the airport n ones on the plane yes?

Namita: the other one is on the plane ... i could see seats behind you

Nicholas: okay

Nicholas: so you have 3 diff ones now yes?

Namita: and it looks like you took the pic urself ... cuz ur arms looked outstretched in front of you holding ...maybe a camera

Namita: no you sent me the one ur sitting in the airport with tony twice ..and one of you cliffhanging

Namita: or something

Nicholas: repelling ok sorry... I'll get this right hold on

Nicholas: looking for the LL photo

Namita: lol ok

Nicholas: I do love your profile photo here... love that look your giving mmhmm

Namita: hehehe ...the look of ... up to no good !!!

Nicholas: lol the look of "my god I'm gonna jump you!!"

Namita: yesss that is the up to no good look ...and im going to jump ur ...umm ...ahem .... im going to jump on ur recliner

Nicholas: lol....

Nicholas: my god I have a lot of photos

Namita: of urself ...or me ?

Nicholas: mmm just photos in general... can never have enf of you

Namita: hehe ..did u find the pic im talking about?

Waiting for ~Namita~ to accept the file "IMG_1911_2.JPG " (738 Kb). Please wait for a response or

Cancel (Ctrl+C)

the file transfer.

Nicholas: there we go

Nicholas: yup

Transfer of file "IMG_1911_2.JPG" has been accepted by ~Namita~. Starting transfer...

Cancel

Namita: ok crossing my fingers ..hehe

Nicholas: lol it should be the right one

Transfer of "IMG_1911_2.JPG" is complete.

Namita: heheok

Nicholas: it was a cropped version on an original.... n yes i took it on the plane, arm stretched out on the way dwn there

Namita: yessssss thats the one !!!

Nicholas: okay good

Nicholas: it's not blurry is it?

Namita: down where ???

Nicholas: to Mexico

Namita: it is kinda

Namita: stretched down in mexico??

Nicholas: the original has Tony in it

Nicholas: lol no silly, on the plane, on our way to Mexico

Nicholas: arms stretched out, holding the camera on the plane to Mexico

Namita: hehehehhee

Namita: ok phewwwww !!!

Namita: uh huh

Nicholas: I was looking for it in the wrong spot, thats why I was having trouble finding it

Namita: uh huh ... i see .. im salivating here ...dont mind me!!

Nicholas: your profile photo is so very hot!!! love it... I know I said that but it was worth saying again

Nicholas: oh good coz there's some salivating going on here too hehe

Nicholas: damn you are soooo awesome!!!

Nicholas: sorry I didn't pass that photo onto you sooner

Nicholas: can you send me this one thats up please?

Nicholas: you still there? or have you passed out?

Nicholas: your status shows you're still online but away..... its been 40 mins.... i'm assuming you got booted, 😊 😊

End Time: 1:47 AM

Chapter 23 November 17

Start Time: 12:15 AM

Nicholas: hey you

Namita: hello

Namita: how are you ?

Nicholas: how've you been?

Nicholas: I'm good

Namita: ohh god ... im trying to come back from the dead !!

Namita: ohhhhh i loveeeee ur pic

Nicholas: I got payed yesterday n I got a $1.00 raise

Namita: my fav

Namita: ohhhh wow ...cool !!

Nicholas: you've been up late w/o me? lol

Namita: that must have been a nice surprise !!

Namita: nooooooo

Nicholas: thx

Namita: ive been sick the last couple of days

Nicholas: it was

Nicholas: awe sorry to hear that

Namita: i think i had food poisoning or something

Namita: it wasnt fun

Nicholas: one of the reasons I've left this pic up... was for you

Namita: aweeee thanks

Nicholas: oooo damn

Namita: i loveeeee it

Namita: loveeeeeeee ur dimples

Namita: hehe

Nicholas: thx *blushing*

Namita: and ur big eues

Namita: eyes i mean

Nicholas: hehe

Namita: hehe

Nicholas: I've missed you..... it was such a nice treat talking to you the other morning

Nicholas: I love all your photos

Namita: ohhh yesss ... i didnt expect you to be on either ... then i saw you when i opened my laptop

Namita: hehe

Namita: but i think thats the nite i was sick

Nicholas: I've been leaving it open while I'm eating breakfast... I started doing that when I went for so long not hearing from you

Nicholas: probly

Nicholas: totally okay... I want you to be healthy

Namita: hehe ..sooo sorry ... ur breakfast has been lonely

Namita: yes im getting there

Nicholas: lol sokay I'll survive

Namita: hehe

Namita: how was your day today ?

Nicholas: as much as I'd like to monopolize ur time you are busy dwn there and u are on holiday

Nicholas: it was good... I think I've finally shaken this silly cough I've had for about 5 weeks now

Namita: ohhh nicholas ur not monopolizing my time everrrrrr

Namita: hehe

Nicholas: okay but I'd like too lol

Namita: omg ... wow thats a longgg time

Nicholas: it was

Namita: hehe you go right ahead !!

Nicholas: ohhhh it snowed here this evening

Nicholas: okay cool thx

Namita: are you serious !!?

Nicholas: yup

Namita: that is pretty early !!

Nicholas: about an inch here at home.... it's gone at work though

Namita: usually coquitlam and port moody gets a huge dump !!

Nicholas: the plow went by after I got out of the shower... startled me a little

Namita: i remember that !!

Namita: hehe ... ohh noo

Namita: yeah they can be quite noisy

Nicholas: took me a couple of mins to figure out what it was... it didn't take me long lol

Namita: i used to hate it when i was a kid ...and shoveling the driveway ...then the plow goes right past us plowing everything from the street onto the driveway !!

Namita: hehee ...pheww im glad ur ok !!

Nicholas: yup that happens here too

Nicholas: I have 3 hills to get out of here.... the drive way 1.... the road I'm on 2.... and Clarke Dr

Nicholas: I called into the last job a few times to say I couldn't get out

Namita: OMG .. yess clark drive is pretty steep !!

Namita: wow ...did they take ur predicament seriously ?

Nicholas: of course... they know I don't screw around when it comes to getting to work

Nicholas: well... people take me seriously most of the time

Namita: ahhh ok ...so they were ok with it !

Namita: hehe ..are you a serious guy ?

Nicholas: playful but serious but pretty laid back

Namita: hehehe ...just the way i like it !!

Nicholas: ppl say I'm easy to be around and put ppl at easy easily

Nicholas: yet another similarity

Namita: ahhhhh good !! I can see that in you Nicholas !!

Nicholas: I'm assuming you're the same?

Nicholas: well that's cool u can see that even through here

Namita: yes im pretty laid back too ... no nonsense !! Im receptive of others and usually present myself as approachable too ..and friendly to ppl who i get good vibes from. But i can also be reserved from ppl who im a little conscious of... or ppl im not too sure about

Nicholas: couldn't have put it better myself.... just like me

Namita: hehehe

Nicholas: I'm very aware of the vibes ppl give off

Namita: really??

Nicholas: yup

Nicholas: very receptive to ppls energy

Namita: yes me too ... im aware of negative or creepy vibes from men ...and usually stay away or be cautious of them

Nicholas: yup

Namita: i have a couple of ppl from work ...who are like that

Namita: hehe

Namita: actually ive been very in tune with this kind of energy since i was a kid

Nicholas: ppl that I stay clear of might think I don't like them, only because I don't say much to them... little do they know it's the vibe they give off

Namita: knowing who isnt quite right ...and who is

Namita: hehehehe

Namita: yesss it is sooo true !!

Nicholas: me too... I've always seen things more and viewed the world diff

Namita: and it is good when we have got that ability to know that about ppl

Nicholas: I think that's why I didn't have much in common w the ppl I went too school w

Namita: because you saw things differently

Nicholas: yes it is... it helps cut dwn on the bs w ppl

Namita: that is good ...you were probably beyond your years then !!

Nicholas: that n because I was quite n did my own thing

Namita: Hehhe i like the way you put that !!

Nicholas: thx

Nicholas: I've been told that before about being older than my age

Namita: it is sooo weird ...that i can feel that from you ...even before you said it !!

Nicholas: like minds

Nicholas: another connection my dear

Namita: even when ive been chatting with you these last several weeks ...i could see that

Namita: hehe

Nicholas: well I'm glad it's coming through and that you pick up on it... another quality I love about you

Namita: aweeeeeeeeeee thanks !! !

Namita: what did you have for dinner today ?

Namita: random

Namita: hehe

Nicholas: I can feel who you're about too

Nicholas: I had a pork chop sandwich

Namita: yess it is kinda good that we can feel who each of us are ...thru dialogue ... instead of working thru it for months

Nicholas: I sometimes buy meat that's on sale from the Safeway up the road... it's like 30 to 50% off

Namita: because ppl usually fall for the physical first

Namita: mmmm never had pork chop sandwich before

Namita: is that the Safeway on Comolake and clark ?

Nicholas: they do... another reason I've enjoyed getting to know you here.... as much as I'm going to love seeing you in person

Nicholas: that's the one

Namita: hehe aweee

Namita: omg i loveee it when you tell me what places you go ...cuz it takes me back to my childhood

Nicholas: the sandwich is a name I just made up for what I made

Namita: thats the grocrey store we went to ...fro groceries

Nicholas: wow, small world

Namita: akk ok

Namita: arghh

Namita: sorry spelling bad

Namita: hehe

Namita: yes small world

Nicholas: I cooked the pack of pork chops n thinly sliced it n put it in a sandwich

Namita: that was the only grocery store we had for years

Namita: before Extra Foods came along

Namita: then superstore on Lougheeed

Nicholas: I've been seeing past the poor spelling, urs n mine for weeks now

Namita: wow ..that is cool ... ive never had pork chop sandwich

Nicholas: I shop at Super Store all the time, was just there the other day

Namita: do you put lettuce n tomato

Namita: hehe ...it is still there !!

Nicholas: not usually... produce usually goes bad before I can eat it all

Namita: yesss ..hows the new fridge ?

Nicholas: well I'll make you one one day then

Namita: mmm

Namita: ok

Namita: i can make good ribs

Namita: for you ... one day

Nicholas: the fridge is awesome... I can keep ice cream now, which is so great coz I put it in my smoothies

Namita: mmmmmmm smoothies

Namita: yummmmmm

Namita: ur making me hungry ..which is probably a good sign

Nicholas: I'll definitely take you up on that one day

Namita: hehe

Namita: do you like BBQ

Nicholas: yah you probly need to eat soon

Namita: no i had soup earlier

Nicholas: LOVE to BBQ n eat it too

Namita: so im still good

Nicholas: oh good

Namita: mmmm loveee bbq

Namita: do you like salmon ?

Nicholas: I can cook a mean rib eye steak but you don't eat beef er haven't tried it I mean

Namita: hehehe

Namita: nooo i havent

Namita: sounds like ur a good cook !!

Nicholas: not a big fan of salmon... I grew up on it.... I like to catch it but I prefer to catch n release

Namita: we will be competing

Namita: ahhhh ok

Namita: i lovee it

Nicholas: I graduated top of the grade 12's for Foods n Nutrition

Namita: OMG really ???

Namita: and you didnt become a chef ?

Nicholas: nope

Nicholas: not my passion

Namita: you know i almost thought about going to culinary school !

Namita: if i ahd nt got in nursing school

Nicholas: working in a kitchen for a living didn't appeal to me

Namita: hadnt *

Namita: yes true ...would be too hot !

Nicholas: I thought about it but decided not to

Nicholas: you sound like a fantastic cook!! n I love that you love to cook

Namita: Yesss i lovee to experiment

Namita: and i dont follow recipes usually

Nicholas: nor do I... just like my dad

Namita: i like to get a general idea ..then twist it to my taste

Namita: hehe

Nicholas: my dad was a fantastic cook... he use to make seafood chowder that was to die for... everybody loved it

Namita: i love cooking indian ,spanish for example pallea ...or asian

Namita: WOW sounds delish !!

Namita: did you remember how to make it ?

Nicholas: yah me too... when I bake I follow recipes coz thats more chemistry

Nicholas: I think I could probably do it justice

Namita: hehe yesss baking is ...like i say it ... cant fuck with baking ... that is different .otherwise ur screwed

Nicholas: yup there's things happening in baking that you can't leave out or sub

Nicholas: you can add spices like to flavor scones but that's about it

Namita: hehehe ... yes ive been a culprit of it

Namita: i follow the recipe exactly for baking

Namita: except i hate it when im making cupcakes ...and they bake and rise one side and over the rim ...then they look like manatees

Nicholas: I've made some pretty bad food before... the worst was dinner for the girls n me.... looked like barf on a plate

Nicholas: lol

Namita: OMG Are you serious !!!

Namita: LOL

Namita: what did you make ?

Nicholas: I like the crust on the top of the cup cakes when they're right out of the oven

Namita: mmm yess me too

Namita: hehe

Namita: or just lick the icing off

Nicholas: lol it was a mix of too many things... it was gross... we laugh about it now

Namita: did you eat it ?

Namita: or had to order in ?

Nicholas: mmmmm I'd like to lick the icing off you!! hehe

Namita: lol

Namita: whip cream too?

Nicholas: we ate it, it didn't taste too bad... wasn't great but edible

Namita: that would be fun

Nicholas: love whip cream!!!... it's a nice light snack lol

Namita: hehehe... yess me too

Nicholas: right out of the can into your mouth mmmm

Namita: with fruits

Namita: yummmm

Namita: hehehe

Namita: i loveee the container one

Nicholas: any excuse to have whip cream

Namita: mmmmmmmmmmmmm

Nicholas: cool whip?

Namita: yess that the one

Nicholas: eeewww don't like that one at all

Namita: really ??

Nicholas: got a be the real thing for me

Namita: i know it does kinda taste oily

Nicholas: never liked cool whip

Namita: you mean the cool whip is not real ???

Nicholas: that's coz it's whipped petroleum product

Namita: eweeeeeeeeeeeeeeeeeeeeeeeeeeeee !!!!!!!!!!

Namita: are you kidding me !!!?

Nicholas: nope check the container

Namita: YUCK PFTTTTTTTTTTT

Namita: i never did

Nicholas: read the ingred

Namita: it looked real to me

Namita: hehee

Namita: which one is real then ?

Nicholas: I put it in the cheeze whiz category

Nicholas: the stuff in the can that says Real Whip Cream on it

Namita: ohhhhhhh god ...im not a cheez whiz fan

Nicholas: coz cool whip comes in a pressurized can now too

Namita: ohhhh ...hehehe of course the one that says real whip !!

Nicholas: lol yup

Namita: hehe

Namita: hmmmm

Nicholas: never liked cheeze whiz... gross

Namita: YUck me either

Nicholas: n adults are always trying to feed it to kids on celery for a snack

Namita: yesss true

Namita: that is pure grosss !!

Nicholas: and if you need a quick pain killer, the propellent in the whip cream can is NOs

Nicholas: laughing gas

Namita: im not huge fan of cheese as is ...on other foods ...like pizza or pasta im ok with

Namita: really ??

Nicholas: good to know... I like a few diff cheses

Nicholas: yup

Namita: how do you know all this

Namita: hehe

Nicholas: steel trap memory.... that n I read the can once

Namita: did you try it?

Namita: you must do well on exams !! LOL

Nicholas: when I had my wisdom teeth out n if I've got a killer migraine

Namita: uh huh

Nicholas: *shakes head* sucked at exams

Namita: lol

Nicholas: well I suppose I could do better now

Namita: well ur past that now

Nicholas: you need to hold the can up right so the whip doesn't come out

Nicholas: that's right... no exams here

Namita: hehehehe

Namita: will you help me ?

Namita: lol

Nicholas: sure

Nicholas: w what?

Nicholas: oh exams?

Namita: hold the can up ?

Nicholas: sure

Namita: nooo with the whip cream

Namita: the can

Nicholas: okay

Namita: hehhe

Namita: and it is all about trying the can ...dont get hanky panky with me

Namita: lol

Nicholas: never

Nicholas: always open to the hanky panky

Namita: hehehe

Nicholas: I will always be packing when I'm w you

Namita: hehehe.. guess id better watch my back

Nicholas: nah I'll watch it for you n your front n sides

Namita: hehhee

Namita: ok i can see ur my bodyguard now !!

Nicholas: sure

Namita: lol

Nicholas: they'll have to go through me first to get to you lol

Nicholas: though ppl find me intimidating sometimes too... not sure why but they do

Namita: hehehe ...i can go thru you too

Namita: is it ur height ?

Nicholas: maybe n coz I don't say much till you get to know me or coz I'm quiet

Namita: well so can i ..be quiet

Nicholas: I watch n am aware of my surroundings... head on a swivel so to speak

Namita: nicholas brb ok

Nicholas: I sometimes think I should've have been a spy

Nicholas: okay

Namita: sorry im back

Nicholas: yeah!!!

Nicholas: so glad

Namita: hehe

Namita: still recovering

Nicholas: was enf time for me to get a drink

Nicholas: I bet.... you didn't speew did you?

Namita: almost

Namita: i got some ginger ale

Nicholas: oooo damn... sorry to hear that

Namita: im ok

Nicholas: good plan

Nicholas: I have some flat 7up in the fridge

Namita: that always helps ...instead of taking gravol ... which would be too drugging

Nicholas: yup

Namita: nooo i font 7up too sweet

Namita: find*

Nicholas: I wish I could just hold you n try to help you feel better

Namita: aweeeee thanks nicholas ....just saying that makes me feel good

Nicholas: I like 7up.... I mix it w my fruit juice for a sparkling drink

Nicholas: oooh good... anything to help you feel better my sweet

Namita: yes mixing it is ok with me

Namita: even sprite is good for mixing

Namita: muahhh thanks

Nicholas: I buy the little short can's of 7up's

Nicholas: welcome... I could almost feel that thx

Namita: ahhh yesss ...less waste

Namita: heheh

Nicholas: yah n I don't need the big cans

Namita: yess the bigger ones are too much

Nicholas: 6 little cans last me quite a while

Namita: ohh wow ...thats good

Namita: sometimes if i have rough day at work ... i crave a soda ... which would probably be my beer ...if i drank

Namita: lol

Nicholas: the girls like the juice/7up drink too n they can split a can n no waste

Namita: and usually i go for the real coca cola

Nicholas: we've had this convo before

Namita: yess ive done the fruit juice and 7up ... it tastes good

Nicholas: or you've told me that before

Namita: have we ??

Namita: really?

Nicholas: I think so

Namita: hehee

Namita: sorry

Namita: hehe

Nicholas: no need to be sorry my dear

Namita: hehe are you making notes then

Namita: i will quiz you on it !

Nicholas: no need... steel trap memory

Nicholas: deal

Namita: lol

Nicholas: I bet I get a lot right even w/o studying

Namita: hehehee

Namita: i could try to take you down !

Nicholas: lol I'd let you esp if you tried to tackle me

Namita: hehehe...which brings me to ur point when you said ur head swivels around .. something to that effect before i had to excuse myself

Nicholas: yes

Namita: so i was thinking ....hmmmm can i even creep up on this guy everrr???

Nicholas: we'll see hehe

Nicholas: you can try as many times as you'd like

Namita: hehehe

Namita: and end up defeated !!!?

Nicholas: and just as you get close enf n think that you've done it w/o me noticing.... I say BOO! n scare you lol

Namita: hehehehe

Nicholas: or I counter attack you

Namita: of course you will catch me off guard and the tables will be turned on me

Namita: lol

Namita: omg ..would you chase me too ?

Nicholas: sure

Namita: hehe

Nicholas: that's if you ran

Namita: what if i crawl under a table or bed?

Nicholas: I'd come in after you lol

Namita: hehehe

Nicholas: we could build a fort while we're there lol

Namita: ohhh myyyy

Namita: yesss ..and i will grab all the pillows in the house

Namita: so there !!!

Nicholas: what?! so no boys allowed in ur fort?

Namita: noooooooooooo

Namita: just me ..and the girls

Nicholas: awe man!

Namita: hehehehe

Nicholas: I would stomp around and be the giant

Namita: get ur own club !!

Nicholas: awe nuts!!

Namita: hahhaa

Namita: ohhh noooo

Nicholas: I love how you put the girls in there... made me smile

Namita: someone is having a meltdown

Namita: hehe...glad you caught it !!

Nicholas: *sighs* I'll be fine... don't worry about me *sighs*

Namita: hehehe ...only if you bring a can of whipped cream or ice cream can you enter the fort

Nicholas: ice cream if the girls are there n whip cream if it's just you hehe

Namita: hehehe

Namita: yesss ... but you have to get the flavor right !!!

Namita: too

Nicholas: mmmm

Nicholas: not sure we've covered that yet

Namita: hehehe

Nicholas: right flavour? hmmm

Namita: ahhh haaaaaaaaaa !!!!!!!!

Namita: you dont know my fav ice cream !! !

Nicholas: chocolate

Namita: yes right flavour

Nicholas: so there!!! ha to you lol

Namita: ARGHHHHHHHHHHHHH

Nicholas: lol nice try woman

Namita: ok ok soooo you had a open sesame moment !!!

Namita: Geeeezzzz

Nicholas: that was like 7 weeks ago but I got it ha

Namita: hehehehe

Namita: i forgot ... and you remembered !!!

Namita: hehehe nice one!!!!!

Nicholas: I did.... well thx shucks

Namita: heheee

Nicholas: side note, how's ur uncle?

Nicholas: when I don't here from you I think something has happened

Namita: right now he seems to be doing ok ... he is still on breathing machine ...but he has a tracheostomy now

Namita: with is a hole in the neck for a different route for a breathing tube

Nicholas: that's where they put a tube

Namita: it can stay in longer

Namita: yes

Nicholas: you beat me to it... like minds

Nicholas: is his heart getting stronger?

Namita: sort of ... he is on blood thinner s right now

Namita: but IV form

Nicholas: i see

Namita: to prevent other clots from happening

Nicholas: yup

Namita: plus he has a filter put in for added protection

Nicholas: so it'll be a long road for him yes?

Nicholas: filter?! like an inline filter?

Namita: i guess so ... only time will tell

Namita: yes inline filter ... it is a small badminton birdie like ..filter that they insert into the inferior vena cava ...ur major vein bringing blood back from ur extremities

Nicholas: didn't know they could do that.... it's kind of like a fuel filter in a car

Nicholas: modern technology got to love it

Namita: hehehe yess sort of

Namita: its like a little umbrella that catches any clots as they come

Nicholas: then what happens to the clots, like how do they get them out?

Namita: they dissolve as the blood rushes against it

Nicholas: ah

Namita: its a science

Namita: its been available since the 90's

Nicholas: I'm picturing a fuel filter n w those you change them but I understand what you mean

Nicholas: oh wow so not that long

Namita: yeah ..eventually they can go in and take it out too ...when they put it in...the patient does not have to be sleep ..or sedated ... they can be awake

Nicholas: wow that is cool... is it painful when they take it out?

Namita: and when they go in ...they usually go in the femoral artery ...around the groin area ....with a wire tool ..and let it swim up with the blood going back to the heart

Namita: to where they want it

Namita: sometimes it can be painful ..but the give local anesthetic

Namita: around the skin

Nicholas: holly.... I've heard of them going in that way for a few diff things

Namita: yesss they angiograms that way too

Namita: to stent the heart vessels

Nicholas: and the filter isn't very big either if it's inside a vein

Namita: or open the vessels up

Namita: without surgery

Namita: yes the filter is half the size of my pinky

Nicholas: there's a vale replacement surgery they can do that way too

Namita: theres a what ?

Nicholas: until I see ur pinky I can only imagine though I'm guessing your pinky or your hands for that matter are pretty petite

Nicholas: valve replacement

Nicholas: I just saw my crappy spelling now

Namita: hehehe thanks

Namita: hmmm i didnt know that !

Namita: are ur hands big?

Namita: yes mine are small

Namita: i wear size small gloves at work

Nicholas: it's a tissue vale and you have to be a good candidate for it.... draw back is it'll wear out

Namita: ohhh

Nicholas: I looked at ur hand in the Moving Day photo.... I love them

Namita: really??

Nicholas: my hands big? hmmm... they're proportionate to my body lol

Nicholas: yes

Namita: hehehe

Namita: hmmmm

Nicholas: they look very ummm sexy

Namita: im sure they do ... you mean ur hands or mine ?

Nicholas: lol

Nicholas: ur hands are sexy

Namita: lol ahhh ok

Nicholas: mine are.... big I guess

Namita: hmmm they are nice though

Nicholas: mine'll look big next to urs

Namita: i like it big

Namita: hehe

Nicholas: mine are a little dry this time of year

Nicholas: I'm just guessing but I think you'll like the rest of me hehe

Namita: mine too ... but i take care of them as well as the rest of my body

Nicholas: I've been imagining our first meeting

Nicholas: I bet you do

Namita: ohhhh i will dont you worry

Namita: what have you been thinking ?

Nicholas: imagining what the first thing I'll say... the first thing I'll hear from you.... if I'm going to play it cool or just attack you

Namita: LOL

Namita: too funny !!! should i wear my armor ??

Namita: nO wait isnt that the guys job?

Nicholas: because you see there will be a lot of firsts in just a few minutes

Namita: yess true

Nicholas: guys job? to wear armor?

Nicholas: first words, first hug, first kiss

Namita: hehehe ... i meant man in shining armor .. i was referring to that

Nicholas: ah gotcha

Nicholas: I get it

Namita: lol

Nicholas: I was thinking body armor lol but I get it now

Namita: hehehehe

Namita: ohh geeez

Nicholas: and after such a long wait all those firsts just might make time stand still even for just a moment

Nicholas: body amour... not that I was thinking I'd be that rough

Namita: hmmm wowwww that would be a good feeling ..like we are the only ones standing there

Nicholas: yesssss.... kind of what I'm anticipating

Namita: taking each other in ..using all our senses ...except taste of course ...we can use that one later

Namita: hehe

Nicholas: seeing you n the world just disappearing

Nicholas: lol yes later n yes we will

Namita: seeing you smile ...seeing ur reaction

Namita: hehee

Nicholas: seeing you smile n your reaction hehe

Nicholas: I went to the gelato place w Amanda on Sat n thought about being there w you... though I think about you being w me quite a lot

Namita: aweeeee sooo sweet !!!

Namita: what did u guys have ??

Namita: what flavour?

Nicholas: I had the berry cheese cake n Amanda had coconut n.... can't remember the other flavor

Nicholas: I think you'll like this place much better than the place on Venables... so much creamier

Namita: mmm sounds sooo good !!

Nicholas: it was

Namita: yeah the venables one ...really sucked ...i was sooo disappointed

Namita: i couldnt figure out what the hype was all about

Nicholas: yah, they need to spend more time perfecting a few flavors instead of having 200 so-so flavours... I think

Namita: when ur in my hood ... i will take u and the girls ...to my fav ice cream shop .... it's gelato too... and it is on the seaside of white rock overlooking the ocean

Nicholas: Compari's has about 16 flavours I think

Namita: when ur in the store ...and look out from the window ...all u see is the ocean ...and waves comin in

Nicholas: cool. looking forward to it

Namita: this one is real small

Namita: it has good flavours though

Nicholas: n I did notice the girls in there again, love it

Namita: hehe

Namita: yes i know they will like it too

Namita: we will have fun

Nicholas: they love ice cream

Nicholas: there isn't much to do at my place when they come so I try to do things that are fun so we're not just sitting around watching tv

Namita: aweee im sure they loveeeee their dad a lot

Namita: these are the things they will remember

Nicholas: *smiles* they do

Namita: i cant remember which one is older ?

Nicholas: Isabel is 13 n Amanda is 11

Namita: ahhh ok. how are they doing in school ?

Nicholas: Amanda is really good in school, things come easy to her. Isabel struggles but she does her best and that's what count

Nicholas: I always knew I'd have kids... always liked kids... was a day camp leader for 3 summers

Namita: yesss ive always liked kids too

Nicholas: it's all I've really ever wanted to be was a dad

Namita: i thought i would have kids ...but it hasnt happened ....ohh well

Nicholas: yes I checked that one off weeks ago lol

Namita: ohhh cool!!! thats soooo good to hear

Namita: checked what off ?

Nicholas: you liking kids

Namita: ohhh hehhee

Namita: what does that mean to you ?

Nicholas: how do you mean?

Nicholas: u liking kids?

Namita: yes

Namita: hehe

Nicholas: that ur open to the possibility of having kids in ur life

Namita: yesss i am

Nicholas: weather they're your own or someone else's

Namita: are you talking about more kids ?

Nicholas: no lol

Namita: hehe

Namita: ok

Nicholas: well if thing progress the way I hope they will then you'll have kids in ur life.... again no pressure

Nicholas: even if it's only every 2 weeks or so lol

Namita: no pressure at all

Nicholas: this might sound silly but I saved our very first convo from LL.... it's pretty cute to read after this many weeks later

Namita: really ? what does it say ?

Nicholas: ANd I still feel as excited about you as I did back then

Namita: aweeeeeeeeeee thanks

Nicholas: just me asking to see your back stage n you asking if I liked indian women

Nicholas: I'll show it to you one day

Namita: hehe ...and what was ur answer ?

Nicholas: I have no barriers when it comes to race

Namita: aweee...sooo nice to say that ... unlike some men on there

Namita: some are downright almost racist

Nicholas: I sensed a lot of caution from you when you asked me that... understandable after some of your experiences on there

Nicholas: as I said then n I'll say it again.... their loss n my gain!!

Namita: yess ..cuz i find ppl can say whatever they want ...but is that the case really?

Namita: lol

Nicholas: my world became sooo much brighter once I found you

Namita: aweeeeee nicholas !!

Namita: if i had passed you on the street ...even before LL would you have noticed ?

Nicholas: it took about a week n a half for it to sink in

Nicholas: oh hell yes!!!!

Namita: hehehee woowwww

Namita: hheehe really??

Nicholas: I would so notice a beautiful woman passing me.. n wonder if she noticed me too

Namita: hehehe...yes i would have ..esp when u have dimples i can see from 5 miles .....and a killer smile

Nicholas: and have that thought of "if she could just get to know me" or "I wonder what she's really like?"

Nicholas: awe thx

Namita: hehehe

Namita: she is a freak in bed and a lady on the street

Namita: thats what she is like

Nicholas: lol yah that too

Namita: lol

Namita: im zoning out

Nicholas: me too a little

Namita: ohh geez

Namita: im lying on my side and typing to you

Namita: awkward

Namita: hehe

Nicholas: was visualizing passing you on the street

Namita: heheh really

Nicholas: one hand typing

Nicholas: yup

Namita: and i look up and smile at you

Namita: a fleeting moment

Namita: yes one hand typing

Nicholas: just strangers on the street

Namita: hmmm yess

Namita: then you follow me

Namita: to see where i go

Namita: i fasten my pace

Nicholas: wondering how I could get your attention or all the things I should have said

Namita: hehehe

Namita: i turn a corner quickly

Namita: away from ur sight

Nicholas: me disappointed that I'd lost you

Namita: and as soon as you turn the corner ..i grab ur collar ...and bring ur face to mine ...and kiss you deeply

Namita: taking ur breath away

Nicholas: ooooohhhh dammmm!!!!

Namita: and we havent even introduced ourselves

Nicholas: that it would

Namita: hehe

Nicholas: lol

Namita: then i say hi ..to you thru ur parted lips

Nicholas: now we can steal those moments all the time

Namita: as we take a breather

Nicholas: n exchange names

Namita: noo

Nicholas: no?

Nicholas: and we part strangers?

Namita: not at first

Nicholas: ah

Namita: we haVE TO GO AGAIN for another round of deep kissing

Nicholas: I'm good w that

Namita: hehehe

Namita: ur hands on my hips

Namita: mine on ur chest

Namita: up ur neck

Namita: steadying myself

Nicholas: so you know deep kissing w you is going to cause me to press into you through me jeans

Namita: hmmmmm yesssss

Nicholas: you'll be able to feel my excitement

Namita: hmmmmmm yessssssssssss

Nicholas: coz we'll be pressed together

Namita: if i do ...i will keep kissing you and run my one hand over that ball of excitement

Namita: and rub it

Nicholas: n I'll let you!!!

Namita: hehe

Namita: right out in the open

Namita: i'll be doing that

Nicholas: w your petit hands it will be a handful

Namita: then you grab one of my leg/thigh as u kiss me

Namita: hehe

Namita: yess it will be

Nicholas: totally okay w that... u can touch me when ever n where ever you like!!

Namita: you pull it up against you as u press into me even more

Nicholas: yessss

Namita: hehe

Namita: would that excite you

Nicholas: yes yes

Nicholas: touching you everywhere will put me over every time

Namita: hehehee

Nicholas: I can't wait for you to have a base line to go on

Namita: what base line

Nicholas: being intimate w me

Namita: hmmmm yessss

Namita: i cant wait either

Nicholas: if you craved it before then I'll be like heroin for you lol

Namita: lol .... yesss and ur my antidote

Nicholas: when I leave work I think how nice it would be to drive to you n spend the night

Nicholas: yes

Namita: hmmmyessss....or have a quickie before you leave ur place ...and a longer session when u get to mine after ur work

Namita: 2 different places

Nicholas: the only way to get ur next fix is to ride me till you can't see straight

Namita: omg im totally shutting down

Namita: cant spell

Nicholas: oh yes... I love how you think

Nicholas: I got it

Namita: hehehe ...omg are you saying im going to go blind with too much sex ??

Nicholas: not blind

Namita: hehe

Namita: isnt that an old wives tale

Namita: too much solo will make u blind

Nicholas: just temporarily blurred vision from the endorphin high

Namita: heheh

Nicholas: yes it is lol

Namita: i loveeee that ... cant wait to experience it

Nicholas: and hairy palms

Namita: eweee really

Namita: didnt hear that one

Namita: lol

Nicholas: I can wait to experience it w you!!

Namita: hmmmm yesssssss

Nicholas: yah that's an old one too

Namita: hehehe

Namita: im heading into dreamland soon ... i wanna tell u beofre i pas out ..and leave you wondering what happened

Namita: like last week

Namita: that was embarrassing enough

Namita: lol

Nicholas: okay

Nicholas: oh don't be embarrased

Nicholas: it's okay

Nicholas: okay I'll talk you you tmw?

Namita: i felt like a total FOOL

Nicholas: same time?

Nicholas: totally ok

Namita: when i woke up however briefly ...and seeing ur face with this pic

Namita: yes will be on here tomorrow

Nicholas: I'll be around at breakfast.. about 9

Namita: ok

Namita: ttyl

Nicholas: glad I could be there when you woke even if only in pic form

Namita: it was awesome

Nicholas: gnight my sweet

Nicholas: *smiling*

Namita: goodnite nicholas

Nicholas:

Nicholas: hope you feel better soon

Namita: yes thnx

Namita: ok bye

Nicholas: night

Namita: nite lol

End Time: 3:32 AM

Chapter 24 November 18

Start Time: 12:07 AM

Nicholas: helloooooo

Namita: hi there

Nicholas: I thought I was going to have to stay late tonight but fortunately I didn't

Namita: i almost fell asleep here ... i was waiting ..and had just closed my eyes

Namita: hehe

Nicholas: oh are you tired enf to skip tonight? he says hoping she says no lol

Namita: hehe .. i am tired but im sure we can chat ..or i can

Nicholas: my brain is a little fried... I was welding all shift

Namita: ohhh

Nicholas: ooohhh good!!

Namita: that must strain ur eyes

Nicholas: I've been looking forward to you all day

Nicholas: a little.. the welding arc is bright even w a helmet

Namita: hehe ... even when u were welding with ur helmut on ...you were looking forward to me

Nicholas: I had to weld over top of someone else's crap

Nicholas: ooo love the red dress... very sexy hehe

Namita: lol ....ohhh nooooooo

Namita: thx hehe

Namita: that is not good !!

Nicholas: I really don't like to do that

Nicholas: this piece has failed x-ray 3 times now

Namita: did they not do a good job the first time?

Nicholas: nope... the first 3 times

Namita: you guys xray stuff

Nicholas: yup

Namita: omg

Namita: really ? Hmmm i never knew !!

Nicholas: have to make sure there's no sand pockets in the castings

Namita: ohhh i see

Nicholas: if there is n we blast them they'll explode

Namita: omg ...nooooooooo we dont want that !!!

Namita: that sounds dangerous

Nicholas: had this one been done right the first time I wouldn't have had to fix it but at least it was something diff

Nicholas: it could be

Nicholas: most of the castings are about $20,000 each

Namita: yes i guess ...something different for a change

Namita: omg wowww

Nicholas: yup

Namita: so you really cant screw things up !!

Nicholas: I don't mind running beads all day it's kind of zen like for me

Nicholas: thats right

Namita: hmmm interesting !!

Nicholas: beads is the term for the weldment or mixture of the base metal n welding rod

Namita: so did the other guy get a talking to ..about his work?

Nicholas: don't know

Namita: ahhhh ok

Nicholas: it would have been nice to start from the beginning. w most of the other guys work they don't seem to have a plan w what they're doing

Nicholas: it looks really bad

Nicholas: and hard to tie onto as well

Namita: hehee

Namita: how many guys work at a time in ur shift ?

Nicholas: in the shop I'm in there's 6

Namita: so theres 6 of you

Nicholas: on the entire shift all 3 buildings there's 12 and 2 guys outside

Namita: ahhhh i see ...any women ? hehe

Nicholas: there's 2 of us in my position

Nicholas: no women... no idea why

Nicholas: women in the office yes

Nicholas: just not on the floor

Namita: what are the 2 guys outside doing ?

Namita: ahhh ok

Namita: is there office personnel too ?

Nicholas: one is grinding and the other is gouging

Namita: ohhh well it must be cold when they are doing that at this time of the year??

Nicholas: yup office staff too... there's about 60 ppl total in our plant

Namita: ohh woww

Namita: so its a busy place !!

Nicholas: the grinder is under a cover and the gouger is in a closable booth

Nicholas: it is

Namita: ahhhh ok

Nicholas: I think there's 9 branches world wide

Namita: with this company ?

Nicholas: most in the States and the main office is in Austria

Nicholas: yup

Namita: ohh wow

Namita: so hopefully its not a company that would go out of business

Nicholas: I just got my company shirt I ordered... long sleeve w the company logo embroidered on the front

Nicholas: oh no they've been around since like the 40's

Nicholas: we have a safety slogan contest at the moment

Namita: wowww ...that is good !! So the shirt ..is it like a uniform ?

Namita: or just a company shirt

Nicholas: nope just something to ware

Namita: ahh ok

Nicholas: it was $20.00 to me that's a steal for a long sleeve w embroidery

Namita: hehehe ...that is a good bargain

Nicholas: I have a couple of ideas... the winner gets $100 gift certificate and the company uses the slogan for the next year

Nicholas: oooo there's another one of my fav photo's of you

Namita: i know our icu is ordering a fleece sweater and a jacket vest ...with our logo on it ..and saying icu on the front corner ...and they are charging 75 to 80 bucks each

Namita: hehe thankx

Nicholas: wow that's pretty steep

Namita: that a good idea

Namita: yesss i was like no thanks ... i can buy something half the price and still stay warm

Nicholas: one of my slogans is "Safety, Get It"

Namita: i dont need to advertise that i work in icu

Namita: hehe

Namita: hehe that is a good one

Nicholas: that's true

Namita: hehe

Nicholas: or "Work Safe Today"

Namita: thats good one too !!!

Nicholas: or "Got Safety?"

Namita: hehehe

Namita: ur very witty

Nicholas: lol thx

Namita: hehehe

Nicholas: I can't decide on which one to submit so some help would be great

Namita: hmmmm

Nicholas: I'll even split the prize w you hehe

Namita: i like the last 2

Namita: hehehehee

Namita: nicceeeeeeeeeee

Nicholas: I'm trying to figure out what the ppl making the decision will want

Nicholas: or like

Namita: yesss you kinda have to get into their minds !

Nicholas: yup

Namita: but so like ...got safety ?

Namita: and the other one was good too

Nicholas: or how they'll interoperate my slogans

Namita: hehe ... are other ppl putting their two bit in as well??

Nicholas: yah

Nicholas: I mentioned the contest to a couple of others n no one seemed too keen on it like they could care less.... less submissions the better my chances

Namita: hehehe thats good for you then !!

Namita: what would u get a gift certificate for?

Nicholas: the place I worked at before my surgery had a contest for a new company logo and my submission won... was $100.00

Namita: omgg ...that is good !!

Nicholas: not sure the posting doesn't say

Namita: ahhh k

Nicholas: I have a hard time turning dwn an opportunity to be creative

Nicholas: and I can't do things just half ass either

Namita: hehehe ... once you start to think about it ...then you kinda get absorbed into it

Nicholas: yup

Nicholas: I have my portfolio on a DVD... it's a slide show w music

Namita: ideas come flying in and stuff

Nicholas: I usually do more than what the client was looking for

Nicholas: not that I've had many clients but one day I will

Namita: hehee ...ohh yesss you will !!

Namita: that day will come

Nicholas: I do have quite a few personal projects I want to build to showcase what I'm capable of doing

Namita: omg ..sorry ...im dozing here

Nicholas: sokay

Nicholas: you must be tired coz we're earlier than usual

Nicholas: do you want to sleep?

Nicholas: as much as I'd like to keep you up longer

Namita: yesss im sure that all those creative juices will start coming out when an idea gets planted in ur head

Nicholas: it's being in bed I bet

Namita: yesss and for once my room is warm

Nicholas: nice

Namita: hehe

Nicholas: the weather warmed up a little here too

Nicholas: it rained most of the day

Namita: ohh really ..the snow all gone now ?

Nicholas: in most places though the guys from Chilliwack said there's about 6 inches out there

Nicholas: didn't stop till about 6 this morning

Nicholas: there was about an inch or so here when I got home but it had stopped by then

Namita: wow those guys in Chilliwack ALWAYS GET huge dumps of snow

Namita: wowww

Nicholas: when was this profile pic taken?

Namita: and its not even winter yet

Namita: umm in july

Nicholas: yah I remember last year when they shut the hiway dwn coz of a big accident

Namita: hmmm there were too many accidents happening

Namita: i hope the new hwy is wayy better

Nicholas: cool... so pretty recent... I'm trying to figure out how to take a pic of me right now to post as I have my glasses on n thought you might want to see

Namita: hehehe ..hmmm i dunno

Namita: you can take it with ur phone then email it to me

Nicholas: damn that didn't work so well lol

Nicholas: now I know why I don't take pics of myself... maybe it's just the lighting in here

Namita: hehe

Namita: is it too dark ?

Nicholas: not really just looks like those profile pics you see on the dating sites lol

Namita: heheheee

Nicholas: I'm working on it

Namita: eweee noooooo

Namita: not those

Nicholas: lol

Namita: not to worry take ur time

Nicholas: so far so good... got to love drag n drop

Namita: hehee...ive never done that before

Nicholas: I hope you like it.. I think it looks kind of sill

Waiting for ~Namita~ to accept the file "Photo 7.jpg" (83 Kb). Please wait for a response or

Cancel (Ctrl+C)

the file transfer.

Nicholas: there you go!!

Namita: ohhh ok ..one sec

Transfer of file "Photo 7.jpg" has been accepted by ~Namita~. Starting transfer...
Cancel

Transfer of "Photo 7.jpg" is complete.

Nicholas: that's as current as can be!!

Namita: lol

Nicholas: oh no silence

Namita: ok one sec

Nicholas: not good lol

Namita: hehe ..thats pretty good !!!

Nicholas: I can't believe the lighting on a plane was better than my living room

Namita: now i can see what ur wearing ...and ur glasses

Nicholas: yup that's my Tigger sweater

Nicholas: from Whinnie the Poo

Nicholas: T-I-double-grr

Namita: ohhh ...does it have the characters on it ?

Namita: lol

Nicholas: sure does... well just Tigger

Nicholas: our tops are made outs rubber, our bottoms are made outa springs coz we're bouncy bouncy fun fun fun fun

Namita: hehehhe ...donttttttttttttt

Namita: otherwise i will get that song stuck in my head

Namita: arghhhhhh

Nicholas: *sighs* okay I wont lol

Namita: hehee

Namita: i remember that song from like grade 1 or 2

Namita: omgg

Nicholas: yup

Namita: lol

Nicholas: I keep forgetting today is friday er I guess Sat now

Namita: ur on ur days off ..yayyy

Nicholas: YESS

Namita: do u have plans ?

Nicholas: thought about how cool it would have been to head to you after work n spend the weekend w you... one day

Nicholas: nope no plans... just make it up as I go along

Nicholas: as usual

Nicholas: did you fall asleep?

Nicholas: silly question coz if you did you can't answer me lol

Namita: hehe ... god my eyes are closing here

Namita: im soooo sorry

Nicholas: its okay

Namita: i think im coming down with a sore throat we well

Nicholas: you should go... you need your sleep

Namita: grrrrr i can feel it

Nicholas: that's not good

Namita: i hate that

Nicholas: me too

Nicholas: I'm almost over this stupid cough

Namita: i havent even got my flu shot yet

Nicholas: you get it?

Namita: get what ?

Nicholas: we're being offered it through work for free.... I don't like injecting stuff into my body so I passed on it

Nicholas: the flu shot

Namita: no i didnt get mine yet

Namita: i almost have to

Nicholas: I guess working in a hospital you would

Namita: cuz if im sick ...with a flu ..work will not pay me for taking sick time

Nicholas: understandable

Namita: ohh god nicholas im dying here

Namita: im soooo tired

Nicholas: okay u should sleep

Nicholas: I'll be on in the morning if you're around

Namita: sooosorry ...ok i will be around too

Nicholas: I didn't get up till 9:30 this morning

Namita: ohh wow

Nicholas: no need to be sorry

Namita: well i wanst up till 11ish

Nicholas: I'll have my msn on while I eat

Nicholas: wow 11

Nicholas: I thought I saw you try to log in about 10:30ish

Namita: ok ... yes this week ive been physically bogged down

Nicholas: but you didn't manage to stay on

Nicholas: yah you've been sick

Namita: stay on what ?

Nicholas: stay logged on this morning

Namita: ohhh i could have hit my keyboard ...cuz my laptop is in bed with me ...and it was open ...so i could have rolled onto the keyboard

Nicholas: lol

Nicholas: almost like sleeping w me hehe

Namita: nice picture eh ??

Namita: yesssss well ur pic is on too

Nicholas: I think you'd look amazing while you're sleeping

Nicholas: *smiling*

Namita: hehehe ..drool and all ?

Nicholas: okay you need to sleep as do I

Nicholas: lol drool

Nicholas: there you go again w the drool talk

Namita: well im asking cuz it could be a deal breaker

Namita: hehe

Nicholas: I doubt it

Nicholas: I sleep w my mouth closed

Namita: hehehe just sometimes

Namita: me too

Namita: but u never know

Nicholas: if you're sleeping w your mouth open while ur w me I'll kiss you or something

Nicholas: though I don't want to startle you, you might belt me

Namita: lol will you eh ??

Namita: hehehe

Nicholas: yup

Namita: i will kiss u back

Nicholas: or just slide up next to you n feel you relax back to sleep

Nicholas: mmmm nice

Namita: mmmmmmmmmmm yesss

Namita: or i can turn into ur chest n curl into you

Nicholas: I have a feeling we'll sleep out of total exhaustion

Namita: and fall asleep

Nicholas: I love the sound of that... n I'll hold you till morning

Namita: hehehe i think so tooo ...there will be no action for a bit

Nicholas: yup we'll just pass out

Namita: hehe

Nicholas: okay I'm getting horny here thinking about sleeping w you

Nicholas: so not helping knowing you're so far away

Namita: hehe are u serious ??

Nicholas: yes aren't you?

Nicholas: it doesn't take much when I talk w you Namita

Nicholas: it seems you've fallen asleep my sweet, not to worry, so please don't.... I'm pretty tired too.... I'll look for you n the morning.... sleep well my indian princess... gnight n pleasant dreams 😊 😊

End Time: 1:32 AM

Chapter 25 November 19 Part 1

Start Time:12:54 AM

Namita: OooOOo hey there

Nicholas: hey!!!!

Namita: can you give me sec ...im just writing an email to a friend

Namita: hehe

Namita: loveeeeeeeeeee the pic !!

Nicholas: sure can

Nicholas: lol thx

Namita: did you get my offline messages ?

Namita: hehe

Nicholas: nope

Namita: whatttttttttttt noooooooooooo

Nicholas: they don't come through

Namita: grrrrr

Nicholas: u saw my last though right?

Namita: i left a message saying i passed out before i said goodnite to you !!

Namita: yes i did see urs

Nicholas: unless they're being stored somewhere n I don't know how to get them?

Namita: like in the middle of the nite when i woke up briefly !!

Namita: arghhh ok ... thats dumb ... i didnt want to think i snubbed you

Namita: i really fell asleep last nite

Namita: lol

Nicholas: I would never think that

Namita: hehe

Namita: phewwwwwwwww

Nicholas: I have no doubt you did other wise

Namita: i was soooo tired ...and drifting off the moment i got on msn !!

Nicholas: you weren't feeling well and you were pretty tired as well

Namita: yeahhh

Nicholas: I could tell

Namita: thanks for understanding

Nicholas: not a problem... I know you better that than to think you do that but thx for saying it

Nicholas: I was pretty bagged too

Namita: hehe ur welcome

Nicholas: so it worked out for the better

Namita: ohh good ...sooo you got some much needed sleep too

Nicholas: in a way that is

Namita: hehe ..in a way ?

Nicholas: I did... slept till after 10

Nicholas: in a way... we both needed some sleep

Nicholas: I want you to be well rested n feel better soon so you need ur sleep

Namita: me too ... i got up once around 4 am ... to get some water ...and thats when i realized i fell asleep on you ... and didnt respond back to ur msn ... i also read ur last messages online too

Namita: i felt bad last nite cuz you were writing soo much ..and i was like uh huh ...hhhhhmmm ... like one liners here and there !

Nicholas: I saw you were still signed in so I sent one last so you knew I assumed u fell asleep

Nicholas: thats how I could tell you were tired

Namita: hehe .... yeah i totally didnt sign off ... all nite... slept on my keyboard again

Nicholas: on nights where I'm not home late we'll have to plan to be on sooner

Namita: yesss

Namita: how was ur saturday ?

Nicholas: I can picture you drifting off... so sweet n peaceful

Nicholas: was okay.... did some straightening up n cleaning... how was urs?

Namita: hehehehe ...with halo around my head ...but wait til she wakes up !!!

Nicholas: have you finished ur email to ur friend yet?

Namita: it was ok .. i did some shopping a bit ... bought some xmas gifts ...since it was cheaper here in the US

Namita: no i havent .. im almost done

Nicholas: I'll smile at you and distract you

Namita: hehehe

Nicholas: you have good timing, I was giving you till 1 then I was going to log out... but here you are so YEah!!

Namita: hehe ... yayyyy !!

Nicholas: ☺

Namita: hehehe

Nicholas: is your mom n dad still dwn there too?

Namita: yeah i thought i should log on and see if ur online ... i was around earlier in the evening ...around 8pm ish ...but u werent

Namita: that was a bit too early from our timeline

Nicholas: ah man... I logged on around 9:30ish I think

Namita: yes mom and dad are still here ..they are retired ...so theyre hanging around

Namita: OMG you did ???

Nicholas: I usually log on anytime I'm sitting around so chances are good at catching me

Namita: ahhhh ok ..will remember that

Namita: i was laying down for a bit around 7pm ... thru past 8 ...so i thought maybe you'd be around

Nicholas: I try to log on early in the eve on the off chance you're around

Namita: hehe ok

Namita: good to know

Nicholas: I wonder what you're up too through most of the day

Nicholas: and just like the other morning we were on at the same time so it does work

Namita: well i went shopping ..bought a few things for myself ... and did some xmas shopping ...had lunch

Namita: yes that was cool !! to touch base that morning

Nicholas: tmw there's a game on at 6 so I'll be watching and I'll leave msn open so you know, if your around

Namita: today i felt like crap ..this morning and couldnt get myself out of bed .... for awhile ...but once i was out i felt kinda better

Namita: which game ..canucks ?

Nicholas: that's good.... sleep is important when ur not feeling well but look who I'm telling.... a nurse lol

Namita: hehehe

Nicholas: I only watch the Canucks

Namita: well ur lucky too that im a nurse ... youll be well taken care of !!

Namita: yes me too .. i watch here and there

Nicholas: I can watch other sports n play them too but watch the Canucks when I can

Namita: i hope they pick up in the season

Nicholas: me too

Nicholas: n I have no doubt that u'll take good care of me hehe

Namita: hehehehe ...yesss you can act like a baby all you want !!

Nicholas: this season has been challenging coz I'm at work when most of the games are on

Nicholas: lol I usually suck it up n carry on when I'm sick.... medicate when needed and move on

Namita: ohhhh yesss ... thats noo good !! Do they not put any tvs up ..or would it be too distracting ?

Nicholas: too distracting n we need to pay attention to what we're doing

Namita: hehe... aweeee well dont worry ur in good hands

Nicholas: I have no doubt they'll be fantastic hands

Namita: yesss true ..at work we work with a computer at each bedside ...we only have one critically ill patient at a time ...so when the games are on ... we log onto the sports channel and watch the games on the computer

Namita: it was awesome during the winter olympics too

Nicholas: I'm sympathetic and helpful w the sick too

Nicholas: I bet

Namita: hehe ... i guess you cant even listen to it on the radio

Nicholas: not sure if that comes across the way I want it to so let's just say you're in good hands too

Namita: cuz ur probably wearing those ear things

Namita: hehe dont know what u call it

Namita: hehe thanks for the clarification !!!

Nicholas: I try to listen but my radio isn't loud enf.... I'm looking at getting earmuff protection that has a radio in it

Namita: ohhhh cool !!

Nicholas: I wear foam ear plugs... I'm very diligent when it comes to protecting myself... I wear ear plugs to concerts

Namita: didnt know something like that existed !! I was going to say earmuff ..but i thought it was reserved for those actual earmuffs that keep one warm

Namita: ohhhh

Namita: yeah concerts can be loud

Nicholas: you're right they call them earmuffs

Namita: what was ur last concert again

Nicholas: that ringing you can get from a concert or any loud exposure is permanent hearing loss

Nicholas: I went to Bon Jovi

Nicholas: back in March

Namita: yeah i can imagine !! good thing i have good hearing

Nicholas: what was the last one you went to?

Namita: march this year?

Namita: ok dont laugh ok ?

Nicholas: we just had hearing tests at work a couple of weeks ago n my hearing is great

Nicholas: yup March this year

Nicholas: okay I wont

Namita: mine was Lady gaga ... summer 2010 .... hehehe

Namita: i went with my youngest sister

Namita: jaya

Nicholas: really?! was she good?

Namita: and we had a great time

Namita: actually i found her to be really good !!

Nicholas: ah yes Jaya... the sis that knows about me lol

Namita: probably the best concert ive been too

Nicholas: she put on a good show then?

Nicholas: really that's cool

Namita: yes a great live singer too

Nicholas: that's always a good time when the band/singer is good live

Namita: she did a few slow songs ... playing the piano ...and she does have a great voice

Namita: she wasnt lip synching either

Nicholas: cool.. I don't mind her stuff

Namita: cuz she sang in different octaves ...to prove she wasnt synching ...plus she was talking in between

Namita: too

Nicholas: I think the audience these days are pretty critical when it comes to lip syncing

Namita: yeah in todays music ... i think she is pretty good for her music

Nicholas: ooo thats a new pic... love it... u look very mature

Namita: well yeah ..but if ur paying soo much money up front for it ... youd wanna hear their talent live

Namita: hehe thanks

Nicholas: yes

Namita: actually we even had vip seats

Nicholas: such a beautiful face

Nicholas: you look so exotic n natural

Namita: we were seated quite close up ...id say 15 to 20 feet away from her

Namita: hehe thanks

Namita: i was at a wedding in this one

Nicholas: wow those would be cool seats

Nicholas: you've been to lots of weddings... when is the next one again? and are you going to be back in time for it?

Nicholas: soooo beautiful... was just admiring it again hehe

Namita: hehehe ...i think im done for weddings ... next big ones are coming next year sometime

Nicholas: you just amaze me

Namita: really?

Nicholas: yes you do

Nicholas: I thought you were going to another wedding in Dec?

Namita: yess the december one is coming up too

Namita: but the other ones are family ones ...that are big

Nicholas: are you going to be back in time?

Namita: this one is friends

Nicholas: oh I see

Nicholas: gothcha

Namita: i hope so

Namita: indian weddings are huge nicholas

Nicholas: I bet

Namita: the festivities last a week

Namita: hehe

Nicholas: so I've heard

Namita: you might as well elope

Nicholas: my hygienist at the dentist went to india one year for 3 weddings n thats what she said, that they last a week

Namita: hehe omg for 3 weddings ???

Namita: that is crazzzyyyyyyy

Nicholas: yup she went for 4 weeks

Namita: my sisters wedding was huge !! There were like 300 ppl in the wedding

Nicholas: holly sh** thats a lot of ppl

Namita: it was utter chaos .... but organized chaos

Nicholas: I don't think I know 300 ppl lol

Namita: and i was in the middle of it ... i was the go to person

Nicholas: oh geeze

Namita: yeah me either ... i dont even know 300 ppl !!!!!!!!

Nicholas: my fam is so small

Namita: i was the last one getting ready on the wedding day

Nicholas: there's like 4 of us including me lol

Namita: and i had like 20 mins to get my getup on !!

Namita: omg serious !!!

Nicholas: geeze that's not much time but when you look like you it doesn't take much to fix u up

Nicholas: yup, me, mom, sis, grampa

Nicholas: and the girls of course

Namita: hehehe aweeee thanks !!! Brownie points !!!!

Namita: wowwwww

Namita: yes mustnt forget the girls

Namita: that was just ur side right ?

Nicholas: aunt is in Sask. don't talk to my cousin her son n the rest of the fam is in England

Namita: ahhhh i seee

Nicholas: there was about 20 ppl at my wedding

Nicholas: if u want to call it that.. it was pretty casual

Namita: i decorated the the entire reception place myself on my sisters wedding

Namita: wow ...that is nice ... in a way ...less hassle

Namita: to have a group of ppl i mean

Nicholas: BY yourself???!!!! u'd think out of 300 ppl there would have been others to help

Namita: hehehe ... just me and 2 little kids

Nicholas: damn *shakes head*

Namita: everyone else was tooo busy doing other ... nothing !!!!!!!!!!

Namita: i was soooooo mad !!!

Nicholas: and I'm sure the kids were a big help lol

Namita: plus i had to pick up her cake !!!

Namita: hehe

Nicholas: geeze!!

Namita: yes child labour !!

Namita: i remember i was running around like a chicken with her head cut off

Nicholas: I bet... it can be a stressful day esp when u have no help

Namita: and i went to pick up the 4 tier wedding cake ...cuz the stupid bakery wont deliver ... so i parked my car ... and i think i put it in neutral or something ...when i went to get out of the car ...it was still rolling forward

Nicholas: or as much help as little kids can be lol

Nicholas: oh geeze

Namita: omg ... it was sooooo screwed up ... i quickly jumped in ... i was half out ...and tried to stop the car before it hit the car parked in front of me

Nicholas: oh god!!

Namita: then put my head on the steering wheel ...in exasperation !!

Nicholas: talk about adding to the stress level geeze

Namita: i was that worked to the bone and stressed

Namita: hehe

Nicholas: I bet

Namita: yes the bride was fine ...and i was stressed

Nicholas: was just going to ask if she new nothing about it n everything was fine as far as she was concerned

Nicholas: which sis got married?

Namita: when the reception was finally underway ... i was sooo tired and stresses ...which i never am...that i slipped away .... and just sat in solitude for an hour or so

Namita: good thing no one sent out a search party

Namita: ohhhh ... priya got married

Nicholas: oh how I wish I could have slipped away w you n relieved that stress w you *wink wink*

Namita: hehehee

Namita: mmmm that would have been welcomes

Namita: welcomed i mean

Nicholas: so Preet and Jaya aren't married then?

Nicholas: hang on

Namita: yes preeti is too ..now ...jaya and i arent

Nicholas: there's only 3 of you?

Namita: huh

Nicholas: ah there's 4 of you

Namita: so pretti and priya are married ...jaya and i arent married

Namita: hehe

Nicholas: was having trouble remembering how many sis you have

Namita: the 2 middle ones are married

Nicholas: gotcha

Namita: hehe

Nicholas: steel trap memory was a little shaky there lol

Namita: yes im sure it is hard to keep tract of all these brown women

Namita: hehehe

Nicholas: lol

Namita: tiny bit of rust

Namita: hehe

Nicholas: well the most important one is right here

Namita: aweeeeeee thanks ...the best for the last

Nicholas: in some spots there might be some rust

Nicholas: yup

Namita: hehehe ... i will get my oil can out !!

Nicholas: deal

Namita: and oil you up

Nicholas: mmmm like the sound of that

Namita: hehehe

Nicholas: careful or u might spill some on you too hehe

Nicholas: or I might rub it on you

Namita: hehehehe... ohhh its all good ...slick is good !!

Nicholas: can never have too much lubrication hehe

Namita: lmao !!!!!

Nicholas: random; what did you have for dinner?

Nicholas: are you close to Fisherman's Warf?

Namita: i had roasted chicken,veges ..and potatoes ... we went to a restaurant for dinner

Nicholas: cool

Namita: umm hmmm it rings a bell

Namita: did u have food from there

Nicholas: famous wharf in Frisco

Namita: ohhh yesss... you know i havent been there yet

Nicholas: we went to a restaurant while we were stopped there on our way to Disneyland

Namita: uh huh

Nicholas: I don't remember a lot about it

Namita: ohhhh ...not even the food ?

Nicholas: I remember Alcatraz and being in the restaurant and my dad having Swordfish but that's about it

Namita: ohh soo are u talking about when you were a kid ?

Nicholas: yeah was grade 6

Namita: ohhh ok ... that was long time ago ...hehhee

Nicholas: sure was

Namita: you know ive never been to disneyland

Namita: do you like roller coasters ?

Nicholas: Fisherman's Wharf is still there

Namita: yeah

Nicholas: not a big fan of roller coasters... makes me sick

Nicholas: been twice

Namita: yessssssssss me toooo !!!!!!! I dont like them at all ...just looking at it makes me sick !!!!

Nicholas: equilibrium is very sensitive

Nicholas: yup that's me

Namita: once when we were kids ..dad put me and preeti on a roller coaster ..at the pne ...guess who was barfing ...?

Nicholas: I could do the scrambler when I was younger but not a chance now

Nicholas: gee ummm you

Namita: im good with the kiddy rides but thats about it !! hehehe

Namita: YESSS !!!

Nicholas: that must have been a great ride for the other passengers lol... not!!

Namita: and i was crying .. i must have been about 8 or 9

Nicholas: I went on the fairs wheel a couple of summers ago n it freaked me out a little

Namita: lol .. i was barfing into a bag ...i dont know how i had a bag

Namita: i think it was the cotton candy bag

Nicholas: licky to have a bag

Nicholas: lucky*

Namita: hehe omg ..it did !!

Nicholas: eeewww wouldn't want that cotton candy after lol

Namita: hehehehe

Namita: good thing im not a fan of cotton candy either

Namita: toooooo sweeet for me

Nicholas: yup... the point where it comes over the top n starts the dwn side makes my stomach drop

Nicholas: me either

Namita: ohhh god !!!

Nicholas: just spun melted sugar

Namita: the ride that dad put us in ...was those bucket looking rides . i think its called the spider spin

Nicholas: so many similarities between us.... so cool

Nicholas: looks like an egg beater?

Namita: yesss i think .. i was googling it

Nicholas: that sound like the scrambler

Namita: lol

Namita: the octopus ride

Namita: yeah thats it

Nicholas: yah makes me sick just looking at it

Namita: heheheh yess me too ..thats why disneyland doesnt appeal to me

Nicholas: the last time I went to the PNE was to see the band that night

Namita: ohhh

Nicholas: there's so much more to DL (Disneyland) than the rides though... so you know

Namita: i went like 6 yrs ago with my lil niece

Namita: yeah ive heard that

Nicholas: and some of the rides are real tame just to take you through it

Namita: but if i go ..it wouldnt be for the rides

Namita: ohhh ok

Nicholas: the pne or DL?

Namita: DL

Nicholas: ah

Nicholas: well I don't think I would call some of the displays "rides" well maybe but they are pretty tame I'd go on them if thats any indication of how tame they are

Namita: hehehe ... i will only take ur word on it for now

Nicholas: I think I'd rather go to Mexico than DL

Nicholas: okay lol

Namita: hehe or costa rica

Nicholas: sure

Namita: hmmm would love to check out that

Nicholas: I told the girls that now that I have this job that I'm going to try to take them to Mexico in maybe Nov next year

Namita: ohhh cool !! im sure they are excited to hear that !!

Nicholas: yes they are

Nicholas: totally!!

Namita: hehe

Nicholas: lol there's an add for LL on tv right now lol

Namita: some of those LL commercials sound sooo chessy

Namita: cheesy i mean ..hehe

Nicholas: it was for the phone version

Namita: hehee

Nicholas: something about you'll find someone so amazing and beautiful that you wont believe it

Namita: hehehe

Namita: do u alway watch tv while ur talking to me ? lol

Nicholas: it's just on in the back ground volume is low or muted

Nicholas: I have trouble sitting in a room w nothing going on, seems strange

Namita: ohh yess ...you need background noise

Nicholas: you always have my undivided attention my dear

Namita: hehee aweeeeeeeee thanks

Namita: i knowwwww

Nicholas: my mom doesn't have anything on in her place n it's always so quiet

Namita: she doesnt have a tv ?

Nicholas: she likes the quiet, i find it strange only coz I'm use to sounds around me

Namita: or just not on ?

Nicholas: she does she just doesn't turn it on very often

Namita: well she is close to the ocean ... can she hear it from her place ?

Nicholas: she actually just got a new one... it's very nice

Nicholas: nope

Namita: ohhh nicee ..a flat screen ?

Nicholas: though she's about 5 mins from it

Nicholas: yup flat

Namita: ahhh sooo nice still

Namita: do you ?

Namita: have a flat screen i mean

Nicholas: I'd like to get a better tv... the one I have is from next door when they moved

Nicholas: it's the old flat type weighs about 200 lbs and big

Namita: oh .. hehehehe

Nicholas: takes up a lot of room too

Nicholas: would be nice to get a newer lighter one

Nicholas: I find the most programs don't fit my screen

Namita: some of them can be quite expensive

Namita: ohhh

Nicholas: they obviously broadcast in a diff format

Namita: ohhh i see

Nicholas: yes they can... I'm not big on spending just for the sake of having the latest n greatest.... I buy what suits my need and is hopefully on sale

Namita: a lot of my friends are into the huge flat screen ..and PVr'S ... and im not ...cuz i dont watch tv much

Nicholas: and I don't need to break the bank w my purchases

Nicholas: me either

Namita: i dont watch ...glee, american idol, or all the other new and hip shows

Nicholas: if it suits my needs and I can make due w it then I'll get it

Namita: yess

Nicholas: noooooo me either.. I can't stand those shows

Nicholas: I remember a time when reality tv was called the NEWS!

Namita: me either !!! ... i hardly ever watched Friends or bachelor ...omg i cant stand reality tv

Namita: or that island one ...ohhhh yess survivor !!!

Namita: like REALLYY ??!

Nicholas: oh god survivor yuck

Namita: survivor to me is Ethiopia or sudan

Nicholas: I like to watch things where they're building something or a good comedy that makes me laugh

Namita: or wherever there ppl living in extreme poverty

Namita: yes i love stand up comedy

Namita: or some of the home shows

Namita: love documentaries

Namita: or animals

Nicholas: yah n the back stabbing n plotting... hate it... n I don't use the word hate very often

Namita: or just about different places

Nicholas: yes documentaries

Nicholas: informative shows

Namita: im proud to say ..ive never watched those stupid shows

Namita: doesnt appeal to me

Nicholas: ones that make you think or tell you something you didn't know before

Namita: yesss love those ones

Nicholas: I watched a couple of them while I was married but since I've been on my own I don't

Nicholas: more similarities gotta love it

Namita: hehehe ..yessss

Namita: 2 peas in a pod !!!

Namita: again

Nicholas: yup

Namita: ok i do gotta admit ...i have one crazy show i love

Nicholas: all this time apart might be a good thing in a way coz once we're together we'll be inseparable

Namita: hehehhee

Nicholas: which one?

Namita: yesss

Namita: well its something ive get so interested in ...im trying f=to find the right word ... well the show is ghost hunters or ghost hunters international ...and i get sooo interested in it

Namita: but i think i do believe in them too ... esp when you work with ppl who are dying ...i would believe it !!

Namita: and aliens too

Nicholas: aliens well we'd be pretty arrogant to think we're the only intelligent life out there... I mean space goes on forever n that's a long time... hard to get ur head around at times

Nicholas: yah you can feel the energy leave someone

Namita: if dinosaurs existed ...im sure there are other things out there that are waiting to be discovered

Nicholas: it you're open to that stuff which we are

Namita: yes i can feel the energy ..and sometimes weird things do happen

Nicholas: yes and aliens... it's just a matter of time before they decide to visit n say hi

Nicholas: I bet they do

Namita: hehehe yess

Namita: ive never seen any ghosts ...but had just weird unexplainable things happen

Nicholas: I've felt a ghost before

Namita: but i havent seen any aliens yet !! hehehe

Namita: you have !!! tell me !!

Nicholas: was dwntwn working on a movie. we were in Punch Lines, the old comedy club in Gastown... I was alone in the corner by the windows cleaning up n felt a cool breeze on my neck n when I turned around there was nothing and no windows open

Namita: ohhhhh ...did u see anything ?

Nicholas: earlier in the day the bartender that opened the place was telling us about encounters ppl had over the years n most described the cool breeze

Nicholas: didn't see anything but felt it

Namita: ohhh wowww .very cool

Nicholas: Gastown is full of spirits

Namita: were you scared ...did u know at the time what it was?

Nicholas: there's a lot of history dwn there

Namita: yesss ive heard

Nicholas: I knew n was n a little spooky but not scared

Nicholas: I did know

Nicholas: sorry now I'm repeating myself lol

Namita: hehe...one time when i was doing my rotation in River View for nursing school

Namita: riverview hospital ..in coquitlam

Nicholas: yup

Nicholas: thats a freaky place I bet

Namita: i was supposed to wrap things up with my patient ...and meet the rest of the group in a different part of the floor

Nicholas: mmhmm

Namita: i think the conference room was 2 floors up from where i was

Namita: the rest of the girls left ...without me

Nicholas: oh geeze

Namita: and i finished up ... and finally left to meet them

Namita: i didnt know where i was going

Nicholas: oh no

Namita: cuz every meeting was somewhere different as room were available

Namita: sooo i went thru a stairwell ... into one wing

Namita: it was fall time soo things were a little eerie for me

Nicholas: oh man the suspense is killing me

Namita: i was walking up the stairs ...and high heel boots on ...we could wear street clothes for that rotation

Namita: hehe

Namita: bear with me

Nicholas: I am

Namita: so once i got to a landing thinking i was in the right place .. i see a lonnnnnnngggggg hallway

Nicholas: the suspense is good

Namita: and i was like i dont ever remember coming this way

Namita: soo i started walking down the hallway ... heels clicking ... and echoing

Nicholas: freaky!!

Namita: and every room door was shut and locked

Namita: it was really really eerie and scary ...my heart was racing

Nicholas: I bet

Namita: then i heard some laughter

Nicholas: omg

Namita: coming in from behind me

Namita: but a little ways away

Nicholas: I have goose bumps

Namita: i thought it was my colleagues

Namita: so i stopped

Namita: and waited ...thinking someone is coming up the stairs

Namita: but no one showed up

Namita: lol

Nicholas: I'm totally there

Namita: so i keep going ... and i got the weird feeling that someone was behind me

Namita: like a shuffled walk

Nicholas: oooohmg

Namita: and when i stopped to turn ...no one was there

Nicholas: geeze

Namita: i was sooooooooooo freaked out ...that i couldnt move

Nicholas: ooommmgggg

Namita: then finally i decided to not venture anymore ... i went back down the stairwell ...and no one was there

Namita: and got myself back to the unit ...and then went to another floor where another group of students were ...to follow them

Namita: when i told the nurses .. there ..they told me that there are no rooms occupied there ...i went the wrong way

Namita: the side i went to was kinda out of bounds ..

Nicholas: yah no kidding

Namita: not being used

Nicholas: oh man

Namita: so i dont know what i heard

Namita: my colleagues were all at the meeting

Namita: longggggg before me

Nicholas: wow so there was no one there in that wing

Namita: noooo that wing was closed

Nicholas: spooky

Namita: that hallway was creepy ...cuz one side was huge windows overlooking a worn out courtyard with dead trees

Nicholas: there are a lot of sprits there so I've heard

Nicholas: very fitting

Namita: and the other side was all these rooms with doors shut

Namita: yes all the more reason i was creeped

Nicholas: wow

Namita: it was grey and dungy too

Nicholas: you're a good story teller but I kinda figured that from your scenario on ur profile

Namita: ohh im sure there are lots of spirits ...they even have this old worn out over gown graveyard in the grounds

Namita: hehehe thanks

Namita: one time i was finished my shift early

Nicholas: omg really?! that would be something to see

Namita: and was waiting for my ride from mom ..she worked in BBy (Burnaby) hospital

Namita: yess you should see it ...you can be there in the day time

Namita: so i was waiting ...and it was only 3 pm ...and she got off at 3 ...by the time she got to me it would be 4 pm

Nicholas: we'll have to venture there one day... during the day though

Namita: and i hated waiting inside with all the crazy ppl

Namita: yesss not at nite ..id be tooo creeped

Nicholas: lol I don't blame you

Namita: ive heard some crazy stories

Namita: sooo i decided to wait outside on the porch of the building

Namita: one sec

Nicholas: okay

Namita: getting a pic

Nicholas: k

Namita: arghhh i can t send it

Nicholas: hmm

Namita: google river view

Namita: go to images

Nicholas: okay did that

Namita: go 20 rows down

Namita: sorry 21 row

Nicholas: okay I'm there

Namita: 6th pic over is west lawn

Namita: west lawn building

Namita: i mean

Namita: the creep entrance to one of the buildings

Nicholas: I don't see a lawn

Nicholas: or should I?

Namita: there is no lawn

Nicholas: okay

Namita: it is a pic of a building

Nicholas: the b/w pic?

Namita: yes i guess so

Namita: it should say west lawn

Nicholas: for me its' the 4th pic

Namita: ohhh it has stairs in the front

Namita: and pillars

Namita: if not then google river view west lawn

Nicholas: white building?

Namita: yes

Namita: cement looking

Nicholas: okay think I've got it

Namita: cement

Namita: does it look creepy ?

Nicholas: yup

Namita: thats the building they put me in

Namita: theres a porch on it

Nicholas: oh geeze

Namita: or a landing

Namita: so im there waiting for mom

Nicholas: yah n a bunch of stairs

Namita: yesss thats the one

Namita: hehe

Nicholas: okay

Namita: and was a windy rainy day

Nicholas: of course it was

Namita: i was not going to stick around right inside with the creeps

Namita: some of the patients could wander themselves

Namita: without nurses

Nicholas: freaky!!!

Namita: and just inside of the door was a smoking room

Namita: and they would be congregated there smoking and arguing or talking to themselves

Namita: or doing gross things

Nicholas: eww like what?

Namita: so i waited outside ...knowing it would be an hour before i see real pp

Namita: like sometimes BJ's (blow jobs)

Nicholas: longest hour I bet

Nicholas: omg really?

Namita: yesssssssssss omg

Namita: yesss ive seen it nicholas ...thats another story

Namita: heheh

Nicholas: right there in front of everyone?

Namita: yesssssssssss

Nicholas: eeewwww

Namita: full on !!!!!!!!!!!

Nicholas: my god!!

Namita: now u see why i waited outside

Nicholas: YAh!!

Namita: so im standing there in this creepy building ...and biding my time

Namita: when i hear the door open behind me

Namita: the huge wooden doors

Namita: and then i hear someone talking to himself

Namita: getting closer and closer to me

Nicholas: geeze

Namita: and i close my eyes and start praying

Namita: like pleaseeeeeeeeeee dont let him come to me ...pleaseeeeeeeeeee

Nicholas: I bet

Namita: and next thing you know

Namita: i feel a hand running down my long hair ...and down my back ...and his face is near the side of my head

Nicholas: grosssss!!!

Nicholas: yuck!!

Namita: talking to me ... saying preetyyyyy lady ... do you have a cigarette

Namita: and a lighter !???

Nicholas: eeeewwwwww

Namita: i was sOoOOOoOoOoOOooOOOOo grossssssssssssssssssssssed out

Nicholas: I can't imagine... grossss

Namita: OMG Nicholas !! You wont even believe this ..the guy looked like one of those bums on the street on hastings

Namita: and he had no teeth

Namita: and he stunk

Nicholas: eeewwww

Namita: like reeked

Namita: and his face was inches from me

Nicholas: like a homeless person I bet

Namita: i jumped back of course

Nicholas: eewww I bet you wanted to shower after

Namita: and i tried not looking surprised ... cause i didnt want to se thim off

Namita: set him *

Nicholas: I got that

Namita: so i politely said no i dont ..and i am sooo sorry that dont ... maybe you can check inside if the others have one

Namita: i had to smile thru all that

Nicholas: ur a brave woman

Namita: when i got home i was in the shower ,,,washing and scrubbing my hair

Namita: a million times

Namita: heheh

Nicholas: ooohhh I bet

Nicholas: grosss

Namita: i was there for 16 weeks ... for the entire rotation ...and counting every min of it

Nicholas: wow 16 weeks

Namita: and that bj stroy

Namita: story ... i mean

Namita: hehe

Namita: do u wanna hear that one?

Nicholas: sure if you want to tell it

Namita: ok ...there are soo many buildings on the grounds of riverview ...one of them was called the PEN ...AND IT WAS A RECREATIONAL BULIDING WITH A (sorry for caps) a small cafeteria ..and a bowling alley and a smoke room

Nicholas: uhuh

Namita: some of the patients who were kinda ok ..and had ground privileges ..meaning they could go on the grounds of with out a nurse or escort

Namita: and soo every lunchtime my student nurse colleagues and i went down to the pen to the cafeteria

Namita: to have lunch

Namita: well the cafeteria was run entirely by patients who are well enough

Namita: and i think they earned a lil money too

Namita: my colleagues would order burgers and fries

Namita: and all sorts of stuff from them

Nicholas: oh no hope it was clean food

Namita: where as i refused to eat from there

Nicholas: good plan

Namita: its not something i would have done

Namita: hehe

Namita: cuz one day ...one of our female patients ..who thought she was bon jovi's wife ..and was going to have his baby

Nicholas: lol

Namita: was in the cafeteria ...right behind our table ... giving a BJ to one of the kitchen staff patient ..who was sitting there having a smoke

Nicholas: oommmgggg

Namita: when we heard the moans ...we turned around ..and full on action was going on

Namita: yesssssssssss

Namita: i was soooooooooooo grossssssssed out

Namita: i could have hurled !!!!!!

Nicholas: holly crap

Nicholas: grosss

Namita: i was like OMFG !!!!!

Nicholas: I can't imagine

Namita: and we were the only ones there as students

Namita: the other patients were cheering them on

Nicholas: omg!!!!

Namita: we had to phone a real nurse in the other building west lawn ...which was like blocks away

Namita: to run over and pry them out

Nicholas: you had to stop them?!

Namita: by then i was outside ... laughing and grosssssssssssssssssed out

Namita: Noooooooooooo i wasnt not going to touch them ...but another nurse had too !!!!!!!!

Namita: it was against hospital rules

Namita: at least for that area of the ground !!

Nicholas: geeze.. can't believe someone had to stop them n I can see it being against the rules

Namita: hehe well in other areas of the grounds they are allowed to

Nicholas: you've def seen ur fair share of stuff

Nicholas: they're allowed to?! wow

Namita: if they deemed they have some thought process and both parties are consensual ...and they have a supply of condoms

Namita: yesss isnt that gross

Nicholas: yeessssss

Namita: it doenst have to be the same partner

Nicholas: ewwww

Namita: as long as they have safe sex

Namita: yes eweeeeeeee is right

Nicholas: good thing... we wouldn't want the crazies breading lol

Namita: hehehe

Namita: omg

Namita: right then and there i knew i didnt want to be a psychology nurse

Nicholas: no kidding

Namita: opened my eyes for sure

Nicholas: uh yah

Namita: after i was done with that rotation ... i was sooooo done

Nicholas: I bet

Namita: hehe

Namita: ohhh the horror

Nicholas: those are brave women that stay in that work environment

Namita: yesss ...we each get a panic button too

Namita: and carried it everywhere we went

Nicholas: I mean men can protect themselves maybe a little better n don't have things that crazy men would want

Namita: just in case you got attacked

Namita: esp the women

Nicholas: a friend of a friend worked at a prison n she carried one of those too

Namita: i only witnessed that once while in was there

Namita: yeah i believe it ...you just never know

Nicholas: oh geeze... was she traumatized from it?

Namita: who me ?

Nicholas: the person who was attacked?

Namita: ohhh yess ...i guess ... im not sure ... cause i didnt stay long after that ... i was actually stationed in one of the dangerous units in RV (River View) ... and that too on ground floor !!!

Namita: so we all carried those panic alarms

Nicholas: I can't imagine trying to work in those conditions

Namita: ohh god me either ... scary

Namita: are you tired ?

Nicholas: hard to enjoy your job w that kind of stress and not very rewarding

Nicholas: I am a little.... you?

Nicholas: its after 4 my god how time flies w you

Namita: yes ... hehe with all the talking ...im such a chatter box tonite

Namita: i just noticed the time

Namita: hehe

Nicholas: I love listening to you

Namita: at least i didnt fall asleep on you

Namita: aweee thanks

Nicholas: that you didn't

Namita: hehe

Nicholas: I love hearing your stories

Namita: brownie points ??

Namita: for me

Nicholas: of course

Namita: ohhhh ive got many

Namita: some are super funny

Nicholas: I wait all day to talk w you

Namita: aweeeeee nicholas !!!!

Namita: ur soooo sweet

Namita: i look forward to talking to you too

Nicholas: one of the reasons I check in through out the day to maybe have a surprise

Namita: hehe

Nicholas: well thx

Namita: ur welcome

Nicholas: I love seeing your profile pic too coz its usually one I don't already have

Namita: hehehe ...ur mesmerized by this one ??

Nicholas: ANd they're all so wonderful

Nicholas: a little... don't think I've seen it before

Namita: aweeee thanks

Nicholas: though I'm always a little mesmerized by you

Namita: hehehe ...im blushing now !!!!

Nicholas: you are too cute

Namita: hehe

Nicholas: I can't help but think how lucky I am

Nicholas: okay I'm getting a little mushy now hehe

Namita: im sure we will have many evenings to share and chat in between or among other activities

Nicholas: yes we will

Namita: ahem !! yes we will

Nicholas: I look forward to hearing and learning all about you Namita

Namita: aweeee thanks !!!

Namita: i think we both got a good feel of who we are as a person so well here

Nicholas: it'll be 8 weeks tmw... not that I've been counting lol

Nicholas: that we have

Namita: lol... wow www

Namita: since from LL?

Nicholas: as we've said before it would have taken months to get this far in person

Nicholas: yup since sept 30th

Namita: yessss soooo true !!!

Nicholas: that was the day I messaged you about ur story

Namita: my LL story ??

Nicholas: yup

Namita: hehehe

Namita: you can complete it when ever u want

Namita: lol

Nicholas: I'm amazed at how you brightened my life

Namita: aweee thanks

Nicholas: will do... we'll work on completing it together

Namita: well im glad to put a smile to ur face

Namita: hehe make it reality

Namita: except no party

Nicholas: yes that will be oh so nice

Namita: in this scenario just us

Nicholas: yes thats right... we'll just skip to the after party part

Namita: hehehe

Namita: make sure u have the fireplace going

Nicholas: I don't think I'll be able to keep my hands off you for the first little while

Namita: hehhee

Nicholas: I can just turn it on lol its electric

Namita: ahhhhhh yessssss

Namita: technology

Nicholas: though the after party should take place at your house coz I'm thinking we'll get naked to finish the story

Namita: hehheee

Nicholas: provided thats the first time

Namita: we can have our own naked party !!

Nicholas: YESSSSS

Namita: colted optional

Namita: omg

Namita: i mean clothes

Nicholas: lol was wondering what colted was lol

Namita: that was sooooo far off ..the spelling

Nicholas: sokay

Namita: lmao

Nicholas: well after today it'll be one more day closer to being able to see you

Namita: heyyyyy its the new thing ok ??!

Nicholas: it can be our code

Namita: aweeeeeeeeeee

Namita: hehhe

Namita: oh god im dozy again ...geezzzz sleep is getting in the wayyyyyyyyy

Nicholas: yah you should sleep so you can feel better

Namita: well so should u

Namita: hehe

Nicholas: we'll have plenty of time to catch up once ur back

Nicholas: yes I should

Namita: i dont want u to catch a cold sitting in ur chair without a blanket

Nicholas: we can talk till we fall asleep n and other activities too

Namita: lol

Nicholas: I hope that made sense

Namita: heheh yesss it did

Nicholas: It will be so much easier when we're face to face

Nicholas: ok good

Namita: yesss it will be ...then we can devour each other

Nicholas: less typing n more... ahem... talking

Nicholas: like minds once again

Namita: yes of course more talking !!!

Namita: hehe

Namita: cuz talking is good !!

Nicholas: devouring yes... I'l gladly have 2nds n 3rds of you anytime or anywhere

Namita: lmaoooooooooooo

Nicholas: talking w you is awesome n i love it!!

Namita: ohhhh myyyyyy

Namita: ohhh yesss mee toooooo

Namita: i enjoy it

Namita: we cover sooo much

Nicholas: that we do

Nicholas: was gonna say something n now its gone

Namita: ohhhh no worries

Namita: it will come

Nicholas: was probly something mushy

Namita: say it !!!

Namita: hehe

Nicholas: can't think of it still lol

Namita: if u remember that is

Namita: hehe

Nicholas: was probly something about you getting ur sexy little ass back here so we can see each other n make this a reality

Nicholas: I love how open n honest you are w me

Namita: ahhhhh

Namita: ohhh thanks nicholas

Nicholas: you're as open n honest w me as I am w you n I love it!!

Nicholas: I never had that before either

Namita: yessss me too ... i like to say whats in my mind

Nicholas: me too

Namita: but not in a bad way ..say if im ticked about something ... i dont like yelling about it ... i like discussing it

Namita: in a calm and civil way

Nicholas: yes totally agree.... take the emotion out of it and resolve the issue

Namita: and im the kind of person who can tell u how much i appreciate u everyday

Namita: in words or subtle ways

Nicholas: I love the sound of that.... me too

Namita: yessss

Namita: totally agree

Namita: i like to get to the point

Nicholas: knowing we're both on the same page is soooo important

Namita: instead of playing mind games

Namita: yessssssssss totally

Nicholas: yes.. so many ppl get hung up on being mad that they never resolve the problem

Namita: uh huh !!!!

Namita: then they forget what they even mad at

Nicholas: yup

Nicholas: as much as I could stay up all night n talk w you we should really get some sleep

Namita: nicholas i dont want to cut u off

Namita: lol

Namita: i was writing something similar

Nicholas: you were going to say the same

Nicholas: lol

Namita: hahhahahah

Nicholas: like minds

Namita: hahhahahahaah

Namita: that is too funny

Nicholas: 😃

Namita: actually what i was going to say was

Namita: shut up nicholas ..not now ...go to bed !!!!!

Nicholas: lol

Namita: hehehehe

Namita: down boy !!

Nicholas: lol

Namita: hehehehe

Namita: i cant beleive i have a sense of humor at 4 30 in the morning

Namita: ohhh look 440 now

Nicholas: surprising what u can find a 4:30 in the morning

Namita: hehehehe

Namita: im giggling in my sleep here

Nicholas: okay so I'll be on at breakfast n through out the day if ur around

Namita: what in like an hour you think ??

Nicholas: not sure when breakfast will be mind you lol

Nicholas: lol

Namita: hehhee

Nicholas: doubt it

Namita: tee hee hee

Namita: we are sooooooooooo bad

Nicholas: I'll be around during the game to at 6

Namita: ok will try to log on and distract you

Nicholas: well there's a diff between bad n naughty lol

Namita: yes yes

Nicholas: fine w me anytime

Namita: hehe

Namita: ok goodnite then ?

Nicholas: okay gnight my darling Namita

Namita: aweeeeeeee

Nicholas: sleep well

Namita: goodnite sweetheart

Namita: you too

Nicholas: *smiling*

Namita: have a good sleep

Nicholas: thx

Namita: ur welcome

Nicholas: you called me sweetheart.. I like that

Namita: hehe ..well u are !!!

Nicholas: u are too

Namita: no u first !!

Namita: hehe

Nicholas: hehe

Namita: 😊

Nicholas: okay i'm going now hehe

Nicholas: night

Namita: ok me too

Nicholas: 😊

Namita: nite nite

End Time: 4:45 AM

Chapter 25 November 19 Part 2

Start Time:11:55 AM

Nicholas: good morning

Namita: hey there

Nicholas: did you sleep well?

Namita: just got out of the shower

Nicholas: mmmm nice

Namita: yes i did ...like a baby !!

Namita: hehe

Namita: how about you ?

Nicholas: me too... woke at 10ish but didn't really get up till 11

Nicholas: yes very sound

Namita: hehe ... wow we had a busy nite last nite ...not the we would want it ..but nonetheless

Nicholas: thought you should know before I fell asleep I fantasized about you riding me

Namita: ohhhhhh wowwwwwww

Nicholas: yes we usually talk the night away

Namita: while u were in bed ??

Nicholas: yes

Namita: hehe....was it good ?

Nicholas: very good... almost like you were there

Namita: hehehe

Nicholas: very intense

Namita: hehe ...i think you enjoy it more if i was on top of you !!

Nicholas: oooohh hell yes!!!

Namita: then you can see almost every inch of me

Namita: what happens to my body as i ride you

Nicholas: yes... thought about seeing how you'll squirm n moan

Namita: mmmmmmmmmmm yesssssssss

Nicholas: n shudder

Namita: taking you in ...every last inch

Nicholas: mmmhmmm

Nicholas: you're turning me on again

Namita: you feel urself disappear inside of me

Namita: hehe

Nicholas: thought about that too... how ur going to feel when I enter u the first time n seeing ur reaction

Namita: mmmmmmm yesssssssssssssssss !!!

Namita: id be in heaven !!

Nicholas: and when you feel ALL of me as u settle dwn on top of me

Namita: ohhh god !! That is quite erotic !!!

Nicholas: thinking there couldn't be more but u soon realize there's so much more

Namita: me rocking slightly back and forth on you !!

Nicholas: mmmhhmmm

Namita: holding ur hands

Namita: fingers entwined

Nicholas: or me holding ur hips... pressing myself DEEeep inside you

Namita: ohh god !!!!

Namita: then i lay down on top of ...face to face ... as you try to penetrate deep into me

Nicholas: rolling my hips so I can touch every inch of you

Namita: you can hear me gasping at each penetration

Nicholas: mmm yessss

Namita: calling out ur name

Namita: holding on to ur shoulders

Namita: my mouth inches from ur face

Nicholas: wrapping my arms around u holding u close so all u need to do is just enjoy the ride

Namita: OMG nicholas !!!!!!!!!!!

Namita: i can almost feel it !!!

Namita: you holding me close to you

Nicholas: we'll have such an awesome time

Namita: taking in my scent ...which makes you wild even more !!

Nicholas: yes it will

Namita: hehe

Nicholas: touching u n feeling u n listening to ur body... telling me what you want next

Nicholas: um starfish this morning?

Namita: mmmmm yesssssss

Namita: hehe

Namita: i dont know why msn changes my pics when i log off

Nicholas: hmmm mine doesn't

Namita: hey you gotta say it is sexy though !!!

Namita: heehehe

Nicholas: I guess it's coz ur special

Namita: yesss of course i am

Nicholas: yes it is

Namita: hehehe

Nicholas: knowing its urs it sure is

Nicholas: insert metaphor here

Namita: hehehee

Namita: you like my starfish ??

Nicholas: oooooo there we go

Namita: and i lovee ur sea cucumber !!!

Nicholas: I LOve ur starfish!!

Namita: hehe

Nicholas: lol good one!

Namita: ok im being silly ?? hehee

Nicholas: go right ahead my dear

Namita: hehehee

Namita: did u have breakfast yet

Nicholas: I did finished about 45 mins ago

Nicholas: have you?

Namita: its a sunday .... and it would be sooo cool to have breakfast in bed together ..and just lounge all day

Namita: no i havent eaten anything yet

Nicholas: ooooo yes it would... was thinking similar when I woke this morning

Namita: i'll go down and have some toast soon ...im sure everyone is up

Namita: and waiting

Namita: mmmmmmmm yesssssssss wouldnt that be sooo cool

Nicholas: wondering why ur only just up hehe

Namita: hehehe

Namita: yes lil old me !! whats taking me sooo long

Nicholas: hehe

Nicholas: good thing no one knows how late u were up hehe

Namita: im sure if we were going anywhere ..we would never make it in time !!

Namita: hehee yesss good thing

Namita: good thing i have my own room

Namita: otherwise im screwed

Nicholas: are the relies playing tour guide?

Nicholas: yes u'd be screwed n not the good kind

Namita: yes ... today they decided to go around town and explore a bit more

Namita: id rather be screwed the proper way

Nicholas: that's good

Namita: hehe

Nicholas: we'll take care of that very soon my dear

Namita: hehehe

Namita: im excited now !!

Nicholas: now?!

Nicholas: lol

Namita: hehee ...yes

Nicholas: you haven't been all a long?! lol teasing

Nicholas: or excited just at this particular moment?

Nicholas: lol

Namita: of course i was !!!!!!!!!!!! LOL

Namita: hehehe

Namita: now it is just starting ...hehe

Nicholas: mmhmm

Nicholas: this is like waking together n carrying on where we left off form last night

Namita: hehehe .. yesss ... and its sooo nice !! it was only like 5ish that we logged off

Namita: actually i have a confession too

Nicholas: yes it was

Nicholas: yes

Namita: hehe

Nicholas: u played last night before u slept too?!

Namita: i did get carried away and pleasured myself

Namita: hehe yessssss

Namita: till i cam hard !!!

Nicholas: mmmmm I thought about that tooo

Namita: came hard !! i mean

Nicholas: mmmmm

Nicholas: love the sound of that

Nicholas: thx for confessing

Namita: hehe

Namita: ur welcome

Namita: it was such a good release

Nicholas: we were so connected we could feel each other even though we're this far apart

Nicholas: yes it was!!

Namita: hehe yesssss

Nicholas: can only imagine how wicked it will be when we're together

Namita: mmmmmm yesssss

Namita: and getting naughtier and naughtier

Nicholas: yes

Namita: hehee

Nicholas: words just can't describe how amazing you're going to feel

Namita: mmmm yessss ... id be wanting more and more ...and be sooo ...umm whats word im looking for ...

Namita: sooooo wonton ? ..is that word ?

Nicholas: thats a word

Nicholas: wanton more of something... sure

Namita: does it mean crave more more and more ...or to be wanton .yesss

Nicholas: and urning

Namita: yesss

Namita: you may be tired though

Namita: i warn you

Namita: hehe

Nicholas: lol... you may be tired sweetie

Namita: hehee

Nicholas: we'll see just how worn out we make each other lol

Namita: mmm im afraid i wont be able to walk

Namita: hehe

Nicholas: you'll be able to walk but you'll feel it hehe

Namita: hahahaa

Namita: do i need crutches

Namita: or i can just lean on you ??

Nicholas: wanton |'wäntn|adjective 2 (esp. of a woman) sexually immodest or promiscuous.

Namita: ahhhhhhhhhhh

Nicholas: u can lean on me anytime!!

Namita: well not promiscuous

Nicholas: no crutches

Namita: hehe

Nicholas: no not that

Namita: im never been promiscuous

Namita: hehe

Nicholas: me either

Namita: but i know the first part does sound right

Nicholas: but it is a word

Namita: so u googled it !!?

Nicholas: I thought it was

Namita: hehe

Namita: awesome!!

Nicholas: dictionary on my laptop

Namita: hehehe

Nicholas: I just highlight it n click look up in dictionary

Nicholas: I use it all the time

Namita: ohhh cool !!!

Nicholas: the fam must be wondering where you are by now?

Namita: hey nicholas ... i have to go soon !!

Nicholas: lol like minds

Namita: we said the same thing !!

Nicholas: we did

Namita: hahaa

Nicholas: okay

Nicholas: have a wonderful day Namita

Namita: you too nicholas

Nicholas: n maybe catch you during the game

Nicholas: thx

Namita: i loveee the way out names start with N

Namita: it is not common in either gender

Nicholas: hehe you've said that before n it is cool

Namita: ohh yesss the game ..i will try to be around

Namita: yesss i have

Nicholas: okay not to worry if ur not but I'll be around

Namita: ok i should run now

Namita: talk to you later

Nicholas: okay see yah 😊

Namita: bye

Namita: have a good day !!

Nicholas: u2

Namita: get some chips or popcorn for the game

Nicholas: lol ok

Namita: bye

Nicholas: bye

End Time: 12:37 PM

Chapter 26 November 23

Start Time: 12:45 AM

Nicholas: hey sweetie how are you feeling?

Namita: heyyy give me sec

Nicholas: k

Namita: hey there... ive been down in the dumps for the last 2 or 3 days

Namita: sorry if i havent been around

Nicholas: that's what I figured

Namita: this cold or flu has me good

Nicholas: sokay

Nicholas: thats what I thought happened... not to worry

Namita: ok phew ...last nite i tried to log on ... but it said ur offline

Nicholas: do you think you're over the worst now?

Nicholas: I've waited till 1 to give you enf time

Namita: but then if im in email inbox it said ur online

Nicholas: strange

Namita: i think my pc was acting weird again

Nicholas: could be

Namita: im still coughing and hacking a lot

Namita: and my voice is gone

Nicholas: mmm is the sore throat gone now though?

Namita: i can only whisper if i talk

Nicholas: one of the nice things about talking here... you can rest ur voice

Namita: nooo the sore throat is till there

Namita: yesss thats right

Namita: hehe

Namita: how have you been

Nicholas: mmmm not good... still contagious when the throat is still sore

Nicholas: I'm good... better now... I've missed you

Namita: yes not good ... good thing we're not close ..or they would have been no kissing

Namita: hehe

Nicholas: that just wouldn't do hehe

Namita: hehe .. that would have been absolute hell !!!

Nicholas: did you plan to go to San Fran on your holidays but ended up going earlier coz of what happened w ur uncle? or did you have other plans for the time?

Nicholas: yes it would be very difficult to be around u n not touch you

Namita: i had other plans at the time ... i was thinking of going to new york with a few of my work friends...we had a plan to go shopping ...and enjoy what new york has to offer ...ive never been

Namita: id have to wear some bubble suit around you ...hehe

Nicholas: wow that would have been cool.... I've never been either

Nicholas: oooo sexy

Namita: alas one day ...maybe we can both go

Namita: hehe

Nicholas: see through n nothing else hehe

Nicholas: I'd be up for that

Namita: hehehee yess all thru ...look but cannot touch !!!

Nicholas: maybe catch a Canucks Rangers or Islanders game while we're there

Namita: ive been in bed just about all day long

Namita: ohhh yesss

Namita: that would be nice too

Nicholas: I pictured you sleeping most of the time the last few days.... I figured you'd be around when you were up for it

Namita: thanks for understanding nicholas

Nicholas: I've been thinking of you n sending good vibes ur way to help u get better

Namita: aweeeeeeeee thanks luv

Nicholas: I'm an understanding kind of guy

Namita: i got that feeling form you long ago ....and all the good vibes too

Namita: how was work for you ?

Nicholas: glad you got them coz they were just for you

Nicholas: works been good... shifts go by quickly which is nice

Namita: hehe ..yes i got them alright ..no airwave interference here

Namita: ohh thats good

Nicholas: I was late home last nite coz I was doing a weld repair n wanted to finish it... was only a half hr later but that should be over time too

Namita: ohh good .. nice to get overtime esp at this time of the year

Namita: is it like double for you ?

Nicholas: I made sure my vibes were directed to you so there's no way anything could stop them hehe

Namita: hehehe

Nicholas: time n a half for the next 4 hrs I think then double after that

Namita: ohhh

Namita: our is always double from start to finish

Namita: and there is a lot of overtime every week

Nicholas: it's only a half hr but the guy I car pool w said they may round it up to a full hr but I'm not holding my breath for that

Nicholas: wow double time is good

Namita: hehe ahhh i see

Namita: do you always car pool with ur coworker

Nicholas: I told my supervisor that I stayed to finish 1 so he knew n 2 to make sure I got payed for it.... I didn't say that part to him though

Namita: most times i bank my OT and take it out when I know a paycheck is going to be less

Nicholas: yah, he catches a ride w me... he's on my way so it's no big deal.... he's the guy that keeps missing days

Namita: good for you to finish the job that u started out to do

Namita: ohhhhhhhh him ...lol

Nicholas: I put money away in a diff account so I have extra to pay myself if I take a day off here or there

Namita: ohhh good idea ... smart move

Nicholas: yah I didn't want someone else to finish it and I wanted to grind it to make sure it was good

Nicholas: well I knew it was good coz I did it lol

Nicholas: I think my standards are higher than most... I care about the quality of my work

Namita: well that s good !! You really love ur job and looks like you have really good work ethics to complete what us tarted

Namita: thats good to hear Nicholas ... you have a dedication to do ur job !!

Namita: I like that

Nicholas: I've been saving money for a while now... I've used some of it sometimes for hot rod parts or little things but I'm good w my money... always have been

Namita: thats good !! It is sooo easy not to for some ppl .... but one does have to save for the future

Nicholas: thx that's nice to hear that someone else appreciates it too

Namita: im very careful too with what im doing with my money

Nicholas: I call it craftsmanship and I don't think there's a lot of it these days

Namita: yess true !

Nicholas: yes you never know when you're going to have a rainy day n need a little extra money

Nicholas: wow this is quite the slide show tonight... I can hardly keep up

Namita: hehe

Namita: keeping you on ur toes

Nicholas: I also like to see a project from start to finish

Nicholas: yes you are

Namita: well once you put all that time and energy into a project ...it is nice to keep at it and see the end result

Nicholas: I just keep this pic up.... seems to be your fav... if you'd like a change just let me know

Namita: nooo lovee it

Namita: hehe

Namita: ok i will

Namita: let you know i mean

Nicholas: it is... if I had been able to start it at the beginning of the shift I would have had lots of time but I got it after lunch

Nicholas: I knew what u meant

Nicholas: hehe

Namita: ohh... im sure ur bosses can see that you are every dedicated to ur projects

Nicholas: it's uncanny how easily I can read you or understand you

Nicholas: I think so too... I seem to be getting more n more things to do

Namita: hehe really ?? How so ?

Nicholas: not only do I get to do the Assemblyman's position, my primary job but I can gouge if need be and I've been doing the weld repair/build up too

Nicholas: so I get to do 3 things... I never know each day what I'll be doing till I'm there, which I don't mine, brakes up the day and makes me valuable to the company

Namita: that is good ..plus you know welding so well from before

Nicholas: yup

Namita: ur a jack of all trades ... that makes you a hot commodity !!!

Nicholas: that's one of the reasons I got this position, for my welding ticket.... it's a very useful skill

Namita: yesss i can imagine !! It is a good skill to have !!

Nicholas: lol I've always been one of those but before I had a ticket I couldn't really get a job doing anything

Namita: yess they all want to see an official certificate ... from an approved school

Nicholas: my dad showed me how to weld n use a cutting torch when I was 15 when I started the hot rod... I went to school to get certified

Namita: ahh yes ... well ur dad taught you a great skill ... and kinda set you up for a good trade

Nicholas: yah... I can do basic plumbing and electrical work too, a little construction n wood working as well but I can only do those things for myself or friends

Nicholas: that he did n inheriting a little of his mind helps me w problem solving too

Namita: i think you have great talent when you can do all those things ... it is very handy !!!

Nicholas: I think I got a little more creative stuff in my brain though

Namita: good for you nicholas !!

Nicholas: thx

Nicholas: even just today I used those skills to figure something out that someone couldn't

Nicholas: okay enf tooting my horn lol

Namita: hehe noooooooooo ur not

Nicholas: I don't like to brag

Namita: it just makes you even more talented with what ur doing

Namita: you know your stuff !!!

Nicholas: I think that's why I want to open my own creative design studio, so I can design n build projects from start to finish

Nicholas: projects to showcase what I can do and projects for others... once they see what I'm capable of building

Namita: that is good nicholas !!! right now ur gaining ur experience and working towards ur dream to do that

Nicholas: I'll show you some of the other projects I have in mind one day

Namita: wooww cool

Nicholas: let me see if I can send one

Waiting for Namita to accept the file "low flow vw bus. psd" (924 Kb). Please wait for a response or

Cancel (Ctrl+C)

the file transfer.

Transfer of file "low flow vw bus .psd" has been accepted by ~Namita~. Starting transfer...

Cancel

Nicholas: I hope it's not too big

Nicholas: I got the idea from a Hot Wheels toy car.... though the toy is based on a regular bus which is too big. So as you can see it's a VW bus, the one w the little windows in the roof. The back is wind blown and pinched at the bottom. I'm going to use the VW so I can scale it dwn into something more manageable.

Transfer of "low flow vw bus .psd" is complete.

Nicholas: I want to put my logo on the roof so it runs all the way from the front to the back

Waiting for Namita to accept the file "3fBQfe.jpeg" (272 Kb). Please wait for a response or

Cancel (Ctrl+C)

the file transfer.

Namita: Wowwww ... did you draw this .??

Transfer of file "3fBQfe.jpeg" has been accepted by Namita. Starting transfer...

Cancel

Namita: Nice concept !!

Nicholas: this one it part of my logo

Nicholas: thx

Transfer of "3fBQfe.jpeg" is complete.

Nicholas: I didn't draw it but I messed w it enf in photo shop to get the idea out

Namita: did you draw the flame one ??

Nicholas: I did come up w my logo on my own though

Waiting for ~Namita~ to accept the file "g7EE8S.jpeg" (91 Kb). Please wait for a response or

Cancel (Ctrl+C)

the file transfer.

Namita: very cool !!!

Transfer of file "g7EE8S.jpeg" has been accepted by ~Namita~. Starting transfer...

Cancel

Transfer of "g7EE8S.jpeg" is complete.

Nicholas: this is what my business cards look like

Namita: ohhh wowwwwwww ..very nice

Nicholas: and a good idea of my tattoo

Nicholas: thx

Namita: you made ur own business cards ?

Namita: where did u get it done ?

Nicholas: It took me a long time to figure out what to call myself coz ppl would ask "what do you do" n I always say "what do you need me to do"

Namita: ohhh i will tell you what you need to do !!!

Namita: lol

Nicholas: I came up w the idea and a graphic artist put it onto a disk for me so I could get them printed

Nicholas: lol I'm sure u will n anytime my dear hehe

Namita: hehee !!

Namita: that is sooo cool !! I loveeee ur logo !!

Nicholas: it was funny coz when the graphic artist was putting my name n # on them she was trying to squish them together on the same side n I said why not put my name dwn one side n the # dwn the other... she said she'd never done that before.... I think it works and I quite like them

Nicholas: thx I love them too

Namita: what was her name ? Does she live in ur area ?

Nicholas: it's so much nicer to hand someone a card rather than writing ur name on a napkin or scrap paper

Namita: yess so true

Nicholas: she worked in PoCo, not sure if she's still there... can't remember her name

Namita: dont think of it n it will come to you

Namita: my sister who makes jewelry on the side ...got her business cards made ...but online ... and it was thru Vista .. i think its called ...they made like 500 cards with logo ... for about 12 bucks

Nicholas: originally I went to her coz the printer I used needed my logo digitized coz all I had was my original drawing, so he pointed me her way

Namita: ohh ok no i dont know her

Nicholas: wow 12 bucks that is cheap er inexpensive

Namita: yesss i was going to tell u to check it out

Namita: its called vistaprint .. i just googled it

Namita: i told another friend of mine ..and they lovee it

Nicholas: I don't even remember how much mine were.... though I did get about 700 coz when the guy in the back was printing them he thought the guy up front said 1000 so I lucked out coz they only charged for the 500

Namita: ohh good for you !!!

Nicholas: I have the disk w all the logo stuff on it

Namita: so you have enough !!

Namita: hehe

Nicholas: lots

Namita: yessss keep the disc in a safe spot

Nicholas: I think I've only just broken into the 500 not too long ago

Namita: ahhh

Nicholas: the printer gave me the foil printing things they use too so I'll go back there again so they don't have to charge me for the set up

Nicholas: hope that made sense

Namita: yes kinda

Namita: hehe

Nicholas: doesn't matter was kind rambling

Nicholas: lol

Waiting for ~Namita~ to accept the file "blueflame bike.psd" (1692 Kb). Please wait for a response or

Cancel (Ctrl+C)

the file transfer.

Nicholas: this is a Blueflame bike I'd like to build one day too

Transfer of file "blueflamebike.psd" has been accepted by ~Namita~ Starting transfer...

Cancel

Nicholas: so many projects n not enf time.. that's always the case

Nicholas: as I say I hope these files aren't too big

Namita: well you do have an artistic mind ...and tons of ideas locked up in ur head ...im sure one day it will be reality

Nicholas: I don't really have a good idea about those things I just send stuff

Namita: no the files are good

Nicholas: ok cool

Transfer of "blueflame bike.psd" is complete.

Namita: OHhhhhhhh WOWWWwwwwwwww that is a cool looking bike !!!

Nicholas: I use to feel bad that I couldn't draw my ideas very well but I like to work 3 dimensionally.. so now I use whatever means possible to get the idea out... even if it means cutting out pics from a magazine n glueing things together

Nicholas: thx

Namita: loveeeeeeee the color

Nicholas: thx me too

Namita: blue !! ...hehe

Nicholas: now that one has a lot of hrs in photoshop. I found a chopper image I liked then lowered the seat and raised the tank then blended them in that wind blown sleek look.

Nicholas: but of course

Namita: well i can see what ur vision is !!

Nicholas: wouldn't be Blueflame Creative w/o some blue in it

Nicholas: that's the idea

Namita: hhehe yesss

Namita: i was thinking just before i was talking to you tonite ..how i love the color blue

Namita: and then the other color that caught my eye in my room was ... and that i lovee is ..orange

Nicholas: I knew you like blue... tis my fav color

Namita: yesss blue is my colour of choice

Nicholas: I do like a deep metallic orange.... still looking for a project to paint orange

Nicholas: one can never go wrong w choosing blue when it comes to me... I go for it every time

Nicholas: funny that my hot rod is green though lol

Namita: yess i totally agree

Namita: and blue and orange kinda go to together

Nicholas: red and blue are very common hot rod colours n I wanted something that would stand out n there weren't a lot of green ones out there at the time I painted it

Namita: green is good too

Namita: well how about the blue and orange flames on it

Nicholas: my god Namita you change ur pic n my heart skips

Namita: hehe

Namita: this is from a couple of weeks ago here

Nicholas: I've always liked blue n white fire so I think w the VW bus project I'll put it on that

Nicholas: wow ur so beautiful

Namita: hmmmm sounds very cool !!!

Nicholas: love how pretty you are... makes me smile

Namita: aweee thanks

Nicholas: and hence Blueflame Creative

~Namita~ would like to send you the file "313004_181844111904582_163153073773686_374..." (70 Kb). Do you want to

Accept

(Ctrl+G) or

Decline

(Ctrl+C) the invitation?

Transfer of file "313004_181844111904582_163153073773686_374..." from ~Namita~ has been accepted. Starting transfer...

Cancel

You have successfully received 313004_181844111904582_163153073773686_374_n.jpg from ~Namita~. Before opening this file, you may want to scan it with a virus-scanning program.

Nicholas: can you send me the one from the other night pls? the one from the wedding

Nicholas: I've run out of room on my screen for all of your photos

Namita: which one

Namita: hehe

Namita: i cant even remember

Namita: hehe

Namita: ur too funny !!

Nicholas: hmmm I'd say the pretty one but they're all pretty

Namita: what was i wearing

Nicholas: cream dress I think

Nicholas: looking to the right med shot

Namita: ohh yess one sec

Namita: I thought u looked very mature

Nicholas: YESSSSS!

Namita: this one

Nicholas: I mean um yah that's the one lol

Namita: hehe

Nicholas: okay so ur not looking to the right but that's it

Namita: one sec .. i have to find it in files

Nicholas: take ur time

Namita: ok but keep talking

Nicholas: you are so photogenic

Nicholas: I'm a little stunned here lol after 2 or 3 days w/o talking w you n now new pics I can't think straight hehe

Namita: awee thanks

Namita: hehe

Namita: ohhhhhhh nicholas !!!!!

Nicholas: even ur candid photos are great

Nicholas: I'll have to do some rearranging to fit you all in on my screen hehe

Namita: hehe ...yesss im miss ever ready here

Nicholas: or all of you in that is

Namita: actually dad says ive always been photogenic ..since i was a baby

Nicholas: I believe it!!

Namita: hehe thanks

Nicholas: *sigh*

Nicholas: you look so much younger

Nicholas: I'd say maybe early 30's at most

Namita: what in the latest pic ?? you mean ?

Nicholas: as thats the most resent then yes

Namita: yes it is

Namita: my parents look young too ..esp mom

Namita: so i think ive got the good genes

Nicholas: mind you I don't think I look 39.. certainly don't feel it lol

Namita: nooo you dont

Nicholas: oh there's those good jeans again hehe

Nicholas: thx

Namita: i think you look around 34 or 35

Namita: hehe

Nicholas: I don't know what it is.. I've seen ppl I graduated w n they look OLD

Nicholas: speaking of graduation did u attend ur reunions?

Namita: hehee really ??

Namita: actually no

Nicholas: oh yah

Nicholas: me either.. couldn't be bothered

Namita: i was working ...plus i wasnt interested in seeing the ppl i wasnt fond of

Nicholas: honestly I didn't really feel the need to talk to them n catch up as I didn't really know them back then

Namita: some of those ppl are still the same as the were in high school i mean ,... and i dont mean physically

Namita: i mean in attitude

Nicholas: I get it

Nicholas: high school for me was a place to go

Namita: uh huh

Nicholas: I didn't socialize much... was working on the hot rod.... of course lol

Nicholas: oooo that's a nice pic too

Nicholas: same hair style, same day? yes

Namita: yesss yess ..you had ur mind on other important stuff

Namita: yes same day

Nicholas: that I did

Namita: im still trying to find the other pic

Nicholas: keen eye here

Namita: arghhh

Nicholas: no worries

Nicholas: how did you get it up to show me but can't find it to send?

Nicholas: I don't get computers sometimes

~Namita~ would like to send you the file "389829_181844745237852_163153073773686_374..." (73 Kb). Do you want to

Accept

(Ctrl+G) or

Decline

(Ctrl+C) the invitation?

Transfer of file "389829_181844745237852_163153073773686_374..." from ~Namita~ has been accepted. Starting transfer...

Cancel

You have successfully received 389829_181844745237852_163153073773686_374_n.jpg from ~Namita~. Before opening this file, you may want to scan it with a virus-scanning program.

Namita: its in my msn chat file but i cant find it in my pictures file to send it to you

Namita: thats where i have to go to send it too

Nicholas: ooo I like that one... shows more of you mmmm mmmm

Nicholas: oh I see

Namita: hehehe

Namita: i will find it

Namita: dont worry

Nicholas: sokay don't stress or worry ur not feeling well n need to take it easy hehe

Namita: hehe i wont

Nicholas: just admiring ur latest photo... mmhmm

~Namita~ would like to send you the file"1289205413.jpg" 20 Kb). Do you want to

Accept

(Ctrl+G) or

Decline

(Ctrl+C) the invitation?

Transfer of file "1289205413.jpg" from ~Namita~ has been accepted. Starting transfer...

Cancel

Namita: ohhhhhhhh brace urself

You have successfully received 289205413.jpg from ~Namita~. Before opening this file, you may want to scan it with a virus-scanning program.

Nicholas: okay

Nicholas: here we goooooo!!

Namita: lol

Nicholas: OOOHH MMMMYYY FFFF******KKin GGGOOD can nicholas say WOW!!!

Now we're talking. Black bra and panties looks like it's right out of a Victoria Secret catalog.

Namita: hehe

Namita: this should make up for the other pic

Namita: it is from last year

Nicholas: and then some thaaaaaank you!!

Namita: which miranda took

Nicholas: ah yes I'll have to thank that Miranda women when I meet her hehe

Namita: hehee

Nicholas: that's like calendar quality

Namita: she is pretty good !!

Nicholas: yyuummmyyyy

Namita: a few friends of hers and i ...we wanted some good pics of ourselves

Namita: so we decided to do some racy ones

Nicholas: well I think it has to do w the model but I'm more than a little bias

Nicholas: yes you did!!

Namita: its more comfortable to do a pic like this than if i was in front of some male photographer ... that i wont do !!

Nicholas: I can imagine

Nicholas: a few friends??? sounds like a photo shoot.... sounds like every guys dream lol

Namita: so we took our opportunity with her talent

Namita: i know some of the boyfriends of the other girls were on cloud nine when they saw their pics

Namita: hehhe

Nicholas: sorry I rambled a bit in that last one

Namita: noooooooo no worries

Nicholas: I bet they were

Namita: i like when u ramble

Nicholas: lol

Namita: hehe

Nicholas: keep showing me pics like those n I'll be a rambling fool hehe

Namita: hahahah

Namita: what did u like about the pic ?

Nicholas: I can picture you on the bed like that when I come home n I turn to pudding inside

Namita: hahhaha !!

Namita: youd be stuttering

Nicholas: the look in your eyes, the outfit, the pose, how I can see your abs

Namita: and clumsy

Namita: hehee

Namita: yeah right !!

Namita: lol

Nicholas: see I can't type proper now

Namita: hehehehe

Nicholas: n those lovely boobs mmm mmm mmm

Nicholas: that cute little bum of yours

Namita: heheh you love em all !!!!!!!!!!

Nicholas: lol yes I do!!!

Namita: im giving you impure thoughts !?

Nicholas: n those hot legs damn

Namita: lol

Nicholas: yes you certainly are

~Namita~ would like to send you the file "148223_182411105103224_160615060616162_654..." (29 Kb). Do you want to

Accept

(Ctrl+G) or

Decline

(Ctrl+C)

the invitation?

Namita: what about this one ?

Nicholas: I'll have to keep those ones in a special file

Transfer of file "148223_182411105103224_160615060616162_654..." from ~Namita~ has been accepted. Starting transfer...

Cancel

You have successfully received 148223_182411105103224_160615060616162_654_n.jpg from ~Namita~. Before opening this file, you may want to scan it with a virus-scanning program.

Namita: hehe yesss in a fault !!

Nicholas: now your just teasing me

Namita: lol

Namita: yes ive been holding out on you !!

Nicholas: please don't send naked ones or partially naked ones.. if you have any that is... I want to see you naked the first time in front of me

Namita: no i dont have any naked ones

Nicholas: yes you have.. I kinda figured you were holding out on me lol

Nicholas: okay

Namita: and i wouldnt do that either

Nicholas: I knew you wouldn't hehe

Nicholas: how resent are those last ones?

Namita: would you consider these partially naked ?

Nicholas: nope

Namita: they are from last year

Nicholas: cool

Namita: if i had to do any naked ones ...id do it with my partner ..not alone

Nicholas: how often do you get together w Miranda to do a photo shoot? n how long do you take?

Nicholas: ah yes well we'll see what we can do about those then

Namita: whenever we meet most times it is her idea ...cuz she is building her portfolio tho these pics arent part of it !!

Namita: sometimes she calls and asks ppl if she can use them as models

Namita: so i help out

Nicholas: oh yes her portfolio... can never have too many

Namita: hehe

Namita: we have been friends for a long time

Nicholas: that's very good of you... and I appreciate it immensely

Namita: awweee ur welcome !!

Nicholas: I only wish I had more to show you but I guess you'll have to wait for the live showing hehe

Namita: hehe ...can i touch ??

Nicholas: absolutely!!!!!

Namita: can i taste ??

Nicholas: yesssssss!!!!!

Namita: hehehe

Namita: can i inspect ??

Nicholas: I'll be a big Nick-sicle for you though I wont be cold

Nicholas: inspect sure just no probing lol

Nicholas: new pictures..... it's a bit like christmas here lol

Namita: hehe i loveeeeeee Nicksicle ...mmmmmmmmmmm yummmmmmm

Namita: hehe too funny !!

Nicholas: oh good I hoped you might

Nicholas: once you get the wrapper off it goes on for ever lol

Namita: mmmm sounds like a no melt Popsicle !!

Nicholas: only my heart

Namita: hehehe good one !!!!

Nicholas: thx I can be quite witty at times lol

Nicholas: esp when I'm up late

Namita: hehe ..your not tired yet ?

Nicholas: oh way past tired my dear but it's been 3 days... was having some Namita withdrawal

Namita: hehehe ...its nice to be in touch with you again ... missed chatting with you !!

Namita: I can imagine if u really came home after work to me

Nicholas: yes it is nice and I have missed you too

Nicholas: ooooo me tooo

Namita: hehheeh

Namita: im sure we would burn up the night

Nicholas: yes we would... we'd find a stride and maximize our time n energy so we got enf sleep and of course play time

Namita: hehe ... yesss we would be soo in tune to each other ... going all night long

Namita: and cuddling close together

Nicholas: n sleep out of pure exhaustion

Namita: not a moment apart

Namita: mmmmm yesssssss

Nicholas: ooh yes the cuddling.. been imagining that

Namita: mmmm yess .. i loveeeeeeeee it !!!!!!!

Nicholas: to have you curled up to my chest my arms around you n we just fall asleep together... love it

Namita: ohhhh yesssssss ... or i swing one leg over ur tummy as we sleep together

Namita: and you holding on to my calf

Namita: or thigh

Nicholas: yyyyesssss

Nicholas: I'll take thigh pls

Namita: while ur on ur back

Namita: hehehee

Namita: ahhh ur a thigh man !!!

Namita: lol

Nicholas: yup legs n ass man here

Namita: and id be curled into the crook of ur neck

Namita: heheheh

Nicholas: I'll probly go for putting my hand on ur bum

Namita: hehe no worries

Namita: im all for it !!!

Nicholas: ur head on my other arm

Namita: im such a touchy person myself that i dont mind at all

Nicholas: or my other arm under you

Namita: mmm yesss

Namita: me breathing quietly after our love making

Nicholas: me too.... love to be touched by my partner

Namita: and sleeping satisfied

Namita: ohhh good to hear

Nicholas: yes quite satisfying

Namita: although i can feel ur still very excited with me ...as ,my leg rubs your ..ummmm manhood

Namita: all over again

Nicholas: if we're not satisfied then we'll do it till we are but I'm sure we'll get it dwn the first time hehe

Namita: nooooooo we would do it again and agian to one up the other

Namita: perfection is the key !! hehehe

Nicholas: oh I'm sure it wont take me long to be aroused physically w such a beautiful woman as you naked beside me

Namita: aweeeeeee nicholas !!

Nicholas: practice makes perfect I say lol

Namita: hehe

Namita: yess it sure does !!

Nicholas: theses new pics make the anticipation of seeing you all the more tortures

Namita: can u imagine if we made love over and over again ... me still wet from the last time !!!

Nicholas: I still keep running through our first meeting in my mind

Namita: ohhhh you really like them !??

Namita: heheh

Nicholas: yes I can n I'm sure we will

Nicholas: very much!!

Nicholas: not complaining but I've been seeing the same ones for 8 well lets say 7 weeks now

Nicholas: it's nice to see diff poses n looks

Namita: lol !!!!

Namita: ur making me laugh !!

Nicholas: were you able to find the one I requested? or you'll look later?

Nicholas: I love making you laugh

Namita: im still looking ... but i have so many pics in my actual file

Nicholas: ANd I can't wait to hear your laugh

Nicholas: I bet you do

Namita: its like 3 or 4 pages of stuff

Nicholas: cool

Nicholas: I can't wait to see them ALL!!!

Nicholas: lol

Namita: hehehe

Nicholas: or maybe just all of you to start

Namita: yesss all of me ....so you can map my body !!

Nicholas: so you know I'm probly going to be bouncing off the walls the day I get to see you the first time... said that before but I thought it needed repeating

Nicholas: I'll commit it to memory that way I can find my way in the dark hehe

Namita: hhehehe ... i have a feeling you will go crazyyy !!!

Namita: hahaha

Nicholas: just might

Namita: and id be laughing and giggling at ur antics !!

Nicholas: and if need be I'll use my body or face to find my way

Nicholas: I may just tickle you a little here n there along the way

Namita: mmmmmmmmmm or mouth!!!

Nicholas: YEssssss

Namita: omg !!! dont tickle me !!!!!

Namita: id go nuts !!!!!!

Namita: hehee

Nicholas: mmmm torture I say!!!

Namita: noooooooooo hehee

Nicholas: just a little inadvertent tickles?

Nicholas: no I wouldn't torture you

Nicholas: torture is all this waiting

Namita: hehehe ... i dont mind... but if u tickle me ...be careful i might scream

Nicholas: inadvertent tickles like when my nose runs under your breast as I work my way around your body

Namita: ommgggg ... i will be ecstatic

Nicholas: or when I glide my fingers up the inside of your arm

Namita: id loveeeeeeeeeee those lil tickles

Namita: and feeling you around me exploring

Namita: mmmmmmm yesssssssss

Nicholas: prepare urself woman coz there'll be a whole lot of those comin' ur way

Nicholas: n breathing in your sent on your neck

Namita: hehehe i loveeeeee when you say that ...woman !! !

Nicholas: you can hear me breathing you in

Namita: ohhhhhh god ..i will go crazzzzzy

Nicholas: ANd you are a woman Namita

Namita: awee thnx

Namita: i would love it when you devour me

Nicholas: you are quite welcome

Namita: and take me in a feverish way

Nicholas: nice n slow to begin with... exploring ever inch of you

Namita: mmmmmmmm yesssssss

Nicholas: I think you'll be quite satisfied when I'm done... then we can carry on w the journey

Nicholas: and work our way to the finally

Nicholas: or intermission if need be

Namita: ohhh god ... im soooo excited

Namita: i can just imagine how its going to be

Namita: we would be inseparable

Namita: day and nite

Nicholas: good to hear.... just wait n see how excited you are when I'm exploring you

Namita: ooooooOOoOOOOoooo i loveeeeeeeeeeee it !!!!!!!!

Namita: ur getting me turned on Nicholas !!

Nicholas: there are so many nuances to your body n not just the obvious ones

Nicholas: oh sorry I can stop hehe (but I wont)

Namita: noooo dont !!!

Namita: i came across another pic you might like

Nicholas: it takes so much more to type what I'm going to do, it'll be so much easier when I show you

Nicholas: cool

Nicholas: send it along pls

Namita: yessss it would be

Namita: this was taken a year ago too

Namita: one sec

Nicholas: k

~Namita~ would like to send you the file "2010-07-21" (69 Kb). Do you want to

Accept

(Ctrl+G) or

Decline

(Ctrl+C) the invitation?

Transfer of file "2010-07-21" from Namita has been accepted. Starting transfer...

Cancel

You have successfully received 2010-07-21from ~Namita~. Before opening this file, you may want to scan it with a virus scanning program.

Nicholas: it didn't come through

Nicholas: it's just a blank page

Namita: ohhh

Namita: one sec

Nicholas: well i must say that I'm more than a little turned on here too but that's nothing new when I chat w you

Namita: aweee ...well im glad ur are turned on ...sooooo sexy !!!

Nicholas: you just have that ability

Namita would like to send you the file "17647_bips_123_ 176l o.jpg" (69 Kb). Do you want to

Accept

(Ctrl+G) or

Decline

(Ctrl+C) the invitation?

Nicholas: there we go... just added ur latest pics to my Namita file in iPhoto

Transfer of file "17647_bips_123_176lo.jpg" from Namita has been accepted. Starting transfer...

Cancel

You have successfully received 17647_bips_123_176lo.jpg from Namita. Before opening this file, you may want to scan it with a virus-scanning program.

Namita: hhehee ...my my im keeping you busy there !!!

Nicholas: uuuhhhh mmmm

Nicholas: yup

Nicholas: OMG Namita WOW!!!

Namita: hehehe are you still in ur seat ??

Nicholas: bearly

Nicholas: I think i'm about 6 inches out of it

Namita: hahahah

Nicholas: or sitting on 6 inches of air

Namita: are u serious ??

Namita: ohhhhhhhhhhhhhhhhhh

Nicholas: yes

Namita: do you know what i thought when u said that ???

Namita: hahhaha

Nicholas: as much as I love them all now I do have a favourite

Namita: thats why i asked you if ur serious

Nicholas: what did you think?

Namita: hehe i thought u meant you are actually out on 6 inches ...meaning ur six inches out ...like 6 inches straight

Namita: hehe

Nicholas: ah well that would be 7 inches lol

Namita: hehe ...yes i know ...but i thought 6 inches ..and one more inch to complete it soon

Nicholas: once my heart started again I was able to regain my senses

Namita: lol

Nicholas: ah gotcha

Namita: so which is ur fav ?

Nicholas: I do love that one

Nicholas: not sure if it's coz ur half naked or not

Namita: this new one you mean ?

Nicholas: I think that's it

Nicholas: yes the new one!!

Nicholas: this is the most I've seen of you... ANd pretty much how I imagined

Namita: wowww cool !!!

Namita: now you can see my assets

Namita: hehe

Nicholas: YEs I can n oh how I love them!!!

Namita: lol

Nicholas: you have a fantastic body Namita

Namita: thanks nicholas ... i do take care of my body ... i do my cardio ..and lots of yoga

Nicholas: ANd you described urself just as in your story from LL

Namita: my grandma taught me to do yoga since i was 4 or something ...long before it was a craze here in vancouver

Nicholas: it shows... damn!!

Namita: yes i did .. i tried to catch the essence of who i am both physically and as a person

Namita: yoga comes from india

Nicholas: yes it does

Namita: and it has been long practiced there for generations

Namita: in conjunction with meditation as well

Nicholas: after 8 weeks I can see you are exactly as u described n I'm so glad

Nicholas: yes

Namita: aweee thanks nicholas ... glad u like it

Nicholas: I learned to meditate when I studied Tai Chi

Namita: i could have sent this pic ages ago... but i want you to know who i am first

Nicholas: was worth the wait

Namita: ohhh cool ... did you enjoy meditation?

Nicholas: I appreciate that and respect that you waited

Nicholas: I did

Namita: ur welcome

Nicholas: was something I did on my own before just learned more tools to help after learning Tai chi

Namita: wowww very good !!!

Namita: ive never done tai chi before

Nicholas: the waiting reassures me that u are as classy as I hoped and you are

Namita: it sure does !!

Nicholas: I like that you waited

Namita: i dont want to portray myself as all the other women do ...desperate or classless

Nicholas: forgot what I was going to say

Namita: ive always had some class i think ...ever since i was aware of my femininity

Namita: if that make sense

Nicholas: you are very classy Namita and I love it

Nicholas: it does

Namita: im not the kind of person to flaunt myself or throw myself at every guy

Namita: im quiet and reserved ... and respectful

Nicholas: some have it n flaunt it.... others have it, know they do but choose to be classy about it n not flaunt

Nicholas: I can totally see that

Namita: yess thats it

Nicholas: another amazing quality I love about you

Namita: couldnt have said it any better

Namita: aweee thanks

Nicholas: oh good I'm glad it made sense

Namita: yes of course ... i get you !! i got that from you the moment we talked

Nicholas: I've always been attracted to women that know they're attractive but choose to be reserved about it

Nicholas: yes you did

Nicholas: and again no one has ever gotten me before

Namita: hehehee

Nicholas: I don't like it when women use their looks to get what they want... total turn off

Namita: ommg me tooo !!!

Namita: i hate it !!

Namita: i have no respect for them

Nicholas: was just thinking that on the drive home how you see me for "me"... the real me

Namita: just before i left ... i heard a rumor from my colleagues

Nicholas: and u appreciate all the things that "are" me

Namita: ohhh yess i have a good feeling about you

Nicholas: n I you

Namita: we have the same values and outlook on life

Nicholas: we do

Namita: well the rumor i was going to tell u was

Nicholas: that's what you said in one of your first emails on LL

Nicholas: oh yes sorry

Nicholas: do go on

Namita: this nurse ...she is probably 20 something

Namita: im thinking 26 or 28

Nicholas: mmmhmm

Namita: real ditz

Namita: if thats how u spell it

Nicholas: I know what u mean

Namita: well she went around and slept with one of the hot doctors at work ... he is in his 30's ... and according to most nurses ...they all think he is a hunk ... i dont think so

Namita: so she goes and sleeps with him multiple times

Namita: and i know she would do that

Nicholas: oh no sleeping w a co-worker not good

Namita: knowing her

Namita: and he is married to someone else...and she knows that too !! Like how classy is that !!!!

Nicholas: OMG not cool... bad form.. shame on her ANd him!!

Namita: yesss i know ...my jaw dropped when i heard it

Namita: wasnt surprised when i found out who the nurse was

Nicholas: not cool... and ppl wonder why the divorce rate is so high

Namita: i really dont know where i was going with this story ..hehehe

Nicholas: sokay

Namita: ohhh maybe being so classless

Nicholas: good story though

Namita: lol

Nicholas: meh I just like hearing you er reading ur words

Namita: hehe

Nicholas: one day, hopefully soon, I'll get to hear that beautiful voice of yours

Namita: going back to what u were saying ...what is it that i emailed you about on LL ??

Namita: ohh yess

Nicholas: don't laugh but I saved it

Nicholas: I'll show you lol

Nicholas: it was all I had of you that early on

Namita: hehehe ok

Nicholas: Wow! Your bio is really cool. Very creative. How are you? And can I see you please? You can see me seems fair... yes?

Nicholas: this was my first contact

Nicholas: and ur reply was

Namita: this is what i wrote to you ?

Namita: ohh

Namita: yess

Nicholas: no that's what I first wrote to u

Namita: yes got it

Nicholas: your reply was this

Nicholas: Hi there ... thank you, glad you enjoyed reading my profile. I enjoyed reading yours as well. I am working the next 2 days ... i work odd hours ...so i wont be around til sunday. So it would be nice to connect with you online and exchange bs. Id rather exchange while we are online. Dont worry ... i described myself exactly as in my story. Have a good next 2 days ... and i look forward to chatting with you !! Cheers ~ N

Namita: hehehehehe yes i remember !!

Nicholas: when you said u work odd hrs I immediately thought nurse

Namita: serious ???

Nicholas: seems so long ago

Nicholas: I did

Namita: what if i worked in a factory or something

Namita: hehe

Nicholas: odd hrs over the weekend, dead give away, for me at least

Namita: hehehe

Namita: ur too smart !!

Nicholas: lol not for the income you posted on ur bio lol

Namita: hahahhaah good one

Nicholas: it's funny I've read our first convo a few times

Nicholas: I'm amazed at how far we've come in just 8 weeks

Namita: hahaha well you never know ... i could work in a factory making i dunno ...chips ??

Nicholas: a few as in 2 or 3 times just to be clear lol

Nicholas: yah yah lol

Namita: wowww ...what did u think of me ? back then

Nicholas: spicy chips!!

Namita: well i will tell you ..it was ur pic that caught my eye first ...a fresh face

Namita: and then i read ur bio ... i was interested ...but hesitant ... i didnt have any credits

Nicholas: I hadn't seen you at that time so I was thinking and hoping for beautiful

Nicholas: credits? you've mentioned that before. what are they?

Namita: but i was sure if i peeked at ur profile ...then it would tell you in the other end that i did and prompt you to see mine

Nicholas: I'm so glad you were interested!!

Namita: the credits you mean ?

Nicholas: yes

Namita: you have to buy points or credits so you can chat online on LL

Nicholas: as I said it was ur story that caught my eye

Nicholas: I didn't

Namita: or send a message

Nicholas: I just paid for a month n started searching n talking

Namita: i dont think we chatted on LL messenger

Nicholas: nope just in email LL

Namita: ohhh so must have had a deal

Namita: ahhhh i seee

Nicholas: must have... it worked out really really well I think.... I'm quite happy w how things turned out

Namita: hehehe me too !!

Nicholas: I still catch myself thinking about you n think "she's real, I'm not imagining her" lol

Namita: hehehe ok i will pinch you when i see you

Namita: on ur butt ??

Nicholas: I would have never in a million years believed I'd meet some one as amazing as you

Nicholas: and as honest as I am

Namita: aweeeeeeeee thanks nicholas

Nicholas: yes you've said that before... I'll be prepared

Namita: hehehe

Namita: im sure you will wear ur steel underwear !!

Nicholas: I gave it a month n it only took a week to find you

Nicholas: not a chance, I'll be easy access for you my dear

Namita: Wowwwww really !!

Nicholas: yup

Namita: mmmmmm loveee the easy access

Nicholas: was giving it a month

Namita: question for you

Nicholas: yes

Namita: kinda off topic ...but youre going to love this

Namita: hehe

Nicholas: cool

Namita: if we were in bed together ...and i woke you up in the middle of the nite ...cuz i was horny ... and ur tired and in deep sleep ...what would you do ?

Nicholas: I'd be all over you!!!!

Namita: hehehe

Namita: you will !!???

Nicholas: hell yah

Namita: i wont have to beg ?

Nicholas: you'll never have to beg

Namita: hehee

Namita: even though ur super uber tired

Nicholas: I'll be ready anytime

Nicholas: I'll always be packing too

Namita: hehe ..cuz i do have a high sex drive

Namita: just warning you

Namita: hehe

Nicholas: so I've heard lol

Namita: hehe

Namita: or how about i do you while ur asleep

Nicholas: well I'll do my best to satisfy

Namita: would u like that ?

Nicholas: fat chance of me sleeping through it lol

Namita: hehhehee

Nicholas: sure would

Namita: or morning lovemaking

Nicholas: to wake thinking I'm having a dream n I'm not actually dreaming

Namita: maybe a 6am lovemaking into the morning

Nicholas: morning love making is awesome

Namita: me too ...would loveeeeeeeeee it

Nicholas: we'll do it 7 ways from sunday

Namita: hehehe ok

Nicholas: this isn't making you out of town any easier

Nicholas: as I say we'll need some time the first go round

Namita: hehe yessss and no interruptions

Nicholas: after that we'll work on wearing each other out n see who falls a sleep first lol

Namita: no phones or pagers or faxes

Namita: or dogs

Nicholas: nope

Namita: or doorbell

Namita: nothing

Namita: hehe

Nicholas: it'll be the sleep over to end all sleep overs

Namita: hahahaha yesssss

Nicholas: the sleep over that lasts all week end !!

Namita: yessssssssssss

Nicholas: big box O condoms some snacks n that's about it

Namita: just hanging out all week

Namita: hehe

Nicholas: oh I'll bring movies too

Namita: if we were very very serious ...would you do it without a condom

Namita: yes movies too

Namita: like we are going to watch it

Nicholas: you not on the pill not sure that'd be wise

Namita: i can go on it

Nicholas: oh I see

Nicholas: I miss read that

Namita: miss read what

Nicholas: I have no problem getting snipped

Nicholas: miss read ur w/o condom message

Namita: no i dont want u to go under the knife

Namita: if i can go on the pill

Nicholas: there's no knife

Namita: i just dont like the side effects of it in the long run

Nicholas: if you were on the pill and we were serious then I would

Nicholas: side effects?

Namita: awee nicholas

Namita: well the chance of heart disease is greater with women who are on pill

Namita: or even blood clots

Nicholas: oh on the pill

Nicholas: thats not good

Namita: yes

Nicholas: much easier for me to get snipped... I've looked into it before

Namita: do you get the same feeling when ur using a condom ?

Nicholas: def something I've thought about

Namita: you have ?

Namita: ohhh

Nicholas: I don't really notice a diff w or w/o

Namita: ohhh good

Namita: is it ultra thins ?

Nicholas: I have... was just after i was separated. went for the prelim visit

Namita: uh huh

Nicholas: I like the Durex Love condoms

Namita: visit to the doctor ?

Namita: i have never bought a condom before ...hehhe

Nicholas: to see the Dr that would do it yes.... not my GP

Namita: what are they like ...the love condoms

Namita: ohh yess

Nicholas: hmm well you wont have to either

Namita: i shy away from that aisle

Namita: at the drugstore

Nicholas: don't know how to describe them... love is just the style of one of the Durex line

Namita: ohhh ok

Nicholas: well if you don't need them then why would you

Nicholas: I'll show you mine

Namita: yesss ... i mean if im browsing at london drugs or somewhere and some other product are right beside the condoms ...than i hurry up and get out of there

Namita: yes you show me urs and i will show mine !! heheheh

Nicholas: they have quite a few cool things in that aisle... diff lubes n toys kind of stuff

Nicholas: lol I knew you'd bite at that one

Namita: in london drugs ??

Namita: hehehe

Namita: you know me too well !!!

Nicholas: stick w me and you'll be well versed w condoms

Namita: hehe mmmmmmm

Nicholas: where ever they sell condoms

Namita: ahhh ok

Namita: i get all red and flustered when im in that aisle ...hehehe

Nicholas: they're just little finger vibrators

Namita: can u imagine someone soo poised like me being like that

Namita: OOoooOoo niceeee

Nicholas: hehe you're cute

Namita: hehe

Nicholas: I think it's kinda fun to look n buy them

Namita: its true ..my cheeks get soo hot

Namita: yess id loveee it with you

Namita: no problem there

Namita: i can hide behind you

Nicholas: it'll be old hat once ur w me a while

Namita: hehe

Nicholas: lol it's not like they're going to jump out n scare you hehe

Namita: hehe im like that even when im buying other products like feminine products

Namita: sorry more than u wanted to know

Nicholas: ah i see

Namita: hehehee

Nicholas: totally fine

Namita: noooo i know ... but i have to get used to it

Nicholas: I had a mom that educated me on those things so when I was grown I would have an understanding on the issue

Namita: ur mom you mean

Namita: what issues ?

Namita: hehe

Nicholas: I'm pretty open about everything.... meaning I can talk about pretty much everything

Nicholas: women issues= monthly cycles

Namita: ohhh i like that !!!

Namita: ohhhhh so ur mom talked to you about it

Nicholas: doesn't gross me out

Namita: ohhhhhh good

Nicholas: pretty much and having a sister

Namita: not that im going to torture you with it

Namita: im not like that

Nicholas: she didn't sit me dwn n have a show n tell

Namita: anyways ..talking about women issues

Namita: hehhee ur mom !!!

Namita: that is too funny

Nicholas: yes.... she was just open about talking about it

Namita: did u know anything before then

Namita: or was it a revelation ?

Nicholas: she figured that one day when I'm w someone I should be informed and sympathetic to the issue

Namita: yesss true

Namita: but i might be an exception sometimes

Nicholas: I had my ideas.... my parents were open about answering our questions when we had them.... and then there was sex-ed to fill in the rest

Nicholas: exception how?

Namita: yesss true !!! i remember those classes

Nicholas: my high school was the very first in BC to have a condom machine

Namita: well remember i told you how i can be even hornier during my time of the month

Namita: ohhh wowww

Nicholas: my mom was on the school board and the chair person for a few years n sex-ed was a big topic

Nicholas: I remember

Namita: wow ... good for your mom !!!

Namita: thats what i meant ... i crave it even more then

Nicholas: I thought that's what you meant

Namita: esp the latter part of the days

Nicholas: do you think you crave it in general coz you haven't had a partner who can satisfy you the way you want?

Namita: i think sooo ... but ive always had a huge sexual appetite since i was in my 20's

Nicholas: me too

Namita: but alot of it is true to what you said

Nicholas: the partner part?

Namita: yes

Nicholas: well you're in for a treat w me my dear

Namita: aweeeeeeee nicholas !!

Nicholas: coz you'll be completely n totally satisfied w me

Namita: you are quite in tune with a woman's body and know how to please

Namita: ohhh god nicholas

Nicholas: that I do

Namita: even though im sick ... im soooo turned on right now

Nicholas: not to toot my horn but I haven't had any complaints

Nicholas: hehe good to know

Namita: hehe i believe that !!

Nicholas: omg it's almost 5!!

Namita: hehehe yes it is ....is it out new high ?

Nicholas: you're not going to get better staying up till the wee hrs

Namita: mmmm yes nicholas

Nicholas: as much as I love talking w you

Namita: im practicing for the real thing

Namita: hehe

Nicholas: lol well there wont be a lot of talking... well may be in relation to the activities

Namita: heheheh

Namita: yess thats for sure !!!

Nicholas: I can't wait to satisfy you the way you've always needed

Nicholas: just throwing that out there

Namita: aweee nicholas ...and of course i for you

Namita: id loveeeeeeee to taste you for a longgg time

Nicholas: hehe thx

Nicholas: mmmhmmm

Nicholas: all in due time

Namita: explore ur body

Namita: feel you

Namita: ur muscles

Namita: kiss you

Nicholas: it's going to be pure magic!!

Namita: mmmmmmyesss

Namita: using all our senses

Nicholas: this last pic will tie me over quite nicely till I get to devour you for real!!

Namita: on each other

Namita: hehe the one in my bra and panties ?

Nicholas: YEssssss

Namita: hehe i always wear something matching

Namita: like this one

Nicholas: can't wait to get our naked bodies together

Namita: i lovee lingerie shopping

Namita: mmmmmmm yesss

Nicholas: you always dress sexy which I love!!

Namita: or how about i sit on top of you

Namita: in my bra and panties

Namita: straddling you

Nicholas: abso-frigin-lootly!!

Namita: and you reach up and undo my bra

Namita: ur hands trying feverishly to undo the hook

Nicholas: I'd be searching those panties for a way in.... w/o using my hands

Namita: hehe

Namita: you can move it aside and enter me

Nicholas: oh yessss

Namita: mmmmmmmmm

Nicholas: love the thought of that!!

Namita: mmm yesss

Namita: me too

Namita: im now face to face with you lying on top of you

Nicholas: you'll be able to feel me bursting to get out of my pants

Namita: ooooooooooh myyyyyyyyyyy

Namita: yesssssss

Namita: i loveeeeeeee to see you hard

Nicholas: and you will

Namita: and pulsating

Namita: waiting for a release

Nicholas: mmmhhmmmm

Namita: that would be soooo hot !!!

Nicholas: watching me cum all over your tits?

Namita: ohhh yesss

Namita: me tasting ur hard cock

Nicholas: that would be fun

Namita: ur cum

Namita: id be sooooo hungry for it

Nicholas: you're driving me crazy woman!!

Namita: cuz its only for me

Namita: hehe

Nicholas: just you

Nicholas: and only you

Namita: mmmmmmm yessss

Namita: you can hear me moaning ...as i take u in deep inside my mouth

Namita: sending vibrations all the way down ur beautiful cock

Nicholas: I'll have to be careful not to knock you over from the back pressure

Namita: making you crazyyy

Namita: hehehehe

Nicholas: sooo crazy

Nicholas: my god

Namita: its ok knock me over

Namita: im ok with it

Nicholas: good to know

Namita: no im all good for it

Namita: i would totally enjoy you ...every bit of you

Nicholas: and I you

Namita: do you like having ur balls played with

Nicholas: a little sure

Namita: do you get amazing sensations on it

Nicholas: hmmm it's more a "oh she's really got me by the balls" kind of feeling lol

Namita: hehehe

Namita: hahaa tooo funny !!!

Nicholas: more sensations when you play w the shaft n head

Namita: ohhhhhhhh i loveee that alright

Nicholas: sorry couldn't resist

Namita: right down to the base

Nicholas: yes that's the sweet spot

Namita: hehe that was funny !! very quick witted

Nicholas: thx

Namita: if i lick and suck there

Nicholas: one of the many features I have to offer

Namita: tasting you ...running my tongue in circles

Namita: right at the base

Namita: at the same time massaging ur hard cock in my hands

Namita: rubbing the tip of my thumb on ur head

Nicholas: that would get you a mouth full of pure Nicholas

Namita: heheeh

Namita: yesssssssss id loveeeeeeeeeeeeeee thatttttttt

Namita: drinking you up !!!!!!

Nicholas: mmmmhmmmm so would I!!

Namita: keeping my mouth on you as you shoot off inside of my mouth

Nicholas: ohhhhh yes

Namita: and then i swallow it

Namita: would you like that ?

Nicholas: feeling my every contraction

Namita: yesssssss

Namita: feeling you pump every drop

Nicholas: I want you to do whatever you're comfortable w

Namita: i would lovvve to please you

Namita: you can hear my moans of pleasure

Nicholas: I can't wait to reciprocate

Namita: im just getting u off like that ,,... expecting nothing in return for myself

Nicholas: that's soooo hot

Namita: just you ..and ur pleasure

Namita: and watching u cum ...cause i made you

Nicholas: I can almost feel your mouth on me

Namita: mmmmm all hot and wet on ur hard cock

Nicholas: mmmmhmmmm

Namita: running my tongue on the the tip of ur penis

Nicholas: that would be soooo awesome Namita

Namita: flicking it

Namita: then sucking on it

Nicholas: tell me you're playing w urself?

Namita: like my mouth just fits onto you

Namita: hehe

Namita: sort of

Namita: are you ?

Nicholas: me too

Namita: ohhh good

Nicholas: hard n no where to put it

Namita: i was on my back for a second and arching my back as if ur on top of me

Nicholas: oh how i'd love to burry it deep inside you right now

Nicholas: ooooo nice

Namita: mmmmmmmmmmmmm yesssssssssssssssss

Namita: ohh god nicholas !!!!!

Nicholas: well I'm pretty damn hard here n slippery

Namita: im quite wet here too

Nicholas: I can almost feel you

Namita: ohh god i loveee the pic ur sending me ... i can imagine

Nicholas: now I'm full on stroking it coz thats the only way it's going to go dwn

Namita: mmmmmmmmmmm nicholas

Namita: i just want it deep inside of me

Nicholas: all the talk about you going dwn has made me this hard

Namita: feel every inch

Nicholas: i just want to bee

Namita: mmmmmmm i kiss ur cock

Namita: run my tongue up and down

Namita: kiss the inside of ur thighs

Nicholas: mmmmm

Namita: run my tongue over there too

Nicholas: it feels so smooth n hard

Namita: and then take ur huge cock ...into my mouth

Nicholas: how I wish you were here helping

Namita: tasting ur precum

Namita: go down like ive been starving for this for a longgg time

Namita: i can hear ur moans

Nicholas: mmmhmmm

Namita: and trying to steady me

Namita: i hear hear you say ...ohhh god baby !!!

Nicholas: oh god yesss

Namita: and i keep going

Nicholas: yes please

Namita: you can feel the hotness of my mouth

Nicholas: i can

Namita: ur precum running and my saliva running down ur hard cock

Namita: and i slurp up every bit of it

Nicholas: yes making me so hot

Namita: laping it up

Namita: you want me sooo bad

Nicholas: yesss i do!!!!

Namita: both of us can see how pink ur cock is from being worked up ... it looks angry

Nicholas: i just want to fuck you till you scream for more

Namita: like it can destroy me at any given moment

Namita: mmmmmmmmmmmmm yesssssssssssss

Namita: ohhhhhhhhhhhh yes nicholas !!!!!!!!

Nicholas: omg!!! namita!!!! yes

Namita: you lay me on my side

Namita: and pull my panties aside

Nicholas: yesss

Namita: and push ur cock right inside of me

Nicholas: oh baby yessss

Namita: ur one hand on my breast

Namita: and the other in my panties playing with my clit

Namita: im arching into you

Nicholas: yes rubbing that hot swollen little clit

Namita: taking you in

Namita: and going wild like a cat

Nicholas: feeling you wither n squirm

Namita: i turn my head and kiss you

Namita: now we are connected from both ends

Nicholas: yes

Nicholas: i kiss u sooo deeply

Namita: i can see ur cock going in and out ...in and out

Namita: mmmmmmmmmmmmm yessssssssss

Namita: it feels sooooooo good

Nicholas: yes it feels sooooo goood!!!

Namita: i can feel every inch of you deep inside

Namita: and there is a lot of hot liquid escaping me

Nicholas: yessssss

Namita: running down my thigh

Nicholas: making me ride you faster n deeper

Namita: and you can feel the squirts against ur cock

Nicholas: yesss

Namita: mmmmmmmmmmmmm yessssssssss

Namita: im grabbing the sheets in front of me to steady myself

Namita: as u thrust me

Nicholas: oh cum for me namita

Nicholas: i want to feel u cum

Namita: ooooh god nicholas !!

Nicholas: cum all over me

Namita: ohhhhhhhhbaby

Nicholas: i'll make u cum

Namita: pleaseeeeeeee

Namita: omggg

Namita: mmmmmmmmmmmmmmmmmm

Nicholas: i'll rub ur clit and fuck you so hard you think ur head will come off

Namita: ommggg nicholas

Nicholas: pressing on ur clit n rubbing little circles till you pop for me

Namita: i can feel my pussy tightening around ur cock

Nicholas: mmmm yesss

Namita: tighter and tighter

Nicholas: which tells me ur ready to cum

Namita: closing in on you

Nicholas: so i fuck you faster

Namita: my breathing rapid and ragged

Nicholas: yess

Namita: mmmmmmmmmmmmmmm nicholas

Namita: u slam into me

Nicholas: omg i'm going to cum.... gonna explode inside you!!!

Namita: making me gasp

Namita: im milking ur cock

Nicholas: you never new sex could be sooooo great

Namita: mmmmmmmmmmmm yesssssssss

Namita: like we were made for each other

Nicholas: oh my god yes

Namita: ohhhh baby im still cumming!!

Nicholas: yessss

Namita: mmmmmmmmmmmm

Nicholas: ride it out.... ride my cock

Namita: ohhhhhhhhhhh nicholas

Nicholas: my god Namita wow

Namita: ommg

Nicholas: my god it's almost 10 to 6

Namita: ohhh fuck

Nicholas: my landlord is just up... I can hear him up stairs

Nicholas: he leaves at 7

Namita: ohhh nooo were u noisy ?

Nicholas: this is a new record

Nicholas: no no

Namita: lol yesss

Nicholas: might have to get an energy drink for tmw er today lol

Nicholas: you are awesome!!!! you know that

Namita: lol ... sorry i was still cumming

Nicholas: no need to apologize

Nicholas: esp for that

Namita: hehe thanks

Namita: did u cum for me?

Nicholas: oh yes

Namita: wowww i would have lapped that up

Namita: and cleaned u off

Nicholas: mmmhmmmm

Namita: then kiss you

Nicholas: you'll get your chance hehe

Namita: hehe

Nicholas: mmhmmm

Namita: would u be ok with that

Nicholas: yup

Namita: good

Namita: you should get some sleep nic

Nicholas: was just thinking that

Namita: hehe

Nicholas: you too

Namita: you must be tired and spent

Nicholas: was thinking we should

Nicholas: yup

Nicholas: haven't been up this late in a long long time

Namita: hehe i hope i didnt overwork you

Nicholas: nah

Nicholas: I can handle it

Namita: ok .... glad

Nicholas: I'll look for you after work tmw?

Namita: yess will be around

Namita: for sure

Nicholas: cool

Nicholas: gnight or should I say gmorning Namita n thx for tonight

Nicholas: oh how i love talking w you

Namita: ohh baby yesss .. i enjoyed every min of it

Nicholas: cool

Nicholas: enjoy ur day tmw n I hope you feel better

Namita: thnx

Namita: goodnite

Nicholas: night 🙂

Namita: 🙂

End Time: 5:58 AM

Chapter 27 November 24 Part 1

Start Time: 12:03 AM

Nicholas: hello there!!

Namita: heyyyyyyyyyyyy

Namita: can u give me a sec

Nicholas: hey you!!

Nicholas: sure can

Namita: im just changing into my ..ahem .... then crawling into bed

Nicholas: mmmm nice

Namita: hehe one sec ok

Nicholas: still hanging on lol

Namita: ok im all urs now

Nicholas: ooo i like the sound of that!!

Namita: hehe

Namita: is this colour bad for ur eyes

Nicholas: I just finished my snack so it worked for everyone lol

Nicholas: nope

Nicholas: is that the pink?

Namita: ohhh what did you have ?

Namita: yes s pink

Nicholas: bowl of Special K almond

Nicholas: looks more like purple

Namita: ohhh sounds good !

Namita: yeah it does

Nicholas: it is... it's funny how I picked it up the first time

Namita: lets go with navy here

Nicholas: oooo GO Navy!!

Namita: picked what up ? the special K

Namita: hehe

Nicholas: yup

Nicholas: is kind of a long story in type

Nicholas: do you still want to hear it?

Nicholas: well not too long but still

Namita: sure if ur up to it

Nicholas: of course

Nicholas: okay was at my moms n she meant to pick up the original special K

Namita: ohhh yess

Nicholas: but when I opened it it turned out to be the Almond kind

Namita: didnt it say on the box ? with almonds ?

Nicholas: so jump to me back over here grocery shopping

Nicholas: she didn't really look she just picked it up

Namita: ohhhh ok

Nicholas: so I reached for the strawberry special K as I usually buy

Namita: uh huh

Nicholas: went to have my before bed snack of Special K Berries and I inadvertently picked up the almond kind by mistake

Nicholas: so now I've been eating it since

Namita: hehehe

Namita: so you mean you never returned it ?

Nicholas: not a really exciting story in type

Nicholas: oh I wouldn't try to return food

Nicholas: turned out to be quite good

Namita: hehehe so now ur stuck with almonds

Nicholas: that was a while ago now

Namita: ohh well ..then thats good !!

Nicholas: I switch it up now n again

Namita: youre liking it now

Nicholas: it was good the first time I tried it so I wasn't disappointed

Nicholas: did the weather clear up dwn there?

Namita: ohh good !!

Namita: sort of ...but it has been raining on and off

Namita: what about over there?

Nicholas: it stopped raining about half way through my shift n actually warmed up a little

Nicholas: did you get my reply email?

Namita: ohhh ...hehe yesss i did get ur email ...im sure it was a nice surprise for you ...also i was concerned if you got enough rest and sleep

Nicholas: it was sooo nice to read when I sat dwn for my break

Namita: anddddddddddddd you didnt tell me you had a doctors appointment !!!!!!!!

Nicholas: I didn't want to stop talking w you

Namita: geeeeez i felt like and idiot

Nicholas: I'll catch up on my sleep on the weekend

Namita: hehee

Nicholas: oh please don't

Namita: yesss well that too ...but i dont want you to not have ur rest

Namita: i was worried

Namita: hehe

Nicholas: lol it was a quick power nap then off to the Dr then home to bed again

Namita: is everything ok

Nicholas: I'm a big boy so not to worry but thx for saying it

Namita: is ur doctor nearby

Nicholas: yup was just the annual cardiologist appointment

Namita: ohh i see

Nicholas: my GP is in Langley

Namita: wow of all days i keep you up all nite on

Namita: hehe

Nicholas: I don't see the Dr very often

Namita: thats a long ways for a doctor GP

Nicholas: it is but he's really good

Namita: mine is ... in coquitlam

Nicholas: oh geeze that far too

Namita: in the plaza medical ..on north road

Namita: hehe

Nicholas: makes sense though as you grew up in this area

Namita: he has been my gp since i was 8

Nicholas: wow how you've changed

Namita: hehehehe

Nicholas: have you ever thought of living in this area again?

Namita: would loveee to

Namita: i always loved that area

Nicholas: it is nice... I like it... as we've said it's very central to pretty much everything

Namita: yess very true

Namita: back in the old days if i said i live in coquitlam

Namita: then ppl would roll their eyes saying omg that is too far !!!

Nicholas: lol

Nicholas: now Maple ridge is too far, for me anyway

Namita: now its like if you say you live in mission or maple ridge that is tooo far

Namita: hahahahhaha

Nicholas: yup

Namita: we said the same thing

Nicholas: yes we did

Nicholas: like minds yet again

Nicholas: I smiled a few times today thinking about you

Namita: i wasnt even looking what u wrote cuz i have to see my keys when i type

Nicholas: me too

Namita: hehehe

Namita: what did you smile at ?

Nicholas: the thought of you

Namita: anything in particular

Nicholas: and how excited I am to talk w you and one day see you

Namita: aweee

Nicholas: just how you seem to fit into my life

Namita: hehe ...and in many other ways too

Nicholas: yes

Namita: hehe

Nicholas: I'm a little apprehensive to tell ppl we met on LL coz I don't want them to be disappointed if they don't meet someone really awesome like I did

Nicholas: side note; I think this is the first time you've been on before me

Namita: yeah they would be thinking he got the best one ...so what are my chances now !!

Namita: lol

Namita: hehe really ??

Nicholas: lol you said it

Nicholas: I think so

Namita: hehe too funny

Namita: ok random now

Nicholas: okay

Nicholas: I can keep up w random

Namita: question ...do you have a middle name ?

Nicholas: why yes I do.... Roy... its my grampa's name

Namita: ohhh ok

Nicholas: do you?

Namita: mine Rainya

Nicholas: I love how exotic Namita Rainya Puranjay sounds

Nicholas: wow now that's cool

Namita: both of us now have an R name

Nicholas: oh my god didn't see that

Namita: like the queen rainya of jordon ...if you head of it ...thats how you pronounce it

Nicholas: NRT and NRP cool

Namita: hehehe

Namita: i almost laughed when you said Roy

Nicholas: haven't heard of it till now?

Namita: cuz my middle name starts with R

Nicholas: you did?!

Namita: google it

Nicholas: ah

Nicholas: and look under wikipedia you mean?

Namita: sure i guess

Namita: i never googled her before

Namita: but i know of her

Nicholas: ooooooh her lol I thought you meant Roy lol duh

Namita: nooooooooooooo

Namita: hehehhee

Namita: omg you really are sleep deprived !!

Nicholas: may be lol

Namita: google jordans queen

Nicholas: lol yah I got it now

Namita: go to images

Nicholas: im there... I've see her before

Nicholas: she's their queen?

Namita: yes so now you know whom im talking about

Namita: yes she is

Nicholas: I do

Nicholas: wow she looks too young to be a queen

Nicholas: she looks like a miss america contestant

Namita: yeah she looks young ... but i think she is about our age

Namita: but her husband looks old

Nicholas: oh well she is young then lol

Nicholas: so she married into royalty?

Namita: yes

Nicholas: ah that makes more sense

Namita: what ?

Nicholas: that she's the queen of a country.... she looks too young

Namita: hehe i think she has 4 kids too if im not mistaken

Nicholas: oh yes the hubby looks very old

Nicholas: cool

Namita: hehee

Namita: yesss of course he has to be old

Namita: as long as they have a good looking wife

Nicholas: and loaded or royalty to land a wife that looks like her lol

Namita: hehehe

Nicholas: I'd rather look at my photo's of Princess Namita

Namita: anyways i wast named after her ...just that the name is same just spelt a lil differently

Namita: hehe aweeeeeee im blushing

Nicholas: I see

Nicholas: I'll stroke your ego anytime my dear

Namita: lol

Nicholas: among other things hehe

Namita: thanks ... no im not like that ... high on myself

Namita: heheh nice one

Nicholas: I know ur not... that's another great quality you have

Namita: ohh thanks nicholas

Namita: that soo nice of you to say

Nicholas: but I'll keep telling you how important you are to me and how beautiful you are

Nicholas: anytime

Namita: hehe... if you do ...i kinda get shy about it

Nicholas: hehe okay well I wont make a big deal about it.... I'll be subtle

Namita: hehe ok

Nicholas: maybe a wink or a smile

Nicholas: or a touch

Namita: ohhh my

Namita: if u wink ...ur going to get a shy smile too

Nicholas: cool

Namita: thats one of my habits

Namita: sometimes strangers wink ...or visitors of patients

Nicholas: or that "up to no good smile"?

Namita: and i totally shy away

Namita: yes i loveeeee those ...cuz it keeps me guessing

Nicholas: I find winking from strangers to be, well, strange

Namita: yes true ... very unexpected

Nicholas: what did you get up to today?

Namita: have women done that to you ?

Nicholas: god no

Nicholas: I don't seem to attract that kind of attention

Namita: not much ..... im taking it easy ...my voice is hoarse and barely audible

Nicholas: ah

Namita: hehe really ?

Namita: have you ever had a bad date ?

Nicholas: I do see women stealing looks though... the girls esp Isabel sees them too

Namita: hahahah

Namita: what do they say ? ur girls

Nicholas: hmm bad date?.... I don't date a lot to really have any that stand out

Namita: hell i would steal a look from under my eye lashes

Nicholas: Isabel doesn't say anything she just looks straight at me to see if I noticed.... which I do and then we smile at each other

Nicholas: one time when the 3 of us were on the ferry

Namita: that is absolutely cute !!

Namita: uh huh

Namita: well you are a handsome hotness !!! ... hehee

Nicholas: I got up to put something in the garbage and when I sat back dwn Isabel said that a young woman a few seat and rows away saw me stand up

Namita: hehe and ??

Nicholas: and watched me go from my seat to the garbage then back to my seat

Namita: hehehehe that is hilarious !!

Nicholas: all I could do was smile... she didn't say anything but I think she thought it was pretty cool

Namita: but i wouldnt blame the woman !!

Nicholas: thx for that 😊 😊

Namita: hehe

Namita: ur welcome

Namita: id do the same thing if i was there ...id drop everything and watch you get up and do ur thing

Namita: and never take my eyes off you

Nicholas: hehe geeze now I'm blushing

Namita: hehehe

Namita: im sure my mouth would be on the floor

Nicholas: I find it funny when I meet the moms of the girls friends the first time.... a look of "oh I get it now"

Nicholas: hehe thx

Nicholas: well I would certainly notice you too

Nicholas: one time a friend of the ex, her mom met me and said something like "oh so there is a dad, was starting to wonder how she had kids"

Namita: hehehehe

Nicholas: or had kids w/o a dad around

Nicholas: yah

Namita: wowww for ppl to say that !!

Namita: do u have a pic of her ?

Namita: i know stupid question

Namita: im just wondering what she looks like

Nicholas: not stupid

Nicholas: no I don't

Nicholas: okay random... what did you change into?

Nicholas: a butterfly?

Namita: what do u mean ?

Nicholas: you changed into your... ahem.... so what did you change into?

Namita: hehehehehe

Namita: im wearing a black nightie

Nicholas: mmmmm black nightie.... satin I suppose?

Namita: yes ...with a lil black lace detailing

Nicholas: I don't know why I torture myself like this

Namita: lol

Namita: i know if i was near you with that on ...it would be on the floor

Nicholas: ur photo's are enf to drive my mad yet I continue to imagine you in bed barely clothed

Namita: hehehe

Nicholas: hehe you know it!!

Namita: feeling me up ?

Nicholas: rubbing my body over yours

Namita: id loveeeeeeeee to have you all over me

Nicholas: one day… or night… or both

Namita: and id be all over you ...rubbing myself all over you

Namita: my scent

Namita: so you remember when u go to work

Namita: hehe

Nicholas: mmmm absolute torture

Namita: im bad !!

Namita: hehe

Nicholas: yes you are

Namita: hehe

Nicholas: I'd love to smell you on me even when we're apart

Namita: mmmmmmmm yesssssssss me too !!!

Nicholas: I've imagined you wearing my clothes like my sweaters

Namita: yesss or ur shirts

Nicholas: or my Canucks jersey and nothing else

Namita: or tshirts

Nicholas: yes

Namita: ohh yesss

Nicholas: w that up to no good look mmm mmm

Namita: id wear ur canucks jersey with nothing else on ...and sit beside you to help cheer them on

Nicholas: seeing how big my sweater looks on you

Namita: and have you wondering what im doing

Nicholas: hehe you ARe bad!!

Namita: hehe

Namita: then id say to you ...WHAT ???

Nicholas: getting my attention is what you'd be doing

Namita: and eat ur popcorn

Nicholas: lol

Namita: hehe

Nicholas: bad bad bad lol

Namita: with a ponytail too

Nicholas: mmmmm

Namita: bat my eyelashes at you while ur trying to watch the game

Namita: are you into movember ???

Namita: lol

Nicholas: nope... lol not into body hair

Nicholas: thought about growing one but was too much work

Nicholas: or facial hair

Namita: hehe good cuz that would be the only thing to deter me to distract you from ur game

Namita: ladies dont like it

Nicholas: too 70's looking eeewwww

Namita: but we know how to get back

Namita: yessss the pornstache

Namita: hehe

Namita: eweee

Nicholas: how do you get back?

Namita: hehe we ..ahem ... we dont shave either

Namita: down there

Nicholas: that's what I thought

Namita: lol

Nicholas: no hair for me

Nicholas: just on your head though

Namita: hehe phewwww

Namita: yes just on my head

Nicholas: ANd I do love your hair

Namita: you do ?

Nicholas: you are such a nice little package.... if you don't mind me referring to you as a package?

Nicholas: sure do

Namita: no not at all

Namita: what do u like about it ?

Nicholas: all your qualities are bundled into a package.... I'll have one Namita package to go please

Nicholas: the CUrls!!

Namita: hehe

Nicholas: how wavy it is

Namita: you love the curls ?

Namita: hehe

Nicholas: yup

Namita: awee thanks

Nicholas: it curls naturally yes? and you straighten when you feel like it

Namita: yes it is naturally curly or wavy ... and sometimes i blow dry it straight tooo

Nicholas: thats what I thought

Namita: im glad i can be versatile with my hair ....my other sisters dont have that

Namita: and it is silky smooth

Nicholas: you are very versatile

Namita: awee thx

Nicholas: mmmmm can't wait to run my finger through it

Nicholas: from your scalp to the very end

Namita: OoOOoOoOOoo im going to purr if u do that ...hehhe

Nicholas: and gently massage my fingers into your scalp

Namita: ohhhhhhh myyyyyyy nicholas

Nicholas: Id love sitting watching a movie or something and playing w your hair

Namita: would you really ??

Nicholas: as I've said I'm not usually still... I usually have a hand moving on your body somewhere

Nicholas: yes

Namita: heheh cool !!!!!!!!

Nicholas: I don't have hair so it's nice to play esp when I know you like it so much

Namita: even if its under my shirt ...or ahem ur canucks jersey ???

Namita: i meant ur hand

Namita: yes i would loveeeee it if u played with my hair

Namita: smelling it ...will drive u wild ?

Nicholas: I'm sure it will

Namita: i always make sure my hair smells nice

Nicholas: if it's possible to be any more wild than I already am for you

Namita: hehehe

Nicholas: yes you've said that.... I love that you take such good care of yourself

Nicholas: that was part of my wish too

Namita: hehe thx

Namita: heres a scenario for you

Nicholas: k

Namita: kinda off topic

Nicholas: sokay

Namita: say if we were out together ... and some other guy smiled at me ....or winked ..or just watched me ...what would u do ? are u ok with it ?

Nicholas: totally fine

Nicholas: I'm comfortable w myself and you know that we're together

Namita: yessss and you would know that from me

Nicholas: I say let them look all they want coz they'll never get to know you the way I do and will hehe

Namita: ok ..so what if ...a guy started making advances at me now

Namita: hehe good one

Namita: and soooo true

Nicholas: he wouldn't... I have a this thing, that I sometimes intimidate other guys... I don't know why

Namita: really ??? good !!!!!

Nicholas: Tony n I have seen it... maybe it's because I'm quiet and watch my surroundings

Namita: ive been in a situation where ive been out with a guy ..and he didnt do anything or stand up for me ..despite me trying to keep the other guy at bay

Nicholas: Tony n I have a good laugh about it most times

Namita: WOw im glad to hear that you have that aura !!

Nicholas: really?! well that wont happen w me

Namita: ok good

Nicholas: you're in good hands

Namita: that was long time ago ...and it wasnt pleasant for me ...needless to say that was the last for him that day

Namita: he laughed cuz he thought it was funny

Nicholas: I bet it wasn't nice... bad form on both of them

Nicholas: very bad form

Nicholas: when we're out ppl will know that we esp you are not to be messed with.... we'll be far too confident to have losers like that approach you like that

Namita: yesss i really hate these sore losers

Nicholas: it's too bad you've had to experience that

Namita: im glad to know that u have a no mess with me aura

Namita: yes .. i was young too

Nicholas: that i do

Namita: and didnt know how to handle the situation

Nicholas: was the guy you were w big? little? skinny? white?

Namita: i have had bad dates ...like one time dates

Namita: and probably the same sore losers too

Namita: he was white ...medium build

Namita: 5 '10"

Nicholas: yah I'm not sure where some guys seem to think that just because you take a woman out, you get to sleep w her

Namita: ohhhhh ive had close calls on that

Namita: thank god i was able to get out of them

Nicholas: or where along the way women became property or that they're just here to satisfy our needs.... I don't get it

Nicholas: yes... that must be difficult for women

Namita: yess there are men like that out there still ...and no wonder they are single

Nicholas: yesss

Nicholas: and they have no idea why either

Namita: yesss well to them it is a game...they will never get it

Nicholas: I've always been respectful of women n treated them as equals ... that's my mom's doing.... and my dad was never disrespectful to women either.... so I had 2 good role models on that front

Namita: ohh good for your parents !! on that !!

Nicholas: I've always treated women and men as I want to be treated

Namita: respectful men ..in my eyes are sexy

Namita: i believe in chivalry too

Nicholas: me tooooo

Namita: although i do my part too

Namita: hehe

Nicholas: always polite and respectful.... I open doors for my partner

Namita: that is super sexy to me nicholas !!

Namita: yesssssss

Nicholas: oh side note

Namita: yes ?

Nicholas: when I left the Dr's office

Namita: yes

Nicholas: I saw an old woman trying to step up onto the sidewalk.... so I headed over and asked if she wanted help, which she did n I helped her onto the sidewalk

Nicholas: was my good deed for the day

Namita: aweeeeeeeeeeee nicholas that is sooooo sweet !!

Namita: muahhhhhhh !!!

Nicholas: A long time ago when I lived dwntwn I helped an old lady across the street

Namita: i open doors for men too

Nicholas: cool

Namita: uh huh

Namita: and i shut them on ppl who are on their cellphones

Nicholas: I also hold it open and look to see if anyone is coming

Namita: hehe

Nicholas: lol

Nicholas: drives me crazy seeing ppl so tuned out to their surroundings

Namita: sometimes i let moms in grocery lineups go ahead of me if they have a crying baby or child

Namita: omg yesss

Nicholas: so are you still looking at coming back in early Dec? and how is your uncle doing?

Namita: it is my pet peeve to see ppl on the cell and coming out of stores and im driving in parking lot ...and these guys come right of the store and in front of my car without looking both ways !!!!

Nicholas: I helped a woman to her car w her groceries once... she would have left her cart n made 2 trips so I offered... she was a little surprised at first then accepted

Namita: he is doing ok

Namita: he is out of icu

Nicholas: OMG!! I hate it when ppl just cross the street n don't look

Namita: yes i always look both ways !!!

Namita: even teach my niece and nephew that !!

Nicholas: that's good he's out of ICU.... must be all the positive wave and having loving family close by

Namita: its one of my peeve

Namita: do u have others ?

Namita: hehehe yess

Nicholas: when an emerg vehicle comes up behind you while you're driving..... you pull over to let it by ANd the ppl behind you race out and not let you back into ur spot

Namita: cell phone and driving is still a big one for me

Namita: yessssssssssss hate that !!!!!!!!

Namita: or they still cross an intersection !!!!!!!

Nicholas: yah.. hard to imagine I use to do it too.... not all the time but when the phone rang I'd answer it

Namita: knowing an ambulance is coming

Namita: yes me too ...but most times i tried pulling over

Nicholas: so are you still looking at coming back in early Dec?

Nicholas: me too

Namita: one of mine is ...when ur in an elevator ...and it stops on ur floor

Namita: the door opens ...and the ppl outside starts barreling in ..not letting you exit !!!

Namita: yes i am

Nicholas: like on the skytrain.. hate that

Namita: im might come back with mom and dad ... but they are still deciding too when to come back

Namita: theyre looking at dates

Namita: ohh yess skytrain too

Nicholas: I don't use the word hate very often, I find it very harsh but those things I hate

Namita: ohhh it bother me sooo much

Namita: sometimes i say something too

Nicholas: silly question but you'll let me know when I can see you, yes?

Namita: yessssssss of course !!!

Namita: hehe

Nicholas: I say your welcome to ppl when I hold the door for them and they haven't said thank you

Nicholas: lol I knew you would er will

Namita: hehe yess thats good one too

Nicholas: the girls think it's funny when I do or say things like that

Namita: hehe im sure they giggle

Namita: i would

Nicholas: I teach them to be aware of their surrounding

Namita: where do i meet on you height wise ?

Nicholas: hang on n I'll check again

Namita: hehehe

Namita: am i making you get up ?? sooo sorry

Nicholas: sokay I needed the stretch

Namita: ohh ok

Nicholas: 5' 7" comes up to my mouth

Namita: oOOOOooOOoooOOoooo

Namita: niceeeeeeeeeee

Nicholas: yup just right

Namita: hehehe

Nicholas: another part of my wish.... 5' 7" or taller

Nicholas: I think 5 7 is prefect

Namita: yess otherwise its a long wayyy down for you

Nicholas: you'll fit perfectly into me

Namita: mmmmmmmmmmmm like the sounds of that

Nicholas: it is... I've dated shorter women n its not great

Namita: i bet !!

Nicholas: you'll be just right... I wont have to squat to reach you n you wont have to stand on your tip toes

Namita: hehe ... too funny

Namita: i can stand on ur feet to reach you perfectly

Namita: and we can walk around like that in ur place

Nicholas: I still can't believe sometimes you're real... sorry just another reality moment

Namita: hehehe no worries

Nicholas: lol

Namita: we can hold on to each other like that

Namita: hehe

Nicholas: I think that's when I smile the biggest

Namita: when ?

Namita: hehe

Nicholas: when the reality of you sinks in a little more

Nicholas: happens now n again

Namita: ahhhhhhhhhhh i see ..hehe

Nicholas: was all the time for the first week lol

Nicholas: its still just as strong

Namita: hehe

Nicholas: but I can let it settle easier now

Namita: i would have loved to see ur first reaction when you saw my pics

Nicholas: lol you'd have laughed I bet

Namita: thats why i didnt send them in an email

Namita: really??

Nicholas: at my reaction sure... coz you're so modest... I like that

Namita: hehe

Namita: can u describe to me ur reaction ?

Nicholas: I often wonder what kind of reaction women have when they see me

Nicholas: well

Namita: hehe ... hmmmm well you are pretty cute !!

Namita: HAWT !!

Namita: mine was ... "who the hell is that" !!!?

Namita: OMG look at his dimples

Namita: me coming closer to the LL screen

Nicholas: cupping my hand over my mouth n saying "oh my f**king god are you serious?! you've got to be sh**ting me!"

Namita: and squinting

Nicholas: hehe

Namita: hhehheehe really?

Nicholas: I do remember shaking and trying to compose myself and my thoughts

Namita: ive always found bald men sexyyy

Nicholas: you've said that

Namita: heheheheh im still laughing here

Nicholas: would you have approached me if I hadn't have messaged you first?

Namita: yesss im always gravitated to them

Namita: yess eventually

Namita: maybe in a couple of days when i was off

Nicholas: I took me a few months to decide if I had a nice shaped head to pull it off

Namita: i had already hot listed you

Namita: the first time

Namita: first time i mean

Nicholas: cool hot list nice hehe

Namita: so i could go back and google

Nicholas: lol

Namita: ohhh yessss babyyyy u were hot listed !!!

Nicholas: NOw you're being silly

Namita: noooooooooo not kidding !!

Nicholas: blushing again

Namita: i was at work a day later

Namita: and on my break i logged onto LL

Namita: and went to my hotlist .... and looked at ur pic again

Nicholas: I wanted to message you but I knew you were at work n I didn't want to pester you or seem needy

Namita: admiring ur eyes

Namita: hehe

Nicholas: awe shucks thx

Namita: i thought well he isnt messaging me ...so he is not all too taken by my profile

Namita: maybe he is dwelling on it mulling it over

Nicholas: I waited all weekend n kept thinking "please let her be hot"

Namita: hmmm i guess i will find out by the weekend

Nicholas: I was sooooo taken by ur profile!!

Namita: hehehe

Namita: really ??

Nicholas: as I said that's why I messaged you coz it was soooo cool n creative

Namita: that is tooo funny

Nicholas: and different

Namita: awee thanks

Namita: hehe

Nicholas: ANd I was so taken back by your photo's that I completely forgot to tell you my name... I remember telling you that in one of my replies too

Namita: hehe i think i remember ...but i purposely signed by ~N~ ...to keep u guessing what my name would be

Nicholas: I liked reading your words in your replies too

Namita: really ??

Nicholas: yes you did

Nicholas: I did

Namita: i dont know what i said in my other emails

Namita: lol

Nicholas: i was captivated... yes that's the right word

Nicholas: lol I'll show you one day

Namita: aweeeeeeeeeee really !!?

Namita: ok

Nicholas: I was

Nicholas: and then to see you... wow!!!!

Nicholas: still catch myself daydreaming of you

Namita: were you sitting in ur recliner ?

Nicholas: I remember waking up the next morning and thinking how cool it would be to wake next to you and in our next convo you said something similar, like you'd been reading my mind

Nicholas: I am

Nicholas: oh no not then

Nicholas: was sitting at the counter where I usually put the laptop

Nicholas: mmmm I have that photo on my screen

Nicholas: I did a little shuffling and fit the new ones on

Namita: hehe i see we had like minds wayyy early on !!!!

Nicholas: yes we did

Namita: this one ?

Namita: hehe

Nicholas: yup

Namita: you must be a collage expert by now

Namita: hehhee

Nicholas: I was amazed to find out we were thinking the same things early on

Namita: hehehe yesss

Nicholas: lol just when it comes to your pics

Nicholas: did you manage to find my fav pic yet?

Nicholas: er the other fav

Namita: ohhh nooo

Namita: i didnt even look today

Nicholas: its okay

Nicholas: all in due time

Namita: i hope i didnt delete it accidently

Nicholas: me tooo don't say that!!

Namita: its in my main pc though at home

Namita: hehe

Nicholas: ah... you have a lap top and home computer then

Namita: yes

Nicholas: I just have a laptop.... well I do have a pc but it's old n slow n I don't use it

Namita: i like to do stuff while im in bed ...like talk to you

Namita: so laptop is handy

Nicholas: I like the sound of that

Namita: hehe

Nicholas: i can be fairly handy in bed too lol

Namita: not nothing naughty !!!

Namita: hehe

Namita: with my laptop

Nicholas: I got it

Namita: do you ?

Namita: lol

Nicholas: I usually just sleep in bed n well play too

Namita: with ur laptop?

Nicholas: noooo

Nicholas: not big on watching TV in bed or eating

Namita: you mean play play ?

Namita: no me either

Nicholas: I mean having sex er making love

Namita: using ur laptop?

Namita: hehe

Nicholas: my thoughts at this moment

Nicholas: no silly

Namita: lol

Namita: ohh come on !!!

Nicholas: having sex is just doing the act w someone.... and making love is sharing yourself physically and emotionally w someone you care a lot about

Namita: pfttttttttt !!! 😜

Namita: yessssssssss i totally agree on that one !!!

Nicholas: nope... the only time I was in bed w the laptop was when Tony was here n you n I were talking

Namita: and i prefer the latter

Nicholas: me too

Namita: hmmmmmmmmmm

Nicholas: wow quarter to 3.. how are you holding up?

Namita: yes im ok ..are you ? just let me know if u need to head off

Nicholas: I'm okay for a little while longer

Namita: can i ask you a personal question

Nicholas: so early Dec eh? is that around the first or is that like the first full week in Dec?

Nicholas: you can

Namita: what turns you on sexually ...as in aides ...visual ...or feel

Nicholas: anything

Nicholas: hmmm...... what gets that tingly feeling started

Namita: are u an adventurous type ?

Nicholas: I'm thinking n trying to put it into words

Nicholas: yes to a degree

Namita: what would it be ?

Namita: if i may ask ?

Nicholas: I'm pretty much ready to go anytime

Namita: we are thinking around the dec 10 timeline

Namita: yesss

Namita: but what would make u adventurous sexually?

Namita: there is no wrong or right answer here... im good with ur answers

Namita: or you could tell me what ur not into

Namita: or not into

Namita: if thats easier

Nicholas: being w someone I'm attracted to.... how she touches me and what she says... when she tells me what turns her on .... and what she wants to do w me and to me.... when she's as into me as I'm into her and she tells me so

Namita: ohhhh you will knowww !!!

Nicholas: I like it outside

Namita: Like the moment you walk into the door after work .... i will come up to you ..give you a hug and kiss

Nicholas: that'd do it!!

Namita: and tell u im going to eat you up

Namita: and undress you right there and then

Namita: you would do it outside ?

Nicholas: yup

Namita: heres what im not into

Nicholas: okay

Namita: swinging

Namita: not that ive done it

Namita: uh ohhh

Namita: is that one of ur good ones ??

Nicholas: mmmm not really into seeing or knowing you're w someone else

Namita: yesss good

Nicholas: the idea of it is cool but to actually do it not too sure

Namita: thats out of the way !! PHEWW

Namita: hehehe

Namita: what would be cool nicholas ...just ur take on it

Nicholas: when I'm w someone I'm WITH her and only her

Namita: not judging you by any means

Nicholas: didn't think so

Namita: hehe noooooooo

Namita: im curious if anything

Namita: whats in ur mind

Nicholas: have to admit my heart jumped a little when you said swinging and not the good jump

Namita: ohhhh you thought im into swinging ??

Nicholas: so you're saying you'd want to swing or no?

Nicholas: yes

Namita: NOoooooo

Nicholas: okay

Nicholas: gOOD

Namita: im NOT into swinging

Nicholas: GOOD me either

Namita: isnt that what i said ?

Nicholas: I want you n only you

Namita: did i type it wrong

Namita: heheh

Namita: yes im a one woman man!!!

Nicholas: I wasn't sure, I just needed the clarification

Nicholas: good

Namita: ohhh good god !! hehehheeh

Namita: Noooooooo !!

Namita: hehehhehehehehehhehehe

Nicholas: yah you typed "here's what I'm into... swinging"

Nicholas: I was like WHAT!!

Namita: no wonder there was a pause from you !!!

Nicholas: lol

Namita: OMFG !!!!!!!!!!!

Nicholas: its all good now

Namita: i did !!!!!!!!!!!!!!

Namita: OMG

Namita: thats not what i meant !!!!!!!!

Nicholas: its clear now

Namita: hehehe im soo sorry to give u a surprise !!!

Namita: like that

Nicholas: its okay I'm good now

Namita: i hope ur smiling or laughing

Nicholas: I am

Nicholas: not to worry

Namita: i feel like a dork !!!

Namita: hehe

Namita: no im definitely not into that

Nicholas: was a little stunned there for a sec but I'm good now

Nicholas: oh please don't

Namita: like i said im a one woman man!!!

Nicholas: It's all good

Namita: i would never ever even think about cheating on my spouse or bf

Namita: its just not me

Nicholas: those situations can be fun to fantasize about but I think they are best left as a fantasy

Namita: yesss true !!!

Nicholas: me either

Nicholas: I don't know if it's healthy for a relationship or not.... I just know that it would make me sick to my stomach to see you w someone else... just the though makes me queazy

Namita: ohh god ... i cant do something like that !!! I know how i would feel if i was in the position and ur with someone else

Nicholas: it's a lot like a 3way... fun to think about but way too strange... and once it's done you cant take it back

Namita: id be sick too

Namita: yesss trueee

Nicholas: you are all I need

Namita: there is no fun in that

Namita: aweeeeeeee nicholas !!!!

Nicholas: I'm much to involved w the woman I'm with to think about another one

Namita: yesss all i need is you too ...one good man ...who knows what he is doing

Nicholas: the woman meaning you

Namita: hehe good !!

Nicholas: yes

Namita: i have eyes only for you

Namita: ive always been that way

Nicholas: well I think I fit the bill of "one good man" very well but I can be a little bias

Nicholas: lol

Nicholas: me too

Namita: hehe ..really ?? how so ??

Nicholas: I know what monogamous means

Nicholas: the one good man part?

Namita: heheh yessss

Nicholas: I know how I am and am pretty aware of myself and how I think and my values I possess... I don't objectify women and I treat them as equals... so yah

I'm a good man and the woman I end up with is very lucky to have me.... end rant lol...

Nicholas: hope that doesn't come off conceded

Nicholas: but I like me and once you know me I think you'll agree

Namita: i feel i have good values too that reflect both my indian heritage and the canadian culture as well. Indian women are well versed to take care of their husbands

Nicholas: or know me better

Namita: no it doesnt sound conceded at all

Nicholas: good

Namita: yesss i already have a good feeling

Nicholas: a mutually respectful relationship has no limits and I think that's where we're headed n I'm so very excited at the possibility of a future with you Namita

Namita: aweeee nicholas ... yess me too ... every relationship is based on respect ,trust, love and sooo much more

Nicholas: we set out to find someone who compliments our lives and I think we succeeded

Namita: and i know we have shared some of it already

Nicholas: yes we have.... it still takes me back at times

Namita: hehe

Namita: i loveeee everything about you so far

Nicholas: the first time you mentioned just looking at nature and taking it in that's when I knew you were someone special

Namita: omg really ??

Nicholas: and i love everything about you too Namita

Namita: wowwowowowwwww

Namita: ive always been like that ..i admire the lil things

Namita: whether is a lil ant crawling away ...or a snow peaked mountain

Namita: to the trees

Nicholas: that's when I knew you were someone that sees the world the way I do.. you're the first person I've met that does

Namita: wow really ..im humbled

Namita: now

Namita: ive always appreciated the things around me ...in awe of things

Nicholas: ANd sees me for who I am... when you said you saw that sparkle in me that was a big one too

Nicholas: me too

Namita: and maybe thats why im single ...cuz im in my own lil world

Namita: heheheh i still see it !!

Nicholas: omg couldn't have said it better and thought that same thing too

Namita: hehe really

Namita: my mom always tells me ... when i was a baby ...she would put me in the yard while she be busy doing stuff near me ...and i was just sitting up by then ...and id be in awe of the grass... touching it and looking at it

Namita: ive always been detail orientated

Nicholas: I'm still like that

Namita: hehe

Nicholas: OMG me too

Namita: hehe see bang on

Nicholas: almost a perfectionist

Namita: i loveee the smell of the grass

Namita: when i used to walk to school ...in grade one

Nicholas: but very detail oriented

Namita: i remember stopping and literally smelling the neighbors roses everyday

Namita: and then skip along

Nicholas: cool

Namita: and i still do

Namita: in my own garden i look at spiders closely

Nicholas: n watch as it builds a new web

Namita: yesss

Nicholas: n how the web just comes out of it n it never stops

Namita: yesssss exactly!!

Namita: i loveee to watch the lil birds coming in to find food

Nicholas: or how the rain water runs away in little streams down the leaves on the bushes

Namita: i love to watch a squirrel at the side of the road or cross my fence

Namita: yessssssssssss that too ...the rain water

Namita: i loveee how when im driving and it is pelting rain ..i turn off my radio to listen to it

Namita: its sooo relaxing

Nicholas: or how the rain collects on the bush next to my car n it looks like diamonds all over the bush

Namita: yesssssss

Namita: i loveeeee how day old snow glistens like stars

Namita: i love star gazing too

Namita: looking at the moon

Nicholas: the city lights reflecting on the car while its raining n ur driving

Namita: yesssssss wowwww

Nicholas: LOVE the moon

Namita: see its all those little things ...that if i said it to anyone else they would laugh

Nicholas: can point out most of the landing sites and their names on the moon too

Namita: yesss me too loveeeeeeeeee the moon

Namita: in various phases

Nicholas: yes no one seems to get it

Namita: ohhhh i dont know that ...but u can teach me

Nicholas: it's almost like they're missing it

Nicholas: sure can

Namita: yessss they are missing life

Nicholas: was going to put it that way

Namita: i loveeeeeeeeee the cheery blossoms in the spring

Nicholas: ran through my head

Namita: hehe

Nicholas: when the wind blows and the blossoms come dwn like rain

Namita: i loveee taking pics of cherry blossoms standing under the tree

Namita: yesssssssssss loveeeeeeeee that nicholas !!!!!!

Namita: i loveeeeee what the earth has to offer

Nicholas: yess

Namita: i lovee getting dirty to plant something

Nicholas: was thinking similar n how most ppl are missing out on it

Namita: and watch the miracle of growth

Nicholas: they get too caught up in the stress of their lives

Namita: yesss ppl get too busy with mundane everyday lives

Nicholas: your awesome!!

Namita: i lovee watching my dog dig a hole in the ground ...as much as i want to stop him from doing it

Namita: i lovee how his ears flop around doing it

Nicholas: I honestly never thought I'd meet someone like you

Nicholas: yes

Namita: and wonder what the hell is going on in his head

Namita: hehehe

Namita: aweeeeeeeeeeee nicholas !!!

Nicholas: lol probly "diggin' a hole diggin' a hole" lol

Namita: hehehee eee ...yess all the way to china

Nicholas: lol

Namita: yess i loveeeeee all of that

Namita: and many more

Nicholas: yessss

Namita: hehhee

Nicholas: it would be so nice to be in bed w you right now

Namita: you should get some sleep soon

Namita: id be talking like this to you

Nicholas: then we could kiss n go to sleep n pick up where we left off

Namita: yesssssss

Nicholas: soon you'll be back in the same city

Namita: or you can kiss me to shut me up and mutter against my lips shut up sweetheart and go to sleep

Namita: hehe

Namita: yessss

Nicholas: hopefully you'll still have some time to yourself when you do get back

Namita: yes i will

Nicholas: lol I would never tell you to shut up

Namita: hehehehehhehe

Nicholas: I will never say anything to hurt or harm you. I know you know that but just wanted to say it again

Nicholas: or raise a hand to you EVER!!

Namita: yeah sure you wont ..esp when ur trying to sleep ....and youd say ..but we covered all that sweety when we first met ...can u pls go to sleep now

Nicholas: lol okay I'll give you that

Namita: ohhhh nicholas i knowww that !!!

Namita: hehe

Nicholas: it's early Alzheimer's testing lol

Namita: thanks for saying that ..it means a lot to me !!

Namita: hehehe

Nicholas: you are quite welcome

Namita: hehe im giggling here

Nicholas: probly coz you're sooo tired lol

Nicholas: I know I'm fading fast here

Namita: yeah i have zero tolerance for physical violence

Nicholas: me either to anyone

Namita: yes we should go to sleep

Nicholas: men women children the elderly

Namita: yesssssss i agree

Nicholas: we should

Namita: and animals

Nicholas: one thing first

Namita: yes

Nicholas: right

Nicholas: in one of your replies on LL

Namita: yes

Nicholas: you said something about " I'm sure we'll have lots of long chats very soon" or something like that

Nicholas: and you were sooo right

Namita: uh huh

Namita: hehhehee

Namita: awwwwe u remember that ??

Nicholas: its in the saved doc

Nicholas: I read it the other day or maybe this morning

Namita: ohhh i havent even looked

Namita: i dont think i have it

Nicholas: my LL account is gone I closed it way long time ago

Namita: cuz LL deletes them after some time

Namita: ahhh ok

Nicholas: I don't need to search anymore

Namita: hehhe nooo?

Nicholas: I saved our convo's before I did though

Nicholas: lol nope.. brat

Namita: ohhhhh

Namita: i wish i thought of that

Nicholas: you can see mine lol

Namita: hehehe

Nicholas: I'll let you

Namita: 😶

Namita: at least one of us did

Nicholas: I wish I had saved ur story too

Namita: i will make new stories with you

Nicholas: yes we will

Namita: everyone has read that one

Namita: we will have our own

Namita: or i will send u on a treasure hunt of me

Namita: hehe

Nicholas: if the hunt is on ur body I'm in!!

Namita: hahahha

Namita: yes i will draw a map for u too

Nicholas: I'll follow it to a T

Namita: and arrows pointing

Namita: hahhaha

Namita: ur too funny!!!

Nicholas: though I'll probly get side tracked at the stops along the way

Namita: hehehehe

Nicholas: n take my time n "see" the sites

Namita: hehehhehehee

Nicholas: take them all in so to speak

Namita: omg look whos witty at 4 am ?????

Nicholas: geeze

Namita: heheh

Nicholas: I need to sleep

Namita: ok luv you need to sleep

Nicholas: I'm crashing fast

Nicholas: you do too

Nicholas: tmw then?

Namita: yes im heading that way

Nicholas: I'll be on w breakfast

Namita: yessss

Nicholas: not sure when that'll be though

Namita: ok will touch base with you tmw sometime

Nicholas: sleep well my sweet

Namita: aweee thanks nicholas

Namita: pleasant dreams

Nicholas: u2 night

Namita: 😊

Namita: and muahhhhh

Nicholas: 😊

Namita: goodnite

End Time: 3:55 AM

Chapter 27 November 24 Part 2

Start Time: 11:54 AM

Nicholas: good morning sunshine!!

Namita: heyy good morning

Namita: i just got out of the shower

Namita: hehe

Nicholas: did you sleep well?

Namita: when did u wake up ?

Nicholas: mmm nice image

Namita: yes i did

Namita: hehe

Nicholas: about 10ish

Namita: i got up around 1130 ...slept in ..but my chest still feels heavy and im coughing alot

Nicholas: mmm sorry to hear that

Namita: hopefully this will pass soon

Nicholas: should be getting better soon though

Namita: i was in the shower and thinking of you

Nicholas: mmmm like that mmmhmmm

Namita: and that was like 5 mins ago

Namita: i just came into my room

Nicholas: I thought how awesome it'll be to wake up next to you

Namita: i was lathering up and thinking ur beside me

Namita: hehe yesss

Nicholas: mmmm

Namita: that would be cool too

Namita: hehe

Namita: have u had breakfast ?

Nicholas: yup

Namita: or lunch ?

Namita: hehehe

Nicholas: I try to eat as son as I get up

Namita: yes that is good !!

Nicholas: lol brunch.. my usual breakfast

Namita: i like to brush my teeth first

Nicholas: ah

Namita: then breakfast then brush gain

Namita: again

Nicholas: wow those are some clean teeth

Namita: hehehe

Namita: nice and white

Nicholas: your oral hygiene shows in your pics

Namita: really?

Namita: hehe

Nicholas: I like good oral..... hygiene lol

Namita: im a picture poster for dentists

Namita: hehehehhe nice one !!!

Nicholas: I take good care of my teeth too... when I get a cleaning the hygienist runs out of things to do coz my teeth are so clean

Namita: hehhe ohhh thats good !!!

Namita: and you have straight teeth too ?

Nicholas: I think so too

Nicholas: yes

Namita: not that it matters

Nicholas: braces

Namita: ahhhh

Namita: i never had braces

Nicholas: I'm multi tasking at the moment

Namita: yes me too

Namita: hehe

Nicholas: yes I remember you said that

Nicholas: what else are you doing?

Namita: im putting face cream on ... moisturizer

Nicholas: ah

Namita: hehe

Namita: and body cream

Nicholas: ooooo body cream nice

Namita: lol..it smells nice tooo

Nicholas: I bet it does

Namita: what are u up to ?

Nicholas: I'm buying Isabel's xmas gift online

Nicholas: and just relaxing before I have to get ready for work

Namita: ahhhh ...what are u getting ?

Nicholas: her mom, my mom and me are getting her a Kitchen Aide mixer in green apple color

Namita: ur getting Isabel a kitchenaide ??

Nicholas: yup

Namita: is she cooking or baking already ?

Nicholas: it's what she wants apparently

Namita: really?

Nicholas: she'd like to be

Namita: does she cook ?

Nicholas: she likes to bake too

Namita: ohhhh

Namita: i have one ..and yes they are handy

Nicholas: not a lot but I'm sure she will

Namita: mine is black

Nicholas: cool

Namita: well i hope it inspires her

Namita: i do lovee it

Nicholas: I hope she'll use it a lot... though she'll have it forever too

Namita: whenever i feel like eating some roti ...and indian bread ...i mix it in there and forget it for a few mins while the dough is mixing ...and do other stuff

Namita: and voila ... i have the dough ready ...and can start rolling it

Nicholas: I love roti!!!

Namita: before i used to make the dough by hands since i was like 14 or something

Namita: i can still do it

Nicholas: cool

Namita: you loveeeeeeeeee roti ???

Nicholas: yessss

Namita: ohhhhhhhhhhh

Namita: niceeeeeee

Namita: well i can make home made ones

Namita: what do u eat roti with ?

Nicholas: I order it every time I go the Banana leaf... it's a Malaysian restaurant in Vancouver

Nicholas: just by it's self

Namita: ohhh yesss ive heard of banana leaf

Namita: with the green chicken curry?

Namita: mmmmmmm

Namita: Malaysian ?

Nicholas: I usually order just appies coz I can get a couple of things n they are really filling

Namita: yesss i can imagine

Nicholas: yes Malaysian

Namita: theres another restaurant on Granville called Red door ..omg the food there is sooo good too

Nicholas: what type of food is it?

Namita: its asian fusion ... sort of indian chinese, and thai

Nicholas: I can't seem to find this promo code on the site I'm on.... I hate it when that happens

Nicholas: oh I see sounds cool

Namita: ohhhh ur trying to order the kitchenaide

Nicholas: yes

Nicholas: there's a spot to enter this "code" but I can't find it

Namita: ohhh

Namita: how much is the kitchenaide ?

Nicholas: it's $299 n change... a little expensive I think for a 13 year old... though there's 3 of us going in on it

Nicholas: I still have no Idea what to get Amanda

Namita: ohhh ...yes they are expensive ... i know when i bought mine it was over 300 dollars ...but i just bought it here !!

Namita: has she given you any clues ?

Nicholas: it's about 200 less in the States

Nicholas: no but the ex has suggestions

Namita: yess ... hehe ... i should have bought it from there

Nicholas: iPad or Ebook or something like that

Namita: ohh nooo what are her suggestions?

Namita: OMG

Namita: serious ??

Nicholas: yah

Namita: sounds like she is going to use it more !!

Namita: wowww

Namita: whats a kid going to do with an ipad ??

Namita: im not into those things

Nicholas: I can see a Kindle or something coz she does like to read

Namita: yes that might be good

Nicholas: I have Tony's old Xbox but I never play it

Namita: ive only heard of the kindle recently

Nicholas: my sis n Shannon have them... don't know if they still use them a lot

Namita: ohhh

Nicholas: when I buy something I really think about how much I'm going to use it... most times I don't think I will so I don't get it

Namita: yesss i do that too

Namita: i hate wasting money for nothing

Nicholas: I do lots of research on what I want

Nicholas: me toooo!!!

Namita: i cant justify spending a lot of money on something i might not use often

Nicholas: yes me too!!

Namita: hehe

Namita: yayyy

Nicholas: even when it comes to parts for the hot rod.... I try to visualize what it'll look like and make sure it's exactly what I want

Namita: yesss that is good !!

Namita: i do that too ...visualize what the end result is going to be

Nicholas: and really think about if I need it or just want it

Nicholas: there's such a big diff between the 2

Namita: yessss hehee thats the same talk i have in my head ....is it a need or want !!!

Namita: i was going to say that earlier

Namita: but you beat me to it

Nicholas: lol like minds

Nicholas: I did

Namita: lol

Nicholas: it's so much more satisfying to be happy w a purchase, knowing you'll use it and it suits your needs

Namita: yesss true

Nicholas: I don't want you to think I'm ignoring you... I'm just filling out shipping info here

Namita: nooo ur not ....im kinda getting ready here too

Nicholas: ok cool

Namita: take ur time

Nicholas: would love to watch you getting dressed but prefer watching you undress hehe

Namita: hehe .... while ur in bed ...and doing my rituals ..in getting dressed and brushing my hair ...and applying a lil makeup

Namita: that would be cool

Nicholas: mmmhmmm so very cool

Nicholas: well that's done just finishing up something else

Nicholas: and the site is dwn for maintenance so I'm all your for a few more minutes

Namita: hehhe

Namita: so u didnt get it ?

Nicholas: oh I got it

Namita: ohhh ok

Namita: green one ?

Nicholas: I was trying to enter a contest w my bank

Nicholas: yes the green one

Nicholas: the contest; you could win 10 grand just by using your TD Visa in the next few weeks

Namita: hehhee thats my bank tooo

Nicholas: lol

Namita: hehee

Nicholas: it's a popular bank, I think for the hrs

Namita: yess it is

Nicholas: I do love this photo of you... the one in your bra n panties.. so very hot!!

Nicholas: I'm just admiring the pic on my screen

Nicholas: thinking about watching you get ready

Namita: the black one ?

Namita: or the white one

Nicholas: the black bra n panties yes

Namita: ahhhhh

Namita: it looks sooo magazine-y

Nicholas: love the part of your tummy below your belly button to the top of the panties

Namita: miranda took it ...she has her own studio

Namita: and background

Namita: hehehe

Nicholas: yessss it does I think that when I look at it too

Nicholas: looks like a Victoria Secret add

Namita: ahhhhhhhhh ..hehehe

Namita: i was thinking what is VS

Namita: and i should know that

Nicholas: lol

Namita: maybe i should try out for them

Nicholas: you don't have any VS (Victoria Secret)?

Nicholas: oh misread that

Nicholas: yes you should

Nicholas: they could use some exotic

Namita: yess i do have a lot of VS stuff

Nicholas: I thought you might

Namita: i just didnt pick up on it right away when u said that ...lol

Namita: nooooo its always the white girls for VS

Nicholas: lol was trying to cut dwn on the typing

Namita: it would throw them off balance

Namita: then there would be an uproar too

Nicholas: i think you'd look fantastic in there

Namita: lol

Namita: well VS only has the all american women in their flyers

Nicholas: I think you'd look fantastic in a garbage bag lol

Namita: to put someone exotic is wayyyyyyyy off the key

Nicholas: that's true

Namita: awee thanks

Nicholas: yah appease the masses

Nicholas: well my dear I should get going

Namita: ohh ok

Namita: when do you leave

Nicholas: I leave at 2 ... I have a little more to do to get ready today as I haven't done my morning routine

Namita: ohhh

Namita: no worries

Nicholas: the day goes by so quickly when I sleep the morning away

Namita: hehe...yes you better get on it !!!

Nicholas: lol

Nicholas: I'd rather be getting on you!!

Namita: hahhahaha

Namita: yes get it on !!!!

Nicholas: okay... I'll talk w you tonight?

Namita: yess ok

Nicholas: enjoy your day

Namita: you too ...take care and drive safe !!!

End Time: 1:07 PM

Chapter 28 November 25

Start Time: 11:53 PM

Nicholas: bing bong!!

Namita: heyyyyyyyyyy

Namita: whos there?

Nicholas: ah Mr Handsome lol

Nicholas: can I come in n play?

Namita: lol ..Ohhhh yesss i know him !!

Namita: tell him to come on in

Nicholas: *smiling* how are you?

Nicholas: oh I will thx

Namita: hehe ... im good !!

Namita: Ur home !!!!!

Nicholas: I am

Nicholas: showered n everything

Namita: hehe safe and sound !

Namita: you usually shower after work right ?

Nicholas: yup

Namita: before too ?

Nicholas: usually shower before bed when I'm not working too

Namita: what about before work ?

Nicholas: nope just at night before bed though in the summer I can shower a few times to cool dwn n stay clean

Nicholas: I feel dirty after work and it helps leave work at work so to speak

Namita: hehe ... i have to shower before work ..even though its 5 am ... it kinda wakes me up ... then again when i get home from the hospital ... to get any cooties off !! Hehhee

Nicholas: I'm a pretty clean guy... I like to be clean

Namita: well sometimes im working in isolation rooms ..and u never know what is in there

Nicholas: I can see that... wash all the hospital "stuff" off

Namita: yesss im glad to hear that ... i loveee a squeaky clean guy

Nicholas: absolutely totally agree

Namita: hehe

Nicholas: then ur in for a treat w me

Namita: there are showers at work too ...but i rather come home to my own shower

Namita: hehe mmmmmmm sounds good !!!

Nicholas: yah... more comfortable at home that way you can relax

Namita: omg my spelling is bad already !!!

Nicholas: I like to relax w the shower n cleans the body and mind

Nicholas: not to worry my dear I understand you perfectly

Namita: yesss me too ... i love just standing under a shower

Namita: i always take my time

Nicholas: yah I have a routine too.... I like to feel clean n refreshed

Namita: but at the same time conscious water wastage not good ... so i do time myself

Namita: yessss me too

Nicholas: lol me too, don't like to waste even water

Nicholas: I don't understand how ppl can take an hr to shower

Namita: omg ...yes i dont understand it either

Nicholas: Tony can shower in like 5 mins.... don't understand how you can get clean in that short a time

Nicholas: I'm about 20 mins when I have to shave

Namita: hehe ...my dad is a 5 min' ter too

Nicholas: wow

Namita: my mom doesnt understand what he does to get out so quickly

Nicholas: lol

Namita: hehe

Namita: hehe yes they are quite funny sometimes

Nicholas: ur parents?

Namita: yes

Namita: hehe

Nicholas: how long have they been married?

Namita: they play fight ..and joke around with each other

Namita: its 44 yrs

Nicholas: that's cool

Namita: just this september

Nicholas: wow!! my parents were married for almost 41

Nicholas: Sept what?

Nicholas: my parents were Oct 21

Namita: woww ... i say if ur married for that ... youve got something good going !!

Namita: ahhhhh

Nicholas: yup

Namita: september 28 for mine

Namita: hehe

Nicholas: cool

Namita: i wanted to do that for sooo long !!

Nicholas: now that's a sexy photos.... haven't seen that one

Namita: which one ?

Nicholas: this one thats up now

Nicholas: do what for so long?

Namita: im seeing my orange flower

Namita: nudge you

Namita: like this

Namita: ohhh ok i see it now

Nicholas: I'm confused

Namita: i had to clear my window

Namita: confused ?

Nicholas: what are you talking about? nudging me?

Namita: arent you getting the online nudges ??

Nicholas: nope

Namita: like it shakes ur msn window ?

Nicholas: do they show up on our screen?

Namita: it shakes ur msn screen

Nicholas: I haven't seen it.. try again n I'll watch n see

Namita: lol

Namita: do you see ...the happy face icon ...then a share a pic icon ...then a video call icon at the bottom of ur msn screen ?

Nicholas: I just have the happy face and the font icons

Namita: ohhhh

Nicholas: the call icon is at the top of mine

Nicholas: maybe it's not compatible w a mac

Namita: maybe u should upgrade ur windows then

Namita: ohhh yess maybe

Nicholas: I'm just finishing an email to Target, the company I bought the mixer for Isabel from... I'll 2 sex k

Namita: ohh ok no worries take ur time

Nicholas: I hate it when a web site doesn't work the way it should

Namita: lol

Namita: yesss another peeve

Nicholas: its asking for a zip code/postal code yet when i give them the postal code is says there's an error

Namita: arggggggggghhhhhhhhhh

Nicholas: they've charged me tax and as I'm out of their country so I shouldn't be

Namita: thats dumb !!!

Nicholas: yes my thoughts exact

Namita: hehe

Nicholas: and the error is saying the zip code should contain numbers, well duh postal codes have numbers

Nicholas: stupid site lol

Namita: lmao

Namita: ohhh noooo its not ur nite !!!

Nicholas: I'll call them tmw

Nicholas: I'm thinking because I gave a US ship to address maybe that's why but who knows

Namita: do you want me to fix em here for you ...the americans i mean !!

Nicholas: PLease!!! n thx lol

Namita: lol

Nicholas: I dislike un-user friendly sites and the one that don't work the way there suppose to

Namita: hehehe ... some ppl here are quite ignorant i find

Nicholas: those good'ol americans

Namita: ohh yesss that drives me crazy too !!!

Namita: hehehe yes damn those americanos

Nicholas: not all of them mind you I have met some really interesting intelligent Americans over the years.

Nicholas: I once heard a comedian say... the americans say it's our land!! yet they stole it from the natives.... forced the chinese to build it and made the blacks maintain it.... yet it's our land

Nicholas: he was an American comedian too

Namita: OMGGG LMAOOO it is sooooooooo trueeeeeeeeeeeeeeee !!!!!!!!!!!!!!!

Nicholas: I thought so too

Namita: wowww couldnt have said it better !!!!!!!

Namita: hehehhe

Nicholas: yah.. good one

Namita: hehehe .. i loveee stand up comedians

Nicholas: me too!!

Namita: lewis black

Nicholas: YESSS!! love him

Namita: hehe

Nicholas: louis ck

Namita: russel peters i can relate to

Nicholas: lol he's funny

Namita: yesssssssss heard of him too

Nicholas: I watch Just For Laughs when I can

Namita: there was another guy i really loved ..and the name is not coming to me

Nicholas: there are some really funny comedians out there

Namita: yes loveee that show

Nicholas: I saw Jeff Dunham at UBC one year

Namita: ohhh dane cook

Nicholas: took Tony for his B-day

Namita: ohhh cool !!!

Nicholas: yes I like Dane's mannerisms

Namita: yes there are good canadian ones too !!!

Nicholas: well RP (Russell Peters) for one lol

Namita: ohh yess

Namita: hehe

Nicholas: my friend is a comedian Damonde Tschritter. he's a friend of my sisters too, she graduated w him

Nicholas: he use to live across the street when we we all in high school

Namita: ohhh cool !! He must be super funny !!

Nicholas: he is.. we saw him at Laugh Lines and dwntwn n was funny both times

Nicholas: let me see if I can find a youtube of him

Namita: ok sure !!

Namita: i was listening to a lil collective soul here

Namita: hehe

Nicholas: http://www.youtube.com/watch?v=vHt1Mpt84wc

Nicholas: oh cool I have one of their cd's

Namita: one of my fav bands

Nicholas: really, cool

Namita: hehe

Namita: hehehehe ...that was good !!!

Nicholas: we'll have to watch some youtube together

Nicholas: comedians on youtube that is

Namita: ohh yesss

Nicholas: together as in the same room lol

Namita: hehe i know what u meant

Nicholas: hehe

Namita: id be giggling all the time

Namita: we can cuddle in bed and watch it

Nicholas: Damonde won first place in the Seattle comedy competition a few years back

Nicholas: he was the first Canadian to win since it started 25 years ago

Namita: ohhhh good for him !!! How long have you known him ?

Namita: WOwwww thats good !!

Namita: he looks pretty young too !!

Nicholas: hmmm.... since I was in grade 9

Namita: wowww

Namita: was he always funny ?

Nicholas: he's 2 years older than us.... same age as my sis

Namita: ahhh ok

Nicholas: always out going and a bit of a showman w/o being cocky... he was very well liked when we were in school

Nicholas: he's a good guy

Namita: well good for him getting ahead in the comedy scene ...i know it is sometimes cutthroat area

Nicholas: I watched his comedy special, the one that clip was from... was cool to see some one I know on tv

Nicholas: though I was on tv a couple of times

Namita: hehe you were ??

Nicholas: yup was an extra in a tv series

Nicholas: in a couple of diff episodes

Namita: which one ?? do u have a clip ?

Nicholas: was called Sliders

Nicholas: I don't

Namita: ohh never heard of it

Nicholas: one episode I was dancing around in an end of the world party in a toga

Nicholas: oh and a balloon hat

Namita: omggggg realllllllllllllyyyyyyyyy !!!!!!!?

Namita: hehhehe

Nicholas: I have 2 movie credits too

Namita: ohh cool !!!!!!

Nicholas: if you go to imdb and search my name I'll come up

Namita: search where ?

Nicholas: imdb international movie data base

Namita: ohhhhh ok

Namita: that is soooo cool

Nicholas: I stumbled upon my name in there

Nicholas: lol

Nicholas: you got to have a look at this

Nicholas: http://www.youtube.com/watch?v=L6KgQPAAVJk&feature=related

Namita: ohh wow .. i just did ... and there are 3 titles that come up with ur name

Namita: gunfighters moon

Nicholas: 3 really oh right that one

Namita: as makeup artist

Nicholas: was my last film I worked on.. was such a nightmare

Namita: hehehhee

Namita: really why ?

Nicholas: the whole crew was really fun except for the woman I worked under... such a bitch

Nicholas: ran out of money

Namita: she ran out of money ??

Nicholas: and didn't have a reg job

Nicholas: no no I ran out of money... that's why it was my last film

Namita: ohhh

Namita: ohh they didnt pay well ? or this was casual work ?

Nicholas: wasn't steady enf... was hard to get into the union and the industry was more who you know not what u know

Namita: yesss im sure that was disheartening to know that it was soooo unfair like that

Namita: did u put makeup on women too?

Nicholas: sure did

Nicholas: yah... I wanted to get into the special fx make up but that was even harder to get in to

Namita: wowww you must have a good eye for that !! Like everyday kinda makeup?

Nicholas: mmm maybe

Namita: hehe ..would you do me too ??

Nicholas: I didn't like doing the straight make ups was very boring

Nicholas: oh I'd do you lol

Nicholas: not really

Namita: LOL

Nicholas: I did it coz it got me closer to doing the spfx make up

Namita: so if a asked you to do my makeup ..would you ?

Namita: yes i understand what ur saying

Nicholas: I'd prefer not too... I haven't done a straight make up in a very long time.. I'm afraid I'd be too rusty

Nicholas: that n I don't like doing straight make up's

Nicholas: I think you do a very good job on your own

Namita: hehe ... ok ... yes leave it to me then

Nicholas: how about you do it n I'll just watch

Namita: aweee thanks

Namita: i try to mix things up

Namita: yes you watch ..and make me laugh

Nicholas: I like it when you can't tell a woman is wearing any

Namita: so i will have the steady hand

Nicholas: oh yes

Namita: hehe

Namita: yesss i like to put it on as naturally as possible

Nicholas: side note; here's some Louis Ck

Namita: i dont like fake lashes and stuff

Namita: its gross

Namita: ohh ok

Nicholas: you don't need them anyway

Nicholas: http://www.youtube.com/watch?v=4u2ZsoYWwJA

Namita: yes i dont ..hehe ...do u like mine though ?

Nicholas: oh yes very much!!!

Nicholas: one of the things I noticed when I first saw ur pics

Namita: really ??

Nicholas: how well your make up accentuates your features

Nicholas: yup

Namita: hehe thanks !!!

Nicholas: welcome

Nicholas: I notice the little things hehe

Namita: yes i can see that ...but im sure you sat there and scrutinized from every angle ...and magnified the pics too

Namita: lol

Nicholas: lol

Nicholas: did not

Namita: yesss you did !!!

Nicholas: well didn't scrutinize but had a really good long look

Namita: 😜

Namita: hehhe

Namita: im bugging you !!!

Nicholas: i know

Nicholas: its all good

Namita: heheh

Nicholas: I can take a little ribbing now n again lol

Namita: hehehehehe

Nicholas: I usually have a good long look at your pics esp when I get new ones

Namita: how about an elbow in ur rib ??

Namita: hehehe ohhhh im sure

Nicholas: as long as it's yours yes

Nicholas: did you check out the link I sent you?

Namita: yes im watching it

Nicholas: this ones funny too

Namita: hehehehe

Nicholas: okay cool

Nicholas: http://www.youtube.com/watch?NR=1&v=CzbURUrgQao

Nicholas: I'll let you watch

Namita: k

Nicholas: have you heard of Danny Bhoy

Nicholas: now he's funny

Nicholas: http://www.youtube.com/watch?v=c2U5IA49eEo

Namita: sounds familiar ... im trying to watch this one ..but there sooo many fbombs that i dont want anyone else to hear from my room ..heheh

Nicholas: oooh oops sorry lol

Namita: heheh

Namita: its hard for me to hear at a low volume

Nicholas: the danny bhoy clip doesn't have any fbombs

Namita: but send them i could hear it later ... i forgot to take my headphones along

Namita: ok will look at his

Namita: one sec

Namita: lmao

Namita: im at the irish part

Nicholas: i've seen a 1 hrs spec of his n it was soooo funny

Nicholas: that's his catch phase

Namita: hehe

Nicholas: http://www.youtube.com/watch?v=aSFMnpDQd18

Namita: http://www.youtube.com/watch?v=SsWrY77o77o this one is one of favs cuz i can relate to it

Nicholas: oh that one wasn't the one I thought it was

Namita: ohh k

Nicholas: checking it now

Namita: ok

Nicholas: lol funny

Namita: hehehe

Nicholas: still on

Namita: k

Nicholas: good one!! you've experienced that ?

Nicholas: with the Danny Bhoy stuff I like how he laughs at his stuff too

Namita: well when i used to have my nails done ... it would always be asians doing it ...no matter where you go !! And most of them cant speak english and they would try anyways ... and the funny thing was they would have english names too ..just like she portrayed

Nicholas: too funny

Namita: a few times the nails would be crooked and id point it out to them and of course it was my fault ...for having a crooked finger

Namita: hehehe

Nicholas: geeze *shakes head* no customer service.. just give us your money n f**k off

Namita: hehehe yes danny bhoy is funny ... yess i lovee how comedians laugh at their own jokes ..cuz it tells me that they are really into it

Namita: hehee

Namita: too fuuunnny

Nicholas: yah there story tellers

Namita: lol

Nicholas: http://www.youtube.com/watch?v=bocezmdGjTw&feature=related

Namita: hehehehe

Nicholas: okay that's enf looking at youtube, more talking w you please

Namita: hehe

Namita: ok

Nicholas: so glad you concur

Namita: yessss i wanna be chatting with you

Nicholas: have you seen the movie Almost famous ?

Nicholas: was just thinking about it n now it's on

Namita: umm nooo ..who is in it ?

Namita: heard of it

Nicholas: though I have this ability to do that... think of something n then it happens

Nicholas: um no one really famous... the guy from My Name Is Earl

Namita: hehe yess it happens to me too ...like a dax song ...and then it comes up on the radio

Nicholas: oh Kate Hudson

Namita: ohhh

Nicholas: I try to think of something difficult to test it and low n be hold it happens

Namita: hehehehe ...ur physic !!!

Nicholas: like a clip in a movie Matilda... and it came on in an add for the station I was watching the other day... I had just thought of it a few days ago too

Namita: woww isnt that strange sometimes ..how thing like that pop out from nowhere ...power of the mind !!!!

Nicholas: don't know if it physic but there's something I'm in tune to... haven't been able to master it yet

Nicholas: power of attraction

Nicholas: anyway this movie is a good one

Namita: OOOOoOOOoOOOOooOOO wowwwwwww

Namita: i havent even heard of that one either

Nicholas: my dreams have a tendency to come true too... when I remember them

Nicholas: it has a good story

Namita: hehhe ... i hardly ever remember them ... forget by the time the day is done

Nicholas: I know I've slept well when I don't remember my dreams

Namita: yesss me too !!

Nicholas: OOOOooooOOOO I like that pic!!

Namita: you do ??

Nicholas: very pretty!!

Namita: hehe

Nicholas: love your smile!!

~Namita~ would like to send you the file "299003_220534 704680998_168160689918400_634..." (80 Kb). Do you want to

Accept

(Ctrl+G) or

Decline

(Ctrl+C) the invitation?

Transfer of file "299003_220534704680998_168160689918400_634..." from ~Namita~ has been accepted. Starting transfer...

Cancel

You have successfully received 299003_220534704680998_168160689918400_634_n.jpg from ~Namita~. Before opening this file, you may want to scan it with a virus-scanning program.

It's a head shot, it makes me think of a shampoo or a face cleanser commercial.

Nicholas: unbelievable simply unbelievable

Namita: hehe ... i knew you would like this one

Nicholas: OOOO wow! and it's huge too!!

Nicholas: Oh My God Namita wow!!

Nicholas: takes up a 3rd of my screen... love it!!

Namita: now you can kiss it

Namita: hehe

Nicholas: damn

Namita: lmao ohhhhhhh nicholas !!!!!

Nicholas: well I don't want to mess up the screen so I'll wait for the real thing

Namita: i can feel ur excitement !!!

Namita: ohh practice !! Live a little !!!!

Nicholas: I can see the colour of your eyes.. all the lines n colours in ur eyes

Namita: this was last year

Namita: i was on my way with miranda and friends to see cirque du soliel .... we stopped by her studio for a photo shoot

Namita: im wearing a white dress

Nicholas: sooo awesome!!

Namita: yes sometimes they look brown ...other times sort of dark grey

Nicholas: I love that you just take pics when ever n you look ravishing so all the time

Namita: heheh aweeee thanks !!!

Nicholas: you're killing me here lol

Nicholas: anytime

Namita: it was kind of candid ...cuz we were laughing and cracking jokes

Namita: so i wasnt ready and posing

Nicholas: I think there's a tie for my fav photo

Namita: but im happy with it

Nicholas: it's very nice, love it

Namita: aweeee im glad you like it

Nicholas: even better that you weren't ready.. very natural

Nicholas: oh I do!!

Namita: hehehe yesss !!

Nicholas: it's very distracting

Namita: hehe

Nicholas: I can add that one to my phone n it should turn out really well on it

Namita: lemme distract you ..have you seen cirque du soliel ?

Nicholas: I have not

Namita: it is very cool .. i think the girls will loveeeee it !!!

Nicholas: thought about it... would have to take the girls.... a little pricey for me when they were here as I didn't have a well paying job then

Nicholas: I think so too

Namita: yes it is pricey unfortunately ...i had to think once twice thrice ..before i went

Namita: well they come every 2 yrs

Nicholas: yeah worth it though I bet

Namita: so maybe next year

Nicholas: really? didn't know that

Nicholas: maybe

Namita: are u distracted then ?

Nicholas: I'm always distracted when I'm w you

Namita: hehhee

Nicholas: it's kind of cool coz I can read ur words n see your photo n it almost like we're in the same room

Namita: heheheh

Nicholas: love your eyes

Namita: yesss i do lovee talking to you ... i imagine that ur nearby when we're chatting like this

Nicholas: me too

Namita: what do u like about them ?

Namita: hehe

Namita: sorry i hope i dont sound like im fishing for compliments

Nicholas: their shape... the sparkle I see in them... the person I've come to know that's in there

Namita: thats not my intention

Namita: hehe

Nicholas: no no

Nicholas: I know you're not like that

Namita: aweeeeeeeee soooo sweeet ... i like to hear what you see

Namita: from ur eyes

Nicholas: i can tell... I know that's why you ask

Namita: hehehe

Namita: we are sooo much like 2 peas in a pod

Nicholas: I see the most beautiful woman I've had the pleasure of getting to know

Nicholas: yes we are

Namita: ohhhhhhh nicholas !!! You are such a sweetheart ... i just want you to know that

Nicholas: thx.. I like hearing you say stuff like that too

Nicholas: I think you're pretty awesome too

Namita: ur very very welcome !!!!!!!

Nicholas: I never thought I'd meet some one on line like you or w so many similarities as me

Nicholas: hope that makes sense

Nicholas: I'm just beside myself most times w how great you are

Nicholas: I think thats what makes me smile the most

Namita: yess it totally does ... that online thing is a hit and miss ...but mostly misses !! Its almost like gambling or rolling a dice !! But im glad to find a real down to earth guy with real values ....a killer smile ..and beautiful eyes ...and hard worker ...and super romantic like me...Values friendships and relationships ...umm what else can i say ...the list is endless about you nicholas !!!

Nicholas: thank you so much ANd I'm so glad you're as excited about me as I am about you... your list goes on and on....

Namita: hehehe it sure does !!!

Namita: i could go on and on and on !!

Nicholas: I keep running through all our similarities too

Nicholas: me too

Namita: hehehe yess me too !!

Nicholas: we'll talk till we're blue in the face but ppl still wont get us

Namita: lol !!!!

Nicholas: similarities right dwn to our work ethics *shakes head*

Namita: yesss we have a silent understanding ...and thats what i like !!

Nicholas: they just wont get it no matter how we explain it

Namita: yesss true !!

Nicholas: yes well said

Namita: no ..you well said it !! hehehhe

Nicholas: and really they don't have too... the ones that are in tune will be able to see it

Namita: ohh heres another pic you might like ...

Nicholas: cool love your pics

Namita: yess true ... the understanding is between you and me ... the looks ..the smiles

Nicholas: the touches

Namita: we know what each of us are thinking

Nicholas: the hand holding

Namita: yessss

Nicholas: mmmhmm

Namita: the touch on the arm ..or a brush of the arm

Namita: eyes locking from far away

Nicholas: a hand on your lower back as we pass through a room

~Namita~ would like to send you the file "38314_416550973811_273777518811_4511052_37..." (48 Kb). Do you want to

Accept

(Ctrl+G) or

Decline

(Ctrl+C) the invitation?

Transfer of file "38314_416550973811_273777518811_4511052_37..." from ~Namita~ has been accepted. Starting transfer...

Cancel

Namita: mmmmmmmm i like that !!!!!

You have successfully received 38314_416550973811_273777518811_4511052_3781302_ n.jpg from ~Namita~. Before opening this file, you may want to scan it with a virus-scanning program.

Namita: its just gives us more closeness

Namita: closeness ...that hand at the lower back i mean !

Nicholas: ppl wondering what just happened

Namita: uh huh !!!

Nicholas: oooOO I love the dress... you were right I do love it

Nicholas: like minds

Namita: hehehe ...ur hand at my lower back ...now that u can see it sort of !!

Nicholas: I love my hand on your lower back... to me it's an intimate moment in public

Namita: you loveee my dress ...thanks !!

Namita: one of my favs actually

Namita: yesss id go crazyyy for that

Nicholas: I can see your lower back in the pic of you lying on ur tummy w no clothes on

Namita: lol

Namita: ohhhhhhh

Namita: hehe

Namita: heyyyy i had some clothes on ...heheh

Nicholas: I like to touch esp in public w/o being all over each other

Namita: yesss me too !!!

Nicholas: lol if you call a towel clothes lol

Namita: not like all over each other

Namita: though

Namita: agree

Nicholas: yes

Namita: ohhhh that one !!!

Namita: heheh

Nicholas: confident n classy

Namita: i thought ur talking about the white bra and underwear one

Nicholas: not that I care what others think but they wonder what our secret is

Namita: yesss totally !!!

Nicholas: white bra n underwear? ur holding out on me again

Namita: noooooooooooo

Namita: the one im on the wooden floor

Namita: on my tummy

Nicholas: wooden floor?

Nicholas: this one looks like like a bed

Namita: ok one sex

Namita: sec

Namita: arghhhhhhhhhhh

Nicholas: lol

Nicholas: I love it when you do that

Namita: hehehe

Namita: im typing in the dark !!!

Nicholas: in the dark... very romantic

Nicholas: your key board doesn't light up?

Namita: lol ..yesss

Namita: no it doesnt ....never did

Nicholas: oh mine does

Nicholas: not bragging lol

Namita: 😜

Nicholas: I keep going over what I'm going to do when I finally see you for the first time

Namita: really what ?? hehe

Nicholas: seeing your face light up.... maybe run to you... sweep you off your feet.... hug you... gently kiss you.... and never let go

Namita: aweeeeeeeeeeee Nicholas !!!!!!!!!!

Nicholas: feeling how great your body will feel next to mine

Nicholas: smelling how awesome your sent is

Namita: hehe ... it would be quite rush for both of us ...taking in everything about each other !!

Nicholas: I haven't quite pictured the setting yet.. it's almost like the rest of the world just disappears around us

Namita: i dont know how we're going to keep our hands off each other

Nicholas: feeling your arms around me

Namita: yesss .. everything is off to oblivion !!!

Nicholas: I don't think we will for some time

Namita: running my hands up ur back

Nicholas: I see it but it's kinda fuzzy

Namita: heheh

Nicholas: so you know, you'll feel all of me when we're that close

Namita: hmmm every inch of you ??

Namita: i think we would be on the floor right there at the doorstep !!

Nicholas: probably... you'll defiantly feel how hard you make me

Nicholas: could very well be

Namita: hehehe ohhhhhhhh nicholas

Nicholas: maybe I should meet you at your place coz I don't know if I'm going to be able to see you n not be naked w you

Nicholas: I can do the gelato n Rocky Point I'm okay w that... we'll just have to make sure it's not too long in between the first and second dates

Namita: hehehe... my place is big enough and has 3 rooms ..and no tenants

Namita: just ballo to cover is ears and eyes

Nicholas: cool

Nicholas: lol

Namita: baloo i mean ...my dog

Namita: hehe

Nicholas: I knew

Nicholas: well we can keep the first date out of the bedroom as we've said all along, if need be but I wont keep my hands off you so you know

Namita: hehehe out of the bedroom being ...in the kitchen or living room??

Nicholas: lol good one!!

Namita: im being cheeky

Nicholas: yes you are.. another great quality!!

Namita: then it might end up on the kitchen table then !!!

Namita: lol

Nicholas: as long as I'm w you nothing else matters

~Namita~ would like to send you the file "393126_185401078207599_143343382413369_386..." (99 Kb). Do you want to

Accept

(Ctrl+G) or

Decline

(Ctrl+C) the invitation?

Transfer of file "393126_185401078207599_143343382413369_386..." from ~Namita~ has been accepted. Starting transfer...

Cancel

Namita: hehe

You have successfully received 393126_185401078207599_143343382413369_386_n.jpg from ~Namita~. Before opening this file, you may want to scan it with a virus-scanning program.

Namita: this is the pic i was talking about

Namita: took me awhile to find it

Namita: hehe

Nicholas: oh that one yes I do have it

Namita: ok

Nicholas: though this one is bigger than the other one

Namita: now you tell me !!

Namita: hehehe

Nicholas: great bum

Namita: this one is better ..the other was an initial pic

Namita: hehehe thanks

Nicholas: the little one is nice... it fits in my collage well but I like the bigger one... can see you better

Namita: hehehe ..bigger butt too !!!

Nicholas: not a chance

Namita: hehe

Nicholas: love the look on your face

Nicholas: can't wait to have that look directed at me hehe

Namita: really ?

Nicholas: yesssss

Namita: i will do that right in front of ur tv as ur watching the canucks game ....and do the come hither look

Namita: and see what happens !!

Nicholas: good bye game!! n hellooooo Namita!!!!

Namita: hehehehheheheeeeeeee

Nicholas: it's a "are you going to just stand there speechless or come over here n love me" look

Namita: youd be like... for fucks sake !!! Ohhhhhhh alright .... i will come to the bedroom with you ...and u say it in defeat !!

Nicholas: I love that you have so many photos

Namita: hehehe

Namita: different looks and angles

Nicholas: lol yeah right

Namita: i get it sent to me by miranda most times

Namita: and others i load up

Nicholas: I'll be "get your sexy little ass over here woman!!"

Namita: lol

Namita: so there you are lying on the bed ...listening to the game with one ear ...and im crawling up on the bed from the foot end

Nicholas: or "meet me half way coz you're far too hot to be over there all by yourself"

Namita: crawl over you like a panther ... but giggling

Namita: hehehee

Nicholas: a giggling panther cool

Namita: like how ur mind works

Namita: hehe

Namita: yessss havent you heard of the giggling panther ???

Nicholas: well I get cold easy coz of the meds I'm on so you can keep me warm w all your hotness

Namita: there is the pink panther ...but giggling one is better

Nicholas: just did, can't wait to see her either

Namita: aweee yess i will keep u warm !!!

Nicholas: much better... very illusive too... I haven't seen one for, well ever

Nicholas: I know you will

Namita: hehehheeh

Namita: ur too funny !!!!!!

Namita: so would you really stop watching ur fav game if i did that ??

Nicholas: seen a few photo's of one but the jury is still out as to weather or not they actually exist

Namita: hehehe .. i will show you one !!!

Nicholas: abso-friggin-lutely!!!

Namita: even if they are winning ??

Nicholas: there is nothing on tv that's more important than you!!

Namita: ohhhhhhhhhhhhhhhhhhh NIcholas !!!!!!!!!!!

Namita: MUahhhhhhhhhhhhhhhhhhhhhhhhhh!!!!!!!!!!!!!

Nicholas: anytime my sweet

Namita: that totally turned me on !!!!!!!!

Nicholas: I've waited 39 years and there is no more time to waste

Namita: hehheehe

Nicholas: glad I can flip your switch

Namita: do u ever go to friends places ..or hang around with buddies or work friends

Nicholas: not really

Nicholas: go out when Tony's in twn

Namita: actually i wont do that to you if ur watching a game ...id cuddle with you !!

Nicholas: get together w Diana now n again

Namita: ahhh k

Namita: who is diana ?

Nicholas: cuddling is good too but I wont mind if the moment strikes you

Namita: hehe

Nicholas: my friend that I've known when I was married... she told me about LL.. sound familiar?

Namita: ohhh i would go for the kill if i have to !!!

Namita: ohhh yesss i remember !!

Nicholas: oh good, wouldn't want you to hesitate coz the "game" is on

Namita: how is she doing

Namita: heheh

Namita: ohhh i would prowl a bit !!

Namita: hide and ambush you !!

Nicholas: good the last time I talked w her... haven't talked to her is a week or so

Namita: ohhh cool !!

Nicholas: I got an image of 2 cats playing .. one jumps on the other... surprising it... n they roll around in a big ball playing

Nicholas: then one takes off and the other chases it

Namita: hehhehehehe exactly !!!!!!!

Namita: and i hide somewhere !!

Namita: maybe under the bed

Nicholas: I know ur somewhere waiting but don't know exactly... on my toes..... senses sharp... listening... waiting

Nicholas: you could spring at any moment

Namita: hehehehe.. im trying not to breath

Nicholas: but then the giggling gives you away!!

Namita: hand over my mouth !!

Namita: hehehe

Namita: yesss but of course

Nicholas: and I jump you from your blind side.. you let out a yelp!!

Namita: AHHHHHHHHHHHHHHHH !!!!!!!!

Namita: i scream !!!!!

Nicholas: and i attack YOu!!

Namita: and run around the room ..jump on the bed and jump out of ur way

Namita: NOOOOooooo!!!!!!! hehhehee

Namita: then you totally pounce on me

Nicholas: lol I haven't played like this since I was a kid.. well not quite like this lol

Namita: hehehe me either !!!!!!!

Namita: i loveeeeee it !

Nicholas: yesssssss

Nicholas: we'll be like a couple of kids but serious when needed

Namita: hehehe ohhh yessssss

Nicholas: I'm getting hungry again

Namita: id loveeeeeee every moment of it !!!

Nicholas: me toooo

Namita: really ..for cereal?

Nicholas: i'm gonna love playing w you Namita

Namita: i can t wait !!

Nicholas: I guess I'll settle for cereal..... would like you but I have to wait till after the 10th boo hoo

Nicholas: that was my pouting

Namita: hehehee

Namita: i can almost hear it !!!

Namita: muahhh!!!!

Nicholas: kissing it better?

Namita: thats what i would do !!

Namita: yesss

Nicholas: well i wont need to pout when you're around

Namita: taking the swelling of ur lips down !!

Namita: hehe

Nicholas: but you can still kiss me whenever

Namita: ahhh ok ...hehhee

Namita: ohhh i will

Nicholas: oooo I can feel it, it seems to be working

Namita: hehehehe

Nicholas: you're awesome!!

Namita: so are you Nicholas !!

Nicholas: there is a word yet to be invented to describe just how amazing you are

Nicholas: thx.. we're in good company

Namita: hehehe ...wow ur thinking that !!

Namita: thats soo sweet

Nicholas: yup

Namita: hehe

Namita: do u want to call it a nite ...since ur hungry

Nicholas: I can eat after

Nicholas: I am getting tired though... you must be fading too

Nicholas: it is 3:35

Namita: yeah my eyes are hurting from the screen and im kinda getting a headache

Namita: from it

Nicholas: oh that's no good

Namita: hehe no

Namita: but i enjoyed every minute of our chat

Nicholas: oh yes me too!!

Nicholas: as I always do

Namita: hehe ..yes as always !!!

Namita: eat ur breakfast with that big huge pic of mine

Namita: watching you

Nicholas: I have the girls tmw, I'll pick them up after my breakfast

Nicholas: i will

Namita: ahhh ok

Namita: any plans ?

Nicholas: I'll see if you're around while I eat

Namita: hehe

Nicholas: Isabel needs an xray on her finger.. it's been 2 weeks now n the Dr wants to see how it's healing

Namita: ohhhhhhh

Namita: her mom didnt take her ?

Nicholas: I might check out a shoe store in new west

Namita: does she even work ?

Namita: ohhh ok

Nicholas: she'll be at work and they're w me

Namita: what does she do ...i cant remember if i asked

Nicholas: yah.. she's a book keeper for a pub

Namita: ohhhh

Nicholas: amazing how i can sense what ur going to ask

Namita: really ? you knew i was going to say that !?

Nicholas: I had a feeling

Namita: i remember

Namita: hehe

Nicholas: we'll probly go to Langely the get the oil changed in the car

Namita: thats a drive and a half !!

Namita: go to white rock then afterwards to the lil town

Nicholas: I'm going to make that pasta dish for them the one I told you about

Namita: yesss i remember

Namita: mmmmmm sounds good !!

Nicholas: I'm thinking I'll make a cheese sauce but w an old cheddar instead of the Tex Mex mix I usually use

Nicholas: the old cheddar will have a stronger flavor

Namita: ohhhh i see

Namita: sounds good though

Namita: does it have meat in it

Nicholas: I'm just going to use the chicken bacon n pasta this time

Namita: ohh ok

Nicholas: that way it's a nice mix of pasta cheese n bacon.. or little bacon bites in a cheese sauce

Namita: mmmmmmmmm bacon

Nicholas: and the chicken to make it well balanced

Nicholas: though I guess bacon is meat too

Namita: after i talked to you this morning i made myself a good cardiac breakfast

Nicholas: brain not working so good now

Namita: hehe

Nicholas: oh yah bacon n eggs

Nicholas: eggs cooked in the bacon fat?

Namita: yesss and sausage and toast with marmalade

Namita: loveeeeeeeee marmalade

Namita: i used to hate it when i was a kid

Nicholas: hmmm not a big fan of marmalade or sausage

Nicholas: I don't like the peel in it

Namita: ohh ur no fun !!! LOL

Nicholas: lol

Namita: i loveee it

Nicholas: well you are special so of course you do

Namita: sausage i can eat one or two ..but i do prefer bacon

Nicholas: bacon over sausage for me

Nicholas: I don't like the sausage burps all day after eating it

Namita: yes thats my preference too but i was a pig this morning ..my appetite returned with a vengeance

Namita: eweeeee Nicholas !!!!!!!

Namita: hehhee

Nicholas: too greasy n I don't like the spices in them either

Namita: lol

Nicholas: thats good you eat lots means you're on the mend

Namita: yeah

Namita: i wasnt even hungry fro lunch

Namita: but had snack instead

Nicholas: so will you be around tonight?

Namita: some veggies and dip

Namita: and apple juice

Nicholas: those are good

Namita: yes i will

Nicholas: ah yes juice love it

Nicholas: okay

Namita: mmmmmm yesss

Nicholas: I'll look for you earlier as I wont be at work n the girls will be in bed by 9

Namita: ok i will be around

Nicholas: I'll still log in at breakfast

Namita: ok

Nicholas: just in case I catch you

Namita: will look fro u

Nicholas: love starting my day talking w you

Namita: hehehe

Nicholas: smiled about that today too

Namita: its like we're not apart

Nicholas: yes

Nicholas: just a reconnect

Namita: uh huh

Nicholas: even though we just spent like 4 hrs talking

Nicholas: I love that!!

Namita: hehehehe i knowwwwwww where does the time go !!!!!!

Nicholas: talking for hrs and can't wait to talk w you again soon

Namita: i think we are getting the talking out of the way !!!

Nicholas: lol

Namita: hmmmmm now i wonder what we're really going to do !!!!!!

Nicholas: my mom thinks we'll be all talked out... I doubt that

Namita: hehhehee

Namita: did u talk to her about me ?

Namita: lol

Nicholas: yes me tooo.. I'm sure we'll cum up w something

Namita: hahhahahahahah niceeee one !!!!!

Nicholas: just whan i originally told her about you

Namita: ahh ok

Nicholas: she's still in Australia for another week

Namita: im sure my juices will be flowing when i try ..ahem ...to chat with you in real

Nicholas: mmmhmmm

Namita: ohhh cool !! i hope she is having a great time !!

Nicholas: me too

Nicholas: yes we'll do what we can to get your juices flowing

Namita: lol

Nicholas: okay I don't want ur headache to get bad

Nicholas: so we should say gnight?

Namita: hehe ... im trying not to stare at the screen

Nicholas: i don't like to hear that you're in pain

Namita: yeah ..i guess so

Nicholas: I not trying .... as your newest pic is up mmmhmmmm

Namita: lmao !!!!!!!

Namita: ur hypnotized by me !!

Nicholas: I am

Nicholas: captivated by you

Namita: aweeeeeeeeeee thx

Nicholas: I'm very lucky

Nicholas: anytime

Namita: one question to think about b4 we go

Namita: hehe

Nicholas: ppl ask if I win money a lot , I tell them my luck comes in diff forms

Nicholas: yes

Namita: just popped into my lil head

Nicholas: pretty little head

Namita: aweee nicholas sooo nicee

Namita: hehe

Namita: ok are you into lovemaking like everyday even multiple times ... so im asking do you have a good drive or stamina ?

Namita: hehe

Nicholas: yes I do

Namita: hehe

Nicholas: and we'll do it as many times as we want to

Nicholas: lol

Namita: hehe

Nicholas: i have both

Namita: i know i have a very strong drive for it ...of course with the right person

Namita: and im asking if ur ok with it

Nicholas: yes that's important

Nicholas: I am sooo okay with it!!

Namita: would i tire you ?

Namita: hehe

Nicholas: that was part of my wish too

Namita: what ?

Nicholas: we'll see

Nicholas: a high sexual drive

Namita: that someone has a naughty sexual appetite ?

Namita: yesss its ME !!!!

Namita: hehhee

Nicholas: I think I said "likes to have sex... is really attracted to me"

Namita: ohhhh ok

Nicholas: we'll see if you tire me

Namita: i dont remember

Nicholas: I wont tire of you

Namita: from LL

Namita: hehehe i know i wont !!

Namita: ur too cute !!

Nicholas: I haven't told you what my whole wish was yet

Namita: ohh ok ....what was it ?

Nicholas: I have a high drive esp when I'm attracted to my partner

Namita: LOVEEEEEEE IT !!!

Nicholas: I think I'll wait n tell you in person okay?

Namita: i think youve kinda knew that about me ..esp when i dropped hints

Namita: ok

Nicholas: I'll be able to do it w you as many times as my equipment will allow me and I'll be able to get you off regardless of if I'm hard or not

Namita: ohhhhhhhhhhhhhhh nicholas !!!!!!!!!!!!

Nicholas: you told me fairly early on about ur high drive

Namita: lol

Nicholas: I'm looking forward to satisfying you.... then you'll know what I've been talking about all this time

Namita: OMG i cant wait !!!

Nicholas: I'm pretty sure you'll have your fill and come back for more

Nicholas: but I'm sure I can wear you out

Namita: ohhh there sno coming back ,,... id be right there beside you the whole time

Nicholas: I certainly going to give it er you my all

Namita: ur making me hot right now

Namita: hehhe

Nicholas: literally and figuratively

Namita: literally !!!!!!!!!!!!!!

Namita: hehhe

Namita: omg im sooo excited for us

Nicholas: me too!!

Nicholas: not just in the bedroom either

Namita: yesss in many ways

Nicholas: we seem to have a great start to a wonderful relationship

Namita: yesss we hit almost every topic and covered soo much !!

Nicholas: yes we have and so easily too.. things just flow n I love it

Namita: yesss me too

Namita: ok we should sleep before we make it 5 am

Nicholas: yes we should

Namita: yesss i feel very comfortable with you

Nicholas: we go off on our chats n next ti's an hr later lol

Namita: hehehehehe

Nicholas: and I w you Namita

Namita: awee thnx

Nicholas: and I'm so glad you feel that way

Namita: i do

Nicholas: okay my brain is shutting dwn

Namita: mine too

Nicholas: gnight my sweet

Namita: goodnite luv

Nicholas: maybe see you later this morning if not tonight

Namita: yep

Namita: will be around

Nicholas: gnight you 😊 😊

Namita: 😊

End Time: 4:19 AM

Chapter 29 November 26

Start Time: 11:43 PM

Nicholas: hello !!!!

Namita: well hello there ..sorry to keep you waiting

Nicholas: you're not even in yet n I've already jumped on you lol

Namita: hehe

Nicholas: sokay you didn't

Nicholas: I was looking at storage cases online

Namita: yes i barely took my next breath and u jumped on me.. hehe

Nicholas: yes i did

Namita: ohhh cool !

Namita: did you find any ?

Namita: what kind of storage ?

Nicholas: I'm looking for an idea for a new tool storage box

Nicholas: I did

Namita: ohh i see

Nicholas: I built one before but I find it hard to move around n it's a little to small

Namita: u talk ..im changing

Namita: ohhhh...for those things you need alot of storage space

Nicholas: for my tools so I can wheel it out n work then close it up n put it away when I'm done

Nicholas: mmmm changing... into something sexy I'm sure hehe

Namita: hehe

Nicholas: I'm trying to keep the storage as compact as possible but easy use too

Namita: mmm if u were here im sure youd be glued to me as ur lying there on the bed !!

Namita: storage for ur tools?

Nicholas: I did find this one place that might work out easier than building something but I need to research it more

Nicholas: yes I would... I would let you put anything back on

Namita: hehe would or wouldnt ?

Nicholas: wouldn't lol... there's that poor spelling again

Nicholas: yes my hand tools... circular saw and router etc

Namita: ahhh i see ..makes sense

Nicholas: as I said I have one I built but it's not as user friendly as I'd like and it's a little too small

Namita: hmmm ...yeah well its good to try and find a good storage online ...its a good investment for those important equipment

Namita: and im sure the tools cost a lot too

Nicholas: these ones I found don't have casters which I want for ease of moving

Namita: yes i was going to ask you that ...if they had the casters

Nicholas: not too much... I'm not looking at storing them somewhere else... it's basically a rolling tool box

Namita: how much are they ?

Nicholas: I'll probly end up building something as always... that way I can customize it n it suits my needs perfectly

Namita: ohh cool !!

Namita: im sure ur handy in many ways like that

Nicholas: no Idea, I don't see a price, I know they aren't cheap

Namita: ohhh

Nicholas: thx.. I made the last one so the next one should be easy

Namita: you know what ur doing ..and thats good !!!

Nicholas: though when I do build it I haven't decided if I'm going to need a table saw... if I do then I'll have to build it at my mom's place where those tools are

Nicholas: thx... but when I go to my mom's I work on the hot rod so I can never win lol

Namita: ohhhh i see ... arent table saws huge ? and heavy ?

Nicholas: though I guess I win

Nicholas: I guess so to a degree

Nicholas: I usually research things online to get a good idea of what I want, then use all the qualities from all the ones I like n make my own

Namita: ohh good for you Nicholas !!

Namita: id still be beating my head trying to figure something out from scratch !!

Nicholas: I've always been that way I can never find exactly what I want n no one seems to make what I want or need so I build it

Namita: Wowww thats what i call handy !!

Nicholas: now you don't have to w me around... you can dream it n I'll make it

Namita: hehe thanks

Nicholas: anytime

Namita: i like when guys are handy like you !!

Nicholas: cool

Nicholas: I'm pretty handy

Namita: hehhee

Namita: how are the girls ?

Nicholas: I enjoy fixing things or building something out of nothing

Nicholas: they're good.. we had fun today I think

Nicholas: was busy

Namita: You did ?? what did you guys do ?

Nicholas: non stop from the time I picked them up...

Namita: im sure they loved every min of it !!

Nicholas: went n got Isabel's finger xrayed.... went to Langely to get the oil changed in the car..... went to Timmy's for lunch.... stopped a Rogers to grab a movie... came home watched the movie... then the game.... made dinner part way through the game and then bed for them about 9... pheeeeewwwww.. that was a lot

Namita: what movie did you guys see ?

Namita: hehe

Nicholas: Gulliver's Travels w Jack Black

Namita: ahhhh ... i havent seen that one !!

Namita: was it good ?

Namita: did they pick it ?

Nicholas: it was cute... not worth owning

Nicholas: they did

Namita: lol

Namita: im giggling here

Nicholas: it looked ok when it came out but didn't do well at the theater

Nicholas: I love it when you giggle

Namita: hehehe ... i guess it was a total miss !!

Nicholas: okay enf about my day.. how was your day and what did you do?

Namita: are they with you tomorrow as well?

Nicholas: they are till 4

Namita: any plans for tomorrow ?

Nicholas: probly just relax n hang out

Nicholas: was funny this morning...

Namita: hehe uh huh

Nicholas: I told them last night I'd be by before 10 to pick them up n I didn't wake up till 10 lol

Namita: hehehehe

Namita: were they wondering ??

Nicholas: oops.. I never know when I'm going to wake up

Namita: ohhhhhhhhhhh well we fell asleep late too !!

Nicholas: they texted to see if I was on my way.. had to tell them I'd be there by 11

Nicholas: yes we did

Namita: hehe ..so sorry to keep u up late !!

Nicholas: i sleep so soundly!! would have loved to wake up w you this morning

Namita: mmmmmmmmmm yessssss

Nicholas: please don't apologize I'm totally cool w it

Namita: with ur one arm over me .....over my tummy ....or holding me close

Nicholas: once we make room in our lives and find a bit of a routine it'll get easier

Nicholas: holding you close yes yes!!

Nicholas: always

Namita: yess

Namita: hehe

Namita: you burying ur face into my hair as we are kinda spooning each other

Nicholas: mmmmm yesss

Nicholas: I know I said this last night but I love these new photos

Namita: mmm my mind is on a roll !! hehhe

Nicholas: okay.... so what did you get up to today??

Namita: hehe were u looking at them today ?

Nicholas: I'd love to roll around w you hehe

Namita: oOOoOOOoo yesss

Nicholas: I was and swapped out the other one for this new one on my phone hehe

Namita: if u suddenly take me into ur arms roll me on top of you as im asleep and then im waking up wondering what happened

Nicholas: I sneek peeks at my phone all the time hehe

Namita: hehee

Namita: i hope ur daughters dont get a hold of ur phone ...hehhee

Nicholas: they don't and they know not too

Namita: hehe

Nicholas: they really have no need to open my phone

Namita: im not worried at all though

Namita: but yes they shouldnt go into ur phone either

Namita: and im sure they wont

Nicholas: neither am I but I'm being careful at the same time too

Nicholas: don't want to rush things

Namita: they sound like wonderful girls though !!

Namita: yes for sure

Nicholas: I'm excited for them to meet you but all in due time

Namita: yesss in due time ...and give them time to adjust too

Nicholas: I think they are... they are pretty special kids... very articulate and respectful

Nicholas: yes

Nicholas: I think they're going to love you

Nicholas: they know how to be in public

Namita: woww cool .. they sound so cute !!

Nicholas: they are though I'm pretty bias

Namita: hehe

Namita: can u describe them to me

Nicholas: I'll see if I can find a pic of them that's recent

Namita: well only if ur ready to do that nicholas

Nicholas: I'm ready just thought it'd be easier but I don't think I have recent pic of them

Namita: no worries at all

Namita: but if i were you ..dont give out their pics online

Namita: only when you have met me then

Nicholas: Isabel is the sporty one, she has a heart of gold.. has to try a little harder at things before she gets them esp in school

Namita: aweee ... does she have brown hair ,blonde ?

Namita: or blue eyes like her dad?

Nicholas: blue eyes blonde hair both

Namita: aweee cutee !!

Nicholas: their mom has blue eyes and had blonde hair

Namita: they must have been adorable when they were vavies

Namita: babies

Namita: i mean

Namita: arghhh

Nicholas: they were

Nicholas: Amanda is the younger one... more fragile than her sis... learning comes easy to her esp school work

Namita: good for her !!!

Nicholas: Amanda is a lot like me in her behavior too very laid back takes things as they come

Namita: im like that too ... hehe

Nicholas: Isabel stresses out easier and likes routine

Namita: ahhh i see

Namita: kinda like her mom?

Nicholas: a little

Nicholas: she Isabel is also at the age where everything is a bother to her

Namita: ohh noo ... i always forget their ages now ... is it 13 and

Namita: ohhhhh

Nicholas: I usually just let them talk about stuff

Namita: yes thats good ... but listen intently even though exteriorly ur nonchalant about it

Namita: i do that with my niece

Namita: when she talks about school ..and ive picked up on alot of thengs

Namita: things*

Namita: sorry im typing in the dark again

Namita: hehehe

Nicholas: it cool

Namita: hehhee

Namita: lol

Namita: question

Nicholas: yes

Namita: why did you guys split ...if you don't mind me asking

Nicholas: it's ok

Nicholas: I think that's a story for another time... a face to face convo

Nicholas: it's too much to type

Namita: oh ok

Nicholas: lets just say she presented herself as someone she wasn't and the type of person she really is played a big part

Namita: the decision to split was probably for the best ..and peace of mind for everyone ... it is not really setting a good example to ur kids if ur relationship was not healthy ... they are girls and they need to know that they shouldnt put themselves in a spot where their emotional and physical well being can be compromised

Nicholas: it worked out in the end... I'm much happier away from her... was kind of my get out of jail free card

Namita: when i said that paragraph above i meant... when ur girls are older and they start forming their own relationships... then they should be strong enough to know when to walk away

Nicholas: yes

Namita: now you know ...and trust ur instincts

Nicholas: yes I really listen to my instincts now

Namita: woww .. that is something though

Nicholas: now I make decisions based on my instincts not coz it's convenient or seems like it'd be fun for awhile

Nicholas: I've learned a lot in the last 5 or 6 year about myself

Namita: yesss cuz ur not doing urself a favour by settling

Nicholas: esp to listen to my instincts coz they're pretty damn sharp

Namita: youve been out on ur own ....about 2 yrs now?

Namita: good for you

Nicholas: and I may not like what my instincts are telling me but they're usually right in the end

Nicholas: been on my own for 6 years

Namita: ohhh its been 6 yrs

Nicholas: yup

Namita: how old were the girls then É

Nicholas: 5 and 7

Namita: arghhh my question maRK button is screwed

Namita: ahhh ok

Nicholas: it's cool I knew what it was

Nicholas: I feel you

Namita: hehe good !!

Namita: you do??

Nicholas: I feel you = I know what ur saying

Nicholas: I'd love to be feeling you

Namita: im using the number 6 button ..the second function is the question mark

Nicholas: so how was ur day?

Namita: but it is throwing me off ...cuz i have to reach for it while laying on my side here

Namita: day was good ... i thought i was getting better ..but ohhh noooooooo

Namita: my sinuses were congested ...and was sneezing alot

Namita: got wet in the rain didnt help

Nicholas: you must be in the home stretch by now

Nicholas: it rained most of the day here too

Namita: well still coughing stuff

Namita: wowww

Nicholas: yah comes w the territory

Namita: i hear strong winds in the forecast

Nicholas: you'll be better before you know it

Nicholas: it was pretty blowy here a couple of days ago

Namita: hehe yess

Namita: im such a baby when im sick too

Namita: even though im a nurse

Nicholas: oh yah

Namita: hehee

Nicholas: not as tough as you sound? hmmm or just when ur sick?

Namita: no just when im sick

Nicholas: you sound pretty tough to me

Namita: im tough in every other way ..at work

Namita: you wouldnt believe

Nicholas: ah... well I don't mind taking care of you

Nicholas: I bet you are

Namita: hehe ... you wont tell me to suck it up ??

Nicholas: you sound like a strong woman

Nicholas: god no!!

Namita: hehe thanks

Nicholas: I'll bring you soup and make sure you're warm

Nicholas: and keep up on your meds if they're needed

Namita: my friends tell me to suck it up buttercup !!!

Namita: hehe nice friends i have !!

Nicholas: yah well that's what friends are for

Namita: aweeeeeeeeeeee thanks nicholas !!!

Namita: lol

Namita: im sure the soup u bring me would be delicious

Namita: and you score brownie points

Nicholas: I hope you like it... probly Timmy's.. chicken noodle

Nicholas: love to score brownie point

Namita: mmm yess they are good too

Namita: lol

Nicholas: or whatever kind of soup you'd like but CN (chicken noodle) works the best

Namita: yess i lovee CN

Namita: and mushroom

Namita: you dont like mushroom right ?

Nicholas: I make chicken soup when I buy the whole chicken... I boil the bones n skin dwn then build a soup off that

Nicholas: I don't mind Campbell's Soup mushroom soup but yes don't like mushrooms

Namita: yess making ur own stock is good ... i do that too and then store it in the fridge to build on it later

Nicholas: yup... I freeze some of the soup too to have later

Namita: yes thats the one i eat ..campbells mushroom soup

Nicholas: I'll eat Money's caned mushrooms but none of the others

Nicholas: can't bring myself to eat a fungi

Namita: heheheheh

Namita: dont say that ..the first time i had mushroom soup was when i was in hospital when i was around 13 or 14 yrs old

Namita: actually royal columbian

Nicholas: for what?

Namita: ohhh i had tonsils out

Nicholas: me tooo!!!

Nicholas: when I was 4 OMG!!

Namita: omg you did too !!!

Namita: hehehe

Namita: i was 13

Namita: woww

Namita: hehe

Nicholas: use to get really bad earaches and that was the treatment

Namita: yesss me too

Nicholas: earaches?

Namita: yes cuz i used to get earaches ...and they used to swell up if i had a cold or flu

Namita: so they took them out at royal columbian

Nicholas: my god ur like the female version of me!! just way better looking hehe

Nicholas: I had mine out when we lived if Fort McMurry

Namita: lol !!!

Namita: omgggg ive been to ft McMurry !!!

Nicholas: I still remember it even though I was so young

Namita: in 2003 or 2004 ish

Nicholas: I know... you've told me

Namita: hehehe

Nicholas: er I remember

Namita: ok i wont bore you

Namita: with that story

Nicholas: your not

Namita: but it was in dead winter too

Nicholas: you just said u'd been to fort Mac

Nicholas: isn't it always the dead of winter there lol

Namita: lol yess

Namita: i really did freeze my ass off there

Namita: that is the coldest temp ive been in

Nicholas: well it grew back very nicely I must say hehe

Namita: lmao

Namita: thanks !!!

Namita: glad you like it !!!

Namita: how long were you there when u were little ?

Nicholas: mmm don't remember maybe a year or 2

Nicholas: ANd yes I do like it... can't wait to hold it in my hands

Namita: ahhh ok ...long time to be in the boonies for !!

Namita: lmao

Namita: hmmmm im sure it will fit right in

Nicholas: yah... my dad was working at Syncrude at the time

Namita: ohh yess

Nicholas: yes I think so too just the right size.. one for each hand

Namita: lol

Namita: i like how we are having 2 diff conversations here !!!

Nicholas: sorry I'm distracting u from ur story.. please go on lol

Nicholas: we've done that before

Namita: noo i didnt have a story .. i thought you did

Nicholas: mm nope mine was done.. wasn't that long

Nicholas: random

Namita: hehehe ok

Nicholas: have you seen the Truman show w Jim Carrey?

Namita: no i havent

Namita: is it good É

Nicholas: you haven't?!! omg we'll add it to the list... yes it's very good

Namita: hehe no i havent ... hmm never even thought of watching it

Namita: but yes add to the list

Nicholas: hmm.. we've got quite a list of movies.. we're going to have to have a few movie nights I see

Namita: hehee ..yesss ...like every other night i suppose

Nicholas: yah n EVery other night we'll be NAKED!!

Nicholas: or we can watch movies naked too

Namita: lmaooooo !!!!!!! I guess clothes is optional !!

Nicholas: yup

Namita: we wont have a problem with it ...less laundry

Nicholas: good thinking

Namita: we will save on the bill and detergent

Namita: see yesss a money saver

Nicholas: yes

Namita: lol

Nicholas: though the condom bill will be quite high lol

Nicholas: so it'll balance out

Namita: Lmao !!!!!!!

Nicholas: I'd take more condoms over more laundry any day

Namita: we may need to go to costco for them ...and stock up

Namita: hehehehe

Namita: ohhh nicholas !!!

Nicholas: yah... wont have to worry about the expiry date that's for sure

Namita: hehe for sure

Namita: i was thinking of the pill today

Nicholas: those poor things wont know what hit them lol

Namita: and was browsing the net

Nicholas: oh yah

Namita: what poor things ...lol?

Nicholas: oh yah

Nicholas: the condoms

Namita: ohhhhhhhhh

Namita: hehe

Namita: giggling

Nicholas: poor things wont know what happened to them lol

Namita: hehe

Nicholas: what did you find out?

Namita: anyways i was browsing the net ..and on yahoo there was a story ..of some family members suing the company of YASMin birth control pills

Namita: cuz the woman of the family ..who was i think in her 20`s ...died from a blood clot

Nicholas: I've heard Yasmin has been having trouble

Nicholas: oh geeze

Namita: i dont pay attention to those things ... so didnt know that that brand was having problems

Nicholas: the reg pill I don't think has those problems but I know there are side effects

Namita: will have to look into it

Nicholas: it's fairly new and a diff type of control

Namita: oh really ?

Namita: whats it called ?

Nicholas: I'm open to talking about it and whatever you decide I'll respect

Namita: it is a pill right ?

Namita: yes me too

Nicholas: I don't know the name of the reg pill that's been used for years n years

Nicholas: yes it's a pill

Namita: ahh ok

Nicholas: out of curiosity, what made you look into it?

Namita: hehe ... well i wasnt really intentionally looking into ...yahoo is one page i browse everyday ...and i saw it there ..and from there i started researching more

Nicholas: oh yah

Namita: im thinking if i should go on it

Nicholas: and why is that? if you don't mind me asking

Nicholas: I would still use condoms, so you know

Namita: well i dont want you to buy mega bulks of condoms ..and id rather be as close to you as possible

Namita: if that makes sense

Namita: yes i know

Nicholas: I see.. it does

Nicholas: form what I see if you were on it, we'd be able to play w/o a condom until it was time to finish, then roll one on n finish

Namita: hmmm thats a thought

Nicholas: you not being on the pill makes playing bare back very dangerous on the pregnancy front

Namita: yess i know

Namita: i wouldnt do that ...and take a risk like that

Nicholas: me either

Namita: its not worth it

Nicholas: even a little pre cum in the right area could be dangerous

Namita: yesss true !!!

Nicholas: no it's not and it's all about being comfortable w each other, which we are.. we just don't need to cause an issue that's totally preventable... hope that doesn't sound callus?

Nicholas: it's hard to convey caring n gentle in type form

Namita: no no it doesnt.. i totally understand what ur saying ... i dont want to be that person in that situation ..at this age ...single and pregnant

Namita: and its not me either ...ive never wanted to be in that situation ever

Nicholas: yes and you wouldn't be single as I'd be there for you

Nicholas: it is totally preventable so we do what we can

Nicholas: we'll do what we can

Namita: well we wont be pregnant in that situation

Nicholas: yes

Namita: yess we are adults ...not teenagers

Namita: so yes i understand

Nicholas: that's right

Nicholas: so if you going on the pill is something you want to do then we'll talk more about it.... the other option as I've said is me getting snipped

Namita: ok

Nicholas: it's all about our respect for each other and open communication

Namita: yes it is !!! Snipping sounds sooo invasive

Nicholas: from what I know it really isn't.. it's like 30 mins to an hr and 3 to 4 days recovery n that's it

Namita: is it covered by medical ?

Nicholas: it's a scalp-less procedure too

Namita: ohh ok

Namita: what do they do ?

Nicholas: mmm not sure, it just might be... would be worth looking into

Nicholas: I think they band the tube the sperm travels up from the testicles... not sure how they do it though... I'm thinking a needle of some sort

Namita: ohhh ok

Nicholas: you still get an ejaculate but there's no sperm in it

Nicholas: that I didn't know.. I thought you just shot blanks

Namita: things change sooo much in as little as a year ...they come up with something different all the time

Nicholas: they do

Namita: no i knew that

Nicholas: it's really quite an easy procedure

Namita: im sure it is ... a lunchtime procedure for some

Nicholas: would be very strange at first to not use condoms... we spend most of our lives trying to not get some one pregnant... then just be able to go for it when ever the mood strikes

Namita: hehehe

Namita: ok not when im cooking though ok ?

Nicholas: lol okay deal

Namita: any other time im game

Namita: like if ur talking on the phone with someone ..and i start coming at you

Nicholas: so you wouldn't want me to slide up behind you while ur in the kitchen n wrap my arms around you.... n slide my hands over ur breasts then maybe into your panties?

Nicholas: n diddle you while ur hands are busy?

Namita: mmmmmmmmm sounds nice already ... ok if you put it that way !! Sureeeeeeee

Nicholas: okay cool

Nicholas: hehe

Namita: hehe...well what if ur talking on the phone

Nicholas: mmhmm

Namita: and i come up and start kissing ur neck

Namita: and open ur zipper and start playing with you

Namita: making you all hard

Nicholas: I will never stop you from having your way w me!!

Namita: hehehe

Namita: and ur on a lengthy conversation

Nicholas: mmmhmmm

Namita: and u watch me kneel down

Namita: and open ur pants even more

Nicholas: mm love the sound of that... yes please!!

Namita: and pull u out ....and start teasing and sucking on ur already hard cock

Nicholas: mmm a thousand times yes!!

Namita: and ur trying hard to keep ur composure

Nicholas: I love the way you think!!

Namita: hehe

Nicholas: I am sooo there my god!!

Namita: and you start to tremble and shake as i take ur entire cock into my mouth

Namita: hehee

Namita: loooooonnng and hardddddddd

Nicholas: mmmm

Nicholas: omg! woman!!

Namita: but you just cant get off the phone

Namita: hehe

Nicholas: oh I'll get off in another way I'm sure of it!!

Namita: i make eye contact with you as ur hard cock is enveloped by my mouth

Namita: hahhahhaa

Nicholas: mmmmm yes please

Namita: you see the twinkle in my eye

Namita: i stick my tongue out at you

Namita: playing in ur precum

Nicholas: *sigh* my god yesssssss

Namita: my hand also doing wonders along ur shaft

Namita: does that turn you on ??

Nicholas: mmmm soooooo looking forward to feeling this too

Nicholas: hehe way past turned on

Namita: hehe

Nicholas: does that turn you on? he asks knowingly

Namita: omg yesss ...to torture you like that

Namita: to take some control from you

Nicholas: mmmm

Namita: ur at my mercy

Namita: hehe

Nicholas: I'd give it willingly esp knowing I'm in good hands

Namita: hehehehe

Nicholas: and mouth hehe

Namita: ohhhh you will literally be in good hands !!!

Namita: hehe yess an mouth

Nicholas: can't wait!!!

Namita: id run my tongue down the shaft

Nicholas: I love that you love doing that

Namita: suck on the base

Namita: and you can hear me ...doing this to you

Namita: now thats what i mean ..when i say im adventurous

Nicholas: I love that you have such an adventurous sexual appetite

Namita: not that swinger thing the other day !! OMG

Nicholas: yes I do

Nicholas: yes not like that

Namita: hehe

Namita: i told you !!

Namita: i have a good appetite

Namita: hehe

Nicholas: just being open to each other and doing what feels good

Namita: i could even open you up in the car ...maybe at nite ..if we`re driving ..and start playing with you

Namita: yesss totally

Nicholas: well I'll feed that appetite all it can handle!!

Namita: hehee

Namita: RArrrrrrrrr !!!!

Nicholas: yes please.. always open to road head hehe

Namita: hehehe

Namita: would u enjoy that ?

Nicholas: I love playing w you while I'm driving or ur driving

Nicholas: oh soooo very much

Namita: mmmmm yesssssss

Nicholas: it'd be sooo much fun

Namita: or park the car somewhere remote ..and just get it on !!!

Nicholas: yes yes

Namita: esp when its raining

Namita: and the windows fog up !!

Nicholas: I look for places like that when I drive around

Namita: im on top of you in the back seat of the car ...and im like a vixen ...and open my top ..so u can see my full breasts

Nicholas: or even a quick one in a parkaide during the day

Namita: yessss at work !!!

Namita: hehe

Nicholas: *deep sigh* yes

Namita: hehehehe

Nicholas: thought about you stopping by my work while I'm on dinner break n jumping you in the parking lot hehe

Namita: hehehe ... wouldnt that be cool !!!!!!!

Nicholas: yes it would

Namita: we have to time our rendezvous

Namita: 30 mins

Nicholas: I'd have such a big smile on my face when I went back to work lol

Namita: hehe

Namita: on my nite shifts i have 2 hrs straight on break

Namita: thats if it is not busy

Nicholas: yup 30, would be the quickest quickie we've ever had

Namita: hehe

Nicholas: OOOoooOOOOO

Namita: ive seen other nurses go for a quickie

Namita: well their 2 hrs

Nicholas: I'd love to jump you at your work

Namita: and they leave their phone numbers

Nicholas: I'd be all over that!!

Namita: hehehee

Namita: it will have to be in the car

Nicholas: sure

Namita: hehe

Namita: no janitor room here !!

Nicholas: they leave their phone numbers? how'd mean?

Nicholas: to get a hold of them if they're needed?

Namita: well i have to as well if im away from the unit ..even to go and get some hot chocolate for myself

Nicholas: ah I see

Namita: just in case an emergency happened with ur patient

Namita: like heart stopped ..or some lethal heart rhythm

Nicholas: I get it

Namita: that kinda of thing ...or ur partner is super busy

Nicholas: I'm gonna start a count dwn on the calender till you get back lol

Namita: then she or he can call

Nicholas: yup totally get it

Nicholas: this is killing me.... I have to find things to occupy my thoughts or they drift to you and how badly I want you

Namita: hehehe

Namita: ohhh nicholas !!

Namita: ok honestly .. how often do u fantasize of me sexually

Nicholas: looking at those big beautiful brown eyes n those amazing lips of yours... damn!!

Namita: heheh

Nicholas: lol per hr or per day

Namita: kissable ?

Namita: ohh wowww

Nicholas: YESSSSS!!

Namita: cool

Nicholas: oh so kissable

Namita: hehe

Nicholas: I fantasize about you probably 90% of the day n sexually about 95%

Nicholas: i'm really looking forward to just being able to spend time w you.. weather it be naked time or just being together

Namita: ohhhhh myyyy ... i do too !! I fantasize you with me in bed ... holding me ...inspecting me ...like my hands or fingers ...which i find endearing

Namita: or making love to me

Namita: aweee yess me too

Nicholas: was just going to ask that ... u beat me to it

Namita: i imagine you on top of me holding me down ... kissing me

Namita: ask what ?

Nicholas: how often you think of me

Namita: hehe

Namita: everyday

Nicholas: I think about you so much that it seems strange to not have you with me

Namita: aweeee so sweet !! nicholas !!

Nicholas: like the first time I see you we'll just carry on where we left off even though we haven't met physically

Namita: i imagine looking into ur deep blue eyes ...for which im a sucker for

Nicholas: cool

Namita: and smiling up at you

Namita: when ur laying on top of me

Nicholas: like we've only been apart for a few minutes

Namita: yessss

Namita: and then i imagine folding my hands behind ur neck

Namita: and we just kinda talk

Namita: for a bit

Namita: and you lay ur head on my chest

Nicholas: I wake in the morning n think "soon she'll be here"

Namita: or my tummy

Namita: hehhe

Nicholas: mmm love the sound of that

Nicholas: lay my head on you boobs mmm mmm

Namita: just those lil moments like that .. are soo intimate ...it doesnt have to be sexual

Nicholas: kiss you right between them

Nicholas: yes exactly!!!

Namita: we could be talking about what to eat fro dinner or something

Namita: mmmmmmmm yesssssss

Nicholas: yah just having such a deep connection

Namita: yesss exactly

Namita: id love it if you lay ur head on my boobs or tummy

Nicholas: I'll love kissing you in those spots coz I know I'm the only one that gets to

Namita: hehe yesssssss

Nicholas: lay my ear on ur tummy.... listening to ur body... love that

Namita: mmmmmmm yesssssss ... such and intimate feeling

Nicholas: yes

Namita: or i lay on ur chest

Nicholas: I love those moments, just being connected and happy

Namita: head on ur chest ...listening to ur heartbeat ...or on ur tummy

Nicholas: my hand on your shoulder or arm mmmhmmm

Namita: mmmm yessssss

Namita: im curled up to you

Nicholas: gently running my fingers up n dwn your arm

Namita: mmmmmmm yessssss

Namita: driving me wild silently !!

Nicholas: talking about whatever is on our minds

Namita: yessss

Namita: til we fall asleep in each others arms

Nicholas: it's going to seem so surreal when we do this

Namita: hehhee yesss

Nicholas: *smiling*

Namita: me too

Nicholas: it's almost like you're here or we're there

Namita: hehe yesssss

Nicholas: you have such a calming effect on me

Namita: really ... a lot of ppl say that about me ...friends and professionally

Namita: even my voice is quiet calm ... and soft

Nicholas: you have this way of making me feel like everything is okay in my world deep inside

Nicholas: I get that too!!

Namita: you do !!!

Namita: cool !!

Nicholas: calming and easy to be around... put ppl at ease

Namita: yesss me too !!!

Nicholas: 2 peas

Namita: hehe once again !!

Nicholas: yup

Namita: heyyy tell me if you have to call it a nite ok ..esp with the girls around

Nicholas: okay i will... I'm good... they're asleep n I'm on the couch tonight so it's all good

Nicholas: you tell me too okay

Nicholas: they usually sleep for 11 or 12 hrs when they're here

Namita: ok ..but i mean if you have to get up early and do stuff with them.

Namita: hehe woww thats good sleep

Nicholas: they catch up on their sleep when they're here, I think coz they can be totally relaxed here n be themselves

Namita: i dont want you to sleep in ..and they are waiting ..hehe

Namita: aweee

Nicholas: I will... we usually just hang out on our sundays but thx for the thought

Namita: ok

Namita: are u watching the grey cup tomorrow

Nicholas: lol I'm usually up before them even the last time we were up late n they were over

Nicholas: yah I'll try n watch

Namita: lol

Namita: i dont even understand football !

Nicholas: I do love this new big photo

Namita: lol

Namita: what do u love about it

Nicholas: the sparkle in your eyes... your wonderful smile... the woman i know and have become sooo very fond of

Namita: hehehe ... aweee thanks !!

Nicholas: how perfect I think you are on the inside too

Nicholas: knowing the woman in these photos is so amazing and wonderful and thinks the same about me too

Namita: do you have a type?

Nicholas: I do... kind, genuine, polite, confident, caring

Namita: most men want blondes

Namita: interesting how you went w qualities ... most ppl list physical

Nicholas: as I've said before I think diff

Namita: im exactly how i have presented myself ..my thoughts, beliefs , values, outlook etc

Nicholas: me too!!!!

Nicholas: I love how open you are we me right from the start... just as I have

Namita: awee thanks nicholas ... and so have you too !

Nicholas: at the start you were so refreshing to talk with...I think thats what drew me to you

Namita: wowww that is sooo nice of you to say that !!

Nicholas: you just put urself out to me as I do or did and it was so cool to get that kind of honesty in return

Nicholas: you are very welcome Namita

Namita: well i wanted to be straightforward with you ..and who i am ...what im looking for etc

Nicholas: I feel so lucky to have found such as amazing woman that sees the world the way I do... I know we said similar things last night but it's very important to me and I want you to know how lucky I feel having you in my life

Namita: ohhh that is sooo sweet of you to say that ...and ur very very welcome !! im blushing right now

Nicholas: *smiling*

Namita: hehehe

Nicholas: it will be 9 weeks tmw... when I do get to see you the waiting as torturous as it's been will be so very worth it... I'm sure it will all disappear once I can hold you

Namita: hehe ..woww its been awhile ... and time has flown by ...but we have covered so much ground by just chatting like this ...whereas it could have taken us more time to open up to each other if we were face to face

Nicholas: yes as we've said before

Namita: in reality i find that i can be reserved and kinda quiet and size a person up ...their behavior ...how the carry themselves ...or how they talk

Nicholas: I can't imagine you not around... not that I ever would

Namita: but i have opened up to you alot

Nicholas: and i love n appreciate it so much... it's difficult and tiresome to keep guessing what my partner is thinking or wants

Nicholas: I love that you've open your life to me

Namita: yes i dont like mind games

Nicholas: nor do I

Namita: and guessing all the time

Nicholas: I think I spent too many years trying to find someone who I was hoping I was right for them instead of deciding if they were right for me.. if that makes sense?

Namita: wowww that does make sense ...sometimes you just have to step back and think about what ur doing ...or try to see urself from third person perspective

Nicholas: yes

Namita: and you find the answers to ur problems

Nicholas: yah, just listening to what you really want in a partner and life itself and not compromising your values for anything.... and really understanding what those values are

Namita: yesss well said !!! esp at 3 am ...hehehe ...couldnt have said it better

Nicholas: side note; we could be the poster couple for LL... lol.... wonder if they'd pay us... hmmm

Namita: hehehe

Nicholas: lol yah I noticed the time too

Namita: yesss we could ...but would it be the orange section or blue or green

Nicholas: lol.. hmmm not sure

Namita: hehe

Nicholas: we'd have such a big disclaimer on our story though lol

Namita: hahahhaa

Namita: hehe ...yes we would have real fine print ..saying results may vary

Namita: or something

Nicholas: yup... not typical results lol

Namita: lol

Namita: thats too funny !!

Nicholas: yah, maybe we'll just keep our success to ourselves lol

Namita: if its orange ..then we could take a pic of me laying on ur chest ..and the pic is taken from ur back

Namita: hehe that too

Nicholas: yes and Miranda can take the photos

Namita: look at me !!! Im already thinking of the shot !!!

Namita: hehe

Nicholas: yesss look at you mmhmmm.. anytime

Namita: heheheee

Namita: im zoning out nicholas

Namita: so sorry

Nicholas: was thinking similar

Nicholas: it cool

Namita: really ?

Nicholas: yup

Nicholas: not zoning just that it's late

Nicholas: n you need ur rest to get healthy

Namita: im sure if were together and we are chatting liek this .. we would trail off mid sentence and fall asleep !!

Nicholas: how is ur uncle doing?

Namita: he is getting better slowly but surely

Nicholas: yes we will... then I can finally wake up next to you... and think mmm there she is

Nicholas: that's good to hear

Namita: and im going to eat her up !!!!!!

Namita: hehee

Nicholas: yes

Nicholas: snuggle next to you n gently touch you w my whole body

Namita: mmmmmmmmmmmm niceeeeeeeeeee

Namita: get me all aroused

Namita: watch my body react to you

Namita: and you smile gently

Nicholas: as much as I want you to sleep I'd want to wake you so I can talk w you some more

Nicholas: yes n touch you all over

Namita: yah right ...TALK !! MY ASS !!

Namita: hehee

Nicholas: mmm that ass of yours mmm

Namita: lmao

Namita: yes my ass what ??

Nicholas: yes that glorious ass of urs.. so nice n firm... so awesome mmmm

Namita: hehehehe ..... nicholas !!!

Nicholas: to run my hand over it.. to watch the goose bumps as ur skin reacts to my touch

Namita: ohh god ..yesss

Nicholas: n feel the heat from your body

Namita: mmmmmmm yesssssss

Nicholas: soon my sweet very very soon

Namita: hehe...yes yes

Namita: ohhhh alright !!

Nicholas: oh all right?

Nicholas: in ref to what?

Namita: i can wait i mean

Nicholas: oh gotcha

Namita: hehe

Nicholas: will be the best thing ever

Namita: i thought u were going to keep going

Namita: hehe

Nicholas: lol I was but ur not here n I was trying to keep it under control

Namita: ok ..down boy !!

Nicholas: I'll keep going when ur w me

Namita: are u hard?

Namita: hehe

Nicholas: sort of

Namita: you are !!!!!!!!!!!

Nicholas: lol I am now

Namita: wooooooooowwwwwwwwwwwwwwwwwww

Namita: hehe

Nicholas: it never really goes away while we're talking

Namita: ohhhhhhhhhhhh wowwwwwwwwwww

Nicholas: it's just at diff stages of hardness

Nicholas: thats the reaction u have on me Namita

Namita: hmmmmmmmmm sounds soooo good

Namita: may i ask

Nicholas: anything

Namita: are u thick

Nicholas: yes... said that before... or you just like me telling you how I'm built I bet hehe

Namita: hehehe

Namita: im blushing again

Nicholas: get ur sexy little ass back here and you can find out for yourself

Namita: hehe ok ok

Namita: hehehe

Nicholas: and try it out er on

Namita: we should get some sleep before something else gets in the way

Nicholas: yes we should

Namita: ohhhh i will be trying it out

Namita: are u going to sleep on the recliner

Nicholas: we'll have plenty of time to play when ur back

Namita: mmmmmm yesssssss

Nicholas: no no I sleep on the couch in my sleeping bag

Namita: ohhh ok

Nicholas: you just can't get back here soon enf for me lol

Namita: lol

Nicholas: I wont be around during breakfast so you know but I'll be on for sure at reg time probly earlier

Namita: ok

Nicholas: only coz the girls are here in the morning

Namita: will be around tomorrow nite

Nicholas: cool

Namita: yes i understand

Nicholas: can't wait

Namita: its their time anyways

Nicholas: it is thx for understanding though I knew you would

Namita: ohhh ur welcome Nicholas !!!

Namita: so goodnite then ?

Nicholas: till tmw then?

Namita: hehe

Namita: yes tomorrow

Nicholas: sorry was just imagining u here w me

Nicholas: 😊

Nicholas: sleep well my sweet and have a great day tmw

Namita: mmmmm i would have done something about ur hardness long ago

Nicholas: yes please

Nicholas: and i would have let you do what u wanted

Namita: hehe ..we should not get into that ...or esle it will be 9am soon

Namita: ohh yesss

Nicholas: lol yes it will.. u started it 😊

Namita: we both get sucked in

Nicholas: that we do

Namita: hehe yess my fault

Nicholas: but it's so much fun w you

Namita: i admit

Namita: hehe

Namita: goodnite Nicholas

Nicholas: okay gnight you

Nicholas:

End Time: 3:26 AM

Chapter 30 November 27

Start Time: 11:27 PM

Namita: heyyy there

Nicholas: heyyyy

Namita: can you give me a moment ... hope ur day was good

Nicholas: sure can

Namita: i just got in

Nicholas: let me know when you're good to talk

Namita: ok

Namita: i shouldnt be too long

Nicholas: ok

11:29 PM

12:24 AM

Namita: oh god soo sorry i got caught up with family ... i was washing my face and got stopped in the hallway

Namita: then i went downstairs to get a drink ....bad move !!

Namita: got caught in with everyone

Namita: sorry to keep u waiting

Nicholas: it's okay, family first

Namita: i keep saying that almost every nite

Namita: hows was ur day ?

Nicholas: its totally fine I'm just hanging out

Namita: ok

Nicholas: was ok... the Lions won the grey cup!!

Nicholas: how was ur day?

Namita: yess i heard !! I hope there wasnt any of those idiots out there destroying the city

Namita: was it a good game ?

Nicholas: yah I hope so too

Nicholas: was good.. the Lions seemed to be the dominant team

Namita: ohh good for them !!

Nicholas: I didn't wake up till 11:20 this morning

Namita: ohh hehehe .. were the girls wondering ?

Nicholas: Amanda was up about an hr before me.. Isabel got up about a half hr after me

Nicholas: I DId have a dream about you last night

Namita: ahhh ... they must have been tired too

Namita: you did!!!

Namita: what did you dream ?

Nicholas: they seem to catch up on their sleep when they're here

Nicholas: it wasn't a long dream but

Namita: wowww ..can u remember any of it

Namita: yeah well thats good for them ... they sound like lil angels

Nicholas: you were beside m n I realized that I could kiss you so I did!!!

Namita: hehee

Nicholas: it felt like the very first time

Namita: hehe ..did i respond ?

Nicholas: and it was as vivid as I've imagined!!

Nicholas: the dream was over too soon to see ur reaction

Namita: aweeee to bad !!

Namita: hehe

Nicholas: it was such a great feeling!!

Namita: well i would have devoured you ...by rolling on top of you ...and pinning you

Nicholas: hehe

Namita: lol

Namita: and you would be like ...what the hell just happened ??

Namita: and you would shake ur head

Namita: hehhee

Namita: and id be giggling like usual

Nicholas: my subconscious reminded me I was on the couch n the girls were here n not too get too carried away w the dream

Nicholas: lol

Nicholas: I'd devour you too

Namita: hehehe ...isnt that weird that even in ur sleep ...you seem to be aware of ur surrounding

Nicholas: there would be nothing left of us.... just a white ball of energy

Namita: hahahaa

Nicholas: yah I do... I'm always aware of my surroundings... makes me wonder if my mind sleeps at all

Namita: hehehe

Namita: yeah

Nicholas: maybe that's why I don't usually remember my dreams

Namita: did you guys do anything after getting up ?

Namita: well they say most ppl dont remember their dreams after 10 mins of waking up

Nicholas: nope.. just hung out.. ate... watched the game

Namita: and it is sooo true

Namita: ahhhh ...hope they had lots of fun !!

Namita: im sure they look forward to next weekend

Namita: you have them every weekend ?

Nicholas: a book I think I told you about said that they think ur mind dreams to file the days events away

Nicholas: usually every other weekend

Nicholas: sometimes it works out that I get to see them 2 weekends in a row

Namita: ahhhh ... that is cool with the dream...probably true

Nicholas: like this coming weekend

Namita: cool ..im sure they love being with you

Namita: ahhh ok

Namita: they look forward to it im sure

Nicholas: they do

Namita: does their mom work every day

Namita: or just weekends

Nicholas: she works thurs to sun but she's going on full time now that she's done some work related upgrading

Namita: ahh i see

Namita: do the girls come home from scool by themselves then ?

Namita: omg ...i cant even spell school ...hehhe

Nicholas: before I was on afternoons I would see them mon and thurs eve and every other weekend

Namita: yes i did go to school !!!

Nicholas: lol

Namita: hehe

Nicholas: their mom's usually done work by 3 and she picks them up

Namita: ahhh good

Namita: these days ..it is sooo different than when we were growing up

Nicholas: she leaves them alone sometimes, which I'm not real keen on, but they're not usually alone for too long

Nicholas: no kidding eh

Namita: i remember ..walking to school thru all my years by myself

Namita: even to charles best ..which is near mariner road

Nicholas: or walking to the store n not thinking twice about it

Namita: yesss

Namita: i did that too ... to get candy

Namita: or when mom sent me to get something she ran out of

Nicholas: I was mindful of my surroundings but more so now

Namita: like a lil corner store run

Namita: i knowww times have changed sooo drastically

Nicholas: yah or ride ur bike around

Nicholas: yah

Namita: uh uh

Nicholas: I always said I'd never be one of those "I just looked away for a second" parents

Namita: omggg me either

Nicholas: I just looked away for a second n they were gone

Namita: even though i dont have kids

Namita: i notice sometimes in a mall

Nicholas: i always knew I'd have kids

Nicholas: I've always like kids

Namita: the parents or mom is walking ahead and the lil 2 or 3 yr old is behind them a few feet away

Namita: yess me too

Namita: and i wonder ..how can they do that .... they seem so confident that no one can walk away with their kid

Nicholas: I relate to kids well too... I know what it was like to be a kid..... and the only thing that kids want to be, is an adult or at least treated as an equal... I talk to them like an equal... not dwn to them or condecending baby talk like some parents do

Namita: when i had my niece or nephew with me ... im always holdign their hand

Namita: with and iron grip

Nicholas: yah

Namita: yeessss soo true

Nicholas: I taught the girls early on that I need to be able to see them where ever and whenever we are out

Namita: yesss that is sooo good !!! Im like that too with my niece and nephew

Nicholas: and that screaming is nasty.... you only scream when someone is trying to steal you or your sister

Namita: ohhh good !!! yes that isss very good that youve instilled that !!

Nicholas: when they were little I could walk into a room full of kids screaming n playing and my kids would be the ones not screaming

Nicholas: I saw it once w Isabel when she was in kindergarden

Namita: heheheeee... wowww that is good !!! Im sure you must be proud of them

Nicholas: kids seem to join in on that gang mentality... like when one kid starts to scream others join in

Namita: then ur like ...noooo thats not my kid !!! hehehe

Nicholas: yup

Namita: yesss it is soooo true ... its a learned behavior

Nicholas: what did you get up to today?

Nicholas: you must be pretty comfortable w your surrounding dwn there

Namita: we decorated the xmas trees ...and helped my aunt ...since most of the family is here ....kinda cheering her up

Nicholas: though anxious to get back I bet

Namita: and bringing some normalcy to her

Namita: yesss i would love to get back to my bed

Namita: hehee

Nicholas: thats good of you.... though you're like that so it seems natural to assume that

Namita: and then we went around town ... visited my moms side of the relatives

Nicholas: oh yah right your own bed... will feel sooooo good

Namita: my grandpas brother is still alive ...but usually not doing well

Namita: i consider them my grandparents

Namita: him and his wife

Nicholas: cool

Namita: who is also elderly

Nicholas: how many relies do you have dwn there?

Namita: well my mom knows them since her childhood and he reminds her of her dad... my real grandfather

Nicholas: yah your family will be around the same age as mine

Namita: omg i lose count ... i have relies from both sides of the family

Namita: my mom has cousins ... and their families

Nicholas: one of the many things I love about you.... there's no generation gap

Namita: then my dad has cousins too

Nicholas: and all that family is in Frisco?

Namita: hehehehe no

Namita: nicholas that is just some of the family !! hehee

Namita: i have some in washington

Namita: in seattle

Namita: in england

Nicholas: yah I bet

Namita: New Zealand

Nicholas: wow!!

Namita: australia

Namita: india

Namita: fiji

Namita: and singapore

Namita: then here as well

Nicholas: we'll have to make sure we give everybody lots of notice if we decide to get them all together lol

Namita: the puranjay clan is huge

Namita: hehehee

Nicholas: no kidding

Namita: a year in advance

Namita: hehe

Nicholas: yah no kidding

Namita: hehhee

Namita: one reason why my sisters wedding was sooo big

Namita: then all the family friends

Namita: omgggg thats never ending too

Nicholas: I'll need some of your family to even out the odds lol

Namita: lol

Namita: it is one huge big happy family

Namita: i think ive told you ... i have cousins whom ive never even met

Nicholas: I have the girls, my sis, my mom, Shannon probly Tony n that's about it

Nicholas: yes you have said that

Namita: hehe ... thats ur clan !!! can u imagine if you met all my family

Nicholas: though I don't mind if you repeat urself lol

Namita: we would have to start in the morning or something

Namita: hehe

Namita: yeah i thought i mentioned it

Namita: i was going to sit down one day and count them all

Nicholas: defiantly and all day meet n greet lol

Namita: smile and wave !!

Namita: hehe

Nicholas: maybe I could just have a QnA session in front of all of them lol

Namita: and dont worry we do have relatives by marriage who are white too

Namita: hehehe

Nicholas: lol funny

Namita: they would grill you ...esp the girls

Nicholas: I bet!! ... I can handle them

Namita: im sorry ... hhehe ... i wasnt sure how to say that ... the polite way of saying it

Nicholas: though I'm sure that by you introducing me to your family they'd know I was someone special and important

Nicholas: totally fine... I don't get offended very easy

Namita: hhee ..they would surround you ..and it will be one interrogation after another ...and i will stand in a distance and smile and wave

Namita: ohhh good !!!

Namita: hehe

Nicholas: lol

Namita: i was going to say caucasian ...then thought that was too proper

Namita: aahhhhhhhhhhh i dunno !!!!!!!!

Namita: hehee

Nicholas: its cool

Namita: arghhh

Nicholas: you did fine

Namita: heheheh

Namita: do i get an interrogation ?

Nicholas: mmmm don't think so... my family knows I'm very selective w who I date and I don't introduce them to just anyone

Namita: ahhh ok ..well thats good !!!

Namita: so im off the hook !!

Namita: hehehehe

Nicholas: you are

Namita: heheh

Nicholas: what are you up to tmw?

Nicholas: you must be running out of things to occupy ur time

Namita: not sure ...usually things happen spontaneously ... i go with the flow .... i do spend time with my uncle every day though

Namita: what about you ...and plans before you go to work ?

Nicholas: thats good, that you spend time w him... tis the reason ur there

Namita: yess thats right ... he is waking up ...but cant talk ... he has a tracheostomy ...a breathing tube thru his neck

Nicholas: mmmm not sure.. nothing major... I'll try to remember to make an appointment w the dentist now that my benefits have kicked in

Nicholas: ooohhh great!!! he's waking up that's awesome news Namita!!

Namita: ohhh good !! that is such a good feeling when you know youve got good benefits thru ur work

Namita: are the girls covered under urs ?

Nicholas: yah n they are good benefits too.. yes they are

Namita: yessss ive been excited but guarded too

Nicholas: 100% basic dental which is awesome

Namita: that is good !!!

Nicholas: I bet

Nicholas: in your professional opinion how do you think ur uncle is doing? or would you rather not answer like that?

Namita: yesterday was the first time i went in to see him ..after being sick all week with a cold

Namita: so i was happy to see him

Nicholas: cool.. yah don't want to give him a cold

Namita: hmmm i think he is doing ok ... but sometimes things happen

Nicholas: I can feel ur enthusiasm

Namita: sooo i do hope he averts any setbacks if he has any

Nicholas: that they do.... I'm sure he can feel the good vibes from having such loving family around him

Namita: yesss mee tooo

Namita: how ur mom doing ? have you talked with her lately ?

Nicholas: coming from a good family was part of my wish too

Namita: aweee really?

Nicholas: haven't heard from her since she arrived dwn there.... she'll be back the end of the week... I think that'll be 3 weeks

Nicholas: yup

Namita: hehe i hope she is having a great time !!

Nicholas: shows me a solid family foundation

Namita: and made the most of her trip

Namita: yess that is important to me

Namita: as well as forming new bonds and relationships

Namita: thats what keeps us together as a unit

Namita: no matter what

Nicholas: me too.. I hope she's able to find a way to move forward in her life... she's still pretty out of sorts w my dad not around

Namita: im sure the void will never go away ....but she will learn to go on

Namita: sometimes you just have to

Nicholas: it's something you never get over but one needs to find ways to move forward

Namita: yesss sooo true

Namita: we kinda said the same thing ...hehhe

Nicholas: I know when I get sad about him not being around I just think of him n can hear him say "don't worry about me, just keep carrying on"

Nicholas: yes we did... we do have a tendency to do that hehe

Nicholas: just typing that choked me up a little

Namita: aweee nicholas !! you know from somewhere ... im sure he is proud of you and who you are ...and who youve become

Namita: ohhhhhhh 😭 😭 😭

Namita: i know if something happened to my parents ..id be lost

Nicholas: my mom said he told her to tell my sis n me that before he died

Namita: i cant imagine

Namita: ohhhh woww

Nicholas: it's the worst thing to happen to me

Namita: ohh im soo sorry to hear that

Nicholas: you just find ways to move forward

Namita: yess

Namita: you must have been real close to ur dad ...probably ur first real friend

Namita: ur buddy

Nicholas: I know my sis had a harder time w it than I did

Nicholas: yah we became real close

Namita: ohh wow ... she was just as close

Namita: i dont hear very often of ppl being close to their parents ...most times i feel they take them for granted ... and to hear that from you ..really shows me the kind of person that you are

Namita: hehehe

Namita: aweee

Nicholas: no my sis was on again off again w my dad... fortunately she was on w him when he died

Namita: ohh i see

Nicholas: awe thx... my dad n I had a lot in common and he taught me so much

Namita: imagine the guilt on her if she wasnt

Namita: that is sooo good to hear

Nicholas: its a shame when ppl don't appreciate their parents

Namita: ive always had a good relationship with my parents

Namita: both of them

Namita: i tell them i love em ...and hug them ...kiss them ...like today ..hehe

Namita: i saw my dad sitting alone waiting for family members

Nicholas: no kidding... I know my cousin felt guilty for not keeping in touch w him... my cousin thought of my dad as a father figure as he was adopted and didn't always have a male role model in his life

Namita: and i went up to him ... gave him a hug and kiss for no reason ..and he was like HUH ??

Namita: ahhh i see

Nicholas: I know being a dad those little things make you feel so good

Namita: hehehe yesssss

Namita: my dad still considers me as his lil baby

Nicholas: I love it when the girls, usually it's Amanda comes over n gives me a hug for no reason

Namita: hehehe

Namita: that is sooo cute

Nicholas: yah as much as ur kids grow up you still see them as those little kids

Namita: lil girls are soooo fun

Namita: at every age

Namita: ur always trying think what is going on in their minds

Namita: yes and Isabel ?

Nicholas: Isabel's not as huggy as Amanda but she shows her feeling in her own ways

Namita: ahhhh ok ..was she ever ?

Nicholas: ummm she was when she was little but she grew out of it quite early

Namita: ahhh ...well it is a girl thing ..it may return at some point

Nicholas: I hope so

Namita: hehe

Namita: well if she doesnt ...you do it ...and keeo doing it

Nicholas: I let her be herself n let her know I'm there for her when she needs me

Namita: keep*

Namita: yessss thats good too

Nicholas: I'm hoping when she's older she'll see that she can be more open w her feelings

Namita: yes ...oh she will see one day or another ...right now her mom is the only close woman figure to be an example

Nicholas: you know, switching subjects, I have so many photo's of you that I have 3 diff screens on my desk top

Namita: hahahhaa

Namita: you just switch from them ?

Nicholas: on a Mac I have what's called Spaces n it lets me have 4 diff screens at the same time

Namita: ohhh cool !!

Nicholas: and yes I can switch to which ever one I want

Namita: ohh wowwww

Namita: i dont have that ...mine is a mere ordinary pc

Namita: hehehe

Nicholas: screen 1 has the lovely red dress you sent the other night and the large pic from the same night

Nicholas: screen 2 has more the same type of pics

Namita: uh huh

Nicholas: but screen 3 has all the hot n sexy photo's!!

Namita: hehehe

Namita: the sizzling ones !!! Yeah keep them at bay !!!

Nicholas: and I love the black bra n panties one

Nicholas: I figured out what I love about it

Namita: ohh yesss

Namita: i forget that i gave u that one

Namita: hehe

Namita: what is that

Nicholas: it's the playful candid look you have... and your amazing body too!!

Namita: hehehe aweeeee thanks !!!

Nicholas: the magazine-y one

Namita: hehehehe

Nicholas: shows lots of skin mmm mmm

Namita: im like that in real life too ..playful ....and stay stress free

Nicholas: nice n you've said that before n I love that about you

Namita: despite my job ... im the opposite

Nicholas: I try to be calm n relaxed all the time too

Namita: i dont drink smoke or do coffee or tea or drugs everrr ..and im still stress free

Nicholas: me too

Namita: i`ll probably live till im 130 or something

Namita: hehhee

Namita: or both of us

Nicholas: well I don't consider one drink when out w Tony being a drinker as I have a drink maybe 4 times a year

Namita: yesss well that is absolutely nothing

Nicholas: you'll always look 39 to me

Namita: a drop in the bucket

Namita: hehehe

Namita: aweeeeeeeeeee thanks

Namita: im cool with being stuck on 39

Nicholas: I don't know how ppl can drink so much or so often

Nicholas: age is all a state of mind

Namita: ohhh god me either

Namita: yess i agree

Namita: ive seen patients drink 40 ouncers or 3 or 4 cases of beer a day

Nicholas: I don't like the taste of alcohol... when I have a drink I drink it coz I like the taste of what I'm having... not to get smashed... was never like that

Namita: and then they come into hospital sick for other related causes ...and then go to alcohol withdrawl

Namita: and it is soooooooooooo bad

Namita: we have to tie them down with their arms and legs

Nicholas: I bet

Namita: ohhh good ... i cant even acquire the taste of alcohol ...even wine

Nicholas: I've never liked wine n don't know why ppl drink it

Nicholas: I guess that's good for us though, one less thing to have to buy lol

Namita: ohhh god me either ..if i take a sip of it ..i wanna spit it out ...it takes me a few mins to even swallow it ... then i tear up

Namita: eweee

Namita: hehehehe yesss

Nicholas: yah I don't see what others see or taste in it

Nicholas: as I've said I'd rather have milk or juice, water

Namita: omg i thought i was the only one on this earth to think that

Nicholas: nope

Namita: juice for me

Nicholas: yes

Nicholas: another similarity

Namita: im not a milk person ...unless its hot chocolate

Nicholas: yes you've said that before

Nicholas: did you not grow up w milk?

Namita: hehe yes

Namita: ohhh my mom tried

Nicholas: as i've said I go through 4 liters in about 5 days I guess

Namita: i did have it with cereal ...but it took awhile for me to even drink the milk at the end

Nicholas: are you not concerned w osteoporosis ?

Namita: hehe .. i try to drink milk in other ways

Namita: like hot chocolate

Namita: or eat fish ..for calcium

Namita: or ice cream

Namita: yogurt

Nicholas: drinking the milk at the end of ur bowl of cereal is important coz there are water soluble minerals in that milk n you miss out on the if you don't drink it

Nicholas: ah okay the ur good then lol

Namita: ohhhhhhhhhhh ok ..if you say so geeeeeeeeeeeeeezzzzzzz why do you have to be soooooo difficult !!!

Namita: hehehee

Nicholas: lol

Namita: hehe

Namita: you can hear the defeat in me

Nicholas: just one of the many features I have to offer... keeps you on ur toes lol

Nicholas: I can

Namita: sitting at the table and you forcing me to drink my milk

Namita: hehe

Nicholas: I hear more sarcasm than anything lol

Namita: the other bad habit i have

Namita: is when im eating a sandwich ... with crusts ...i peel them off

Nicholas: sarcasm?

Namita: cuz i dont like them

Namita: noooo no sarcasm

Namita: hehe

Nicholas: OH no you don't eat ur crusts tisk tisk lol

Namita: yesss i admit

Nicholas: ha I can hear it in ur reply lol

Namita: and i was the stickler when my sisters wouldnt eat them as kids

Nicholas: what will I do w you *shakes head*

Namita: well i try to eat it

Namita: i will nibble on the crust at the end when i feel im still hungry after i devoured the sandwich

Nicholas: I just might have to send you to bed w no desert lol

Namita: lmao

Namita: heyyyyy i can have it in bed !!!

Namita: wink wink

Nicholas: eat ur crusts n u could have desert IN bed

Namita: lol

Nicholas: same thing again we on a roll tonight

Namita: heheheh i knowwwwwwww

Namita: like minds again !!!

Nicholas: yet again... so cool!!

Namita: hhehee

Namita: giggling !!!

Nicholas: *smiling*

Namita: ahhhh we are a duo !!!

Nicholas: we are... unstoppable!!

Namita: hehehe

Nicholas: I know I keep asking n you keep answering but... you still looking at coming back on or around the 10th?

Namita: yes i am

Nicholas: okay *sighs*

Namita: my pc keeps freezing on me …arghh

Namita: i knowww sounds far away still

Nicholas: oh no, that's no good

Namita: its ok now

Nicholas: you know if the girls hadn't have had a pro-d day the fri before you left we might have been able to see each other before you left

Nicholas: yes it does sound far away but it's only 2 more weeks

Namita: hehe yeah i guess so ... i forgot about that

Nicholas: in all reality it's been 9 weeks today since we met Cyberly so 2 weeks more is or will be nothing

Namita: you will survive !! Hehhee for both of us !

Nicholas: it'll go by before we know it you'll be in my arms soon enf

Nicholas: yes we will

Namita: aweeeeee yesss

Nicholas: my dream last night will carry me through a little bit further

Namita: hehe ... hope u dream tonite ...or i come into it ... the one and only

Nicholas: I'm sure you will

Namita: hehehe

Nicholas: you know I don't usually dream about someone.... so you must be really prominent in my mind

Namita: im ur subconscious and invaded every corner

Namita: hehe

Nicholas: well I know I think of you most of the time

Nicholas: yes you have and I'm ok w that

Namita: yeah me either ... i dont dream anything in particular

Namita: i do have a lot of dreams of my childhood home in coquitlam though

Nicholas: if I can't have you w me physically then I'll take subconscious anytime

Namita: i dont know why ...probably cause it doesnt exist anymore... they tore it down

Nicholas: maybe coz it was such a big factor in ur life

Namita: i was soooo sad to see another house in its place ... it wasnt like it was run down

Namita: it was probably close to 45 or maybe 50 yr old house

Namita: yess maybe

Nicholas: I know I think about the house I grew up in sometimes.. I concentrate on all the details n travel through the whole house in my mind

Namita: yessss me too !!

Namita: every nook and cranny

Nicholas: I do that w my grandparents house from Falkland too

Nicholas: yes!!

Namita: even exactly where the floors creeked

Namita: hehehe wooow cool

Nicholas: the grandparents house was so, um, I felt so loved and comfortable in it, it make some feel safe and calming

Namita: woowww that is sooo good ...it is still around ?

Nicholas: *makes me feel

Namita: still there

Nicholas: yup

Namita: are you tired

Nicholas: yah it is both of them I think

Namita: ohhh ok

Nicholas: sorry just saw an add for a museum in ontario that the gov might close, so I was signing the petition to try to keep it open.... its a building that built planes for WW2 then turned it into a museum

Namita: ohhh cool !!!

Namita: i loveee old history

Nicholas: do you want the site to sign it?

Namita: i studied world history in school ...esp the WW1 WW2

Namita: etc

Namita: sure

Nicholas: okay cool

Nicholas: http://casmuseum.org/

Nicholas: the petition is in the top right hand corner

Namita: ohh ok

Namita: stupid pc is freezing up

Namita: i will do it later

Nicholas: oh geeze, I thought you were signing the petition

Namita: i was tring to ..but pc froze up on the page

Nicholas: damn

Namita: yess damn !!! is there a time limit

Nicholas: I don't know. I just saw the add so I'm thinking you have a little bit of time

Namita: ohhh ok

Nicholas: I'm trying to post the youtube add from the site to FB to promote the cause but I can't seem to find the add on youtube

Namita: ohhhh ...hehe i cant help u ...dont look at me ! hehee

Nicholas: lol

Namita: lol

Nicholas: I'm going to look at you all the time my dear

Namita: hehehe

Nicholas: well any chance I get I will

Nicholas: I figured it out

Nicholas: it's posted and all is well again lol

Namita: http://www.youtube.com/watch?v=3KsF6khzsUU here watch this ...totally cracks me up when i look at this

Namita: ok phewwwwwwwwwww

Namita: crisis averted

Nicholas: you showed me this site before

Nicholas: still funny though

Namita: i did !!!!

Namita: omg

Nicholas: yup

Namita: i think the reason why is stuck on me..is cuz ...i actually seen it in stires

Namita: stores

Nicholas: did you get a chance to see the other youtube links I sent the other night?

Namita: like the snuggle blanket

Nicholas: yah I've seen them too and the infomercial too

Namita: hehhe eyes i did

Namita: yes

Namita: i mena

Namita: mean ....fuckkkkkkkkkk

Namita: hehhee

Namita: ARGHHHHH

Nicholas: holy sh** this one was on the side bar of the link you sent. check this out

Nicholas: what's got you so riled up?

Namita: what do u mean ?

Namita: hehehee

Namita: i cant see my keys

Nicholas: what's w the cussing and ARHHH?

Namita: cuz my spelling is wayyyyyy off sometimes

Namita: hehe

Nicholas: can you not turn a light on?

Namita: seen before that

Nicholas: it's all good... I know what you're meaning

Namita: hmmm well thats an idea !!

Namita: thanks nicholas !!

Namita: hehhee

Nicholas: lol I'm full of ideas. not always good ones lol

Namita: no i dont have a lamp ... i dont want to turn the big floodlights on

Namita: hehehehe

Namita: thanks though

Nicholas: yeah I wondered about that

Namita: what were you holly sh***ting about

Nicholas: oh this vid that was on. lemme send it

Nicholas: http://youtu.be/Mp0B8HPDSNQ

Nicholas: very strange indeed

Namita: ok

Nicholas: someone came up w that

Nicholas: weird eh?

Namita: OMG weird !!!

Nicholas: there is some wired shit on there

Namita: ya i know ... i thought they keep an eye out on bad videos

Nicholas: just the nudity I think

Namita: yeah ...im not sooo sure about that

Nicholas: really?

Nicholas: I haven't seen any not that I'm looking lol

Namita: i saw a video of some homemade music with lots of nudity ...and it was in the sidebar of one of my fav songs

Nicholas: really wow

Namita: that was like 3 weeks ago too

Nicholas: geeze

Nicholas: crazy

Namita: yes i was surprised

Namita: i dont see it now

Nicholas: yah it surprises me what some ppl put on there or out there

Namita: yeah reALLy

Nicholas: they're usually pretty quick about deleting it

Namita: lol

Nicholas: *shakes head* some really wired stuff

Namita: uh huh !!!

Nicholas: find anything interesting?

Namita: wackos out there i tell ya

Namita: heheh nooo

Namita: i didnt find that crazy video

Nicholas: oh well

Namita: im zoning out though

Nicholas: oh okay do you want to sleep

Nicholas: oh geeze its 3 wow

Namita: hehehe

Nicholas: didn't notice till now

Namita: hehehe

Namita: are u tired ?

Nicholas: was just like 1ish not too long ago

Namita: dont you get cold sitting out there in ur recliner

Nicholas: a little but as I say I only get a few hrs w you so I take them when I can

Namita: yes time flies when we are chatting

Nicholas: nope I dress warm

Namita: ohh yes

Nicholas: I'll be around when I have breakfast as usual just not sure when I'll be up though

Namita: ohh ok

Namita: make sure you get enough rest though

Nicholas: we should get some sleep though

Namita: before work

Nicholas: yes u 2

Namita: yes

Namita: i will

Nicholas: if I don't see you in the morning I'll look for u after work

Namita: i lovee how at the end of our conversation ..the sentences get shorter and shorter ...then one or 2 words

Nicholas: lol yes they do

Namita: ok i will be around

Namita: hehhee

Nicholas: we wind dwn

Namita: hehe ... its like uh huh ...hmmmm

Namita: oh yes

Namita: right

Nicholas: yup... lol

Nicholas: *smiling*

Namita: nice touch !

Namita: with urs there

Nicholas: like minds

Namita: yup !

Nicholas: was my intention... I knew you'd see it

Namita: oh i didnt miss it

Nicholas: even in ur tired state

Namita: uh huh !!!

Nicholas: lol

Namita: hehehhee

Nicholas: I love how playful you are

Nicholas: even in your state of tiredness

Namita: aweee thanks ... im glad

Nicholas: you're so nice to talk with

Namita: im always like that !!

Nicholas: me too

Namita: even at work

Namita: joke around ...crack a few jokes

Nicholas: we're going to have so much fun together

Namita: hehe im sure

Nicholas: alright then we should sleep Namita

Namita: yes nicholas dear

Nicholas: sweet dreams my sweet

Namita: awee thanks ...and you too literally

Nicholas: I'll dream some more of you tonight

Namita: heheh ok

Nicholas: I hope

Namita: hehehe

Namita: invite me and i will come over in ur dreams

Nicholas: will be so much more fun when you're w me finally

Nicholas: I'll try it

Namita: then we dont have to dream of each other

Namita: hehe ok

Nicholas: would be really cool if I dreamed about you n you dreamed about me

Nicholas: or was the same dream

Namita: hehehee i will pray to thr dream gods

Nicholas: now that would be a connection we wouldn't be able to explain to others

Namita: hehehehe yessssss

Namita: they will think we`re joined at the hip !!

Nicholas: okay sleep well my sweet

Namita: ok

Nicholas: lol yah the hips

Namita: you too

Nicholas: thx

Nicholas: night 😊 😊

Namita: nite 😊

End Time: 3:13 AM

Chapter 31 December 3

It's been five days since our last chat. Maybe her uncle passed away? If he did, I can only imagine what Namita and her family are going through. I'll check in tonight after the Christmas party — if she's around.

I was back and forth about going to the Christmas party right up until I headed out the door. I already handed in my deposit, a little something to cover the empty seat if you were a no show. I planned on taking Namita but, with her in San Francisco that's not happening. I decided to go for the free meal but mostly because I didn't want to lose fifty dollars. Having not met Namita in person yet, I really didn't want our first meeting to be a social gathering, especially with my co-workers. Some of them I don't really know all that well so, it's sort of okay she can't make it. I'm hoping the party will be a good distraction and help take my mind off not hearing from her.

The hour long drive out to Richmond seems to take forever. I found a place to park and walk the couple of blocks to the hotel where the dinner is being held. Being a little nervous I scan the banquet room and spot a table with some familiar faces. "Do you mind if I join you?" I ask the table as a whole. "Not at all, For sure, Absolutely!" Are the replies.

I find a seat between Michael, who's my supervisor and a woman I assume is Chris's wife, Chris works the day shift. The other guests at the table are Jim and Cheryl along with Michael's wife Dana and, I was right Chris's wife, Parjeet. I worked with Jim at a previous job. He was the one that told me about the opening with this company. I've socialized with him and consider him a friend. I feel a little more at ease once I realize we are all a little nervous as we're not used to making dinner conversation. As we get deeper into the evening and everyone has more to drink the conversations flow more easily.

I start chatting with Parjeet, Chris interjects now and again but our conversation is mostly the two of us. She mentions she and Chris, being an Indian couple, were an arranged marriage. I've always wondered how an arranged marriage works. What if you don't like the other person? Are you stuck with them? Parjeet explains they did have a choice. When she met Chris they liked each other so they dated to be sure it was going to work.

Eventually our conversation progresses to what we do for a living. Parjeet says she's a nurse and works at St. Paul's Hospital. "Does the name Namita Puranjay sound familiar?" Shaking her head she says, "No it doesn't." She explains that it's a big hospital and the departments usually keep to themselves. I rave about Namita and how awesome she is and how I think I've found the perfect partner — so much for taking my mind off her. As she doesn't recognize the name I'm more than willing to show her the picture on my phone. She doesn't recognize it either so she shows Chris. He says, "She looks familiar."

He pulls out his phone and searches Google images, then passes his phone to me. "They're close and could pass for sisters or cousins," I say, holding them next to each other, "But they're not a spot on match."

Unbeknownst to me, others at our table have been listening in on our conversation and want to compare the images. As our phones go around the table I explain what we're doing, who Namita is and how I met her. The volume of the room around me fades to nothing. Deep in my mind a quiet voice softly whispers, *"What if Namita doesn't turn out to be who I think she is?"* The consensus is they're close but not the same.

With dinner over and the rest of the night under way, I manage to leave the party quickly without looking like I'm in a hurry. The drive home seems twice as long as the drive in while I keep repeating the name given to me by Chris.

Finally home I can hardly get my key in the door to unlock it. I go straight to my laptop. As I type, the Google suggestions show up in the drop box. Click on the name, then Images and anxiously wait as the page opens. Not being immersed in the Indian culture I don't know anything about her. As the images start popping up one after another my mind turns to quicksand. I feel like I'm being sucked into a swirling vortex of nonsense. My stomach churns as my head spins. "What the fuck is going on!" After somewhat collecting my thoughts I email Namita.

> Hey you! How are you?... I haven't heard from you in awhile.... I've waited for you all week... The work Christmas dinner tonight was really good, too bad you weren't able to come with me would have been nice to show you around... One of my co-worker's wives works at St. Paul's. She works in the CCU unit... I mentioned your name but she didn't recognize it as the departments keep to themselves... I showed her the photo of you I have on my phone but she didn't recognize it... Her husband said you look a lot like the Bollywood actress Bipasha Basu... sound familiar? I'm sure you get mistaken for her all the time... When I got home I googled her and much to my shock I found 14 of the same photos you sent me! Including the ones you used as your messenger profile pic AND the ones from your Lava Life profile... yah your friend Maranda took them, right.. the deist goes right back to our first contact... I saw you managed to crop the words off the magazine pic's too... thinking back to our first conversation you wanted to wait till we were both online so you could witness my reaction... you were so interested in whether I believed you'd described yourself so well. And you said all along that you were just as you described... remember when you asked what I was looking for? do you remember what I said? I can't believe after all our great conversations and all the "similarities" you're not who you presented yourself to be... Not sure what your game was here but words alone can not describe how extremely hurt and disappointed I am... I can't believe I stayed up to the early morning hours talking to someone as horrible and deceitful as you... what you did was down right mean and shitty!! I would appreciate an explanation Namita if that is your real name? Though I don't expect to hear from you now that I know the truth...

It hurt to say such cruel things to her. I just needed to settle... clear my head... absorb this...

The rest of the night I was in a bit of a haze but I did find my way to bed.

Opening my eyes it was morning. I pulled my covers off and as my feet hit the floor reality punched me in the stomach. *This can't be happening?!* Once fully coherent I decided this time, I will call St. Paul's Hospital and see if I was imagining the last 12 hours. I looked up the number and dialed.

"Thank you for calling St. Paul's Hospital, how may I direct your call?" Asked the voice from the switchboard.
"The ICU desk please."
"One moment." There was a click and I was connected.
"ICU this is Lisa."
"Hi there, is Namita Puranjay at work today?" I asked tentatively.

I could tell from the slight pause the name didn't sound familiar. Then Lisa inquired, "Is that a nurse?"

"Yes it is."
"There's no one that works here by that name."
"Oh... Okay... Thank you..." And I hung up.

There's no one that works here by that name, echoed through my mind and solidified the reality revolving around me.

I feel as though something has reached inside my chest and squeezed the life out of my heart.

I came to know Namita quite well and intimately over these last 9-1/2 weeks. As far as I knew she was a 39 year old East Indian woman, was 5' 7" and lived in White Rock. She owned a house with a two car garage that had a big yard front and back with a huge flower garden. She had a Golden Retriever named Baloo, like the bear character from the Jungle Book. She worked as an ICU nurse at St. Paul's Hospital in Vancouver. She told me stories from her childhood, her time in nursing school and things from her daily life. I thought she was as open and honest with me as I was with her. I saw my future with her falling into place and I was really looking forward to it. I couldn't believe she was as beautiful on the inside as she was on the outside. I learned of her morals, her values and her interests. She was turning out to be everything I was looking for in a partner.

My first experience with internet dating turned out to be quite the rollercoaster ride. Maybe this time I'll finally delete all the pictures and conversations and try to convince myself she never existed — on some level she never did.

I guess the fairytale does only exist on tv or in the movies.

Whenever I look back on this all I can do is, LOL!

The End

Epilogue

It took me about 3 months to separate my emotions from the images and personality I had come to know as Namita Puranjay. Our conversations were always natural, respectful and pretty hot at times. There were never any long pauses that made it seem like she was thinking of what to say next or any obvious deflecting or dodging replies. We had the perfect opportunity to get to know each other without the physical distractions. I thought I was experiencing an undeniable chemistry, blossoming into what could be a long and loving life together.

I feel there was a lot of truth to what she had been sharing but, it was all built on a lie. The bread crumbs lined up during my many editing sessions. For example, the name and size of some of her photo files, compared to the ones I sent her, were remarkably long. And she never sent me any from her laptop camera while we were chatting like I did. Somewhere between Chapter 8 and Chapter 25 Sonia, one of her sisters, became Pryia, something I didn't notice until a friend pointed it out. In Chapter 26 one of the photos she sent has "_bips_" in the file name. Bips is what people close to Bipasha call her. She never asked me for money or gifts so in that aspect I guess I got lucky.

I still get a little pull in my heart if I see photos of Bipasha but I'm quickly reminded of what happened.

To this day I have no idea who I was talking to or what would motivate someone to do this. At the time of this publishing I still have the perfume I bought for her. I decided to turn this experience into a book to have closure.

I've never heard from Namita again.

Thank you for reading.

About the Author,

Nicholas Tombs grew up in Parksville British Columbia, Canada and lives in Maple Ridge. He's a welder, an artist and an inventor. He's been creating ever since he was a kid. He works in a multitude of mediums ranging from but not limited to metal, wood, fabric, clay... and now writing.

Love On Line? A Tale Of Internet Dating is Nicholas's first book. He is intimately connected to the story and brings a gentlemen's unique perspective.

To contact the author:
blueflame_creative@hotmail.com
blueflamecreative.ca

www.ingramcontent.com/pod-product-compliance
Lightning Source LLC
Chambersburg PA
CBHW071112080526
44587CB00013B/1317